Constitutional Innovation and Same-Sex Desire in D'Annunzio's Fiume, 1919–1920

The Fairleigh Dickinson University Press
Series in Italian Studies

General Editor: Dr. Anthony Julian Tamburri,
Dean of the John D. Calandra Italian American Institute

The Fairleigh Dickinson University Press Series in Italian Studies is devoted to the publication of scholarly works on Italian literature, film, history, biography, art, and culture, as well as on intercultural connections, such as Italian-American Studies.
On the Web at http://www.fdu.edu/fdupress

Recent Titles

Aleardo Zanghellini, *Constitutional Innovation and Same-Sex Desire in D'Annunzio's Fiume, 1919–1920* (2024)
Massimo Castoldi, *Teaching Freedom: Stories of Anti-Fascist Teachers in Italy* (2024)
Sabrina Vellucci, *Italian American Poetics of Place: An Environmental Perspective* (2024)
Paola Irene Galli Mastrodonato, *Emilio Salgari: The Tiger Is Still Alive!* (2024)
Emanuele Pettener, *When We Were Bandini: Humor and Satire in John Fante's American Dream* (2024)
Julianne VanWagenen, *Mythologist in Microgroove: A Study of Italian Myths and Cultural Shifts with Fabrizio De André on Lead Vocals* (2023)
Cristina Perissinotto, *Marco Paolini: A Deep Map* (2023)
Raymond Angelo Belliotti, *Italian Rebels: Mazzini, Gramsci, and Giuliano* (2022)
Anna Camaiti Hostert and Enzo Antonio Cicchino, *Trump and Mussolini: Images, Fake News, and Mass Media, Weapons in the Hands of Two Populists* (2022)
Raymond Angelo Belliotti, *Heroism and Wisdom, Italian Style* (2022)
Joseph Francese, *The Unpopular Realism of Vincenzo Padula:* Il Bruzio *and Mariuzza Sbrìffiti* (2021)
Marie Orton, Graziella Parati, and Ron Kubati (eds.), *Contemporary Italian Diversity in Critical and Fictional Narratives* (2021)
Giorgio Linguaglossa, *Alfredo de Palchi: The Missing Link in Late Twentieth-Century Italian Poetry* (2020)
Daniela Bini, *Portrait of the Artist and His Mother in Twentieth-Century Italian Culture* (2020)
Cinzia Russi, *Sicilian Elements in Andrea Camilleri's Narrative Language: A Linguistic Analysis* (2020)
Raymond Angelo Belliotti, *Values, Virtues, and Vices, Italian Style: Caesar, Dante, Machiavelli, and Garibaldi* (2020)
Elio Attilio Baldi, *The Author in Criticism: Italo Calvino's Authorial Image in Italy, the United States, and the United Kingdom* (2020)

Constitutional Innovation and Same-Sex Desire in D'Annunzio's Fiume, 1919-1920

Aleardo Zanghellini

FAIRLEIGH DICKINSON UNIVERSITY PRESS
Vancouver • Madison • Teaneck • Wroxton

Published by Fairleigh Dickinson University Press
Copublished by The Rowman & Littlefield Publishing Group, Inc.
4501 Forbes Boulevard, Suite 200, Lanham, Maryland 20706
www.rowman.com

86-90 Paul Street, London EC2A 4NE

Fairleigh Dickinson University Press gratefully acknowledges the support received for scholarly publishing from the Friends of FDU Press.

British Library Cataloguing in Publication Information Available

Library of Congress Cataloging-in-Publication Data

Library of Congress Cataloging-in-Publication Data
Names: Zanghellini, Aleardo, author.
Title: Constitutional innovation and same-sex desire in D'Annunzio's Fiume, 1919-1920 / Aleardo Zanghellini.
Description: Lanham: Fairleigh Dickinson University Press, [2025] | Series: The Fairleigh Dickinson University Press series in Italian studies | Includes bibliographical references and index. | Summary: "This book tells the story of decadent poet Gabriele D'Annunzio's occupation of Fiume in 1919–1920. It provides the most comprehensive and detailed analysis to date of D'Annunzio's visionary Constitution for Fiume, arguing that the sublimation of same-sex desire was a key driver of political and legal innovation during the occupation"—Provided by publisher.
Identifiers: LCCN 2024041036 (print) | LCCN 2024041037 (ebook) | ISBN 9781683934356 (cloth) | ISBN 9781683934363 (ebook)
Subjects: LCSH: Rijeka (Croatia)—History—Siege, 1919. | Rijeka (Croatia)—Politics and government—20th century. | D'Annunzio, Gabriele, 1863–1938—Political activity. | Carta del Carnaro. | Italy—Politics and government—1914–1922. | Homosexuality—Croatia—Rijeka—History—20th century. | Italy—Politics and government—1914–1922.
Classification: LCC DR1645.R54 Z36 2025 (print) | LCC DR1645.R54 (ebook) | DDC 949.72/02—dc23/eng/20241003
LC record available at https://lccn.loc.gov/2024041036
LC ebook record available at https://lccn.loc.gov/2024041037

∞™ The paper used in this publication meets the minimum requirements of American National Standard for Information Sciences—Permanence of Paper for Printed Library Materials, ANSI/NISO Z39.48-1992.

A mia madre

Contents

Acknowledgments

Several colleagues, relatives, and friends indulged me by taking (or convincingly feigning) an interest in this project. Staff at Reading University Library promptly actioned countless requests for interlibrary loans. Reading Law School funded the trips that enabled me to carry out my archival research. Staff at the National Archives, Parliamentary Archives, and the Archives of Il Vittoriale degli Italiani kindly assisted with sources: Charlotte Smith and Alessandro Tonacci were especially hospitable and liberal with their time. Discussions with Karin Lesnik-Oberstein helped clarify some key points in Freud's writings. During the acquisition process, Anthony Tamburri, in addition to offering invaluable practical assistance, supported me through his generous assessment of the manuscript. My heartfelt gratitude to each and every one of you.

Writing generally makes me a sorry excuse for a partner, and this book was no exception. Hideki tolerated my neglect and, together with Kerberos, kept me grounded. Your patience and your love mean the world to me.

Introduction

In September 1919, not three months since the Peace Treaty had been signed at Versailles, Gabriele D'Annunzio—decadent poet, refined wordsmith, consummate Don Juan, patriotic haranguer, and war hero—led a contingent of volunteers to occupy Fiume, now Rijeka, in coastal Croatia. Fiume had been left to its own devices by the departing Hungarian governor in October 1918, upon the dissolution of the Habsburg Empire, to whose authority the town had been subject for the best part of five centuries. Because of its nature as an Italian enclave within Yugoslav territory, and because of uncompromising views about where it properly belonged, determining Fiume's fate had proved an intractable problem at Versailles, despite the Italian delegation's efforts to have it assigned to Italy.

D'Annunzio installed himself in Fiume with his 'legionnaires' in a bid to embarrass the Italian government into declaring its annexation. From Rome, British diplomatic sources observed that D'Annunzio had, 'despite his unsavoury past, theatrical manners and colossal conceit, the power of swaying the Italian people to an extraordinary degree'.[1] Twelve days into the occupation, they reported, enthusiasm had reached fever pitch, 'as is only possible with this excitable race':

> It may no doubt be thought inconceivable that a first class European power should have drifted into a situation, which must forfeit her the sympathy of her Allies and which may lead to serious internal trouble. . . . One has, however, to reckon with the temperament of the Italian people. . . . [The] saner point of view [adopted initially by the moderate press] has . . . completely disappeared by no argumentative process, and has given way to the present wave of unreasoning enthusiasm. . . . It is true, of course, that, with this emotional people, there may be at any time a 'révirement' but for the moment the country has practically become demented and beyond control.[2]

The Italian government, caught between the risk of large-scale military insubordination if it proceeded to forcibly remove D'Annunzio and the certainty of alienating the Allies and antagonising the Yugoslavs if it unilaterally declared Fiume's annexation, was only too aware of the impossible situation D'Annunzio had put it in. That situation dragged on for sixteen months, during which D'Annunzio, despite the need for compromise he periodically seemed to experience, did his best to fashion Fiume into the image of an ideal (his ideal) political community. Then, at the end of 1920, the Italian government put an end to the poet's unique social and political experiment in a show of force pitting Italians against Italians. D'Annunzio called it 'the bloody Christmas'.

The political legacy of the whole episode is widely regarded as out of proportion to its nature as a relatively minor insurrection. Among other things, D'Annunzio's Fiume is variously considered to have paved the way to fascism[3] to have imparted on Italian politics a violent bend that made itself felt well beyond the *ventennio fascista*;[4] to have prejudiced Britain in its diplomatic dealings with Italy for decades afterwards;[5] to have inaugurated a new way of doing mass politics;[6] to have been the first occasion on which an organised, global movement briefly emerged for the liberation of the Third World;[7] and to have prefigured the sexual revolution and counterculture of the 1960s and 1970s.[8]

This book tells the story of D'Annunzio's occupation of Fiume, before turning to a close analysis of the Constitution the poet promulgated there in September 1920. D'Annunzio's Constitution, the *Carnaro Charter*, is the most remarkable normative outcome of the occupation; nonetheless, it has remained relatively understudied, despite some revival of scholarly interest in Italy in recent years. The central part of the book provides the most detailed textual, contextual, comparative, and intertextual analysis of the *Charter* to date, in any language. In its final part, the book argues that the sublimation and discursive circulation of same-sex desire was integral to sustaining the political and legal order of the occupation. Accounts of the occupation cursorily mention that homosexuality was openly tolerated in D'Annunzio's Fiume. That same-sex desire, in structuring both D'Annunzio's Fiume speeches to the legionnaires and the political commitments of prominent legionnaires, was key to sustaining Fiume's political and legal order during the occupation has entirely escaped scholarly attention. The final part of the book addresses this serious oversight.

TELLING THE STORY OF THE OCCUPATION FROM, OR DESPITE, THE BRITISH POINT OF VIEW

The story of D'Annunzio's occupation has only been thoroughly told once in English, nearly fifty years ago, by Michael Leeden.[9] Leeden's work has been argued to privilege the aesthetic qualities of the endeavour, as a spectacle led by D'Annunzio's showmanship, at the expense of focusing on its political significance.[10] Leeden's book perhaps invited this criticism through its chapter headings ('The Star', 'The Stage', 'Setting the Stage', etc): these are as misleading as the book's provocative title (*The First Duce*), which implies a likeness between D'Annunzio and Mussolini that Leeden in fact denies.[11] Chapter headings aside, I do not think the criticism is justified in substance. If anything, Leeden's book is superior to most treatments of D'Annunzio's Fiume for both breadth of coverage and balance in interpretation.

The reason why, despite Leeden's admirable book, I retell the story of D'Annunzio's Fiume is threefold. First, telling it provides the necessary context to the law- and affect-centred analyses undertaken in the rest of book. Secondly, based as I am in Britain, I have the benefit of easy access to British archival material. The National Archives and Parliamentary Archives hold a wealth of Foreign Office and War Office documentary evidence about Fiume in the immediate postwar years. Some of these archival sources have been used selectively in Woodhouse's biography of D'Annunzio[12] and have informed diplomatic history books about the peace negotiations at Versailles. Until this book, however, there was no dedicated treatment of the Fiume question that drew systematically and in detail on this material. As I explain shortly, this material helps round out our understanding of key aspects of the occupation, particularly the leadup to it. Thirdly, much has been published in Italian since Leeden's book, with more archival evidence unearthed and analysed. Owing to the one-hundredth anniversary of the occupation, in recent years Italy has witnessed a resurgence of popular and historical interest in D'Annunzio's Fiume. Alongside its use of original British archival sources, *Constitutional Innovation and Same-Sex Desire in D'Annunzio's Fiume, 1919–1920* relies on a synthesis of this literature to provide an up-to-date English-language account of the Fiume endeavour.

My reconstruction in the initial part of the book (chapters 1 through 5) makes an attempt at comprehensiveness, seeking to present the relevant events in their multiple historical dimensions: diplomatic, political, social, intellectual, and legal. These dimensions are often treated separately, or at any rate rather more selectively than I do, in existing literature. I also devote considerable attention to the relevant contextual background (Fiume's pre–World War I history, interethnic relations in the town, D'Annunzio's political career, etc.), including the leadup to the occupation, on which British archival sources are especially rich and illuminating.

It may be natural to assume that British sources coeval to the occupation provide a relatively uninvolved and hence impartial perspective on a politically fraught issue that did not concern Britain directly. In practice, that assumption proved, as often as not, mistaken. British archival sources should be approached with, at times, a degree of scepticism—an attitude which required perhaps less effort on my part than it would for a British scholar handling the same material. Foreign Office sources, specifically, must be read keeping in mind that, as I will explain at length in due course, Britain was home to a vocal and influential pro-Yugoslav lobby. D'Annunzio's anti-British rhetoric also did nothing to skew British observers in his favour.

War Office records must be treated with caution too. When approaching reports issuing from Fiume-based British military sources, one must take into account that, by the time D'Annunzio arrived in Fiume in September 1919, Italo-British relations in town—then occupied by an Inter-Allied force—were strained at best. For the British ambassador in Rome, Rennell Rodd—whose letters and reports, unlike virtually any other Foreign Office source, invariably seek to understand the Italian viewpoint—English officers in Fiume assimilated a pro-Yugoslav stance as a result of consorting with French troops, whose language, unlike Italian, they could sometimes speak.[13] The naval attaché to the embassy, who visited Fiume, ascribed British troops' Yugoslav sympathies to the fact that the Yugoslavs 'are certainly very hospitable to English and Americans, and entertain a good deal, which the Italian Fiumani never do.'[14] Writer Lina Waterfield, who had worked for the programme of British propaganda in Italy during the war and who visited the town three months before D'Annunzio's arrival, had a more sophisticated sociopsychological explanation:

> Our men understand the Croat and Austrian temperament better than the Latin—they are tired to death of [Italian-style] flag waving and patriotic talk on the top note. . . . They are even more sick of hearing so much about how Italy saved Europe and of her 'glorious' victory on the Piave. . . . They do not at present regard the Italian as a 'white man', and they bitterly resent his being 'top dog' in Fiume which is supposed to be an interallied affair . . . they say that we have lost prestige by the way we have had to knuckle under the Italians. . . . The English like the Croats, and show it. They find them hospitable and sager to entertain them . . . and they all talk English perfectly. When Croats talk politics they start on a basis of facts (often incorrect . . .) but the impression is reposeful. In short they, our people, are not bored by them. Then remember that the Croat ladies are exceedingly handsome, amiable and often very amusing. . . . It is now the fashion for Italians to boast to being perfectly open and frank in their conversations with us, which consists of telling us that we are traitors. People of the highest official rank talk in the wildest way against England. . . . [W]hen a review was held in Fiume and English and French . . . troops took part, not a single cheer, or the murmur of a cheer, was given for the Allies.[15]

In a context fraught with such mutual antipathy and distrust, assessing the credibility of purportedly factual reports coming from British military sources can at times be challenging. In some sources the virulent nature of certain comments woven through factual claims gives a clue to the (un)reliability of the latter. An egregious example is a January 1919 letter from the British director of military intelligence, Plunkett, who, after accusing Italian troops in Fiume of all manner of malfeasance, capped his report with: 'All Britishers, whether soldiers, civilians or diplomats, with experience in this part of the world, have a feeling of loathing for [the Italians] and their ways'.[16] Serendipitously, a comment on the folder containing the letter, scribbled by Rodd (to whom the letter had been forwarded), reads: 'I think Plunkett cannot have got over the trouble he got into last time he came to Rome, and he is evidently extremely prejudiced.'

In other cases, assessing credibility is not quite as straightforward, but other clues can be relied upon to guide one's judgement. An important example is Lieutenant Colonel Peck's diary of the British Mission in Fiume, preserved in the records of the War Office, and his reports to the director of military operations, which were regularly shared with the Foreign Office. Facts reported by Peck turn out to be interwoven with the author's political judgements, in which anti-Dannunzian sentiment is palpable. Many such facts also turn out to be not directly observed but secondhand accounts, as often as not by D'Annunzio's sworn political adversaries, such as Riccardo Zanella. The diary also takes seriously Italian newspaper articles whose reports are clearly distorted by ideological affiliation (as in the claim that D'Annunzio's Fiuman supporters were only women and children—a misogynistic, if inherently implausible, hobby horse among D'Annunzio's most virulent critics, used to discredit his politics).[17] I will return to Peck's testimony before the end of the introduction; for the time being, suffice to say that in *Constitutional Innovation and Same-Sex Desire in D'Annunzio's Fiume, 1919–1920* I did my best to navigate this evidentiary minefield in pursuit of what I hope turned out to be a reasonably objective account. As I explain shortly, the conclusions to the book speak to some of these methodological challenges.

LAW

In September 1920 D'Annunzio promulgated a Constitution called *La Carta del Carnaro* (*The Carnaro Charter*), after the name of the gulf on whose shore Fiume nestles. In the event, the Constitution proved to be exceedingly short lived, for the Italian government itself put an end to the occupation in December 1920. Yet the *Charter* is the most intellectually momentous and politically valuable outcome of an enterprise whose overall political legacy must be considered mixed at best. First, the *Charter* grapples (and does so imaginatively) with problems and dilemmas that continue to characterise contemporary societies, including gender equality, protection of minorities, freedom of religion, and political representation. Secondly, it belongs to the generation of interwar Constitutions that set in motion the process that would lead to the welfare state.[18] Thirdly, because of its unapologetic constitutionalisation of aesthetic commitments and intrinsic values, the *Charter* is a unique constitutional document—certainly the most fascinating I have ever set eyes upon.

We cannot formulate a historical assessment of the Fiume occupation without a detailed examination of the *Charter*. As I will argue, there also are good reasons for treating the *Charter* as the centrepiece of D'Annunzio's political thought. Although the Fiume endeavour cannot be reduced to D'Annunzio's own political priorities, it would have been a profoundly different affair if someone else had led it. To the extent that it provides insight into D'Annunzio's political and normative commitments, a detailed study of the *Charter* is indispensable to an accurate historical interpretation of the Fiume endeavour. Conversely, the decision to make the *Charter* a central object of study in this book provided a further reason for making the preceding reconstruction of events quite as detailed as it is. A proper appreciation of the *Charter* requires a thorough understanding of the leadup to and context of its genesis. These are as unique in the world of constitutional law making as the authorship of the *Charter* itself.

If, when it comes to historical reconstructions of the occupation, the problem is to reconcile and synthesise a multiplicity of first- and second-hand accounts, literature on the *Charter* itself is rather less abundant. One of the chapters in Leeden's 1977 book provides virtually the only English-language treatment. In Italy, a fair degree of scholarly attention was paid to D'Annunzio's Constitution in the two decades following its promulgation,[19] culminating in Mirabella's 1940 monograph—the first book fully devoted to a study of the *Charter*.[20] Generally, however, analyses during this period are clouded by a contingent ideological preoccupation with either recuperating the *Charter* into fascism or with insisting that it contributed nothing to it.[21] Since the end of the regime, constitutional law studies on the subject have been relatively scant.[22] To be sure, a number of short, more or less descriptive pieces—both old and new—have been published.[23] Generally, though not invariably, they address select parts of the *Charter*. Since the turn of the century, lengthier and/or more searching analyses have appeared, offering keen insight into disparate aspects of the Fiuman Constitution.[24] However, with the exceptions of Stendardi and Costa's hard-to-find 1971 essay[25] and now Agrí's 2023 book,[26] there is no truly comprehensive analytical commentary. Accordingly, the central part of *Constitutional Innovation and Same-Sex Desire in D'Annunzio's Fiume, 1919–1920* (chapter 6) engages in what I believe to be the most extensive and detailed textual, intertextual, comparative, and contextual analysis of the *Charter* (as a whole) to date.

LOVE-LORE

The analysis in the final three chapters of the book is centred on *eros*, and specifically the ways in which D'Annunzio harnessed homoerotic affect to sustain and inspire his legionnaires' loyalty for Fiume's political cause and political and legal structures. These discursive deployments of same-sex desire partake of a broader rhetoric of Love (not specifically homosexual) which D'Annunzio used when addressing the Fiuman population itself, rather than his legionnaires. Despite some analyses of D'Annunzio's speeches and dialogues with the crowd in Fiume,[27] there is no analysis of how D'Annunzio deployed homoerotic imagery for political purposes in these discourses, let alone an examination of how these rhetorical moves articulate with broader homoerotic concerns in his literary production. The final part of the book (chapters 7 through 9) fills this interpretive gap.

The analysis in this part was inspired by Giovanni Comisso's largely autobiographical novel *Harbour of Love* (1924),[28] set in Fiume at the time of its occupation by D'Annunzio's forces. Comisso was one of D'Annunzio's legionnaires, as was Guido Keller, whom the narrative voice in *Harbour of Love* describes as 'my friend', without ever directly identifying him. Keller played a much more significant role than Comisso in the Fiume endeavour, though one would not know it from *Harbour of Love*. What one does learn from *Harbour of Love* is that its author was deeply infatuated with Keller and that he managed to construct virtually the whole book around a series of incidents involving, in one way or another, same-sex desire. I felt that there was enough in *Harbour of Love* to suggest that homoerotic investments might not have been an entirely contingent aspect of political and military dynamics in occupied Fiume and set out systematically to chart, in an exploratory spirit, the entanglements of law, political power, and same-sex desire in D'Annunzio's Fiume.

The line of enquiry suggested by Comisso's book was even more fruitful than I anticipated. A wide ranging analysis into D'Annunzio's biography and literary production revealed his genuine and abiding interest in same-sex desire. This was somewhat startling, considering D'Annunzio's reputation as a Don Juan. Existing criticism, despite two notable English-language exceptions addressing homosexuality in some of D'Annunzio's works,[29] is oblivious to this aspect of D'Annunzio's literary production. Predictably, D'Annunzio's homoerotic concerns were not set aside during the occupation; rather they infused and invigorated that distinctive oratorial practice that is considered D'Annunzio's most innovative contribution to the craft of politics. D'Annunzio's Fiume speeches, in conjunction with the published testimonies of both Comisso and Léon Kotchnitzky (a young Belgian intellectual who for a time shaped the foreign affairs policy of D'Annunzio's command), as well as evidence relating to Guido Keller held in the archives of the Vittoriale in Italy, attest to the discursive circulation of sublimated same-sex desire in occupied Fiume and show how this worked as a driver of political and even legal innovation. As we will see, D'Annunzio claimed that the *Charter* itself was the offspring of his platonic intercourse with the legionnaires.

D'ANNUNZIO'S POLARISING FIGURE

When D'Annunzio led the Fiume expedition in 1919, there was more than one plot afoot to seize the town. If he had not accepted to lead the march on Fiume, somebody else might well have done so. For a while a different candidate was considered to lead it—another soldier and man of letters, Captain Sem Benelli.[30] Eventually, Benelli was openly offered the command of the local Fiume militia[31] but declined,[32] probably because he caught wind of the fact that D'Annunzio was tipped to lead the occupation itself. As occupied Fiume would have looked profoundly different under a different leadership, this book is necessarily as much about D'Annunzio and his political thought as it is about Fiume.

To this day, D'Annunzio remains a deeply controversial figure. During his lifetime, and from a young age, he deliberately cultivated an unconventional and sometimes scandalous public persona. After his death, his (purported) association with fascism did nothing to enhance his reputation. In his book *The Fifth Season*, published shortly after his experience in Fiume, Kotchnitzky gives a snapshot of widespread anti-Dannunzian bias around 1919.[33] This ranged, Kotchnitzky explains, from manufactured claims in the press, through the *ressentiment* of rivals who could not forgive D'Annunzio his success, to the opposition of the Italian political establishment. Foreign visitors to Italy also played their part. Among others whom Kotchnitzky singles out for ridicule there was 'the sexagenarian Miss, presbyterian and sentimental, a reader of Marion Crawford and Pre-Raphaelite fanatic, [who] does not love D'Annunzio and proclaims him a *most wicked man indeed.*'[34]

But one need not have fit that particular demographic to proclaim D'Annunzio wicked in his own lifetime. No less than universally respected Italian philosopher Benedetto Croce, fifteen years earlier, had declared D'Annunzio a captive to 'sensualism and cruelty'.[35] Forty years after the end of the Fiume occupation, anti-fascist Professor Augusto Monti's diagnosis was, again, that D'Annunzio was devoid of moral and common sense.[36] Today, nothing much has changed. D'Annunzio was 'devoid of moral qualm, lacking in genuine kindness and compassion',[37] declares eminent Italian historian Lucio Villari in a recent book. Moral judgements, as I argue in the conclusions to the book, are not necessarily out of place in historical scholarship, but moral indignation may compromise historical objectivity. At a minimum, the deep-rooted sentiments transpiring from the kinds of categorical pronouncements reported earlier make clear that writing about D'Annunzio's politics is fraught with risks. Inadvertent misrepresentations and interpretive pitfalls are not uncommon.

Consider Woodhouse's 1998 study, 'the first fully documented biography of D'Annunzio in any language'.[38] Woodhouse underscores early on D'Annunzio's polarising personality, implying awareness of the risk of providing partisan accounts. Yet the pages of the biography dealing with Fiume regularly treat as credible and objective the highly suspect testimony of one Father Macdonald, who in 1921 published a book on Fiume based on his recent experiences there.[39] Macdonald's book is a veritable catalogue of factual inaccuracies,[40] misleading statements,[41] gossip,[42] speculation dressed up as fact,[43] improbable theorising,[44] patent anti-Italian prejudice,[45] prissy moralising (even making allowances for his religious office),[46] misogyny,[47] and sheer fabrications.[48] All of this tells strongly against treating it as remotely reliable. One might agree with Osbert Sitwell, who quipped that D'Annunzio's Fiume 'was a unique adventure that deserved a more sympathetic study than it would obtain from an English clergyman at the time of the poet's escapade'.[49] Sitwell mentions no names, but the dig at Macdonald is unmistakable through the choice of word 'escapade': Macdonald's account was entitled *A Political Escapade*.

As we dig a little deeper, we discover that Macdonald was more than an inconsequential amateur writer of *memoirs*. Let me return, here, to the diary of Lieutenant Colonel Peck, chief of the British Mission in Fiume. As I surveyed the archival evidence, I was perplexed at Peck's comment on D'Annunzio's annulment of the popular vote on the *modus vivendi*, a compromise agreement with the Italian government that would have solved the town's political *impasse* to the satisfaction of the Fiumans. Rather than being surprised at D'Annunzio's *volte-face* about the referendum he himself had called, Peck professed surprise at the fact that the results of the vote had not been engineered to reflect D'Annunzio's preferred outcome. Peck maintained that *every* vote held in town since the Italians had taken over, even before D'Annunzio's arrival, had been rigged; he wondered why the result of the plebiscite on the *modus vivendi* 'was not managed in like manner.'[50] Such a confident, blanket appraisal of 'Italian methods' (as Peck calls them elsewhere)[51] seems extreme even among D'Annunzio's opponents; but it does distinctly echo the fantastic allegations that Father Macdonald's book makes about D'Annunzio and the National Council of Fiume. This, it turns out, is not by coincidence. An entry in Peck's diary from 13 January 1920 mentions the findings of an information-gathering mission by one Captain Macdonald, whose preposterous claims (treated as entirely credible by Peck) happen to tally with those made in Father Macdonald's book, down to the relish for dwelling on very specific lurid (and fabricated) detail.[52] A 1921 book on the birth of Yugoslavia corroborated my theory that Father Macdonald and Captain Macdonald were one and the same person: after praising Father Macdonald as very well informed, the author mentions in passing that 'he appears to have been a member of the British Mission'.[53]

To what extent did Macdonald's cavalier approach to facts shape the international policy of the British government, via its influence on Peck's diary entries and reports shared with the War Office and Foreign Office? Woodhouse, who himself considers Peck's reports 'models of sage objectivity', plausibly notes that they must have been treated as an 'invaluable . . . guide for Foreign Office decisions', given the words of praise to be found in Foreign Office staff's marginal notes on his reports.[54] The problem, clearly, was the same for Foreign Office personnel in 1920, as it is for academic researchers one century later: if we come to our subject matter precommitted to feeling moral indignation about the human agents we choose to write about, we become less adept at sifting the evidentiary wheat from the chaff exemplified by Macdonald's book. While virtually all historical research faces these kinds of issues, they present themselves particularly starkly in connection with polarising figures such as D'Annunzio.

THE ARGUMENT

The first two chapters of the book deal with the leadup to D'Annunzio's occupation. Surprisingly, given its geographical location, Fiume's Italian character was not due to Venetian domination. Originally founded as a Roman colony and destroyed by the Francs in the eighth century, Fiume was reestablished in the High Middle Ages as a dominion of vassals of the Sacred Roman Empire. In the fifteenth century it came under Habsburg control. Its Italianization was a centuries-long process connected to the town's economic and political development. Italians brought a tradition of seafaring, commerce, and sophisticated legal training; additionally, the Italian language, because of Venetian dominance in the Adriatic, was that sea's *lingua franca* of commerce and politics. In 1776, Fiume was made part of Croatia and, through it, joined with Hungary; but the Fiumans, suspicious of their Croat neighbour, remonstrated, and three years later Fiume was joined directly to Hungary, without the intermediation of Croatia. Between 1848 and 1867 the town came under Croat control, during a period in which Croatia managed to assert its independence from Hungary; but Hungary reestablished direct control over both Fiume and Croatia severally at the end of that period. Thereafter, Hungarians encouraged the town's further Italianization, in part to keep in check Croat ambitions for another takeover; later, they offset this through its Magyarization, leading to Italian irredentism. Meanwhile, the Slav element was being marginalised through educational and other policies.

In late October 1918, Yugoslavs from nearby Sušak and Italian Fiumans (organised in a National Council) vied to fill the power void created by departing Hungarian authorities. The National Council, who on 30 October had unilaterally proclaimed Fiume's desire to be annexed to Italy, prevailed thanks to the backing of Italian troops. Fiume, unlike parts of the Dalmatian coast further south, had not been promised to Italy in the event of a victory; thus, at the end of hostilities, Italy had not immediately proceeded to occupy it. However, when the French, who had strategic interests in supporting the new Yugoslav state at the expense of Italy, dispatched Serbian troops to Fiume to preempt a possible Italian occupation in November 1918, the Italians responded by sending in their own (more numerous) troops and claiming control in the name of the Allies, on the basis of the Villa Giusti Armistice. Ostensibly Inter-Allied, in practice Fiume's occupation force was Italian, both because it was under Italian command and because of the vast preponderance of Italian troops.

The Italian presence in Fiume must be seen as an insurance policy against Yugoslavs seizing control and against the Allies assigning the town to them. The message is clear: Fiume was Italian, Italian troops had responded to the Fiumans' call for protection, and Italy expected Versailles to determine Fiume's fate accordingly. But the 1915 Treaty of London had not promised Italy Fiume in the event of a victory, and the strategic calculations that had determined the territorial arrangements provided for in the treaty no longer held after the unanticipated dissolution of Austria-Hungary and Russia's changed foreign policy following the revolution. This made everything that the treaty provided for with respect to territorial concessions to Italy in the eastern Adriatic open to being revisited. The US president was adamant that Italy must not have Fiume, which was Croatia's natural outlet to the sea, arguing that an application of self-determination principles was inappropriate in the case of Fiume. Britain's foreign policy was particularly receptive to Yugoslav claims thanks to an influential pro-Yugoslav lobby that had ties with the Foreign Office, and a commercial one that feared Italy's acquisition of a monopoly on shipping business. The French, for their part, aspired to acquire dominant influence in the region by sponsoring Yugoslav claims and established a parallel military authority structure (under the guise of a base to supply the Army of the Orient) in Fiume.

The months between autumn 1918 and summer 1919 were characterised by dissensions between Italian and French officers and incidents between Fiumans and French troops, as well as Italian and French troops. These culminated in disturbances leading to the death and injury of several French soldiers, only days after the Treaty of Versailles had been signed, leaving Fiume's future undecided. An Inter-Allied Commission of Inquiry found fault with the Italian command's failure to keep order and defuse tensions and made recommendations to the effect that the occupation be made genuinely Inter-Allied. The president of the National Council, the local governing authority backed by the Italian command, had indicated that if the outcome of the inquiry were to amount to a departure of the Italian occupation forces, Fiume would take matters into its own hands and seek the assistance of an army of volunteers. This is precisely what transpired when, on 12 September 1919, Gabriele D'Annunzio marched on Fiume at the head of his army of 'legionnaires'.

Having set out this context in the first and second chapters, and before turning to D'Annunzio's occupation in the fourth chapter, the book discusses D'Annunzio and his politics in chapter 3. This is necessary because not only popular but also academic representations often paint a distorted picture of D'Annunzio's politics, as well as his personality, the two being argued to be intertwined. Without a relatively detailed and nuanced assessment of D'Annunzio's politics, it is impossible to appreciate the complex and at times contradictory nature and legacy of D'Annunzio's occupation of Fiume, and particularly its politically radical, progressive, and visionary qualities, alongside its more reactionary (imperialistic and ethnocentric) ones.

D'Annunzio had had his political debut with the Liberals two decades before the occupation of Fiume. This had been followed by something of a love affair with the Socialists, until his concerns had become more nationalistic and interventionist. At the end of the war he established a reputation as a passionate advocate for the (dubious) Adriatic cause, championing the interests of ethnically Italian populations in Dalmatia (and of Italy in ruling over Dalmatia). D'Annunzio's political practice, most notably in Fiume itself, is sometimes said or assumed to have been proto-fascist. This characterisation is unhelpful. It obscures the fraught relationship between D'Annunzio and Mussolini, who made sure to harass D'Annunzio's political movement out of existence after the end of Fiume's occupation. It also overlooks the considerable ideological discontinuities between D'Annunzio's *Fiumanesimo* and fascism including their vastly different brands of corporatism and antiparliamentarianism. D'Annunzio's antimaterialism is also alleged to be reactionary; but far from rejecting the socialist call for improving the material conditions of the working classes, it simply expresses D'Annunzio's conviction that well-being has ineliminable spiritual as well as material dimensions. Some of the most objectionable political commitments ascribed to D'Annunzio—such as a ruthless will to power and incurable elitism—are often imputed to him as a result of methodological moves that treat his literary production as a political manifesto, ignoring the function of his *oeuvre* and the evolution of

D'Annunzio's normative vision. The *Carnaro Charter* is by far the most fully worked out and serious enunciation of D'Annunzio's political commitments; it should take precedence over other sources when a reconstruction of his political thought and legacy is attempted.

Chapters 4 and 5 discuss D'Annunzio's occupation. The march on Fiume was planned with Fiume's own National Council. At least two plots to occupy Fiume were afoot. One involved a vast network of nationalist forces conspiring for the occupation not only of Fiume but also Dalmatia and was being watched by the Italian government. The other was a comparatively more *impromptu* affair, led by officers who had been obliged to leave Fiume following the Inter-Allied Commission's report into the July 1919 disturbances. The latter plot overtook the former, and D'Annunzio marched on Fiume on 12 September 1919. The Inter-Allied occupation forces left after D'Annunzio's arrival, on the understanding that Italy would deal with the situation. In Fiume, D'Annunzio and the National Council agreed on a power-sharing arrangement. The council remained largely independent of D'Annunzio's command, and serious dissensions sometimes ensued, none of them more significant than the one attending to the *modus vivendi*. This was a compromise agreement where the Italian government proposed to take over from D'Annunzio's troops until such time as the desired goal of annexation became politically viable. The National Council and a referendum of Fiumans were both in favour of the proposed solution, but D'Annunzio annulled the vote and stayed on in Fiume, reorienting the occupation to the Left in 1920.

D'Annunzio now aspired to make of Fiume a social and institutional laboratory modelling the kind of political renewal and innovation that he had vaguely called for in his attacks against Italy's political establishment virtually ever since entering the world of politics two decades previously. He appointed the revolutionary syndicalist Alceste de Ambris to head his cabinet in January 1920, and in September they proclaimed the Carnaro Regency, ushered in by the brand new Constitution they devised for Fiume. The project had been delayed because it met with the opposition, among others, of the National Council. Like the Italian government, the council was concerned that a Republic might be instituted in Fiume, with Bolshevist leanings at that. The regency was short lived. In November 1920, Italy and Yugoslavia finally reached an agreement about the future of Fiume, but D'Annunzio refused to recognise it. Together with the legionnaires that had remained loyal to him, he was forcibly ousted at the end of December.

There was never a policy of persecution while D'Annunzio held Fiume, but incidents of violence and bullying are recorded against Yugoslavs and anti-annexationists on the part of fanatical annexationists and legionnaires. Yugoslavs undoubtedly experienced the atmosphere in Fiume as oppressive, both during D'Annunzio's time and the Italian occupation that preceded it;

many left. Some ordinances of D'Annunzio's command are sometimes cited as evidence of D'Annunzio's tyrannical leanings, but these were *verbatim* reiterations of relevant wartime Italian laws (for instance on political crimes) and were hardly ever applied in Fiume. One of the most noteworthy political innovations of D'Annunzio's Fiume is the (ultimately unsuccessful) League of Fiume, or *l'Anti-Societé des Nations*, hailed as the first time sections of the Third World came together in a (short-lived) global movement of anticolonial resistance. It was the brainchild of Léon Kotchnitzky, one of a large number of radical intellectuals of various stripes flocking to the political and intellectual melting pot that was D'Annunzio's Fiume. This vibrant political and cultural *milieu* was enabled by the poet's openness to coeval movements of political contestation and his receptivity to the aspirations of a new generation of national revolutionaries.

It is, however, the *Charter*, discussed in chapter 6, that is the most signal achievement of D'Annunzio's Fiume—for all that many Fiumans (prime among them the fairly conservative National Council) did not ask for it and would have rather done without it. It is not chiefly in practical terms that the *Charter* was an achievement, for Fiume never experienced a government truly under it. To appease those who opposed it, the application of the *Charter* was suspended while special committees studied its articles; and between its proclamation in September 1920 and the demise of the regency at the end of December, a caretaking government ruled the town. Nor was the *Charter* much of an achievement in terms of its political legacy. True, it was adopted in the early 1920s as the manifesto of the National Federation of Fiume Legionnaires, which did much to prevent the confluence into fascism of many *Arditi* (wartime Italian *élite* corps) and legionnaires. But in the latter half of the decade, the federation (by then known as the Dannunzian Spiritual Union) was suppressed by Mussolini, and the *Charter* became no more than a historical curiosity. In terms of intellectual history, nonetheless, the *Charter* stands out as a highly significant and original legal document for several reasons. Uniquely, it gives expression to the concerns of European syndicalist and corporatist thought. It is one of the three Constitutions to have inaugurated, all in 1920, the practice of constitutionality review in Europe. It gives imaginative treatment to problems that continue to beset contemporary liberal societies—from welfare rights, through minorities protection, to representative politics. And it is quite unlike any other Constitution for its attention to aesthetic values, not only because it is the most literary Constitution ever written but also because it constitutionalises aesthetic concerns as intrinsic goods.

D'Annunzio's critics continue to misinterpret its provisions and have dismissed the *Charter* as ridiculous, a distraction, and an exercise in virtue signalling. The close textual analysis offered in chapter 6 points to erroneous interpretations in existing literature and to how favourably the *Charter* compares with coeval constitutional equivalents. It also reveals the textual promiscuity of the *Charter* with sources as different as Plato's dialogues, Fiuman irredentist writing, the manifesto of revolutionary syndicalism and D'Annunzio's own poetry, as well as the influence of numerous constitutional traditions. This leaves little doubt about either the intellectual seriousness of the document or De Ambris and D'Annunzio's earnestness in using it to give expression to their normative vision.

D'Annunzio maintained that the *Charter* was an 'act of life' and a labour of love. He claimed that in the *Charter* he brought to light what had been sown by the legionnaires, after a nine-month gestation period that had started with the rejection of the *modus vivendi* and ended with the promulgation of the *Charter*. The homoerotic subtext of this claim, suggesting the intellectual generativity of same-sex desire, is not a whimsical, isolated element in D'Annunzio's oratorial practice in Fiume. Rather, it articulates with D'Annunzio's veritable and abiding (but near-universally unremarked) preoccupation with same-sex desire. More specifically, it links with the way in which he believed same-sex desire was, unlike different sex desire, capable of sublimation into either creative or active, but invariably fruitful and worthwhile, pursuits. D'Annunzio thematised this sublimation in his novels and enacted it in his Fiume speeches to the legionnaires. Rather than D'Annunzio's unilateral harnessing of same-sex desire, however, what we witness in Fiume is a discursive circulation of same-sex desire as a means of quickening and invigorating politics, as well as sustaining legal innovation. This is discussed in chapters 7, 8, and 9. Together, they make up the third and final part of the book.

As argued in chapter 7, D'Annunzio fraternised with famously same-sex attracted personalities, adopted a gender presentation that left his heterosexuality open to challenge, and routinely expatiated on the beauty of the male form. If this were not enough, he wrote a play on Saint Sebastian, whose main concept is to portray religious ecstasy in the terms of masochistic homoerotic passion. Same-sex desire also features in all his novels, initially as a potentially destructive force (not unlike heteroerotic passion) but later as a promising alternative to different-sex desire. Same-sex desire—as represented in these works—is liable to sublimation, or may otherwise successfully be harnessed in the pursuit of creative and active life projects, in contrast with the self-referential and fruitless ones characteristic of a life ruled by heterosexual desire.

Chapter 8 examines a selection of D'Annunzio's speeches to the legionnaires to show that D'Annunzio practiced what he preached. The speeches show a skilful and deliberate, more or less subtle use of homoerotic affect—ranging from declarations of love, through praises of the legionnaires' beauty, to phallic and mating metaphors—to consolidate the legionnaires' loyalty to the Fiume cause, and their investment in Fiume's social, political, and legal forms. Everything about the speeches—including the ways in which they articulate with concerns expressed in his novels—militates against treating them as instances of manipulation rather than genuinely communicative action. Indeed, the earnestness and intensely personal feeling transpiring from D'Annunzio's speeches to the legionnaires can at times be quite disarming. As I argue drawing on Freud, some relatively overt homoerotic passages in the speeches may have been counterproductive, interfering with group cohesion among the legionnaires, and with their willingness to sublimate libidinal energy into commitment to D'Annunzio's Fiume.

In the final chapter, I analyse the published writings and private correspondence of authors Léon Kotchnitzky and Giovanni Comisso, as well as D'Annunzio's action secretary, Guido Keller. I use these sources to show that the *milieu* of D'Annunzio's Fiume was genuinely receptive to expressions of same-sex desire and conducive to a political practice fed and sustained by it. Some legionnaires' political commitments (such as Kotchnitzky's and Henry Furst's interclass solidarity) and normative vision (such as Keller's and Comisso's antimaterialism) were in part driven by their experience of homoerotic affect—for each other, for D'Annunzio, and, in a more diffused, Whitmanesque fashion, for *Arditi*, workers, and soldiers. The intellectual synergies between these young Italian and foreign intellectuals, and between them and D'Annunzio, in conjunction with the poet's deliberate sublimation of same-sex desire in his oratorial practice, testify to the circulation of homoerotic affect in D'Annunzio's Fiume, and to its role as a driver of political and legal innovation.

A NOTE ON TRANSLATIONS

Whenever the source I quote from is in a language other than English (which will be apparent from the bibliographical information in the citation), the English translation is mine. This applies to all sources: archival material, legal material, D'Annunzio's speeches, his works of literature, or the *Carnaro Charter*. I do not rely on published English translations of D'Annunzio's literary works but render them in English myself, including their title. So the novel *Il Piacere* is widely known as *Child of Pleasure* in English, while *Il Fuoco* has been translated as *The Flame*. I see no good semantic-aesthetic reason for these choices and accordingly refer to them as *Pleasure* and *Fire*, respectively.

NOTES

1. Fiume and the Adriatic: 51/2: Letter from H. W. Kennard to Earl Curzon of Kedleston (21 September 1919), The National Archives, FO170/1248.

2. Fiume and the Adriatic: 51/2: Letter from H. W. Kennard to Earl Curzon of Kedleston (24 September 1919) The National Archives, FO170/1248.

3. Franco Gaeta, *Il Nazionalismo Italiano*, second edition (Roma and Bari: Laterza, 1981), quoted in Paolo Alatri, "La Storiografia sull'Impresa Dannunziana a Fiume," in *D'Annunzio e il Suo Tempo: Un Bilancio Critico*, ed. Francesco Perfetti, vol. 1 (Genova: Sagep, 1989), 39.

4. Alatri, "La Storiografia," 29, 38.

5. John Woodhouse, *Gabriele D'Annunzio: Defiant Archangel* (Oxford: Clarendon Press, 1998), 351.

6. Michael A. Leeden, *The First Duce* (Baltimore and London: John Hopkins University Press, 1977), 202.

7. Marco Cuzzi, "Tra Autodeterminazione e Imperialismo: La Lega di Fiume," in *L'Italia e la "Grande Vigilia": Gabriele D'Annunzio nella Politica Italiana Prima del Fascismo*, ed. Romain H. Rainero and Stefano B. Galli (Milano: FrancoAngeli, 2007), 164; Marco Cuzzi, "'La Nostra Bandiera è la più Alta': La Politica Esteriore di D'Annunzio e la Lega di Fiume," in *Fiume 1919–2019: Un Centenario Europeo tra Identitá, Memorie e Prospettive di Ricerca*, ed. Giordano Bruno Guerri (Milano: Silvania Editoriale, 2020), 324.

8. Claudia Salaris, *Alla Festa della Rivoluzione: Artisti e Libertari con D'Annunzio a Fiume* (Bologna: Il Mulino, 2002).

9. Leeden, *The First Duce.*

10. Enrico Serventi Longhi, "La Dittatura Sovrana di Fiume: Innovazioni Politiche, Sociali ed Economiche (1919–1920)," *Mondo Contemporaneo* 2 (May 2016): 143–44.

11. Leeden, *The First Duce*, 201.

12. Woodhouse, *Gabriele D'Annunzio.*

13. Prime Minister: Letter from R. Rodd to E. J. Harding (14 December 1918), Parliamentary Archives, LG/F/200/1/20.

14. Fiume and the Adriatic: 51/1: Report by NW Diggle to R. Rodd (12 July 1919), The National Archives, FO 170/1247.

15. Prime Minister: Report from L. Waterfield to A. Thorold (5 June 1919), Parliamentary Archives, LG/F/43/7/13.

16. Fiume and the Adriatic: 51/1: Letter from G. A. Plunkett to [unspecified] (29 January 1919), The National Archives, FO 170/1247.

17. Fiume: Diary of the British Military Mission, Fiume (4–10 January 1920), The National Archives, WO 106/853.

18. Giovanni Michele Palmieri, "Sulla Tutela dei Diritti dell'Uomo e delle Libertá Fondamentali nella Carta del Carnaro," in *Lo Statuto della Reggenza Italiana del Carnaro tra Storia, Diritto Internazionale e Diritto Costituzionale*, ed. Augusto Sinagra (Milano: Giuffré, 2009), 178.

19. For a comprehensive review of the literature between 1920 and 1940, see Alessandro Agrì, *La Costituzione della Reggenza Italiana del Carnaro* (Torino: Giappichelli, 2023), 219–59.

20. Tommaso Mirabella, *La Carta del Carnaro* (Palermo: Libreria D'Agata, 1940). For a discussion, see Alessandro Agrí, "Tommaso Mirabella e la Carta del Carnaro (1920–1940)," *Rivista di Storia del Diritto Italiano* 93, no. 2 (2020).

21. Agrì, *La Costituzione della Reggenza*, 223.

22. Giuseppe De Vergottini, "Prassi e Utopia nel Disegno Costituzionale Dannunziano," *Rivista AIC* 3 (2019): 603. See also Davide Rossi, "D'Annunzio, la Carta del Carnaro e la Crisi dello Stato Liberale, tra Rappresentanza e Antiparlamentarismo," *Giornale di Storia Costituzionale* 38, no. 2 (2019): 145.

23. Alessandro Fricano, "Cento Anni dalla Carta del Carnaro: Nuove Suggestioni Costituzionali," *Forum di Quaderni Costituzionali* 1 (2021); Giovanni Zucchini, "La Pubblica Aministrazione nelle Carta del Carnaro," and Davide Lo Presti, "Cittadino e Pubblica Amministrazione nella Costituzione Dannunziana," in *La Cittá di Vita Cento Anni Dopo: Fiume, D'Annunzio e il Lungo Novecento Adriatico*, ed. Davide Rossi (Padova: Wolters Kluwer—Cedam, 2020); De Vergottini, "Prassi e Utopia"; Rossi, "D'Annunzio, la Carta del Carnaro e la Crisi"; Silverio Annibale, *La Questione di Fiume nel Diritto Internazionale* (Rovigno, Fiume, and Trieste: Centro di Ricerche Storiche Rovigno, 2011); Carmelo Ferlito, "Principi Economici della Carta del Carnaro," *StoriaVeritá* 52 (2008); Nereo Bianchi, "La Carta Costituzionale della Reggenza Italiana del Carnaro," *Fiume: Rivista di Studi Fiumani* 1, no. 1 (1982); Nereo Bianchi, "La Carta Costituzionale della Reggenza Italiana del Carnaro," *Fiume: Rivista di Studi Fiumani* 1, no. 2 (1982); Nereo Bianchi, "La Carta Costituzionale della Reggenza Italiana del Carnaro," *Fiume: Rivista di Studi Fiumani* 2, no. 1 (1982); Vittorio Frosini, "D'Annunzio e la Carta del Carnaro," *Nuova Antologia* 2041 (January 1971).

24. Federico Lorenzo Ramaioli, "Res Publica Fiumana: Elementi Medievali nella Concezione Giuridica della Fiume D'Annunziana," in *D'Annunzio Legislatore: Costituzioni, Visioni, Utopie dell'Impresa Fiumana*, ed. Giordano Bruno Guerri (Milano: Silvana Editoriale, 2022); Francesco Margiotta Broglio, "Tra Laicitá e Credenze Religiose 'Supreme'. Fiume 'Stato Libero' e il 'Vaticano Cittá Libera'. Il Diritto Ecclesiastico della Reggenza di Fiume," in *D'Annunzio Legislatore*, ed. Guerri; Alessandro Agrí, "Gabriele D'Annunzio e l'Ora Sociale: Dalla Carta del Carnaro al Patto Marino (1920–1924)," in *D'Annunzio Legislatore*, ed. Guerri; Leonardo Tosoni, "Carta del Carnaro: Diritti di Libertà e Prospettive di Giustizia Sociale nella Fiume Dannunziana," *Historia Constitucional* 22 (2021); Giuseppe De Vergottini, *La Costituzione secondo D'Annunzio* (Milano: Luni, 2020); Giuseppe Franco Ferrari, "La Carta del Carnaro: Un Centenario in Sordina," *Nomos: le Attualitá del Diritto* 3 (2020), https://www.nomos-leattualitaneldiritto.it/wp-content/uploads/2021/02/Ferrari-3-2020-REV-2.pdf; Davide Rossi, "La Carta del Carnaro, Antidoto Contro le Tossine del Parlamentarismo," in *La Cittá di Vita Cento Anni Dopo*, ed. Rossi; Alessandro Agrì, 'D'Annunzio Politico: La Carta del Carnaro (1920)," *Atti e Memorie dell'Accademia di Scienze, Lettere e Arti di Modena serie viii* XVII, no. I (2014); Alessandro Agrì, "La Carta del Carnaro: Un Disegno Costituzionale

Incompiuto," *Fiume: Rivista di Studi Adriatici* 27 (2013); William Klinger, "La Carta del Carnaro: Una Costituzione per lo Stato Libero di Fiume (1920)," *Quaderni* (Centro di Ricerche Storiche-Rovigno) XIV (2002) (despite some inaccuracies and sweeping conclusions). Renato Lombardo, *Sui Fondamenti Culturali della Carta del Carnaro: Aristotele, Vico, Nietzsche* (Pescara: Tracce, 2011), discusses some possible intellectual influences over the *Charter*, but pays little attention to the *Charter* itself.

25. Nicolino Flaminio Costa and Gian Galeazzo Stendardi di Montebenichi, "La 'Carta del Carnaro'," in Gabriele D'Annunzio, *Reggenza Italiana del Carnaro: Disegno di un Nuovo Ordinamento dello Stato Libero di Fiume* (Milano: Perelli, 1973).

26. Agrí, *La Costituzione della Reggenza.*

27. George L. Mosse, "The Poet and the Exercise of Political Power: Gabriele D'Annunzio," *Yearbook of Comparative and General Literature* 22 (1973); Natalia Skradol, "Carnival of Exception: Gabriele D'Annunzio's 'Dialogues with the Crowd'," *Rhetorica: A Journal of the History of Rhetoric* 30 (2012).

28. Giovanni Comisso, *Al Vento dell'Adriatico*, second edition (Torino: Ribet, 1928), 103 (originally published as *Il Porto dell'Amore* in 1924).

29. Jared N. Becker, *Nationalism and Culture: Gabriele D'Annunzio and Italy after the Risorgimento* (New York: Peter Lang, 1995); Derek Duncan, *Reading and Writing Italian Homosexuality* (Aldershot, UK, and Burlington, VT: Ashgate, 2006).

30. Leeden, *The First Duce*, 50.

31. Fiume and the Adriatic: 51/1: Letter from R. Rodd to Earl Curzon of Kedleston (16 June 1919), The National Archives, FO 170/1247; Fiume and the Adriatic: 51/2: Commission Interalliée D'Enquête de Fiume, Procés-Verbaux et Rapport (1919), 44, The National Archives, FO 170/1248.

32. Leeden, *The First Duce*, 51.

33. Léon Kotchnitzky, *La Quinta Stagione: o, I Centauri di Fiume*, trans. Alberto Luchini (Bologna: Zanichelli, 1922), 15–17.

34. Kotchnitzky, *La Quinta Stagione*, 16.

35. Benedetto Croce, "Gabriele D'Annunzio, Parte II," *La Critica* 2 (1904): 98, quoted in Enrico Serventi Longhi, *Il Faro del Mondo Nuovo: D'Annunzio e I Legionari a Fiume tra Guerra e Rivoluzione* (Udine: Gaspari, 2019), 21.

36. Serventi Longhi, *Il Faro*, 21.

37. Lucio Villari, *La Luna di Fiume—1919: Il Complotto* (Milano: Ugo Guanda, 2019), 16.

38. Woodhouse, *Gabriele D'Annunzio*, vi.

39. Woodhouse, *Gabriele D'Annunzio*, 327, 331.

40. For example, the claim that upon the dissolution of Austria-Hungary, Fiume's political status 'reverted to the *Status quo ante*, i.e., it was re-incorporated in the Kingdom of Croatia'. J. N. Macdonald, *A Political Escapade: The Story of Fiume and D'Annunzio* (London: John Murray, 1921), 23. This is wrong as a matter of international law: Fiume, which had been (an unwilling) subject to Croat rule for an interlude of only two decades in its centuries-long history, remained formally dependent on Hungary when the Habsburg Empire broke up. Annibale, *La Questione di Fiume*, 45–50.

41. For example, the claim that, having taken charge of the government of Fiume in 1918, the Italian National Council proceeded to artificially Italianise the town by replacing 'the old names of the streets and public squares.' Macdonald, *A Political Escapade*, 37. Many of those 'old' names dated from 1915, when Hungarians had renamed Fiume's formerly Italian-named streets. William Klinger, *Un'altra Italia: Fiume 1724–1924*, ed. Diego Redivo (Rovigno, Fiume, and Trieste: Centro di Ricerche Storiche Rovigno, 2018), 279, https://crsrv.org/wp/wp-content/uploads/2020/03/N.45-Klinger-Fiume.pdf.

42. For example, claims about the dubious reputation of prominent members of the Italian National Council of Fiume. Macdonald, *A Political Escapade*, 27.

43. For example, the claim that those who took part in marches in favour of annexation of Fiume to Italy were 'actors' in the pay of the 'Italian propaganda department', whose 'retaining fees . . . must have amounted to no inconsiderable sum'; Macdonald, *A Political Escapade*, 118–19. Another example is the statement that 'no one had the slightest doubt that had force been even so much as threatened . . . [D'Annunzio's] rebels would one and all have evacuated the town within a quarter of an hour.' Macdonald, *A Political Escapade*, 146. This supposition was amply disproved by the conflict that eventually put an end to the occupation.

44. For example, the claim that D'Annunzio's 'constant orgies, and the disease from which he was commonly reported to be suffering, so affected his brain as to render him irresponsible alike for his words and for his actions.' Macdonald, *A Political Escapade*, 128. The vacuity of this comment is apparent from the fact that D'Annunzio had made a career of posing as irresponsible and outrageous from a young age, well before the time he might be supposed to have contracted syphilis.

45. For instance, Italy's claims over Fiume were due to Italy's victory which 'had upset the mental balance of a section of her people'. Macdonald, *A Political Escapade*, 522. D'Annunzio's followers were largely made up of the 'riff-raff of the Italian army', an abundant commodity given the 'laxity of discipline that prevail[s] even among the best Italian regiments'. Macdonald, *A Political Escapade*, 113. '[H]istory . . . provided many examples' of 'Italian duplicity'. Macdonald, *A Political Escapade*, 119. It was easy for D'Annunzio to captivate 'a "temperamental" Latin race' and make it 'shriek frenzied *Evvivas'*. Macdonald, *A Political Escapade*, 129.

46. For example, the claim that the 'poet actor had succeeded in attaching to his touring party' a 'stage chorus of loose women and licentious soldiery'. Macdonald, *A Political Escapade*, 126. Or: 'even members of previously respectable households fell victims to the wave of license which pervaded' D'Annunzio's Fiume, and 'Italian officers were not ashamed to appear abroad painted and powdered like street walkers'. Macdonald, *A Political Escapade*, 135.

47. Consider: 'the main body [of pro-annexation marches] consisted of women, for the greater part fanatical, hysterical, and pleasure-seeking, to use no plainer and more vulgar terms'. Macdonald, *A Political Escapade*, 118. Or: elections held in Fiume under D'Annunzio should be regarded as farcical on account not just of voting irregularities but also because 'out of 6700 votes recorded, 4500 were cast by female voters'. Macdonald, *A Political Escapade*, 133. Or: D'Annunzio's political project in Fiume was entirely discreditable, as proven by the fact that 'the crowd [of

his followers] was . . . composed in six-tenths of women . . . and only in one tenth of men who had come as spectators'. Macdonald, *A Political Escapade*, 146.

48. No details need be given of Father Macdonald's explanation for D'Annunzio's renaming a certain restaurant in Fiume 'The Platypus Tavern'. Suffice to say that the actual reason is much less imaginative but in better taste: a platypus taxidermy had been placed there by a group of legionnaires who had chosen it as their unofficial headquarters. Giordano Bruno Guerri, *Disobbedisco: Cinquecento Giorni di Rivoluzione. Fiume 1919–1920* (Milano: Mondadori, 2019), 150.

49. Osbert Sitwell, *Discursions on Travel, Art and Life* (London: Grant Richards, 1925), 218.

50. Fiume: Diary of the British Military Mission, Fiume (4–10 January 1920), The National Archives, WO 106/853.

51. Fiume: Diary of the British Military Mission, Fiume (12–18 January 1920), The National Archives, WO 106/853.

52. Fiume: Diary of the British Military Mission, Fiume (12–18 January 1920), The National Archives, WO 106/853. This refers to the 'Platypus Tavern', about which see note 48.

53. Henry Baerlein, *The Birth of Yugoslavia*, vol. II (London: Leonard Parsons, 1922), chapter VI, footnote 44.

54. Woodhouse, *Gabriele D'Annunzio*, 328.

Chapter 1

Fiume and the Treaty of London

INTRODUCTION

The occupation of Fiume by D'Annunzio was preceded by a sequence of events that—with the benefit of hindsight and given the context—appears to have been more or less bound to result in just that kind of outcome, even if the poet had played no part in it. This chapter and the next trace this sequence of events. In this chapter I begin to do so along two parallel chronological perspectives. One peers into Fiume's more distant past, to clarify the centuries-long leadup to its distinctive prewar political status, as well as to its claims to Italianness. The other perspective is focused on more recent circumstances and events. These include the way in which the application of the 1915 Treaty of London, which did not include Fiume among the territorial concessions made to Italy in the event of a victory, was called into question at the end of the conflict; the Yugoslavs' occupation of the town, which stirred Fiuman notables into action and into declaring the town's annexation to Italy; and—something less obvious from existing literature—the way in which France sought to prevent Italy from establishing de facto control in Fiume in autumn 1918, while effectively catalysing Italian efforts to do so. The upshot was that between November 1918 and September 1919 Fiume experienced an ostensibly Inter-Allied but practically Italian occupation—so much so that it would not be inaccurate to look at D'Annunzio's as a second (officially unendorsed) Italian occupation.

THE TREATY OF LONDON (1915)

At the outbreak of World War I, Italy had been a party to the Triple Alliance with Germany and Austria-Hungary for more than three decades. Italy did not, however, consider itself bound to join its allies, and it opted for neutrality. This is because the Alliance was essentially a defensive affair, while Austria-Hungary (apart from failing to consult Italy before sending its ultimatum to Belgrade) was engaged in a war of aggression against Serbia.[1] Intense and multipronged efforts were made by foreign powers, particularly Britain, to get Italy involved in the conflict.[2] Prime Minister Antonio Salandra, with his Minister for Foreign Affairs Sidney Sonnino, engaged in negotiations with both warring parties. They made territorial demands in exchange for either maintaining Italy's neutrality to the benefit of the Central Powers (Germany, Austria-Hungary and the Ottoman Empire, later joined by Bulgaria) or joining the conflict alongside the *Entente* or Allies (Russia, Britain, France, and Japan).[3]

While joining the *Entente* would have involved a 'betrayal' of much-admired Germany, which gave some Italian diplomatic and military elites pause, there was little love lost between Italy and its other ally, but historical foe, Austria-Hungary. In the years before the war, Austria-Hungary's military leaders had been speaking of preemptive strikes against the Latin country. Its diplomats now complained of Italy's excessive demands during the negotiations about its position in the conflict, while covertly planning not to honour whatever concessions they might have been induced to make in exchange for Italy's continued neutrality.[4] It is not entirely surprising, therefore, that Italy eventually chose to join the Allied Powers by signing the Treaty of London in 1915, though other factors also played a role. On the one hand, a less antagonistic relationship between Italy and France had been transpiring with respect to each other's colonial interests in Africa. One the other hand the catastrophic prospect loomed of Italy's long coastline coming under attack by British naval power if Italy remained allied with Germany, given the worsening of Anglo-German relations in the years leading up to 1914.[5]

Internally, Salandra's reactionary Liberal government was hoping that victory alongside the Allies would strengthen the monarchy and political status quo, staving off democratic reform.[6] Internationally, Italy's priorities were to reclaim Italian-populated lands from Austro-Hungary, to guarantee its strategic security by extending its northern border up to the Alps, to contain a nascent Slav (and specifically Serb) threat, and not to be sidelined by the Allies in the event of a partition of Ottoman lands.[7] Of all these goals, the foremost was reclaiming Italian-populated lands still under Austria-Hungary's control—so-called *terre irredente* (unredeemed lands)—thus completing the process of national unification.[8] However, strategic security also loomed large: when Italy had wrestled the Lombardy and Veneto regions back from Austria during its second and third independence wars (in 1859 and 1866), not only had Austria been left to rule over lands still largely populated by Italians, but the Italian frontiers with Austria had been purposely drawn in a way unfavourable to Italy.[9] Austria retained control of the bastions of the Dolomites and Julian Alps, which functioned as 'a screen for offensive operations against the Italian plains'; meanwhile, Austrian control over the Adriatic islands and its northeastern ports 'converted that sea into an Austrian lake dominated by the Austrian navy.'[10]

The Treaty of London promised, in the event of a victory, that Italy would be awarded territories making up parts of present-day northeastern Italy, as well as the Istrian peninsula (now largely in Croatia) and, to its south, part of the Dalmatian coast and islands (also in present-day Croatia).[11] Some of these regions (those in present-day Trentino and other northeastern Italian territories, but also some enclaves in present-day Croatia)[12] had predominantly Italian populations. Others—notably, present day South-Tyrol, but also much of the portion of Dalmatia promised to Italy in the Treaty—did not. Any Italian claim over them could only be justified—if at all—on grounds of strategic security, not ethnology.[13] The promise of a portion of Dalmatia to Italy, in particular, had caused Russia to object vigorously during the treaty negotiations.[14] However, Italy indicated to the Allies that only the reward of strategic security in the Adriatic through control of a portion of the Dalmatian coast could justify its entry into war, hinting that its other claims could be obtained merely in exchange for neutrality.[15]

The town of Fiume (present-day Rijeka) in the Carnaro Gulf area, nestled between Istria and Dalmatia, was not included in the treaty's concessions to Italy, despite being predominantly inhabited by Italians, some of whom had advocated its annexation to Italy even before the war.[16] Exact figures are disputed, but irredentist writers cited census figures from 1915 putting the Italian population at 27,000 out of a total of 50,000,[17] with Slavs the second largest group at 15,000.[18] A note to article V of the Treaty of London stated: 'The Adriatic Territories enumerated below shall be attributed by the four Allied Powers to Croatia, Serbia and Montenegro,' listing Fiume as one such territory.[19]

It was sometimes stated that the Treaty of London's provision with respect to Fiume was a concession to Russia's design.[20] Russia had advocated the creation of two Slav nation-states—one of Catholic Slavs (roughly, Croatia) and the other of Southern Slavs, led by Serbia. In Russia's vision, Fiume would function as Croatia's trade outlet to the sea, while the port towns further down the eastern Adriatic coast would serve the same function for the Serbs.[21] It seems, however, that rather than making any concession to Russia's designs, Britain, France, and Italy were keen to contain the risk of Russia's hegemony.

Italy, which so far had had to contend with the threat of Austria-Hungary, expected that after the war its security might be put at risk rather by a Russia-backed Serbia. The Tsarist Empire's support of a larger Serbia was driven by its desire to replace Austria-Hungary as the leading power in the eastern Mediterranean, with an eye on the Adriatic ports.[22] Assigning some of Dalmatia's coastal towns to Italy in the Treaty of London was intended to offset this projected increase in Russian power in the Mediterranean.[23] For the same reason (keeping Russia's imperialistic ambitions at bay), Britain, France, and Italy were not necessarily keen to see the Habsburg Empire and its presence in the Mediterranean disappear after the war: until 1917 all the Allies would consider the continued existence of Austria-Hungary a crucial stabilising force in the region.[24] This explains why Fiume was excluded from the concessions to Italy. Fiume would serve as the main port town of Croatia,[25] which Britain, France, and Italy foresaw would either remain part of a much-reduced Austria-Hungary or possibly of Hungary alone (in the event of its separation from Austria). The plan was to ensure that the postwar successor of the Habsburg Empire would retain a portion of northern Adriatic coastline (including Fiume) to prevent Croatia from being absorbed into Russia-backed Serbia[26] and to not deprive it of its sole sea outlet for trade.[27]

REVISITING THE TREATY AT THE CONCLUSION OF HOSTILITIES

When the Allies managed to secure victory against the Central Powers despite Russia's exit from the war in December 1917, the assistance they received from the United States proved to be 'the deciding factor'.[28] This gave the United States tremendous clout at the Paris Peace Conference. The Allies, therefore, could not afford taking lightly President Woodrow Wilson's intention to regard the Treaty of London as a private affair that did not bind him, on the ground that he had never been formally notified of it (despite being made aware of its terms by Lord Balfour in 1917).[29] As a secret agreement, there is indeed a strong argument that the treaty was a political, rather than a legally binding, document.[30] Italy's foreign affairs minister, however, was quick to point out Wilson's double standard, as the US president was willing to admit the binding nature of the secret agreement between England, France, and Japan with respect to Shantung.[31]

Whatever its validity at international law, a number of developments called into question the wisdom of following through with the treaty at the end of the war. First, the Austro-Hungarian Empire was no more. Guaranteeing its survival to counteract Russian influence in the Balkans had no longer been necessary after Russia, following the 1917 revolution, had negotiated a separate peace with the Central Powers. The threat of an imperialistic Russia gaining influence over the eastern Mediterranean via its support for Serbia seemed to have evaporated. So had, therefore, Britain's and France's strategic incentive for ensuring that the Treaty of London be followed through.[32] Additionally, with Austria-Hungary out of the picture, the clauses of the London Treaty that Italy had insisted on for reasons of strategic security were deprived of their original (if not necessarily of any) rationale.[33]

Secondly, at the Peace Conference Italy had to reckon with a new entity: the nascent Kingdom of the Serbs, Croats, and Slovenes. The coming into being of the new Yugoslav state had been facilitated by Bolshevik Russia's renouncing its ambitions in the Adriatic[34] and prompted by its revealing the content of the (secretly negotiated) Treaty of London. This induced the Croats to side with the Serbs, even in an asymmetrical alliance, if that was the price to pay to put up an effective resistance to Italian claims in the eastern Adriatic.[35] The new kingdom declared any treaty null and void to the extent that it conflicted with the Yugoslavs' right to self-determination.[36] At the Paris Peace Conference, the committee representing the Yugoslav National Council in Zagreb insisted on drawing the line between Italy and Yugoslavia roughly where the 1914 frontier had been between Italy and Austria—a position that raised the eyebrows of even the most impassioned British pro-Yugoslavs and alienated potential supporters the Yugoslavs might otherwise have had in Italy.[37]

Indeed, Yugoslav claims sometimes encompassed not only Istria and Dalmatia but even portions of northeastern Italy that had been part of it since shortly after the country's unification, more than half a century before.[38] These claims were based in part on the outcomes of the Congress of Oppressed Nationalities, which Italy itself had hosted in 1918. The congress had been organised precisely in response to the terms of the Treaty of London, after these had been leaked to the leaders of the nascent Yugoslavia.[39] Whatever declaration or commitment was adopted at the congress did not technically bind the Italian government,[40] none of whose members had signed it; moreover, Italian prime minister Vittorio Emanuele Orlando, in addressing the congress, had made mention of Italy's need to secure 'defensible frontiers' and its intention to protect all 'Italian peoples'.[41] All the same, the congress had reaffirmed the right of people under foreign rule to organise themselves into politically independent nation-states. The Italian and Yugoslav delegates had specifically committed to recognise each other's sovereignty and to resolve amicably any territorial disputes on the basis of self-determination principles.[42] Burgwyn states that the 'impression left behind was that the Italians were prepared to renounce Dalmatia while the Yugoslavs would renounce Trieste and Istria.'[43]

In practice, however, until 1920 Italy—which had simply not anticipated, when negotiating the Treaty of London, that the emergence of a Yugoslav state might be in the cards—would refuse to recognise the new state and would maintain the diplomatic fiction that its interlocutor was the Kingdom of Serbs.[44] The Serbs had fought with, rather than against, the Allies; conversely, Italy had been confronted with fierce fighting from Croat troops in the service of the Austro-Hungarian Army until, and even after, the signing of the Armistice.[45] Prime Minister Orlando in late 1918 resented being pressed by the Allies to extend immediate recognition to a state which, in accordance with what had been established by its National Council in Zagreb, had unilaterally defined its own northwestern boundaries in a way that limited Italy to the line of the river Isonzo.[46]

Thirdly, if Croatia was now to be united with the southern Slavs, granting it Fiume might no longer be considered a matter of economic necessity. Even without Fiume, the Kingdom of Serbs, Croats, and Slovenes would 'possess an abundance of other ports in this same sea' to cater to its trade needs.[47] Conversely, Italy had suffered greater losses and borne greater burdens than reasonably anticipated as a result of revolutionary Russia's exit from the conflict and Austria-Hungary's redeployment of its forces against Italy; granting Italy Fiume could be seen as due compensation for this.[48] Having said this, no other Yugoslav port was nearly as well developed and well connected to the railway lines of the hinterland as Fiume; thus, if Yugoslavia was to be deprived of Fiume, an arrangement would have to be made for Yugoslav access to its port for several years, until such time as ports further south were developed and became fully operational.

Finally, and most crucially for our purposes, a key factor prompting a reevaluation of Italy's demands at the Peace Conference was the National Council of Fiume proclaiming the town's annexation to Italy on 30 October 1918.[49] Despite some irredentist advocacy,[50] Fiume had hardly been on the radar of the general Italian population and government until then,[51] explaining why it could be so easily omitted from Italy's demands in the Treaty of London. This all changed with the proclamation of annexation—a dramatic act that is liable to be misunderstood (as it was by Italy's Allies at Versailles) unless we peer at least briefly into Fiume's past.

FIUME/RIJEKA, FROM ROMAN COLONY TO ITALIAN ENCLAVE

The original town, Tharsatica, had been founded by the Romans around the second century AD, at the estuary of a river overlooked by a fortified hilltop settlement dating from the bronze age.[52] As a colony of the Roman Empire, the town enjoyed self-government: supreme political power was vested in two magistrates elected by a popular assembly.[53] Guarding Italy's eastern boundary in the fifth century, Tharsatica fell to the Goths, until Justinian drove them away and claimed the town as part of the Eastern Roman Empire in the sixth century. The town, suffering from incursions by the Avars, was destroyed by the Francs at the turn of the eighth century. Political organisation was only reestablished when, having been rebuilt as Fiume or Rijeka (both of which mean 'river'), it became a feudal possession of vassals of the Sacred Roman Empire in the twelfth to thirteenth centuries.[54]

By the fifteenth century the government of Fiume resembled the autonomous Italian mediaeval city-states (*comuni*), with two magistrates endowed with the executive power and a council of affluent and authoritative citizens which elected them and adopted the laws. But Fiume remained integrated into a feudal political structure, and as such the head of political power was formally the captain, who represented the emperor and had general oversight functions.[55] In 1530 Fiume received its statute from the Habsburgs, of whom the town had become a feudal possession in the 1460s.[56] The statute systematised, reelaborated, and updated several acts and statutes already in force.[57] Albeit reflecting elements of the constitutions governing Italian *comuni*, the 1530 statute fell short of granting the genuine political autonomy enjoyed by the latter, or by free imperial towns.[58] Nonetheless, the prerogatives and privileges articulated in the statute formed the basis of the future political autonomy of the town.[59]

Fiume sought to exercise a degree of not only internal but even external sovereignty, maintaining consular representatives in some Italian towns. It also paid homage to the emperor upon condition that its laws, freedoms, and immunities were preserved, and it did so in its own right, not as part of a broader province.[60] While many polities within the Habsburg Empire enjoyed (varying) levels of autonomy, Fiume's case is distinctive in that its municipal government managed to retain it for longer than most, even as other localities lost their powers to the empire's centralising tendencies in the seventeenth and eighteenth centuries.[61] Despite the population living largely off industry and trade already in the fifteenth century,[62] until the seventeenth century Fiume remained a military post of limited commercial importance, used to ward off the threat of invasion from central Asia. This strategic importance continued even after its economic development and into the twentieth century—particularly in terms of containing a Russian threat.[63]

It remains somewhat unclear exactly how the Italian cultural heritage and identity of Fiume took root and developed,[64] particularly because the town never came under the direct control of Venice.[65] There is, however, evidence of a bilingual tradition in Fiume that goes back centuries.[66] Toponyms indicate the coexistence of two civilizations—an Italian one associated with the town itself, seafaring and trade, and a Slav one in the hilly hinterland.[67] Disparate documentary sources indicate the presence, and possibly prevalence, of an Italian element already in the fourteenth and fifteenth century.[68] Fiume's legal officials and public notaries all came from Italy,[69] and the legal privileges granted in the 1530 statute began attracting a commercial class, including from the Italian coastline facing, across the sea, the Carnaro Gulf.[70] By the end of the sixteenth century the ruling classes bore almost entirely Italian surnames.[71] In the seventeenth century Fiume was being classified as Italian, as opposed to Croatian, in geographical scholarship.[72] Meanwhile the Habsburgs were relying on the Church of Rome to reestablish and consolidate order and orthodoxy in their dominions; this brought Jesuits and their educational institutions to Fiume in the seventeenth century, resulting in further Italianization.[73] In general, the Italian element increased over time and came to clearly predominate by the early twentieth century, through processes of immigration and acculturation.[74]

FIUME, CROATIA, AND HUNGARY

Croatia had entered a personal union with the kingdom of Hungary in the twelfth century,[75] meaning that the king of Hungary was also the king of Croatia. Hungary, after being defeated by the Ottomans, came under the protection of the Habsburgs in 1525,[76] and Croatia itself did so in 1527.[77] Although the Habsburgs had to proceed with caution in their dealings with both Hungary and Croatia so as not to alienate their loyalty,[78] with time the Habsburgs consolidated their power over both.[79]

Up to 1776, Fiume had been directly dependent on the Austrian monarchy, without being incorporated into one of the territorial entities that made up the Archduchy of Austria.[80] However, by this time it had become an increasingly important commercial outlet for Hungarian produce.[81] Thus, in 1776 Maria Theresa joined Fiume and its district to Croatia, and therefore Hungary.[82] Fiume had long feared the ambitions of neighbouring Croats to extend their control over the town,[83] and its highest officials made remonstrations, desiring the town to retain its provincial autonomy.[84] Three years later the arrangement was altered so as to annex Fiume—as *corpus separatum*—directly to Hungary, without its incorporation into Croatia (though the 1776 rescript providing for incorporation into Croatia was not expressly repealed).[85] The new situation pleased the Hungarians, who could thereby exert a more direct influence over Fiume through their governor. It also pleased the Fiumans, who had been historically suspicious of the Croats, and who would enjoy considerable autonomy thanks to Fiume's treatment as *corpus separatum*. This meant that, unlike other Hungarian towns, Fiume would not be within the purview of a local aristocratic committee represented in the Hungarian Diet—a committee which would, by geographical necessity, have been a Croatian one.[86] But this arrangement was not accepted by the Croats, resulting in a dispute about the town's political status, which explains much of the context to D'Annunzio's occupation after the war.[87]

Croatia did hold control of the town between 1848 and 1867. At the beginning of this period, Croatia was rebelling against Hungary's attempts at suppressing its former autonomy. In this, Croatia was in part supported by Austria, which had an interest in consolidating its own control over Hungary. In its attempt to establish itself as a separate political entity, Croatia demanded the annexation of both (Austrian) Dalmatia and Fiume.[88] Croat troops occupied Fiume after the Croat Diet claimed it for Croatia. Austria appears to have acquiesced, regarding Fiume 'as the reward of the Croatians for their fidelity to the Emperor' at a time when Hungary had tried to resist Austria's control.[89]

The Croats reassured the Fiumans that both municipal freedoms and the use of Italian would be preserved; no egregious abuses or inequities were recorded, for all that Fiuman and Hungarian historiography later tended to portray this period as one of unmitigated oppression.[90] Yet some of the political privileges of the town were abolished, its council was dissolved and replaced with a new body, and a process of Croatization began.[91] Both government and trade in Fiume had been carried out in Italian, 'the lingua franca of Adriatic urban culture',[92] but the Croat authorities made it clear that the preservation of Italian was a temporary concession and that the long-term goal would be to eliminate it from public use.[93] The Croats' attempts to normalise the status of Fiume as a Croat town by having it send representatives to their Diet in Zagreb was met with obstructionism by both the town representative authority and the population.[94] Economic considerations also contributed to the discontent with Croat rule. The Croats lacked the means to develop the port of the town, while neighbouring Trieste was flourishing thanks to the Austrians developing its infrastructure, thereby attracting businesses formerly operating from Fiume.[95]

In 1867, after Austria had experienced considerable setbacks as a result of Italy's independence wars and the Austro-Prussian war, Hungary was able to negotiate the institution of a double Austro-Hungarian monarchy. With their power increased, Hungary forced Croatia to give up its claims to independence from Hungary and regained control of Fiume.[96] Paragraph 66 of the document settling their differences (known as the *Nagoda*) was drafted in two different versions. Whereas the Croat version left the future of the town to further negotiations, the Hungarian version reinstated its status as Hungary's *corpus separatum*.[97] However, the original Croat document has a slip of paper pasted over the relevant passage, bearing a Croat translation of the Hungarian version of paragraph 66. The Croat Diet, so the story goes, had voted for Fiume's future to be determined at a later point in time, as per the original Croat text. After this, a falsification occurred, with the consequence that royal approval was given—in both the Hungarian and (falsified) Croat versions of paragraph 66—to Fiume's being Hungary's *corpus separatum.*[98] The story even has a name for the culprit of this forgery: Count Julius Andrassy.[99]

Research into the Diet records, if still in existence, might confirm to what version of the *Nagoda* the Croat Diet agreed. The story of the falsification of the *Nagoda*, however, smacks apocryphal—an account of events that it was politically expedient for Croat nationalists to consecrate as official history. Robert Willaim Seton-Watson, as we will see, was notoriously a passionate supporter of Yugoslavia's claims over Fiume, and he popularised the story in Britain. Yet even he had to use tentative language when endorsing this account: 'It thus *appears* that the definition of Fiume as "separatum sacrae regni coronae adnexum corpus" has never received the sanction of the Croatian Diet, and is a one-sided claim of Hungary' (emphasis added).[100]

Alternative explanations are both possible and plausible. The Croat version of the document may be patched at paragraph 66 simply because an amendment was agreed at the eleventh hour. After all, paragraph 66, in the version of the *Nagoda* receiving the royal approval and incorporated into article XXX of the Hungarian Constitution, does reaffirm Fiume's status as *corpus separatum* but expressly specifies that its legislative and governmental autonomy would be decided by agreement between the Hungarian Parliament, the Croat Diet, and the town itself.[101] Thus, according to the terms of the agreement receiving the royal approval, the Croat Diet retained a say in the practical political implications of Fiume's special status: this may have been an acceptable compromise for the Croats at the time. The very fact that, as Seton-Watson notes, the 'interpolated passage is not even in the same handwriting as the rest of the document',[102] far from supporting the theory of a forgery, may rather suggest that the change was a regular, if perhaps last minute, amendment.[103]

Be that as it may, Fiume effectively returned into Hungary's direct political orbit. In 1872 the Statute of the Free Town of Fiume and its District was passed, which each new governor of Fiume, upon his appointment by the king of Hungary, was required to solemnly promise to respect. The promise was delivered in Italian before the town's Municipal Council, which retained competence to rule over matters pertaining to the town's life and organisation.[104]

Hungarian rule in the last three decades of the nineteenth century was responsible both for modernising Fiume's infrastructure, leading to a thriving economy,[105] and for its further Italianization, as a result of Italian businessmen and entrepreneurs being encouraged to settle in town. At the same time, the development of Fiume caused Hungarians to take an ever-increasing interest in the port town, whose administration and education system they came to dominate. Accommodations were made for Italians (who tended to belong to the wealthier classes), with the marginalisation of (often less prosperous) Croats.[106]

For as long as Hungary was prepared to preserve the autonomy of the *corpus separatum*, Hungarian rule had suited Italian/Italianised Fiumans. This no doubt explains why Fiume witnessed no more than 'a rather moderate and nuanced irredentist practice in the second half of the 19th century'.[107] But in the last decade of the nineteenth century relations between Fiume and Hungary started to deteriorate, as a result of Hungary's changing policy orientations, connected with the influx of Hungarians into town.[108] This Hungarian population staffed the civil service and did not tend to settle long term;[109] yet the overall number of Hungarians 'was increasing fairly rapidly before the war.'[110] The perception amongst Italian Fiumans seems to have been that if Hungarian rule over Fiume were to end, the Hungarian population (reported to have grown from 379 to 6,400 between 1880 and 1915) would leave, as they were not truly invested in local life.[111]

FIUME'S DEMOGRAPHICS IN THE EARLY TWENTIETH CENTURY

In the Italian academic literature on Fiume's occupation, there is surprisingly little discussion of the complex demographics and ethnolinguistic politics of the town population in the years leading up to the war. Some Italian-language accounts dating from the war or immediate postwar years tend to give the impression of a sharp division between Fiumans properly so called—portrayed as Italian, middle class, and making up the majority of the town citizenry—and Croats, who tend to be othered as invariably working class and/or migrant and/or politically disengaged and/or dwelling in nearby Sušak, across the river, or in the hills rather than Fiume proper. While in many parts of the Habsburg Empire urban centres existed whose main language was different from that spoken in the surrounding countryside,[112] and while this linguistic pattern was also apparent in Fiume, it obscures a more complex reality.

In terms of ethnic preponderance, it has been estimated in a recent study that at the turn of the century almost 50 percent of the population was Italian and more than 30 percent Croat.[113] According to census figures, in 1910 49 percent of the population identified Italian as their first language and 73 percent was able to speak it.[114] A 1919 confidential handbook prepared under the direction of the historical section of the British Foreign Office suggests a higher figure, close to 55 percent: Fiume's 'population in 1910 was 49,806, of which 26 per cent spoke Serbo-Croatian, 13 per cent Magyar, 4.7 per cent German, and the rest, with few exceptions, Italian or Italian dialects'.[115] Whatever the exact figures, it does not seem in contention that Italians were by far the largest ethnic group, and those who advocated Fiume's annexation to Italy made much of this.

The political significance of the annexationists' claim about the town's predominantly Italian character was frequently challenged on two different grounds. First, it was claimed that large numbers of Italians present in Fiume were the artificial and recent result of a colonisation orchestrated by the Hungarians in the second half of the nineteenth century.[116] This was a *pièce de résistance* of Yugoslav nationalist propaganda,[117] but recent research indicates that the increase in the Italian population was a centuries-long, organic, and gradual process.[118] It is of interest that the Yugoslavs' charge of an orchestrated increase in the Italian population of the town is perfectly mirrored by the way in which annexationists made sense of the exponential growth of the Croat population since 1900. After the percentage of the Croat population halved in the last two decades of the nineteenth century as a result of a rapid growth in other ethnic elements, it had risen again by nearly 40 percent in a single decade between 1900 and 1910.[119] Just like Yugoslav nationalists claimed that Fiume's Italians had been artificially introduced by Hungarians, so Italian annexationists argued that this increase in the Croat population was less than spontaneous. They pointed out that 'thirty years ago [Sušak] was a little village with no special national character', and that it developed into a Croat stronghold only after the Croat government deliberately established offices there,[120] with the result that Croat businesses were now encroaching on the old town, bringing about undesirable demographic changes.[121]

Secondly, those who challenged the annexationists' reliance on Fiume's predominantly Italian population frequently argued that Croats outstripped Italians if the populations of Fiume and nearby Sušak, which functioned as a single economic unit and were only separated by a stream, were pooled.[122] It was estimated, specifically, that in 1918 the compound unit of Fiume-Sušak had a population composed of 41 percent Italians and 42 percent Slavs.[123] But this argument had no bite to the extent that the annexationists' official programme was confined to Fiume and its district (the *corpus separatum*), which had never included Sušak. The Italian government, too, in endorsing the demand for annexation, maintained that the river had 'always been a national and state boundary, the old city of Fiume being regarded as Hungarian, the eastern bank as Croatian'.[124]

Economically speaking, it made sense to treat Fiume and Sušak as interdependent. The latter had developed relatively recently as a result of Fiume's industrialization: the area on the other side of the river offered the flat land required for industrial establishments that Fiume itself lacked.[125] The timber wharves so important to Fiume's economy were in Sušak.[126] This led some

Italian anti-annexation political analysts to recommend the creation of an autonomous city-state around Fiume-Sušak,[127] but at times it also led annexationists to include the harbour alongside Fiume and its district in their territorial demands.[128] Thus, some annexationists wanted to have it both ways: to have Fiume annexed to Italy without Sušak and its majority Croat population, while also claiming for Fiume the part of the port that pertained to Sušak. Croats rightly complained about 'divid[ing] the town . . . while counting the harbour as a whole'.[129]

ETHNOLINGUISTIC IDENTITY AND POLITICS IN EARLY TWENTIETH-CENTURY FIUME

The growth of nationalist sentiment in the latter half of the nineteenth century complicated interethnic relations in Fiume. Simplifying somewhat, those who saw Fiume as pertaining to Croatia by right often conceptualised nationality in the essentialist terms of 'natural' belonging: Fiume was Croat *despite* its (purportedly) nonautochthonous Italian element. Conversely, those who claimed it as Italian emphasised an elective or voluntaristic conception of nationality: Fiume was Italian because it chose to be, despite being physically located in foreign territory.[130] These attitudes are still to some extent apparent in contemporary historiography. Italian historians (whether or not they approve of D'Annunzio's occupation) generally take at face value the postwar self-identification of many Fiumans as Italians. Meanwhile, their Croat counterparts confidently assert that 'Italy was not the homeland of Rijeka natives (Fiumams/*Fiumani*) on any basis whatsoever'[131] and that they were 'Italians who actually had nothing to do with Italy'.[132]

In the second half of the nineteenth century, Hungarians, interested in retaining control of the town and in warding off another Croat takeover, had set up an educational system with primary education provided in Italian and secondary education in Hungarian. During the period of Croat rule, secondary education had been exclusively in Croat; after Hungarians regained control, the Croat gymnasium was moved to Sušak.[133] Fiume's professional middle classes—who occupied the town centre in greater and greater numbers—were thus either Hungarians or Italian/Italianised Fiumans fluent in Hungarian. Croats who did not speak Italian were effectively cut off from these educational and professional opportunities,[134] as well as from political ones, for Hungarian law restricted suffrage to the Hungarian and Italian elite.[135] By 1915 the majority of the Slav population (some of them economic migrants from Croatia, and many indeed residing in Sušak) may well, as annexationist voices remarked, have had little involvement in the political life of the town;[136] but it seems clear that this was not by choice.

At the same time, the narrative of Fiumans as essentially Italian and middle class obscures the presence of an Italian working class,[137] a Croat middle class, and the fact that many Fiuman Italians were actually Italianised Croats.[138] It was not uncommon for Fiumans who qualified (for the purposes of the census, but also socially and politically) as Italians to have borne surnames of Slavic origin. A look at the names of the members of the (Italian) National Council, in its different incarnations prior to and during D'Annunzio's occupation, is instructive. Fiumans, apparently, made no assumptions about your national affiliation purely on the basis of your surname.[139] The process worked both ways, for we see many Italian names in the clandestine organisation *Galeb*, whose goal was to put up armed resistance against D'Annunzio's occupation in the name of Yugoslav interests.[140]

Yet there are reasons to interrogate, specifically, the process of Italian acculturation in Fiume. This appears to have been ongoing, spontaneously, for the previous several centuries,[141] aided by intermarriages and by the fact that Italian was the language of schools, courts of law, politics, trade, and seafaring.[142] The emergence of nationalist movements in the nineteenth century seems to have ideologically inflected this phenomenon in ways that made it for some more compulsive and for everyone more politically fraught. Badurina, for instance, draws attention to the coercive elements—anti-Slav prejudice, discrimination, and stereotyping (generally around the *topos* of civilised Italian townsfolk versus uncouth Croat hill people)[143]—that induced some Croats to Italianise as a matter of survival strategy. She notes the political and social advantages attaching to being Italian, access to which was contingent on electing to be Italian rather than proof of ancestry.[144]

Apart from these more coercive processes, we can also speculate that, starting from the second half of the nineteenth century, when the activities of Italian cultural circles aimed at raising patriotic awareness intensified, Italian Fiumans had become particularly effective ambassadors of their own culture. As a result, a number of elite Fiumans of Croat heritage appear to have experienced feelings directed at Italians and their culture which ranged from allophilia (comfortably coexisting with their own Croat national pride) to xenocentrism.

An example of allophilia is Rikard Lenac, who, as we will see, briefly held power in Fiume on behalf of the new Yugoslav kingdom upon the dissolution of the Habsburg Empire in autumn 1918. Lenac's genuine love of Italian culture and his commonplace use of the Italian language with family members did not displace a strong sense of Croat national belonging, and of Croatia's rights over Fiume.[145] Indeed, he and other Croat intellectuals in Fiume even credited the Italian *Risorgimento* that had led to unification of the country with modelling and inspiring their own patriotic sentiment for a free and self-ruling Croatia.[146] On the other hand stands Lenac's cousin, Lionello

Lenaz, who drafted the text of Fiume's National Council's 30 October 1918 proclamation of annexation to Italy[147] and would be appointed rector for education in D'Annunzio's 1920 provisional Fiume government. Lenaz demonstrated complete cultural alienation with respect to Croatia and a xenocentric identification with the Italian community, accompanied by palpable anti-Slav sentiment.[148] Although for many Fiumans a non-Italian heritage was no bar to qualifying as fully Italian, people such as Lenaz were ridiculed by their Croat-identifying fellow townsfolks as 'elective Italians', 'renegade Yugoslavs', and traitors.[149]

The terminological choices of some Croat-identifying Fiuman Croats are also interesting: by using interchangeably either the word Italians or terms (sometimes pejorative ones) that modify the words 'Fiumans' and 'Italians' to connote informal membership of an informal group,[150] they synecdochically imply that (all) the Italians of Fiume were really Croats acting under false pretences. This implication is factually incorrect,[151] but it is consistent with the views of some nineteenth-century Croat intellectuals, who subscribed to a strictly essentialist view of nationality, and who were thus able to explain away the Italian language and culture of the Fiumans as form rather than substance. These might go so far as to claim that even if the Fiumans may have spoken in Italian, their thoughts were Croat.[152] Father Macdonald too, whom we have already met in the introduction, in his account of pre-Dannunzian and Dannunzian Fiume switches back and forth between the expression 'Italians' and 'Italianophiles'.[153] In line with the sentiments of some Croats (whose exaggerations at least can be excused by their having genuine reasons to feel aggravated),[154] Macdonald claimed that Italian-identifying Croats in Fiume were allochthonous opportunistic fraudsters and unscrupulous adventurers motivated by personal gain,[155] that the town's Italian political leaders were 'well-known Croatian renegades who made no scruple to turn their coats to suit the times',[156] and that 'the vaunted *Italianity* of Fiume' was 'artificial and evanescent'.[157]

Such claims are contradicted by the endurance and fanaticism of the patriotic sentiments of several Italianised Croats and other Italianised southeastern Europeans who were at the forefront of Fiume's annexationist movement. Nonetheless, Kirchner Reill notes that the specific performance of Fiuman Italianness orchestrated by Fiume's National Council between autumn 1918 and the end of D'Annunzio's occupation in late 1920 involved a number of political leaders and citizens whose nationalistic fervour is open to dispute.[158] She takes this as indicating, along with other factors (such as the deliberately piecemeal and partial, rather than abrupt and wholesale, Italianization of the legal system),[159] that the National Council had not just ideological but also pragmatic-opportunistic reasons for advocating annexation to Italy. Essentially, Reill argues that the National Council chose the most eligible candidate to replace Hungary as Fiume's patron and sponsor,[160] and its understanding of annexation and nation remained exquisitely Fiume-centric.[161] To the extent that much of the town citizenry (for very many of whom Italian was not their first language)[162] went along with this performance of Italianness, it was because it shared these pragmatic-opportunistic motivations and assumed that annexation would be on Fiume's own terms.[163]

FIUME IN THE PREWAR AND WAR YEARS (1898–1918)

With these contextual points in mind, we can return to the leadup to the proclamation of annexation to Italy by Fiume's Italian National Council in 1918. From the end of the middle ages until the mid-nineteenth century and beyond, Liburnia, to which Fiume geographically belonged, had rarely been seen as part of Italy in political circles.[164] In the process that led to Italy's unification (and apparently even as far back as the time when the town was briefly under the control of Napoleon),[165] Fiume had been occasionally considered by Italian political elites as belonging to Italy, marking as it did—so it was believed—Italy's natural eastern boundary.[166] But these are exceptions, and several statements are documented from prominent *Risorgimento* men showing that they regarded Fiume to lie beyond Italy's rightful borders.[167] Hungarian policies directed at altering the town's cultural identity set in motion a process that would change all this. These policies appear to have been largely driven by the new ideology of the nation-state, which demanded congruence between the political organisation of the state and its cultural identity, replacing the political and ethnic pluralism characteristic of old European empires.[168]

In 1898 the Hungarian government set up a local Hungarian administrative authority with the power to review the decisions of the traditional governing body of the town—the (Italian) Municipal Council. After four years of activism, Fiume's Autonomist Party managed to have the new authority abolished.[169] The Autonomist Party had been created in 1896 to oppose Hungary's new centralising tendencies, although the party remained formally committed to recognising Hungary's rule as the best way to avert a Croatian takeover.[170] Its brand of irredentism was, in this sense, cultural rather than political[171]—something that Hungary might, in its own interest, have worked with rather than against.

But the policy of Magyarising the town continued. Hungarians took over all state primary and secondary education, limiting movement between Fiume and both Italy and Istria, requiring tertiary education to be undertaken in Hungary, making it easier to remove Italian nationals resident in Fiume, and expelling political activists.[172] The result was a deepening of Italian patriotic sentiment in a town that had not had any serious irredentist tradition to speak of.[173]

Much of the contest between Hungarians and Italians played out around symbolic spaces—such as the Municipal Council's decision to rename some streets in 1910 after the names of famous Italian personalities, and popular protests against bilingual signage in the new streetcars.[174] There was a flurry of activity among cultural groups and networks devoted to the cultivation of Italian patriotic values,[175] whose work had begun in the second half of the nineteenth century.[176] *La Giovine Fiume* (Young Fiume), which had been created around 1905 by young irredentists, advocated annexation to Italy. Some of its members had been university students in Italy; their ranks were increased by 'hot-blooded secondary schoolers who first and foremost longed for physical altercations [with Croats] on Rijeka's streets'.[177] The organization clashed with what it saw as the lukewarm patriotism of the Autonomist Party and was dissolved by the Hungarian government in 1912.[178] During World War I, several Fiuman volunteers enlisted in the Italian Army.[179]

In 1913 the Municipal Council was dissolved after its vote of no confidence for the Hungarian government. Hungarian police forces were posted in the town; with their connivance, a purportedly Italian terrorist attack was simulated in 1914, as a pretext to justify repression, although the plot was uncovered by the Autonomist Party.[180] Despite the fact that Hungarians—making up a relatively small percentage of the population—had at their disposal nearly half of the votes, at the elections of 1914 it was determined more prudent to leave the floor to Italian lists, and the Autonomist Party gained control of the Municipal Council.[181] However, the Hungarians dissolved it again the following year and installed an administration more sympathetic to Hungary.[182] The new municipal authority now included a number of Hungarian councillors.[183] The following year the streets of the town received new Hungarian names.[184]

In 1916, the Hungarian border police was replaced by the Hungarian state police and took over from the local municipal police forces.[185] Hungarian police abuses intensified during the war years, when many Fiumans came under suspicion of disloyalty to the Hungarian government.[186] Italian cultural associations were dissolved, and Italian citizens resident in Fiume were deported[187] or interned along with irredentists.[188] This was consistent with Austria-Hungary's wartime policies towards its Italian-language subjects: where not conscripted, they were variously subjected to surveillance, deprivation of liberty, mass deportations, and detention in concentration camps. Such policies, rather than any widespread and genuine irredentist feeling, are argued to have been chiefly responsible for the growth of support for Fiume's annexationist movement during the war years and its immediate aftermath.[189]

A secret committee with the mission of organising and mobilising the citizens to ensure an Italian future for Fiume was created in 1918.[190]

In the autumn of 1917, the Hungarian councillors considered further increasing their number within the municipal authority, requiring that one of the vice presidents should be Hungarian, permitting the use of Hungarian during the authority's discussions and in citizens' paperwork, and requiring the use of Hungarian alongside Italian for all public notices. However, as shown in a remarkable confidential document—reproduced in a book authored by the irredentist Edoardo Susmel[191] (later secretary general of the regency proclaimed by D'Annunzio in Fiume in 1920)[192]—the councillors determined that under the circumstances these moves would be counterproductive. Fiume's political autonomy no longer exceeded that enjoyed by any Hungarian town; thus, the population's steadfast attachment to the Municipal Council's Italian character had symbolic but no practical value, except for its vital function of constraining the political influence of the Croats.[193]

THE CROAT NATIONAL COMMITTEE AND THE YUGOSLAV OCCUPATION

Plans to make the town more Hungarian and to root out Italian dissent came to an abrupt halt when Fiume became free of Hungarian control, as a result of Hungary's new minister for external affairs requesting a separate armistice with the Allies on 28 October.[194] Croat troops proceeded to occupy the town, while a Croat National Committee constituted itself in Sušak (which, as we have seen, lay across the river, outside Fiume's traditional *corpus separatum*) and took possession of Fiume's governor's palace.[195] The committee did so in the name of the National Council of Zagreb, which—having constituted itself on 6 October 1918[196]—had unilaterally declared Fiume part of the new Kingdom of Serbs, Croats, and Slovenes.[197] The Zagreb government charged Rikard Lenac with assuming power in Fiume.[198] Reassurances were given that everyone's personal liberty and property would be respected regardless of nationality.[199]

For all that the brand of Croat nationalism cultivated by the Croat intelligentsia in Fiume did not always sit comfortably with the Yugoslav national mythology underpinning the new Yugoslav state, there were great expressions of patriotic enthusiasm coming from the Croat population of Fiume.[200] The reaction of Italian Fiumans was muted.[201] Only ten days before, Andrea Ossoinack, member of the Hungarian Parliament for Fiume, had declared—to the outrage of the Hungarian press—that Fiume asserted its right to be Italian in light of President Wilson's self-determination principle.[202] This had been as much in reaction to Hungary's increasingly heavy-handed rule since the turn of the century as to ward off the very peril that had now materialised: the town's absorption into Croatia and, via it, Yugoslavia.

Some Fiumans later reported to British observers Yugoslav attempts to introduce 'harsh repressive measures' and to intimidate the population through continuous 'rattle of rifles and machine guns' during nighttime.[203] While the latter sounds probable on the part of occupying troops,[204] the former would be wholly uncharacteristic of what we know of Lenac. Allegations of repression at the hands of the Yugoslav authorities appear to have been either manufactured or considerably inflated, in a bid to justify Italian control of the town. Indeed, British military sources report that, while Lenac himself admitted that looting and stealing (which he had tried to control) had taken place, Italians who alleged oppression and ill treatment during Lenac's short rule were 'unable to produce any facts'.[205] Lina Waterfield had it on the authority of an Italian admiral that, while looting had occurred, the population, when questioned, had reported no deaths or cases of ill treatment.[206]

Italian Fiumans had, nonetheless, well-founded fears of being made to lose their cultural and linguistic identity in the event of Fiume being incorporated into the Yugoslav state. Indeed, the Yugoslav delegation itself at Versailles submitted that 'Fiume, if left to herself, would be Slav again in less weeks than it took the Magyars years to Italianize her'.[207] The statement betrays a determination to ignore the town's centuries-long Italian heritage, as well as to treat its Italian character as an artefact of Hungarian politics; and it implies that no efforts were contemplated, or indeed considered desirable, to preserve such character in the event of absorption into Croatia. The Fiumans' deep mistrust of the Yugoslavs was also due to the fact, as remarked by British observers, that the Croat troops that now ensured Lenac's hold on power had been fighting against Italy in the army of Austria-Hungary up until the signing of the Armistice.[208]

Yet alongside such legitimate concerns, there is evidence of xenophobic motivations playing a role in Fiumans' opposition to Croat control.[209] British observers declared that the 'Hungarians and Italians apparently agree in being equally contemptuous of the Croats.'[210] The irredentist Susmel, for example, wrote that it was essential that the world understood that 'the will of [Fiume's] people could not be handed over and be at the mercy of an inferior race who tended desperately to prey upon this, our Fiume, which had always escaped its contact like a beautiful woman instinctively flees a boorish touch'.[211] Indeed, the tradition of Italian irredentism in the eastern Adriatic cannot easily be disentangled from anti-Slav sentiment and outright xenophobia.[212] According to Lloyd George, this antagonism was largely due to the Habsburgs using the Croats to 'hunt, imprison and execute Italian patriots', burning 'into the Italian heart [the conviction] that the Croat was the instrument of Austrian tyranny'.[213]

Responding to the appeals of Fiuman irredentists/annexationists, an Italian destroyer moored at Fiume's wharf on 4 November 1918, later joined by two more ships, but the crew received the order not to disembark.[214] A Serb battalion then entered the town and occupied Fiume's public buildings on either 14 November[215] or 15 November.[216] It is not generally remarked that this belonged to the Army of the Orient, under French command, and had been dispatched by order of General Franchet D'Espèrey.[217] The timing here is crucial: on 13 November the Allies had signed the Belgrade Armistice with Hungary,[218] which could be interpreted as authorising them to occupy Fiume. Significantly, it was Franchet D'Espèrey himself who had been chiefly responsible for negotiating the Belgrade Armistice, and he took the view that Fiume was 'included in the territory comprised in the terms of the Armistice concluded with the Hungarian forces'.[219] Franchet D'Espèrey no doubt knew that Italian naval forces were in Fiume's harbour ready to—but as yet instructed not to—disembark. Clearly, the French sought to preempt the Italian move by sending the Serb battalion as soon as the Belgrade Armistice gave them the semblance of a legal basis to take swift action.

Predictably, Italy sent more troops to Fiume by sea. The Serbs threatened to fire on them if they attempted to disembark, with French naval forces on site 'supporting, or at least tolerating the Serbians'.[220] On 17 November, Admiral Rainer gave the Serbs an ultimatum to withdraw and ordered his men to disembark, antagonising French and British naval officers, who opposed Italian landing, partly on the ground that the only lawful justification they saw for it—the risk of Serb troops looting the town—was nonexistent.[221] The Italian landing remained controversial, and a commission of enquiry on Fiume was later established as part of the Inter-Allied Commission of Admirals for the Adriatic. In January 1919 the British delegate, Rear Admiral Kiddle, would complain that the 'Italian Government is making every effort to prevent the whole circumstances of the Italian landing at Fiume from being put on official record. No doubt they fear that their landing had no justification and was carried out in direct breach of faith.'[222] His Italian counterpart, Admiral Mola, maintained that the landing had 'put an end to the unjust and dangerous state of things which was brought about by the constitution at Fiume of a Croatian Government.'[223]

THE ITALIAN OCCUPATION

While Admiral Rainer ordered his men to land, General di San Marzano, commanding one of the columns which were marching on the town by land, announced, at the Italian prime minister's behest, that he was taking charge in the name of the Allies. He thereby relieved an unwilling but compliant Lenac of the town's control.[224] While di San Marzano purported to take control in the name of the Allies, it seems clear that the Italians were acting practically unilaterally. The occupation became Inter-Allied—or ostensibly Inter-Allied—in an attempt to normalise the situation. Pichon, French minister for foreign affairs, later declared that Britain and France had managed, not without difficulties, to establish the Inter-Allied character of the occupation.[225]

Note that the Fiumans had been clamouring for the Italians to disembark for two weeks, but the Italian troops had been holding off. The decisive factor that prompted the Italian occupation was the French sending Serb troops to occupy the town. As Rear-Admiral Kiddle noted in his reports to Britain, 'The Italians had to act rapidly as General Franchet Espèrey had already decided to occupy Fiume, and his Serbian troops actually arrived on 15th November and French troops were following them.'[226] Italian self-restraint (quite remarkable up to then, considering that later the Allies accused Italy of all manner of excesses) was thrown to the wind the moment its political and strategic expediency appeared undermined by Franchet D'Espèrey's preemptive move. No wonder that, once the Italians did descend upon town, British officers remarked that the 'Italian occupation has all the appearance of an annexation to the Italian crown'.[227]

Britain and France quickly resolved to send in their own troops, the view being taken, particularly in French political quarters, that 'the only way to prevent real trouble is as far as possible to associate English and French troops with Italian troops in any occupation on the eastern shore of the Adriatic'.[228] Even so, one month later British sources would comment that the 'occupation is entirely Italian, it is an Allied occupation in name only'.[229] In January the British delegate to the Inter-Allied Commission of Admirals for the Adriatic, Rear-Admiral Kiddle, together with his French and American colleagues, would try to remedy this situation. They proposed a reduction of the Italian contingent in Fiume and the dispatch to town of a Serb battalion and a French one, to join the American and British battalions already present.[230] The British government was in favour of implementing these recommendations,[231] yet it appears that there was no follow-up. Presumably, the other Allies were persuaded that a change might do more harm than good in the politically fraught climate of Fiume and given the delicate negotiations underway at Versailles.

The Serbian government, in protesting with the British foreign secretary against the arrival of the Italian troops, dubiously portrayed what appears to have been undoubtedly inconvenient measures—such as the closing of schools or taking over of the ferry service—as making 'life so utterly impossible for the population that it will not be surprising if serious civil strife ensues.'[232] But the worst that the mayor of Sušak had to report by early January 1919 was that Italian 'troops were arbitrarily billeted without reference to him, and that in some cases they took school-houses'; while Croat residents of occupied local villages, when interviewed, 'all said they hated the Italians . . . but they had no complaints against the behaviour of the soldiers.'[233]

Having said this, British reports indicated the Italian forces' heavy handedness in managing the situation,[234] the Italian command's politically motivated uses of censorship powers,[235] and a permissive attitude towards anti-Slav propaganda and demonstrations.[236] In practice, it seems that many of the more objectionable measures or actions were taken, rather than by the troops, by young militant organizations[237] or by Fiume's autochthonous (Italian) civil authorities, generally with the Italian command's tolerance.[238] Yet the latter is also reported to have followed up on requests from the Allies to curb some of the most egregious actions of fanatical annexationists.[239] Either way, British reports note that 'Serbians and Yugo Slavs . . . look upon [the French] and us as their natural protectors against the rudeness and insolence of the Italians.'[240] Ironically, as Lina Waterfield remarked in connection with reports of the Italian authorities' politically motivated expulsion orders and their arbitrary use of censorship powers, the 'suppression of any national life was [just] what Italians suffered in Dalmatia and Trieste from Austria who used the Croats as a thorn in their flesh.'[241]

Captain Henderson's perceptive remarks about the Italo-Slav relations in Cattaro (Kotar) throw light on the mutual distrust and dislike between Yugoslav residents and Italian troops in the area. There, he reported, the Italians had 'shown a remarkable lack of tact at the very outset . . . march[ing] through the town with a much superior force [than the other Allied troops], with colours flying and the band playing the national Anthem'. However, Henderson continued,

> They certainly had some provocation. They see every Allied flag flown by the inhabitants except their own, every Allied officer saluted except theirs. Having beaten Austria, thus rendering the Jugo Slav movement possible, and having done much for the Serbians, the Italians profess their inability to understand this hostile attitude. The Italians are perhaps less inclined than some Nations might be to make allowances which in the circumstances would appear to be so necessary. They tend to become themselves excited and to consider their honour offended.[242]

In Fiume, such dynamics between the local Slav population and the occupying Italian troops were no doubt exacerbated by two circumstances that emboldened the troops in their proprietary attitude and intensified Yugoslav fears that the town would indeed end up being assigned to Italy. The first was the town's Italian identity. The second was the fact that Fiume's Italian National Council had formally announced their and the Fiumans' intention that Fiume should be annexed to Italy. We will return to this shortly. For the time being, suffice to say that the National Council was Fiume's 'revolutionary government',[243] which the French, American, and British delegates of the Inter-Allied Commission of Admirals for the Adriatic recommended should be deprived of any executive power,[244] and which the former two would have liked to abolish altogether.[245]

THE LEGAL BASIS OF THE OCCUPATION

The legal basis for di San Marzano's occupation was, according to Italian generals, 'the faculty permitted to the Italian Command to occupy strategic points located beyond the Armistice line'.[246] This appears to refer to article 4 of the Villa Giusti Armistice. Indeed, it has been argued that the legal basis of the occupation was either article 4 or article 6 or both.[247] Article 4 authorised the Allied Powers to occupy any strategic point in Austria-Hungary where it was necessary in order to maintain order or make possible military operations. Article 6 provided that local authorities, under the control of Inter-Allied troops, would provisionally administer the 'evacuated territories of Austria-Hungary'.[248]

If these articles, however, authorised di San Marzano's occupation, it would appear that they would have authorised an occupation as soon as the first Italian ships reached Fiume on 4 November, for the Armistice had been signed on 3 November. However, for a time the view was apparently taken that Italian troops did not have permission to occupy territories not included in the concessions made to it by the Treaty of London, which excluded Fiume.[249] Before di San Marzano took over control of the town, British naval officers were expressing the similar view that 'Fiume, being outside Istria, cannot be occupied within the terms of the Armistice'.[250] The fact that the French did not send Serb troops sooner suggests that they may have taken a similar view of what the Villa Giusti Armistice authorised them to do with respect to Fiume. On a literal reading, such restrictive interpretation appears hard to justify with respect to article 4, which is phrased very broadly and would seem to have lawfully authorised either the French-Serb or Italian occupation. Yet everyone concerned appears to have interpreted article 4, initially, in a more restrictive way.

Conversely, the suitability of article 6 to legitimate either the Italian or French-Serb occupation is open to doubt. This is because the expression 'evacuated territories of Austria-Hungary' may have excluded Fiume. Article 6 provided that local authorities would provisionally administer the 'evacuated territories of Austria-Hungary' under the control of Inter-Allied troops.[251] The expression 'evacuated territories of Austria-Hungary' appears to refer to article 1, which required Austria-Hungary not only to evacuate any foreign territories invaded since the beginning of the war but also to withdraw behind a certain line specified in the article, effectively requiring it to vacate some of its own former territories.[252] Notably, article 1 did not expressly either include Fiume among these territories, or exclude it from them.

Franchet D'Espèrey apparently took the view that the Belgrade Armistice had solved the matter. The Belgrade Armistice was a military convention regulating the conditions under which the Villa Giusti Armistice was to be applied in Hungary. As such, it can be read as qualifying the Villa Giusti Armistice. As we have seen, the French general is reported to have 'considered Fiume as included in the territory comprised in the terms of the Armistice concluded with the Hungarian forces'.[253] But was he correct? Article 1 of the Belgrade Armistice required Hungary to withdraw from, among others, 'Croatia-Slavonia' and authorised the Allies to occupy the evacuated territories of Hungary (including 'Croatia-Slavonia') 'on the conditions laid down by the general commander in chief of the Allied Armies.' But like the Villa Giusti Armistice, article 1 of the Belgrade Armistice made no mention of Fiume. While Fiume had certainly been evacuated *de facto* by the Hungarians, whether or not it was *de jure* one of the 'evacuated territories of Austria-Hungary' for the purposes of article 1 of the Belgrade Armistice (and hence, arguably, for the purposes of article 6 of the Villa Giusti Armistice) would seem to depend on whether Fiume was part of 'Croatia-Slavonia' (article 1 of the Belgrade Armistice). But whichever way one looks at it, the answer seems to be that it was not. If Fiume, as Hungary maintained, was *corpus separatum* of Hungary, then it was clearly not part of 'Croatia-Slavonia' and was thereby not one of the 'evacuated' territories of Austria-Hungary; it therefore could not be legitimately occupied pursuant to either article 1 of the Belgrade Armistice or article 6 of the Villa Giusti Armistice. If, on the other hand, after 1867 Fiume had not returned to its status as *corpus separatum* of Hungary, then the status of the town had remained indefinite, to be decided at a future point (in accordance with the original, unamended Croat version of the *Nagoda*). This would have left Fiume in a limbo, but the implication is the same: it could not be lawfully occupied because whatever Fiume was, it still was not (unlike its pre-1867 status) part of 'Croatia-Slavonia'.

Thus, although both French-Serb and Italian troops proceeded to occupy the town on the basis, apparently, of the Belgrade Armistice, the surest (and only) lawful basis for their occupation preexisted that Armistice and was article 4 of the Villa Giusti Armistice.

THE NATIONAL COUNCIL'S PROCLAMATION OF ANNEXATION

Even before the arrival of di San Marzano and the Inter-Allied forces, Italian Fiumans had anticipated the Croats' move to take control at the end of October and stirred into action. By this time even many supporters of the Autonomist Party had become convinced that the only way to effectively protect Fiume's identity was by annexing it to Italy.[254] The day before Lenac assumed power on behalf of Zagreb, Italian Fiumans had instituted a civic militia, largely made up of volunteer teenage boys.[255] After that, Fiume's newly constituted Italian National Council had taken swift action. Gathering in the municipal palace on 30 October, the National Council had declared not to recognise its Croat counterpart—the Croat National Committee in Sušak—and invoked the right to self-determination to declare the town's annexation to the 'motherland' Italy.[256] The National Council added that it considered the current administration of the town a provisional solution and entrusted its fate to the United States, 'mother of freedom and universal democracy.'[257] As the National Council put it to the US Senate approximately one year later, the town, upon the dissolution of the Austro-Hungarian Empire, could have joined Italy by historical right, but 'it acknowledged a superior and more universal right in the self-determination principle proclaimed by your President'; its decision to have Fiume annexed to Italy, the National Council argued, was then 'fully valid on the legal plane'.[258] The National Council also insisted, in a subsequent letter to US senator Lodge, that annexation was genuinely desired by the town itself, rather than demanded by Italy.[259]

When Italian troops made Lenac resign its powers, General di San Marzano effectively entrusted the National Council with the government of the town, which it would retain until and throughout D'Annunzio's occupation. It is almost certainly false that the National Council was guilty of all the evildoing with which many of its detractors charged it. I have already had reason to question the credibility of Father Macdonald, and the testimony of a number of others is also suspect. For example, much as one is inclined to believe that he must have had some reason for complaint, it is hard to take entirely seriously the testimony of Ruggero Gotthardi, founder of Fiume's Autonomist Democratic Party (not the same as the much older Autonomist Party discussed earlier). Gotthardi, who claimed to be 'homeless, fugitive, persecuted and menaced by death', described the National Council as 'hyenas greedy of gold, malefactors of the worst kind', 'not even born in the country', 'for the most part sons of Slav fathers, hence renegades of the worst kind [whose] . . . sole object . . . is to rob the town'. They 'suppressed by terror' 'any protesting voice' and 'inflamed the minds of idealistic youths and captivated the hearts of susceptible maidens with handsome soldiers'.[260] Gotthardi's overblown rhetoric has much in common with Croat propaganda. His insistence that the National Council had made themselves rich at the expense of Fiume and wanted annexation merely to hold on to power and to finance a luxurious lifestyle makes the allegation that he was being paid by the Belgrade government not improbable.[261]

Nonetheless, there is evidence of the National Council's anti-Slav propaganda and discrimination, both before and after D'Annunzio's arrival.[262] Discriminatory measures include cases of not granting business permits to Croats,[263] police charging Croats who denied that Fiume was Italian with inciting hatred among nationalities,[264] and abuses in the use of expulsion orders.[265] At the same time, there is also evidence that measures directed at Italianising the town were either optional (as in the case of laws providing for the conversion of non-Italian surnames to Italian ones)[266] or, where technically compulsory (as in the case of using Italian in business paperwork), that they were not strictly enforced. Kirchner Reill shows that, for all the rhetoric of its propaganda office,[267] the National Council was more concerned with displaying Italianness to outsiders than eliminating non-Italianness and converting the citizens' souls.[268]

ORIGINS OF THE NATIONAL COUNCIL

There are different accounts of how the Italian National Council came into being. Klinger argues that the National Council was the entity that could be seen as continuing Fiume's prewar municipal representation.[269] Leeden shares this view, arguing that the National Council was the new name Fiume's previous governing body, the Municipal Council, gave itself on 30 October, the day after its membership had been expanded considerably.[270] Other accounts, on the other hand, emphasise discontinuity, rather than continuity, between the National Council and the previous constitutional order. De Vergottini states that the National Council constituted itself on 17 October 1918, quick on the heels of the Austrian emperor's attempt to salvage the monarchy by providing for the transformation of the empire into a federation of independent states under the Habsburgs.[271] Martini states that the National Council came into being on 30 October following a vote of the people on that date.[272] Susmel provides perhaps a particularly reliable account, given that he was actively involved in the processes of pro-Italian mobilisation in those days. According to him, on 29 October the first Italian flag was displayed from the balcony of the Philarmonic Hall, where citizens spontaneously began to congregate, forming 'the first hard core of what was to be the National Council.'[273] Ossoinack gave the same date to the Peace Conference, explaining that it was the day when the Hungarian authorities had left. The National Council had been created in protest against the Croat occupation, and its Constitution had been approved by acclamation in the public square thronged with several thousand people, which, Ossoinack argued, made it a legitimate and representative body.[274] In short, the National Council was a body claiming to rightfully represent the people of Fiume, it supervened on both the Hungarian administration and the previous municipal representative authority, the Municipal Council, and its membership at least partly overlapped with the latter.

The Hungarian governor of Fiume, upon leaving town prior to the impending arrival of Croat troops in late October, had handed over his powers to the mayor of Fiume, Antonio Vio, on the understanding that the following day they would be formally transferred to the Croat National Committee, if only to avoid bloodshed.[275] Vio—who would shortly become a member of the Managing Committee of the National Council[276]—failed to follow through with the transfer.[277] Nonetheless, the Zagreb Council, in whose name the Croat National Committee had taken control of Fiume's Governor Palace, purported to be the legitimate successor of the dissolved Austro-Hungarian Empire. The Italian National Council, unable to assume authority over the seat of government of the former Hungarian administration (now occupied by the Croats), set up a 'city government', effectively taking over from and replacing the previous municipal authority.[278] Lenac confirmed that, on assuming the governorship of Fiume, he had left the 'Municipal Government as it was'.[279]

The result was a fortuitous arrangement of divided powers—with the Croat National Committee succeeding the Hungarian governor and the Italian National Council succeeding the Municipal Council. This may have offered di San Marzano, when he occupied the town in the name of the Allies less than three weeks later, a pretext to legally rationalise his support for the National Council's claims to authority, at the expense of those of the Croat National Committee. After all, those who carried forward the legacy of Fiume's traditional municipal authority, the Municipal Council, had, *prima facie*, a rather straightforward claim to being regarded as the kind of 'local authority' to which, in accordance with article 6 of the Armistice, provisional administration of the formerly imperial territories should be entrusted. Conversely, it was less clear that the Croats, who had supervened on the imperial administration in the name of a council based in Zagreb, could be so regarded. This assumes, however, that article 6 of the Armistice applied to Fiume. The assumption is, as we have seen, questionable.

In June 1919 the Yugoslav delegation petitioned the president of the Peace Conference, asking for a dissolution of the National Council and a declaration of invalidity of all its laws. Its case rested on the purported private character of the National Council,[280] prompting the National Council to attempt to establish its legitimacy (representativeness), as well as its continuity of power both de facto and de jure. Andrea Ossoinack, whom the National Council had appointed as its delegate at Versailles, argued that the National Council had been left free to operate during Lenac's rule, and that this constituted tacit recognition of its continuous existence between the day of its Constitution and 17 November, the day of the arrival of Italian troops.[281] As to the National Council's Constitution, Ossoinack explained, it had been effected pursuant to one of the last proclamations of the emperor, who had accorded to all the peoples of the empire the option to create their own National Councils.[282]

De Vergottini, however, argues that the Constitution of the National Council at the end of October 1918 amounted to a break with the preexisting constitutional status quo and that the National Council was a transitional government engendering a new state entity to replace the political order swept away by the defeat of Austria-Hungary.[283] Indeed, the circumstances of the appropriation of political power by the Italian National Council indicate that its claim to legitimate authority was not grounded in legal continuity with the immediate constitutional past but on self-standing empirical and normative facts. Accordingly, when in January 1919 the National Council gave itself a formal organisation, it rationalised the legitimacy of its power, and of the constitution of Fiume into an independent state the previous October, by appealing to both the popular will and its century-old constitutional traditions as '*libero comune*' (free city-state).[284]

However, the fact that the National Council regarded itself as a legitimate authority on the basis of its *de facto* power combined with relevant principles of political morality (popular consent, self-determination, etc.) does not mean that at international law Fiume was a new political entity. From the perspective of international law, Fiume remained part of Hungary, which had not formally given up its authority over it yet, and which continued to exist despite the dissolution of the Austro-Hungarian Empire. It has been argued that at international law the circumstances in which the National Council assumed and maintained power were too fluid and contested to allow its *de facto* control to displace Hungarian sovereignty and beget a new *de jure* state of affairs with Fiume as a sovereign entity.[285]

CONCLUSIONS

In assigning Italy part of the Dalmatian coast but not Fiume, the Treaty of London sought to improve Italy's strategic security, as well as to ensure an appropriate postwar balance of power in Europe. These provisions had been negotiated on the basis of two assumptions. First, it was predicted that the Austro-Hungarian Empire would come out of the hostilities merely pared down, rather than shattered, and that Croatia (as part of Hungary) would need Fiume as an outlet to the sea. Secondly, it was assumed that Russia's imperialistic ambitions in the Adriatic, through its backing of a greater Serbia, must be kept in check. Both these assumptions turned out to be incorrect at the end of the war.

The dissolution of Austria-Hungary and Russia's changed foreign policy gave space for a new political entity to emerge—the Kingdom of Serbs, Croats, and Slovenes. This made it no longer necessary for Italy to have part of Dalmatia: neither Russia (through it proxy, Serbia) nor Austria-Hungary seemed now to threaten Italy's security and an appropriate balance of power in southeastern Europe. Nor was it any longer necessary for Croatia to keep Fiume, which was culturally an Italian enclave, with a majority Italian population: the new Yugoslav kingdom would now have plenty of ports, though these would take years to suitably develop, and so Yugoslavia's free use of Fiume must be secured at least for the medium term.

The Yugoslavs, however, were determined to have Fiume. The town had been under the authority of Austria between the fifteenth and eighteenth centuries and then directly annexed to Hungary as its *corpus separatum*, except for a period of two decades during the nineteenth century, when Croats had gained, and then again lost, control of it. But throughout the centuries Croatia had always regarded Fiume as rightfully its own, despite the gradual process of Italianization of its culture and population.

Fiumans became increasingly decisive in jealously guarding the Italian character of the town and of its municipal authority in the late nineteenth and early twentieth centuries. When the Yugoslavs seized control of the town with the help of Croat troops at the end of October 1918, a self-constituted and purportedly representative body of Fiuman notables, the National Council, protested by proclaiming Fiume's annexation to Italy. On the strength of this and of Fiumans' appeals for help after Serb troops also occupied the town, Italians sent in their own troops and deposed the Yugoslav provisional authority.

Italy's and Yugoslavia's rival claims to Fiume, and the way in which the Yugoslav provisional authority maintained control, while it did, with the support of Croat and, later, Serb troops obscure the role that a third power played in this sequence of events: France. Nearly fifty years ago Leeden unequivocally argued, on the basis of research in Italian archives, that in autumn 1918 the contest between Italians and Croats over Fiume quickly turned into a contest between the former and French.[286] But British archival material sheds light on the specific dynamics through which this occurred. In contrast to what might be naturally assumed, the Serb troops were not dispatched by the new Yugoslav kingdom: rather, they belonged to the Army of the Orient and were under French command. General Franchet D'Espèrey, who had negotiated the Belgrade Armistice with Hungary, lost no time sending Serb troops to Fiume as occupation forces, on the basis of his interpretation of what was authorised under the newly signed Armistice. The French military was, manifestly, attempting to preempt a similar move on the Italians' part. As we will see in the next chapter, France had its own ambitions in the Mediterranean, and it was in its interest to prevent the creation of a status quo that might facilitate Italy's acquisition of strategically important (whether in an economic or military sense) points in the eastern Adriatic.

The Italians themselves had been poised to occupy Fiume but had been detained by a perception that the Villa Giusti Agreement with Austria did not authorise such a move. The arrival of the Serb troops dispatched by Franchet D'Espèrey rid the Italians of any such scruples. The Italian occupation that followed was purportedly in the name of the Allies, but British military sources would regularly complain that it was Inter-Allied only in name. As we will see in the next chapter, the catalyst for D'Annunzio's own march on Fiume was just the fact that the occupation was, after ten months, finally about to be made a genuinely Inter-Allied affair.

NOTES

1. Maxwell H. H. Macartney and Paul Cremona, *Italy's Foreign and Colonial Policy, 1914–1937* (New York: Howard Fertig, 1972), 14–16; René Albrecht-Carrié, *Italy at the Paris Peace Conference* (Hamden, CT: Archon, 1966), 10.
2. Stefano Marcuzzi, *Britain and Italy in the Era of the Great War: Defending and Forging Empires* (Cambridge, UK: Cambridge University Press, 2020), 60–61.
3. Mario Mondini, *Fiume 1919: Una Guerra Civile Italiana* (Roma: Salerno, 2019), 16.
4. Mondini, *Fiume 1919*, 18–20.
5. H. James Burgwyn, *The Legend of the Mutilated Victory: Italy, the Great War, and the Paris Peace Conference, 1915–1919* (Westport, CT, and London: Greenwood, 1993), 8–9.
6. Stanley G. Payne, *A History of Fascism* (Madison: University of Wisconsin Press, 1995), 85–86.
7. Macartney and Cremona, *Italy's Foreign and Colonial Policy*, 21; Albrecht-Carrié, *Italy at the Paris Peace Conference*, 26.
8. David Lloyd George, *The Truth About the Peace Treaties*, vol. II (London: Gollancz, 1938), 761.
9. Lloyd George, *The Truth*, 762; Albrecht-Carrié, *Italy at the Paris Peace Conference*, 5.
10. Loyd George, *The Truth*, 762–63.
11. Marina Cattaruzza, *L'Italia e la Questione Adriatica: Dibattiti Parlamentari e Panorama Internazionale (1919–1926)* (Bologna: Il Mulino, 2014), 19.

12. In 1910 Indigenous Italians made up 37 percent of the population of Istria, Fiume, and Zara (a Dalmatian port town) taken together. Croats were the second largest ethnic group at 35 percent. Olinto Mileta Mattiaz, "Ipotesi sulla Composizione Etnica in Istria, Fiume e Zara: Ieri e Oggi," *Ricerche Sociali* 11 (2002): 17.

13. Lloyd George, *The Truth*, 767.

14. Cattaruzza, *L'Italia e la Questione Adriatica*, 19–20.

15. Albrecht-Carrié, *Italy at the Paris Peace Conference*, 28.

16. Roberto Vivarelli, *Storia delle Origini del Fascismo: L'Italia dalla Grande Guerra alla Marcia su Roma*, vol. 1 (Bologna: Il Mulino, 1991), 234–35; Alberto Pellegrino, "Lettere e Telegrammi di D'Annunzio a Riccardo Gigante," in *D'Annunzio Politico: Atti del Convegno (Il Vittoriale, 9–10 Ottobre 1985)*, ed. Renzo De Felice and Pietro Gibellini (Milano: Garzanti, 1987), 77; Enrico Burich, *Fiume e L'Italia* (Milano: Ravá, 1915), 11–13; Giovanni Stelli, "L'Irredentismo a Fiume," in *L'Irredentismo Armato: Gli Irredentismi Europei Davanti alla Guerra*, vol. 1, ed. Fabio Todero (Trieste: IRMSL, 2015), 152–61.

17. Burich, *Fiume e L'Italia*, 17.

18. Edoardo Susmel, *La Cittá di Passione: Fiume negli Anni 1914–1920* (Milano: Treves, 1921), 182.

19. Treaty of London (26 April 1915), reproduced in Macartney and Cremona, *Italy's Foreign and Colonial Policy*, 46.

20. Fiume and the Adriatic: 51/1: Letter from Italian Delegation to the Peace Conference to G. Clemenceau (7 July 1919), The National Archives, FO 170/1247; Memorandum by H. Nelson Gay (15 December 1918), enclosed in letter by the US Ambassador in Italy to the Secretary of State, in *Papers Relating to the Foreign Relations of the United States, The Paris Peace Conference, 1919*, vol. I, ed. Joseph Fuller (Washington: United States Government Printing Office, 1942), 442, https://history.state.gov/historicaldocuments/frus1919Parisv01/d356.

21. Memorandum by H. Nelson Gay, 442–43.

22. Vivarelli, *Storia delle Origini*, 169–70.

23. Albrecht-Carrié, *Italy at the Paris Peace Conference*, 230–31.

24. Andrea Carteny, "From the Lusanne Congress to the Rome Pact Until the Fiume League: Nationalists and Nationalism (1916–1920)," in *War, Peace and Nation-Building (1853–1918)*, ed. Aleksandar Rastović, Andrea Cartney, and Biljana Vučetić (Belgrade: Institute of History, 2020), 36.

25. Cattaruzza, *L'Italia e la Questione Adriatica*, 19.

26. Vivarelli, *Storia delle Origini*, 173, 234; Macartney and Cremona, *Italy's Foreign and Colonial Policy*, 57.

27. Macartney and Cremona, *Italy's Foreign and Colonial Policy*, 77–78.

28. Albrecht-Carrié, *Italy at the Paris Peace Conference*, 36.

29. Macartney and Cremona, *Italy's Foreign and Colonial Policy*, 52.

30. Silverio Annibale, *La Questione di Fiume nel Diritto Internazionale* (Rovigno, Fiume, and Trieste: Centro di Ricerche Storiche Rovigno, 2011), 51–52.

31. Fiume and the Adriatic: 51/2: Letter from H. W. Kennard to Earl Curzon of Kedleston (20 October 1919), The National Archives, FO 170/1248.

32. Vivarelli, *Storia delle Origini*, 186–87.

33. Lloyd George, *The Truth*, 791.

34. Vivarelli, *Storia delle Origini*, 190 (note 90).

35. Raoul Pupo, "La Questione di Fiume e le Vicende del Confine Orientale," in *Fiume 1919–2019: Un Centenario Europeo tra Identitá, Memorie e Prospettive di Ricerca*, ed. Giordano Bruno Guerri (Milano: Silvana Editoriale, 2020), 18.

36. Lloyd George, *The Truth*, 800.

37. Albrecht-Carrié, *Italy at the Paris Peace Conference*, 108–11; Pupo, "La Questione di Fiume", 23; Burgwyn, *The Legend*, 204, 257.

38. Cattaruzza, *L'Italia e la Questione Adriatica*, 20; Geoffrey A. Haywood, *Failure of a Dream: Sidney Sonnino and the Rise and Fall of Liberal Italy, 1847–1922* (Firenze: Olschki, 1999), 489; Macartney and Cremona, *Italy's Foreign and Colonial Policy*, 81; British Delegation: Enclosure 2 to Communication from DMI to Under Secretary of State for Foreign Affairs (5 August 1919), The National Archives, FO 608/39.

39. Macartney and Cremona, *Italy's Foreign and Colonial Policy*, 53.

40. Macartney and Cremona, *Italy's Foreign and Colonial Policy*, 79.

41. Albrecht-Carrié, *Italy at the Paris Peace Conference*, 45.

42. Carteny, "From the Lusanne Congress," 40–42; Cattaruzza, *L'Italia e la Questione Adriatica*, 23–24.

43. Burgwyn, *The Legend*, 151.

44. Pupo, "La Questione di Fiume," 15–16.

45. Prime Minister: Report from L. Waterfield to A. Thorold (5 June 1919), Parliamentary Archives, LG/F/43/7/13.

46. Prime Minister: Letter from R. Rodd to A. Balfour (11 November 1918), Parliamentary Archives LG/F/200/1/20.

47. Memorandum by H. Nelson Gay, 443; see also Albrecht-Carrié, *Italy at the Paris Peace Conference*, 239.

48. Macartney and Cremona, *Italy's Foreign and Colonial Policy*, 80.

49. Cattaruzza, *L'Italia e la Questione Adriatica*, 21.

50. Stefano B. Galli, "Irredentismo Trentino e l'Impresa di Fiume nel Nome di Cesare Battisti," in *Fiume 1919–2019*, ed. Giordano Bruno Guerri, 93–94.

51. Stelli, "L'Irredentismo a Fiume," 155; Albrecht-Carrié, *Italy at the Paris Peace Conference*, 102; Raoul Pupo, *Fiume Città di Passione* (Bari: Laterza, 2018), 37; Thea Pičić, *Rijeka Ili Smrt! D'Anunzijeva okupacija Rijeke, 1919–1921 / Rijeka or Death! D'Annunzio's Occupation of Rijeka, 1919–2019* (Rijeka: Naklada Val, 2019), 24; Mondini, *Fiume 1919*, 17.

52. William Klinger, *Un'Altra Italia: Fiume 1724–1924*, ed. Diego Redivo (Rovigno, Fiume, and Trieste: Centro di Ricerche Storiche Rovigno, 2018), 18, https://crsrv.org/wp/wp-content/uploads/2020/03/N.45-Klinger-Fiume.pdf.

53. Edoardo Susmel, *Fiume Attraverso la Storia: Dalle Origini Fino ai Nostri Giorni* (Milano: Treves, 1919), 19–20.

54. Klinger, *Un'Altra Italia*, 23–26; Susmel, *Fiume Attraverso la Storia*, 24–32.

55. Susmel, *Fiume Attraverso la Storia*, 37, 44–45.

56. Klinger, *Un'Altra Italia*, 35; Susmel, *Fiume Attraverso la Storia*, 39, 55.

57. Susmel, *Fiume Attraverso la Storia*, 55–56.

58. Klinger, *Un'Altra Italia*, 40, 42.
59. Klinger, *Un'Altra Italia*, 43.
60. Susmel, *Fiume Attraverso la Storia*, 58–59; Alessandro Agrì, "Lo 'Stato di Fiume' e il Suo Diritto (1918–1924)," *Historia et Ius* 19 (2021): 11, http://www.historiaetius.eu/uploads/5/9/4/8/5948821/agri_19.pdf.
61. Agrí, "Lo 'Stato di Fiume'," 10.
62. Susmel, *Fiume Attraverso la Storia*, 46.
63. Klinger, *Un'Altra Italia*, 27, 35.
64. Klinger, *Un'Altra Italia*, 36.
65. Klinger, *Un'Altra Italia*, 37.
66. Albert Merdžo, "Nuove Conoscenze sulla Composizione Etnica della Popolazione di Fiume Attraverso i Secoli," *Quaderni* (Centro di Ricerche Storiche-Rovigno) XXX (2019): 292.
67. Klinger, *Un'Altra Italia*, 38.
68. Susmel, *Fiume Attraverso la Storia*, 50–51; Giovanni Stelli, "Per una Storia di Fiume," *Fiume: Rivista di Studi Adriatici* 29 (2014): 5; Pupo, *Fiume Città di Passione*, 5.
69. Klinger, *Un'Altra Italia*, 40.
70. Klinger, *Un'Altra Italia*, 36.
71. Pupo, *Fiume Città di Passione*, 5.
72. Luigi Peteani, "Testimonianze sull'Italianitá di Fiume," *Fiume: Rivista di Studi Fiumani* II, no. 1 (1982): 1–4.
73. Klinger, *Un'Altra Italia*, 54–56.
74. See generally Merdžo, "Nuove Conoscenze."
75. Klinger, *Un'Altra Italia*, 21.
76. Klinger, *Un'Altra Italia*, 35.
77. Annibale, *La Questione di Fiume*, 11 (note 1).
78. Klinger, *Un'Altra Italia*, 49.
79. Klinger, *Un'Altra Italia*, 49, 56–57.
80. Annibale, *La Questione di Fiume*, 12.
81. Klinger, *Un'Altra Italia*, 83.
82. Klinger, *Un'Altra Italia*, 85; Annibale, *La Questione di Fiume*, 11–12.
83. Klinger, *Un'Altra Italia*, 52.
84. Annibale, *La Questione di Fiume*, 12; Susmel, *Fiume Attraverso la Storia*, 70; Stelli, "Per una Storia," 9.
85. Annibale, *La Questione di Fiume*, 12.
86. Klinger, *Un'Altra Italia*, 85, 86, 105, 110, 274; Michael A. Leeden, *The First Duce* (Baltimore and London: John Hopkins University Press, 1977), 17.
87. Klinger, *Un'Altra Italia*, 274.
88. Pupo, *Fiume Città di Passione*, 12.
89. Croatia-Slavonia and Fiume (March 1919), The National Archives, FO 373/1/10, 34.
90. Pupo, *Fiume Città di Passione*, 13–14.
91. Annibale, *La Questione di Fiume*, 13; Leeden, *The First Duce*, 19; Burich, *Fiume e L'Italia*, 8, 23; Susmel, *Fiume Attraverso la Storia*, 85–87.

92. Dominique Kirchner Reill, *The Fiume Crisis: Life in the Wake of the Habsburg Empire* (Cambridge, MA: Harvard University Press, 2020), 25–26.
93. Stelli, "Per una Storia," 11; Merdžo, "Nuove Conoscenze," 299–300.
94. Susmel, *Fiume Attraverso la Storia*, 87–89; Pupo, *Fiume Città di Passione*, 14.
95. Pupo, *Fiume Città di Passione*, 14.
96. Pupo, *Fiume Città di Passione*, 14–15.
97. Leeden, *The First Duce*, 19.
98. Croatia-Slavonia and Fiume (March 1919), The National Archives, FO 373/1/10, 35; Leeden, *The First Duce*, 19.
99. Fiume and the Adriatic: 51/1: Report ('Weekly Proceedings') of Captain HWW Hope (29 November 1918), The National Archives, FO 170/1247.
100. Croatia-Slavonia and Fiume (March 1919), The National Archives, FO 373/1/10, 35 (quoting R. W. Seton Watson, *The Southern Slav Question*, 81, 82).
101. Croatia-Slavonia and Fiume (March 1919), The National Archives, FO 373/1/10, 90 (reproducing an English translation of article XXX[66] of the Hungarian Constitution); Annibale, *La Questione di Fiume*, 18 (note 15).
102. Croatia-Slavonia and Fiume (March 1919), The National Archives, FO 373/1/10, 35 (quoting R. W. Seton Watson, *The Southern Slav Question*, 81).
103. At the time of writing, an image of the patched document can be found at https://upload.wikimedia.org/wikipedia/commons/c/ce/Rijecka_krpica_HDA_300109.jpg.
104. Susmel, *Fiume Attraverso la Storia*, 91–92.
105. Kirchner Reill, *The Fiume Crisis*, 26; Susmel, *Fiume Attraverso la Storia*, 94–97; Pupo, *Fiume Città di Passione*, 19.
106. Leeden, *The First Duce*, 19–23.
107. Milou Van Hout, "In Search of the Nation in Fiume: Irredentism, Cultural Nationalism, Borderlands," *Nations and Nationalism* 26, no. 3 (2019): 5.
108. Stelli, "L'Irredentismo a Fiume," 149.
109. Memorandum by H. Nelson Gay, 446.
110. Croatia-Slavonia and Fiume (March 1919), The National Archives, FO 373/1/1, 9.
111. Burich, *Fiume e L'Italia*, 20–21.
112. Pupo, *Fiume Città di Passione*, 17.
113. Merdžo, "Nuove Conoscenze," 291.
114. Kirchner Reill, *The Fiume Crisis*, 139.
115. Croatia-Slavonia and Fiume (March 1919), The National Archives, FO 373/1/10, 9. Because the inhabitants of Fiume were largely polyglots, these percentages must refer to first language.
116. J. N. Macdonald, *A Political Escapade: The Story of Fiume and D'Annunzio*, (London: John Murray, 1921), 16; Adriatic, Italian Desiderata: A. Balfour, Memorandum of Interview with the Italian Ambassador (13 April 1919), The National Archives, FO 608/28/2.
117. Kierchner Reill, *The Fiume Crisis*, 146.
118. See generally Merdžo, "Nuove Conoscenze."

119. Croatia-Slavonia and Fiume (March 1919), The National Archives, FO 373/1/10, 36.

120. Italy: Aims in Dalmatia and Croatia: The Future of Fiume (Memorandum by A. Ossoinack) (23 January 1919), The National Archives, FO 608/15/8.

121. Susmel, *La Città di Passione*, 22.

122. Macdonald, *A Political Escapade*, 35; Lloyd George, *The Truth*, 809, 817, 831; Albrecht-Carrié, *Italy at the Paris Peace Conference*, 92–94 (summarising the Report of the American Territorial Experts in January 1919) and 100–101; La Question de Fiume: Plan of Fiume-Susak, with notes on population (Comité Yougoslave, Paris), The National Archives, FO 925/33014; Italy: Aims in Dalmatia and Croatia: A. W. A. Leeper's minutes on The Future of Fiume (Memorandum by A.) (23 January 1919), The National Archives, FO 608/15/8; Prime Minister: Letter from D. Lloyd George to V. E. Orlando (28 May 1919), Parliamentary Archives, LG/F/55/4/39; Prime Minister: Note handed to V. E. Orlando on April 24 [1919] by the President of the United States and the Prime Ministers of Great Britain and France, Parliamentary Archives, LG/F/158/1/11; Adriatic, Italian Desiderata: A. Balfour, Memorandum of Interview with the Italian Ambassador (13 April 1919), The National Archives, FO 608/28/2; Adriatic, Italian Desiderata: R. Lenac, The Question of Fiume (Reka), The National Archives, FO 608/28/4; Fiume, Statistics: A. W. A. Leeper's minute on letter from S. Sonnino to A. Balfour (1 March 1919), The National Archives, FO 608/35/4; Italy, Rebellion: Letter from Lieutenant Colonel S. C. Peck to D. M. O., War Office (10 October 1919), The National Archives, FO 608/41/1; Italy: Aims in Dalmatia and Croatia: H. Nicolson, The Question of Fiume (15 January 1919), The National Archives, FO 608/15/8.

123. Carlo Maranelli and Gaetano Salvemini, *La Questione dell'Adriatico* (Firenze: La Voce, 1918), 63–64.

124. Prime Minister: Letter from R. Rodd to D. Lloyd George (6 May 1919), Parliamentary Archives, LG/F/200/1/20.

125. Maranelli and Salvemini, *La Questione dell'Adriatico*, 63.

126. Prime Minister: Report from L. Waterfield to A. Thorold (5 June 1919), Parliamentary Archives, LG/F/43/7/13.

127. Maranelli and Salvemini, *La Questione dell'Adriatico*, 63, 66.

128. Adriatic, Italian Desiderata: Fortnightly Intelligence Summary of the British Military Mission, Fiume (5 November 1919), The National Archives, FO 608/28/2.

129. Prime Minister: Report from L. Waterfield to A. Thorold (5 June 1919), Parliamentary Archives, LG/F/43/7/13.

130. Pupo, *Fiume Città di Passione*, 16–17.

131. Pičić, *Rijeka or Death*, 8.

132. Pičić, *Rijeka or Death*, 18.

133. Pupo, *Fiume Città di Passione*, 14–15.

134. Federico C. Simonelli, "La Costruzione di un Mito: Rituali, Simboli e Narrazioni dell'Impresa di Fiume (1919–1921)" (PhD diss., Università degli Studi di Urbino Carlo Bo, 2014–2015), 38, https://ora.uniurb.it/bitstream/11576/2630991/1/phd_uniurb_257536.pdf.

135. Pupo, *Fiume Città di Passione*, 32.

136. Burich, *Fiume e L'Italia*, 18–19.

137. Merdžo, "Nuove Conoscenze," 272.

138. See generally Natka Badurina, "I Croati di Fiume," *Qualestoria* 48, no. 2 (2020).

139. Kirchner Reill, *The Fiume Crisis*, 198–99.

140. Ervin Dubrović, "L'Organizzaione *Galeb* (Gabbiano) Contro D'Annunzio," in *Fiume 1919–2019*, ed. Giordano Bruno Guerri, 61–72.

141. Stelli, "Per una Storia," 7; Giovanni Stelli, "La Lunga Storia dell'Autonomia Fiumana," in *La Cittá di Vita Cento Anni Dopo: Fiume, D'Annunzio e il Lungo Novecento Adriatico*, ed. Davide Rossi (Padova: Wolters Kluwer—Cedam, 2020), 2.

142. Merdžo, "Nuove Conoscenze," 271.

143. Badurina, "I Croati di Fiume," 67.

144. Badurina, "I Croati di Fiume," 62–63.

145. Badurina, "I Croati di Fiume," 57.

146. Badurina, "I Croati di Fiume," 59–60, 67. Similarly, elsewhere on the eastern Adriatic coast, in Split, the existence is documented in the latter half of the nineteenth century of Italian-speaking local populations who identified as either Croats or Serbs rather than Italians. This had largely to do with the fact that Italian had been established as the language of bureaucracy, education, and culture during the time of Venice's domination and had remained so even under Austrian domination. Maranelli and Salvemini, *La Questione dell'Adriatico*, 89.

147. Pupo, *Fiume Città di Passione*, 46.

148. Badurina, "I Croati di Fiume," 60–61. Nonetheless, it is worth recalling that when in 1939 Lenaz was invited to illustrate to Fiuman Fascists, of which by that time he was one, the racial politics of fascism he declared that all the scientific knowledge he possessed as a physician led him to the exact opposite thesis and to dispute the fascist claim that race was a problem in the first place. Giordano Bruno Guerri, *Disobbedisco: Cinquecento Giorni di Rivoluzione. Fiume 1919–1920* (Milano: Mondadori, 2019), 348.

149. Badurina, "I Croati di Fiume," 63–64, 67.

150. Badurina, "I Croati di Fiume," 63–64.

151. Merdžo, "Nuove Conoscenze," 271.

152. Stelli, "Per una Storia," 20–21.

153. Macdonald, *A Political Escapade*, 24, 25.

154. See, for example, Kirchner Reill, *The Fiume Crisis*, 71–72.

155. Macdonald, *A Political Escapade*, 17.

156. Macdonald, *A Political Escapade*, 27.

157. Macdonald, *A Political Escapade*, 107.

158. Kirchner Reill, *The Fiume Crisis*, 72.

159. Kirchner Reill, *The Fiume Crisis*, 123–31.

160. Kirchner Reill, *The Fiume Crisis*, 80.

161. Kirchner Reill, *The Fiume Crisis*, 212–18.

162. Kirchner Reill, *The Fiume Crisis*, 74.

163. Kirchner Reill, *The Fiume Crisis*, 132–33, 224.

164. Maranelli and Salvemini, *La Questione dell'Adriatico*, 272–73.

165. Luigi Peteani, "Irredentisti Fiumani del Risorgimento," *Rivista di Studi Politici Internazionali* 17, no. 2 (April–June 1950): 284.
166. Peteani, "Irredentisti Fiumani," 285.
167. Maranelli and Salvemini, *La Questione dell'Adriatico*, 273.
168. Stelli, "La Lunga Storia," 3.
169. Burich, *Fiume e L'Italia*, 9–10; Susmel, *Fiume Attraverso la Storia*, 99–10.
170. Stelli, "L'Irredentismo a Fiume," 150–51; Stelli, "Per una Storia," 22; Pupo, *Fiume Città di Passione*, 26–27.
171. Giovanni Stelli, "Gli Autonomisti Fiumani e l'Impresa Dannunziana," in *Fiume 1919–2019*, ed. Giordano Bruno Guerri, 38.
172. Burich, *Fiume e L'Italia*, 10–11; Susmel, *Fiume Attraverso la Storia*, 100; Pupo, *Fiume Città di Passione*, 36–37.
173. Maranelli and Salvemini, *La Questione dell'Adriatico*, 65–66.
174. Pupo, *Fiume Città di Passione*, 28–29; Pičić, *Rijeka o Morte*, 22.
175. Susmel, *Fiume Attraverso la Storia*, 100–102.
176. Giuseppe Gerini, *Omaggio a Gabriele D'Annunzio: Gabriele D'Annunzio e la Passione di Fiume* (Fiume: Termini, 1939), 9–10 (reproducing an extract from the Fiuman irredentist daily newspaper *La Vedetta D'Italia*); Peteani, "Irredentisti Fiumani," 286; Stelli, "L'Irredentismo a Fiume," 146–47.
177. Pičić, *Rijeka or Death*, 23–24.
178. Giulio Benedetti, *La Pace di Fiume: Dalla Conferenza di Parigi al Trattato di Roma* (Bologna: Zanichelli, 1924), 8–11; Stelli, "L'Irredentismo a Fiume," 161–74; Pupo, *Fiume Città di Passione*, 31.
179. Susmel, *Fiume Attraverso la Storia*, 103; Susmel, *La Cittá di Passione*, 101.
180. Stelli, "L'Irredentismo a Fiume," 174–75; Burich, *Fiume e L'Italia*, 15–16.
181. Burich, *Fiume e L'Italia*, 15.
182. Mario Maria Martini, *La Passione di Fiume: Diari, Cronache, Documenti* (Milano: Sonzogno, 1919) 103; Leeden, *The First Duce*, 24.
183. Susmel, *La Cittá di Passione*, 122 (note 1).
184. Klinger, *Un'Altra Italia*, 279.
185. Susmel, *La Cittá di Passione*, 67.
186. Susmel, *La Cittá di Passione*, 61–74.
187. Susmel, *Fiume Attraverso la Storia*, 104.
188. Pupo, *Fiume Città di Passione*, 45.
189. Mondini, *Fiume 1919*, 25–26.
190. Susmel, *La Cittá di Passione*, 138–39.
191. Susmel, *La Cittá di Passione.*
192. Gerini, *Omaggio*, 92.
193. Susmel, *La Cittá di Passione*, 123–33.
194. Susmel, *La Cittá di Passione*, 149.
195. Leeden, *The First Duce*, 26, 28.
196. Annibale, *La Questione di Fiume*, 16–17.
197. Memorandum by H. Nelson Gay, 444.
198. Susmel, *Fiume Attraverso la Storia*, 108.
199. Pičić, *Rijeka or Death*, 28.

200. Badurina, "I Croati di Fiume," 55–59.
201. Badurina, "I Croati di Fiume," 56.
202. Adriatic, Italian Desiderata: Stenographic report of the speech delivered by the Deputy of Fiume in the Hungarian Parliament on 18 October 1918, enclosed to letter from A. Ossoinack to A. Balfour (13 March 1919), The National Archives, FO 608/35/3; Susmel, *Fiume Attraverso la Storia*, 107–8; Susmel, *La Cittá di Passione*, 146–47.
203. 1918 Embargoes: Extracts from a Report by Lieutenant Colonel Bromhead, British Military Cinema Mission, to Lieutenant Colonel Alexander, British Propaganda Mission in Rome, The National Archives, FO 170/1134.
204. Fiume, Zagreb, and Laibach: Report from Major A. C. Temperley to Lieutenant General T. Bridges (29 November 1918), The National Archives, WO 106/1394.
205. Fiume and the Adriatic: 51/1: Report of Rear Admiral E. B. Kiddle to the Secretary of the Admiralty (5 January 1919), The National Archives, FO 170/1247.
206. Prime Minister: Report from L. Waterfield to A. Thorold (5 June 1919), Parliamentary Archives, LG/F/43/7/13.
207. British Delegation, Correspondence and Papers Relating to Austria-Hungary (Political): Future of Fiume, comm.d by Serb-Croat-Slovene Delegation (29 March 1919), The National Archives, FO 608/8.
208. 1918 Embargoes: Extracts from a Report by Lieutenant Colonel Bromhead, British Military Cinema Mission, to Lieutenant Colonel Alexander, British Propaganda Mission in Rome, The National Archives, FO 170/1134.
209. Pičić, *Rijeka or Death*, 8.
210. Fiume and the Adriatic: 51/1: Report ('Weekly Proceedings') of Captain H. W. W. Hope (29 November 1918), The National Archives, FO 170/1247.
211. Susmel, *La Cittá di Passione*, 172–73.
212. Luca Giuseppe Manenti, "Geografia e Politica nel Razzismo Antislavo: Il Caso dell'Irredentismo Italiano (Secoli XIX–XX)," in *Fratelli al Massacro: Linguaggi e Narrazioni della Prima Guerra Mondiale*, ed. Tullia Catalan (Roma: Viella, 2015).
213. Lloyd George, *The Truth*, 783–84.
214. Pupo, *Fiume Città di Passione*, 47.
215. Pičić, *Rijeka or Death*, 44; Burgwyn, *The Legend*, 207.
216. 1918 Embargoes: "Martin's" Despatch to Commodore Commanding, British Adriatic Force (16 November 1918), The National Archives, FO 170/1134.
217. Fiume and the Adriatic: 51/1: Report of Rear Admiral E. B. Kiddle to the Secretary of the Admiralty (26 December 1918), The National Archives, FO 170/1247.
218. Convention Regulating the Conditions Under Which the Armistice, Signed between the Allies and Austria-Hungary, Is to Be Applied in Hungary (13 November 1918), art. 1.
219. Fiume and the Adriatic: 51/1: Report of Rear Admiral E. B. Kiddle to the Secretary of the Admiralty (26 December 1918), The National Archives, FO 170/1247.

220. 1918 Embargoes: "Martin's" Despatch to Commodore Commanding, British Adriatic Force (16 November 1918), The National Archives, FO 170/1134.

221. 1918 Embargoes: "Martin's" Despatch to Commodore Commanding, British Adriatic Force (17 November 1918), The National Archives, FO 170/1134.

222. Adriatic: Letter from Rear Admiral E. B. Kiddle to the Secretary of the Admiralty (14 January 1919), The National Archives, FO 608/27/9.

223. Inter-Allied Organisation of Fiume: Letter from Admiral Mola to all the Admirals of the Naval Committee for the Adriatic (12 January 1919), The National Archives, WO 32/5129.

224. Annibale, *La Questione di Fiume*, 19; Susmel, *La Cittá di Passione*, 166–70.

225. Fiume and the Adriatic: 51/1: Communication from the French Ambassador in London (30 December 1918), The National Archives, FO 170/1247.

226. Fiume and the Adriatic: 51/1: Report of Rear Admiral E. B. Kiddle to the Secretary of the Admiralty (5 January 1919), The National Archives, FO 170/1247.

227. 1918 Embargoes: "Martin's" Despatch to Commodore Commanding, British Adriatic Force (19 November 1918), The National Archives, FO 170/1134.

228. Prime Minister: Letter from the Earl of Derby to A. Balfour (21 November 1918), Parliamentary Archives, LG/F/52/2/48.

229. Fiume and the Adriatic: 51/1: Report of Rear Admiral E. B. Kiddle to the Secretary of the Admiralty (26 December 1918), The National Archives, FO 170/1247.

230. Adriatic: Telegram from Venice (Rear Admiral E. B. Kiddle) to Admiralty (16 January 1919), The National Archives, FO 608/27/9; Adriatic: Enclosure 1 to letter 9 from Rear Admiral E. B. Kiddle to the Secretary of the Admiralty (14 January 1919), The National Archives FO 608/27/9. There also were French troops already established in Fiume, as we will see, but they purported to be there as the personnel of a military base to supply the Army of the Orient, rather than in an Inter-Allied capacity as occupation forces.

231. Adriatic: Letter from [unsigned] (for Mr. Balfour) to the Earl of Derby (27 January 1919), The National Archives, FO 608/27/9.

232. Fiume and the Adriatic: 51/1: Telegram from Serbian Minister to the Foreign Secretary (18 December 1918), The National Archives, FO 170/1247.

233. Fiume and the Adriatic: 51/1: Report of Rear Admiral E. B. Kiddle to the Secretary of the Admiralty (5 January 1919), The National Archives, FO 170/1247.

234. Fiume and the Adriatic: 51/1: Report of Rear Admiral E. B. Kiddle to the Secretary of the Admiralty (26 December 1918), The National Archives, FO 170/1247.

235. Fiume, Zagreb, and Laibach: Report from Major A. C. Temperley to Lieutenant General T. Bridges (29 November 1918), The National Archives, WO 106/1394.

236. Adriatic: Letter from Rear Admiral E. B. Kiddle to the Secretary of the Admiralty (14 January 1919), The National Archives, FO 608/27/9.

237. Fiume, Desiderata: Enclosure (II) to letter from Lieutenant Colonel S. C. Peck to G. H. C., British Forces in Italy (8 June 1919), The National Archives, FO 608/35/6.

238. Adriatic, Italian Desiderata: Report from Captain R. J. Baird to D.M.I., Military Section, British Delegation (12 May 1919), The National Archives, FO 608/35/3; Adriatic, Italian Desiderata: Letter from the S.H.S. National Council of Fiume-Sušak to D. Lloyd George (14 May 1919), The National Archives, FO 608/35/3; Adriatic, Italian Desiderata: Letter from the Yugoslav National Council to the General Commanding the British Troops in Fiume (27 April 1919), The National Archives, FO 608/35/3.

239. Adriatic, Italian Desiderata: Report from Lieutenant Colonel S. L. Whatford to C.I.G.C. (30 April 1919), The National Archives, FO 608/35/3.

240. 1918 Embargoes: "Martin's" Despatch to Commodore Commanding, British Adriatic Force (19 November 1918), The National Archives, FO 170/1134.

241. Prime Minister: Report from L. Waterfield to A. Thorold (5 June 1919), Parliamentary Archives, LG/F/43/7/13.

242. Fiume and the Adriatic: 51/1: Report on Situation in Cattaro Area by R. F. Henderson (24 November 1918), The National Archives, FO 170/1247.

243. Fiume and the Adriatic: 51/1: Report of Rear Admiral E. B. Kiddle to the Secretary of the Admiralty (5 January 1919), The National Archives, FO 170/1247.

244. Adriatic: Telegram from Venice (Rear Admiral E. B. Kiddle) to Admiralty (16 January 1919), The National Archives FO 608/27/9.

245. Adriatic: Enclosure 1 to letter 9 from Rear Admiral E. B. Kiddle to the Secretary of the Admiralty (14 January 1919), The National Archives FO 608/27/9.

246. Fiume and the Adriatic: 51/2: Commission Interalliée D'Enquête de Fiume, Procés-Verbaux et Rapport (1919), 6, The National Archives, FO 170/1248.

247. Annibale, *La Questione di Fiume*, 20–21 (note 21).

248. Armistice Convention with Austria-Hungary, Protocol of Conditions of the Armistice between the Allied and Associated Powers and Austria-Hungary (3 November 1918), art. 4, 6.

249. Pupo, *Fiume Città di Passione*, 47.

250. 1918 Embargoes: "Martin's" Despatch to Commodore Commanding, British Adriatic Force (16 November 1918), The National Archives, FO 170/1134.

251. Armistice Convention with Austria-Hungary, Protocol of Conditions of the Armistice between the Allied and Associated Powers and Austria-Hungary (3 November 1918), art. 4, 6.

252. Armistice Convention with Austria-Hungary, Protocol of Conditions of the Armistice between the Allied and Associated Powers and Austria-Hungary (3 November 1918), art 4, 6.

253. Fiume and the Adriatic: 51/1: Report of Rear Admiral E. B. Kiddle to the Secretary of the Admiralty (26 December 1918), The National Archives, FO 170/1247.

254. Stelli, "La Lunga Storia," 13; Adriatic, Italian Desiderata: Telegram from R. Zanella to A. Balfour (17 May 1919), The National Archives, FO 608/35/3.

255. Susmel, *La Cittá di Passione*, 150.

256. Renzo De Felice, *D'Annunzio Politico, 1918–1938* (Roma and Bari: Laterza, 1978), 41; Susmel, *Fiume Attraverso la Storia*, 108–9.

257. Proclamation of the National Council (30 October 1920 [mistakenly dated 30 September]), reproduced in scanned form in *La Carta del Carnaro e Altri Scritti su Fiume*, ed. Marco Fressura and Patrick Karlsen (Roma: Castelvecchi, 2009), 85.

258. Martini, *La Passione di Fiume*, 103.
259. Martini, *La Passione di Fiume*, 66.
260. Fiume, Desiderata: Letter from R. Gotthardi to G. Clemenceau (3 October 1919), The National Archives, FO 608/35/6.
261. Italy, Rebellion: *La Vedetta d'Italia* (15 October 1919), enclosed to Diary of the British Military Mission, Fiume (15–19 October 1919), The National Archives, FO 608/41/1.
262. Badurina, "I Croati di Fiume," 54, 66.
263. Badurina, "I Croati di Fiume," 54.
264. Kirchner Reill, *The Fiume Crisis*, 134–35.
265. Kirchner Reill, *The Fiume Crisis*, 152, 162–63; British Delegation, Fiume: Report from Lieutenat Colonel S. C. Peck to D.M.O., War Office (24 July 1919), The National Archives, FO 608/36.
266. Kirchner Reill, *The Fiume Crisis*, 199–200.
267. Kirchner Reill, *The Fiume Crisis*, 211.
268. Kirchner Reill, *The Fiume Crisis*, 180–92, 220–23.
269. Klinger, *Un'Altra Italia*, 295.
270. Leeden, *The First Duce*, 26.
271. Giuseppe De Vergottini, *La Costituzione secondo D'Annunzio* (Milano: Luni, 2020), 53.
272. Martini, *La Passione di Fiume*, 103.
273. Susmel, *La Cittá di Passione*, 151–52.
274. Adriatic, Italian Desiderata: Letter from A. Ossoinack to G. Clemenceau (8 July 1919), The National Archives, FO 608/35/3.
275. Annibale, *La Questione di Fiume*, 18 (also note 14).
276. Danilo L. Massagrande, "I Governi di Fiume Indipendente, 1918–1924," *Fiume: Rivista di Studi Adriatici* 5 (2002): 11–12.
277. L. Massagrande, "I Governi di Fiume," 7.
278. Pičić, *Rijeka o Morte*, 40–41; Fiume, Administration: Letter from N. P. Pachitch to G. Clemenceau (23 June 1919), The National Archives, FO 608/35/5.
279. Fiume and the Adriatic: 51/1: Report of Rear Admiral E. B. Kiddle to the Secretary of the Admiralty (5 January 1919), The National Archives, FO 170/1247.
280. Fiume, Administration: Letter from N. P. Pachitch to G. Clemenceau (23 June 1919), The National Archives, FO 608/35/5.
281. Adriatic, Italian Desiderata: Letter from A. Ossoinack to G. Clemenceau (8 July 1919), The National Archives, FO 608/35/3.
282. Adriatic, Italian Desiderata: Letter from A. Ossoinack to G. Clemenceau (8 July 1919), The National Archives, FO 608/35/3.
283. De Vergottini, *La Costituzione*, 54.
284. Preamble to Ordinance no. 407 (22 January 1919) Concerning the Provisions for the Operation of Fiume Italian National Council, in *La Bilancia, Bollettino Ufficiale del Consiglio Nazionale* 20 (25 January 1919), reproduced in Massagrande, "I Governi," 29.
285. Annibale, *La Questione di Fiume*, 50, 56.
286. Leeden, *The First Duce*, 29.

Chapter 2

Fiume and the Paris Peace Conference

INTRODUCTION

At the Paris Peace Conference Italy put forward what the Allies rightly regarded as an extravagant set of demands, asking for the integral application of the Treaty of London as well as Fiume—the latter on self-determination grounds. The moderate Socialist Bissolati maintained that Italy's government approached the negotiations asking 'for twenty in order to obtain ten' but ended up being held hostage to public opinion, which 'they had allowed . . . to be whipped up into demanding twenty as a due'.[1] Indeed, Mondini has recently argued that the Italian delegates' position and conduct at the Paris negotiations can only be properly understood in light of developments in the role of mass media. These made the delegates accountable to a burgeoning but ill-informed reading public, whose views were actively being shaped by the print media in ways that had been unprecedented prior to the war.[2]

The Allied Powers were quite unwilling to grant Italy Fiume, which must serve as a port to Croatia and the hinterland. The British delegation at Versailles included a particularly fervid pro-Yugoslav contingent, who would repeatedly off-handedly dismiss any argument in favour of assigning Fiume to Italy. But President Wilson was the most formidable opponent the Italians had to contend with. The farthest he was prepared to compromise involved the creation around Fiume of a buffer state between Italy and Yugoslavia. Italy, not unreasonably, feared this solution would lead to the rapid de-Italianization of Fiume.

France's interests in ensuring a postconflict balance of power in the Mediterranean that would keep Germany and Italy from acquiring undue influence kept the Gallic nation busy in Fiume itself—where it established a parallel military authority structure not subject to the Inter-Allied Command of General Grazioli. Long-drawn uncertainty over Fiume's future (which the Treaty of Versailles failed to determine) exacerbated enmity between Fiumans and Italian troops on the one hand and pro-Yugoslav French troops on the other, leading to fatal incidents in July 1919. These paved the way to the second and unofficial Italian occupation—the one led by Gabriele D'Annunzio on 12 September 1919.

FIUME AND DALMATIA IN ITALY'S POSTWAR POLITICAL DISCOURSE

Those who had advocated Italy's intervention in the war fell broadly between two camps. On the right of the interventionist spectrum were the Nationalists and more conservative element of the Liberal establishment. On the left were so-called democratic interventionists, including Democrats, Republicans, and some Socialists, who viewed the conflict as a decisive step in protecting and asserting democracy against (Germanic) imperialism and reaction in Europe.[3]

At the end of the war, everybody agreed that Italy must complete its unification by obtaining those parts of northeastern Italy, such as the Trentino region, that had been under Austrian control and had long and rightly been mourned as *'terre irredente'* ('unredeemed lands'). But this is where consensus ended. Democratic interventionists advocated renouncing any indefensible territorial claims, especially those over Dalmatia and South Tyrol, arguing that Italy should model moral leadership for the rest of Europe.[4] The Nationalists, on the other hand, championed a politics of national will to power and anti-Slav sentiment that made them demand much of the eastern Adriatic coast on cultural and historical grounds.[5]

But the characterisation and perception of Dalmatia as one of Italy's unredeemed lands was a recent affair. According to Maranelli and Salvemini, no one in the mid-nineteenth century would have dreamed of claiming Dalmatia for Italy.[6] The belief that Dalmatia belonged to Italy by right had been the outcome of a campaign waged during the war years by the Nationalist press, as well as Nationalist politicians and military leaders. It was based on false or misleading claims about the prevalence of Italian elements in the local populations,[7] and ones to the effect that Austrians had introduced Slav populations in Dalmatia to displace Indigenous Italians.[8] During the war, this crusade, duly exploited by Austrian military leaders, backfired by galvanising Croat troops in fighting against the Italians with special tenacity.[9] Yet after the Armistice was signed, propaganda about Dalmatia only increased.[10] American observers noted that the Italian press had adopted a tone 'regarding Italy's claims and rights along the northern and eastern Adriatic' which might not be 'imperialistic, but has a tendency in that direction.'[11] The Nationalist press manufactured new claims about Slavs slaying Italian women and children in Dalmatia; meanwhile, military leaders of Italian troops that had occupied Dalmatia deflected attention away from their own mistreatment of the local Slav populations by representing them as a case of the *bon sauvage* awaiting Italy's civilising influence.[12] The self-serving nature of such claims was of course less easy to appreciate at a time when it was still respectable to speak of 'backward people to be taken in hand by more efficient nations'[13]—these being Lloyd George's words at the Paris conference when discussing international mandates.

If different political forces had radically different views about Dalmatia, all interventionists were in agreement, however, on the subject of Fiume. Indeed, much of Italy's public opinion was, throughout 1919, in favour of its annexation. This was largely thanks to Fiumans' own activism and advocacy.[14] The cause of Fiume resonated with those who felt aggravated by the frustration of patriotic aspirations and believed in self-determination principles; and it loomed large for those nationalists who saw in an occupation of the town the potential for triggering a political crisis in Italy and a turn to the Right.[15] Even those who, later, were quick to condemn D'Annunzio's occupation regarded Italy's claims over Fiume as a matter of justice.[16]

On the afternoon of the date on which the National Council proclaimed that it desired annexation to Italy, thousands of Fiumans are said to have marched through the streets and ratified the proclamation through acclamation in a plebiscite held in a public square.[17] While this did not have a direct effect on the Croat occupation, the news caused ripples of patriotic euphoria in Italy. Neutralist Socialists were virtually alone in failing to jump on the bandwagon.[18] For everyone else, the town's mainly Italian population and its vote in favour of annexation to Italy made it nearly incomprehensible that its fate should be tied to any other country.[19] The cause of Fiume had captured the nation's patriotic imagination.[20]

ITALY'S DEMANDS AT THE PARIS NEGOTIATIONS

Italian democratic interventionists had challenged the Nationalist narrative about Dalmatia, arguing that it was not in Italy's interest to obtain control over territories where the Slavs were bound to see Italians as foreign dominators.[21] Yet when the Italian delegation (led by five diplomats, including the current and former prime ministers and the minister for foreign affairs)[22] articulated its position at the Paris Peace Conference, it turned out to mirror the Nationalist demand: Italy should receive all the lands promised in the Treaty of London, as well as Fiume. This, as Nicolson's analysis makes clear, was the effect of disagreements between Minister for Foreign Affairs Sidney Sonnino and Prime Minister Vittorio Emanuele Orlando.[23]

Sonnino thought that the point of Italy going to war, at the cost of ruining its economy and industry (which had just started taking off in the prewar years), had been to obtain more than a policy of neutrality would have yielded. The Treaty of London specified exactly what the reward was to consist of.[24] Italy should therefore give up any claims over Fiume, lest they should imperil the other powers' willingness to comply with the treaty, which secured the greatest gains for Italy. Conversely, Orlando would have traded Dalmatia (whose absorption into Italy could lead to Slav irredentism) for Italian-populated Fiume. Not only would the annexation of Fiume please public opinion, but its possession, alongside the mountain that overlooked the town, Montenevoso, was also more important than Dalmatia to Italy's strategic security, now that it had to share a land frontier with a thirteen million–strong Yugoslav neighbour.[25] Sonnino disagreed, thinking that compromising on the Treaty of London would lead to a Yugoslav state strong enough to contend with Italy over control of the Adriatic, yet not strong enough to resist Germany, who would then secure a de facto hegemonic position in the Balkans.[26] The fact that the danger posed by Yugoslavia loomed large in both Orlando's and Sonnino's calculations is consistent with the report that Italians dreaded 'pan-Slav union as a far more formidable neighbour than the decadent Austrian Empire.'[27] The result of Orlando and Sonnino's disagreement, and of the former's inability to get the latter to compromise,[28] was to officially demand both Fiume and full compliance with the Treaty of London—the very maximalist outcome sought by the Nationalists.[29]

At Versailles, the Italian case for granting Italy Dalmatia pointed to the significant influence of Italian culture on the shores of the eastern Adriatic[30] and to past policies of arbitrary and coercive de-Italianization.[31] While the claim about Italian cultural heritage was not seriously contestable, claims about Austrian suppression of Italian elements in Dalmatia were exaggerated.[32] The delegates also argued that assigning Italy the portion of Dalmatia promised in the Treaty of London was vital to ensuring Italian strategic security, as the western Adriatic was, by its natural attributes, highly vulnerable to attack, while the morphology and water depths of the eastern Adriatic coast provided a natural defence from attack.[33] Such arguments fell on deaf ears among the Allies. The British ambassador in Rome was an exception in taking the view that Italy could not 'feel safe with much less than was secured to her by the London agreement'. According to him, in 1915 there had been a consensus that 'it was essential to Italy to make her coasts secure by establishing herself on the opposite shore, which nature has made practically impregnable, and preventing that line of islands and succession of ports from being used against her in the future as it had been in the past.'[34]

With respect to Fiume, the Italian delegates appealed to both the town's predominantly Italian ethnic composition and the outcome of the National

Council's 30 October 1918 annexation vote, in light of the principle of self-determination.[35] Italy's argument was that the Treaty of London was based on principles of equilibrium, rather than justice, but the announcement and acceptance of the self-determination principle now made justice the key consideration here.[36] Yet economic arguments are also said to have underpinned Italian demands: the prosperity of Trieste could only be assured if Fiume was not assigned to a foreign power, which would have an interest in making it a strong competitor to the former.[37] The Yugoslav delegation seized on and distorted such arguments, claiming that Italians' 'exclusive object is . . . to let Italian Fiume die and her hinterland suffer for the sake of Italian Trieste.'[38] While British Foreign Office personnel credited, and British military observers and delegates at Versailles rehashed, the Yugoslav account of Italian economic interests,[39] Wilson, Clemenceau, and Lloyd George rightly discounted them in a note they sent to Orlando: 'We cannot believe that the owners of Trieste have anything to fear from Fiume as commercial rival.'[40] Indeed, the economic argument for assigning Fiume to Italy (or at any rate for not assigning it to Yugoslavia) was not (as Yugoslav propaganda and pro-Yugoslav diplomats maintained) that Fiume must be impoverished for the sake of Trieste; rather, it was that Trieste should not be impoverished for the sake of Fiume. The idea was that, because Yugoslavia would control Trieste's as well as Fiume's hinterland and their railway system, the Yugoslavs could, in the event of Fiume being assigned to them, manipulate the railway tariff system to redirect virtually all trade traffic to Fiume and away from Trieste.[41]

In general, the Italian claims at Versailles came across to the Allies as imperialistic. The British under secretary of state for foreign affairs commented, in January 1919, that 'Sonnino's stubbornness and the extravagant nature of Italy's claims have had as a result that it is now literally true that Italy has not a friend in Europe except ourselves, and she is doing her best to make her isolation complete.'[42] In fact, the British thought that they must get Italy to abandon its claims over both Fiume and Dalmatia.[43] Although both principled and strategic arguments underpinned Italy's claims, it is clear that they were also driven by imperialistic ambitions. These had partly to do with Italians being desperate to be taken seriously by the rich European nations that had been exploiting its emigrant labour and regarded their impoverished southern neighbour as a *parvenu* on the stage of the world's great powers.[44]

The Italian negotiators' attempts to convince the Allies to grant Fiume to Italy were mistakenly taken as evidence that Italy had been acting in concert with Fiume's National Council and directing its moves to put the international community before a *fait accompli*.[45] In reality, the National Council had acted unilaterally in proclaiming annexation. Even when Gabriele D'Annunzio later occupied Fiume, Prime Minister Nitti, who had succeeded Orlando, had no involvement in it. Though he knew that something was afoot,[46] and although even some Italian military authorities at times assumed the government must have been party to the conspiracy to occupy Fiume,[47] Nitti was only guilty of indecisiveness in the state of semi-anarchy in which the country found itself at the time.[48]

THE US POSITION AT VERSAILLES

Italy's allies were not disposed to give way to her demands. The United States having joined the *Entente* in 1917, Italy had to face, first of all, President Wilson's opposition.[49] Wilson declared that US assistance had been indispensable to end the war, and that upon joining the war effort against the Central Powers the United States had made clear the principles by which the country stood.[50] Wilson affirmed that in the forthcoming era of the League of Nations, strategic considerations were no longer appropriate to determining postconflict territorial arrangements.[51] In any case, neither chaos-ridden Russia nor dissolved Austria-Hungary posed any threat to Italy's territorial security, so the territorial arrangements provided for in the Treaty of London no longer stood.[52] To the extent that Italy was concerned about a security threat coming from the Yugoslav state, it could be contained through such measures as limiting the number of Yugoslav weaponry and fortifications on the eastern Adriatic Coast.[53]

Point 9 of Wilson's famous 14 Points, which were to inform the peace negotiations, expressly stated that Italy's frontiers should be readjusted 'along clearly recognisable lines of nationality.'[54] Wilson, specifically, opposed Italian rule over Dalmatia and eastern (inland) Istria, whose population was largely made up of Slavs. While his belief in the principle of self-determination might have made him sympathetic at least to Italy's claim over Fiume, he also rejected this, on the ground that assigning the port town to Italy would give the impression of a foreign power having control over territories that were not part of its natural borders.[55] Because the Italian population of Fiume was not continuous with Italy's population (that is, it was surrounded by Slav populations), its annexation to Italy would have been arbitrary.[56] Wilson also believed that the National Council was not a legitimately elected body, and that its annexationist programme did not represent the will of the Fiumans.[57] There was some truth in the former, if not necessarily the latter, point: even after the initially self-constituted National Council called for elections so as to reconstitute itself into a democratic body, voting rights were enjoyed only by those with 'pertinent' status, in accordance with Austro-Hungarian law. This had the effect of making the National Council a body representing overwhelmingly middle-class concerns.[58] Additionally, because at international law Fiume remained part of Hungary, it seems legally correct to say that the

National Council was not a legitimate political entity, which would explain why its members were never given a seat at the negotiating table in Paris.[59] Finally, Wilson invoked economic considerations: Fiume served as a vital port to Yugoslavia, Hungary, Romania, and Czechoslovakia.[60]

While Orlando approached the negotiations with much rhetorical flair and little hard data, Wilson had been thoroughly primed by expert researchers charged with providing him with advice.[61] Only one such specialist had been originally assigned to study the Italian question, but eventually others became involved.[62] The chief Italian specialist, joined by some other experts, passionately advocated Fiume's assignation to Yugoslavia 'on the basis of ethnography, self-determination, historical ties, and economic needs.'[63] A careful consideration of all these grounds hardly compelled the recommendation the chief specialist insisted on, but the experts were perhaps working with partial information. Indeed, it has been noted that many specialists on Wilson's inquiry developed their expertise as a result of, rather than possessing it prior to, the inquiry.[64] Other advisers to the US delegation favoured Fiume's assignation to Italy as the least between two evils.[65] But the former group of experts sent direct appeals to Wilson, urging him not to relent. They claimed that war would be unavoidable if the town was not granted to Yugoslavia, that no political or economic arrangement could rectify the injury of depriving Yugoslavia of Fiume, that assigning it to Italy would bring the League of Nations 'down to [Italy's] level', and that Italy's claims to such an 'aggressive and unjust settlement' stemmed purely from a determination to 'emerge from the Conference with loot for their people', 'to carry home an ample bag of spoils'.[66] As Albrecht-Carrié points out, this appeal was 'far removed from being a technical statement of local conditions, the primary task of the territorial experts'.[67]

The upshot is that, while the US delegation as a whole appeared divided on the issue of Fiume,[68] the president came to the negotiations precommitted to the outcome that the town should be assigned to the Yugoslav state, so as to facilitate its trade by sea, and because Fiume's multicultural population made an application of the nationality principle impossible.[69] Wilson also feared that assigning Fiume to Italy might thrust the Yugoslavs, disappointed with an unjust peace, into the embrace of the Bolsheviks.[70] Lastly, the US president is said to have put up a strong opposition to Italian demands simply because he could (in a way precluded to him with British and French equally imperialistic claims),[71] and because he was xenophobically inclined to consider Italians as essentially untrustworthy.[72] The reciprocal dislike between the American president—'with a nature rich and varied in animosities'[73]—and the Italian negotiators only entrenched him into his aversion.[74] Lloyd George spoke of a clash between 'Italian emotionalism' and Wilson's 'rigid and frigid idealism'.[75]

For a time, Wilson proposed that Fiume should be part of Croatia, while retaining some autonomy.[76] Soon, however, he came to accept a different position, from which later he would never budge. This was, as Burgwyn notes, 'a compromise of sorts', departing from the advice of the president's most vociferous experts; however, the Italians, '[a]bsorbed as they were in their own injuries', failed to appreciate this.[77] According to Wilson's plan, Fiume should be incorporated into a buffer state between Italy and the new Yugoslav state. This would be called the 'Free State of Fiume' and would comprise a territory wider than Fiume and the district that had constituted the historical *corpus separatum.* Its population would amount to approximately 200,000 Croats and 40,000 Italians.[78]

According to Wilson's proposal, the state of Fiume would be administered by a government appointed by a special Commission of the League of Nations. A referendum would eventually be called to determine permanent institutional arrangements. If Italy objected to the results of the referendum (where Italian Fiumans would be much in the minority), the League of Nations would be solely responsible for determining the state's future, always ruling out annexation to Italy, but taking care to preserve for Fiume 'a degree of autonomy exactly similar to that which it enjoyed under Hungarian domination'.[79] Because similarity by definition rules out exact correspondence, it is not clear what 'exactly similar' might have meant. It is also unclear that the practical implications of Fiume retaining this autonomy would be much to Fiume's advantage. As we have seen, Fiume's autonomy had shrunk considerably in the years preceding the war. It seems that Wilson's guarantee of autonomy might therefore have been fairly empty. This explains why, even after a change of guard in Italy's government brought about a more conciliatory attitude in the negotiations, the Italians still insisted that 'the town of Fiume, besides the privileges of Maria Teresa, should receive a special statute . . . [to] safeguard its absolute independence',[80] or at least 'a statute efficaciously safeguarding its "Italianitá", which, owing to the great Slav majority in the Free State, would be more threatened than it was under Hungary.'[81] The Americans, however, were firmly opposed to this on the ground, among others, that it would 'open the door to every sort of Italian intrigue, open or disguised, for the annexation of Fiume to Italy.'[82]

Fiume's own emissaries in Paris met Wilson, but to no avail.[83] The National Council had appointed Andrea Ossoinack (who had been the last member of the Hungarian Diet for Fiume) as their official representative at Versailles. Ossoinack, however, was not granted admission to the official proceedings, only private audiences.[84] The transcript of a meeting sponsored by Orlando between Ossoinack and Wilson on 14 April 1919 shows them debating the economic reasons for and against assigning Fiume to Italy.[85] Among other things, Ossoinack argues that Italy would be well placed to make the necessary investments to develop the port, so that, in accordance with the Fiumans' wishes, it would serve the whole hinterland as a free port. Wilson's response is informed by free market dogmatism: the countries interested in using the port, he says, could make the necessary investments. Ossoinack's answer sounds prescient (considering the recent rise of China's political power in the western Balkans as a result of its Belt and Road Initiative): 'This means that Fiume will be dependent on the country to which it would own the most money. What kind of free State would that be?'[86]

FRANCE AND BRITAIN AT VERSAILLES

France and Britain, unlike the United States, did consider themselves honour bound to respect the Treaty of London.[87] When Prime Minister David Lloyd George clearly stated this before Wilson, he moved Orlando to tears of gratitude.[88] Yet France and Britain also made it clear that Italy had to choose between either the full concessions of the Treaty or Fiume; it would not be granted both.[89] In practice, Britain felt its hands were tied by the Treaty of London but looked to the United States to do what it considered was precluded to itself—namely, to energetically promote a territorial settlement that would depart from the arrangements contemplated in the treaty, while also not granting Italy Fiume.[90]

Both France and Britain were fundamentally committed to *realpolitik* in international relations.[91] Yet they claimed that Italy, in insisting on the application of the Treaty of London, was impervious to the new principles that were to determine postconflict territorial arrangements in a new Europe.[92] But for all their appeal, who was to say that Wilsonian principles of self-determination would work to guarantee peace as effectively as the century-old principles of the balance of power familiar to Europeans? As Nicolson put it, 'The defensive value of armaments, strategic frontiers, alliances and neutralization could be computed with approximate accuracy: the defensive value of "virtue all round" could not thus be computed.'[93] Indeed, the nationality principle was often honoured in the breach at Versailles, as in the case of Hungary, Romania, and Czechoslovakia.[94] Britain and France did not appear to have any qualms over dividing between them the spoils of the German colonial dominions and Ottoman lands, with the blessing of Wilson.[95] The Italian Socialist Salvemini argued that colonial partitions between France and Britain, no less than the United States's jealously guarded Monroe Doctrine (which had evolved from an instrument to resist European colonialism to a device for maintaining American hegemony in the Western Hemisphere), were inconsistent with Wilsonian self-determination principles: only Italy was expected to strictly bow to these principles.[96] Nicolson is eloquent: 'We had accepted a system for others which, when it came to practice, we should refuse to apply to ourselves.'[97]

To the extent that the treatment afforded to Italy implies a double standard and a reluctance to treat Italy as a major European power on a par with France and Britain, the situation was in part of Italy's own making. First, Italy's tardiness in committing not to sign a separate peace and in declaring war against Germany[98] did nothing to reassure the Allies that Italy was a reliable partner.[99] British archival materials also provide evidence of other reasons for complaint. A letter sent from the British delegation in Paris to the foreign secretary cites—as one reason for rejecting Italy's claims regarding Fiume and the Adriatic—two incidents where Italian military or political authorities had thwarted the execution of decisions of the Supreme Council even when 'concurred in by their own plenipotentiaries.'[100]

Secondly, when signing the Treaty of London, the Allies had expected—in part through Italy's own 'reticence on its fighting capability'—a more significant contribution from Italy to the conflict. [101] Later, the British ambassador in Rome, Rennell Rodd, lamented 'disparaging remarks . . . too freely made by allied officers regarding the military effort of Italy', which suggested 'a want of perception and appreciation among the Allies of the really great sacrifices endured by a young people with very limited resources.'[102] But Rodd was often the odd one out among relevant British civil servants. According to Burgwyn, 'the British would attempt to curtail their new ally's treaty rights as punishment for what appeared to them as poor military performance.'[103]

Thirdly, Italy did not do itself any favour with its occupation policies in Dalmatia following the Armistice with Austria-Hungary. These involved imprisonment and exile of elements regarded as hostile, censorship, and replacement of local authorities with more amenable governing bodies.[104] Arbitrary requisitions and arrests were also carried out, as reprisals against the looting and destruction of Italian property by retreating Croat troops at the end of the war.[105] These harsh occupation policies antagonised the Allies,[106] who also complained that Italian occupation forces 'are doing everything to make the Yugo-Slavs feel that they (the Italians) are landing in their Country as Conquerors, and by unnecessary parading of troops, colours and playing the band, are making it extremely difficult for the remainder of the Allies to carry out [their] duties'.[107]

France and Britain also had reasons to be sympathetic to the new Yugoslav state. France's interests in the eastern Adriatic meant that it was determined to keep Germany in check, and this required the establishment of strong states, including a strong Yugoslavia, to fence Germany in.[108] Having strategic interests in the region, which they were hoping to promote by bringing the Yugoslavs within their sphere of influence, the French quickly sent ships and soldiers to Fiume to protect Croat interests and openly advocated the justice of a Yugoslav Fiume.[109] Indeed, Italy's insistence during the negotiations on being granted the portion of Dalmatia promised in 1915 was partly due to its apprehensions about a future Slav-French alliance proving hostile to Italy.[110]

A strengthened Italian presence in the Mediterranean is also said to have run counter to British imperial interests.[111] Archival material alludes to concerns of this sort: 'We realised that the territorial arrangements contemplated by [the Treaty of London] could not be realised without gravely affecting, not to our advantage, the whole situation in the Adriatic'.[112] In British military quarters, the fear was also expressed that assigning Fiume to Italy would make Yugoslavia attempt to retaliate against Italy at a future point. This in turn would require Italy to maintain a large standing army, which would drive France to do the same, and Italy itself to seek the protection of Germany, forming a new 'Mittel Europa, which [would] be a serious menace to the peace of the world.'[113]

BRITAIN'S PRO-YUGOSLAV LOBBY

Although the British felt honour bound to apply the Treaty of London if Italy so demanded, they much preferred disapplying it in favour of a solution which would take Yugoslav interests seriously, assigning it both Dalmatia and Fiume. London was home to the headquarters of the Yugoslav Committee, whose work the British government had supported during the war for its potential to destabilise Austria-Hungary.[114] The committee, formally constituted by a group of South Slavs in 1915, represented and defined the political aims, aspirations, and strategies of the emerging Yugoslav nation and had branches in all major capitals.[115] When the Treaty of London had not yet been made public but rumours about its existence started circulating, the committee immediately denounced it.[116] In 1915 it published *The Southern Slav Programme*, which explicitly argued—among other things—for annexing Fiume to the future Yugoslav state.[117]

British economic interests also advised against assigning Italy Fiume, lest the Latin country should acquire commercial dominance in the area.[118] After Hungary and Austria, British ships were, by volume of exports and imports, the most active in Fiume. Britain and its colonies were recipients of the vast majority of the sugar exported from Fiume—by far the town's most important export, alongside timber—and supplier of its main commercial imports (cereals and textile raw materials).[119] The organ of British ship owners, the *Shipbuilding and Shipping Record*, argued that the lucrative business of ferrying emigrants from Fiume to New York and South America might be lost to Britain if Fiume were assigned to Italy.[120] Italians also gave credit to stories to the effect that a British navigation company had secured a practical monopoly at Fiume if it were to be assigned to the Yugoslavs, and hence that British commercial interests were behind the vociferous pro-Yugoslav position of part of the British press.[121] The fact that the British ambassador in Italy in March 1919 wrote to the foreign secretary advising that 'some denial should be given at once to story [circulating in the Italian newspapers] if possible'[122] suggests that even he could not quite rule out the falsity of these allegations. Nor did the allegations go away. True, it was primarily to American interests that George Herron was referring when he wrote, in an article published in *Epoca* in May, of the 'intrigues of several international financiers having diplomatic privileges', who were 'trying to obtain concessions for the development of Fiume and the Dalmatian ports, and to buy all the lines of navigation in the Adriatic'.[123] But the British ambassador in Rome noted that rumours circulating in the Italian press spoke of 'powerful financial interests which contemplate the development of Jugo-Slavia with American and perhaps international capital', implying that Britain remained under suspicion too.[124]

It was, however, primarily through the efforts of journalist Wickam Steed (diplomatic correspondent and later foreign editor for *The Times*) and political activist R. W. Seton-Watson that British public opinion and the British government came to support the creation of a Yugoslav state and to resist the attribution of Fiume to Italy. With experience and knowledge of relevant geopolitical realities, Steed and Seton-Watson advocated in favour of self-determination for national entities ruled by the Habsburg Empire.[125] Steed believed that the surest way to end the war was to weaken the Central Powers by engendering disaffection among the 'subject races' of Austria-Hungary—something that could be achieved if such populations became convinced of the Allies' intention to support their self-determination. However, the Treaty of London patently undermined the Allies' commitment to self-determination.[126]

In 1916 Steed and Seton-Watson sponsored the creation of a Serbian Society in Britain, aiming to promote the cause of a Yugoslav state.[127] Three years later Steed introduced the campaign directed against Austria-Hungary in the work of the Foreign Office programme of Propaganda in Enemy Countries,[128] enlisting Seton-Watson as his assistant.[129] Because of their ties to the Foreign Office, Steed and Seton-Watson 'were in a position to slant British and American foreign policy in favour of Yugoslavia at the expense of Italy'.[130] As a result, the British delegation at Versailles included several intellectuals who became impassioned and sometimes dogmatic supporters of a Yugoslav nation-state.[131] Steed himself, with Lord Northcliffe (who owned *The Times*, where Steed's views were aired), was 'very busy at Paris in the "*coulisses*."'[132]

Neither the United Italy Society of Great Britain (whose executive committee, as they made a point of specifying, consisted 'exclusively of British subjects')[133] nor the British Italian League[134] were a match for Steed and Seton-Watson's influence. These bodies, which favoured Fiume's annexation to Italy, have left few traces of their activities, and archival sources show that no notice of their arguments was taken by the nonplenipotentiary delegates, technical advisers, and technical experts that supported the British plenipotentiary delegates at Versailles.

Through Seton-Watson and Steed's efforts (and even, it must be said, their intrigues) the British press also came to exhibit a pro-Yugoslav bias. Italy's reformist Socialist Gaetano Salvemini was a strong advocate of Italy's renouncing its indefensible claims over Dalmatia and firmly believed that Italian Nationalist propaganda over Dalmatia was the main reason why Italy was 'morally isolated' in the *Entente*.[135] In 1917, nonetheless, Salvemini declined Seton-Watson's invitation to contribute to the recently founded publication *The New Europe*: while the periodical 'rightly throws light on the mistake of the inflated demands of certain Italian imperialists,' Salvemini wrote, 'it seems to ignore those of Slav imperialists . . . [and] that on the Slav or philo-Slav side there is much to condemn too'.[136] Salvemini and other Italian democrats did eventually agree to collaborate with *The New Europe* but resigned one after the other between the end of 1918 and January 1919, in protest against the unabashedly pro-Yugoslav sentiments the periodical by then came to express.[137]

Meanwhile, leading articles in Italian moderate newspapers complained of the way in which Lord Northcliffe's *The Times*, of which Steed was described as 'the leading light', sought to control both public opinion and governmental policy, at home as well as abroad, 'by increasing agitation against Italian aspirations [in the Adriatic] in the name of England and the United States'.[138] From diplomatic correspondence, it transpires that in contention was no less than a punitive press campaign orchestrated by Steed and Northcliffe in response to Italy's failure to satisfy their wish that it should immediately recognise the Yugoslav state. In addition to owning *The Times*, Northcliffe was director of propaganda in enemy countries and Italy, and in early November 1918 he had written a letter (actually authored by Steed) addressed to the Italian commissioner for aeronautics, who was 'practically a minister'.[139] Northcliffe calls the commissioner his friend[140] and purports to write in a private capacity, but it seems obvious that he counted on the commissioner to disclose the contents of the letter to Orlando (something the commissioner duly proceeded to do), with a view to influencing Italian foreign policy. Having described himself as 'not a member of the British Government', Northcliffe/Steed in their letter nonetheless take it upon themselves to insist on Italy's recognising the Yugoslav state without delay, threatening by indirection a damaging press campaign in the event that Italy does not. The document is quite extraordinary for its bullying tone:

> I cannot sufficiently strongly insist on the necessity of Italy's official policy [with respect to the Yugoslav question] being without any delay raised to that lofty level to which President Wilson has brought the whole allied cause with the enthusiastic support of the great mass of the British public.
>
> If this is carried out, *immediately publicly spontaneously*, it may be of great advantage to Italy. But . . . it will not be tolerated that any obstacles should be placed in the way of an equitable peace settlement through any kind of secret treaty or by any contrivances of antiquated diplomacy. The allied and associated peoples who have won the war despite the errors of their Governments will see to it that the peace will be such a one as they have fought for.[141]

The British ambassador in Rome, Rodd, wrote to Balfour (foreign secretary) that Steed had developed (and passed on to Northcliffe) his 'mania for being a protagonist in the creation of Jugo-Slavia' primarily as a result of his long-term involvement and co-habitation with Madame Rose, a 'brilliant . . . journalist' who had helped launch Steed's journalistic career.[142] Rodd worried that the English tended to 'be led by the press to take an almost disproportionate interest in the Jugo-Slavs and a large section of the press is in the hands, vicariously at any rate, of one of the most rabid partisans, inspired by a domestic Jugo-Slav connection.'[143]

Ironically—given Rodd's appeal to the foreign secretary—the delegates that supported the British plenipotentiaries at Versailles, many of whom were drawn from the Foreign Office,[144] were themselves implicated in the one-sided nature of British press reporting. Archival material suggests that these men did not have any qualms about sharing anti-annexation testimony with British propaganda staff (who saw to it that it would be distributed to the press in London and Paris)[145] despite their rating the source of the information as 'mediocre'.[146]

In archival sources, the most recurrent names among the British representatives at Versailles that dealt with the Fiume question are those of Harold Nicolson, Allen W. A. Leeper, Eyre A. Crowe, and Harold W. V. Temperley. All of them sat in one or the other of the five advisory territorial committees created by the Supreme Council to redesign European frontiers.[147] Nicolson, Leeper, Temperley, and Crowe customarily wrote down minutes on intelligence, submission, and correspondence received on Italy and the Adriatic question. Their manifest anti-Italian bias in the minutes relating to the Fiume question makes for fascinating reading. The position of Fiume was peculiar and messy enough that reasonable people might disagree on how it should be solved: yet the minutes reveal both an unbreakable consensus among the four representatives, and their steadfast unwillingness to concede that the annexationists had even an arguable case.

The minutes are invariably scathing in their assessment of Italian claims and enthusiastic about material that had a tendency to undermine them. The use of loaded language is commonplace: Italy's treaty-based territorial concessions are described as 'the Italian *grab*', [148] the Italian prime minister's telegram is a 'hysterical outburst',[149] etc. Equivalent expressions are never applied to Yugoslav or pro-Yugoslav claims, even when overblown or suspect. A double standard is apparent from the dismissive treatment of relevant evidence or perspectives if they came from either Italy, Fiume's National Council, non-Italian supporters of Italy's claims to Fiume, or British voices inclined to compromise and conciliation with Italy. Thus, 'the statistical game is played by . . . Italians with . . . disregard of all honesty';[150] 'I do not think any suggestion from Grazioli! [to wit: the Italian general in command of Fiume's occupation forces] can be entitled to any serious consideration';[151] 'There is nothing fresh in this [submission from the National Council] and it means nothing';[152] 'Professor Herron is an unreliable, bolshevistically-inclined, American agent';[153] 'This is an old trick of Sir Rennell Rodd';[154] 'In spite of his misspelt Croat name, [Ossoinack] is a thoroughly sound Italian Jingo. No good purpose could be served by an interview';[155] 'It is satisfactory that Pres Wilson took the occasion to answer the absurd arguments of this very suspect Italianised Croat.'[156]

Bias can also be garnered from other circumstances, including relevant personnel's ability to misread information in a way that confirms the pro-Yugoslav outcome to which they are precommitted. A fairly egregious example is to be found in a minute addressed by the director of military intelligence, General Thwaites, to Crowe. Thwaites transmutes General Watts's opinion that the National Council is a 'Regime' oppressing the majority of the 'population'[157] into the conclusion that 'General Watts states that the Italians are very much in the minority as regards population in Fiume.'[158] Shortly thereafter, Lieutenant Colonel Peck's entirely impressionistic (and, on a literal reading, logically impossible) statement that 'it is becoming obvious that the Italian element in Fiume certainly does not reach to more than 40%, and probably not more than 50%'[159] is enthusiastically greeted by Crowe with: 'This amply confirms what we have always contended'.[160]

In sum, the British delegation adopted a palpably pro-Yugoslav stance at the Paris Conference. The Italian delegates were disappointed at best, outraged at worst, at the Allies' willingness to afford this treatment to the demands of the new Yugoslav state, particularly when the Croats had been fighting against the Allies and with Austria-Hungary until Habsburg troops had finally been routed.[161]

NEGOTIATIONS IN CRISIS AND THE FALL OF ITALY'S GOVERNMENT

On 23 April 1919 Wilson decided to directly appeal to the Italian people and bypass their intractable government. First, he suspended the provision of any further financial aid to Italy.[162] Secondly, in the French press he publicly announced his opposition to what he regarded as imperialistic Italian demands,[163] setting out his vision about the right territorial arrangements in the eastern Adriatic and urging Italy to negotiate on the basis of principles of justice rather than self-interest.[164]

This direct appeal to public opinion while negotiations were ongoing was unprecedented in the history of international negotiations.[165] The fallout from Wilson's move is reported to have left the US ambassador in Rome 'in a state of complete dejection'.[166] The publication of Wilson's manifesto—which British prime minister Lloyd George privately declared to have been due to a mixture of idealism and vanity[167]—was taken by the Italian delegates as a ruse to manipulate them into accepting the American president's position. Orlando critiqued Wilson's attempt to pit the Italian people against their government,[168] and the Italian delegates left the conference in protest on 24 April 1919 to seek the confidence of the Italian Parliament.[169] Sonnino saw the risks involved in this move and unsuccessfully tried to avert it by declaring himself prepared to compromise on the Treaty of London,[170] of which, as we know, he had been the most intransigent defender.[171]

Despite a ban on all demonstrations issued by Fiume's Inter-Allied Command, the National Council responded to Wilson's published announcements by staging a large demonstration. This the Yugoslavs described, and the British naturally accepted, as not being representative of the majority of the population; allegedly, the National Council had used coercive practices to engineer a show of popular support.[172] The National Council also invited General Grazioli—who was then in command of Fiume's Inter-Allied occupation forces—to assume all powers and swore that Fiumans would have their will to be annexed to Italy honoured 'until the last'. But Grazioli—alive to the complications that his acceptance would have created for the Italian government and for himself—declined. He noted that the Italian government had not yet declared Fiume's annexation[173] and argued that the Fiuman people's legitimate representatives must remain in charge.[174] Some weeks later, the National Council addressed an official communication to Italian prime minister Orlando to the effect that they would not tolerate Fiume's destiny being bargained away without the town's own consent.[175]

Visiting Fiume at the end of May, and commenting on how Italians had 'completely lost their heads' to a patriotic fervour that made them willing to shed blood, Lina Waterfield declared that 'Wilson has done as much to unite Italy as the Risorgimento.'[176] The delegates returning from Versailles were greeted with widespread public demonstrations of support in all large towns.[177] *Arditi* used ropes to carry Orlando's car to the king's palace in Rome,[178] and the government thought it prudent to place a guard around the American embassy.[179] The writer Giovanni Comisso's unedifying experience reveals, however, that participation in such public demonstrations may have often been less than spontaneous and quite uninformed.[180]

In any case, virtually all political forces, including moderate Socialists, made a united front in support of the government.[181] Even the Socialist Filippo Turati, in speaking for the forty neutralist Socialists who had not voted in support of the government in the confidence vote, conceded that Fiume had a right to self-determination. However, he went on to state that Italy did not have a right to demand it when it had tolerated the self-determination principle to be disapplied to the detriment of Russia and in favour of France, Britain, and the United States. The latter two, Turati declared, were notably Wilsonian in advocating the nationality and self-determination principles when other countries were concerned and imperialistic when it came to their own interests.[182]

William Erskine, counsellor at the British embassy in Rome, reported that while six months previously the general sentiment had inclined towards compromise, now public opinion about Fiume had become more rigid: the Fiume question had been postponed for so long at the Peace Conference that Italian Nationalists had had ample time for their propaganda. This propaganda had been 'greatly helped by the exaggerated claims put forward by the Jugo-Slavs' leaders at the Peace Conference, and also by the irritation due to the attitude of Mr Steed and the Northcliffe press'. Primarily, however, the public's new intransigence about Fiume was due to the perception that Wilsonian principles had been 'cast aside' when it came to the settlement of questions affecting other Allies.[183]

Erskine went on to note that even if, as some claimed, Italians were not a majority in Fiume, for the Italian public

> it would be an act of treachery to hand them over to the tender mercies of a Balkan people . . . whose soldiers they accuse of the greater part of the atrocities and devastations alleged to have been committed in the districts invaded by the Austrian Armies. The argument that Fiume is necessary as an outlet for Croatia and Hungary does not appeal to them when they are told that the retention of Danzig by Germany on the ground of the population being German is not regarded as an obstacle to its serving as adequate outlet for Poland.[184]

There was 'no doubt', Erskine continued, that Wilson's announcement to the French press, prompting the Italian delegates to leave the negotiating table, had 'been the prime factor in producing [this] remarkable unanimity'.[185]

The Italian delegates' walkout, however, only had the effect of France, Britain, and the United States continuing the negotiations amongst themselves.[186] The former two proceeded to formally acknowledge the new Yugoslav state, which, unlike the United States, they had hitherto refrained from doing at Italy's request.[187] On 3 May, Orlando was offering Lloyd George to return to the negotiating table on condition that the Treaty of London be 'confirmed' at the Peace Conference (leaving Fiume to Croatia), but reserving the right for Italy to negotiate directly with Croatia at a later stage for a cession of Fiume in exchange for other territories.[188] Lloyd George apparently made no such commitment. Rather, he informed Orlando that if the Italian delegates did not return, he would no longer consider himself bound by the Treaty of London,[189] prompting the British ambassador to write to him that Orlando had found his message 'rather peremptory' and 'may return really with a certain sense of humiliation'.[190]

Indeed, though the show of multipartisan support to the government briefly convinced some in Italy that the delegates would now enjoy greater clout at the Peace Conference,[191] the way the Nationalist press reported on their return eventually managed to damage Orlando's leadership.[192] Rumour spread that the return was due to an ultimatum from Paris, and the British ambassador in Rome reported that 'the military organizations which have been allowed to influence public opinion are said to be assuming a menacing language towards delegates should they return without satisfactory compromise.'[193] The Orlando government fell in June 1919, when the prime minister was asked to account for his external affairs policy, leading to the appointment of a new prime minister, Francesco Saverio Nitti.[194]

Nitti quickly strove to reestablish good diplomatic relations with the Allies. He saw that economic reconstruction was dependent on it, as well as on containing both the most outlandish ambitions of the Nationalists and the political activities of certain sectors of the Army. Consequently, he facilitated troops' demobilisation and the transfer of power from the military to the civil administration. He failed, however, to manage the country's expectations over the Adriatic question and to respond to national sentiment over Fiume.[195] The Treaty of Versailles, signed by Italy shortly after the new government took office,[196] secured for Italy Trento and Trieste (traditional *terre irredente*), but not Fiume.

An economist and statistician by training, it has been argued that Nitti was inclined to assess the Fiume problem in terms of cost-benefit analysis, yielding the rational conclusion that patriotic sentiment should give way to the more urgent need of postwar economic recovery. He believed that pursuing further national unification was likely to prove politically destabilising and to risk impoverishing the country.[197] Alienating Wilson might jeopardise Italy's financial security, with repercussions, among other things, on its ability to secure foodstuffs from abroad, at a time when it was experiencing serious food shortages.[198] Nitti apparently assumed that the people of Italy would, as rational economic actors, come to see this. But he overestimated the extent to which the country was prepared to follow him.[199] A contemporary observer argued that he 'was an economist, that is a monocle who, like many students of that science, studying men as workers, producers, savers, account-keepers and profit-makers, easily falls into the trap of believing that they should do nothing else'.[200]

FIUME'S ITALIANIZATION DURING THE OCCUPATION

Italian troops, as we saw, had entered Fiume on 17 November 1918. According to British military observers, this marked the beginning of trouble. In late January 1919, Brigadier General Gordon, commanding the British contingent in Fiume, remarked that 'no matter what the Peace Conference may decide about the fate of Fiume a bitter hatred between these people will remain, as a result of the Italian occupation and the various hostile acts committed by both sides during the past 2 ½ months.'[201]

On 7 December 1918 the National Council constituted itself as an official law-making body, with its managing committee as the executive, assuming the governmental functions formerly attributed to the Hungarian governmental authority. This arrangement was intended to last until Italy would ratify the annexation. The relevant decree was conveyed to the Allied Powers in Versailles. The functions of the old Municipal Council were instead assumed by the new office of the mayor.[202]

The 22 January 1919 law on the functioning of the National Council reiterated Fiume's right to self-government without external interference and was followed by a number of laws addressing public order and the town's economic and political recovery.[203] The self-constitution of the National Council into an official governing body attracted critiques from both democratic and Slav political minorities, but it was recognised as legitimate by General Grazioli—who is said to have privately supported, and intended to facilitate, the National Council's and radical young Fiumans' design to have Fiume annexed to Italy.[204]

Grazioli had supervened, as Allied commander at Fiume, on General di San Marzano after the latter had occupied the town on 17 November. Admiral Rainer, who had ordered the landing of Italian seamen on the same day in circumstances that had antagonised his French and British counterparts, had also been replaced. According to Rear-Admiral Kiddle, of the Inter-Allied Commission of Admirals for the Adriatic, 'in the middle of November, the Italian residents and press worked up supposed disorders in Fiume and desired the occupation of the town by Italian troops'. Italian forces had seized on this pretext, but the officers whose ruthlessness had been an asset in launching the occupation had then been swiftly replaced by ones whose personal style would be less grating on the Allies.[205] This change of guard, however, did not prevent tensions from continuing within the Inter-Allied command. In March 1919, Brigadier-General Gordon, after reporting his standing up to Grazioli in the matter of politically motivated expulsions and other decisions likely to cause frictions with Yugoslavia, voiced his 'impression that [Grazioli] is acting under instructions'.[206] On a visit in late May, Lina Waterfield said of Grazioli that he 'has a difficult time being evidently pushed by his Government in the present policy—the English says he is insincere—what else can he be with Sonnino behind him—and the Allies to be dealt with.'[207]

The National Council provided for the Hungarian flag to be replaced by the Italian one[208] and passed a number of other measures intended to entrench the Italian character of the town. In spring the National Council passed a law repealing Hungarian criminal laws and regulations and replacing them (with effect from 1 July) with their (more liberal) Italian equivalents;[209] it also expressly abolished the death penalty.[210] Not only the former but also the latter move was clearly intended to pay homage to the elective Italianness of Fiume, Italy having been one of the first European countries to have abolished capital punishment, in 1889.

The significance of these legal changes, when reported by the Fiume British Military Mission, was not lost on the British nonplenipotentiary representatives and technical advisers at Paris. The changes sent them into a minute-writing spree taking up an unusual two and a half pages, denouncing variously the illegality, invalidity, *ultra-vires* character, and extraterritoriality of the National Council's move. Their comments betray an initial conflation between the National Council of Fiume and the Italian occupying forces, effectively ascribing (wrongly) the legal changes to the latter. The conflation is easily explained by the way in which these representatives give proof, again and again, to have thoroughly assimilated Steed and Northcliffe's pro-Yugoslav propaganda. This would condition them, for example, to take at face value such mischaracterisations of the National Council, by pro-Yugoslav voices, as 'the executive office of the Inter-Allied Command',[211] or as an 'administrative body of the occupying power',[212] or, conversely, such speculations dressed up as facts by British observers who claimed that 'the Italian military authorities are virtually under [the National Council's] thumb'.[213] The conflation was later rectified, albeit only half-heartedly. It was conceded that the National Council was 'technically independent' of Grazioli's Allied command, save for declaring that the difference between the local authority and the occupying forces was 'no doubt more apparent than real' and that the legal changes remained 'equally illegal in either case'.[214] In the event, Nicolson and Crowe (foreign under secretary) decided to take no action on the assumption that Fiume would be constituted into an autonomous state and then these questions would 'settle themselves'.[215]

In an imaginative move that symbolically reaffirmed the National Council's commitment to annexation to Italy and signalled its determination to be recognised as an official governing body, a special issue of Fiume stamps bearing the Italian flag was also produced, and requests were sent to the postal authorities of different countries to treat the stamps as valid.[216] The National Council even managed to enlist the cooperation of the Italian Postal Services, as the Britain General Post Office found out upon receiving a circular from the International Bureau of the Postal Union, sent on behalf of the Italian Postal Services, announcing that Fiume had been provisionally constituted into an autonomous state (!) and that its postage stamps should be regularly recognised.[217] In a show of supremely British pragmatism, the Foreign Office eventually decided not to acknowledge these requests at all, but to continue to deliver letters bearing the stamps without surcharge, that is, as if the stamps were valid.[218]

On 2 June, Ossoinack wrote to the president of the Peace Conference that if the powers at Versailles chose to settle the Fiume question in a way contrary to the wishes of the Fiumans, the town would not recognise their decision. This was not only because Fiume had been denied a voice at the negotiating table but also because its political autonomy had always been based on an inherent right to self-determination, which the town had managed to assert even against absolute monarchies.[219]

FRENCH AND ITALIAN TROOPS IN FIUME

Tensions in Fiume arose not only between Italians and Croats but, particularly, between Italian and French troops. British military sources dating from December 1918 detail serious bickering and point scoring between French and Italian officers about requisitioning of ships under the French flag. Conflict was facilitated by the fact that French officials, being in Fiume under the military authority of the Army of the Orient, did not recognise the Italian Inter-Allied command. The reports identify the Italian military occupation as a chief cause of disturbances and critique Italians' aggressive behaviour, but they are also scathing of the French, whom they accuse of behaving in a manner calculated to cause incidents.[220]

When, on 17 November 1918, the Italian troops had managed to displace the Serb battalion dispatched by Franchet D'Espèrey, the French had not found it expedient to insist, as Serbia had requested them to, on Italian troops departing from Fiume.[221] But neither had they, thereby, resigned themselves to relinquishing control of the town and seeing it annexed to Italy. The establishment, one month after the National Council had constituted itself into a governing body, of a French naval base in the harbour, to supply the Army of the Orient under General Franchet D'Espèrey, must be seen in this context—although it generally isn't, because of a failure (with rare exceptions)[222] to appreciate the role played by France in the events that had precipitated the Italian occupation in the first place.

It is significant that a communication from the Italian embassy states that 'as a result of recent communication from the Italian Government to the French Government, the latter have agreed to the principle of maintaining an Italian occupation of that port together with the existence of a naval base for the Army of the East.'[223] The French base, albeit officially established only in order to supply the Army of the Orient, in practice meant a large presence in Fiume of French soldiers not under the authority of Grazioli's Allied command. It seems clear that Italy and France had, effectively, worked out a compromise that afforded each a degree of influence over local events, while the town's destiny was being deliberated in diplomatic circles. It is telling, in this respect, that the French demanded immediate accommodation for 2,000 men, and a total of 7,000 eventually—a number that matched exactly the Italian forces stationed in town and that could have only been accommodated if the Italian troops in Fiume had been considerably pared down.[224] It is also telling that the British reported French troops in Fiume to have been 'very much in evidence'.[225]

This should be seen in light of Italy's and France's competing foreign policy ambitions. In December 1918, Ambassador Rodd wrote to the foreign secretary that in Italy there was 'a growing conviction . . . that the French are supporting the Jugo-Slavs, not from any ideal of equity but with a view to the isolation of their chief Mediterranean rival.'[226] In a later letter he himself somewhat cautiously endorsed the view that 'the French are at the bottom of a good deal of the trouble and are endeavouring to extend their influence everywhere on the other side of the Adriatic, and stir up the Jugo-Slavs.'[227] As he had elaborated in another missive, ostensibly Italy and France were 'on the best of terms', but 'individual Frenchmen in authority in the Adriatic' deliberately made 'difficulties for the Italians' and encouraged the Yugoslavs.[228] Rather than from Balfour himself, the answer to Rodd came from the foreign under secretary. Albeit no fan of 'the greediness of Italian Foreign Policy', at whose door he squarely laid the present difficulties, he conceded 'that the French are not always tactful in their dealings with the Italians, and that they also have an exaggerated appetite'.[229]

The National Council clearly had an inkling of all this and protested against the establishment of the French base. The French insisted that it implied no assertion of political right over Fiume,[230] but the Fiumans were not reassured. Many felt that the French base was a pretext, specifically, to introduce Serb elements into town.[231] One can hardly accuse them of outright paranoia. General Tranié, who had been sent to open the base, was in command of the Franco-Serb battalions of the Army of the Orient,[232] and had been ordered to occupy Fiume with one French and one Serb battalion. In the event, the latter remained stationed elsewhere 'for reason of convenience' and also because the Italian occupation meant that it could not be accommodated.[233] Yet approximately 250 Serbs ended up among the French troops at the base, with a high proportion of officers, which made General Grazioli worry about possible espionage activities[234] and resulted in serious dissensions between him and the commander of the French forces in Fiume, General Savy.[235] It did not help matters that, around the same time, the Italian press had been stridently critical of France, who was 'regarded to have secured most of her essential objects [at Versailles], one of which was the opposing of a barrier to the eventual rivalry of a more powerful Italy in the Mediterranean.'[236]

The French were widely perceived by the Fiumans to side with the Yugoslavs.[237] British archival material sheds light on this point. Military reports from December 1918 state that Yugoslav deputations in Fiume and Istria 'laid special stress on the friendliness of the French, and some of them went so far as to say that they would have welcomed French occupation. . . . The more anti-Italian they were the stronger they expressed their French sympathies';[238] and that Yugoslavs in Fiume 'hate the Italians and look to the Allies . . . especially the French, who are fraternising closely.'[239] Later, Fiumans would complain that French soldiers regularly provoked the Italian population with the acquiescence of the French command.[240] British military reports testify to enmity between French and Italian troops on the eastern Adriatic coast generally—that is, beyond Fiume—and to US and British corps having to 'act as buffer'.[241] As early as mid-December 1918 it was reported that 'tension between the Italians and the French in the Adriatic is evidently becoming disconcertingly acute.'[242] In Fiume, the Italian command's fears of an open conflict erupting with France are manifest in its dispatches to Rome.[243]

JULY 1919 DISTURBANCES

In early July 1919, public order disturbances involving Italian troops and their French counterpart culminated in the death of nine French officers and the wounding of forty-one French soldiers. In the first such disturbance, as news spread around town of a French soldier ripping an Italian cockade off the breast of a young local woman, French soldiers were set upon in several locations by young Fiumans, aided by Italian soldiers. All those involved were apparently between sixteen and twenty-one years of age.[244] The Croat Club was also trashed. Only three days before, upon the signing of the Treaty of Versailles, French soldiers had cheered France and Yugoslavia and, apparently, they had booed Italy.[245]

French and pro-French voices claimed the cockade incident was staged by the Italians as a pretext to attack the French.[246] Conversely, the Italian press claimed the French had engineered it all to bring Italians into disrepute.[247] But there is very little reason to doubt the spontaneous nature of the incident. The Supreme Command of the Inter-Allied Forces recorded incidents on seven different occasions between December 1918 and July 1919, the majority of which involved Fiumans overreacting to their aggravation at French soldiers' disorderly or provoking behaviour.[248] A February 1919 report from Brigadier-General Gordon, in command of the British contingent in Fiume, refers to several riots and incidents in December and January, including the killing of a French sailor by an Italian soldier, lamenting that 'the Italian authorities cannot produce any of the Soldiers' involved.[249] Thus, scuffles between Italians and French soldiers had been the order of the day for many months.

The young Fiuman woman involved in the first July incident claimed that the French soldier had ripped off and trampled upon her cockade; the soldier himself claimed instead that, in his drunkenness, he had raised his hand and made as if to touch her breasts, without actually making contact.[250] It is far from improbable that the assaulted woman's account was truthful, because—although this appears a little-known fact in the secondary literature—incidents involving cockades were very frequent. Comisso's memoirs report that it was as common for French sailors to cross the bridge to Sušak to visit Croat young women and to come back sporting Yugoslav cockades, as for young Fiuman women to pin cockades with the town colours on Italian soldiers' uniforms. Fiuman young women themselves conspicuously displayed Italian cockades, and during the evening *passeggiata* those self-same French sailors, having drunk one too many in Sušak, would attempt to rip off those cockades.[251] Roles were also reversed: British War Office and other correspondence from December 1918 and January 1919 reports Yugoslav women having their national colours torn from their dresses by Italian civilians or soldiers on a daily basis and French soldiers and sailors wearing Yugoslav badges in retaliation.[252]

In any case, both Italian and Yugoslav literature have sometimes exaggerated the importance of the cockade incident that sparked the first July disturbance, as if the apportioning of blame depended on its exact dynamic. Clearly it does not: the attacks on other (uninvolved) French soldiers were unjustified whether or not the French soldier misbehaved (and whether he misbehaved, specifically, in a nationalistic or a sexual way). At the same time, it does not strain credibility that a single—in itself relatively insignificant—incident should spark such widespread disturbances in the Fiuman context of French-Italian enmity at this particular point in time. Numerous such incidents, as we saw, had previously occurred generally (though not invariably) without lethal consequences, and on a smaller scale. But as British and American sources in Fiume opined, by this time both uncertainty over the future of the town and the campaign of the local press and agitators had resulted in tensions reaching breaking point.[253] Commander Diggle spoke of 'propaganda which has been going on on all sides, save the British for months past.'[254]

Further attacks on French troops, including lethal ones, followed a few days later. The timing is significant, as the targets of the attack appear to have been 'French bluejackets from a torpedo boat and a destroyer' that had just arrived[255]—suggesting that the Fiumans were violently protesting against what they saw as an intensification of foreign 'interference' with their national destiny. The attacks were sparked by French soldiers firing their weapons (without injuring anyone) in the context of either altercations with Fiumans or their feeling threatened by the latter's numerical preponderance and hostile behaviour. Once again, Fiumans savagely overreacted and Italian troops actively partook in one of the attacks.[256] Reports of aggression against French colonial (specifically, Annamese) troops detail horrific violence on the part of Fiumans.[257] Rear Admiral Sinclair pointed out that 'it is impossible to believe that the mild natured Annamese, who have been the greatest sufferers, would do anything aggressive' to provoke the Fiumans.[258] Only one week before, these troops had been racially abused in the local press and reported to have harassed Fiuman women, in line with an established nationalist *topos* of foreigners endangering native women's honour.[259] Even conceding that, as the naval attaché at Rome noted, French soldiers would from time to time deliberately provoke the Fiumans by loudly parading their pro-Yugoslav sympathies and anti-Italian sentiments, without French officers making any serious efforts to curb their behaviour,[260] the sheer disproportion in death and injuries as between the two sides 'told heavily against' the Italians.[261]

In an interview with Admiral Sinclair, General Grazioli stated that he had not been able to keep order because this would have required him to fire on civilians, which put him in an impossible situation; but he now planned to send away trouble-making *Arditi* companies. He added that the National Council was trying to make the French leave, prompting Sinclair to observe, in a letter to the admiralty, 'This is probably a fact and judged by his own behaviour and that of the troops under his command, it would appear that this is his policy also.'[262]

Colonel Peck believed that the disturbances had been 'organised with the full knowledge of the Italians [meaning the Italian command], if not by the

Italians themselves'.[263] Given, however, that the predictable outcome of a concerted, successful, and unequal attack on the French, to which Italian troops partook, would be to impeach the Italian command and Italian military presence in Fiume, it is hard to see the logic of this inference. Peck could hold on to his theory by assuming that something had gone wrong with the plan: the disturbances had been organised, but they were organised 'badly', so that the outcome was the opposite of what had been desired. But this is more informative about Peck's penchant for believing anything anti-Italian and anti-Fiuman than about the nature of the disturbances. The evidence Peck had to show for his thesis was twofold. First, there was intelligence elicited by a British spy from Major Canevari, but Canevari had been dismissed from Grazioli's staff and his testimony appears unreliable, showing he had a serious grudge against Grazioli borne of wounded pride. And, secondly, there was intelligence elicited by a Fiuman lieutenant in the Italian Army, but this had done no more than assent in conversation to the spy's own suggestions about the organised nature of the riots and how they could have been better organised.[264]

More credible is the Fiume British Mission's report, dating from a few days after the incidents, that Grazioli was still making 'no determined effort to keep order in the town.'[265] The report suggested that the factors leading to the incidents included 'the lack of serious attempts to keep order', 'young Fiumani' being encouraged to drill 'as military units' and having their acts of violence systematically overlooked, civilians being allowed to carry arms, a 'press campaign against the French', and 'drunken French troops' reportedly expressing 'anti-Italian views publicly on several occasions'.[266] At the end of June, before the July incidents, serious frictions had also occurred between General Grazioli and General Savy, who claimed French soldiers in Fiume were under his exclusive orders and those of his superior, General Franchet D'Espèrey.[267]

From the embassy in Rome, Rodd, commented that it was 'impossible to judge from either Italian or French sources with whom fault really lies'.[268] Nitti facilitated the constitution of an Inter-Allied inquiry and its fact-finding work about the role of Italian troops in the disturbances.[269] General di Robilant was appointed as the Italian member of the Commission of Inquiry. The commission's report is exemplary for its balanced treatment of the evidence and in its assessments. It argued that the factors that enabled the present state of hostility between the French and Italians/Fiumans were the Allies' recognition of the new Yugoslav state without Italy's concurrence, the fact that the peace of Versailles postponed to a date to be determined the settlement of all questions relating to Fiume, and Italy's conviction that France was intent on recreating a Gallic version of the Habsburg Empire. In such circumstances, the report noted, all civil and military authorities should have collaborated to defuse tensions. Instead the National Council had proclaimed annexation, discriminated against Croats, and permitted the activities of young radical annexationists; the Croat National Committee in Sušak continued in existence with the sole purpose of spreading Croat propaganda; the Italian command failed to take any action against Fiumans threatening public order, openly supported the National Council, and made arbitrary use of its censorship powers to favour Italian viewpoints; and the French command and French officers failed to conceal their Yugoslav sympathies. The report concluded that if all these authorities shared responsibility for generating a climate conducive to the serious events under investigation, the Italian command was solely responsible for the failure to keep order.[270]

The report's main recommendations were a change of personnel in the Italian command and in the troops that had partaken in the disturbances; a reduction of the Italian contingent; a change in personnel of the French base, with an eye to its disestablishment; the replacement of the National Council with an interim elected body under the control of the Allies; the dissolution of Fiume's local militia; the establishment of an Inter-Allied military administration under either US or British command; and an American or British police force to maintain order.[271]

Concerning the last recommendation, Léon Kotchnitzky (a young Belgian intellectual who would play an important role in D'Annunzio's Fiume command in 1920) would later quip, 'we all knew what that meant: for several years now, English forces have been "maintaining order" in Cyprus, Cairo, Gibraltar, Hong-Kong, Zanzibar.'[272] The recommendations were certainly greeted with outrage by the National Council, some of whose members were quite convinced that the British had an interest in securing a port in the Adriatic, and from there to take control of the Balkan route to Constantinople.[273] The outgoing Italian troops, for their part, were positive that following through with the report recommendations meant that Fiume would be lost to Italy.[274] Mario Maria Martini (later head of D'Annunzio's special secretariat in Fiume)[275] declared that the departure of the Italian troops hailed 'a very bitter tomorrow'.[276] According to Comisso, suspicious deaths of French soldiers continued even after the report of the Inter-Allied Commission.[277]

CONCLUSION

A serious commitment to the nationality and self-determination principles would have recommended a deceptively simple solution to the territorial arrangements in the eastern Adriatic: Fiume should be assigned to Italy, while Dalmatia, except for a few Italian enclaves, to Yugoslavia. The problem is that the Italian delegation was all for self-determination so long as it concerned Fiume, but not with respect to Dalmatia. And Wilson defended self-determination as it concerned Dalmatia, but not when it came to Fiume.

Wilson's intransigence was the greatest obstacle to a solution of the Fiume question in favour of Italy, but France and Britain also had strategic and/or economic interests in opposing it. Italy's maximalist set of demands at the Peace Conference made it easier to challenge the Italian position in its entirety—even with respect to Fiume, where an application of self-determination principles may have militated in favour of assigning it to Italy. In the event, the Treaty of Versailles was signed without the fate of the town having been determined.

While some literature has previously alluded to the pro-Yugoslav position of the British press and of the British delegation at Versailles, archival evidence shows just how entrenched and dogmatic that position could be. British archival evidence also casts light on two other matters. First, as we saw in the previous chapter, the Inter-Allied occupation of Fiume between November 1918 and September 1919 was, for all intents and purposes, an Italian occupation. Secondly, France played a more significant role than is generally appreciated in shaping the occupation, by maintaining a parallel military authority structure independent from the Inter-Allied Command. This was widely—and, given France's interests in engineering a particular balance of power in the Mediterranean, probably rightly—perceived by the Fiumans as a ruse to frustrate the goal of annexation.

The July 1919 disturbances, far from being a fluke, should be seen in the context of Italy's manifest and France's more covert (and, admittedly, probably not as single-minded) attempts at influencing the local balance of power in Fiume in a way conducive to their foreign policy priorities. The outcome of the disturbances, in line with the recommendations of the Inter-Allied Commission of Enquiry, was that after ten months the Italian occupation was poised finally to become genuinely Inter-Allied. This, of course, frustrated the Italians' ongoing attempt at creating a status quo that might facilitate a formal settlement of the Fiume question in their favour, explaining the timing of D'Annunzio's own occupation of Fiume, a few short weeks after the Inter-Allied report was published.

NOTES

1. British Delegation: Telegram from R. Rodd to Earl Curzon of Kedleston (17 May 1919), The National Archives, FO 608/39.

2. Mario Mondini, *Fiume 1919: Una Guerra Civile Italiana* (Roma: Salerno, 2019), 38–43.

3. Maxwell H. H. Macartney and Paul Cremona, *Italy's Foreign and Colonial Policy, 1914–1937* (New York: Howard Fertig, 1972), 25.

4. Geoffrey A. Haywood, *Failure of a Dream: Sidney Sonnino and the Rise and Fall of Liberal Italy, 1847–1922* (Firenze: Olschki, 1999), 475.

5. Marina Cattaruzza, *L'Italia e la Questione Adriatica: Dibattiti Parlamentari e Panorama Internazionale (1919–1926)* (Bologna: Il Mulino, 2014), 29–32; Roberto Vivarelli, *Storia delle Origini del Fascismo: L'Italia dalla Grande Guerra alla Marcia su Roma*, vol. 1 (Bologna: Il Mulino, 1991), 237–41.

6. Carlo Maranelli and Gaetano Salvemini, *La Questione dell'Adriatico* (Firenze: La Voce, 1918), 89–90.

7. Vivarelli, *Storia delle Origini*, 175–77, 192–93, 216–17.

8. Maranelli and Salvemini, *La Questione dell'Adriatico*, 87.

9. Maranelli and Salvemini, *La Questione dell'Adriatico*, 217–18.

10. René Albrecht-Carrié, *Italy at the Paris Peace Conference* (Hamden, CT: Archon, 1966), 69.

11. Letter from the Ambassador in Italy to the Special Representative (15 November 1918), enclosed in letter from the Ambassador in Italy to the Secretary of State (15 November 1918), in *Papers Relating to the Foreign Relations of the United States, The Paris Peace Conference, 1919*, vol. I, ed. Joseph Fuller (Washington: United States Government Printing Office, 1942), 448, https://history.state.gov/historicaldocuments/frus1919Parisv01/d356.

12. Margaret Macmillan, *Peacemakers: Six Months that Changed the World* (London: John Murray, 2001) 294, 300–301.

13. David Lloyd George, *The Truth about the Peace Treaties*, vol. II (London: Gollancz, 1938), 873.

14. Vivarelli, *Storia delle Origini*, 541

15. Renzo De Felice, *D'Annunzio Politico, 1918–1938* (Roma and Bari: Laterza, 1978), 8–10.

16. See, for example, Guglielmo Ferrero, "Sessanta Anni Dopo" (27 September 1919), in Guglielmo Ferrero, *Da Fiume a Roma: Storia di Quattro Anni (1919–1923)* (Milano: Athena, 1923), 11.

17. Edoardo Susmel, *Fiume Attraverso la Storia: Dalle Origini Fino ai Nostri Giorni* (Milano: Treves, 1919), 109; Edoardo Susmel, *La Cittá di Passione: Fiume negli Anni 1914–1920* (Milano: Treves, 1921), 155–56.

18. Vivarelli, *Storia delle Origini*, 236–37.

19. Vivarelli, *Storia delle Origini*, 527,

20. Haywood, *Failure*, 475–78.

21. Vivarelli, *Storia delle Origini*, 178–80, 215, 201 (note 115).

22. Gian Luigi Cecchini, "La Reggenza Fiumana nella Storia e nell'Ordinamento Giuridico Internazionale," in *Lo Statuto della Reggenza Italiana del Carnaro tra Storia, Diritto Internazionale e Diritto Costituzionale*, ed. Augusto Sinagra (Milano: Giuffré, 2009), 82.

23. Harold Nicolson, *Peacemaking, 1919* (London: Constable, 1933), 178–80.

24. British Delegation: Enclosure 2 to communication from DMI to Under Secretary of State for Foreign Affairs (5 August 1919), The National Archives, FO 608/39.

25. Nicolson, *Peacemaking*, 178–80.

26. H. James Burgwyn, *The Legend of the Mutilated Victory: Italy, the Great War, and the Paris Peace Conference, 1915–1919* (Westport, CT, and London: Greenwood, 1993), 202–3.

27. British Delegation: Enclosure 2 to communication from D.M.I. to Under Secretary of State for Foreign Affairs (5 August 1919), The National Archives, FO 608/39.

28. Haywood, *Failure*, 488.

29. Vivarelli, *Storia delle Origini*, 248–51.

30. Lloyd George, *The Truth,* 811–12.

31. V. E. Orlando's response to President Wilson (24 April 1919), published in Giulio Benedetti, *La Pace di Fiume: Dalla Conferenza di Parigi al Trattato di Roma* (Bologna: Zanichelli, 1924), 248; Lloyd George, *The Truth*, 844–45.

32. Albrecht-Carrié, *Italy at the Paris Peace Conference*, 98–99.

33. Macmillan, *Peacemakers*, 294.

34. Prime Minister: Letter from R. Rodd to [E. J. Harding] (14 December 1918), Parliamentary Archives, LG/F/200/1/20.

35. Cattaruzza, *L'Italia e la Questione Adriatica*, 35–37; Lloyd George, *The Truth*, 811.

36. Daily Italian Political Notes (14 November 1918), enclosed in letter from the Ambassador in Italy to the Secretary of State (15 November 1918), in *Papers Relating to the Foreign Relations of the United States, The Paris Peace Conference, 1919*, vol. I, ed. Joseph Fuller, 445.

37. Macmillan, *Peacemakers*, 303; Nicolson, *Peacemaking*, 179.

38. British Delegation, Correspondence and Papers Relating to Austria-Hungary (Political): Future of Fiume, comm.d by Serb-Croat-Slovene Delegation (29 March 1919), The National Archives, FO 608/8.

39. British Delegation, Correspondence and Papers Relating to Austria-Hungary (Political): A. W. A. Leeper's minutes on Future of Fiume, comm.d by Serb-Croat-Slovene Delegation (29 March 1919), The National Archives, FO 608/8; Italy: Aims in Dalmatia and Croatia: H. Nicolson, 'The Question of Fiume' (15 January 1919), The National Archives, FO 608/15/8; Italy, Rebellion: Letter from Lieutenant Colonel S. C. Peck to D.M.O., War Office (10 October 1919), The National Archives, FO 608/41/1.

40. Prime Minister: Note handed to V. E. Orlando on April 24 [1919] by the President of the United States and the Prime Ministers of Great Britain and France, Parliamentary Archives, LG/F/158/1/11.

41. Maranelli and Salvemini, *La Questione dell'Adriatico*, 70–72.

42. Prime Minister: Letter from R. Cecil to R. Rodd (3 January 1919), Parliamentary Archives, LG/F/200/1/20.

43. Adriatic, Italian Claims in Adriatic: H. Nicholson's minute (14 February 1919), The National Archives, FO 608/27/9.

44. British Delegation: Enclosure 2 to communication from D.M.I. to Under Secretary of State for Foreign Affairs (5 August 1919), The National Archives, FO 608/39.

45. Leeden, *The First Duce*, 30.

46. Nino Valeri, *Da Giolitti a Mussolini: Momenti della Crisi del Liberalismo* (Firenze: Parenti, 1957), 66.
47. Letter from General M. A. N. Di Robilant to F. S. Nitti (12 September 1919), in Valeri, *Da Giolitti a Mussolini*, 69–70.
48. Valeri, *Da Giolitti a Mussolini*, 71.
49. Macartney and Cremona, *Italy's Foreign and Colonial Policy*, 80, 84.
50. Lloyd George, *The Truth*, 820.
51. Cattaruzza, *L'Italia e la Questione Adriatica*, 41.
52. Haywood, *Failure*, 482.
53. Cecchini, "La Reggenza Fiumana," 83.
54. Lloyd George, *The Truth*, 785.
55. Cattaruzza, *L'Italia e la Questione Adriatica*, 41, 44.
56. Lloyd George, *The Truth*, 814.
57. William Klinger, *Un'Altra Italia: Fiume 1724–1924*, ed. Diego Redivo (Rovigno, Fiume, and Trieste: Centro di Ricerche Storiche Rovigno, 2018), 299, https://crsrv.org/wp/wp-content/uploads/2020/03/N.45-Klinger-Fiume.pdf.
58. Léon Kotchnitzky, *La Quinta Stagione: O, I Centauri di Fiume*, trans. Alberto Luchini (Bologna: Zanichelli, 1922), 46–48.
59. Silverio Annibale, *La Questione di Fiume nel Diritto Internazionale* (Rovigno, Fiume, and Trieste: Centro di Ricerche Storiche Rovigno, 2011), 56.
60. Lloyd George, *The Truth*, 814.
61. Mondini, *Fiume 1919*, 34–35.
62. Lawrence E. Glefand, *The Inquiry: American Preparations for Peace, 1917–1919* (New Haven, CT, and London: Yale University Press, 1963), 327–28.
63. Glefand, *The Inquiry*, 328.
64. Glefand, *The Inquiry*, 48.
65. Glefand, *The Inquiry*, 329.
66. Second Appeal of the American Experts to Wilson (17 April 1919), in Albrecht-Carrié, *Italy at the Paris Peace Conference*, 129–30.
67. Albrecht-Carrié, *Italy at the Paris Peace Conference*, 130–31.
68. Glefand, *The Inquiry*, 329.
69. Dominique Kirchner Reill, *The Fiume Crisis: Life in the Wake of the Habsburg Empire* (Cambridge, MA: Harvard University Press, 2020), 28–30; Pupo, *Fiume Città di Passione* (Bari: Laterza, 2018), 61.
70. Burgwyn, *The Legend*, 278.
71. Kirchner Reill, *The Fiume Crisis*, 40–41.
72. Leeden, *The First Duce*, 13; Macmillan, *Peacemakers*, 296.
73. Lloyd George, *The Truth,* 828.
74. Haywood, *Failure*, 481, 483, 490.
75. Lloyd George, *The Truth*, 827.
76. Cattaruzza, *L'Italia e la Questione Adriatica*, 41.
77. Burgwyn, *The Legend*, 274.
78. Memorandum between G. Clemenceau, F. L. Polk, and E. A. Crowe (9 December 1919), in Benedetti, *La Pace di Fiume*, 269.

79. Copy of President Wilson's final proposal, in Benedetti, *La Pace di Fiume*, 260.

80. Prime Minister: Memorandum enclosed in telegraphic message from F. S. Nitti to D. Lloyd George (via G. Imperiali) (27 October 1919), Parliamentary Archives, LG/F/55/4/39.

81. Prime Minister: Letter from F. S. Nitti to D. Lloyd George (6 January 1920), Parliamentary Archives, LG/F/55/4/39.

82. Adriatic, Italian Desiderata: A. W. A. Leeper, Memorandum (reporting conversation with Dr. Bowman of the US Delegation) (14 November 1919), The National Archives, FO 608/28/2.

83. Susmel, *La Cittá di Passione*, 180.

84. Benedetti, *La Pace di Fiume*, 29.

85. Susmel, *La Cittá di Passione*, 187–90; Benedetti, *La Pace di Fiume*, 237–42.

86. Susmel, *La Cittá di Passione*, 188.

87. Lloyd George, *The Truth*, 793–94.

88. Lord Riddell, *Intimate Diary of the Peace Conference and After* (London: Gollancz, 1933), 53.

89. Macartney and Cremona, *Italy's Foreign and Colonial Policy*, 59; Lloyd George, *The Truth*, 816–17.

90. Fiume and the Adriatic: 51/2: Letter from E. A. Crowe to Earl Curzon of Kedleston (3 November 1919), The National Archives, FO 170/1248.

91. Haywood, *Failure*, 483–84.

92. Cattaruzza, *L'Italia e la Questione Adriatica*, 45; Haywood, *Failure*, 507.

93. Nicolson, *Peacemaking*, 192.

94. Mondini, *Fiume 1919*, 40.

95. Cattaruzza, *L'Italia e la Questione Adriatica*, 46; Haywood, *Failure*, 499; Albrecht-Carrié, *Italy at the Paris Peace Conference*, 95; Burgwyn, *The Legend*, 281.

96. Adam Tooze, *The Deluge: The Great War and the Making of Global Order, 1916–1931* (London: Penguin, 2014), 310.

97. Nicolson, *Peacemaking*, 193.

98. Initially Italy only declared war against Austria-Hungary, avoiding to do so against Germany and the Ottoman Empire. Maurizio Serra, "Il Contesto Diplomatico dell'Impresa Fiumana," in *D'Annunzio Legislatore: Costituzioni, Visioni, Utopie dell'Impresa Fiumana*, ed. Giordano Bruno Guerri (Milano: Silvana Editoriale, 2022), 12.

99. Cecchini, "La Reggenza Fiumana," 93–94. Ironically, however, it was then Britain and France that engaged in covert dealings to sign a separate peace with Austria-Hungary. Burgwyn, *The Legend*, 97–104.

100. Fiume and the Adriatic: 51/2: Letter from E. A. Crowe to Earl Curzon of Kedleston (3 November 1919), The National Archives, FO 170/1248.

101. Burgwyn, *The Legend*, 20.

102. British Delegation: Letter from R. Rodd to Earl Curzon of Kedleston (23 May 1919), The National Archives, FO 608/39.

103. Burgwyn, *The Legend*, 20.

104. Albrecht-Carrié, *Italy at the Paris Peace Conference*, 66; British Delegation: Report from Major General A. C. Temperley to Major General W. Thwaites (31 January 1919), The National Archives, FO 608/38.

105. Haywood, *Failure*, 492.

106. Haywood, *Failure*, 480.

107. 1918 Embargoes: "Glasgow's" Despatch to Commodore Commanding, British Adriatic Force (18 November 1918), The National Archives, FO 170/1134.

108. Haywood, *Failure*, 484; Albrecht-Carrié, *Italy at the Paris Peace Conference*, 67; Pupo, *Fiume Cittá di Passione*, 60.

109. Leeden, *The First Duce*, 29, 32.

110. Lloyd George, *The Truth,* 807.

111. Raoul Pupo, "La Questione di Fiume e le Vicende del Confine Orientale," in *Fiume 1919–2019: Un Centenario Europeo tra Identitá, Memorie e Prospettive di Ricerca*, ed. Giordano Bruno Guerri (Milano: Silvania Editoriale, 2020), 19.

112. Fiume and the Adriatic: 51/2: Letter from E. A. Crowe to Earl Curzon of Kedleston (3 November 1919), The National Archives, FO 170/1248.

113. Fiume and the Adriatic: 51/1: Extracts from letter from A. Kelly, Commodore Commanding, British Adriatic Force, to British Commander-in-Chief (13 December 1918), The National Archives, FO 170/1247.

114. Klinger, *Un'Altra Italia*, 286; Ervin Dubrović, "L'Organizzaione *Galeb* (Gabbiano) Contro D'Annunzio," in *Fiume 1919–2019*, ed. Giordano Bruno Guerri, 65.

115. Prime Minister: C. A. Hereshoff Bartlett, *Italy and the Jugoslavs: A Question of International Law* (Paris: La Cootypographie, 1919), 14, Parliamentary Archives, LG/F/200/1/20.

116. Hereshoff Bartlett, *Italy and the Jugoslavs*, 15–17.

117. Dubrović, "L'Organizzaione *Galeb*," 62.

118. Leeden, *The First Duce*, 31.

119. Croatia-Slavonia and Fiume (March 1919), The National Archives, FO 373/1/10, 70–71, 73–74.

120. This would be as a result of Italy's zealous application of its stringent laws designed to protect emigrants' well-being onboard. British shipping companies operating in Italian ports had been found in breach of such laws in the past. Adriatic, Italian Desiderata: Letter from R. Rodd to Earl Curzon of Kedleston (22 May 1919), The National Archives, FO 608/35/3. The interests of British shipping companies in the emigrant traffic from Fiume are also stated in Foreign Office sources. Fiume, Desiderata: C. Tufton's minute on letter from Earl Curzon of Kedleston to Admiralty, Board of Trade, Ministry of Shipping (2 April 1919), The National Archives, FO 608/35/6.

121. Burgwyn, *The Legend*, 274; Fiume and the Adriatic: 51/1: Letter from R. Rodd to A. Balfour (29 March 1919), The National Archives, FO 170/1247.

122. Fiume and the Adriatic: 51/1: Letter from R. Rodd to A. Balfour (29 March 1919), The National Archives, FO 170/1247.

123. Fiume and the Adriatic: 51/1: G. Herron, "Behind the Scenes," translated from the *Epoca* (3 May 1919), The National Archives, FO 170/1247.

124. Prime Minister: Letter from R. Rodd to D. Lloyd George (6 May 1919), Parliamentary Archives, LG/F/200/1/20.

125. M. L. Sanders and Philip M. Taylor, *British Propaganda During the First World War, 1914–18* (London and Basingstoke, UK: Macmillan, 1982), 222.

126. Sanders and Taylor, *British Propaganda*, 224.

127. Burgwyn, *The Legend*, 125.

128. Sanders and Taylor, *British Propaganda*, 222.

129. Sanders and Taylor, *British Propaganda*, 223.

130. Burgwyn, *The Legend*, 254.

131. Mondini, *Fiume 1919*, 34.

132. Prime Minister: Letter from R. Rodd to A. Balfour (11 November 1918), Parliamentary Archives, LG/F/200/1/20.

133. Fiume and the Adriatic: 51/2: Resolution passed by the Executive Committee of the United Italy Society of Great Britain, enclosed in letter from V. Fisher to the British Ambassador in Rome (15 October 1919), The National Archives, FO 170/1248.

134. Adriatic, Italian Desiderata: *Italy and Her British Critics* (26 April 1919), The National Archives, FO 608/28/2.

135. Maranelli and Salvemini, *La Questione dell'Adriatico*, 218.

136. Letter from G. Salvemini to R. W. Seton-Watson (10 February 1917), printed in appendix to Vivarelli, *Storia delle Origini*, 593 (in French).

137. Burgwyn, *The Legend*, 214.

138. Fiume and the Adriatic: 51/2: Letter from G. Buchanan to Earl Curzon of Kedleston (1 December 1919), The National Archives, FO170/1248.

139. Prime Minister: Letter from R. Rodd to A. Balfour (12 November 1918), Parliamentary Archives, LG/F/200/1/20.

140. Prime Minister: R. Rodd's translation of letter from Lord Northcliffe to E. Chiesa (3 November 1918), enclosed in letter from R. Rodd to A. Balfour (12 November 1918), Parliamentary Archives, LG/F/200/1/20.

141. Prime Minister: R. Rodd's translation of letter from Lord Northcliffe to E. Chiesa (3 November 1918), enclosed in letter from R. Rodd to A. Balfour (12 November 1918), Parliamentary Archives, LG/F/200/1/20.

142. Prime Minister: Letter from R. Rodd to A. Balfour (11 November 1918), Parliamentary Archives, LG/F/200/1/20.

143. Prime Minister: Letter from R. Rodd to A. Balfour (11 November 1918), Parliamentary Archives, LG/F/200/1/20.

144. Jason Tomes, "British Empire Delegation at the Paris Peace Conference" (24 May 2007), in *Oxford Dictionary of National Biography*, https://doi.org/10.1093/ref:odnb/95641.

145. Italy, Rebellion: A. Thorold's minutes on letter from R. Gotthardi (23 October 1919), The National Archives, FO 608/41/1.

146. Fiume, Desiderata: A. W. A. Leeper's minute on letter from R. Gotthardi to G. Clemenceau (3 October 1919), The National Archives, FO 608/35/6.

147. Tomes, "British Empire Delegation."

148. Fiume, Statistics: E. A. Crowe's minute on letter from S. Sonnino to A. Balfour (1 March 1919), The National Archives, FO 608/35/4 (emphasis added).

149. Italy, Rebellion: A. W. A. Leeper's minute on telegram from G. Buchanan to Foreign Office (27 October 1919), The National Archives, FO 608/41/1.

150. Fiume, Statistics: E. A. Crowe's minute on letter from S. Sonnino to A. Balfour (1 March 1919), The National Archives, FO 608/35/4.

151. Adriatic, Italian Desiderata: H. W. V. Temperley's minute on extracts from Report by the Naval Attaché to Rome (16 July 1919), The National Archives, FO 608/35/3.

152. Adriatic, Italian Desiderata: A. W. A. Leeper's minute on Future of Fiume: Letter from National Council (22 February 1919), The National Archives, FO 608/35/3.

153. British Delegation: E. A. Crowe's minute on telegram from R. Rodd to A. Balfour (5 May 1919), The National Archives, FO 608/39.

154. British Delegation: E. A. Crowe's minute on telegram from R. Rodd to A. Balfour (14 June 1919), The National Archives, FO 608/39.

155. Adriatic, Italian Desiderata: A. W. A. Leeper's minute on letter from A. Ossoinack to A. Balfour (13 March 1919), The National Archives, FO 608/35/3.

156. Adriatic, Italian Desiderata: A. W. A. Leeper's minute on Report of the Conference between President Wilson and the A. Ossoinack (14 April 1919), The National Archives, FO 608/35/3.

157. British Delegation, Fiume: Letter from General H. Watts to General W. Thwaites (22 July 1919), The National Archives, FO 608/36.

158. British Delegation, Fiume: Minute by W. Thwaites on letter from General H. Watts to General W. Thwaites (22 July 1919), The National Archives, FO 608/36.

159. British Delegation, Fiume: Report from S. C. Peck's to D.M.O., War Office (24 July 1919), The National Archives, FO 608/36.

160. British Delegation, Fiume: Minute by E. A. Crowe on S. C. Peck's Report to D.M.O., War Office (24 July 1919), The National Archives, FO 608/36.

161. Lloyd George, *The Truth,* 787, 803–4; Albrecht-Carrié, *Italy at the Paris Peace Conference*, 66–67.

162. Tooze, *The Deluge*, 309.

163. John Woodhouse, *Gabriele D'Annunzio: Defiant Archangel* (Oxford: Clarendon Press, 1998), 317; Kirchner Reill, *The Fiume Crisis*, 36.

164. Wilson's message to the Italian people, republished in Benedetti, *La Pace di Fiume*, 242–45.

165. Albrecht-Carrié, *Italy at the Paris Peace Conference*, 141.

166. British Delegation: Telegram from W. Erskine to A. Balfour (3 May 1919), The National Archives, FO 608/39.

167. Lord Riddell, *Intimate Diary*, 60–61.

168. V. E. Orlando's response to President Wilson (24 April 1919), republished in Benedetti, *La Pace di Fiume*, 246; Lloyd George, *The Truth*, 841, 847.

169. Lloyd George, *The Truth*, 847–48; Cattaruzza, *L'Italia e la Questione Adriatica*, 44–45.

170. Cecchini, "La Reggenza Fiumana," 89.

171. Archival evidence, however, shows he had already been prepared to barter part of Dalmatia for Fiume at least as early as the previous March. Prime Minister:

Letter from S. Sonnino to D. Lloyd George (11 March 1919), Parliamentary Archives, LG/F/55/4/39.

172. Adriatic, Italian Desiderata: Letter from the Yugoslav National Council to the General Commanding the British Troops in Fiume (27 April 1919), The National Archives, FO 608/35/3; Adriatic, Italian Desiderata: H. W. V. Temperley's minute on Lieutenant Colonel S. L. Whatford's report to C.I.G.C. of 30 April 1919 (17 May 1919), The National Archives, FO 608/35/3; Report from Lieutenant Colonel S. L. Whatford to C.I.G.C. (30 April 1919), The National Archives, FO 608/35/3.

173. Adriatic, Italian Desiderata: Telegram from Willaim Erskine to Arthur Balfour (28 April 1919), The National Archives, FO 608/28/2.

174. Susmel, *La Cittá di Passione*, 197–201.

175. Susmel, *Fiume attraverso la Storia*, 114–15.

176. Prime Minister: Report from L. Waterfield to A. Thorold (5 June 1919), Parliamentary Archives, LG/F/43/7/13.

177. Adriatic, Italian Desiderata: Telegram from W. Erskine to A. Balfour (26 April 1919), The National Archives, FO 608/28/2; Adriatic, Italian Desiderata: Telegram from W. Erskine to Earl Curzon of Kedleston (29 April 1919), The National Archives, FO 608/28/2; Vivarelli, *Storia delle Origini*, 519–23; Haywood, *Failure*, 498; Susmel, *La Cittá di Passione*, 195.

178. Ferdinando Cordova, *Arditi e Legionari Dannunziani* (Padova: Marsilio, 1969), 40.

179. Macmillan, *Peacemakers*, 309.

180. Giovanni Comisso, *Le Mie Stagioni* (Milano: Longanesi, 1963), 24–25.

181. Vivarelli, *Storia delle Origini*, 526; Nicolson, *Peacemaking*, 177–78; Albrecht-Carrié, *Italy at the Paris Peace Conference*, 145–47.

182. Adriatic, Italian Desiderata: Telegram from R. Rodd to A. Balfour (30 April 1919), The National Archives, FO 608/28/2.

183. Adriatic, Italian Desiderata: Telegram from W. Erskine to Earl Curzon of Kedleston (29 April 1919), The National Archives, FO 608/28/2.

184. Adriatic, Italian Desiderata: Telegram from W. Erskine to Earl Curzon of Kedleston (29 April 1919), The National Archives, FO 608/28/2.

185. Adriatic, Italian Desiderata: Telegram from W. Erskine to Earl Curzon of Kedleston (29 April 1919), The National Archives, FO 608/28/2.

186. Haywood, *Failure*, 500.

187. Cecchini, "La Reggenza Fiumana," 90.

188. British Delegation: W. Erskine's telegram to D. Lloyd George (3 May 1919), The National Archives, FO 608/39.

189. Lloyd George, *The Truth*, 869.

190. Prime Minister: Letter from R. Rodd to D. Lloyd George (6 May 1919), Parliamentary Archives, LG/F/200/1/20.

191. Adriatic, Italian Desiderata: Telegram from W. Erskine to Earl Curzon of Kedleston (1 May 1919), The National Archives, FO 608/28/2.

192. Cattaruzza, *L'Italia e la Questione Adriatica*, 45, 53–55; Vivarelli, *Storia delle Origini*, 532–33, 538; Haywood, *Failure*, 504.

193. British Delegation: Telegram from R. Rodd to A. Balfour (7 May 1919), The National Archives, FO 608/39.

194. Macmillan, *Peacemakers*, 311; Albrecht-Carrié, *Italy at the Paris Peace Conference*, 198–99.

195. Vivarelli, *Storia delle Origini*, 550–53.

196. Haywood, *Failure*, 504.

197. Cattaruzza, *L'Italia e la Questione Adriatica*, 73.

198. Leeden, *The First Duce*, 15–16, 131; Woodhouse, *Gabriele D'Annunzio*, 322.

199. Vivarelli, *Storia delle Origini*, 556–57.

200. Ferrero, *Da Fiume a Roma*, 19.

201. Brig-Gen Gordon Commanding British Troops in Fiume: Report from H. Gordon to the Commander-in-Chief, British Forces in Italy (26 January 1919), The National Archives, WO 106/858.

202. Susmel, *Fiume Attraverso la Storia*, 111–13; Susmel, *La Cittá di Passione*, 176; 1918 Embargoes: Letter from R. Rodd to A. Balfour (17 December 1918) and enclosure, The National Archives, FO 170/1134.

203. Ester Capuzzo, "Da Corpus Separatum a Provincia: Amministrazione e Legislazione a Fiume nel Primo Dopoguerra," in *Fiume 1919–2019*, ed. Giordano Bruno Guerri, 30.

204. Enrico Serventi Longhi, "La Dittatura Sovrana di Fiume: Innovazioni Politiche, Sociali ed Economiche (1919–1920)," *Mondo Contemporaneo* 2 (2016): 146–48; Enrico Serventi Longhi, *Il Faro del Mondo Nuovo: D'Annunzio e i Legionari a Fiume tra Guerra e Rivoluzione* (Udine: Gaspari, 2019), 62–63.

205. Fiume and the Adriatic: 51/1: Report of Rear Admiral E. B. Kiddle to the Secretary of the Admiralty (26 December 1918), The National Archives, FO 170/1247.

206. Letter from G.H.Q. Italy to C.I.G.S. Brigadier General Gordon Commanding British Contingent Fiume: copies of reports and map received: Report from Brigadier-General H. Gordon to the Commander-in-Chief, British Forces in Italy (8 March 1919), The National Archives, WO 106/861.

207. Prime Minister: Report from L. Waterfield to A. Thorold (5 June 1919), Parliamentary Archives, LG/F/43/7/13.

208. Alessandro Agrì, "Lo 'Stato di Fiume' e il Suo Diritto (1918–1924)," *Historia et Ius* 19 (2021): 29, http://www.historiaetius.eu/uploads/5/9/4/8/5948821/agri_19.pdf.

209. Agrì, "Lo 'Stato di Fiume'," 33–34; Adriatic, Italian Desiderata: Report from Captain R. J. Baird to D.M.I., Military Section, British Delegation (12 May 1919), The National Archives, FO 608/35/3; Adriatic, Italian Desiderata: Report from General Spears (16 May 1919), The National Archives, FO 608/35/3.

210. Agrì, "Lo 'Stato di Fiume'," 33–34.

211. Adriatic, Italian Desiderata: Letter from the Yugoslav National Council to the General Commanding the British Troops in Fiume (27 April 1919), The National Archives, FO 608/35/3.

212. Fiume, Desiderata: Letter from Fiume barristers to the Inter-Allied Headquarters, Fiume (31 January 1919), The National Archives, FO 608/35/6.

213. British Delegation, Fiume: Letter from General H. Watts to General W. Twhaites (22 July 1919), The National Archives, FO 608/36.

214. Adriatic, Italian Desiderata: H. W. V. Temperley's, J. H. Morgan's, and H. W. Walker's minutes on Report from Captain R. J. Baird to D.M.I., Military Section, British Delegation (12 May 1919), The National Archives, FO 608/35/3.

215. Adriatic, Italian Desiderata: H. Nicholson's and E. A. Crowe's minutes on Report from Captain R. J. Baird to D.M.I., Military Section, British Delegation (12 May 1919), The National Archives, FO 608/35/3.

216. Fiume, Administration: Letter from General Post Office to the Under Secretary of State, Foreign Office (7 March 1919), The National Archives, FO 608/35/5.

217. Fiume, Administration: Letter from W. E. Parsons to V. A. A. H. Wellesley (14 April 1919), The National Archives, FO 608/35/5.

218. Fiume, Administration: Letter from L. Mallet to Earl Curzon of Kedleston (1 May 1919), The National Archives, FO 608/35/5.

219. Adriatic, Italian Desiderata: A. Ossoinack's letter to G. Clemenvceau (2 June 1919), The National Archives, FO 608/35/3.

220. Fiume and the Adriatic: 51/1: Extracts from letter from A. Kelly, Commodore Commanding, British Adriatic Force, to British Commander-in-Chief (13 December 1918), The National Archives, FO 170/1247; Fiume and the Adriatic: 51/1: Report from Rear Admiral E. B. Kiddle to the Secretary of the Admiralty (18 December 1918), The National Archives, FO 170/1247.

221. Fiume and the Adriatic: 51/1: Communication from the French Ambassador in London (30 December 1918), The National Archives, FO 170/1247.

222. Leeden, *The First Duce*, 29–32.

223. Fiume and the Adriatic: 51/1: Communication from the Italian Embassy (18 December 1918), The National Archives, FO 170/1247.

224. 1919 Fiume and The Adriatic, Part 1: Decypher of Telegram from Senior Naval Officer, Venice, to Admiralty (24 December 1918), The National Archives, FO 170/1247.

225. Fiume and the Adriatic: 51/1: Report of Rear Admiral E. B. Kiddle to the Secretary of the Admiralty (5 January 1919), The National Archives, FO 170/1247.

226. Prime Minister: Letter from R. Rodd to A. Balfour (5 December 1918), Parliamentary Archives, LG/F/200/1/20.

227. Prime Minister: Letter from R. Rodd to A. Balfour (26 December 1918), Parliamentary Archives, LG/F/200/1/20.

228. Prime Minister: Letter from R. Rodd to E. J. Harding (14 December 1918), Parliamentary Archives, LG/F/200/1/20.

229. Prime Minister: Letter from R. Cecil to R. Rodd (3 January 1919), Parliamentary Archives, LG/F/200/1/20.

230. Susmel, *Fiume Attraverso la Storia*, 113–14.

231. Disturbances at Fiume (1919): Note to General F. Grazioli from the National Council, published in *Il Popolo*, July 5 (resume), The National Archives, WO 32/5004.

232. Fiume and the Adriatic: 51/1: Report of Rear Admiral E. B. Kiddle to the Secretary of the Admiralty (26 December 1918), The National Archives, FO 170/1247.

233. Fiume and the Adriatic: 51/2: Commission Interalliée D'Enquête de Fiume, Procés-Verbaux et Rapport (1919), 6, The National Archives, FO 170/1248.

234. Fiume and the Adriatic: 51/2: Commission Interalliée D'Enquête de Fiume, Procés-Verbaux et Rapport (1919), 7, The National Archives, FO 170/1248.

235. Fiume, Desiderata: General Savy's Report (24 June 1919), The National Archives, FO 608/35/6.

236. British Delegation: Letter from R. Rodd to Earl Curzon of Kedleston (23 May 1919), The National Archives, FO 608/39.

237. Susmel, *La Cittá di Passione*, 211; Francesca Rolandi, "A Never Requested Triumph? Reframing Gender Boundaries in Fiume and Sušak after 1918," *Italia Contemporanea Yearbook 2020* (2021): 16; Albrecht-Carrié, *Italy at the Paris Peace Conference*, 237; Thea Pičić, *Rijeka Ili Smrt! D'Anunzijeva okupacija Rijeke, 1919–1921 / Rijeka or Death! D'Annunzio's occupation of Rijeka, 1919–2019* (Rijeka: Naklada Val, 2019), 43.

238. 1918 Embargoes: Enclosure in R. Rodd's letter to A. Balfour (5 December 1918), The National Archives, FO 170/1134.

239. Fiume and the Adriatic: 51/1: Report from Rear Admiral E. B. Kiddle to the Secretary of the Admiralty (18 December 1918), The National Archives, FO 170/1247.

240. Disturbances at Fiume (1919): Note to General F. Grazioli from the National Council, published in *Il Popolo*, July 5 (resume), The National Archives, WO 32/5004.

241. 1918 Embargoes: "Glasgow's" Despatch to Commodore Commanding, British Adriatic Force (18 November 1918), The National Archives FO 170/1134; Fiume and the Adriatic: 51/1: Report from Rear Admiral E. B. Kiddle to the Secretary of the Admiralty (18 December 1918), The National Archives, FO 170/1247.

242. 1918 Embargoes: Letter from R. Rodd to A. Balfour (15 December 1918), The National Archives, FO 170/1134.

243. Leeden, *The First Duce*, 32.

244. Fiume and the Adriatic: 51/1: Report by J. Strick to R. Rodd (7 July 1919), The National Archives, FO 170/1247.

245. Fiume and the Adriatic: 51/2: Commission Interalliée D'Enquête de Fiume, Procés-Verbaux et Rapport (1919), 124, The National Archives, FO 170/1248.

246. J. N. Macdonald, *A Political Escapade: The Story of Fiume and D'Annunzio* (London: John Murray, 1921), 61; Fiume and the Adriatic: 51/1: Report by J. Strick to R. Rodd (7 July 1919), The National Archives, FO 170/1247 (reporting General Savy's opinion).

247. Disturbances at Fiume (1919): Telegram from R. Rodd (8 July 1919) (2.a.), The National Archives, WO 32/5004.

248. Disturbances at Fiume (1919): Summary of Comando Supremo's Account of All the Fiume Incidents from Occupation Till July 8th, The National Archives, WO 32/5004.

249. Fiume and the Adriatic: 51/1: Report of Brigadier-General H. Gordon to the Commander-in-Chief, British Forces in Italy (10 February 1919), The National Archives, FO 170/1247.

250. Fiume and the Adriatic: 51/2: Commission Interalliée D'Enquête de Fiume, Procés-Verbaux et Rapport (1919), 59, 62–63, The National Archives, FO 170/1248.

251. Comisso, *Le Mie Stagioni*, 22.

252. Fiume and the Adriatic: 51/1: Extracts from letter from A. Kelly, Commodore Commanding, British Adriatic Forces, to British Commander-in-Chief (13 December 1918), The National Archives, FO 170/1247; Fiume and the Adriatic: 51/1: Report from Rear Admiral E. B. Kiddle to the Secretary of the Admiralty (18 December 1918), The National Archives, FO 170/1247; Adriatic: Letter from Rear Admiral E. B. Kiddle to the Secretary of the Admiralty (14 January 1919), The National Archives, FO 608/27/9; 33014; Italy: Aims in Dalmatia and Croatia: Situation at Fiume: Extracts from Letter from General H. Gordon to C. de Graz (17 January 1919), The National Archives, FO 608/15/8.

253. Fiume and the Adriatic: 51/1: Report by N. W. Diggle to R. Rodd (12 July 1919), The National Archives, FO 170/1247.

254. Fiume and the Adriatic: 51/1: Report by N. W. Diggle to R. Rodd (12 July 1919), The National Archives, FO 170/1247.

255. Fiume, Desiderata: Letter from Rear Admiral E. S. A. Sinclair to the Admiralty (6 July 1919), The National Archives, FO 608/36.

256. Fiume and the Adriatic: 51/2: Commission Interalliée D'Enquête de Fiume, Procés-Verbaux et Rapport (1919), 124–26, The National Archives, FO 170/1248; Disturbances at Fiume (1919), The National Archives, WO 32/5004; Woodhouse, *Gabriele D'Annunzio*, 326–27.

257. Pičić, *Rijeka or Death*, 58.

258. Fiume, Desiderata: Letter from Rear Admiral E. S. A. Sinclair to the Admiralty (11 July 1919), The National Archives, FO 608/36.

259. Rolandi, "A Never Requested Triumph?," 23.

260. Fiume and the Adriatic: 51/1: Report by N. W. Diggle to R. Rodd (12 July 1919), The National Archives, FO 170/1247.

261. Macdonald, *A Political Escapade*, 78–79.

262. Fiume, Desiderata: Letter from Rear Admiral E. S. A. Sinclair to the Admiralty (7 July 1919), The National Archives, FO 608/36.

263. Fiume, Disturbances: Letter from Lieutenant Colonel S. C. Peck to D.M.O., War Office (31 July 1919), The National Archives, FO 608/36/2.

264. Fiume, Disturbances: Letter from Lieutenant Colonel S. C. Peck to D.M.O., War Office, and enclosures (31 July 1919), The National Archives, FO 608/36/2.

265. Disturbances at Fiume (1919): Telegram from British Mission, Fiume (10 July 1919) (22.a.), The National Archives, WO 32/5004.

266. Disturbances at Fiume (1919): Telegram from British Mission, Fiume (12 July 1919) (21.a.), The National Archives, WO 32/5004.

267. Disturbances at Fiume (1919): Telegram from General C. Delme Radcliffe (6 July 1919) (14.a.), The National Archives, WO 32/5004.

268. Disturbances at Fiume (1919): Telegram from R. Rodd (8 July 1919) (2.a.), The National Archives, WO 32/5004.

269. Vivarelli, *Storia delle Origini*, 554; Leeden, *The First Duce*, 56.

270. Fiume and the Adriatic: 51/2: Commission Interalliée D'Enquête de Fiume, Procés-Verbaux et Rapport (1919), 127–28, The National Archives, FO 170/1248.

271. Fiume and the Adriatic: 51/2: Commission Interalliée D'Enquête de Fiume, Procés-Verbaux et Rapport (1919), 127–28, The National Archives, FO 170/1248.

272. Kotchnitzky, *La Quinta Stagione*, 50.

273. Mario Maria Martini, *La Passione di Fiume: Diari, Cronache, Documenti* (Milano: Sonzogno, 1919), 157; Susmel, *La Cittá di Passione*, 226–27.

274. Roberto Chiarini, "L'Impresa di Fiume nelle Carte del Maggiore Carlo Reina," in *D'Annunzio Politico: Atti del Convegno (Il Vittoriale, 9–10 Ottobre 1985)*, ed. Renzo De Felice and Pietro Gibellini (Milano: Garzanti, 1987), 51.

275. Martini, *La Passione di Fiume*, 145.

276. Martini, *La Passione di Fiume*, 11.

277. Comisso, *Le Mie Stagioni*, 38–39.

Chapter 3

Gabriele D'Annunzio's Politics

INTRODUCTION

The World War I veterans and other volunteers that marched into Fiume on 12 September 1919 did so under the command of Gabriele D'Annunzio. At that time D'Annunzio was already an international celebrity, as much for his consummate skills as a poet and wordsmith as for his amorous exploits,[1] not to mention his wartime daredevilry[2] and his patriotic oratory. Having harnessed the power of art, and occasionally downright ugly criminal incitement,[3] in the service of nationalist concerns before and during the conflict, D'Annunzio has been considered chiefly responsible for creating the collective mood that facilitated Italy's entry into war. This did not escape even his contemporary foreign observers.[4] In 1919, Captain Goad, liaison officer with the Italian Expeditionary Force in Bulgaria, wrote, quite truthfully, that Italy 'was dragged into the war by little short of revolution' through 'the work of a small group young idealist patriots, headed by D'Annunzio.'[5]

For Mosse, the rise of nationalism and mass politics in the nineteenth century created the enabling conditions for poets such as D'Annunzio to take an active role in politics *qua* poets. The new political subject—the nation—called for a symbolic system to represent it, and the cult of nation called for a priest to officiate it. Poets' sensibilities were best placed to provide both.[6] From this point of view, it is not by accident that D'Annunzio's tinkering with politics was unremarkable until he turned to nationalist and interventionist discourses. Yet we cannot appreciate the significance of the Fiume endeavour and of its most significant achievement, the *Carnaro Charter*, if we write D'Annunzio's politics off as those of a war-mongering Nationalist, or, worse, a proto-fascist. This chapter dwells on D'Annunzio's political biography and critically examines claims about the ideological continuity between *Fiumanesimo* and fascism.

BEFORE THE WAR

D'Annunzio had not been a stranger to Italian politics in the two decades preceding the outbreak of war. In 1898, in his mid-thirties, he had been elected to the Chamber of Deputies of the Italian Parliament, after the Liberals had invited him to run in a by-election.[7] His parliamentary activities, however, were conspicuous by his absenteeism.[8] In 1900, after joining those intent on thwarting the passing of laws directed at restricting political freedoms,[9] he crossed to the benches of the Extreme Left, in protest against an incident involving the speaker of the house silencing a Republican member of Parliament.[10] On that occasion D'Annunzio declared that he applauded 'the Extreme Left for defending its ideas with fervour and tenacity' and its members for being 'alive', in contrast with the 'dead' majority of the Chamber.[11]

Thanks to Left obstructionism, the Pelloux government's assault on civil and political liberties (with a view to suppressing popular discontent at rising inflation) failed. In the elections that followed shortly thereafter D'Annunzio ran with the Socialists.[12] His political speeches appealed to the 'intellectual forebears of aesthetic-socialist humanism, from Ruskin to Swinburne to Morris', in order to rationalise his conversion.[13] Though he failed to secure a mandate, he attracted many more votes than the previous Socialist candidate and demonstrated an apparently genuine and even enthusiastic endorsement of socialist principles. This resulted in something of an idyll between the poet and the Left, lasting until 1906, when D'Annunzio's art and politics started looking towards nationalism[14] though nationalist concerns had surfaced in his writings as far back as 1888.[15]

After his brief experience in office at the end of the nineteenth century, D'Annunzio came to the conclusion that the committed intellectual could best deliver his political contributions outside formal state institutions.[16] He did so through his poetry and art, which he used as a medium to express nationalist concerns, though the Nationalists themselves largely dismissed his brand of nationalism as too aestheticized, too spiritualised, and divorced from industrial interests.[17]

The plight of Italian-populated lands yet to be liberated from foreign rule (*terre irredente*) was a distinct preoccupation of D'Annunzio's. If, as we have seen, the Nationalist press started constructing a narrative about the Italian character of Dalmatia only during the war years, D'Annunzio's concern with 'recovering' the eastern Adriatic had been longstanding. This concern was largely bound up with the mythical place that Venice occupied in

D'Annunzio's imaginary.[18] This is especially apparent in his 1898 novel *Fire*, which credits 'the heroic and voluptuous City that carried and smothered the richest Latin dream in her marble arms'[19] with 'the virtue of stimulating the potency of human life . . . exciting all desires to fever pitch', as nowhere else in the world.[20]

Shortly after penning *La Nave* (*The Ship*), a drama on the theme of national grandeur, the poet travelled to Fiume, in 1907, to read it in his own voice to the cast of actors that would stage it.[21] The performance itself was a triumph no less in Fiume than in Venice and Rome, where, at a party organised to celebrate him, D'Annunzio seized the chance to toast the Adriatic lands lost to Italy, much to the embarrassment of the invited politicians.[22]

D'ANNUNZIO'S INTERVENTIONISM

Starting with an '*Ode pour la Résurrection Latine*', published in *Le Figaro* on 13 August 1914,[23] D'Annunzio advocated Italy's entry into the conflict in articles, poetry, and public speeches; he continued to address the nation and Army recruits throughout the war years.[24] On the eve of the war, he had invoked it as the only opportunity for the Latin race to redeem itself from the torpor into which the rule of the masses had thrust it.[25] Here D'Annunzio shares in a broader discourse developed by both nationalist and liberal intellectuals, who variously saw war—with the prospect of death for those sent to the front—as a unique opportunity for the Italian people to redeem themselves from century-old serious failures of character and moral courage, which had enabled their domination by foreign powers ever since the fall of the Roman Empire. The same logic would enable Italian generals to subject mutinous troops to the practice of decimation for their own 'good'.[26] For D'Annunzio himself, this belief in the redemptive power of war was not predicated on denial or glossing over the deathly horrors of war; rather this horror, just because it was so unmitigated, could be transfigured into something genuinely ennobling (utmost sacrifice) and, through it, the experience of war could be spiritualised.[27]

Beyond this conviction that war would ennoble the character of the nation, it was, as D'Annunzio wrote in another French article in 1915, a question of civilizational conflict. As the martial logic of domination was sweeping through Europe, the Germanic race of the Central Powers was bent on enslaving the Latin race and other Mediterranean nations and on asserting economic dominance by claiming possession of the eastern Adriatic and its ports; one stood to watch at one's peril.[28] Likewise, it was imperative to resist the coercive, legalised Slavicisation of Dalmatia.[29] There is continuity between these arguments for intervention against 'pan-Germanism and pan-Slavism'[30] and concerns that D'Annunzio had started conceiving nearly two decades earlier. At the time, he had had written that we must 'fight the destruction, contagion, and violation of beauty which the barbarians bring with them . . . if the Latin races are to preserve themselves, it is time they returned to the healthy prejudice which created the grandeur of Greece and Rome—to believe that all others are barbarians.'[31] As Rhodes explains, this dreaded 'barbarian invasion' alludes to 'Anglo-Saxon and Teutonic commercial and imperial superiority'.[32]

Importantly, entering into war with Austria was also a question of people of Latin lineage regaining possession of what was quintessentially Latin soil:

> [The Adriatic] belongs to us by divine right and by human right: By God, who fashioned earthly shapes in such a way that each race can recognise within them its destiny, and by man, who has multiplied the beauty of the seashore in erecting the monuments of its nobility and in engraving upon it the signs of his highest hopes. . . . Under the Latin power of Rome, of the Popes, of Venice, no less than under the barbarian power of the Goths, the Langobards, the Francs, the German Ottonians, the Byzantines, the Hungarians, the Austrians, civil life on the two Adriatic coasts has constantly been Italian in both its origin and essence.[33]

In the ethnically fluid and politically unsettled geographies of the immediate aftermath of World War I, such impressionistic and metaphysical arguments seem to have carried quasi-normative weight, at least judging by Osbert Sitwell's curious remark that the claim that Fiume 'is Italian "by right of landscape", though strange, is true enough. [Fiume] belongs to the same order as Genoa or Naples. With its spur of hills sinking into the opalescence of the far sea, and the quivering, misty outlines of the islands, the traveller feels that he is once more in Italy, whereas Trieste is a different and alien bay.'[34]

THE WAR YEARS

When Italy declared war on Austria, D'Annunzio immediately joined the armed forces—the oldest lieutenant in the Army.[35] It has been argued that the attraction of war for D'Annunzio was chiefly that it spoke to his egomania, and the need for a theatre in which to perform it.[36] In his study on D'Annunzio and the Great War, Bonadeo makes a more compelling argument to the effect that, despite D'Annunzio's nationalist concerns, his eagerness to fight was dictated largely by his own 'personal needs', his 'emotional and intellectual problems'.[37] Through fighting and war, D'Annunzio sought to escape from himself, or from the part of himself—his libido—at whose mercy he felt thrust upon, and by which he felt thwarted in his wish to realise the spiritual and transcendental values he extolled.[38] After the Armistice, D'Annunzio, apparently grateful for the chastity that war had enforced on him, would write to General Badoglio that he owed 'the highest and purest conquests of [his] spirit to the bloody and muddy war'.[39]

Bonadeo's perceptive analysis is supported by echoes of such concerns in D'Annunzio's novels. For example, Stelio Effrena, the main character in the novel *Fire*, worries that his addiction to love making drains his creative powers and robs him of the time to write. While he was busy giving way to his lust, he reasons, 'someone else, in that very hour, had completed some high work or found, eventually, a heroic reason for living.'[40] From this perspective, one might say that there was a fair deal of projection in D'Annunzio's conviction that war was necessary for the spiritual salvation of the nation.

By the end of the conflict D'Annunzio had been upgraded to the rank of major[41] and was widely seen as the epitome of patriotic values, particularly by young officers.[42] The government had been using him for years in order to stir up patriotic sentiment.[43] His prestige now embraced—in addition to his prewar reputation as a dandy and socialite, Italy's most illustrious living writer, and patriotic orator—the status of a war hero.[44] Among other wartime stunts, he had performed a raid in Dalmatia designed to ridicule the Austrians and their defences (the so-called Buccari joke)[45] and flown over Zara (also in Dalmatia) dropping leaflets promising its liberation: 'Oh Zara, for your Venetian grace, for all your Italian beauty, believe in the promise, believe in the joy of your second spring'.[46] On 24 October 1918, he published an article in *Corriere della Sera* bearing the title 'Victory, Thou Shall Not Be Maimed', which was to become a battle cry for nationalists and irredentists clamouring for Italy being given its 'due' at Versailles.[47] In November D'Annunzio wrote an ode celebrating victory over Austria and claiming Dalmatia for Italy.[48]

By 1919, D'Annunzio was well enmeshed in the web of irredentist movements in the eastern Adriatic[49] and known as the most authoritative and impassioned advocate of the Adriatic cause.[50] Serventi Longhi argues that D'Annunzio's immediate postwar political advocacy should be understood in the context of a subversive movement involving sectors of the Italian Army, who aspired to lead the process of social transformation then underway by engaging emerging political, social, artistic, and labour forces. D'Annunzio, given his prestige, was singled out as an eminent spokesman for this movement, which sought to transfer political leadership into the hands of military hierarchies and to lead Italy into an imperialistic programme of foreign policy.[51] This may overstate D'Annunzio's involvement in this movement. Everything about D'Annunzio, including the way in which the Fiume occupation eventually panned out, shows that he was too much his own man to ever adhere to any kind of political project that he did not himself direct. Yet it seems obvious that there was convergence between the subversive projects Serventi Longhi refers to and D'Annunzio's concerns with political renewal and his nationalistic preoccupations. D'Annunzio's political rhetoric was undoubtedly serviceable—if not necessarily directly intended to facilitate—these projects.

His writings celebrating the Latin heritage of Dalmatian towns in late 1918[52] were followed in mid-January 1919 by the better-known 'Letter to the Dalmatians'. In it, the poet claimed that peace was a smokescreen: 'As the Allies embrace, they bite hard each other's ear, like Sicilian rivals', and 'when they speak of fraternity and new sacrifices, . . . the word . . . alludes to someone else's abnegation'.[53] Each nation's will to power, that is, remained as strong as ever. He asserted the right of 'straight heroic wills'—as opposed to the 'secrets of belaboured [diplomatic] negotiations'[54] favoured by weaklings—to reclaim 'that [Eastern Adriatic] swathe of country that was constantly Italian, in both its origin and essence'.[55] He rejected peace if it meant the imposition of terms suitable to the interests of foreign powers: only a *pax romana* would do for Italy—not a *pax 'gallica'* or *'britannica'*.[56] The letter first appeared on 14 January in the *Gazzetta di Venezia*, a pro-Venetian establishment newspaper with which D'Annunzio had a close collaborative relationship.[57] The following day, on 15 January, the letter was published on the first page of Mussolini's *Il Popolo d'Italia*, with the following headline: 'Italians! Pay Heed to the Message of the Fearless'. Ironically, D'Annunzio had only turned to Mussolini's newspaper in protest against the refusal to publish the letter that came from his longstanding collaborator, the director of *Corriere della Sera*, Luigi Albertini.[58]

More articles and public speeches followed, including the famous Quarto oration.[59] In April 1919, as we know, the Italian delegates left the negotiating table in Paris, in protest against Wilson's breach of diplomatic and political etiquette in announcing to the French press his firm position on the Adriatic issue. D'Annunzio held a speech in Rome on 4 May, where, predicting an imminent Italian occupation of Istria and Dalmatia, he declared: 'We want to glow. We won't be quenched. Our destitution glows and sparks. And all the transatlantic gold [which Wilson uses as leverage to impose peace on his own terms] is dim before it.'[60] Among other things, in his Rome speech D'Annunzio linked the way in which the future of Fiume and Dalmatia was being bargained away to the way in which Britain, France and the US were making 'themselves hoarse as they contended over the boon of the world'. D'Annunzio alluded to a series of suspect, self-interested, or unfair dealings with respect to claims over the German fleet (which was shortly to be scuttled by Rear Admiral Ludwig von Reuter to prevent it from being redistributed among the Allies). He also referred to inadequate war reparations to Belgium for German atrocities; to the Allies profiteering from Germany's economic crisis; to colonial economic exploitation in Africa, Asia, and the Pacific; and to British repression in both Egypt (which was then experiencing the Egyptian revolution against colonial rule) and Ireland (which had just started its war of independence, leading to the establishment of the Irish Free State in 1922). Two further incidents were denounced by D'Annunzio. First, Britain had broken its commitment to grant Palestinian Arabs independence in exchange for Arabs' supporting the Allies against the Ottomans during the war.[61] Secondly, Versailles had denied 'against the Yellow Ally the equality of human lineages'.[62] This refers to the rejection of Japan's racial equality proposal (which sought equal treatment of all members of the League of Nations regardless for race or nationality), largely due to strong opposition from the British Empire's delegation—particularly the Australian delegate—and Wilson's own lack of support.[63]

It is of interest that Comisso, who was present at the Rome speech, records his and the crowd's curiosity rather than—at that stage—any real feeling of being politically stirred by D'Annunzio's words and theatrics (the poet had laid down an Italian flag and threw onto it a black ribbon to signify mourning).[64] Yet visiting Fiume three months before D'Annunzio's expedition, Lina Waterfield declared that 'D'Annunzio is more than ever the voice of Italy'.[65] Some British sources also laid the responsibility for the anti-French July disturbances in Fiume (as well as other anti-French incidents occurring in Genoa at about the same time) squarely—if only partly—at D'Annunzio's door, citing his 'press campaign' in the previous three months.[66]

D'Annunzio's public advocacy about Italy's rights over the eastern Adriatic made him the obvious candidate for Fiume's annexationists, who were seeking someone to champion their cause. Bonadeo argues, nonetheless, that D'Annunzio's motivations for accepting the annexationists' invitation had ultimately less to do with his professed irredentism (about which D'Annunzio felt more conflicted than is generally supposed) than with the 'lure of heroism and with the life-enhancing spectre of death'.[67]

JOHN THE BAPTIST OF FASCISM

Becker argues that it is wrong to dismiss D'Annunzio's move to the Left, at the time we he was a member of Parliament, as political exhibitionism and theatrics; rather, it enacted a synthesis of Left and Right that was paradigmatically proto-fascist.[68] This is in fact a claim well rehearsed in Italian historiography—one that Zani argues is paradoxical to the extent that, rather than finding elements of D'Annunzio's politics in fascism, retrospectively reads fascism into D'Annunzio's political ideology or his political leadership in Fiume.[69] This tendency to project fascist ideology onto D'Annunzio was particularly prominent in the scholarship of postliberation Italy[70] but has by no means disappeared. As the favourite expression goes, D'Annunzio would be the 'John the Baptist of fascism'.[71]

The argument is based primarily on the Fiume experience itself. This is purported to have functioned as a 'petri dish' for the fusion of nationalism and populism through corporatist ideology, creating a common ground between supporters of reactionary nationalism and Left revolutionary interventionism.[72] This synthesis, it is argued, 'will be fully accomplished by fascism'.[73] Dannunzian Fiume was the birthplace of fascism because it 'was the place and moment of confluence of all the factors that undermined the liberal state'—namely, 'right-wing subversivism, a generic discontent with the allied powers' "betrayal", nationalistic expansionism, the myth of [Italy's] maimed victory, the myth of youth, anti-socialism, anti-parliamentarism'.[74] In Fiume, D'Annunzio undermined the national and international credibility of Italian liberal-democratic institutions and showed the power of patriotic appeals to divide Italy's ruling classes; as such, the Ronchi march and Dannunzian Fiume are argued to be a 'necessary' precedent for the march on Rome and Mussolini's coup.[75] D'Annunzio's irreverent verbal attacks on Italy's constituted power catalysed the political fractures that enabled Mussolini to seize control, by precipitating the 1922 Fascist march on Rome, to whom it fell to bring to fruition 'all the drunken excesses and inventions of D'Annunzio's muse'.[76] As a prominent exponent of early twentieth-century irrationalism, whose ideologically inflected literary production and political oratory manipulated audiences into embracing violently subversive ends, D'Annunzio is also said to be chiefly responsible for the degeneration of Italian political life well into the latter half of the twentieth century.[77] The not-so-veiled implication here is that even the terrorist attacks that marred Italy's so-called leaden years—between the late 1970s and early 1980s—could reasonably be laid at the poet's door.

A rather more rarefied line of argument maintains that D'Annunzio was the inventor of fascism because both the poet's Fiume endeavour and Mussolini's movement relied on the logic of redemption, whereby sacrifice promises the future restoration of a mythical happy state at some indefinite point in the future, which does not coincide with the completion of the sacrifice. That logic, we are told, is characteristic of fascism in a way in which it was not of 'other political movements which relied on teleological models of continuous development toward a final historical goal.'[78]

Given the poet's prestige as a war hero and ultimate patriot, the Fascist regime itself—thanks to its control of the press—actively built the myth that D'Annunzio supported the regime. The myth of a proto-fascist D'Annunzio has thus proven difficult to dislodge,[79] in both Italian literature (Villari's 2019 book for example speaks of 'the augmentation of Dannunziansesimo into fascism')[80] and non-Italian literature. Notably, it provides the dominant lens through which the Fiume occupation continues to be read in Croat historiography,[81] as apparent from Tea Perinčić's recent book.[82]

FIUMANESIMO AND FASCISM

The claims set out here rhetorically establish a seemingly natural progression from D'Annunzio's ideology and political practice to fascism, but they do so at the cost of more abstraction than sound, persuasive argument admits. Barbara Spackman confronted this problem when offering her critical reading of D'Annunzio's novels and other works of literature in *Decadent Genealogies*. There she noted that such texts 'can be held to be in the proto-Fascist camp only if all aspects of modernism itself are held to be proto-Fascist. But at such a level of generality, proto-fascism no longer has any specificity at all'.[83] To hold on to the hypothesis of a proto-fascist D'Annunzio, one must turn one's eyes away from evidence that points to a more complex picture of both the context within which the Fiume occupation occurred and of D'Annunzio's own politics.[84]

Nationalists and Fascists (with the support of elements of the Army and those sectors of industry that had a stake in an indefinite continuation of the war) had been actively concocting subversive plots in the immediate aftermath of hostilities.[85] D'Annunzio was widely hailed as a prophet by those on the Extreme Right who were hoping to see the constitutional order dismantled, and he was in contact with prominent subversive elements around the time when Nitti replaced Orlando as prime minister.[86] D'Annunzio's own subversivism, however, cannot be equated with or reduced to such projects. Perfetti argues that whenever D'Annunzio toyed with the idea of a march on Rome, for example, his 'perspective . . . had nothing to do with the project contemplated by fascism'.[87] Indeed, disparate projects for such a march were recommended to him by people of different political orientations,[88] and it seems significant that one that D'Annunzio appears to have taken particularly seriously smacks more of Left-wing rather than Right-wing subversivism.[89]

If we turn to *Fiumanesimo*, the political orientation that developed during D'Annunzio's occupation of Fiume, and which should be regarded as D'Annunzio's main political legacy, the discontinuities with fascism become apparent. This is so even if we grant that understandings of *Fiumanecimo* are contested. Serventi Longhi defines it as a military revolutionary movement aiming at social renewal and the 'nationalisation of the masses', which developed organically as a result of the communal practices of D'Annunzio's legionnaires and their induction into a form of patriotic mysticism.[90] Some have argued that rather than a political or philosophical doctrine,

Fiumanesimo was a spiritual, idealistic, and revolutionary movement aspiring to change society.[91] Others call it an 'anti-theoretical ensemble of actions and aspirations begotten out of [D'Annunzio's] revolutionary project' in Fiume.[92]

At least for some time after the end of D'Annunzio's occupation of Fiume, however, *Fiumanesimo* had a clear political programme. Umberto Foscanelli, De Ambris's secretary,[93] defined it along two main lines. In terms of external relations, it was the 'attempt to build a coalition, against imperial and capitalist powers, of all peoples of any nationality subjected to foreign dominion'. Domestically, it was the commitment to establish a 'social republic' based on the principle that 'those who do not work [the leisure classes] will not eat'.[94]

Colseschi encapsulated the tenets of *Fiumanesimo* into a more detailed manifesto of sorts:

1. The struggle against any kind of tyranny and defence of all oppressed peoples.
2. The defence of the principles of nationality and self-determination against any influence coming from selfish and particularistic interests.
3. The use of violence against all forms of oppression.
4. Brotherhood and free association of all peoples and all races.
5. The struggle until the last against Anglo-Saxon imperialism and militarism, which seeks to smother the world in its embrace.
6. Hard opposition against the Treaty of Versailles, which must be abolished and against the *Society of Nations*—an agency of global finance and speculators.
7. Abolition of the parliamentary system and institution of the government of all organised workers.[95]

Foscanelli's and Colseschi's accounts of *Fiumanesimo* may or may not have been shared by all those who gravitated towards it; and it is ironic that Colseschi would later become the driving force behind the (unsuccessful) creation of a fascist international movement.[96] But it is apparent that Foscanelli's and Colseschi's accounts make *Fiumanesimo* look more akin to Left revolutionary movements than anything else. Even a cursory look at what became the official political manifesto of *Fiumanesimo*—the *Carnaro Charter*—makes clear the radical irreducibility of *Fiumanesimo* to fascism. I will engage in a close analysis of the *Charter* in a subsequent chapter. Here suffice to say that, as Woodhouse aptly puts it, 'its statements are the exact antithesis of anything that was to be promulgated by Mussolini's government'.[97]

Ultimately, the only way to maintain that D'Annunzio is proto-fascist and that *Fiumanesimo* was a prelude to fascism is by explaining away D'Annunzio's openly professed commitment to freedom and individual rights as rhetorical insincerity;[98] his endorsement of the progressive principles of the *Charter* as a result of either short-lived, unthinking enthusiasm,[99] or theatrical virtue signalling;[100] the *Charter* itself as merely a propaganda tool with which D'Annunzio's deftly exploited the convergence of Right- and Left-wing subversivism through 'ridiculous' promises of wholesale social renewal;[101] and the radical Left-wing elements in his Fiume entourage as an insignificant minority,[102] and in any case as exponents of 'a washed out variety of Bolshevism, more literary than political'.[103] But such dismissive moves are more informative about the ideological precommitments of their authors than about either D'Annunzio's politics or *Fiumanesimo*.

D'ANNUNZIO AND MUSSOLINI

The personal and political relationship between D'Annunzio and Mussolini is also pertinent to the question of the poet's alleged proto-fascism. While Fiume's occupation was ongoing, Mussolini deliberately exploited and appropriated the nationalist combat mythology elaborated by D'Annunzio, with a view to increasing the *Fasci*, unite them ideologically, and legitimise them politically and culturally.[104] Yet the relationship between D'Annunzio and Mussolini was ambivalent during the Fiume occupation and outright troubled thereafter.[105]

Even some of D'Annunzio's detractors concede that after the end of the occupation and the Fascists' march on Rome, D'Annunzio strove to oppose fascism and Mussolini.[106] Only a few months after the end of the Fiume adventure, during the May 1921 Italian elections, the poet threatened his followers with expulsion from the National Federation of Fiume Legionnaires if they adhered to Fascism;[107] some weeks later he was instructing Italy's *Arditi* not to mix up with Mussolini's followers.[108]

In 1920–1921, D'Annunzio was critical of the Fascist movement on a number of occasions and did not accept candidature in the National Block,[109] which saw Fascists, Nationalists, and Liberals allied against the red menace, paving the way to Mussolini's political takeover. When, before the march on Rome, the Fascists had occupied by force the Socialists-controlled City Hall in Milan, they ambushed D'Annunzio (on private business in the city) to make him deliver a speech in their support. But he studiously avoided any reference to (let alone praise for) Mussolini's movement. Instead he decried 'a false Italy, which does not wish to live as we did in Fiume, a false Italy which lives, not with its spirit, but with its stomach,' and predicted that a new one will arise 'to fulfil our destiny. This is the Italy of the plough, the hammer and the scythe'.[110] The circumstances under which the address was delivered—from a building waving the fascist flag—made many jump to the conclusion that the address was pro-fascist.[111] But Rhodes puts it aptly where he states that the poet's words were rather 'a paen of praise to Goodness, Fraternity, Peace, with a side reference to communism.'[112] Significantly, Mussolini complained in his newspaper *Il Popolo d'Italia* that the poet had pointedly failed to cheer the Fascists' seizure of the City Hall.[113]

Afterwards, throughout the fascist years, D'Annunzio lived in a sort of political no man's land, careful not to publicly endorse the regime, with numerous points of attrition evident in the private correspondence between the poet and Mussolini.[114] He called the Fascists' signature black shirts 'soiled shirts' and snubbed the regime's anniversaries.[115] Only towards the end of 1933 did D'Annunzio signify his satisfaction with Mussolini's politics, on the occasion of Italy's contemplated rapprochement with France at the expense of 'the uncouth villain' and 'fierce clown' Adolf Hitler.[116] And only later still, when the poet's physical and mental health was rapidly deteriorating towards the end of his life, did D'Annunzio praise Mussolini's political leadership, this time on the occasion of the successful military campaign in Ethiopia.[117] But as Bonadeo notes, the ideology of conquest and imperialistic assertion of power that made D'Annunzio acclaim the Ethiopia campaign in the 1930s was quite removed from the 'dream of national and individual redemption' that had made him a forceful advocate of Italy's rights in the eastern Adriatic fifteen years before.[118]

D'ANNUNZIO'S *ÜBERMENSCHLICH* POLITICS

There are also methodological problems with the claim that D'Annunzio's ideology was a precursor of fascism. That ideology is not extrapolated from D'Annunzio's most exquisitely political programme—the *Carnaro Charter*—but from other sources, including not only his political speeches but even his works of literature. Even in recent, otherwise well-documented scholarly work,[119] D'Annunzio's literary works are often treated as if intended to set out a straightforward political ideology. Passages from D'Annunzio's poetry or literary prose writing are taken almost to speak for themselves, on the strength of a generic claim that his political positions and literary works mirror each other,[120] or on the basis of D'Annunzio's own claim that 'art and politics were never disconnected in my thought.'[121] Yet such a claim is a far cry from an invitation to read his literary work as if it set out political prescriptions.

If D'Annunzio's political thought is so clear and straightforward that 'the accents contained in [his political stances] are regularly reflected in the majority of [his works of literature]',[122] it is hard to see why an analysis of the latter is not redundant for the student of D'Annunzio's political thought. The reason why such an analysis is carried out is that D'Annunzio's works of literature are in fact used by his critics to independently establish certain political commitments they ascribe to him—particularly an ideological investment in the *Übermensch*. The commitments are then used to inform the scholar's interpretation of D'Annunzio's more political and less literary interventions. Through this dubious process, the marks of elitism, a will to power, and even a cult of violence are purported to be detected in D'Annunzio's political texts.

Such takes on D'Annunzio impute to him a certain reading of Nietzsche's philosophy (save for arguing that he had already independently elaborated analogous positions) and go so far as to explicitly claim that his *oeuvre* can only be meaningfully read as a celebration of the Nietzschean *Übermensch*. This, they argue, is constitutive of his whole literary production to such an extent that it admits of no alternative reading, and certainly not one that might unearth any inner tensions within D'Annunzio's own work.[123] On this reading, the key ideological link between D'Annunzio and fascism is forged of an *Übermenschlich* alloy. D'Annunzio's celebration of the *Übermensch* implies a hierarchy and a logic of force that are necessarily at odds with 'human dignity' and 'civil rights'; it seeks to establish the despotic rule of an ostensibly aristocratic figure, who nonetheless responds to a bourgeois worldview and bourgeois preoccupations, summoned in the service of empire and great capital.[124]

Such interpretive moves are highly questionable because they bracket all-important questions about the functions of D'Annunzio's literary writings. As Spackman notes when critiquing the converse tendency to read D'Annunzio's texts in light of his life, 'drawing literary conclusions from biographical data, like drawing biographical conclusions from literary data, depends on elision and an ignorance of the rhetorical nature of the literary text. Either tactic may be useful for indicting or absolving authors and their works, but neither helps us to understand the texts in question.'[125]

No critic who draws adverse inferences about D'Annunzio's political ideology from his texts of literature has attempted to explain how their conclusions square with the much more straightforward statement of that ideology represented in the *Carnaro Charter*. As Foscanelli noted as far back as 1952, the *Charter*, because of its nature as a constitutional document intended to give official expression to D'Annunzio's creed, should be treated as the central text to determine his political legacy.[126] With this in mind, it is significant that Mussolini publicly stated that fascism could not found itself on the *Charter* because it was the product of a 'man of genius', a 'man of the extraordinary times, not the man of day-to-day practice'; privately, he dismissed it as 'less than nothing' as a 'social programme'.[127]

Some recent scholarship has shown more nuance in its treatment of D'Annunzio's literary work for the purpose of understanding his political ideology. On the one hand, discontinuities have been noted between Nietzsche's solipsistic *Übermensch*, invested in his exceptional status as a source of meaning, and D'Annunzio's active *Übermensch*, intent on a political project of asserting his power over the moribund and philistine multitudes.[128] On the other hand, it has been noted that both in his novels and dramas, D'Annunzio's so-called *Übermenschen* often fail at their projects of domination,[129] and that D'Annunzio's appropriation of the Nietzschean *Übermensch* is polemical rather than strictly political, being deployed for aesthetic effect[130] and sometimes as a self-conscious exaggeration. This has been argued to be the case with respect to *The Triumph of Death*,[131] a novel frequently used to distil and indict D'Annunzio's political thought.[132] It is true that Giorgio Aurispa, the central character, extensively cites Nietzsche, his works, and his philosophical concepts in his solipsistic mental gymnastics.[133] But we have simply no ground for reading those gymnastics as a statement of D'Annunzio's political ideology, especially when Giorgio's longing to live the 'Dionysian ideal' is described in the novel itself as *'aspirazioni fittize'*—'false aspirations'![134] Attention has also been drawn to evidence that *The Virgins of the Rocks*—another novel treated by D'Annunzio's critics as especially revealing of his political creed[135]—was regarded by the writer as having no more than incidental political content, notable mainly for its instrumental value: it helped with publicity and sales.[136]

D'ANNUNZIO, BAD BOY

For D'Annunzio's biographer Woodhouse, it is less any ideological continuity (whether mediated by Nietzsche or otherwise) between fascism and the poet's political thought that is to blame than the poet's own 'attitude, inculcated by example into the youth of Italy at a crucial time, which provided all that Mussolini later needed'.[137] By this Woodhouse means D'Annunzio's 'anarchic life-style and his complete disregard for authority'.[138] Yet Italian institutions and authorities had come into disrepute by the time of the march on Rome, quite regardless of D'Annunzio's undeniable contributions to the process of delegitimising them.

Additionally, D'Annunzio's rebel spirit and his disregard for authority (including the authority of convention, opposition to which shows up in his libertinism) are the very antithesis of fascist authoritarianism rather than being continuous with it. Not only were D'Annunzio's and Mussolini's sensibilities at odds on this, but D'Annunzio's normative vision clearly rejected the kind of totalitarianism characteristic of fascism.[139]

D'Annunzio himself saw this clearly. In 1923, Mussolini remonstrated with D'Annunzio that the French press pointed to the poet as a high-profile opposer of the Fascist government and invited him to issue a public and categorical denial, taking the opportunity to remind him that 'what Italians expect from you is—Poetry'. D'Annunzio replied, 'Your telegram has that singular note which is perhaps fundamental to fascism, but which is completely foreign to my spirit life. No one shall influence me—not the least of my opinions and resolutions.'[140] These are words entirely consistent with a man who Kotchnitzky aptly described as 'in open revolt against anything that in the universe might be constraint, hierarchy, settled convention.'[141] Rainero perhaps puts it best where he says that if it may be debatable whether fascist doctrine bears some similarity with D'Annunzio's ideas, it is entirely inappropriate to suggest that fascist ideology sprang out of *Dannunzianesimo*.[142]

Ballinger notes that unlike Mussolini's tight control over Fascist ranks and fascist ideology, 'D'Annunzio proved unable to guide Fiume in a sole direction or manipulate the many different messages and themes which emanated from the city.'[143] Rather than seeing this, as Ballinger apparently implies, as D'Annunzio's failure to realise his wish, it is appropriate to wonder whether such aspiration for ideological control was in fact fundamentally alien to some core part of D'Annunzio's sensibility. An affirmative answer to that question need not deny that the success of the Fiume endeavour might at times have appeared to its protagonists to be dependent on something like ideological control, or that D'Annunzio's outsized ego might at times have lured him (ambivalently) towards it.

D'ANNUNZIO'S ANTIPARLIAMENTARISM

To return to D'Annunzio's stint as a member of Parliament in the late 1890s, when he moved to the benches of the Extreme Left he was very clear that he did not share their ideology[144] but approved of their potential for destroying the political and institutional status quo.[145] D'Annunzio saw representative democratic institutions as conducive to corruption and a politics of feebleness, of deadened mediocrity out of touch with the deeper feelings and aspirations of the people; and he consistently insisted on what he called his 'fierce individualism'[146] and his independence from political parties and ideologies.[147]

Some critics reduce D'Annunzio's critique of parliamentarism to reactionary nationalist politics[148] and conflate antiparliamentarism with anti-socialism, antidemocracy, and elitism.[149] Judging from the political allegiances of some of the best-known European political sociologists and theorists associated with the critique of parliamentarism in the years before and after the war,[150] one might excuse scholars who choose to treat D'Annunzio's own antiparliamentarism with suspicion.[151] Not only, however, is it possible to disentangle at least some of the key arguments of these critics of parliamentarism from their political biographies, but in Italy the critique of parliamentarism also preceded their scholarly contributions by decades. Such a critique had wide currency among disparate sectors of the political and cultural world of postunification Italy,[152] particularly between 1876 and 1890.[153] A decade or so later, the critique of parliamentarism became distinctive, among others, of the groups that made up the revolutionary Left after the reception of the Socialist Party within mainstream politics and before these groups were absorbed into the Italian Communist Party (founded in 1921).[154]

Arguments against parliamentary democracy around the time of D'Annunzio's experience as a member of Parliament were wide ranging. By making the executive accountable to the legislature, and the legislature to the people, parliamentary democracy tends to result in a demagogic politics;[155] in being reliant on the contest between political parties, parliamentary democracy splinters the public good into private interests, rewards politicians who profess the 'correct' ideology over technically competent ones, unduly favours friends of the party, and oppresses its adversaries;[156] parliamentary democracy makes state interests represented by such institutions as the Upper House subservient to those of the Lower House, which is free to make or unmake governments at will and even to compromise the most fundamental laws;[157] parliamentary democracy is built on an assumed, but false, identity between the will of the people and the interest, or common good of the people;[158] the very foundation of parliamentary democracy—the majority principle as the criterion for appointing political leaders—is fundamentally flawed.[159] This and more was adduced against parliamentarism.

The critique of parliamentary democracy became widespread among European intellectual elites of the early twentieth century, resonating with elements of both the radical Left and bourgeois nationalism.[160] Even liberal commentators were fully aware of the crisis of legitimacy bedevilling the representative model of government at the very time when the principle of popular sovereignty and universal suffrage had gained ground in Europe.[161] D'Annunzio's vaguely denouncing the low quality of members of Parliament and parliamentary work, political patronage, ideological stultification, and the failure of the current system to channel all the vital forces of the country into a vibrant forum generating virtuous policy making added little to the well-established critique of parliamentary democracy of his times.[162] As we will see, D'Annunzio did, however, attempt to practically grapple with these problems when designing the law-making body in the *Carnaro Charter*. The key point is that concern with, and denunciation of, the shortcomings and limitations of parliamentary democracy need not normatively commit one—and they did not commit D'Annunzio in the *Charter*—to the view that fascism or other forms of authoritarianism are the remedy.

D'ANNUNZIO'S ELITISM

Long before putting his mind—when designing the *Carnaro Charter* with Alceste De Ambris—to the problem of how to make representative politics work, D'Annunzio had set out an idea of political leadership that he hoped might mobilise the country towards change. Before entering politics, he had predicted the necessary decline of democratic institutions built on the logic of *ressentiment* and on the multitudes' purely materialistic aspirations, and the advent of an unequal world, where criteria for membership in the noble and plebeian classes would be redefined away from wealth and lineage and towards love for, and ability to, self-rule: a 'nobleman' would then be a law unto himself, and a plebeian would be enslaved by his own lack of will and imagination.[163] Later D'Annunzio presented this 'aristocratic' attachment to the ideal of self-rule and one's breaking free from heteronomous law as the very precondition to participation in politics; they were the very qualities that would enable one to communicate and cathect with the multitudes, without thereby debasing oneself.[164]

When campaigning in the late 1890s, D'Annunzio had envisaged the advent of a new political leadership that would finally succeed in grasping the Italian genius's unique commitment to beauty: a veritable cult of the beautiful, on which the destiny of the Nation depended.[165] The same idea was conveyed in *Fire*, the novel D'Annunzio published the year after his election: '"It's true, it's true" thought Stelio Effrena. "Italy's fortune is inseparable from the fortunes of Beauty, to which she is mother." . . . Should not [the new art] synthesise within itself all the latent powers in the hereditary constitution of the nation . . . [and] point to the men who shared in government the original truths to inform the laws of the new statutes?'[166]

We are so conditioned to thinking of politics as the domain of utility that D'Annunzio's remarks will strike many readers as quaint or ludicrous. No doubt this is how many of his contemporaries also received them. Yet Pireddu demonstrated how Italian anthropology—a newly established discipline in Italian universities at the time—was pursuing lines of inquiry that lent some credit to D'Annunzio's identification of beauty as the central guiding principle of political action. Paolo Mantegazza, in particular (with whose ideas D'Annunzio was familiar), treated the beautiful as an ethical principle bound up with a noncalculating logic of gift giving, spontaneous enjoyment, and appreciation of the transience of things.[167]

If at the time of his election D'Annunzio claimed that a rediscovery of beauty had the potential for regenerating politics, a few years before, in the presentation D'Annunzio wrote to introduce a new literary and artistic magazine, beauty had been an antidote to politics.[168] In any case, from now on beauty was to remain an abiding element—if not the *leitmotif*—of D'Annunzio's normative and political vision. Consistent with this, when he informally promulgated the *Carnaro Charter* in Fiume on 30 August 1920, he declared, 'We are for creating . . . a voice of beauty and a form of beauty over the world forgetful of things high and things eternal, over the decrepit world destined to fall down and inexorably fall apart'.[169]

D'Annunzio may have been unusual in articulating so unapologetically the normative primacy of beauty in politics. But Woodward aptly points out that in D'Annunzio's time, disappointment with the direction in which postunification Italy had drifted, as a result of 'unscrupulous bourgeois entrepreneurs with the sullen connivance of a debased proletariat', was widespread among different sectors of Italian society, including 'frustrated Mazzinian idealists, belated Garibaldi hero-worshippers, nostalgic conservatives, atrabilious aesthetes'.[170] It is apparent here how such sentiments were linked with an antimaterialist perspective setting store by higher (spiritual) values—the object of analysis in the next section—as well as with an elitist one that assumed (rightly or wrongly) the masses to be impervious to such values, at least if left to their own devices.

D'Annunzio's vision of an intellectual avant-garde redeeming politics by leading the polity in the pursuit of spiritual-aesthetic values articulates with his earlier reflections on the role of the artist as 'interpreter and harbinger of his time'. This role could be fulfilled thanks to the artist's ability to speak to the multitudes through the language of passion rather than rational persuasion, but only on condition that the artist's soul was allowed 'to come into contact with the collective soul, so as to feel its dim, but constant and unstoppable, undercurrents'.[171] This, again, echoes a point we find in the novel *Fire* (1898), whose lengthy first part is devoted to the protagonist steeling himself for, and delivering, an address to a crowd in Venice: 'The confused feeling arose within [the crowd] of a truth dimly familiar, which the poet now suddenly revealed in the form of an unheard message.'[172]

This suggests a complex conception on D'Annunzio's part of the writer's political role and his relationship with the public. Becker argues that D'Annunzio's literary production sought to appeal to the multitudes because the resultant cachet would increase his own power and influence; the poet's contempt for the masses allowed him to treat them merely instrumentally, manipulating their easily predictable emotional responses for self-aggrandising purposes.[173] But this kind of reductionism trivialises the more idealistic dimension of D'Annunzio's conception of the artist's political role, obscuring his clearly articulated two-way relationship between the artist and the general public. D'Annunzio imagined specific political commitments to take shape within the context of that relationship rather than being unilaterally imposed by an artistic elite. Specifically, in both his political speeches and works of literature, the poet claimed that there is a hidden beauty in the crowds that a capable orator (a poet or a hero) could cause to flash.[174] This is clearly not a Machiavellian argument about manipulating crowds. Not only is the work of the artist-leader-orator oriented towards intrinsic value (beauty), but value is also not something he implants into the people: the multitudes already possess it as a quality that the leader can draw out.

D'Annunzio's conception of the politically committed artist, thus, seems to have sought to transcend the dichotomy between the artist's desire and contempt for the masses. Indeed, during the war years and the Fiume occupation, D'Annunzio may well have personally succeeded at that kind of transcendence. Perfetti, De Felice, and La Rosa argue that the experience of war had an impact on D'Annunzio's elitist individualism, teaching him camaraderie and bringing him face to face with common people's capacity for endurance and sacrifice, with a consequent shift in how he conceptualised the relationship between leaders and subalterns.[175] In line with this, in 1921 he wrote in a letter to Alceste de Ambris that 'those who shovel and till the earth, those who dig coal and metals, those who melt iron, those who consume themselves in the heat of workshops, they carry eternal life like I carry it.'[176]

At the same time, we should treat as a heuristic simplification the idea of D'Annunzio's conversion from prewar elitism to a postwar stance embracing the 'noble people' as 'the best possible antidote to the challenges of the new politics'.[177] This is because, as we have seen, D'Annunzio's prewar deliberative (as distinct from his novelistic) reflections on the relationship between the masses and the artistic/political avant-garde are far from articulating an outright contempt for the masses. Even in his novels—which, as argued, should be treated with caution as sources of information about D'Annunzio's political thought—the elite is idealised not for enjoying lineage-based social privilege but only insofar as it uses its privilege to cultivate cultural and artistic refinement.[178] Democratising processes were similarly critiqued not in themselves but to the extent that they tend to cause the disappearance of a cultivated elite.[179] Serventi Longhi calls D'Annunzio's political thought at the turn of the century a 'combination of elitism and populism'.[180] The incoherence implied by this characterisation is only apparent, for D'Annunzio neither rejected nor praised either the masses or the elite as such but judged them on the basis of their willingness to respond to aesthetic and spiritual values.

D'ANNUNZIO'S ANTIMATERIALISM

The emphasis on beauty and spiritual value in D'Annunzio's political thought shares in a newly emerging nationalist discourse in late nineteenth-century Europe, which rejected the materialist outlook of socialism in the name of spiritual values and virtues.[181] Much has been made of this to argue that D'Annunzio's politics is distinctly proto-fascist. Becker argues that the flip side of D'Annunzio's appeal to aesthetic and spiritual values is a rejection of socialist materialism;[182] consequently, this appeal, inasmuch as it is addressed to the working classes,[183] encourages them to give up the struggle for improving their material conditions.[184] D'Annunzio, on this view, exhorts them to set aside class conflict[185] and instead to find fulfilment in an imperialistic project aimed at establishing Italy's supremacy in the Mediterranean and beyond,[186] including through the use of force.[187]

This analysis is problematic in many ways. D'Annunzio's literary production was multifarious, and one might as well point to works in which he celebrated workers and peasants, equality and justice.[188] Becker overinterprets his sources where he reads D'Annunzio as exhorting the working classes to give up material concerns for spiritual and aesthetic ones. It is telling, for example, that the brand of Dannunzian antimaterialism in the *Carnaro Charter* specifically appealed to some Socialists.[189] Besides, socialist materialism is primarily a thesis about the primacy of 'nature' and 'being' over 'spirit' and 'thought',[190] of the priority of 'nature, matter, the physical, the external world' (as opposed to 'consciousness, mind, sensation . . . the psychical') 'in the solution of philosophical problems'.[191] Opposing this kind of methodological materialism need not normatively commit one to asceticism and to recommending foregoing material concerns—and there is no evidence that D'Annunzio was so committed.

This is not to deny that it is distinctive of D'Annunzio's political thought (as we will see when discussing the *Charter*) to maintain that improving material well-being does not exhaust the goals of political action, and that intangible values are just as important and deserving of being promoted. D'Annunzio was an enemy of, as Woodhouse puts it, 'anti-intellectual materialism'.[192] Where he describes the United States and Britain as 'the governments of insatiable materialism and eternal scepticism',[193] the poet makes clear that the companion of an excessive concern with economic well-being (insatiable materialism) is scepticism—lack of commitment to normative ideals. The objections to democracy D'Annunzio voiced in 1892 were essentially to the way in which the political subject of democracy—the people—only appeared to care for an increase in their physical and material well-being. This necessarily corrupted the political process, for in pandering to a political subject thus constituted, electoral politics and the work of government were encouraged to discount any kind of ideal or higher values.[194] Of course, by the time D'Annunzio stood for election as a self-styled 'candidate of beauty' he no longer believed that the people were incapable of responding to appeals to spiritual values. And when he advocated entry into war he was able to reinvent 'the people as citizens and warriors, as worthy of playing a role in the life of the nation':[195] in other words, as capable of responding to his appeals to sacrifice themselves for a worthy cause. Afterwards, the whole Fiume enterprise was based on the presupposition that the people could be brought round to recognising the importance of idealism and spiritual values and to revolt against a political class that did not give them their due.

In Fiume, the poet coined for Nitti the defamatory nickname 'Cagoia'—untranslatable, but best rendered as 'shit-scared'.[196] D'Annunzio went on to elaborate on Cagoia being a character given to excessive eating, whose moving principle is 'I but think through the belly'.[197] The allusion here is to Nitti's willingness to pacify the Allies in order to obtain aid and credit, for which he was prepared to trade Italy's claims over Fiume.[198] Indeed, Wilson was peremptory and explicit in declaring to Nitti that the US government would not assist the economic reconstruction of any country that failed to adhere to its political programme.[199] When, upon leaving the negotiating table in Paris, Orlando had declared that Italy knew 'the ways of hunger, but not those of dishonour',[200] he encapsulated the idea that Italy was being blackmailed into accepting less than her due through the threat of material deprivation. This set the stage for the perception that Orlando's successor, Nitti, who was more prepared to accommodate the Allies' position, would trade honour for the sake of material well-being—a full belly.

In a notorious Fiume speech, D'Annunzio repeated the motto he ascribed to Cagoia—'I but think through the belly'—over and over again in Trieste vernacular, to the hilarity of the crowd. This served to denounce Nitti's (an economist) lack of idealism. Some tortured, recent interpretations claim that D'Annunzio here must be misquoting the original source of the speech act (Nitti himself), rhetorically exploiting the distance between the original utterance and the poet's subsequent distortion of it.[201] But this is a misunderstanding. In reiterating 'I but think through the belly,' D'Annunzio was not purporting to (mis)quote anyone: he was making up a motto and falsely attributing it to Nitti in a game of fancy in which he very openly invited his audience to follow him. The game involved not only made-up mottoes but also fanciful names (Cagoia) and invented life histories (a habit of excessive eating) for his political adversaries. The audience understood that all this was make believe. It followed D'Annunzio in the game because the made-up name, motto, and life history seemed a revealing metaphor of Italy's prime minister's ideological commitments: his economic utilitarianism, his lack of idealism. No one would have been duped into thinking Nitti might have actually said something such as 'I but think through the belly'; it is preposterous to think that this would have escaped D'Annunzio. The point is important. What I called the tortured interpretation ascribes to D'Annunzio an intent to manipulate the crowd into believing a distortion of the truth. In fact, D'Annunzio is openly using make believe to convey to the crowd what he takes to be the actual truth of the matter.

The metaphor of food filling one's belly, at the expense of cultivating normative ideals and spiritual values, is a leitmotif of D'Annunzio's speeches about Nitti and Italy's treatment of Fiume, from the first to the last day of the occupation. On the day of his arrival in Fiume, the local newspaper *La Vedetta d'Italia* published a speech where D'Annunzio harshly criticised Nitti and Italy's willingness to appease Wilson: 'The slashing thief admonishes every day with a terrible but paternal snigger, letting out every day, within its bight buckle, his belt by one hole: "If to-day thou wilt not prostate thyself, tomorrow thou shalt not eat." The docile chorus answers: "Wherever food is to be eaten, thither let thy wisdom lead us."'[202]

Italy was 'intent on consuming with the American cadets the ungraciously conceded victuals in propitiatory banquets',[203] all the while forgetting about the future of the Fiumans. As a result, the Fiumans' 'sanguinary oath' ('Italy or death!') was 'now no more than a rumpled, faded scrap of paper which the good bourgeois [in Italy] will fasten down with a pin, between the splinter of a shell and the little pebble from Mount Grappa, in his domestic war-museum.'[204] This was all the more reproachable when Fiumans had themselves gone hungry to assist Italian prisoners of war led to town by the Habsburg armies.[205]

Likewise, at the end of the occupation, following the so-called bloody Christmas of 1920, D'Annunzio attacked the bourgeois philistinism that had made, he claimed, Italian people occupy themselves with Christmas festivities, indifferent to the fate of the Fiume legionnaires bombed by the Italian government.[206] Conversely, to his legionnaires in Fiume, he said, 'You are not flesh. You are a form of superhuman will, a weightless momentum, a measureless offering, a fistful of incense thrown into embers, the fragrance of pure spirit.' Against this army of volunteers fighting for an ideal stood the regular Italian Army, following orders out of base self-interest: 'a people shamed by the fulness of their stomach and their suspect honorarium: people well-fed and well-paid,' but 'hands that have felt Cain's recompense are poor at handling rifles'.[207]

These examples illustrate that D'Annunzio's preoccupation with a politics that subordinated ideals to material interests was an abiding one, and that it applied across the board, often targeting specifically the mainstream: the Army, the government, and the bourgeoisie. It is thereby entirely implausible to read into it a bourgeois concern with distracting the working classes from improvement of their material conditions. In fact, D'Annunzio in Fiume famously weighed in on the side of workers during a serious labour dispute, until their demands were met. On that occasion he wrote a piece in support of the legitimate claims of the working classes:[208]

> Were we disputing with hunger and deprivation?
> A fat man [namely, the employers] said: 'This suffices.'
> A thin man [namely, the workers] said: 'This does not suffice'.
> . . . And in that well-appointed room there really was the figure of hunger, there really was the figure of deprivation.[209]

During thc negotiations,

> Every 'no' made the other party [that is, the employers] shake their head, but it made yours convulse, the closer the night came.
> 'Another handful of flour?'
> 'No. We want to live.'
> 'Another piece of bread?'
> 'No. We want to live.'
> 'Another dish of soup? Another bone?'
> 'No. We want to live.'
> . . . I felt a sudden great strength, as if fate had made me leader of another army, different from that of my legionnaires. . . .
> 'We grant all your demands.'
> 'We want to live.'[210]

While D'Annunzio's intervention has been chastised for showing a kind of paternalistic concern rather than an 'authentically socialist' stance,[211] the key point for the purposes of my argument is that D'Annunzio did not advocate that the working classes should give up their aspirations for improving their material welfare. Both in his immediate reflection upon the labour dispute and when reminiscing on it one year later, D'Annunzio did insist that the negotiations were not just about 'the belly' but 'also' about 'the soul', that he and De Ambris had 'also' been doing a 'work of the soul'.[212] But the choice of word 'also' (repeated twice in the relevant passages) makes it amply clear that spiritual and material concerns went hand in hand for D'Annunzio, and that the former were never intended to replace the latter.

The manifesto of revolutionary syndicalism itself explicitly stated, 'The materialism of [class] interests must be subordinated to a superior conception of life'; and 'Every social transformation should be directed above all to the moral and intellectual betterment of the members of the association'.[213] Yet no one could seriously accuse revolutionary syndicalists of not championing the material interests of the working classes. Given the continuity—which will be explored shortly—between D'Annunzio's economic and political thought and revolutionary syndicalism, as well as his cooperation with revolutionary syndicalists D'Annunzio's idealism must be seen as condemning the pursuit of material concerns divorced from spiritual and aesthetic values—not as a rejection of the necessity or justice of workers' claims to improve their material conditions. Indeed, in 1921 De Ambris and D'Annunzio's Federation of Fiuman Legionnaires declared, 'We acknowledge that the proletariat has an absolute right to rise, but we are also convinced that its rise cannot be purely materialistic. Only if improvement in material conditions is accompanied by a spiritual growth—only then will the working classes be able to say that they have won their struggle.'[214] It is thus a serious misrepresentation to portray D'Annunzio's concern with spiritual values as a reactionary rejection of the need to improve the material well-being of the masses.

Finally, if the critique of materialism was an ideological position D'Annunzio shared with the nationalist Right, it was also championed by no less a liberal philosopher than Benedetto Croce, who used it to critique D'Annunzio's own writings. For Croce, the determinism of the natural sciences, combined with the relentless pursuit of material self-interest both by the bourgeois and the working classes, had robbed the social world of its spiritual dimension and of concern for values of mutual concern and cooperation, leaving such authors as D'Annunzio to write books where the self is the source of all meaning.[215]

D'ANNUNZIO'S CORPORATISM

It is true, as we will see in the chapter devoted to the *Carnaro Charter*, that D'Annunzio's political vision, as it concretised itself in Fiume, institutionalised corporatism, and that corporatism later became a distinctive feature of Italian fascism.[216] But the corporatism intended to be instituted in Fiume did not aim, unlike its Fascist equivalent, at domesticating the working classes.

De Vergottini argues that the corporatist model of representation envisaged in the *Charter* was meant as an alternative not only to traditional Parliaments, which the revolutionary Left saw as a kind of liberal hangover unsuited to the twentieth century, but also to Marx's class conflict.[217] Similarly, Hughes Hallett, in a nonacademic context, claims that the distinctive aspiration of corporatism is to transcend class conflict in the name of the national interest.[218] But these claims obscure the discontinuities between D'Annunzio and De Ambris's corporatism on the one hand and Mussolini's on the other. It is rarely remarked that only the latter, but not the former, aspired to transcend class conflict.[219]

The revolutionary syndicalist De Ambris was chiefly responsible for the political programme adopted in Fiume after the first six months and for the constitutional design that intended to institutionalise corporatism as a mode of political representation. A few years later, De Ambris drew attention both to Mussolini's plagiarism in appropriating the vocabulary of corporatism devised in Fiume and to the differences between the two systems. Only Mussolini's brand of corporatism, for De Ambris, implausibly aspired to subsume conflicting class interests under a superior 'national interest'. It was, at that, not an original move, as the Catholic Church had already championed that idea when it had started its work of organising the masses. But despite the Church's powerful means of persuasion, 'white trade unions' had been practicing class struggles in just the same way as 'red trade unions'.[220] For De Ambris, in other words, there was no trade unionism or corporatism that could do away with class conflict.

D'Annunzio had his own reasons for aligning himself with De Ambris on this point. As he remarked when reflecting about the labour dispute he had led in Fiume, 'the crude dispute changed into a vigorous lyrical movement. . . . The new order can only arise from the turmoil of fervour and struggle'.[221] This is consistent with revolutionary syndicalism which, in the formulation of its main philosopher, conceived of the nation as an agonistic forum in which interest groups clashed over their particular interests and came together over the general interest—a process that had its own dynamic logic, which could neither be predetermined nor forcibly controlled.[222]

Thus, the main argument that could be used in support of the view that D'Annunzio was in the business of domesticating the working classes and distracting them from material concerns—namely, the argument that in Fiume the poet anticipated Mussolini's corporatism—flounders. There is no basis for assuming that D'Annunzio's corporatism shared the same orientation towards deradicalising workers' material demands exhibited by Fascist corporatism, and indeed strong evidence to the contrary.

D'ANNUNZIO, MANIPULATOR OF CROWDS

It is a mistake to (dis)credit D'Annunzio with inventing the sacralisation of politics that Gentile has demonstrated was characteristic of Fascism. As Gentile himself notes, the search for a civil religion capable of uniting the Italian people dates to the *Risorgimento*, was a chief preoccupation of Giuseppe Mazzini, was shared by all postunification political actors concerned with awakening the Italian people's national awareness, and had already dawned on Mussolini while he was still a militant atheist and revolutionary Socialist.[223] However, it is widely and correctly acknowledged that D'Annunzio's leadership style as commandant in Fiume and the rituals, symbolism, and theatrics of political power he devised were plagiarised by Fascism, partly thanks to the confluence of many of D'Annunzio's Fiume legionnaires into Mussolini's movement.[224]

One of D'Annunzio's techniques of governance, which Italy's dictator later emulated, was the careful use of public speeches to create a quasi 'mystical relationship' between the leader and the crowd.[225] Especially during the second part of the occupation, D'Annunzio and his entourage became more and more aware of the need to carefully choreograph his public appearances.[226] Senardi captures the views of many where he declares that D'Annunzio's Fiume speeches anticipate Fascism by deploying 'the strategies of emotional coercion, the modes of an irrational and mystical relationship, which remains instead hierarchical and unidirectional, between the Leader and the masses.'[227]

D'Annunzio makes it easier for commentators to reach such conclusions through his own overblown reflections about his oratorial practice and public addresses. Consider the following, from the Poet's *Taccuini*:

> Truly the half hour lived by my spirit and my will to power before I appeared at the railing—that interval of time was to me sublime. . . . Under my windows the human multitude, yet shorn of its humanity [*disumanata*]—flowing, ebullient, spluttering like molten matter. I must respond to its anguish, I must exalt its hope, I must make its devotion ever more blind, and ever more scorching its love for me, me alone. . . . I know not what kind of fluorescence or phosphorescence must have blown though my teeth and lips, then. . . . Did I go to beasts? To souls and minds? Yes, to the people.[228]

From a superficial reading, the parts that stand out most from this passage are no doubt the likening of the crowd to beasts and nonhuman matter awaiting D'Annunzio's demiurgic touch. It is easy to draw the implication that the poet had no respect for his audience and merely intended to manipulate it for his own ends. But if the implication is easy to draw, it also facile. A more sensitive reading would note that in the *Taccuini* D'Annunzio noted down his thoughts, flashes of imagination, and flights of fancy with a view to their future use in works of literature. This suggests both that a literal meaning of the observations recorded in these works is inappropriate, and that D'Annunzio may have emphasised or exaggerated the aspects of his impressions and ideas that would later make for good literary treatment. A further, important point is that in the previous passage D'Annunzio is not describing the moment at which he engages the crowd. Rather he records (and that clearly *ex post facto*) his feelings during the solipsistic, anxiety-ridden, emotionally charged time that precedes the dialogue with the crowd, where the orator's own self-preoccupations, rather than any other-regarding orientations, predominate in him.

With these contextual points in mind, once we set aside our distaste for the apparently instrumentalist portrayal of the crowd, we can readily notice that D'Annunzio's words here convey something rather more complex. Through the use of the literary techniques of oxymoron ('human multitude, yet shorn of its humanity', 'beasts' / 'souls and minds') and contradiction ('I must respond to its anguish' / 'I must make its devotion ever more blind') D'Annunzio is making an important philosophical point. The point conveyed is that—to borrow from Habermas—our real-world communicative practices participate of both genuinely 'communicative' aspects typical of the 'ideal speech situation' and of 'linguistically mediated strategic action'.[229] But then D'Annunzio's candid refusal to disavow the tension between the genuinely communicative and strategic aspects of political oratory may be seen as just that which facilitates, rather than undermines, the possibility of an ethical communicative engagement with his audience—at least once he has stepped out of the solipsistic flights of fancy he indulges in during precommunicative moment ('before I appeared at the railing') and into the actual oration-dialogue.

Indeed, it seems that D'Annunzio's speeches in Fiume were embedded in a communicative practice that was recognisably dialogic.[230] Mosse and others, while acknowledging that the dialogue with the crowds became an essential part of D'Annunzio's speeches, suggest nonetheless that the contributions from his audience were formulaic and that D'Annunzio managed the setting so as to ensure that they were.[231] But this is not the picture we get from those who witnessed his speeches. Colseschi, his personal secretary (and, for a time, minister of external relations), described 'conversations between the Commandant and the people . . . who interrupt the Commandant's speeches, who ask questions, who ask for clarifications, who express their decisions and their will'.[232] Sitwell's account confirms this, reporting D'Annunzio's own description of his dialogic practice: 'When a crowd assembled, he would go out and asked them what they wanted. . . . [G]radually a direct intercourse would thus be built up between the people and their ruler.'[233] This is consistent with other reports of D'Annunzio's dialogic practice (including with subordinates) in more private settings, even in momentous contingencies.[234] It seems to me that to assert with any degree of confidence that D'Annunzio's oratory was a precursor of the ruthless manipulative techniques deployed by Fascism, one must read the sources both selectively and simplistically.

CRUEL MEN BREED CRUEL POLITICS

'What I learned from translating D'Annunzio's novel (and from reading his other novels and plays) is that there is a direct link between personal cruelty and the cruelty of political systems',[235] wrote Susan Bassnett in 2020. It is plausible to assume that a person who lacks moral sensibility will make a bad political leader. Naturally, critics of D'Annunzio's politics tend therefore to take a dim view of his morals and personality. The problem is that his morals and personality—like his political convictions—are often inferred from his literary production, without regard to its chiefly aesthetic function. On other occasions, D'Annunzio's moral character is indicted on the basis of biography. Does this provide firmer foundations for the conclusion that D'Annunzio was a bad man, and so his politics must be too?

Consider the claim that 'there is no evidence that D'Annunzio ever showed regret or compassion or even consideration for others once they had gratified a temporary whim; selfish egoism governed his every action'.[236] One can easily disprove this claim. To give one example, for several years D'Annunzio kept a mutually respectful and sometimes emotional correspondence with the former president of Fiume's National Council, Grossich, well after the old physician had ceased to be of any use to the poet, and despite some serious contrasts between them during Fiume's occupation.[237] The argument about D'Annunzio's callousness continues: 'One of the most significant legacies [D'Annunzio] left to Fascism was the vulgar, indeed obscenely dismissive motto *Me ne frego*, ['I couldn't care less'] which had adorned his letterhead for several years already, and which he would send even in friendly letters to innocuous acquaintances.'[238] A footnote explains: '*Fregarsi*, the plebeian expression for "to masturbate", has now become so much a part of everyday Italian that the most strait-laced matrons will use it to express their indifference, without a thought for its original meaning.'[239] It is useful to closely examine these claims, not as a matter of point scoring but because it serves to illustrate how pronouncements about D'Annunzio's cruelty and immorality tend to function like truth by fiat.

The previous quotes fail to contextualise the origin and use of *Me ne frego*, giving the impression that D'Annunzio gratuitously popularised an obscene expression and that nowadays Italians are so inured to it that we fail to register its obscene character. It is indeed the case that 'strait-laced matrons'—and just about anyone else in Italy lacking an interest in etymology—are, today, blissfully unaware of the fact that *fregarsi* or *fregarsene* ('not to give a damn') has its roots in the Latin *fricare* ('to have sexual intercourse'). But in D'Annunzio's own time, Italians were equally oblivious to the original obscenity of the expression. The 'obscene' connotations of the verb had already been long lost, it appears, by 1869, if novelist Francesco Mastriani could use the expression in his popular work, *Mysteries of Naples*,[240] without anyone batting an eyelid. At that time, the expression was indeed 'vulgar', but less because of any recognisable sexualised overtones than because of its class connotations. *Fregarsi* features in Mastriani's work precisely because of the *milieu* he chose to describe—an exchange between two characters who are manifestly socially deprived and do not belong to polite society. The point is that Mastriani would not have used the expression in his 1869 novel if it could have registered as obscene rather than merely vernacular.

More importantly, D'Annunzio borrowed this working-class expression from the *Arditi*, Italian shock troops formally instituted in 1917 as an alternative combat model to trench warfare.[241] The *Arditi* had taken to writing *Me ne frego* as a motto on the bandages they used to dress their wounds with. It appears to have started on 15 June 1918, when Captain Zaninelli, being assigned a suicide mission by Major Freguglia, is said to have declared: 'Commandant, *me ne frego*, one does what one must for King and country.'[242] What Zaninelli did was die. Such stories about the 'beautiful death' of heroic *Arditi* belong, of course, to the national and military mythology that Italian generals, through their rhetorical exercises, were actively promoting during the war in order to motivate servicemen.[243] This, however, does not alter the point that, whatever other connotations *Me ne frego* acquired after Mussolini's Fascists appropriated it, in the circumstances when D'Annunzio borrowed that expression from the *Arditi*, the words conveyed willingness to die for a worthy cause. So much for D'Annunzio's gratuitously inflicting obscenities on unsuspecting letter recipients and corrupting the *buoncostume* of strait-laced matrons. If the badness of D'Annunzio's politics is ultimately a function of his personal badness, we had better stop and think just how strong the evidence of his badness really is.

CONCLUSIONS

Without evidence that D'Annunzio's nationalism and corporatism, even coupled with his rejection of socialist materialism and parliamentarism, was also committed in some definite way to a rejection of both individualism and class consciousness, and/or to the systematic suppression of dissent, and/or to a tightly regimented economy and society, the case for deeming D'Annunzio's politics proto-fascist is not well made. Cingari's observation, here, is illuminating. He argues that the main difference between fascism (and its violent methods) and the political ideology established by D'Annunzio in Fiume is that the former did away with the contradictions that characterised the latter. Fascism did not care for offsetting its nationalistic will to power with 'any possibility of transvaluation . . . and of realising D'Annunzio's rhetoric of "love".'[244]

NOTES

1. Giordano Bruno Guerri, *D'Annunzio: L'Amante Guerriero* (Milano: Mondadori, 2009), 187.
2. Alfredo Bonadeo, *D'Annunzio and the Great War* (Madison and Teaneck: Farleigh Dickinson University Press; London: Associated University Presses, 1995), 14; Guerri, *D'Annunzio*, 237, 246, 250, 253, 255, 256.
3. Gabriele D'Annunzio, "Arringa al Popolo di Roma in Tumulto, la Sera del xiii Maggio MCMXV," in *Scritti Politici di Gabriele D'Annunzio*, ed. Paolo Alatri (Milano: Feltrinelli, 1980), 143–45; John Woodhouse, *Gabriele D'Annunzio: Defiant Archangel* (Oxford: Clarendon Press, 1998), 290; Lucio Villari, *La Luna di Fiume—1919: Il Complotto* (Milano: Ugo Guanda, 2019), 33–35.
4. Osbert Sitwell, *Discursions on Travel, Art and Life* (London: Grant Richards, 1925), 227; Jared M. Becker, *Nationalism and Culture: Gabriele D'Annunzio and Italy After the Risorgimento* (New York: Peter Lang, 1994), 2.
5. British Delegation: Enclosure 2 to communication from D.M.I. to Under Secretary of State for Foreign Affairs (5 August 1919), The National Archives, FO 608/39.
6. George L. Mosse, "The Poet and the Exercise of Political Power: Gabriele D'Annunzio," *Yearbook of Comparative and General Literature* 22 (1973): 32–33.
7. M. F. N. Giglioli, "'Il Deputato della Bellezza': Gabriele D'Annunzio's Aesthetic Politics in the Fin-de-Siècle Crisis," *Journal of Modern Italian Studies* 18, no. 4 (2013): 509.
8. Francesco Perfetti, "D'Annunzio, Ovvero la Politica Come Poesia," in *D'Annunzio e il Suo Tempo*, vol. 1, ed. Francesco Perfetti (Genova: Sagep, 1989), 369; Giglioli, "'Il Deputato della Bellezza'," 514.
9. Enrico Serventi Longhi, *Il Faro del Mondo Nuovo: D'Annunzio e i Legionari a Fiume tra Guerra e Rivoluzione* (Udine: Gaspari, 2019), 49.
10. Perfetti, "D'Annunzio, Ovvero la Politica," 370; Stefano B. Galli, "Il Sentire Politico di Gabriele D'Annunzio per una 'Grande' Italia: Patriottismo, Nazionalismo, Interventismo," in *L'Italia e la "Grande Vigilia": Gabriele D'Annunzio nella Politica Italiana Prima del Fascismo*, ed. Romain H. Rainero and Stefano B. Galli (Milano: FrancoAngeli, 2007), 72–73.
11. Quoted in Umberto Foscanelli, *D'Annunzio e l'Ora Sociale* (Milano: Carnaro, 1952), 82. See also Enrico Serventi Longhi, "The Triumph of the Noble People: Gabriele D'Annunzio and Populism between Literature and Politics," *Qualestoria* 2 (2020): 205, and Giglioli, "'Il Deputato della Bellezza'," 515.
12. Foscanelli, *D'Annunzio e l'Ora Sociale*, 81–82, 84; Giglioli, "'Il Deputato della Bellezza'," 514–15.

13. Giglioli, "'Il Deputato della Bellezza'," 515.
14. Antonio Alosco, "Il Percorso Socialista di Gabriele D'Annunzio tra Storia e Letteratura," *Forum Italicum* 54, no. 1 (2020): 379–84.
15. Bonadeo, *D'Annunzio and the Great War*, 15–16.
16. Galli, "Il Sentire Politico," 74.
17. Serventi Longhi, *Il Faro*, 47.
18. Roberto Vivarelli, *Storia delle Origini del Fascismo: L'Italia dalla Grande Guerra alla Marcia su Roma*, vol. 1 (Bologna: Il Mulino, 1991), 517.
19. Gabriele D'Annunzio, *Il Fuoco*, in *Romanzi e Novelle*, vol. II (Milano: Mondadori, 1942), 603.
20. D'Annunzio, *Il Fuoco*, 574.
21. Guerri, *D'Annunzio*, 187.
22. Guerri, *D'Annunzio*, 188–89.
23. Marja Härmänmaa, "Gabriele D'Annunzio and War Rhetoric in the 'Canti della Guerra Latina'," *Annali d'Italianistica* 33 (2015): 33.
24. Vivarelli, *Storia delle Origini*, 514–55; Becker, *Nationalism and Culture*, 61; Serventi Longhi, "The Triumph," 208; Galli, "Il Sentire Politico," 79–91; Härmänmaa, "Gabriele D'Annunzio and War Rhetoric," 31–51.
25. Guerri, *D'Annunzio*, 223 (citing a letter D'Annunzio sent to the French ambassador in St. Petersburg).
26. Bonadeo, *D'Annunzio and the Great War*, 79–81.
27. Bonadeo, *D'Annunzio and the Great War*, 73–79, 93.
28. Gabriele D'Annunzio, "Aux Italiens, un Italien," *Journal* (30 September 1914), in *Scritti Politici*, ed. Alatri, 124–26. See also Härmänmaa, "Gabriele D'Annunzio and War Rhetoric," 41.
29. Gabriele D'Annunzio, "La Très Amère Adriatique," *Le Figaro* (25 April 1915) in *Scritti Politici*, ed. Alatri, 129.
30. Woodhouse, *Gabriele D'Annunzio*, 286.
31. Anthony Rhodes, *The Poet as a Superman: A Life of Gabriele D'Annunzio* (London: Weidenfeld and Nicolson, 1959), 50 (quoting from one of D'Annunzio's letters to his translator Hérelle; no date provided).
32. Rhodes, *The Poet as a Superman*, 50.
33. D'Annunzio "La Très Amère Adriatique," 130.
34. Sitwell, *Discursions*, 231.
35. Guerri, *D'Annunzio*, 236.
36. Mario Mondini, *Fiume 1919: Una Guerra Civile Italiana* (Roma: Salerno, 2019), 47, 51.
37. Bonadeo, *D'Annunzio and the Great War*, 10.
38. Bonadeo, *D'Annunzio and the Great War*, 20, 33, 116–17, 122–23.
39. Quoted in Bonadeo, *D'Annunzio and the Great War*, 126.
40. D'Annunzio, *Il Fuoco*, 693.
41. Guerri, *D'Annunzio*, 256.
42. Michael A. Leeden, *The First Duce* (Baltimore and London: John Hopkins University Press, 1977), 12.

43. Pietro Badoglio, *Rivelazioni su Fiume* (Roma: Donatello de Luigi, 1946), 32; Galli, "Il Sentire Politico," 88; Villari, *La Luna*, 25–30.

44. Vivarelli, *Storia delle Origini*, 510–11, 514–15, 536; Leeden, *The First Duce*, 10–11; Pamela Ballinger, "Rewriting the Text of the Nation: D'Annunzio at Fiume," *Quaderni* XI (1997): 135.

45. Woodhouse, *Gabriele D'Annunzio*, 308–9.

46. Rhodes, *The Poet as a Superman*, 158.

47. Nino Valeri, *Da Giolitti a Mussolini: Momenti della Crisi del Liberalismo* (Firenze: Parenti, 1957), 36.

48. Woodhouse, *Gabriele D'Annunzio*, 314.

49. Cristina Benussi, "D'Annunzio e l'Adriatico: Dal Brigantino *Irene* all'Irredentismo," *Archivio D'Annunzio* 2 (2015): 172, https://edizionicafoscari.unive.it/media/pdf/article/archivio-dannunzio/2015/0/art-10.14277-2421-292X-AdA-2-15-11_vcYw6ip.pdf.

50. Vivarelli, *Storia delle Origini*, 518; David Lloyd George, *The Truth about the Peace Treaties*, vol. II (London: Gollancz, 1938), 761.

51. Serventi Longhi, *Il Faro*, 58.

52. Vivarelli, *Storia delle Origini*, 238–39.

53. Gabriele D'Annunzio, *Lettera ai Dalmati* (Venezia: Squadra di San Marco, 1919), 26, https://archive.org/details/digabrieledannvn00dann/page/n19/mode/2up.

54. D'Annunzio, *Lettera ai Dalmati*, 20.

55. D'Annunzio, *Lettera ai Dalmati*, 23.

56. D'Annunzio, *Lettera ai Dalmati*, 30.

57. Giovanni Sbordone, "Il Poeta e la Gazzetta: D'Annunzio nello Sguardo della Classe Dirigente Veneziana," *Archivio D'Annunzio* 2 (2015): 189, https://edizionicafoscari.unive.it/media/pdf/article/archivio-dannunzio/2015/2/il-poeta-e-la-gazzetta/art-10.14277-2421-292X-AdA-2-15-13.pdf.

58. Vito Salierno, "Gabriele D'Annunzio: Il Disprezzo per i Fascisti e il Rapporto con Mussolini," in *L'Italia e la "Grande Vigilia,"* ed. Rainero and Galli, 201.

59. Woodhouse, *Gabriele D'Annunzio*, 286–91.

60. Guerri, *D'Annunzio*, 262 (quoting from the speech delivered on 4 May in Rome). The point about transatlantic gold was made more clearly, if less poetically, in a letter to the US Senate sent by the National Council of Fiume in early September, shortly before D'Annunzio's march into town. The National Council argued that the new territorial arrangements emerging from the Paris negotiations had little to do with law and right and much to do with force: the nations that undertook disproportionate sacrifices relative to their capabilities were now held hostage to the power of richer countries, who might make their offer of aid for economic recovery conditional on the former giving up the very irredentist claims that had motivated them to enter into war. Mario Maria Martini, *La Passione di Fiume: Diari, Cronache, Documenti* (Milano: Sonzogno, 1919), 40.

61. The commitment had been made in the Husayn-McMahon correspondence. It was broken through the Sykes-Picot agreement with France (providing for the internationalization of Palestine) and the Balfour declaration of 1917 (supporting the establishment of a Jewish homeland in Palestine).

62. Gabriele D'Annunzio, "Gli Ultimi Saranno i Primi: Discorso al Popolo di Roma nell'Augusteo" (4 May 1919) in *Scritti Politici*, ed. Alatri, 193.

63. Margaret Macmillan, *Peacemakers: Six Months that Changed the World* (London: John Murray, 2001), 325–30.

64. Giovanni Comisso, *Le Mie Stagioni* (Milano: Longanesi, 1963), 34–35.

65. Prime Minister: Report from L. Waterfield to A. Thorold (5 June 1919), Parliamentary Archives, LG/F/43/7/13.

66. Fiume, Desiderata: Letter from Commander N. W. Diggle to Commodore Sinclair (13 July 1919), The National Archives, FO 608/36.

67. Bonadeo, *D'Annunzio and the Great War*, 131.

68. Becker, *Nationalism and Culture*, 37.

69. Luciano Zani, "Introduzione: I Reazionari di Sinistra e l'Impresa Fiumana," in Serventi Longhi, *Il Faro*, 9.

70. Romain H. Rainero, "Introduzione," in *L'Italia e la "Grande Vigilia,"* ed. Rainero and Galli, 14; Giuseppe Parlato, "Fiumanesimo e Fascismo," in *La Cittá di Vita Cento Anni Dopo: Fiume, D'Annunzio e il Lungo Novecento Adriatico*, ed. Davide Rossi (Padova: Wolters Kluwer—Cedam, 2020), 340; Amleto Ballarini, Relazione, in *Lo Statuto della Reggenza Italiana del Carnaro tra Storia, Diritto Internazionale e Diritto Costituzionale*, ed. Augusto Sinagra (Milano: Giuffré, 2009), 15–16.

71. Natalia Skradol, "Carnival of Exception: Gabriele D'Annunzio's 'Dialogues with the Crowd'," *Rhetorica: A Journal of the History of Rhetoric* 30, no. 1 (Winter 2012): 75. The expression derives from Antonio Aniante, *Gabriel D'Annunzio: Saint Jean du Fascisme* (Paris: Mercure de France, 1934).

72. Ernesto Ragionieri, "La Storia Politica e Sociale," in *Storia D'Italia*, vol. IV(iii): *Dall'Unita' a Oggi* (Torino: Einaudi, 1976), quoted in Paolo Alatri, "La Storiografia sull'Impresa Dannunziana a Fiume," in *D'Annunzio e il Suo Tempo*, ed. Perfetti, 27.

73. Alatri, "La Storiografia," 27.

74. Franco Gaeta, *Il Nazionalismo Italiano* (Roma and Bari: Laterza, 1981), quoted in Alatri, "La Storiografia," 39.

75. Alatri, "La Storiografia," 36–37.

76. Valeri, *Da Giolitti a Mussolini*, 42.

77. Alatri, "La Storiografia," 29, 38.

78. Hans Ulrich Gumbrecht, "On Fiume's Place in the Genealogy of Fascism," *Journal of Contemporary History* 31, no. 2 (April 1996): 255–56.

79. Foscanelli, *D'Annunzio e l'Ora Sociale*, 20–21.

80. Villari, *La Luna*, 17.

81. Davide Rossi, "La Carta del Carnaro, Antidoto Contro le Tossine del Parlamentarismo," in *La Cittá di Vita Cento Anni Dopo*, ed. Rossi, 277.

82. Thea Pičić, *Rijeka Ili Smrt! D'Anunzijeva okupacija Rijeke, 1919–1921 / Rijeka or Death! D'Annunzio's occupation of Rijeka, 1919–2019* (Rijeka: Naklada Val, 2019), 6, 10, 204.

83. Barbara Spackman, *Decadent Genealogies: The Rhetoric of Sickness from Baudelaire to D'Annunzio* (Ithaca, NY: Cornell University Press, 1989), 211–12.

84. Leeden, *The First Duce*, 201–2.

85. Vivarelli, *Storia delle Origini*, 491–509, 533–35.

86. Vivarelli, *Storia delle Origini*, 536–38.

87. Perfetti, "D'Annunzio, Ovvero la Politica," 384.

88. Valeri, *Da Giolitti a Mussolini*, 48–50.

89. This was proposed to the poet by the secretary of the Federation of Sea Workers, Giuseppe Giulietti, who maintained that in order to create a society capable of preventing more wars, a 'social republic' must be established where all workers could enjoy fully the fruits of their labour. Guglielmo Salotti, "I Rapporti D'Annunzio-Giulietti: Dall''Idillio Fiumano' al 'Pactum Sine Nominem'," in *D'Annunzio Politico: Atti del Convegno (Il Vittoriale, 9–10 Ottobre 1985)*, ed. Renzo De Felice and Pietro Gibellini (Milano: Garzanti, 1987), 25. The trade unionist's project was intended to include Italian revolutionary Socialists and Anarchists, and to bring about a socialist economic order, but floundered before the Socialists' reluctance. Foscanelli, *D'Annunzio e l'Ora Sociale*, 120–21; Leeden, *The First Duce*, 141–42.

90. Serventi Longhi, *Il Faro*, 20.

91. Marino Micich, "L'Impresa di D'Annunzio e la Città Esule: Echi e Suggestioni Dannunziane nella Costituzione del Libero Comune di Fiume in Esilio (1966–1969)," in *Fiume 1919–2019: Un Centenario Europeo tra Identitá, Memorie e Prospettive di Ricerca*, ed. Giordano Bruno Guerri (Milano: Silvania Editoriale, 2020), 485–86.

92. Marco Cuzzi, "'La Nostra Bandiera è la più Alta': La Politica Esteriore di D'Annunzio e la Lega di Fiume," in *Fiume 1919–2019*, ed. Guerri, 315.

93. Giordano Bruno Guerri, *Disobbedisco: Cinquecento Giorni di Rivoluzione. Fiume 1919–1920* (Milano: Mondadori, 2019), 315.

94. Foscanelli, *D'Annunzio e l'Ora Sociale*, 128–29.

95. Note by Eugenio Colseschi (27 July 1920), in *La Carta del Carnaro nei Testi di Alceste De Ambris e Gabriele D'Annunzio*, ed. Renzo De Felice (Bologna: il Mulino, 1973), 128–29.

96. Marco Cuzzi, "Tra Autodeterminazione e Imperialismo: La Lega di Fiume," in *L'Italia e la "Grande Vigilia,"* ed. Rainero and Galli, 131; Cuzzi, "'La Nostra Bandiera è la più Alta'," 316.

97. Woodhouse, *Gabriele D'Annunzio*, 345.

98. Alatri, "La Storiografia," 27.

99. Alatri, "La Storiografia," 41 (quoting Fulvio Senardi, *Il Punto su D'Annunzio* [Roma and Bari: Laterza, 1989]).

100. Budislav Vucas Jr. "La Carta del Carnaro nell'Opus di Ferdo Čulinović," in *La Città di Vita Cento Anni Dopo*, ed. Rossi, 307 (reporting Čulinović's opinion).

101. Villari, *La Luna*, 46–47, 72.

102. Alatri, "La Storiografia," 34–35.

103. Emilio Gentile, *Le Origini dell'Ideologia Fascista (1918–1925)* (Roma and Bari: Laterza, 1975), quoted in Alatri, "La Storiografia," 43.

104. Federico C. Simonelli, "La Costruzione di un Mito: Rituali, Simboli e Narrazioni dell'Impresa di Fiume (1919–1921)" (PhD diss., Universita' degli Studi di

Urbino Carlo Bo, 2014–2015), 190–91, 193–97, https://ora.uniurb.it/bitstream/11576/2630991/1/phd_uniurb_257536.pdf.

105. Salierno, "Gabriele D'Annunzio: Il Disprezzo," 201–24.

106. *Scritti Politici*, ed. Alatri, 254 (editor's remarks).

107. Renzo De Felice, "Introduzione," in *Sindacalismo Rivoluzionario*, ed. De Felice, 123–24.

108. Alberto Pellegrino, "Lettere e Telegrammi di D'Annunzio e Riccardo Gigante," in *D'Annunzio Politico: Atti del Convegno*, ed. De Felice and Gibellini, 107.

109. Roberto Chiarini, "Reina, D'Annunzio, Mussolini: Il Ragionevole, lo Scalmanato, l'Opportunista," in *Fiume 1919–2019*, ed. Guerri, 131.

110. Quoted in Rhodes, *The Poet as a Superman*, 228; Foscanelli, *D'Annunzio e l'Ora Sociale*, 187.

111. Rhodes, *The Poet as a Superman*, 229; Foscanelli, *D'Annunzio e l'Ora Sociale*, 190.

112. Rhodes, *The Poet as a Superman*, 228.

113. Foscanelli, *D'Annunzio e l'Ora Sociale*, 188.

114. Perfetti, "D'Annunzio, Ovvero la Politica," 383; Romain H. Rainero, "Gabriele D'annunzio: Il Mito e i Suoi Limiti," in *L'Italia e la "Grande Vigilia,"* ed. Rainero and Galli, 44; Salierno, "Gabriele D'Annunzio: Il Disprezzo," 217.

115. Guerri, *Disobbedisco*, 514.

116. Quoted in Perfetti, "D'Annunzio, Ovvero la Politica," 384.

117. Perfetti, "D'Annunzio, Ovvero la Politica," 385; Rainero, "Gabriele D'Annunzio: Il Mito," 45. The poet's celebration of the campaign in Ethiopia was due as much to the victory it represented for Italy as to the diplomatic failure it represented for Britain. Perfetti, "D'Annunzio, Ovvero la Politica," 385. Britain had sent strong signals of being prepared to take action against Italy, and had been ready to go to war over the Ethiopian question, but was unable to persuade France to join it. Jason Davidson, "Italy, British Resolve and the 1935–1936 Italo-Ethiopian War," *Cahiers de la Méditerannée* 88 (2014); Frank Marzari, "La Questione Etiopica," *Rivista di Studi Politici Internazionali* 39, no. 3 (1972): 425.

118. Bonadeo, *D'Annunzio and the Great War*, 154.

119. For example, Serventi Longhi, *Il Faro*, 45–47.

120. For example, *Scritti Politici*, ed. Alatri, 11 (editor's remarks).

121. From *La Tribuna* (20 June 1902), quoted in *Scritti Politici*, ed. Alatri, 11.

122. For example, *Scritti Politici*, ed. Alatri, 11 (editor's remarks).

123. *Scritti Politici*, ed. Alatri, 14–15, 17, 22 (editor's remarks, quoting approvingly Federico Roncoroni, "Introduzione," in Gabriele D'Annunzio, *Poesie* [Milano: Garzanti, 1978]).

124. *Scritti Politici*, ed. Alatri, 21 (editor's remarks, quoting approvingly Angelo Jacomuzzi, *Una Poetica Strumentale: Gabriele D'Annunzio* [Torino: Einaudi, 1974]).

125. Spackman, *Decadent Genealogies*, 214.

126. Foscanelli, *D'Annunzio e l'Ora Sociale*, 137.

127. Guglielmo Salotti, "Nuovi Studi sulla Carta del Carnaro," *Fiume: Rivista di Studi Fiumani* XIX–XX (1973–1974): 92.

128. Stefano B. Galli, "Alla Ricerca dell'Übermensch: Il Mito del Superuomo nel Pensiero Dannunziano," in *L'Italia e la "Grande Vigilia,"* ed. Rainero and Galli, 18–19, 27–28, 30–31.

129. Marja Härmänmaa, "Anatomy of the Superman: Gabriele D'Annunzio's Response to Nietzsche," *The European Legacy* 24, no. 1 (2019); Giorgio La Rosa, "Il Disprezzo delle Classi Subalterne," in *L'Italia e la "Grande Vigilia,"* ed. Rainero and Galli; Galli, "Il Sentire Politico," 67–68; Jessica Wood, "The Art of Dying in Trionfo della Morte," *Forum Italicum* 51, no. 2 (2017).

130. La Rosa, "Il Disprezzo," 52–53.

131. La Rosa, "Il Disprezzo," 56.

132. For example, Alatri, "La Storiografia," 49 (citing G. Luti's contribution in *D'Annunzio a Cinquant'Anni dalla Morte: Atti dell' XI Convegno Internazionale di Studi Dannunziani*, ed. Edoardo Tiboni [Pescara: Centro Nazionale di Studi Dannunziani, 1988]).

133. Gabriele D'Annunzio, *Il Trionfo della Morte*, in *Romanzi e Novelle*, vol. I (Milano: Mondadori, 1942), 951–60.

134. D'Annunzio, *Il Trionfo della Morte*, 956.

135. See Rossi, "La Carta del Carnaro," 138.

136. La Rosa, "Il Disprezzo," 49–50.

137. Woodhouse, *Gabriele D'Annunzio*, 350.

138. Woodhouse, *Gabriele D'Annunzio*, 1.

139. Chiarini, "Reina, D'Annunzio, Mussolini," 131–32.

140. Quoted in Rhodes, *The Poet as a Superman*, 235.

141. Kotchnitzky, *La Quinta Stagione*, 112.

142. Rainero, "Gabriele D'Annunzio: Il Mito," 39.

143. Ballinger, "Rewriting the Text," 144.

144. Perfetti, "D'Annunzio, Ovvero la Politica," 371.

145. Becker, *Nationalism and Culture*, 49; Guerri, *D'Annunzio*, 149–50.

146. Guerri, *D'Annunzio*, 150.

147. Guerri, *D'Annunzio*, 132, 149–51.

148. *Scritti Politici*, ed. Alatri, 29 (editor's remarks).

149. For example, *Scritti Politici*, ed. Alatri, 32 (editor's remarks).

150. These include: Vilfredo Pareto, *The Rise and Fall of the Elites: An Application of Theoretical Sociology* (Totowa, NJ: The Bedminster Press, 1968) (originally published in 1901); Robert Michels, *Political Parties: A Sociological Study of the Oligarchical Tendencies of Modern Democracy*, trans. Eden and Cedar Paul (New York: Hearst's International Library 1915) (originally published in 1911); Carl Schmitt, *The Crisis of Parliamentary Democracy*, trans. Ellen Kennedy (Cambridge, MA, and London: MIT Press, 1988) (originally published in 1923).

151. Becker, *Nationalism and Culture*, 49.

152. Perfetti, "D'Annunzio, Ovvero la Politica," 372; William Klinger, "La Carta del Carnaro: Una Costituzione per lo Stato Libero di Fiume (1920)," *Quaderni* (Centro di Ricerche Storiche-Rovigno) XIV (2002): 277.

153. Pier Filippo Gomez Homen, *Antecedenti Teorici del Corporativismo Fascista* (Palermo: Sandron, 1929), 6.

154. Günter Berghaus, *Futurism and Politics: Between Anarchist Rebellion and Fascist Reaction 1909–1944* (Providence, MA, and Oxford: Berghahn, 1996), 52–53.

155. Gomez Homen, *Antecedenti Teorici*, 9.

156. Gomez Homen, *Antecedenti Teorici*, 10–12, 19.

157. Gomez Homen, *Antecedenti Teorici*, 79.

158. Gomez Homen, *Antecedenti Teorici*, 109.

159. Galli, "Il Sentire Politico," 71.

160. Patrick Karlsen, "La Carta Rivoluzionaria di D'Annunzio e De Ambris," in *Fiume, D'Annunzio e la Crisi dello Stato Liberale in Italia*, ed. Raoul Pupo and Fabio Todero (Trieste: IRSML, 2010).

161. Guglielmo Ferrero, *Da Fiume a Roma: Storia di Quattro Anni (1919–1923)* (Milano: Athena, 1923), 17, 34–40, 68.

162. Galli, "Il Sentire Politico," 70–72.

163. Perfetti, "D'Annunzio, Ovvero la Politica," 372–73; Guerri, *D'Annunzio*, 109 (both citing passages from the 1892 article "The Electoral Beast").

164. Guerri, *D'Annunzio*, 151.

165. Guerri, *D'Annunzio*, 135–36.

166. D'Annunzio, *Il Fuoco*, 661.

167. Nicoletta Pireddu, "'Il Divino Pregio del Dono': Andrea Sperelli's Economy of Pleasures," *Annali d'Italianistica* 15 (1997).

168. Andrea Lombardino, *Lo Sguardo della Folla: Sighele, D'Annunzio e il Linguaggio della Modernitá* (Milano and Udine: Mimesis, 2020), 385.

169. Gabriele D'Annunzio, "Lo Statuto Letto dal Comandante al Popolo," in *La Carta del Carnaro e Altri Scritti su Fiume*, ed. Marco Fressura and Patrick Karlsen (Roma: Castelvecchi, 2009), 104.

170. Anthony Woodward, "Aestheticism and Politics: Gabriele D'Annunzio's Le Vergini delle Rocce," *English Studies in Africa* 42 (1999): 13.

171. Guerri, *D'Annunzio*, 55 (citing an unidentified writing dating from 1893).

172. D'Annunzio, *Il Fuoco*, 623.

173. Becker, *Nationalism and Culture*, 9, 20–23, 26–28.

174. Woodhouse, *Gabriele D'Annunzio*, 170 (quoting from a passage of *Il Fuoco* and noting that identical sentiments were expressed in D'Annunzio's electoral speech "Il Discorso della Siepe" ["The Speech of the Hedge"]).

175. Perfetti, "D'Annunzio, Ovvero la Politica," 375; Renzo De Felice, "D'Annunzio Politico," in *D'Annunzio Politico: Atti del Convegno*, ed. De Felice and Gibellini, 17; La Rosa, "Il Disprezzo," 64–65; Alberto Gelpi, *Gabriele D'Annunzio Legislatore Costituente* (Roma: Ugo Pinto, 1957), 41–42.

176. Letter from G. D'Annunzio to A. De Ambris (11 May 1921), in *Sindacalismo Rivoluzionario*, ed. Renzo De Felice, 255.

177. Enrico Serventi Longhi, "The Father of 'Sovereignism': D'Annunzio in Fiume between the Crisis of Liberalism and the Critique of Democracy," *Modern Italy* 27 (2022): 38.

178. Gabriele D'Annunzio, *Il Piacere*, in *Romanzi e Novelle*, vol. I (Milano: Mondadori, 1942), 35.

179. Gabriele D'Annunzio, *Il Piacere*, in *Romanzi e Novelle*, vol. I (Milano: Mondadori, 1942), 35.
180. Serventi Longhi, "The Triumph," 206.
181. Becker, *Nationalism and Culture*, 3, 37, 42, 210.
182. Becker, *Nationalism and Culture*, 60, 200.
183. Becker, *Nationalism and Culture*, 50–52.
184. Becker, *Nationalism and Culture*, 60–67, 200.
185. Becker, *Nationalism and Culture*, 54, 187–89.
186. Becker, *Nationalism and Culture*, 61, 96–100, 210–11.
187. Becker, *Nationalism and Culture*, 124–26.
188. Alceste De Ambris, "D'Annunzio e il Proletariato," *L'Internazionale* (3 December 1922), in *Sindacalismo Rivoluzionario e Fiumanesimo nel Carteggio De Ambris—D'Annunzio*, ed. Renzo De Felice (Brescia: Morcelliana, 1966), 348.
189. Guglielmo Salotti, "La Valorizzazione del Lavoro nella Carta del Carnaro," *Clio* 27 (1991): 94–103 (discussing Adelchi Baratono's 1923 commentary on the *Charter*).
190. Vladimir I. Lenin, *Materialism and Empirio-Criticism* (London: Wellred Books, 2021), 74.
191. Lenin, *Materialism and Empirio-Criticism*, 283.
192. Woodhouse, *Gabriele D'Annunzio*, 167.
193. "Satana all'Ombra della Croce," in Comando della Cittá di Fiume, *Atti e Comunicati dell'Ufficio Relazioni Esteriori dal 28 Novembre 1919 al 1 Maggio 1920* (Fiume, 1920), 23, quoted in Cuzzi, "'La Nostra Bandiera è la più Alta'," 314.
194. Bonadeo, *D'Annunzio and the Great War*, 70.
195. Bonadeo, *D'Annunzio and the Great War*, 73.
196. John Dickie, "Review of John Woodhouse, Gabriele D'Annunzio. Defiant Archangel, Clarendon Press, Oxford, 1998," *Modern Italy* 3, no. 1 (1998): 142.
197. Gabriele D'Annunzio, "Cagoia e le 'Teste-di-Ferro'" (27 Settembre 1919), in *Scritti Politici*, ed. Alatri, 212–15.
198. As recorded in the memoirs of General V. E. Pittaluga, quoted in Giuseppe Moscati, *Le Cinque Giornate di Fiume: X Anniversario del Natale di Sangue* (Milano: Carnaro, 1930).
199. Letter from W. Wilson to F. S. Nitti (received by Nitti on 9 November 1919), published in Giulio Benedetti, *La Pace di Fiume: Dalla Conferenza di Parigi al Trattato di Roma* (Bologna: Zanichelli, 1924), 56–57.
200. Ferdinando Cordova, *Arditi e Legionari Dannunziani* (Padova: Marsilio, 1969), 40.
201. Skradol, "Carnival of Exception," 90–91.
202. Gabriele D'Annunzio, *Italy or Death*, trans. Henry Furst (Fiume: La Vedetta D'Italia, ca. 1919).
203. D'Annunzio, *Italy or Death*, 6.
204. D'Annunzio, *Italy or Death*, 8.
205. D'Annunzio, *Italy or Death*, 8–15.
206. Gabriele D'Annunzio, "Agli Italiani, Fiume" (26 Decembre 1920), in *Scritti Politici*, ed. Alatri, 253.

207. Gabriele D'Annunzio, "Siete Tutti Eroi" (28 December 1920), in Moscati, *Le Cinque Giornate*, 133.

208. Serge Noiret, "D'Annunzio a Fiume e i Socialisti Massimalisti: Il Ruolo di Nicola Bombacci (1919–1920)," in *D'Annunzio Politico: Atti del Convegno*, ed. De Felice and Gibellini, 178–79; De Ambris, "D'Annunzio e il Proletariato," 350.

209. Gabriele D'Annunzio, "Questo Basta e Non Basta," in *Scritti Politici*, ed. Alatri, 217

210. D'Annunzio, "Questo Basta e Non Basta," 220.

211. Noiret, "D'Annunzio a Fiume," 179.

212. D'Annunzio, "Questo Basta e Non Basta," 218; Letter from G. D'Annunzio to A. De Ambris (11 May 1921), in *Sindacalismo Rivoluzionario*, ed. De Felice, 249.

213. De Ambris, "Precisiamo il Nostro Concetto Rivoluzionaro. Il Manifesto dei Sindacalisti e la Costituzione Fiumana," *La Gioventu' Sindacalista* (1 September 1921), republished in *Sindacalismo Rivoluzionario*, ed. De Felice, 327.

214. Federation of Fiuman Legionnaires, "Fiumanesimo e Proletariato," *La Riscossa dei Legionari Fiumani* (5 March 1921), quoted in Cordova, *Arditi e Legionari Dannunziani*, 119.

215. See James T. Chiampi, "'Un Dolore Pacato e Equale': Eternally Mourning Ippolita in 'Trionfo della Morte'," *Italica* 87, no. 4 (2010): 582.

216. Law of 5 February 1934, on the constitution and functioning of *corporazioni*.

217. Giuseppe De Vergottini, *La Costituzione secondo D'Annunzio* (Milano: Luni, 2020), 38. See also Alessandro Agrí, *La Costituzione della Reggenza Italiana del Carnaro* (Torino: Giappichelli, 2023), 88–89: 'The primary goal of Fiuman *corporazioni* . . . consists in the transformation of class conflict in collaboration between ctizen-producers'.

218. Lucy Hughes Hallett, *The Pike: Gabriele D'Annunzio: Poet, Seducer and Preacher of War* (London: HarperCollins, 2013), 525; Leonardo Tosoni, "Carta del Carnaro: Diritti di Libertà e Prospettive di Giustizia Sociale nella Fiume Dannunziana," *Historia Constitucional* 22 (2021): 874–75, 879.

219. Parlato, "Fiumanesimo e Fascismo," 353.

220. Alceste De Ambris, "Il Fascismo al Bivio," *La Riscossa dei Legionari* (12 September 1922), republished in *Sindacalismo Rivoluzionario*, ed. De Felice, 339.

221. D'Annunzio, "Questo Basta e Non Basta," 219.

222. Foscanelli, *D'Annunzio e l'Ora Sociale*, 152 (quoting from Oliviero Olivetti, *Il Sindacalismo come Filosofia e come Politica* [Milano: Alpes, 1934]).

223. Emilio Gentile, "Fascism as Political Religion," *Journal of Contemporary History* 25, no. 2/3 (1990): 231–32.

224. Leeden, *The First Duce*, 201; D'Annunzio, "Questo Basta e Non Basta," 45; Salierno, "Gabriele D'Annunzio: Il Disprezzo," 212–13; Klinger, "La Carta," 290; Salvatore Cingari, "Virtuosa Gioia: Di Alcuni Aspetti Utopistici nella Carta del Carnaro," *Giornale di Storia Costituzionale* 10 (2005): 156; Ballinger, "Rewriting the Text," 122.

225. Claudia Salaris, *Alla Festa della Rivoluzione: Artisti e Libertari con D'Annunzio a Fiume* (Bologna: Il Mulino, 2002), 10–11.

226. Simonelli, "La Costruzione di un Mito," 147–49.

227. Fulvio Senardi, "Introduzione," in *Il Punto su D'Annunzio*, ed. Fulvio Senardi (Bari: Laterza, 1989), 69.

228. Gabriele D'Annunzio, *Cento e Cento e Cento e Cento Pagine del Libro Segreto di Gabriele D'Annunzio Tentato di Morire* (Milano: Rizzoli, 2010), 181.

229. See generally Jűrgen Habermas, *The Theory of Communicative Action*, trans. Thomas McCarthy (Cambridge, UK: Polity Press, 1987).

230. Skradol, "Carnival of Exception," 77.

231. George L. Mosse, "The Poet and the Exercise of Political Power: Gabriele D'Annunzio," *Yearbook of Comparative and General Literature* 22 (1973): 37; Federico Carlo Simonelli, *D'Annunzio e il Mito di Fiume: Riti, Simboli, Narrazioni* (Pisa: Pacini, 2021), 259–61; Ballinger, "Rewriting the Text," 140–41.

232. Note by Eugenio Colseschi (27 July 1920), in *La Carta del Carnaro*, ed. De Felice, 128.

233. Sitwell, *Discursions*, 239.

234. Comisso, *Le Mie Stagioni*, 95.

235. Susan Bassnett, "Translating Gabriele D'Annunzio for the Twenty-First Century Reader" (6 March 2020), Decadence and Translation Network, Glasgow University, https://dandtnetwork.glasgow.ac.uk/translating-gabriele-dannunzio-for-the-twenty-first-century-reader/.

236. Woodhouse, *Gabriele D'Annunzio*, 338.

237. Ettore De Franchi, "Gabriele D'Annunzio e Antonio Grossich, Presidente del Consiglio Nazionale di Fiume," in *D'Annunzio e il Suo Tempo*, ed. Perfetti, 115–39.

238. Woodhouse, *Gabriele D'Annunzio*, 338.

239. Woodhouse, *Gabriele D'Annunzio*, 338 (note 50).

240. Francesco Mastriani, *I Misteri di Napoli: Studi Storico-Sociali*, vol. 1 (Napoli: Nobile, 1869), 8.

241. Cordova, *Arditi e Legionari*, 1.

242. Corrado Castiglione, "Cent'anni di Me Ne Frego," *Il Mattino*, October 17, 2018, https://www.ilmattino.it/blog/batman_e_di_destra/manuale_politichese_giornalismo_politica_giornalese_corrado_castiglione-4045669.html?refresh_ce.

243. Cordova, *Arditi e Legionari*, 11.

244. Cingari, "Virtuosa Gioia," 156.

Chapter 4

D'Annunzio's Occupation of Fiume (1919–1920)

INTRODUCTION

D'Annunzio's house in Venice had been regularly visited by Dalmatians and Fiumans since November 1918.[1] Despite toying with projects of 'liberation' involving Dalmatia,[2] he did not seriously consider becoming directly involved in a Fiume expedition until he was invited to lead it by prominent figures within Fiume's political and military class,[3] and it took considerable effort to convince him.[4] The project of a march on Fiume was chiefly driven by forces within Fiume itself. A Fiume-born *Arditi* captain, Nino Host-Venturi, played a leading role. At a later stage the National Council itself became involved in the plot, following the Italian government's reluctance to unilaterally proclaim the town's annexation.[5] There were significant differences between Host-Venturi and the more conservative National Council about who should lead and man the expedition, as this would affect the town's social and political realities during the following occupation.[6] Host-Venturi favoured D'Annunzio and eventually had his way, after the National Council membership was extended to include him and four other veterans, who had protested that they, so instrumental to the success of the enterprise that was afoot, were not being represented.[7]

When D'Annunzio's contingent of volunteers staged the occupation of Fiume on 12 September 1919, its ranks were in part made up of the very Italian occupation troops that had been ordered to leave following the July disturbances, as well as recently demobilised World War I veterans.[8] These included *Arditi*—Italian elite assault troops established during the war, who had played a key role in the Austrian army's defeat—whose units were being disbanded by Nitti.[9] Soon, regular, nondemobilised troops also started joining in the occupation. Among them was naval personnel of the ship *Dante*

Alighieri, which, ordered to leave Fiume's port in accordance with the recommendations of the Inter-Allied Inquiry, had been unable to sail because four hundred crew members had absconded in town with parts of the ship's engine.[10] By November 1919, D'Annunzio's army was 11,000 strong.[11] The occupation also inspired insubordination on the part of Italian troops and officers elsewhere in the eastern Adriatic.[12] Nitti believed that the involvement of sections of the military was due to officers' anxieties about their irrelevancy and unemployment after the war. But many officers were also concerned with the implications for Italy's security and strategic interests of the territorial arrangements being decided at Versailles.[13]

The occupation of Fiume put the Italian government in an impossible position. As the liberal historian Guglielmo Ferrero wrote only a few days into the occupation, Fiume's occupants were largely soldiers (whether or not demobilised) of the Italian Army; yet the government lacked the authority to persuade them to desist, lacked the power to force them, and was expected by the Allies to honour its international commitments.[14] Wilson was particularly incensed, letting the occupation distract him from 'vastly more important subjects which were still awaiting decision.'[15]

The occupation did not cause the Italian government to annex Fiume. It dragged on for sixteen months, until D'Annunzio and his legionnaires were forcibly removed by the Italian Army. By that time, D'Annunzio had lost the support of much of the National Council and many Fiumans. Approximately three months into the occupation, these had already made clear their preference for the situation to be resolved through compromise rather than insisting on immediate annexation. Divisions also arose between D'Annunzio's radical followers (who were hoping to exploit the occupation for ulterior, subversive goals) and the moderate ones (who only sought Fiume's annexation), as well as within the former group. Subversives in Fiume were of many colours, from reactionary (monarchical, militaristic, imperialistic, antidemocratic, and antisocialist) to progressive (syndicalist, trade unionist, republican, internationalist), with hybrid permutations of the two. Changes in D'Annunzio's Fiume command between the end of 1919 and the beginning of 1920 signalled a turn of the enterprise decidedly to the Left, eventually resulting in Fiume's remarkable but more or less stillborn Constitution, the *Carnaro Charter*.

THE FIUMAN ARMY

Host-Venturi, who had been one of the first Fiuman youths to enlist in the Italian Army,[16] believed that defending Fiume and its Italian identity from foreign interference and from Yugoslav attacks was primarily a task for Fiumans themselves.[17] He had started work towards organising an army of volunteers as early as April 1919.[18] In May a section of the Patriotic Society 'Sursum Corda' was established in Fiume with the chief aim of forming a Fiuman volunteer battalion; it started off, ostensibly, as a gymnastic society (which soon proceeded to harass the town's Slavs and Wilson's supporters),[19] which was later inducted into military training.[20] Sonnino even authorised General Grazioli to support the local militia, as long as it was done 'with tact', so as not to give rise to the 'Allies' recriminations.'[21]

The Allies did recriminate against the militia's drills. Grazioli dealt with the situation with obvious ambivalence,[22] caught between the need to appease the Allies and his own personal allegiance to the Fiuman cause. Later, Grazioli would declare to the Inter-Allied Commission of Inquiry into the July disturbances that he could not deny Fiume the right to have and train its own soldiers when Yugoslavia, even before its formal recognition, had openly established an Army and carried out recruitment activities in Fiume.[23] Ossoinack similarly wrote to the Peace Conference that the chief reason for the militia was to provide protection against the Yugoslav Army, which was being provisioned through the use of Fiume's own port, and whose size hardly suggested its being raised for peaceful purposes.[24]

The militia was regularised as a Fiuman Army, formally instituted through a law of the National Council in June 1919,[25] and paraded daily for three weeks in June and July.[26] The drills were interrupted when the last and most lethal of the July disturbances occurred. This is unsurprising, if Rear Admiral Sinclair was right in claiming that the 'Young Fiumani Battalion . . . was the active aggressor in the recent riots.'[27] By August, however, the drills resumed—one imagines in anticipation of the findings of the Inter-Allied Inquiry, submitted by the commission on 9 August.

On 19 August, Lieutenant Colonel Peck reported that, according to what 'he consider[ed] a reliable source, . . . the "Fiume volunteers" are paid five lire a day to wear their uniforms in the street. This is very high pay for such a service, especially considering the state of the finances of the town.'[28] Assuming the volunteers were indeed being paid (the patriotic fanaticism of Young Fiumans suggests they may not have required financial incentives to strut around in the militia uniform), it clearly was as part of an intensification of activities in preparation for the town's plotted occupation by irregular Italian forces. Indeed, the president of the National Council, Grossich, had been entirely candid about it, though no one seemed to take too much notice: 'I do not know what the decision will be at Paris [with respect to the July disturbances], but I exclude the possibility of a withdrawal of Italian troops from Fiume. If this should take place, the city would defend itself with arms. Our men would form the first nucleus of resistance and we should call for volunteers from Italy.'[29]

Here Grossich publicly announced an act exactly like D'Annunzio's expedition two months later, if the response to the July incidents turned out to be such as to make the Fiumans feel undermined in their national aspirations. As it happens, in the highly charged climate that had settled in town, the commission's recommendations, once they became public knowledge, could not fail to be widely perceived by the Fiumans to be a ruse to frustrate the goal of annexation.[30] Accordingly, in August the local press announced that the 'Fiume Volunteers'—as a special corps (identified by their *Arditi* uniform) within the Fiuman Army—were undertaking 'long parades in military discipline, in order to undergo any hardship which might be necessary in defence of our country'.[31] The Army, which according to the Inter-Allied report should have been disbanded, on 27 August was reported to have continued to increase.[32]

Throughout this time, Host-Venturi had been networking with *Arditi* units in Italy,[33] and by late June his correspondence was already alluding to 'the great day when the great movement will be initiated in the name of Italy'.[34] While the initiative to institute a local militia was owed to Host-Venturi, by this time Giovanni Giurati, president of the National Trento e Trieste Association, had become heavily involved in its organisation, in concert with the National Council.[35] Other irredentist associations, such as the Trentino Legion (created in 1917 to support soldiers from Trentino who resisted drafting for the Austrian Army), were also instrumental in providing manpower.[36]

The Trento e Trieste's aim had been, since the turn of the century, to liberate Austrian-occupied lands in present-day northeastern Italy. During the war, the association had been used by the Italian government for propaganda purposes; strong ties had thereby developed between it and Italy's echelons of power.[37] Even before the war, the association had been training paramilitary 'battalions' of volunteers, which were later framed within the regular Army; now it put its infrastructure in the service of the Fiuman cause.[38] Charged by the National Council with training volunteers for the defence of Fiume, it set up recruitment centres in several Italian cities.[39] A circular from the secretary of the Trieste branch to the presidents of its sections even stated that the Ministry of War would provide 'arms, munitions and military instructions'.[40]

By the middle of August, many volunteers had already made their way to Fiume,[41] and British sources estimated the numbers of the Fiuman Army at three hundred.[42] D'Annunzio, who had been asked to help with the organization of the Fiuman Army and to lead it as early as 23 June,[43] was visited in Venice by Host-Venturi,[44] to whom the poet sent a letter expressing his support for his 'bold enterprise' and his willingness to be part of it.[45] Meanwhile, Fiume-based annexationists blamed the Italian ruling classes and mass political parties for foregoing, in the name of public order and economic self-interest, the ideal of completing national unity. They urged decisive, 'young' ex-combatants—whether young in 'age' or 'soul'—to save not only Fiume from foreign domination but also Italy from itself.[46] In September public protests were recorded against the British in Fiume.[47]

THE RONCHI MARCH

British military sources noted, only ten days after D'Annunzio's entry into Fiume, that although there was nothing to show Italy's war minister was privy to the plot, it was 'impossible to believe that there were not several highly placed officers who knew of it.'[48] Indeed, the scheme was encouraged by some Italian military leaders, who had made no mystery of their support for a policy of Italian expansion in the Adriatic.[49] The president of the Trento and Trieste, Giurati—who would later become D'Annunzio's first head of cabinet in Fiume—also played a key strategic role in planning the occupation.[50] All this must be seen in the context of the climate of combatant subversivism that was palpable in Italy in the immediate aftermath of the war. British sources eloquently describe this phenomenon two months before D'Annunzio's expedition:

> There is in this country at present a remarkable political movement among the demobilised soldiers who are organized and act under a direction which, while apparently openly avowed, has possibly also an occult inspiration . . . there is a possibility of a sort of revolutionary movement—a revolution in the interests of order rather than the opposite. . . . There is reason to believe that there is some contact between the officers in the active army and those who direct the movement of the demobilised organisations.[51]

As early as 17 June the British Foreign Office had been notified by the British embassy in Rome of the US ambassador's conviction that 'some measure may be taken by [the] military who will make annexation of Fiume an accomplished fact'.[52] In a minute on the coversheet of this telegram, the intelligence was dismissed by Harold W. V. Temperley as 'a bluff, like all Italian policy, only we don't call it.'

The project of a march on Fiume also enjoyed the support of various Nationalist leaders and organizations and elements of the industrial world;[53] even D'Annunzio was not fully aware of all the different forces and interests involved.[54] Recent scholarship goes a considerable way in documenting the involvement, particularly, of the Nationalist steelworks magnate Oscar Sinigaglia, also vice president of the Trento e Trieste[55] (who would soon bridle at D'Annunzio's independence, as commandant in Fiume, from the network that had facilitated the occupation).[56] Sinigaglia had been actively seeking to influence the negotiations at Versailles on behalf of an 'Action Committee' he had constituted with Giurati and others on the occasion of

Orlando and Sonnino's temporary departure from the Paris negotiation table, following Wilson's indiscretion to the French press.[57] British sources throw some light, indirectly, on the kinds of economic interests that may have motivated Sinigaglia's support for a scheme that might well result in the fall of the government and the advent of a more protectionist one. Several months before, when Nitti was still a minister in Orlando's government, the Italian 'financial and commercial world' had been 'much upset' by the state monopoly schemes Nitti had introduced (probably 'in a bid for Socialist support.')[58] Shortly after D'Annunzio's occupation of Fiume, the Nitti government was said to be negotiating with US international corporations to develop ports and electric power stations in Italy and to electrify its tramways. The British remarked that the scheme was 'unpopular with the large Italian industrial trusts, which would therefore welcome Signor Nitti's fall.'[59]

Eventually, it is from a small town west of Trieste, Ronchi, that D'Annunzio set forth for Fiume in September. From Gino Berri's 1920 account, it appears that what occurred was the convergence, as it were, of two parallel projects for an expedition to Fiume.[60] More than one plot was simultaneously afoot, involving different, albeit at times partly overlapping, sets of agents. One was the broader plot mentioned earlier, whose driving force appears to have been Host-Venturi, who had already made contact with D'Annunzio[61] and was acting in concert with Giurati, Sinigaglia, and their network of Nationalist forces. These were conspiring not only for the occupation of Fiume but also for actions in Dalmatia and for the overthrow of the Nitti government.[62] A second, more confined, and more impromptu project was being organised in Ronchi by Major Reina and seven subaltern officers ('the Ronchi seven') of the Sardinian Grenadiers, who had been ordered out of Fiume following the public order disturbances of July 1919.[63] The Grenadiers, as the first Italian troops to take control of Fiume the previous November, had become a symbol of Fiume's Italian future.[64] They were, in Susmel's words, 'utterly Fiumanised';[65] and when they had left town in late August a demonstration had been staged, with the population standing in their way.[66] Leaflets had been scattered bearing the message: 'The grenadiers swear: either Fiume or death!'[67] From Ronchi they had later written to the Fiumans, 'We live off your memory, your thoughts . . . your faith . . . is ours . . . pay us the honour of trusting us.'[68]

British diplomatic sources are clear in identifying two distinct plots too—one led by the National Trento e Trieste Association, which was known to the government and was being closely watched, and a more spontaneous one on the part of the Grenadiers. Effectively, the latter plot overtook the former, catching the government by surprise.[69] The reason may be simply logistical: Reina put at D'Annunzio's disposal a ready-made contingent in Ronchi, when otherwise the expedition would have had to assemble volunteers dispersed in different localities.[70]

A 'small room' in Ronchi had been 'the secret base of meetings, discussions and plotting' before the seven officers sought to involve D'Annunzio.[71] Only one week before the march, the poet was suggesting that a symbolic act, where he would march into town alongside the seven conspirators, might be preferable to a full-blown expedition and occupation.[72] Italian scholars argue that General Grazioli played a key role in securing D'Annunzio's participation.[73] Having been accused in the Italian Senate of plotting the Fiume expedition with D'Annunzio not long after its occurrence, Grazioli is on record for vigorously denying any involvement.[74] This would seem consistent with his claimed preference (expressed in a private capacity to a British commander) for a solution to the Fiume crisis that fell short of annexation. It would involve the town coming 'nominally under the Italian flag, with an Italian Governor and a mixed police force, and the municipal governing body to be composed of equal numbers of Italian and Yugoslav Fiumani.'[75] The chief of the British Mission in Fiume, however, was firmly convinced of Grazioli's complicity in D'Annunzio's plot.[76]

With the march starting from Ronchi, the plot of the Ronchi seven became the visible face of D'Annunzio's gesture, remaining so in Italy's collective imagination and obscuring the broader network of conspirators that had mobilised in parallel to it. On the one hand, the eventual failure of the occupation and the fact that under D'Annunzio's leadership it quickly took a turn to the Left must have made the Nationalist network that had been initially backing the endeavour wary of drawing attention to their involvement. On the other hand, when Fascism retrospectively appropriated the Fiume enterprise to construct its national and party mythologies, it must have realised that the endeavour of a few brave men made for more powerful material than a committee of industrial magnates and Army leaders.

The Ronchi march was coordinated with Host-Venturi, eluding the intelligence activities of the Allies based in Fiume.[77] D'Annunzio's Army—known as legionnaires—increased along the way, as more and more ex-combatants and volunteers joined,[78] adding up to seven whole battalions, five armoured vehicles, as well as soldiers and officers from different units.[79] This amounted to an Army more than two thousand strong,[80] among which about thirty officers.[81] The vast majority were reservists, and most of the officers were low ranking.[82]

Many *Arditi* had reached the gates of Fiume independently, awaiting D'Annunzio's arrival before entering town.[83] Indeed, in the days prior to the march, *Arditi* leaders had already travelled to Fiume and back, to coordinate the endeavour.[84] The poet's army continued to grow after he took control of the town,[85] attracting demobilised soldiers as well as personnel defecting from the land and naval regular forces—occasionally whole battalions (despite their being threatened with desertion charges),[86] and distinguished generals.[87] D'Annunzio urged such defections, arguing, in a letter 'to the soldiers of Italy', that 'true discipline is not a dry, constrictive formula', that Latin discipline is rather 'acknowledging a sovereign will towards which all other wills flow self-contained', and that such a sovereign will is today the will of the free nation, of which soldiers are both the conscience and youthful creators.[88]

Youthful they certainly were: the average age of D'Annunzio's followers in Fiume is estimated at twenty-two—including many teenagers who, steeped in the belligerent rhetoric that had been targeted at them during the war years, felt they had missed out, because of young age, on the chance to do their part for the nation.[89] In a few days the volunteers are said to have reached ten thousand.[90] Eventually, the poet had to ask soldiers to stop flooding to Fiume, given the logistical difficulties of managing them.[91]

THE FIRST FEW MONTHS OF THE OCCUPATION

Entering Fiume on 12 September 1919, D'Annunzio and his legionnaires were welcomed by Italian Fiumans as liberators,[92] with festivities lasting the whole day.[93] The enterprise also attracted accolades from military personalities, politicians, and intellectuals from around Europe,[94] and even much of the international press was initially sympathetic.[95] But Fiumans were not universally supportive. A dissenting minority believed that the negotiations at Versailles would have led to arrangements 'satisfactory from the Italian point of view' and that D'Annunzio's action might do 'more harm than good';[96] only three weeks into the occupation, the Autonomist Party of Fiume (led by Riccardo Zanella) was campaigning in favour of Wilson's free state solution. The town inhabitants soon started looking askance at the antics and radical politics of some of the occupants.[97]

No violence occurred between the legionnaires and the occupying foreign forces,[98] who were unwilling to interfere with the prevalent sentiment.[99] The night of the day following the occupation, however, one grenadier shut down the headquarters of the Croat newspaper *Primorske Novine*, which had condemned the occupation, and handed the keys over to the National Council.[100] Though reassurances were officially given that everybody's physical integrity and property would be respected regardless of ethnicity, many Croats feared persecution and relocated to Sušak.[101] Croat 'inhabitants from the environs', however, are reported to have continued to bring produce to Fiume every morning and did 'not seem disturbed by the recent events.'[102]

The day of the 'sacred entry', D'Annunzio had a long conference with General Pittaluga,[103] who had replaced Grazioli after the findings of the

Inter-Allied Inquiry into the July disturbances. Pittaluga had been instructed by Nitti to use every means to prevent just the sort of *coup de main* D'Annunzio effected.[104] Yet the following day he announced the dissolution of the Inter-Allied occupation Army 'through force of circumstances'[105] and left town.[106] D'Annunzio gave reassurances that foreign troops would come to no harm, but Pittaluga could not guarantee this to the Allies.[107] Soon telegrams from Fiume were reporting that the 'position of British troops in billets in the town [has] rapidly become impossible owing to marked hostile attitude of rebel troops'.[108] The chief of the imperial general staff had been prescient when, six months before, he had advocated withdrawal of British troops, as the British detachment was 'too small to take effective action, and might become involved in a very difficult situation.'[109] The British, who wondered how to 'eject' D'Annunzio, considered the despatch of further Allied troops 'out of the question' and concluded that 'it remains only to work through the Italians'.[110]

Having received orders from the Italian government to stamp out the rebellion at whatever cost, General di Robilant (who, it will be remembered, had been the Italian representative on the Inter-Ally Commission of Inquiry into the summer disturbances) invited French and British forces to leave, as he could not guarantee their safety.[111] The British—having long been instructed by the Admiralty that in any conflict between the Italians and others in the Adriatic they should 'proceed to sea rather than be drawn into active interference'[112]—left soon thereafter. The initial understanding was that the withdrawal was temporary.[113] However, Britain would not send in its troops again for the whole duration of D'Annunzio's occupation, not even when urged by its own Admiralty (which feared D'Annunzio's destabilising activities in Dalmatia)[114] and by the Yugoslav delegation[115] (which at one point falsely claimed that the Italian Ministry of War had instructed D'Annunzio to invade Montenegro and attack the Yugoslav front).[116]

French troops followed suit within two weeks,[117] with some reluctance.[118] Initially, they had resolved to remain 'at Fiume as a guard for the base of the Army of the Orient', asking the Allies to commit to come to their defence should they be attacked. But the British did not provide any such guarantee, taking the view that the French should 'put to sea and . . . keep out of reach of an attack, especially in view of the Italian guarantee that nothing is to prejudice the question of the future occupation of Fiume.'[119] The executive committee of the United Italy Society of Great Britain passed a resolution condemning the Allied troops' withdrawal, which 'left to the Italian Government the unendurable responsibility of coercing its own nationals.'[120]

By the time of D'Annunzio's entry into town, the National Council had long formally given itself institutional organization and functions. A decree dating from the previous January provided that the National Council, whose declared mission was to seek the annexation of Fiume to Italy, would act like an interim law-making body. Its competences would encompass all state functions, including those previously exercised by the Hungarian administration; its managing committee would act like the executive; and preexisting laws remained in force.[121]

D'Annunzio had not contemplated governing the town, expecting that his dramatic gesture would by itself stir Rome and Versailles into action.[122] But his eccentric and enterprising 'action secretary', Guido Keller, whom D'Annunzio had met during the war[123] and who had lately been playing a key role in D'Annunzio's entourage,[124] convinced the president of the National Council that a power transfer was by far the most promising course of action. He argued that with D'Annunzio in charge, the eastern Adriatic would come under the control of Fiume, with attendant economic benefits.[125] Keller also convinced D'Annunzio that he must take control of internal affairs, alongside the external ones that commanded the poet's attention.[126]

Some continue to labour under the misapprehension that D'Annunzio assumed full powers and the National Council was left in place merely for form.[127] Instead the National Council transferred all powers to D'Annunzio, commandant of Fiume, on 20 September, but on the same date D'Annunzio issued an ordinance to the effect that the National Council would continue in office, although its decisions 'regarding public order and [those] pursuing political effects' would require his approval.[128] D'Annunzio argued that the National Council had a duty to remain in office in the face of its dissolution by the Inter-Allied Commission into the July disturbances, for 'one doesn't remove from the square the bell of congregations and fightbacks.'[129] The vagueness of the formula used in the ordinance about power sharing between the command and the National Council facilitated the conflict that would later follow between them.[130]

In order to address the concern that the National Council was not a legitimate representative body—having constituted itself spontaneously at the end of the war—elections were called for a new representative body, to which would accrue the powers of the National Council, and which would exercise them under the same name (National Council).[131] Peck observed in his dairy that 'Jugoslavs would not dare to vote, not even those that remained.'[132] The newly elected National Council proceeded to reassert Fiume's annexation to Italy and the power-sharing arrangement with D'Annunzio.[133] Formal judicial organs were also instituted, with further specialised bodies established in 1920.[134]

When elections were held for the new National Council, the British Military Mission reported all manner of irregularities and coercion geared towards engineering 'a large majority in favour of D'Annunzio'.[135] The allegations are dubious for three reasons. First, the British Mission's report ignores the independence of the National Council from D'Annunzio's command. This had already manifested itself in a 'clean separation' between their respective policies[136] and would soon lead to serious dissensions between the two. Secondly, the British Military Mission had long left Fiume and relied on informants who had every reason to portray the occupation in its worst light. Thirdly, the report of electoral irregularities is laced with statements about other matters that show the British Mission's credulity for the implausible and even the preposterous, so long as it reflected badly on Italy in general, and D'Annunzio specifically. These include the story that Italy's elite corps (many of whom had enthusiastically supported D'Annunzio's action) were recruited from convicted criminals, the claim that D'Annunzio's followers were animated by no patriotic sentiments but were rather soldiers who defected from the regular Army in retaliation for inflicted or threatened punishment during their time in service, and the conclusion that 'Italy . . . countenances' and 'encourages' defections from the regular Army in support of D'Annunzio's cause.[137] The latter, fantastic inference was drawn from one single case, where a judge had failed to convict one sergeant who had left his regiment and gone to Fiume.[138]

Meanwhile, D'Annunzio's command and the town notables had a document delivered to the Italian delegation at the Peace Conference demanding the recognition of the 30 October 1918 referendum, Fiume's annexation, and the institution of a regime of freeport. The freeport was intended to assuage any concerns that Italian control of Fiume would result in damage to the trade of the hinterland economies that had been relying, or looked forward to relying, on Fiume's port.[139] On the same day—the anniversary of the National Council declaring its wish to be annexed to Italy—its president addressed the town, protesting against the negotiations in Versailles and against the Treaty of London, contesting the right of foreign powers to determine the town's destiny without its consent, and noting that even when Fiume had been under foreign rule, the town had the right to intervene on matters of public law that affected it, in accordance with the principle *'nil de nobis sine nobis'*: nothing shall be decided about us without us.[140] Nonetheless, from a strictly legal point of view, Annibale argues that at international law the National Council's consolidation of its authority, D'Annunzio's occupation, and the departure of Inter-Allied troops signalled the emergence of an insurrectional government with *de facto* powers rather than a new legitimate sovereign entity.[141]

D'ANNUNZIO'S RULE IN FIUME

D'Annunzio appointed Giurati, president of the Trento e Trieste, as head of his cabinet. Alongside the formal structure of D'Annunzio's command, however, a special secretariat operated, independent of it. It was tasked with facilitating a direct relationship between D'Annunzio and the soldiers—the 'legionnaires'—and staffed with some of the most energetic, faithful, and zealous of D'Annunzio's collaborators, including Keller, Colseschi, Passavanti, Foscanelli, and Piffer[142]—about each of whom a few words have been or will be spent.

An ordinance issued by the command a little over one month into the occupation is sometimes used as evidence of D'Annunzio's authoritarian and proto-fascist tendencies. Alatri, reproducing verbatim from a previous article by Peteani, tells us that 'beyond his lush and seductive oratory, [D'Annunzio felt] absolute intolerance towards any adversary. . . . To strike down any opposition, D'Annunzio's Command issued very serious repressive ordinances', such as one that 'prescribed the penalties provided for by the military Penal Code for the crime of espionage, adding that it should "be considered an enemy, for the purposes of said code, anyone who professes hostile feelings towards Fiume's cause. The death penalty will be immediately carried out."'[143]

In fact, there are serious distortions and omissions in this account. Martini reproduces the full text of the ordinance in his firsthand account of the events of 1919:

> Seeing that around Fiume a military blockade is being kept that no right justifies;
> . . .
> 1. As of today, the town of Fiume will be considered, for all purposes of law, wartime fortified town.
> 2. The crime of espionage, committed in Fiume, will be punished in conformity with and in the cases identified in articles 78, 79, 239, 546 of the Penal Code for the Army.
> 3. It will be necessary to regard as an enemy, for the purposes of the above mentioned articles, anyone who professes hostile feelings towards Fiume's cause.
> 4. The death penalty will be immediately carried out.
> Fiume, 16 October 1919.[144]

Alatri and Peteani misquote the ordinance ('for the purposes of said code' instead of 'for the purposes of the above mentioned articles') in a way that makes it look considerably broader and more arbitrary than it is. From their account, one could be forgiven for concluding that D'Annunzio intended anyone who did not share his opinions on Fiume to be immediately put to death without trial! In reality, articles 78 and 79 set out fairly narrowly that someone was guilty of espionage if they were members of the Army who knowingly sheltered a spy or other enemy agent; or who provided the enemy with information or documents to their advantage (or which would endanger the safety of an Army place or establishment); or who obtained, or sought to obtain, or accessed a place in order to obtain such information or documents; or who accessed such a place in disguise, unless they could prove their disguise was for a legitimate purpose. The prohibition to access such a place in disguise also applied to civilians (art. 239) and members of an 'enemy army' or agents 'in the service of an enemy government' (art. 79), and in all cases they would be under the jurisdiction of military tribunals (art. 546).[145]

It is apparent from a textual and contextual reading of the two sets of provisions (the ordinance and the relevant articles of the code) that the ordinance only addressed members of the Army, except in the unlikely case of civilians wearing a disguise; that only actual espionage, and not generally the status of being an enemy, was targeted; that, despite the death penalty being due to be carried out expeditiously, there was no intention to dispense with a trial (albeit carried out by military tribunals); and that the ordinance definition of 'enemy' as all those professing sentiments hostile to Fiume's cause was meant to apply to governments or *armies* (primarily Italy, which had imposed the blockade).

Another ordinance is sometimes cited as evidence of D'Annunzio's authoritarianism. According to this, those who 'performed an act that might "depress the public spirit or otherwise undercut resistance in the occupied territory"' could be punished with jail term of up to 10 years.[146] The ordinance does little credit to D'Annunzio's leadership, but we might also note that it was issued late into the occupation, in October 1920[147] (when things were rapidly unravelling), and that it did no more than reproduce a 1917 Italian royal decree. If D'Annunzio was a proto-fascist tyrant for issuing this ordinance, so had been Italy for the last five years.

When Italy had declared war on Austria in May 1915, in the parts of the country that were declared to be in a state of war, military leaders were immediately invested with law-making powers for the duration of the war. The declaration of war also triggered an extension of the jurisdiction of military courts, while the Court of Cassation authorised the applicability of military law even in the ordinary courts. The form of delegated legislation enjoyed by military authorities was subject to another one: this was the so-called full powers of the king's executive to make laws for the whole territory, including the power to prescribe new criminal punishments. This power (which remained in force also in the immediate postwar years) quickly led to restrictions on freedom of movement, expression, assembly, and association.[148] Some such restrictions even predated the formal declaration of war by two months, targeting, among others, publications deemed to damage the national interest by depressing public spirit.[149] An executive decree dating from June 1915 criminalised any communication made to more than one person, whether jointly or severally, either on military operations, if the communication differed from the official ones, or on any matter of public interest, if the communication were untrue and able to perturb the population.[150] Then, in 1917 the so-called decree Sacchi introduced what came to be known as the crime of 'defeatism'. It punished with a term of up to ten years anyone 'who in any way performs, or incites the performance of, an act that may depress the public spirit or that may otherwise undercut the country's resistance or that may damage the interests connected with the war, or with the internal or external situation of the State'.[151]

D'Annunzio's 1920 ordinance is a verbatim reproduction of the decree Sacchi. If it proves D'Annunzio's authoritarianism, it is sobering to realise that his authoritarianism did not exceed that of mainstream Italian institutional actors, or indeed their European counterparts: for the war years had seen the introduction across Europe of a spate of repressive measures directed at controlling public opinion and ferreting out the enemy within.[152]

Additionally, even D'Annunzio's detractors concede that such repressive ordinances as were issued by D'Annunzio command in Fiume were scarcely applied.[153] No one was ever sentenced to the death penalty,[154] and in many cases involving political crimes, such as defeatism, proceedings were either not pursued, or the accused were merely fined, or benefitted from amnesties.[155] When an American journalist was found to have published false (according to the command) news that members of the red cross were ill treated and that British families had been expelled, he was detained, searched, and escorted out of town[156]—hardly a response in the style of the Blackshirts. Indeed, D'Annunzio was notoriously lenient,[157] and whatever control he maintained in Fiume was due more to rhetorical excesses than actual coercion.[158]

Giurati, as the Right-wing nationalist that he was, lamented that D'Annunzio was incapable of severity and for this very reason unsuited to be the dictator that Nationalists were plotting to install in Rome.[159] Similarly, General Ceccherini reported that it was not possible to make military authority and discipline prevail in Fiume 'where the somewhat blind generosity of D'Annunzio permitted all manner of infraction'.[160] The treatment of Reina is instructive. After his role in organising the Ronchi March, Reina had been appointed head of military staff in Fiume. Some months into the occupation, he and his supporters were believed to have sabotaged Fiume's cause by entertaining secret intercourse with the Italian government, in order to facilitate the acceptance of a compromise. Only Reina was found guilty (of not following orders concerning troops movement), and his sentence—two months' arrest—was quickly followed by permission to leave his room freely.[161] It has been argued that the patently political nature of Reina's conviction could not justify a prolonged incarceration and therefore he was made to leave town;[162] and the whole episode is sometimes adduced as evidence of D'Annunzio's oppressive regime and heavy handedness.[163] But in the ideologically charged circumstances of postwar Fiume, Reina's treatment shows the very opposite. To put this in context, consider that the Italian Army leadership during the war formally encouraged and even demanded both summary justice (including summary executions) and the practice of decimation for its soldiers' collective crimes; and that the Italian military tribunals—compared to their French, British, or German counterparts—disproportionately inflicted the death penalty on soldiers convicted of capital crimes (typically desertion).[164]

Importantly, after D'Annunzio's arrival, the town did not register a notable increase of anti-Slav nationalistic violence,[165] despite exaggerated and sensationalistic reporting in the Yugoslav press.[166] No doubt, both before and during D'Annunzio's occupation, Fiume was flooded with a kind of ethnonationalist rhetoric that must have been grating at best and intimidating at worst for the many non-Italians inhabiting the town.[167] After D'Annunzio's arrival in autumn 1920, more than 1,500 people fled.[168] There were daily examples of legionnaires engaging in bullying of the civilian population and hooliganism, which the command was both indignant about and largely ineffective at curbing.[169] Ethnically motivated discrimination and violent incidents also occurred, both before and after D'Annunzio's arrival.[170] In the latter case, they were generally due to xenophobic legionnaires acting on their own initiative, rather than D'Annunzio's and his command's orders,[171] though D'Annunzio rhetoric sometimes facilitated these outbreaks.[172] One specific attack in late 1920 by Fiuman Fascists on the *Sedi Riunite*—the local Socialist and multiethnic trade union—stands out for being openly tolerated and possibly even encouraged by elements within the command,[173] with D'Annunzio half-heartedly reprimanding those responsible for their excesses.[174] But these moments amount to surprisingly little violence,[175] particularly when compared to post–World War I contexts of organised persecution and interethnic violence in Europe.[176]

Kirchner Reill argues that Fiume's Italianness, even after D'Annunzio's arrival, rather than being enforced trough the violent and physical obliteration of the other, was elaborately performed through the National Council's deliberate manipulation of 'the city-state's infrastructures to make a professed citywide Italianness sustainable for a deeply heterogenous society'.[177] Those infrastructures remained accessible to, and were accessed by, even those who expressly did not identify as Italian.[178] This is consistent with Badurina's findings that there does not appear to have been discontinuity in the way non-Italian Fiumans—whose emotional responses to the occupation ranged from boredom through indignation and resentment to disillusion—experienced the whole period under which the town was under Italian control (November 1918–December 1920).[179]

ITALY'S RESPONSE TO THE OCCUPATION

Prime Minister Nitti had been aware that projects to take over Fiume had been afoot, but he had not expected they would be successful.[180] The occupation did not prompt the Italian Parliament immediately to declare the town's annexation. Liberal commentators argued that it would amount to declaring war to half the world,[181] and even the Nationalists feared the risk of Italy's diplomatic isolation.[182] In Parliament, Nitti described D'Annunzio's action as 'deplorable', an infrequently used expression that—so the British ambassador in Rome took pains to explain to the foreign secretary—carries more serious connotations in Italian than in English, conveying 'the strongest expression of condemnation'.[183]

Yet the Nitti government did not send in the regular Army to oust D'Annunzio. A show of force appears to have been contemplated at the beginning,[184] and General di Robilant even gave D'Annunzio's forces an ultimatum on pain of the use of artillery fire. But the order was countermanded by General Badoglio, deputy chief of the Army's High Command, who was put in charge of dealing with the situation.[185] The reason for a more cautious approach was that there was no guarantee that military sedition in favour of D'Annunzio's cause could be avoided.[186] Many of the younger soldiers, particularly, sympathised with D'Annunzio's dramatic act and the social and political rebirth that it portended.[187] The British Military Mission in Fiume mistook this, through the distorting lens of its customary anti-Italian prejudice, as the government's lack of 'desire to bring the rebels to reason'. They claimed that 'the steps taken against D'Annunzio are merely nominal' and that 'the Italians consider that the state of affairs that has been brought about will cause a settlement of the Fiume question in their favour.'[188]

Effectively, Nitti opted for a policy of deference to Badoglio, who managed the risks of sedition by avoiding recourse to force and by giving reassurances to Army leaders that the government was actively seeking a solution that took due account of the Fiumans' sentiments.[189] When the organisers of the Fiume expedition had previously sought the military's approval for their mission, they had specifically contacted Badoglio, who had, to their surprise, indicated his firm opposition and ordered heightened monitoring of Fiume's borders to prevent the movement of subversive groups.[190] It is not surprising, therefore, that the government's choice fell upon him. An ad hoc office was created to give Badoglio the necessary authority: he was appointed extraordinary military commissary for Venezia Giulia (with competence over the region spanning from Italy's then eastern border up to and including Fiume).[191]

Badoglio's line of action was to avoid any open and likely fatal confrontation between Italy's and D'Annunzio's Armies, to set up a blockade to isolate the town, to facilitate the Allied troops' departure, and to get D'Annunzio's rebel soldiers to desist upon pain of desertion charges.[192] The blockade, which was manned with men receiving double pay and double rations to dissuade them from going over to D'Annunzio's side,[193] was imposed so as to prevent further regular troops from defecting to D'Annunzio's forces and 'to reduce the latter to submission by starvation'.[194] However, the latter objective was never seriously pursued, at least for the first few months—according to British sources, because 'the Italian troops surrounding the town are in sympathy with the rebels.'[195] Meanwhile, the government imposed a regime of censorship with respect to the publication of news regarding Fiume's occupation.[196] British diplomatic sources stated, initially, that 'all communication with town is cut off',[197] but within a few weeks they reported the Italian prime minister's embarrassment at the laxity of the censorship authorities.[198]

It has been argued that it might have been preferable to bring the tensions between the Army and the government into the open rather than for the government to accommodate insubordination and allow its authority to be undermined.[199] But Badoglio had no confidence, at least in the early stages of the occupation, that the regular Army would have followed his order to march against D'Annunzio.[200] The British reported that the Italian Navy appeared 'to be wholly sympathetic with D'Annunzio', so much so that, if the Serbs launched an attack on Fiume—as at one point they seemed poised to do—the Navy would 'assist in the defence of the place.'[201] Three days after D'Annunzio's entry into town, Badoglio wrote to Nitti, asking an unmistakably leading question: 'What are the precise intentions of the Government? To act with much tact, not to force things, attempt to procrastinate the situation? Or rather, decisive use of force, with all the very grave consequences that this may cause, both in Italy and especially here?'[202] Nitti agreed not to use force for the time being.[203]

Nitti made a serious *faux pas* in Parliament by dismissing the occupation, and by implication the patriotic sentiments of those with whom it resonated, as pure folly.[204] The British called it a 'tactical blunder' and noted that he was roundly criticised for his emphasis on Italy's material needs (coal and grain), by which he was seen to be held hostage to the Allies.[205] This was because '[f]oolish observations . . . to the effect that Italy can quickly be brought to reason [regarding its demands at Versailles] by cutting off supplies' had been 'overheard' in the Latin country[206] and made much of by the press some months previously.[207] While conscious of Nitti's unpopularity, however, the British regarded him as the lesser evil: no other statesman could 'deal with the situation less ineffectually.'[208]

Rightly or wrongly, both the Italian Right and the Left attacked Nitti for his dithering, neither assenting to D'Annunzio's demand that the town be unilaterally annexed nor forcing the legionnaires out. From the pages of his *Il Popolo d'Italia*, Mussolini—who soon, however, was to take his distance from D'Annunzio's occupation[209]—proclaimed, 'Italy's capital is on the Carnaro, not on the Tiber. There is our government, to which henceforth we will obey. The government of Nitti—that pernicious man—is over.'[210]

The economic consequences of the occupation made themselves felt immediately, as foreign lenders became unwilling to provide Italy with credit lest the country should be brought into a new war.[211] Attempts to negotiate with D'Annunzio proved fruitless in the early stages, the poet making it known that he did 'not recognise Francesco Saverio Nitti's anti-Italian Government'.[212] From his perspective, the occupation offered Nitti a pretext to credibly claim with foreign powers that he must declare annexation so as to avoid throwing Italy into civil war: why was the prime minister failing to seize his chance?[213] Indeed, Badoglio, concerned that the Army was supportive of D'Annunzio's cause and would prove intractable, urged the government to proceed with the annexation demanded by D'Annunzio.[214] But Nitti took the view that Italy had no choice but to appease Wilson, seeing the superiority of US economic and military power.[215] For his part, Wilson saw the Fiume occupation as an attempt to test his own will and was convinced D'Annunzio had been acting in concert with the Italian government.[216]

The newspapers in Italy—except for Nationalist or militarist ones, which were exploiting the events to discredit the government—had, to the satisfaction of British observers, initially condemned D'Annunzio's action as counterproductive, despite sympathising with its spirit.[217] The Italian population, however, were largely in favour,[218] and soon even the moderate press had jumped on the bandwagon.[219] The British feared that widespread popular discontent with the government might result in Nationalist forces and/or the Army seizing power, which in turn might mean a war with Yugoslavia; the reaction to that, it was feared, might well be the country's turn to Bolshevism.[220]

But public sentiment over Fiume in Italy did not in fact run so deep that meaningful protest was ever staged at the failure of the government to annex it following D'Annunzio's occupation.[221] The November 1919 elections are generally taken to provide further evidence of how Italians felt about Fiume. The elections were the first to have been held in accordance with proportional representation, intended to facilitate the conversion into parliamentary formations of newly emerging ideological blocks resulting from the influence of mass political parties.[222] Ferrero claims that the elections were called specifically in order to gauge the people's feelings over Fiume.[223] The elections yielded remarkable results for the Socialists and the newly formed Popular (Christian democratic) Party: between them, they won more than half the seats, though power remained in the hands of the Liberals.[224] The Church and the Socialists having advocated a position of neutrality during the war, the election results were a defeat for interventionist forces, suggesting that any enthusiasm for the Fiume enterprise had cooled down.[225]

While all relevant secondary sources are in agreement on the significance of the November elections with respect to what they conveyed about public opinion, an interesting document from the British embassy in Rome suggests that the results did not mean that Italians had ceased to care about Fiume. This was because the leaders of official Socialism had never made their campaigning turn upon any particular approach to the Fiume question; and, in any case, the approach all such leaders favoured was based on 'the right of the Fiumans to dispose of themselves and of the Italians to go to meet them.' The document goes on to explain that public opinion was very much in support of resolving the Fiume question along the lines proposed by Italy's minister for foreign affairs, Tittoni.[226]

Tittoni had been formulating several compromise proposals over Fiume's future, which he hoped would be acceptable both to Italian public opinion and foreign powers, and particularly President Wilson, but without success.[227] This is so in spite of D'Annunzio being for a time prepared to compromise, and Lloyd George declaring his willingness to personally intercede with the US president,[228] taking into account 'the moderation of the views of [Nitti's] government as compared with those of [its] predecessors'.[229]

THE *MODUS VIVENDI* AND ITS AFTERMATH

In late autumn 1919, Nitti (on the basis of a design of which Badoglio claimed paternity)[230] was proposing to D'Annunzio that the town of Fiume and its district should be a sovereign state whose territorial integrity would be guaranteed by Italian troops. The state would be adjacent to Italian territory, in view of a future annexation to Italy 'when this no longer constitutes an insurmountable obstacle to obtaining the fruits of victory, to peace world and to the survival of the Nation'.[231] Effectively, the plan, known as *modus vivendi*, provided for regular Italian troops to replace D'Annunzio's legionnaires in Fiume, without firmly committing Italy to Fiume's annexation. Territorial contiguity with Italy and a commitment to not let Fiume's independence be undermined, however, were a key part of the plan.[232]

The negotiations between D'Annunzio's command and the Italian government did not take place in a climate conducive to success, with hard-core annexationists spreading misinformation.[233] D'Annunzio's counterproposals to the government resulted for a time in a breakdown of negotiations and in Nitti authorising Badoglio to tighten the blockade around Fiume, this time encompassing the port. This had the effect of exacerbating divisions between moderate and radical elements within D'Annunzio's following.[234] By the middle of December the blockade had begun taking its toll: legionnaires' accounts from those days mention that many of them felt disheartened.[235]

The pressure on D'Annunzio to compromise—given the town's crisis in terms of its stagnant economic activity, damaged or inoperative infrastructure, chaotic finance, and popular discontent—was significant.[236] A further attempt was made in December 1919 on a new text of the *modus vivendi* (involving some important shifts in emphasis, if not substance), which was initially acceptable to D'Annunzio.[237] The final text of the compromise agreement was approved by a large majority of Fiume's National Council,[238] despite Host-Venturi, President Antonio Grossich, and Riccardo Gigante voting against it.[239] The local press also regarded it as a victory for the town.[240]

When rumours went about, however, that D'Annunzio would be secretly forced to leave town and that the National Council was imposing on him, a protest was staged, orchestrated by intransigent annexationists and radical legionnaires. This gave D'Annunzio, caught between opposing factions, a reason to call a popular vote of the citizens of Fiume.[241] He wrote to Grossich on 17 December 1919, 'the passion of the people infects my soldiers and stirs them,' and that the protest showed a lack of consensus. This meant that before he could endorse the National Council's decision in favour of the *modus vivendi*, a plebiscite should be called.[242]

Posters were put up around town, in which D'Annunzio addressed the Fiumans thus: 'I shall never of my own free will abandon Fiume. I have promised to remain amongst you to await the fruits of our victory and so I will unless you wish me to do otherwise. . . . Meet me at the theatre tonight. I shall speak to you freely and you will decide if I must stay or go.'[243] Two public gatherings were held in the Phoenix Theatre on 16 and 17 December to debate the merits of the compromise proposal.[244] Then on 18 December the citizens were asked if they accepted the *modus vivendi*, thereby absolving D'Annunzio and his legionnaires from their sworn obligation to hold the town unto death until its annexation.[245]

The British Mission in Abbazia (where it had relocated from Fiume) reported that 'Italian Military authorities here are perturbed as they fear that the large majority of women voters will result in retention of D'Annunzio'.[246] We may legitimately doubt the veracity of this. As argued elsewhere in this book, the role of women in supporting D'Annunzio's cause was a pet preoccupation less of the Italian military than of the British Mission itself (especially Father Macdonald), as well as of the local Yugoslav propaganda (for which most of the British Mission's informants appeared to have been conduits).

As it turned out, the majority of Fiumans (women and all) voted for accepting the *modus vivendi*, despite some legionnaires' coercive attempts to engineer a vote against it.[247] According to the legionnaire and writer Giovanni

Comisso, some supporters of the compromise managed to falsely convince voters that 'Yes' meant approval of D'Annunzio's continuing presence in town, but even he conceded that many voted 'Yes' in full knowledge of what it actually meant.[248] When it became apparent that a large majority of voters were in favour of the proposal, pro-annexation extremists created further disturbances, leading the National Council to suspend the vote counting; D'Annunzio himself declared that any result reached under such an inflammatory context could not be binding.[249]

This was not in itself a definitive rejection of the *modus vivendi*, as negotiations with the Italian government continued until 22 December, and until the last D'Annunzio appeared to be on the point of reaching an agreement.[250] In his justifications to the Fiumans for not honouring the popular vote, he made much of the fact that an illustrious patriotic minority within the National Council had rejected the *modus vivendi*.[251] He also appealed to a kind of *force majeure*: the legionnaires could simply not be expected to pack up and go when they had come determined to carry out a heroic enterprise, as heroic impulse does not tolerate disappointment.[252]

D'Annunzio's cavalier treatment of the popular will on this occasion is widely and rightly seen as the low point of his leadership. Leeden argues that in hindsight, to the extent that D'Annunzio's change of heart was dictated by his lack of confidence in Italy's following through with the promises made in the *modus vivendi*, his assessment was vindicated. This is because an Allied memorandum from 9 December shows that there was no international support for the arrangement being negotiated between Italy and Fiume.[253] It is consistent with this that in a leaflet distributed in Fiume on 4 January 1920, D'Annunzio stated that he 'cancelled the plebiscite not for personal ambition, not for pigheadedness or desire for power, but because my departure meant the vanishing for ever of our dream'. As he explained, Clemenceau and Lloyd George's proposal to make of Fiume and the surrounding country a buffer state showed that there was no international commitment to the eventual annexation implicitly envisaged in the *modus vivendi*.[254]

Apart from any misgivings about Italy's ability to get the Allies to agree to any commitments it had made in the *modus vivendi*, other reasons explain D'Annunzio's behaviour. First, in one of his counterproposals during the negotiations on the *modus vivendi*, he had sought explicit guarantees 'that no solution will be accepted to the Adriatic question, which does not provide for our direct military and political control on the lands occupied pursuant to the armistice agreement'.[255] In other words, D'Annunzio had sought to tie the Italian future of Fiume to an Italian future for Dalmatia. The government had rejected this, and there was no mention of this clause in the final version of the *modus vivendi*.[256] If for a time D'Annunzio must have been prepared to give up on this demand, by the time he called for the referendum in an attempt to reverse the approval given by the National Council, he had returned to his original position. As he explained to Grossich and two other councillors, he was troubled that the *modus vivendi* provided a solution for Fiume but not one for Dalmatia.[257]

Secondly, De Felice cites reports of Italian intelligence agents operating in Fiume at the time, corroborated by allusions in the memoirs of Giurati and a letter by Host-Venturi, to argue that D'Annunzio's choice was the result of the sway that radical legionnaires had acquired over him.[258] A tug of war between moderate and radical forces within D'Annunzio's support base had been ongoing. Affected by the advice of the former, at one point D'Annunzio was about to recall his decision not to honour the vote of the National Council on the *modus vivendi*, but a group of radical legionnaires eventually proved more influential on his decision making.[259] These were politically militant young officers—largely intellectuals and/or upper class, many former *Arditi*. Moderates such as Reina had been unable to send them away from Fiume (as they had done with other lower-profile 'undesirables') because of their *éclat* and their personal relationship with D'Annunzio. Despite Giurati not permitting them to play an official role in the command and its policies, they were grouped in the command's special secretariat, in charge of D'Annunzio's appointments, reception of journalists and guests, etc.[260] Largely responsible for the revolutionary character that the Fiume enterprise assumed in 1920, it was these officers who, in concert with Fiume's most intransigent annexationists, orchestrated the derailment of the *modus vivendi*.[261]

Thirdly, and relatedly, these militant legionnaires could not have had their way if D'Annunzio had not let them. His eventual acquiescence to their position, as his previous oscillation between seeking and rejecting a compromise, was probably due to a genuine inner conflict. On the one hand was the object he had set forth with—to have the town annexed to Italy, which the *modus vivendi* may not have brought about in and of itself, yet all but promised to do. On the other hand was the seducing possibility that the occupation of Fiume might turn, after all, into something much more ambitious: it might become a laboratory for new forms of politics as well as social life. It might be used to trigger a political crisis in Italy itself, creating the conditions to engage in these self-same novel forms of life and politics on a much wider scale.[262] Fiume might even be, as D'Annunzio himself explained to the National Council, at the head of a global movement of resistance by all oppressed peoples against the yoke of foreign rule.[263] Indeed, by this time, as we will see, D'Annunzio's command was knee deep in the organisation of the (eventually failed) 'League of Fiume'.

The decision to disregard the will of the National Council and the subsequent annulment of the popular referendum resulted in the departure of moderate and Right-wing nationalist elements among D'Annunzio's collaborators.[264] This included Giurati, who, from Zara, went on to plot for Italy's control of Dalmatia, in coordination with Fiume's command.[265] Some officers, who had always been aware of the seriousness of their defection from the regular Army, also left.[266] According to Badoglio, there were now less than half of the volunteers that the city had seen at the height of enthusiasm about the occupation.[267]

The annulment of the referendum also brought to an end the love affair between the Italian population of Fiume and the commandant with his legionnaires,[268] as well as deepening the rift between the command and the National Council.[269] A diary entry from 8 January 1920, by the chief of the British Mission in Fiume, runs as follows: 'Civilians from Fiume stated that there were only two political parties in the town: (i) Republican; (ii) Free Town.'[270] This seems to suggest that, only three weeks after the referendum, and even before D'Annunzio appointed (as he would, two days later) Alceste De Ambris as his new head of cabinet, the town had appreciated that the goal of annexation no longer defined and unified the *Fiumans'* political landscape. Many former annexationists by now were in favour of a free state solution, as contemplated in the *modus vivendi* or Tittoni's proposals (which sought to mitigate the problems in Wilson's own free state proposal). Meanwhile, those who opposed this solution in the name of annexation were in fact pursuing a different and more radical (namely, a republican) political project, at which many Fiumans looked askance. As we will see, De Ambris's project to constitute the town into a republic met with particular resistance, especially from Fiume's political and economic elite, forcing him to go out of his way to rationalise, more or less convincingly, how such a move was not incompatible with the goal of annexing the town to the Italian monarchical state.

FURTHER NEGOTIATIONS IN PARIS

It is not hard to see why Italy objected to the buffer state (or 'free state') solution in the form contemplated by Wilson. Because of how the boundary of the free state were proposed to be drawn, Italian Fiumans would be a small minority of the overall population. The outcome of the referendum that after five years was to decide the fate of the free state, and Fiume within it, would therefore be a foregone conclusion. Italy clearly did not feel, either, that leaving the last word to the League of Nations instead of the outcome of the referendum (as had been proposed in order to assuage Italian objections) offered sufficient guarantees. Thus, Italy had insisted on making Fiume, as the capital of the buffer state, independent within it, while leaving the port and railway to the free state. But Wilson, as well as Britain and France, felt that this would invalidate the whole design of the free state, which had been devised with 'the double object of safeguarding Italian security and the prosperity and development of Fiume'.[271] Fiume, in their view, should have no more than the limited autonomy it had enjoyed under Austrian rule.[272]

This disagreement had proved to be a sticking point. Exploiting Wilson's absence from Paris, three-way negotiations between Italy, France, and Britain led to a consensus on a different solution, which, after some back and forth with Yugoslavia, resulted, in mid-January 1920, in an ultimatum to the latter. This was to the effect that Fiume and its *corpus separatum* would become a fully independent city-state adjacent to Italian territory, while its port and railway would be administered by the League of Nations. Much of the surrounding land, which would have been part of the buffer state, would now go to Yugoslavia.[273] Yugoslavia played for time, and Wilson, having sought information about the new proposal, vetoed it, insisting on Fiume as the capital of a free state, with the town itself fully integrated within it.[274] A serious rift between France and Britain on the one hand and the United States on the other hand was narrowly averted. Wilson pontificated, 'The Adriatic issue as now it presents itself raises the fundamental question as to whether the American Government can on any terms cooperate with its European associates in the great work of maintaining the peace'.[275] Wilson was displeased that the free or buffer state solution—which he had clearly indicated was his last and best offer—was being set aside by France and Britain. He complained that the two European powers were bullying Yugoslavia into accepting the new proposal by threatening an application of the Treaty of London. Britain and France replied that neither Yugoslavia nor Italy had really wanted the buffer stat and that the threat to apply the Treaty of London put equal pressure on both Yugoslavia and Italy, for the former stood to lose Dalmatia and the latter Fiume.[276]

Wilson continued to reject the new proposal but declared that he would not object if Italy and Yugoslavia could agree on a mutually agreeable settlement, so long as it affected only their own nationals. He even conceded that the free state could be limited to Fiume and its *corpus separatum* but must be under the sovereignty of the League of Nations.[277] The Allies at Versailles were now disposed to let Yugoslavia and Italy settle their differences without interference.[278] This formed the basis for direct negotiations between Italy and Yugoslavia, the latter starting to feel the urgency of reaching a settlement before the star of Wilson, which was waning in the United States, sunk below the horizon.[279]

By March 1920 even committed legionnaires were lamenting the lack of progress: 'We've been here for six months, playing the fools for the world, without ever reaching a conclusion!', wrote one of them home.[280] In the spring, Nitti was replaced by Giolitti as prime minister of Italy. The country was in the midst of a crisis: the Socialists had come to be dominated by the philo-Soviet Maximalist current, advocating violent proletarian revolution, and strikes and land seizures by labourers and dwarfholders were the order of the day,[281] with military mutinies and factory occupations following in the latter part of 1920.[282] Nitti had also come under criticism in the Nationalist press for draconian responses to public order disturbances (including an order to arrest all citizens of Dalmatia and Fiume on the Italian territory, issued after news had reached the government that subversive elements from Dalmatia were making their way to Italy).[283]

The Liberals turned to Giolitti, the old, experienced, reformist leader of many a prewar government.[284] Giolitti had been a convinced supporter of neutrality. He appointed Carlo Sforza as minister of foreign affairs. Sforza had been an under secretary during the Nitti government and had advocated a more decisive handling of both the occupation and the Adriatic question—one that treated it as part of Italy's internal affairs rather than a matter of international politics. The hallmarks of Sforza and Giolitti's policy were ensuring the integrity of Italy's 'natural borders' up to the Montenevoso area (the plateau overlooking Fiume)—whether or not Wilson liked it; compromising about Dalmatia, so as to ensure good relations with Yugoslavia, whose cooperation would be necessary to resist attempts at reconstituting the Habsburg Empire or German expansionism; and consenting to Fiume and its *corpus separatum* being an independent state, but not (as Wilson would have liked) under the sovereignty of the League of Nations.[285]

CHANGES IN D'ANNUNZIO'S COMMAND

Meanwhile, D'Annunzio had replaced his own head of cabinet after Giurati's departure. We have seen that D'Annunzio's rejection of the *modus vivendi* was symptomatic of his becoming ever closer to more radical elements among the legionnaires. It is not surprising, then, that on 10 January 1920 D'Annunzio should choose, as a replacement for Giurati, Alceste De Ambris.[286] De Ambris was Italy's most notable exponent of revolutionary syndicalism a legally trained journalist and trade union leader known to and convicted by Italian authorities as a subversive agitator.[287] D'Annunzio had called to Fiume this 'Socialist of virulent type'[288] (to use the language of British secret military documents) specifically to assist the command and to head his cabinet.[289]

Syndicalism was a political praxis born of the experience of workers' activism and the power of general strikes in 1904–1906, in opposition to the ineffectual parliamentary practices of reformist Socialism.[290] It claimed that trade unions should have no party affiliation and should reject any compromise with political and institutional forces: only through direct action such as strikes and even violence—rather than the deliberative processes of Parliament—could anticapitalist social change be brought about.[291] As De Ambris understood it, syndicalism was a new way of political life, which could not be brought into being through a single, violent revolutionary act. A revolution, however, could pave the way for it by dismantling the obsolete bourgeois economic and political structures that facilitated violence, fraud, and corruption.[292]

While De Ambris had opposed Italy's war in Libya in 1911 (on the ground that colonial wars did not have the potential to inspire heroic and revolutionary mobilisation), he became an advocate of revolutionary interventionism in World War I, coming to see the war as a key opportunity for destabilising the forces of reaction, imperialism, and global capitalism.[293] The February 1917 Russian Revolution, born of the war, confirmed him in this belief.[294] Even before it, he had argued that the defeat of the Central Powers—with their militarist, reactionary, and authoritarian politics and their 'feudal' political organisation—was necessary: not only to prevent a further layer of domination (that of Germanic colonial rule) on Italian workers but also as a step towards European economic and political progress, paving the way to the emancipation of the working classes.[295]

These positions broadly aligned with the thought not only of other revolutionary syndicalists but also of the first self-avowedly Nationalist party in Italy, the Italian National Association, founded in 1910, which had its roots in the thought of the radical Left. Both Revolutionary syndicalists (such as Arturo Labriola) and this brand of nationalists (whose political creed was developed primarily by Enrico Corradini) believed that even more fundamental than the oppression of workers within Italy was the inequitable political and economic balance and structures of power at the international level. These, effectively, relegated Italy as a whole, not only its working classes, to proletarian status.[296] From this perspective, aggressively and violently championing the interests of Italy through its participation in the war could be seen as the international equivalent of a revolution of the working classes within the national boundaries of the state.

With regard to Fiume, De Ambris thought that assigning it to Italy was dictated by considerations of strategic security, the principle of nationality (that is, the ethnic identity of the majority of its population), and the economic and political interests of the adjacent Istrian peninsula; Italy could usefully give up the Treaty of London concessions over Dalmatia in exchange for sovereignty over Fiume.[297] But he had also applauded D'Annunzio's occupation because he saw in it, yet again, an opportunity to trigger a revolutionary mobilisation against Italy's political and economic status quo.[298]

De Ambris had visited Fiume in November 1919. At that time, D'Annunzio had been particularly close to Giulietti, a trade unionist president of the

Federation of Sea Workers. Giulietti's influence on D'Annunzio had made the poet particularly receptive to Left revolutionary concerns, as much for intrinsic as for strategic reasons (his hope to garner support from the Italian Left).[299] The tell-tale signs of this openness to the Left had been in the air since late October 1919, when D'Annunzio's public speeches started entering into more internationalist and anticapitalist territory; at this time, D'Annunzio's then head of cabinet, Giurati, had found the commandant increasingly reluctant to involve him in key decisions.[300]

By the time of the December referendum on the *modus vivendi*, De Ambris had already infiltrated the ideological universe of occupied Fiume through a document titled 'Renewal', circulated as a maxi-leaflet among the legionnaires. It expressly articulated the notion that Fiume—far from the imperialistic and militaristic project that its detractors claimed it was—had now become 'an ideal beacon' poised to model freedom and justice for the rest of the world. This document laid the foundations of what would later be known as *Fiumanesimo*: it insisted that the Fiume endeavour had grown into something that much exceeded, and could not end with, the realisation of the annexationist goals that had prompted the Ronchi march.[301]

De Ambris's appointment to replace Giurati consolidated the swerve to the Left in Fiume's politics—one that, among other things, cooled Mussolini's initial enthusiasm for the occupation.[302] The moderate and conservative National Council was not pleased either. The new head of cabinet would often be in dispute with the National Council over matters of town administration, lamenting their inaction to the detriment of the population.[303] Despite vocal protests from the National Council, De Ambris adopted an interventionist approach in the economy of Fiume.[304]

However, De Ambris's radical zeal also meant that measures directed at ensuring ideological control of the town intensified during his time in office (from January to September 1920). These were rationalised by declaring a 'state of defence', and as a response to the Italian government's own reintroduction of censorship. They included certain restrictions on the freedoms of assembly, expression, and the press[305] and expulsions of Socialist and antiannexationist activists.[306] Three Italian Socialist newspapers were banned from circulation because they were believed to deliberately and systematically misrepresent the situation in Fiume and refused to publish retractions or corrections.[307] While De Ambris was receptive to trade unions' requests to redress abuses by the town's civil police forces, which during his time in office were engaged in surveillance, imprisonment, and expulsion of Slav workers and Bolshevik sympathisers, he did not accede to the requests to ease restrictions on political rights.[308]

It is unclear at best that the measures adopted by the command at this time were proportionate to the severity of the threats that motivated them. All the same, there is evidence, even predating De Ambris's appointment, that the command had sincerely held concerns that Fiume might come under attack from Yugoslav, as well as French and British, troops.[309] At the end of September 1919, British sources had reported '40,000 regular Serbian troops, apart from volunteers, in the vicinity of Fiume and Zagreb',[310] and a concentration of Yugoslav troops in the nearby localities of Ogulin and Porto Re.[311] Later, a January 1920 entry of the diary of the British Mission reports that according to their leader, Maylander, Fiume's Socialists were considering organising 'riots' (as opposed to 'strikes') in Fiume.[312] And at least one clandestine pro-Yugoslav association was actively plotting to force D'Annunzio out of town through military means in the late summer of 1920.[313] Activist groups in Zagreb and Bakar had also been agitating for armed intervention against the occupation, organising in bands that sought confrontations with the legionnaires guarding the town's borders, with a view to prompting regular Serbian troops into action.[314]

THE *CARNARO CHARTER* AND THE REGENCY OF CARNARO

De Ambris became D'Annunzio's most significant and trusted collaborator.[315] Through his efforts and inspiration, D'Annunzio gave Fiume, albeit for a brief time, a frankly innovative and progressive Constitution, the *Carnaro Charter*. Revolutionary syndicalism, as De Ambris himself clarified, called for independence of productive workers from political parties, their recourse to direct action against other social classes and public powers (without intermediaries), their representation in law-making bodies, strong local autonomy, and progressive abolition of centralised state functions and state bureaucratic structures.[316] Most of these principles directly inform the design of the *Charter*.

On 30 March 1920, De Ambris addressed the Fiumans, explaining the reasons that called for formally constituting Fiume into a new sovereign entity. First, annexation to Italy was unlikely to occur in the short term, and secondly, the town was in dire economic straits. To rejog Fiume's economy it was necessary to obtain credit, but lenders were unwilling to provide services to an ill-defined and provisional entity. Fiume therefore required a proper and precise state organisation, which would provide sufficient guarantees of orderly and secure development.[317] The buffer state solution debated at Versailles would result in a state of affairs where 40,000 Italians would be 'smothered' by 200,000 Slavs. Regardless of whether this solution, the Treaty of London, or past projects negotiated at Versailles were implemented, the League of Nations (that 'international capitalistic "trust"' serving the interests of 'Anglo-American plutocracy') was bent on controlling the port and railway system of Fiume. Within one or two decades, De Ambris argued, this would result in demographic changes leading to the loss of Fiume's Italian identity.[318] All of this could be staved off by formally constituting Fiume into an independent state.

Through the *Charter*, however, De Ambris was also hoping to achieve something bigger than securing an Italian future for the town: he sought to inspire a national revolutionary movement. If Italy would not annex Fiume, then, as he liked to put it, Fiume should annex Italy. He believed that the times were ripe for a new political order in the motherland. The working classes had seen neither the fulfilment of the promises that the bourgeois had made them during the war nor the revolution promised by the Socialists. Meanwhile the bourgeois themselves were at the mercy of popular discontent, the police being powerless to protect them from threats to property and personal safety, and the Army was driven to be apologetic for the victory it had delivered to the country. D'Annunzio, De Ambris believed, was the man capable of uniting these disparate social forces, and the novel social and political order envisioned in the *Charter* would be his rallying cry.[319]

It has been argued that D'Annunzio's primary aim in promulgating the *Charter* was rather less ambitious than De Ambris's. He sought to cause difficulties to Giolitti in his negotiations with the Yugoslavs, an agreement with whom threatened D'Annunzio's grandiose vision of Italy's place in the eastern Adriatic.[320] As D'Annunzio's command disclosed to the National Council, it was necessary to preempt Fiume and the surrounding territory being constituted into a free state as a result of the Italian government's negotiations with foreign powers, because this would come at the cost of Italy giving up its claims over Dalmatia. Italy should insist on Dalmatia at Versailles, while Fiume would take care of itself.[321] Yet alongside these instrumental considerations, D'Annunzio also declared that, even if the *Charter* were to be short lived (in the event of Fiume's annexation, which remained his ultimate goal), it would still offer a model of political aspirations 'for the whole world'.[322]

De Ambris drafted the first version of what was to be the *Charter* and sent it to D'Annunzio in March 1920, with an accompanying letter quoting back to D'Annunzio his own words:

> Let us give the word the model of a Constitution offering a home, within itself, to all the liberties and all the daring of modern thought, yet reviving too all the noblest and most glorious traditions of our lineage. A truly Latin Constitution, forging and tempering into our people's ancient civilization that which other people offer to us as truest in the norms of communal life.[323]

Indeed, the *Charter* turned out to be a syncretic but surprisingly coherent document. It is variously argued to have drawn on perspectives and precedents as different as the revolutionary Roman Constitution of 1848, Helvetic institutional arrangements, common law constitutionalism, Venetian constitutional traditions, anarchic syndicalism the statutes of mediaeval Italian city-states, mediaeval legal pluralism, ancient Roman juridical institutions, and both the US and Soviet legal systems.[324]

De Ambris clarified in his letter to D'Annunzio that the decision to constitute Fiume into a free republic through a new Constitution was forced on them by the vanishing of the prospect of its annexation to Italy, combined with the need for the town to be able to function fully, particularly on the economic plane.[325] He added that if the constitutional text was not bolder, it was because he sought to be realistic. In a passage of distinctly Marxian flavour, he clarified that law cannot bring about social change but may at least open the way to the 'novel forces and facts that are begot of mass consciousness and the needs that push it forward . . . in the interplay of economic forces and with the emergence of new technical and moral capabilities.'[326]

Rumours got abroad that D'Annunzio and De Ambris were plotting a radical democratic experiment antipathetic to capitalist concerns,[327] and even a 'Soviet-style communist republic'.[328] In March 1920 military reports to Italy's prime minister ominously referred to a forthcoming attempt to establish in Fiume 'a regime of extreme democracy which is not unlikely to set aside current institutions ' (to wit, the monarchy in Italy), possibly in connection with other planned 'anticonstitutional' activities in different regions of Italy.[329] Such rumours alarmed the National Council, as well as conspicuous sections of the citizenry and moderate legionnaires.

On 21 March General Caviglia (who had replaced Badoglio at the command of Italian troops in the northeastern Adriatic region in December)[330] wrote to Nitti—in an access of wishful thinking—that the project of a republic in Fiume had been aborted because of the resistance put up by officers and carabinieri within D'Annunzio's legion.[331] In April D'Annunzio confirmed that he was contemplating constituting Fiume into a sovereign state but emphasised that the long-term goal remained annexation.[332] In a letter to D'Annunzio dating from 13 May 1920, De Ambris complained of the National Council's prejudiced opposition to the *Charter*, whose content they had not even learnt yet. He was also displeased with the National Council's objections to the command making overtures to the Socialist Party of Fiume.[333] That month the National Council even reached out directly to Nitti, bypassing D'Annunzio, in an attempt to negotiate.[334] These controversies explain why D'Annunzio felt the need to move cautiously.[335] In the event, six months passed between the *Charter*'s first draft and its promulgation.

The economic crisis resulting from the prolonged occupation and blockade had also worsened in the spring. This caused serious tensions between workers and employers and between trade unions and the National Council, making it a delicate time for D'Annunzio to promulgate the *Charter*, given its radical content. It did not help that the support he was seeking from the Italian Socialists (on whose authorisation the Fiuman Left's own support was dependent) was not forthcoming.[336] At this time Nitti's correspondence decries D'Annunzio's 'criminal' attempt to constitute a 'Republic of the Soviets' in Fiume, which he saw as a U-turn in the ideological drivers of the occupation, from patriotic value to anarchy.[337] In a telegram to the minister of the Navy, he claimed that Fiume's workers were ready to 'knock down the National Council applauding D'Annunzio as head of the Bolshevik organisation.'[338]

The plan to constitute Fiume into a republic was especially controversial—as much as, as De Ambris noted, it was hard to see what else Fiume could have been as an independent state, given that there was no monarchy to claim sovereignty over it.[339] The fact that the designation of republic for a time elicited the interest of the Socialists[340] no doubt only contributed to alarm the more conservative elements of the National Council and D'Annunzio's followers. Some legionnaire officers made contact with the Italian military to indicate they were prepared to switch sides and oppose Fiume's republican movement and ended up leaving.[341] Serious internal divisions among the legionnaires resulted in a lethal clash between conservative *carabinieri* and radical *Arditi*.[342] This played out a well-established rivalry between custodians of law and the status quo and elite corps whose members—trained to perform deeds requiring great courage—had, by the end of the war, become invested in their exceptional status and considered themselves above the constituted order.[343]

The controversy over the future status of Fiume as a republic explains D'Annunzio's notable change in terminology in the *Charter*: from de Ambris's Republic of Carnaro to D'Annunzio's Regency of Carnaro. D'Annunzio invoked metrics: 'I think tonight I was favoured with the inspiration of a visiting presence: I'll call the Free State *Italian Regency of the Carnaro*. . . . Besides, it's an endecasyllable! Rhythm is always right.'[344] It is widely agreed that the choice was dictated by a desire not to unduly alarm or antagonise the Italian government, with which D'Annunzio was still hoping to negotiate for Fiume's annexation. Similarly, D'Annunzio was seeking not to alienate the legionnaires and citizens of moderate and monarchic persuasion and those insisting on annexation to Italy.[345] Not only was the terminology of 'regency' ostensibly less inconsistent with the monarchic form of the Italian state,[346] but it also gave the impression of a less definitive, more transitory constitutional arrangement.

Because of these difficulties, it was not until August that D'Annunzio announced that, on 12 September 1920, Fiume would start its new life.[347] Either Italy would formally annex Fiume by then, or the town would constitute itself into an independent state, through the promulgation of a new Constitution.[348] Reassurances were given to the National Council and the citizens of Fiume that they had an 'inalienable' right to freely determine their destiny, that their legitimate representatives' approval of the project would be sought, and that the constitutional text would be submitted to the judgement of the people.[349] On 24 August De Ambris lifted provisions relating to censorship to allow everyone to freely and fully debate the new Constitution.[350] On 29 August copies of the *Charter* were shared with the National Council.[351] The text of the new Constitution was published the day after.[352] On the night of the following day, the poet read the *Charter* to a thronged Phoenix Theatre—access, for that day, being reserved to the Fiumans alone.[353]

In his prefatory speech D'Annunzio spoke of the Constitution as an act of begetting (*'atto di vita'*), through which the people engineered their own 'rebirth in a higher form of life, a superior order of freedom and justice'.[354] In the closing lines he made clear that the goal of annexation had not been displaced, cheering both 'the Italian Regency of the Carnaro' and 'the annexation to Italy, whether forthcoming or not, but certain to happen'.[355] One week later he similarly wrote to Grossich that the *Charter* was the 'vigorous and rigorous confirmation of the will to annexation'.[356] At the end of the reading in the Phoenix Theatre, he told his audience that in the Italian democratic city-states of the eleventh through thirteenth centuries, after a statute had been publicly read, the citizens, gathered in assembly, would approve it by declaring, 'I swear'. 'But we are not,' he added, 'in a Mediaeval assembly of the citizens. We are in the town of restlessness and diversity. We will fight; and perhaps we will, once more, deceive one another and tear one another apart. But don't forget, for your own peace, that your Commandant can be deposed and banished.'[357] Reportedly, the crowd shouted, 'Never!'[358]

According to the findings of a report of the Information Office of D'Annunzio's command, the working and less affluent classes had not grasped the content of the *Charter* after D'Annunzio's reading; De Ambris therefore set out to arrange further public events in which he would explicate it.[359] In the event, D'Annunzio had to proclaim the Italian Regency of Carnaro on 8 September, four days before the appointed date, in order to preempt the (by now well and truly hostile) National Council's thwarting of his project. That very morning the National Council had resigned and transferred its powers to its management committee, charging it with summoning a constitutional assembly in order to discuss D'Annunzio's proposal.[360] D'Annunzio turned the National Council's resignation to his advantage by appealing directly to the people of Fiume. From the balcony of the Palace of Government, with

De Ambris at his side, he addressed the crowds he had summoned and proclaimed the regency.[361] The legionnaires had been instructed not to leave their barracks until half-way through the public meeting, to counter accusations that the public gathering would not be a genuine assembly of the Fiumans.[362]

Commentators deny (and some of D'Annunzio's own collaborators at the time of the regency disputed)[363] that the approbation of the *Charter* expressed by the Fiumans (whether the crowd in the Phoenix Theatre or in the public square overlooked by the palace) was a meaningful deliberation.[364] For all that the text of the *Charter* makes much of the people's sovereign will, popular ratification of the new Constitution followed a model typical of authoritarian states, where a unilateral decision of the ruler is afforded the semblance of popular legitimacy through a plebiscite presented as perfecting the ruler's *pouvoir constituant*.[365] D'Annunzio himself, in a letter dated 6 December 1920 aimed at persuading the National Council to approve the *Charter*, does not refer to any formal vote on the part of the people approving the *Charter*; rather, the document, he vaguely states, had attracted 'the consensus of the people of Fiume in more than one public gathering'.[366] This new mode of doing politics ('an authority that worked through assemblies in which decisions were made by acclamation') became characteristic of Fiume,[367] though no such model was institutionalised within the *Charter* itself with respect to the workings of representative law-making bodies.

The regency was a precarious affair. Not only were there reservations about the *Charter* within D'Annunzio's command and misgivings among the Fiumans,[368] but the regency existed, while it did, at the pleasure of the Allies. While the Inter-Allied troops had long departed, Italy had undertaken to resolve the situation on behalf of the Allies and maintained a blockade around the town. Under such circumstances, it has been argued that at international law the proclamation of the regency did not alter the status of the town as an insurrectional government. Legally speaking, sovereignty over Fiume still belonged to Hungary, with the Allies' power to exercise it on the basis of the Armistice.[369] For others, however, who subscribe to the view that other states' recognition has declaratory rather than constitutive value in the establishment of a new state entity, the declaration of the regency brought into being a new subject of international law.[370]

THE PROVISIONAL GOVERNMENT OF THE REGENCY

The proclamation of the regency prompted the Yugoslav state to protest to the president of the Peace Conference that the act was unlawful, void, and an abuse of the right to self-determination.[371] Undeterred, D'Annunzio proceeded to appointed an interim administration.[372] This was the provisional government of the regency, made up of seven rectors, amongst whom, in the first month, D'Annunzio himself (for external affairs).[373] The provisional government was intended to remain in office until elections for the regular government provided for in the *Charter* were held in early 1921, after which the legionnaires should leave town.[374]

The appointment of this provisional government was accompanied by a reorganisation of D'Annunzio's command, which from now on was to be a technical and administrative body rather than a political one.[375] It was also preceded by the resignation of the managing committee of the National Council.[376] The committee had written to D'Annunzio to note the impossible position it was in. On the one hand it was charged by the National Council with the task of calling for a constitutional assembly to deliberate on the *Charter*; on the other hand it was delegitimated by D'Annunzio's bypassing it through the proclamation of the regency.[377] D'Annunzio wrote to President Grossich words to the effect that just like Fiume's occupation had brought 'liberation' to the town, now the *Charter* brought 'liberty' to it. The proclamation of the regency was 'a revolutionary act' consistent with the spirit of 'revolt' that had animated the Ronchi march. Indeed, the whole of the previous year in Fiume had been itself an 'act of revolt', but the managing committee seemed to have forgotten it, seemed to be 'afraid of words'. The committee, 'without the backing of the now dissolved National Council', was like 'an amputated limb, from which vigour is draining'; as such, it could not 'contribute to the act of life'—namely, to be part of the interim government whose task it was to lead the regency to elections of the new legislature.[378] The committee took the hint and resigned.[379]

In practice, however, D'Annunzio proceeded cautiously, in a conciliatory manner. Not only did one of the first decrees of the regency provide that the *Charter* would not be applied until its provisions were studied and approved by ad hoc committees,[380] but, with the exception of the rectorate for finances (entrusted to the Italian economist Maffeo Pantaleoni), all the rectors were annexationists chosen from Fiume's traditional political elite.[381] The National Council reconstituted itself and took on the role of local municipal authority (*Comune* or *Consiglio Comunale*) provided for in the *Charter*.[382] In this capacity, headed by D'Annunzio's loyal friend, mayor Riccardo Gigante, it ratified the *Charter*.[383]

The short-lived interim government did little to act consistently with the progressive spirit and content of the *Charter*—particularly considering how the new Constitution empowered trade unions and afforded robust protections to minorities and individual rights. With Pantaleoni as rector of finances, workers' political empowerment took a backseat to promoting efficiency and freedom of enterprise. Meanwhile, the rector for justice and internal affairs reintroduced draconian measures for political crimes (death penalty for espionage, expulsion of those guilty of depressing the public spirit) and induced many Slavs to depart by announcing their imminent forcible removal as noncitizens (even if the relevant decree never came into force).[384] The rectors appear to have acted largely on their own initiative. D'Annunzio later declared, 'Out of *trust*, rather than carelessness, I have left the Rectors attend to their tasks without interference. I am ill-rewarded.'[385]

THE TREATY OF RAPALLO

Over the summer of 1920—after the *Charter* had been drafted but before it was promulgated—divisions within the town had grown and the financial and economic crisis had worsened. This had made the prospect of attempting a radical constitutional experiment less and less viable, and De Ambris had convinced D'Annunzio to attempt to negotiate with Giolitti.[386] At this time De Ambris was even prepared to compromise on the buffer state solution, so long as a Canton system was instituted to preserve the Italian identity of the *corpus separatum*.[387] D'Annunzio himself remained intransigent. In a letter from the commandant to his head of cabinet dating from 17 July, he continued to oppose the replacement of his troops with a regular contingent of the Italian Army (a point he considered nonnegotiable). He even instructed De Ambris to relay to the Italian minister of war (with whom De Ambris was liaising in Rome) that he would resort to bombarding 'the blissful Kingdom' (Italy) if the blockade was not immediately removed.[388] But by this time the internal situation in Fiume had become intractable, public opinion in Italy was experiencing indifference induced by fatigue, and the command's negotiating power had accordingly diminished.[389]

Shortly after the proclamation of the regency, the poet reoriented himself to the Right, in a bid not to lose the support of Nationalists and military leaders, putting some distance between himself and De Ambris.[390] The provisional government having been installed, De Ambris himself could devote his energies to his project of exporting *Fiumanesimo* and the revolution to Rome.[391] By mid-November 1920 he was writing letters to the poet complaining of being left out of all important decision making.[392] Meanwhile, D'Annunzio's manoeuvres to the Right proved fruitless. His hopes that the proclamation of the regency would scuttle Sforza and Giolitti's diplomatic efforts turned out to be misplaced.

By February 1921, both Italy and Yugoslavia had ratified the Treaty of Rapallo, deciding on the disputed territories on the eastern Adriatic coast. The lack of progress in negotiations at Versailles in 1920 had resulted in the Allies inviting Italy and Yugoslavia to directly negotiate between themselves.[393] After some false starts,[394] the Rapallo Treaty was the outcome.

The Yugoslavs showed more willingness to compromise after Wilson, their champion, had disappeared from the scene and the Republicans had won at the US presidential elections of 1920.[395] Wilson's cachet in the United States had diminished after the Senate had refused to ratify the Treaty of Versailles for a second time, and his health prevented him from running for a second term.[396] It also helped that Britain and France had informed the Yugoslavs—despite Wilson's protests—that they would support a territorial arrangement in accordance with the Treaty of London if the Italians felt that Yugoslav unwillingness to compromise over Fiume left them no option but to insist on a strict application of the treaty.[397]

The Treaty of Rapallo was signed on 12 November 1920. 'It was in this manner, eighteen months after the Conference of Paris, that, while Wilson was dying in Washington, Italy obtained her desires,' wrote Nicolson.[398] But this way of putting it obscures how different the Rapallo outcome was from what the Italians had initially demanded. Neither Fiume nor Dalmatia were to be assigned to Italy. According to the treaty, Italy would get the Istrian peninsula up to the strategically important Montenevoso plateau (article 1) while giving up its claims to Dalmatia, except for Zara and some islands. Italian Dalmatians, however, could opt to obtain Italian citizenship, while being allowed to retain their domicile in Dalmatia (article 7[2]). Fiume and its district (the historical *corpus separatum*) would become an independent city-state adjacent to Italian territory, a result achieved by annexing to it a small portion of formerly Istrian land (article 4).[399]

D'Annunzio opposed the treaty. He particularly resented misrepresentations made to him by the Italian government about the future of the town's Baross port,[400] which had been built in 1889 on the estuary of the river dividing Fiume from Sušak[401] and was of key importance to the town's economy. He deemed that its concession to the Yugoslavs effectively nullified the independence of Fiume.[402] The treaty itself, as signed by Italy and Yugoslavia, did not mention Baross port, and it gave the impression that it would naturally accrue to Fiume. But it had been covertly agreed that its status would be determined at a later stage, and intelligence obtained by D'Annunzio's command indicated that the Yugoslavs had received representations from Italy that it would be granted them.[403] It is not quite clear whether Baross port pertained to Sušak or rather was part of the territory belonging to the traditional *corpus separatum*.[404] If the former, it would undermine the legitimacy of D'Annunzio's taking umbrage at the misrepresentation. In reality, however, because the port was built on a small plot of triangular land created by sandbanks at the point where the river bifurcated before reaching the sea, it is likely that nobody had ever given a second thought to the question of whether or not it formally belonged to the *corpus separatum*. The issue probably only arose when the Treaty of Rapallo was being drafted, the port having by then acquired economic significance unsuspected until two decades before.

De Ambris pointed out to D'Annunzio that both Fiuman and Italian public opinion was in favour of the treaty—a situation quite unlike the time of the Ronchi march, when D'Annunzio could count on the support of both these 'moral forces'. He therefore advised dilatory tactics, until the situation turned out to be more conducive to the success of their goals.[405] He specifically tried to dissuade D'Annunzio from following through with new projects the commandant had threatened, inspired by some of his collaborators. De Ambris warned that they had an agenda of their own and were trying to commit D'Annunzio to certain actions until the point of no return,[406] despite the fact that the commandant lacked the means and men to carry them out without taking a battering.[407] De Ambris was alluding to the Nationalists, who at the time had D'Annunzio's ear and were advising a surprise action in Dalmatia—as much for its own sake (Dalmatia being something of a Nationalist fixation) as to distract him from any revolutionary project in Italy. 'My Dearest Commandant, seeing as it's not very easy to speak to you, I entreat you to read what I believe is my duty to write you.'[408] Thus did De Ambris preface one of his letters from this time, without producing much effect. Indeed, D'Annunzio—despite formal protests sent to him by his own regency[409]—proceeded to occupy two islands that the Rapallo Treaty had assigned to Yugoslavia.[410] Serventi Longhi argues that by this time an unofficial change of guard had occurred in D'Annunzio's command, and De Ambris's missions in Rome to attempt negotiations with the government were largely designed to keep him out of Fiume.[411]

On 25 November a delegate from Rome left Fiume with D'Annunzio's demands in return for recognising the treaty—namely, the clarification of the status of Baross port, guarantees that the legionnaires would incur no punishment, and recognition that the free state provided for in the Rapallo Treaty would be the regency itself. D'Annunzio's legionnaires would then leave the town after election of the new legislature in accordance with the *Charter*.[412] This was perhaps the kind of dilatory tactic recommended by De Ambris: if the constitutional arrangements of the *Charter* were to remain in force as compatible with, rather than being displaced by, the Rapallo Treaty, the provisions that allowed the legislature to appoint a commandant in the event of military emergencies might then be lawfully relied upon to further prolong D'Annunzio's permanence in Fiume.

THE END OF THE OCCUPATION AND ITS AFTERMATH

The Italian government refused to recognise the regency, this being something not stipulated in the treaty.[413] This amounted, implicitly, to a failure to acknowledge D'Annunzio's and his legionnaires' role in furthering national interests.[414] D'Annunzio therefore refused to recognise the treaty, unless and until the regency itself had ratified it.[415] He also refused to remove his troops from the islands he had occupied.[416]

Giolitti then ordered General Caviglia to put an end to the occupation.[417] By this time, despite the misgivings of the most fervent Fiuman annexationists over the territorial arrangements provided for in the treaty, and their effectiveness in safeguarding Fiume's Italian identity,[418] the majority of the population of Fiume desired life to go back to normal. Italian public opinion had also shifted, in part because Giolitti's carefully managed press propaganda had succeeded in portraying D'Annunzio and the legionnaires as the sworn enemies of family, order, civility, decency, and morality.[419] D'Annunzio's Army had also nearly halved compared to one year before,[420] although he still enjoyed some support in military quarters. While the mission against D'Annunzio's command in Fiume was successful, some elements of the Army appear to have followed through with it somewhat half-heartedly;[421] and almost until the last the regular Army recorded spectacular defections, notably of a number of ships that were part of the blockade.[422]

Although many of D'Annunzio's close collaborators had tried to get him to avoid a violent confrontation,[423] the radical intelligentsia still present among the legionnaires expected the poet to oppose the treaty.[424] Not until an armed confrontation led to approximately sixty casualties, over two hundred wounded,[425] and destruction of part of town in the so-called bloody Christmas did D'Annunzio give in. De Felice argues that this stubbornness can be explained both by his adoption of a principled stance to defend the cause of Fiume, 'beautiful beyond all beautiful ones', and by conflicting (mis)calculations. These led him to believe, alternatively, both that the Italian government would not dare open fire on Italians soldiers and that any attack would gain Fiume the sympathies of the Italian public and tip the scales in his favour.[426]

On 28 December the Italian military authorities informed D'Annunzio they had orders to start bombarding the town at 9:00 am the following day. The poet summoned an emergency meeting with some of the rectors, and with the Municipal Council headed by the faithful Gigante. The consensus was that the town must surrender to avoid further loss of life, particularly civilian. D'Annunzio renounced his military powers, except the command of the Ronchi legionnaires. More significantly, he resigned all his political powers and announced that the provisional government also stepped down with immediate effect.[427]

Host-Venturi and Gigante negotiated the peace agreement, signed on 31 December, requiring all legionnaires to depart and to withdraw from the two recently occupied islands.[428] The preamble stated that 'the State of Fiume is coerced to submit to the application of the Treaty of Rapallo to avoid any military operation against the town.'[429] On the same evening, the Municipal Council headed by Gigante, having assumed full state powers, ratified the agreement.[430] The ratification document[431] again underscores 'the brutal threat of destruction of the town, without even permitting the evacuation of women and children' as the reason for acceptance of the Treaty of Rapallo. And it takes care to specify that the *corpus separatum* of Fiume had always included the areas of the Baross port (whose status, as we have seen, appeared ambiguous in the treaty).[432] It has been argued that because the regency was not a legitimate sovereign entity at international law, the legionnaires were not lawful combatants, and the conflict between the Italian Army and D'Annunzio was not technically a war. This would explain why the peace agreement did not even provide for a cessation of hostilities.[433]

D'Annunzio continued to act and be treated (by his followers as well as the government) as a dissident military leader throughout much of 1921.[434] But despite orders he issued *in absentia*, and his impassioned appeals to the Fiumans to reject the new order (claiming, 'you could not tear me away from you without uprooting your very own reason for living'),[435] the destiny of Fiume was now well out of his hands. By September, fatigue had set in, and he was complaining with his former followers of their intrusive harassment, declaring that the legionnaires were now absolved of their sworn promise to defend Fiume unto death.[436]

In the spring of 1921, elections were held for Fiume's Constitutional Assembly, but the situation remained politically unstable. Fascists staged a violent coup and seized power in the town one year later.[437] In the autumn of 1922, Mussolini became Italy's prime minister, as well as minister for both internal and external affairs.[438] Negotiations with Yugoslavia for the partition of the independent city-state of Fiume began soon thereafter, leading to the Pact of Rome (1924). The town of Fiume finally came under Italian sovereignty, satisfying nationalist aspirations, but the Kingdom of Serbs, Croats, and Slovenes was assigned control over Baross port in accordance with the covert representations made to the Yugoslavs at the time of the Rapallo Treaty.[439] In 1934 D'Annunzio wrote to Riccardo Gigante, mayor of Fiume before and during the occupation, 'Today's Fiume . . . is alien to me, more remote than Marco Polo's Cathay.'[440]

CONCLUSIONS

Many Italian historians argue that the occupation had devastating consequences for Italy's democratic institutions.[441] State authority was undermined when the Italian government was forced to negotiate with seditious military leaders.[442] Furthermore, the occupation is said to have functioned as a touchstone for subversive mobilisation for both the Left and the Right,[443] and even for subversive forces to join efforts across the political divisions of Right-wing Nationalism, anarchic Socialism, and the radical revolutionary democratic tradition.[444] In doing so, it facilitated the ascent of fascism, which saw the usefulness of appropriating the rituals and symbolism of power established by D'Annunzio in Fiume.[445] Alatri argues that D'Annunzio's occupation also did not help Italian interests in the Adriatic, which history proved to have been contingent. It only entrenched Wilson in his unwillingness to accommodate Italian requests.[446] Other political historians, however, argue that with more *savoir-faire* Nitti could have exploited the occupation in Italy's favour.[447] The occupation gave Rome a degree of leverage in the Paris negotiations that up to that point had been lacking. This, in turn, paved the way to the Rapallo outcome—one that achieved the goal of the free state's territorial contiguity with Italy—preventing at least for a time Fiume's absorption into Croatia.[448]

NOTES

1. Roberto Vivarelli, *Storia delle Origini del Fascismo: L'Italia dalla Grande Guerra alla Marcia su Roma*, vol. 1 (Bologna: Il Mulino, 1991), 539; Michael A. Leeden, *The First Duce* (Baltimore and London: John Hopkins University Press, 1977), 62.

2. Leeden, *The First Duce*, 48, 52.

3. Vivarelli, *Storia delle Origini*, 541–46; Leeden, *The First Duce*, 61–62.

4. Leeden, *The First Duce*, 61–65.

5. Vivarelli, *Storia delle Origini*, 543–44.

6. Leeden, *The First Duce*, 50.

7. Leeden, *The First Duce*, 51.

8. Marina Cattaruzza, *L'Italia e la Questione Adriatica: Dibattiti Parlamentari e Panorama Internazionale (1919–1926)* (Bologna: Il Mulino, 2014), 74.

9. Cattaruzza, *L'Italia e la Questione Adriatica*, 72–73; Leeden, *The First Duce*, 34.

10. Edoardo Susmel, *La Cittá di Passione: Fiume negli Anni 1914–1920* (Milano: Treves, 1921), 228, 235.

11. Emanuele Cerutti, "Ricerca del Consenso e Dissenso nelle Truppe Dannunziane," in *Fiume 1919–2019: Un Centenario Europeo tra Identitá, Memorie e Prospettive di Ricerca*, ed. Giordano Bruno Guerri (Milano: Silvania Editoriale, 2020), 150.

12. Cattaruzza, *L'Italia e la Questione Adriatica*, 92.

13. Gian Nicola Amoretti, "Gabriele D'Annunzio ed Emanuele Filiberto di Savoia nei Documenti dell'Archivio Savoia-Aosta," in *D'Annunzio e il Suo Tempo*, vol. 1, ed. Francesco Perfetti (Genova: Sagep, 1989), 289.

14. Guglielmo Ferrero, "Sessanta Anni Dopo" (27 September 1919), reprinted in Guglielmo Ferrero, *Da Fiume a Roma: Storia di Quattro Anni (1919–1923)* (Milano: Athena, 1923), 11.

15. David Lloyd George, *The Truth About the Peace Treaties*, vol. II (London: Gollancz, 1938), 809–10.

16. Susmel, *La Cittá di Passione*, 101.

17. Leeden, *The First Duce*, 50.

18. William Klinger, *Un'Altra Italia: Fiume 1724–1924*, ed. Diego Redivo (Rovigno, Fiume, and Trieste: Centro di Ricerche Storiche Rovigno, 2018), 306, https://crsrv.org/wp/wp-content/uploads/2020/03/N.45-Klinger-Fiume.pdf.

19. Fiume, Desiderata: Enclosure 2 to Report from Rear Admiral E. S. A. Sinclair to the Admiralty (11 July 1919), The National Archives, FO 608/36.

20. Fiume, Desiderata: Report from Lieutenant Colonel S. C. Peck to D.M.O., War Office (25 July 1919), The National Archives, FO 608/36.

21. Quoted in Raoul Pupo, *Fiume Città di Passione* (Bari: Laterza, 2018), 77.

22. Fiume, Desiderata: Report from Lieutenant Colonel S. C. Peck to D.M.O., War Office (25 July 1919), The National Archives, FO 608/36.

23. Fiume and the Adriatic: 51/2: Commission Interalliée D'Enquête de Fiume, Procés-Verbaux et Rapport (1919), 22, The National Archives, FO 170/1248.

24. Adriatic, Italian Desiderata: Letter from A. Ossoinack to G. Clemenceau (8 July 1919), The National Archives, FO 608/35/3.

25. Silverio Annibale, *La Questione di Fiume nel Diritto Internazionale* (Rovigno, Fiume, and Trieste: Centro di Ricerche Storiche Rovigno, 2011), 68–69; Fiume, Desiderata: Report from Lieutenant Colonel S. C. Peck D.M.O., War Office (25 July 1919), The National Archives, FO 608/36.

26. Fiume, Desiderata: Report from Lieutenant Colonel S. C. Peck to D.M.O., War Office (25 July 1919), The National Archives, FO 608/36.

27. Fiume, Desiderata: Report from Rear Admiral E. S. A. Sinclair to the Admiralty (11 July 1919), The National Archives, FO 608/36.

28. Fiume and the Adriatic: 51/2: Letter from Lieutenant Colonel S. C. Peck to D.M.O., War Office (19 August 1919), The National Archives, FO 170/1248.

29. Fiume, Desiderata: "The Troubles and Hopes of Fiume. An Interview with the President of the NC at Rome" (*Il Popolo*, 5 July 1919), enclosed in Lieutenant Colonel S. C. Peck's Report to D.M.O., War Office (6 July 1919), The National Archives, FO 608/36/2.

30. Susmel, *La Cittá di Passione*, 215–16.

31. Fiume, Desiderata: "Our Volunteers" (extract from the *Giornale*, 4 August 1919), The National Archives, FO 608/35/6.

32. Fiume, Desiderata: Delegation Française, "Incidents de Fiume" (27 August 1919), The National Archives, FO 608/36.

33. Leeden, *The First Duce*, 49.

34. Fiume, Desiderata: Letter from N. Host-Venturi to the volunteer battalion Negrotto (24 June 1919), The National Archives, FO 608/36.

35. Leeden, *The First Duce*, 54–55.

36. Stefano Bruno Galli, "Irredentismo Trentino e L'Impresa di Fiume nel Nome di Cesare Battisti," in *Fiume 1919–2019*, ed. Guerri, 88.

37. Pupo, *Fiume Città di* Passione, 74.

38. Pupo, *Fiume Città di Passione*, 75.

39. Fiume, Desiderata: Report from Lieutenant Colonel S. C. Peck to D.M.O., War Office (25 July 1919), The National Archives, FO 608/36; Renzo De Felice, *D'Annunzio Politico, 1918–1938* (Roma and Bari: Laterza, 1978), 5, 7; Vivarelli, *Storia delle Origini*, 542–44, 558; Leeden, *The First Duce*, 54–55; Pupo, *Fiume Città di Passione*, 76–77; Enrico Serventi Longhi, *Il Faro del Mondo Nuovo: D'Annunzio e i Legionari a Fiume tra Guerra e Rivoluzione* (Udine: Gaspari, 2019), 67.

40. Fiume, Desiderata: Enclosure no. 5 to Report from Lieutenant Colonel S. C. Peck D.M.O., War Office (25 July 1919), The National Archives, FO 608/36.

41. Vivarelli, *Storia delle Origini*, 558–59.

42. Fiume, Desiderata: Report from Lieutenant Colonel S. C. Peck to D.M.O., War Office (25 July 1919), The National Archives, FO 608/36.

43. Fiume, Desiderata: Letter from A. Vio to G. D'Annunzio (23 June 1919), The National Archives, FO 608/36.

44. Nino Valeri, *Da Giolitti a Mussolini: Momenti della Crisi del Liberalismo* (Firenze: Parenti, 1957), 44.

45. Mario Maria Martini, *La Passione di Fiume: Diari, Cronache, Documenti* (Milano: Sonzogno, 1919), 15–16.

46. Martini, *La Passione di Fiume*, 16–18 (quoting from a comment by Orazio Pedrazzi).

47. Fiume, Desiderata: Telegrams from British Mission, Fiume, to War Office (5 July 1919), The National Archives, FO 608/36.

48. Fiume and the Adriatic: 51/2: Letter from Lieutenant Colonel C. Rocke to D.M.I., War Office (22 September 1919), The National Archives, FO 170/1248.

49. Vivarelli, *Storia delle Origini*, 546; Leeden, *The First Duce*, 37, 53; Valeri, *Da Giolitti a Mussolini*, 44; Serventi Longhi, *Il Faro*, 72; Fiume: Diary of the British Military Mission, Fiume (4–10 January 1920), The National Archives, WO 106/853.

50. Federico C. Simonelli, "La Costruzione di un Mito: Rituali, Simboli e Narrazioni dell'Impresa di Fiume (1919–1921)" (PhD diss., Universita' degli Studi di Urbino Carlo Bo, 2014–2015), 47, https://ora.uniurb.it/bitstream/11576/2630991/1/phd_uniurb_257536.pdf.

51. Disturbances at Fiume (1919): Letter from Foreign Office to War Office, enclosing letter from R. Rodd (9 July 1919) (13.a.), The National Archives, WO 32/5004.

52. Adriatic, Italian Desiderata: Telegram from R. Rodd to Earl Curzon of Kedleston (17 June 1919), The National Archives, FO 608/28/2.

53. Vivarelli, *Storia delle Origini*, 558; Klinger, *Un'Altra Italia*, 308–9; Leeden, *The First Duce*, 49, 53–54; Valeri, *Da Giolitti a Mussolini*, 44.

54. Leeden, *The First Duce*, 36.

55. Andrea Ungari, "'La Borghesia Nazionale' nel Primo Dopoguerra," in *La Cittá di Vita Cento Anni Dopo: Fiume, D'Annunzio e il Lungo Novecento Adriatico*, ed. Davide Rossi (Padova: Wolters Kluwer—Cedam, 2020), 37–63; Serventi Longhi, *Il Faro*, 64–65.

56. Lucio Villari, *La Luna di Fiume—1919: Il Complotto* (Milano: Ugo Guanda, 2019), 121–22.

57. Villari, *La Luna*, 74–92, 98–99, 113–14, 118–19.

58. Prime Minister: Letter from R. Rodd to A. Balfour (19 December 1918), Parliamentary Archives, LG/F/200/1/20.

59. Fiume and the Adriatic: 51/2: Letter from H. W. Kennard to Earl Curzon of Kedleston (21 September 1919), The National Archives, FO 170/1248.

60. Gino Berri, *La Gesta di Fiume: Storia di una Passione Inesausta* (Firenze: Bemporad, 1920), 16.

61. Berri, *La Gesta di Fiume*, 16.

62. Leeden, *The First Duce*, 53–55.

63. Berri, *La Gesta di Fiume*, 14–16.

64. Leeden, *The First Duce*, 59.

65. Susmel, *La Cittá di Passione*, 217.

66. Susmel, *La Cittá di Passione*, 220, 221; Giuseppe Moscati, *Le Cinque Giornate di Fiume: X Anniversario del Natale di Sangue* (Milano: Carnaro, 1930), 12.

67. Martini, *La Passione di Fiume*, 21.

68. Martini, *La Passione di Fiume*, 34.

69. Fiume and the Adriatic: 51/2: Letter from R. Rodd to Earl Curzon of Kedleston (30 September 1919), The National Archives, FO 170/1248.

70. Berri, *La Gesta di Fiume*, 14–16.

71. Martini, *La Passione di Fiume*, 226–27 (from the diary of the Grenadiers Battallion); John Woodhouse, *Gabriele D'Annunzio: Defiant Archangel* (Oxford: Clarendon Press, 1998), 329–30; Moscati, *Le Cinque Giornate*, 13–14.

72. Simonelli, "La Costruzione di un Mito," 100.

73. Vivarelli, *Storia delle Origini*, 561–63; Roberto Chiarini, "L'Impresa di Fiume nelle Carte del Maggiore Carlo Reina," in *D'Annunzio Politico: Atti del Convegno (Il Vittoriale, 9–10 Ottobre 1985)*, ed. Renzo De Felice and Pietro Gibellini (Milano: Garzanti, 1987), 52; Simonelli, "La Costruzione di un Mito," 48.

74. Fiume: Diary of the British Military Mission, Fiume (4–10 January 1920), The National Archives, WO 106/853.

75. Fiume and the Adriatic: 51/1: Report by N. W. Diggle to R. Rodd (16 July 1919), The National Archives, FO 170/1247.

76. Letter from Lieutenant Colonel S. C. Peck to the Secretary, War Office (6 January 1920), The National Archives, WO 106/853.

77. Martini, *La Passione di Fiume*, 68, 77–78 (from the diary of Lieutenant Cattol).

78. Susmel, *La Cittá di Passione*, 240–41; Moscati, *Le Cinque Giornate*, 17.

79. Pietro Badoglio, *Rivelazioni su Fiume* (Roma: Donatello de Luigi, 1946), 21.

80. Leeden, *The First Duce*, 66.

81. Moscati, *Le Cinque Giornate*, 18.

82. Mario Mondini, *Fiume 1919: Una Guerra Civile Italiana* (Roma: Salerno, 2019), 78–79.

83. Leeden, *The First Duce*, 49.

84. Serventi Longhi, *Il Faro*, 70–71.

85. Susmel, *La Cittá di Passione*, 258–64.

86. Martini, *La Passione di Fiume*, 86–87; Vivarelli, *Storia delle Origini*, 563–64; Badoglio, *Rivelazioni*, 30, 58–59, 67, 122.

87. Leeden, *The First Duce*, 92.

88. Martini, *La Passione di Fiume*, 109 (D'Annunzio's letter of 22 September 1919).

89. Paolo Cavassini, "La Sentinella dell'Eden: Le Lettere Fiumane di Gastone Canziani," in Gastone Canziani, A *Fiume con D'Annunzio: Lettere 1919–1920* (Ravenna: Longo, 2008), 17–18; Mondini, *Fiume 1919*, 75, 84, 87–88; see also, anecdotically, Osbert Sitwell, *Discursions on Travel, Art and Life* (London: Grant Richards, 1925), 229.

90. Susmel, *La Cittá di Passione*, 17.

91. Leeden, *The First Duce*, 92.

92. Vivarelli, *Storia delle Origini*, 564; Martini, *La Passione di Fiume*, 75–77 (from the diary of Lieutenant Cattol); Leeden, *The First Duce*, 67; Berri, *La Gesta di Fiume*, 31–32.

93. Leeden, *The First Duce*, 68.

94. Susmel, *La Cittá di Passione*, 271.

95. Susmel, *La Cittá di Passione*, 254–55.

96. Fiume and the Adriatic: 51/2: Report from Captain Gibson (19 September 1919), The National Archives, FO 170/1248.

97. Badoglio, *Rivelazioni*, 63–65.

98. Susmel, *La Cittá di Passione*, 249.

99. Berri, *La Gesta di Fiume*, 37.

100. Berri, *La Gesta di Fiume*, 52, 70.

101. Giordano Bruno Guerri, *Disobbedisco: Cinquecento Giorni di Rivoluzione. Fiume 1919–1920* (Milano: Mondadori, 2019), 86.

102. Fiume and the Adriatic: 51/2: Report from Captain Gibson (19 September 1919), The National Archives, FO 170/1248.

103. Berri, *La Gesta di Fiume*, 36.

104. Pupo, *Fiume Città di Passione*, 83.

105. Fiume and the Adriatic: 51/2: Communication from General V. E. Pittaluga to General Savy, Colonel Peck, Admiral Andrews (13 September 1919), The National Archives, FO 170/1248.

106. Vivarelli, *Storia delle Origini*, 564.

107. Fiume and the Adriatic: 51/2: Telegram from Rear Admiral, Third Light Cruiser Squadron to Commander-in-Chief, Malta (13 September 1919), The National Archives, FO 170/1248.

108. Fiume and the Adriatic: 51/2: Telegram from Rear Admiral, Third Light Cruiser Squadron to Commander-in Chief, Malta (14 September 1919), The National Archives, FO 170/1248.

109. British Delegation, Correspondence and Papers Relating to Austria-Hungary (Political): Letter from Chief of Imperial General Staff to Under Secretary for Foreign Affairs (13 March 1919), The National Archives, FO 608/8.

110. Fiume, Desiderata: Minute by H. Nicolson on telegrams from R. Rodd to Astoria (12, 13 September 1919), and on telegrams from British Mission, Fiume to Astoria (12 September 1919), The National Archives, FO 608/36.

111. Fiume and the Adriatic: 51/2: Report from Rear Admiral G. Hope to the Commander-in-Chief, Mediterranean (15 September 1919), The National Archives, FO 170/1248; Temporary Withdrawal from Fiume to Malta: Memorandum from A. A. Crosby for D.O.D. Admiralty (15 September 1919), The National Archives, WO 106/865.

112. Fiume and the Adriatic: 51/2: Report from Rear Admiral G. Hope to the Commander-in-Chief, Mediterranean (15 September 1919), The National Archives, FO 170/1248; Temporary Withdrawal from Fiume to Malta: Telegram from Admiralty to Commander in Chief, Mediterranean Afloat (7 May 1919), The National Archives, WO 106/865.

113. Fiume, Desiderata: Telegram from British Mission, Fiume to Astoria (14 September 1919), The National Archives, FO 608/36.

114. Adriatic: Letter from the Admiralty to the Under Secretary of State, Foreign Office (1 December 1919), The National Archives, FO 608/27/9.

115. Adriatic: Letter from Delegation of the Kingdom of Serbs, Croats, and Slovenes to the Secretariat General of the Peace Conference (3 December 1919), The National Archives FO 608/27/9.

116. Adriatic: Letter from P. Pachitch to G. Clemenceau, President of the Peace Conference (3 December 1919), The National Archives, FO 608/27/9.

117. Fiume and the Adriatic: 51/2: Letter from H. W. Kennard to Earl Curzon of Kedleston (26 September 1919), The National Archives, FO 170/1248.

118. Fiume and the Adriatic: 51/2: Letter from [illegible] to D.M.O., War Office (22 September 1919), The National Archives, FO 170/1248; Fiume and the Adriatic: 51/2: Report from Rear Admiral G. Hope to the Commander-in-Chief, Mediterranean (15 September 1919), The National Archives, FO 170/1248.

119. Fiume and the Adriatic: 51/2: Communication from Acting Under Secretary of State to the Director of Naval Intelligence (19 September 1919), The National Archives, FO 170/1248.

120. Fiume and the Adriatic: 51/2: Resolution passed by the Executive Committee of the United Italy Society of Great Britain, enclosed in letter from V. Fisher to the British Ambassador in Rome (15 October 1919), The National Archives, FO 170/1248.

121. Articles 1, 2, 10, 20 of Ordinance 407 (22 January 1919), concerning the provisions for the functioning of Fiume Italian National Council, *La Bilancia, Official Bullettin of the National Council* 20 (25 January 1919), in Danilo L. Massagrande, "I Governi di Fiume Indipendente, 1918–1924," *Fiume: Rivista di Studi Adriatici* 5 (2002): 29–33.

122. Leeden, *The First Duce*, 72.

123. Giovanni Comisso, *Le Mie Stagioni* (Milano: Longanesi, 1963), 59.

124. Susmel, *La Cittá di Passione*, 229; Moscati, *Le Cinque Giornate*, 15–16.

125. Leeden, *The First Duce*, 69; Comisso, *Le Mie Stagioni*, 42–43.
126. Leeden, *The First Duce*, 78.
127. Mondini, *Fiume 1919*, 82.
128. Martini, *La Passione di Fiume*, 103, quoting article 2 of an Ordinance from 20 September 1919; Klinger, *Un'Altra Italia*, 309; William Klinger, "La Carta del Carnaro: Una Costituzione per lo Stato Libero di Fiume (1920)," *Quaderni* (Centro di Ricerche Storiche-Rovigno) XIV (2002): 291.
129. Cited in Susmel, *La Cittá di Passione*, 268 (20 September 1919).
130. Leeden, *The First Duce*, 78–79.
131. Massagrande, "I Governi," 8–9; Law 6560 (21 October 1919), concerning the power transfer to the municipal representative body, *La Bilancia, Official Bulletin of the National Council* 238 (21 October 1919), in Massagrande, "I Governi," 35–36.
132. Italy, Rebellion: Diary of the British Military Mission, Fiume (15–19 October 1919), The National Archives, WO 608/41/1.
133. Susmel, *La Cittá di Passione*, 282, 293–94.
134. Annibale, *La Questione di Fiume*, 62–67.
135. Fiume and the Adriatic: 51/2: Report from Lieutenant Colonel [illegible] to D.M.O., War Office (29 October 1919), The National Archives, FO 170/1248.
136. Leeden, *The First Duce*, 118.
137. Fiume and the Adriatic: 51/2: Report from Lieutenant Colonel [illegible] to D.M.O., War Office (29 October 1919), The National Archives, FO 170/1248.
138. Fiume and the Adriatic: 51/2: Report from Lieutenant Colonel [illegible] to D.M.O., War Office (29 October 1919), The National Archives, FO 170/1248.
139. Giulio Benedetti, *La Pace di Fiume: Dalla Conferenza di Parigi al Trattato di Roma* (Bologna: Zanichelli, 1924), 51–52.
140. A. Grossich's speech (20 October 1919), in Giuseppe Gerini, *Omaggio a Gabriele D'Annunzio: Gabriele D'Annunzio e la Passione di Fiume* (Fiume: Termini, 1939), 28.
141. Annibale, *La Questione di Fiume*, 56–61.
142. Serventi Longhi, *Il Faro*, 95.
143. Luigi Peteani, "I Connotati del Regime Dannunziano a Fiume," *Quaderni del Vittoriale* 19 (1980): 43; Paolo Alatri, "La Storiografia sull'Impresa Dannunziana a Fiume," in *D'Annunzio e il Suo Tempo*, ed. Perfetti, 28.
144. Martini, *La Passione di Fiume*, 182.
145. Penal Code for the Army of the Kingdom of Italy (Firenze: Stamperia Reale, 1869).
146. Alatri, "La Storiografia," 28.
147. Alessandro Alessandro Agrì, "Lo 'Stato di Fiume' e il Suo Diritto (1918–1924)," *Historia et Ius* 19 (2021): 35 (note 141), http://www.historiaetius.eu/uploads/5/9/4/8/5948821/agri_19.pdf.
148. Carlotta Latini, "Una Giustizia 'D'Eccezione': Specialitá della Giurisidizione Militare e Sua Estensione durante la Prima Guerra Mondiale," *Deportate, Esuli, Profughe* 5–6 (2006): 73–77.
149. Latini, "Una Giustizia 'D'Eccezione'," 78–80.

150. Viceroyal Decree 885 (20 June 1915).

151. Royal Decree 1561 (4 October 1917).

152. Giulio Francisi, "La Legislazione di Guerra e i Diritti della Popolazione," in *Parlamenti di Guerra (1914–1945): Il Caso Italiano e il Contesto Europeo*, ed. Marco Meriggi (Napoli: FedOA—Federico II University Press, 2017), 185–88; Giorgio Agamben, *Lo Stato di Eccezione* (Torino: Bollati-Boringhieri, 2003), 23; Ida Ferrero, "Libertá Limitata in Tempo di Guerra: Memorie del Tribunale Territoriale di Torino (1915–1918)," *Italian Review of Legal History* 4, no. 4 (2108): 3, 13; Francesca Chiarotto, "'Effetto Caporetto': Sconfitta Italiana e Vittoria Bolscevica nel Dibattio Pubblico Italiano," in *Il Trauma di Caporetto*, ed. Francesca Belviso, Maria Pia de Paulis, and Alessandro Giacone (Torino: Accademia University Press, 2018).

153. Peteani, "I Connotati," 43; Alatri, "La Storiografia," 29.

154. Enrico Serventi Longhi, "La Dittatura Sovrana di Fiume: Innovazioni Politiche, Sociali ed Economiche (1919–1920)," *Mondo Contemporaneo* 2 (2016): 150.

155. Guerri, *Disobbedisco*, 160–62, 212–14, 226.

156. Fiume: Diary of the British Military Mission, Fiume (3–9 November 1919), The National Archives, WO 106/853.

157. Fiume: Diary of the British Military Mission, Fiume (3–9

158. November 1919), The National Archives,

159. WO 106/853.

e First Duce, 91.

160. Quoted in Leeden, *The First Duce*, 147.

161. Chiarini, "L'Impresa di Fiume," 56–57.

162. Roberto Chiarini, "Reina, D'Annunzio, Mussolini: Il Ragionevole, lo Scalmanato, l'Opportunista," in *Fiume 1919–2019*, ed. Guerri, 122.

163. As in Chiarini, "L'Impresa di Fiume."

164. Giorgio Giannini, *La Giustizia Militare "Sommaria" nella Grande Guerra* (Centro Studi Difesa Civile, 2018), http://www.pacedifesa.org/wp-content/uploads/2020/11/Quaderno-n.1-2018-G.Giannini.pdf.

165. Dominique Kirchner Reill, *The Fiume Crisis: Life in the Wake of the Habsburg Empire* (Cambridge, MA: Harvard University Press, 2020), 70.

166. Berri, *La Gesta di Fiume*, 86.

167. In a letter dated 1 May 1919, British Rear Admiral Alexander Sinclair, after referring to posters appearing overnight in town in late April, bearing a 'proclamation' whose content he does not describe, concluded that 'by posters and proclamations the Italian authorities [meaning, presumably, the National Council] are doing all in their power to excite the population and to arouse racial animosity.' Overseas: Italy: Letter from Rear Admiral E. S. A. Sinclair to the Secretary of the Admiralty (1 May 1919), The National Archives, WO 32/5129.

168. Natka Badurina, "D'Annunzio in Rijeka, 1919: Representations in the Yugoslav Press," in *Fiume 1919–2019*, ed. Guerri, 111.

169. Guerri, *Disobbedisco*, 164–66.

170. Thea Pičić, *Rijeka Ili Smrt! D'Anunzijeva okupacija Rijeke, 1919–1921 / Rijeka or Death! D'Annunzio's occupation of Rijeka, 1919–2019* (Rijeka: Naklada Val, 2019), 170, 179; Natka Badurina, "D'Annunzio in Rijeka," 111; Natka

Badurina, "D'Annunzio a Fiume: La Violenza Politica, l'Etica e la Storia," in *Fiume 1919–2019*, ed. Guerri, 201, 204.

171. Guerri, *Disobbedisco*, 157.

172. See, for example, Ervin Dubrović, "L'Organizzazione *Galeb* (Gabbiano) contro D'Annunzio," in *Fiume 1919–2019*, ed. Guerri, 62–63; Davide Rossi, "La Carta del Carnaro, Antidoto Contro le Tossine del Parlamentarismo," in *La Cittá di Vita*, ed. Rossi, 276; Comisso, *Le Mie Stagioni*, 83.

173. Guerri, *Disobbedisco*, 360–62.

174. Serventi Longhi, *Il Faro*, 158.

175. Dominique Kirchner Reill, "How to Survive in a Holocaust City: D'Annunzio and Fiume," in *Fiume 1919–2019*, ed. Guerri, 76.

176. Kirchner Reill, *The Fiume Crisis*, 70–71; Pupo, *Fiume Città di Passione*, 93.

177. Kirchner Reill, *The Fiume Crisis*, 15.

178. Kirchner Reill, "How to Survive," 82.

179. Natka Badurina, "I Croati di Fiume," *Qualestoria* 48, no. 2 (2020): 46.

180. Leeden, *The First Duce*, 73.

181. Ferrero, *Da Fiume a* Roma, 14.

182. Cattaruzza, *L'Italia e la Questione Adriatica*, 81; Vivarelli, *Storia delle Origini*, 572.

183. Fiume and the Adriatic: 51/2: Letter from R. Rodd to Earl Curzon of Kedleston (14 September 1919), The National Archives, FO 170/1248.

184. Fiume and the Adriatic: 51/2: Letter from R. Rodd to Earl Curzon of Kedleston (14 September 1919), The National Archives, FO 170/1248.

185. Fiume and the Adriatic: 51/2: Telegram from Rear Admiral, 3rd Light Cruise Squadron to Admiralty 144 (15 September 1919), The National Archives, FO 170/1248.

186. Giancarlo Giordano, "Sforza e D'Annunzio," in *D'Annunzio e il Suo Tempo*, ed. Perfetti, 102–3; Vivarelli, *Storia delle Origini*, 575–77.

187. Leeden, *The First Duce*, 76.

188. Fiume and the Adriatic: 51/2: Letter from [illegible] to D.M.O., War Office (21 September 1919), The National Archives, FO 170/1248.

189. Vivarelli, *Storia delle Origini*, 569–70.

190. Leeden, *The First Duce*, 55.

191. Badoglio, *Rivelazioni*, 19, 23.

192. Badoglio, *Rivelazioni*, 24–25.

193. Italy, Rebellion: Telegram from British Mission, Fiume, to Astoria (19 September 1919), The National Archives, FO 608/41/1.

194. Fiume and the Adriatic: 51/2: Letter from H.W. Kennard to Earl Curzon of Kedleston (21 September 1919), The National Archives, FO 170/1248.

195. Fiume and the Adriatic: 51/2: Enclosure (A)(1) in letter of proceedings from Rear Admiral G. Hope to the Commander-in-Chief, Mediterranean (2 October 1919), The National Archives, FO 170/1248.

196. Fiume and the Adriatic: 51/2: Letter from R. Rodd to Earl Curzon of Kedleston (15 September 1919), The National Archives, FO 170/1248.

197. Fiume and the Adriatic: 51/2: Letter [from R. Rodd?] to Earl Curzon of Kedleston (17 September 1919), The National Archives, FO 170/1248.

198. Fiume and the Adriatic: 51/2: Letter from G. Buchanan to Earl Curzon of Kedleston (31 October 1919), The National Archives, FO 170/1248.

199. Vivarelli, *Storia delle Origini*, 578–78.

200. Badoglio, *Rivelazioni*, 33.

201. Fiume and the Adriatic: 51/2: Enclosure (A)(1) in letter of proceedings from Rear Admiral G. Hope to the Commander-in-Chief, Mediterranean (2 October 1919) The National Archives, FO 170/1248

202. Badoglio, *Rivelazioni*, 34.

203. Badoglio, *Rivelazioni*, 39.

204. Ferrero, *Da Fiume a Roma*, 21; Badoglio, *Rivelazioni*, 32.

205. Fiume and the Adriatic: 51/2: Letter from H. W. Kennard to Earl Curzon of Kedleston (21 September 1919), The National Archives, FO 170/1248.

206. British Delegation: Letter from R. Rodd to Earl Curzon of Kedleston (23 May 1919), The National Archives, FO 608/39.

207. British Delegation: Letter from R. Rodd to Earl Curzon of Kedleston (17 May 1919), The National Archives, FO 608/39.

208. Fiume and the Adriatic: 51/2: Letter from H. W. Kennard to Earl Curzon of Kedleston (24 September 1919), The National Archives, FO 170/1248.

209. Francesco Perfetti, "D'Annunzio, Ovvero la Politica Come Poesia," in *D'Annunzio e il Suo Tempo*, ed. Perfetti, 379–80.

210. B. Mussolini, "Governo Vile!," *Il Popolo d'Italia* 253 (15 September 1919), quoted in Giordano, "Sforza e D'Annunzio," 102.

211. Cattaruzza, *L'Italia e la Questione Adriatica*, 100.

212. From a poster printed in Fiume, quoted in Badoglio, *Rivelazioni*, 57.

213. Badoglio, *Rivelazioni*, 75.

214. Badoglio, *Rivelazioni*, 59–65.

215. Cattaruzza, *L'Italia e la Questione Adriatica*, 84; Badoglio, *Rivelazioni*, 59–60.

216. Leeden, *The First Duce*, 76.

217. Fiume and the Adriatic: 51/2: Letter from R. Rodd to Earl Curzon of Kedleston (14 September 1919), The National Archives, FO 170/1248; Fiume and the Adriatic: 51/2: Letter from R. Rodd to Earl Curzon of Kedleston (15 September 1919), The National Archives, FO 170/1248; Fiume and the Adriatic: 51/2: Letter from H. W. Kennard to Earl Curzon of Kedleston (21 September 1919), The National Archives, FO 170/1248.

218. Fiume and the Adriatic: 51/2: Letter from H. W. Kennard to Earl Curzon of Kedleston (21 September 1919), The National Archives, FO 170/1248.

219. Fiume and the Adriatic: 51/2: Letter from H. W. Kennard to Earl Curzon of Kedleston (24 September 1919), The National Archives, FO 170/1248.

220. Fiume and the Adriatic: 51/2: Letter from H. W. Kennard to Earl Curzon of Kedleston (24 September 1919), The National Archives, FO 170/1248.

221. Badoglio, *Rivelazioni*, 82–83.

222. Davide Rossi, "D'Annunzio, la Carta del Carnaro e la Crisi dello Stato Liberale, tra Rappresentanza e Antiparlamentarismo," *Giornale di Storia Costituzionale* 38, no. 2 (2019): 137.

223. Ferrero, *Da Fiume a Roma*, 21–22.

224. Stanley G. Payne, *A History of Fascism* (Madison, WI: University of Wisconsin Press, 1995), 88–89.

225. Cattaruzza, *L'Italia e la Questione Adriatica*, 94; De Felice, *D'Annunzio Politico*, 121; Badoglio, *Rivelazioni*, 110.

226. Fiume and the Adriatic: 51/2: Letter from Paymaster Lieutenant Commander [unnamed] to the Director of Naval Intelligence (12 December 1919), The National Archives, 170/1248.

227. Giordano, "Sforza e D'Annunzio," 102–6; René Albrecht-Carrié, *Italy at the Paris Peace Conference* (Hamden, CT: Archon, 1966), 244–55; Italy, Rebellion: British Delegation, Adriatic Question and Future of Fiume (11 October 1919), The National Archives FO 608/41/1.

228. Badoglio, *Rivelazioni*, 105.

229. Prime Minister: Telegram from D. Lloyd George to F. S. Nitti (via G. Buchanan) (31 October 1919), Parliamentary Archives, LG/F/554/39.

230. Badoglio, *Rivelazioni*, 111–12.

231. *Storia Documentata dei Confini del Regno d'Italia*, vol. 4 (*Confine Italo-Jugoslavo*), ed. Vittorio Adami (Roma: Istituto Poligrafico dello Stato, 1931), 169.

232. Susmel, *La Cittá di Passione*, 321.

233. Berri, *La Gesta di Fiume*, 197; Message from G. Keller to G. D'Annunzio (28 November 1919), Fondazione Il Vittoriale degli Italiani, Archivio Fiumano, Serie Corrispondenza, Keller, Guido.

234. Badoglio, *Rivelazioni*, 121–23.

235. Canziani, *A Fiume con D'Annunzio*, 48 (letter from G. Canziani to his sister Romy [13 December 1919]).

236. Leeden, *The First Duce*, 133.

237. Badoglio, *Rivelazioni*, 127–31; Leeden, *The First Duce*, 134; Susmel, *La Cittá di Passione*, 324–25.

238. Cattaruzza, *L'Italia e la Questione Adriatica*, 93–94; Badoglio, *Rivelazioni*, 132; Susmel, *La Cittá di Passione*, 324–28.

239. Ettore de Franchi, "Gabriele D'Annunzio e Antonio Grossich, Presidente del Consiglio Nazionale di Fiume," in *D'Annunzio e il Suo Tempo*, ed. Perfetti, 117; Susmel, *La Cittá di Passione*, 332; Simonelli, "La Costruzione di un Mito," 134.

240. Berri, *La Gesta di Fiume*, 205.

241. Berri, *La Gesta di Fiume*, 200–205; Badoglio, *Rivelazioni*, 133–34; Leeden, *The First Duce*, 136–37; Susmel, *La Cittá di Passione*, 329; Guerri, *Disobbedisco*, 146–49.

242. Letter from G. D'Annunzio to A. Grossich (17 December 1919), in De Franchi, "Gabriele D'Annunzio e Antonio Grossich," 124.

243. Italy, Rebellion: Telegram from British Mission, Abbazia to E. A. Crowe (17 December 1919), FO 608/41/1.

244. Berri, *La Gesta di Fiume*, 209–12.

245. Badoglio, *Rivelazioni*, 134.

246. Fiume and the Adriatic: 51/2: Telegram from British Military Mission, Abbazia, to War Office (17 December 1919), The National Archives, FO 170/1248.

247. Guerri, *Disobbedisco*, 152–53.

248. Comisso, *Le Mie Stagioni*, 55.

249. Leeden, *The First Duce*, 137; Woodhouse, *Gabriele D'Annunzio*, 337; Susmel, *La Cittá di Passione*, 332–33; Simonelli, "La Costruzione di un Mito," 140–41; Guerri, *Disobbedisco*, 152–55.

250. Berri, *La Gesta di Fiume*, 215–18.

251. Simonelli, "La Costruzione di un Mito," 141; Guerri, *Disobbedisco*, 154.

252. Alfredo Bonadeo, *D'Annunzio and the Great War* (Madison and Teaneck: Farleigh Dickinson University Press; London: Associated University Presses, 1995), 135.

253. Leeden, *The First Duce*, 137–38.

254. Enclosure to letter from Lieutenant Colonel S. C. Peck to the Secretary, War Office (6 January 1920), The National Archives, WO 106/853.

255. D'Annunzio's counterproposal, in Susmel, *La Cittá di Passione*, 323.

256. Susmel, *La Cittá di Passione*, 324–28.

257. Susmel, *La Cittá di Passione*, 381.

258. De Felice, *D'Annunzio Politico*, 53–55; see also Badoglio, *Rivelazioni*, 145.

259. De Felice, *D'Annunzio Politico*, 54–55.

260. Simonelli, "La Costruzione di un Mito," 139, 154.

261. Simonelli, "La Costruzione di un Mito," 140.

262. De Felice, *D'Annunzio Politico*, 53.

263. Berri, *La Gesta di Fiume*, 217.

264. Leeden, *The First Duce*, 138; Badoglio, *Rivelazioni*, 144.

265. Simonelli, "La Costruzione di un Mito," 156–57.

266. De Felice, *D'Annunzio Politico*, 25–27.

267. Badoglio, *Rivelazioni*, 144.

268. De Felice, *D'Annunzio Politico*, 12–13, 57.

269. De Felice, *D'Annunzio Politico*, 121.

270. Fiume: Diary of the British Military Mission, Fiume (4–10 January 1920), The National Archives, WO 106/853.

271. Albrecht-Carrié, *Italy at the Paris Peace Conference*, 262.

272. Albrecht-Carrié, *Italy at the Paris Peace Conference*, 262.

273. Albrecht-Carrié, *Italy at the Paris Peace Conference*, 268–75.

274. Cattaruzza, *L'Italia e la Questione Adriatica*, 113–15.

275. Albrecht-Carrié, *Italy at the Paris Peace Conference*, 278 (quoting from W. Wilson's note of 9 February 1920).

276. Albrecht-Carrié, *Italy at the Paris Peace Conference*, 275–80.

277. Albrecht-Carrié, *Italy at the Paris Peace Conference*, 281–84.

278. Leeden, *The First Duce*, 189.

279. Albrecht-Carrié, *Italy at the Paris Peace Conference*, 285.

280. Canziani, *A Fiume con D'Annunzio*, 58 (letter from G. Canziani to his family [17 March 1920]).

281. Payne, *A History of Fascism*, 89.

282. Payne, *A History of Fascism*, 93.

283. Cattaruzza, *L'Italia e la Questione Adriatica*, 107; Benedetti, *La Pace di Fiume*, 68.

284. Payne, *A History of Fascism*, 89.

285. Giordano, "Sforza e D'Annunzio," 107–9; Albrech-Carrié, *Italy at the Paris Peace Conference*, 300–301.

286. De Felice, *D'Annunzio Politico*, 119.

287. Renzo De Felice, "Introduzione," in *Sindacalismo Rivoluzionario e Fiumanesimo nel Carteggio De Ambris—D'Annunzio*, ed. Renzo De Felice (Brescia: Morcelliana, 1966), 10–33.

288. Fiume: Diary of the British Military Mission, Fiume (4–10 January 1920), The National Archives, WO 106/853.

289. Leeden, *The First Duce*, 140.

290. De Felice, "Introduzione," 18.

291. Giovanni Michele Palmieri, "Sulla Tutela dei Diritti dell'Uomo e delle Libertá Fondamentali nella Carta del Carnaro," in *Lo Statuto della Reggenza*, ed. Sinagra, 154.

292. Alceste De Ambris, "Precisiamo il Nostro Concetto Rivoluzionaro: Il Manifesto dei Sindacalisti e la Costituzione Fiumana," *La Gioventu Sindacalista* (1 September 1921), in *Sindacalismo Rivoluzionario*, ed. De Felice, 313.

293. De Felice, "Introduzione," 33–35, 41; Payne, *A History of Fascism*, 81–82.

294. De Felice, "Introduzione," 47–48.

295. De Felice, "Introduzione," 37, 42–43.

296. Klinger, "La Carta," 277–79.

297. De Felice, "Introduzione," 55.

298. De Felice, "Introduzione," 62–63.

299. De Felice, "Introduzione," 64–66.

300. Leeden, *The First Duce*, 119–21.

301. Serventi Longhi, *Il Faro*, 106–7.

302. Perfetti, "D'Annunzio, Ovvero la Politica," 381. Support for the Fiume endeavour on Mussolini's part has been said to have always been more about nationalist posturing than genuine endorsement, as Mussolini doubted the success of D'Annunzio's enterprise. Payne, *A History of Fascism*, 92–93.

303. Leeden, *The First Duce*, 155–56.

304. Serventi Longhi, "La Dittatura Sovrana," 158–60.

305. Serventi Longhi, "La Dittatura Sovrana," 155; Simonelli, "La Costruzione di un Mito," 159–60, 164; Cerutti, "Ricerca del Consenso," 148; Paolo Palminteri, "I Diritti Umani nella Carta del Carnaro," in *La Cittá di Vita*, ed. Rossi, 261, 263.

306. Kirchner Reill, *The Fiume Crisis*, 153–54.

307. Agrì, "Lo 'Stato di Fiume'," 35; Léon Kotchnitzky, Report (30 April 1920), Fondazione Il Vittoriale degli Italiani, Archivio Fiumano, Kotchnitzky, Léon—1–129.

308. Serventi Longhi, "La Dittatura Sovrana," 155–57.

309. Fiume, Desiderata: Report of Lieutenant Colonel S. C. Peck to the Secretary, War Office (21 November 1919), The National Archives, FO 608/35/6.

310. Fiume and the Adriatic: 51/2: Letter from H. W. Kennard to Earl Curzon of Kedleston (26 September 1919), The National Archives, FO 170/1248.

311. Italy, Rebellion: Telegram from British Mission, Fiume, to Astoria (28 September 1919), The National Archives, FO 608/41/1.

312. Fiume: Diary of the British Military Mission, Fiume (12–18 January 1920), The National Archives, WO 106/853.

313. Dubrović, "L'Organizzazione *Galeb*," 65.

314. Berri, *La Gesta di Fiume*, 125–27.

315. De Felice, "Introduzione," 69.

316. De Ambris, "Precisiamo," 313. For a detailed discussion of the relationship between the *Charter* and the Manifesto of Revolutionary Syndicalism, see Alessandro Agrí, *La Costituzione della Reggenza Italiana del Carnaro* (Torino: Giappichelli, 2023), 166–79.

317. A. De Ambris's speech delivered in Fiume (30 March 1920), in *Sindacalismo Rivoluzionario*, ed. De Felice, 273.

318. A. De Ambris's speech delivered in Fiume (30 March 1920), in *Sindacalismo Rivoluzionario*, ed. De Felice, 274.

319. Letter from A. De Ambris to G. D'Annunzio (18 September 1920), in *Sindacalismo Rivoluzionario*, ed. De Felice, 209–10.

320. De Felice, *D'Annunzio Politico*, 85, 88, 125–26; Perfetti, "D'Annunzio, Ovvero la Politica," 380.

321. Susmel, *La Cittá di Passione*, 351–55.

322. G. D'Annunzio's interview with a Hungarian journalist, *La Vedetta d'Italia* (14 April 1920), in *La Carta del Carnaro e Altri Scritti su Fiume*, ed. Marco Fressura and Patrick Karlsen (Roma: Castelvecchi, 2009), 141.

323. Letter from A. De Ambris to G. D'Annunzio (18 March 1920), in *La Carta del Carnaro e Altri Scritti su Fiume*, ed. Fressura and Karlsen, 126.

324. Mauro Ferri, "Appunti per una Riflessione sulla 'Carta del Carnaro'," in *D'Annunzio Politico: Atti del Convegno*, ed. De Felice and Gibellini, 37–39; Salvatore Cingari, "Virtuosa Gioia: Di Alcuni Aspetti Utopistici nella Carta del Carnaro," *Giornale di Storia Costituzionale* 10 (2005): 155; Guglielmo Negri, "La Carta del Carnaro tra De Ambris e D'Annunzio," in *D'Annunzio e il Suo Tempo*, ed. Perfetti, 62; Federico L. Ramaioli, "Lo Statuto della Reggenza Italiana del Carnaro tra Innovazione e Tradizione: A Cento Anni dalla Costituzione di Fiume," *Fiume: Rivista di Studi Adriatici* XLI (2020): 93–98; Leonardo Tosoni, "Carta del Carnaro: Diritti di Libertà e Prospettive di Giustizia Sociale nella Fiume Dannunziana," *Historia Constitucional* 22 (2021): 859; Nicolino Flaminio Costa and Gian Galeazzo Stendardi di Montebenichi, "La 'Carta del Carnaro'," in Gabriele D'Annunzio, *Reggenza Italiana del Carnaro: Disegno di un Nuovo Ordinamento dello Stato Libero di Fiume* (Milano: Perelli, 1973), 45; Giuseppe de Vergottini, "Prassi e Utopia nel Disegno Costituzionale Dannunziano," *Rivista AIC* 3 (2019): 599–600.

325. Letter from A. De Ambris to G. D'Annunzio (18 March 1920), in *La Carta del Carnaro e Altri Scritti su Fiume*, ed. Fressura and Karlsen, 126.

326. Letter from A. De Ambris to G. D'Annunzio (18 March 1920), in *La Carta del Carnaro e Altri Scritti su Fiume*, ed. Fressura and Karlsen, 133.

327. Umberto Foscanelli, *D'Annunzio e l'Ora Sociale* (Milano: Carnaro, 1952), 130.

328. Valeri, *Da Giolitti a Mussolini*, 56.

329. Letter from General E. Caviglia to F. S. Nitti (14 March 1920), in Valeri, *Da Giolitti a Mussolini*, 76.

330. Italy, Rebellion: Telegram from G. Buchanan (12 December 1919), The National Archives, FO 608/41/1.

331. Telegram from General E. Caviglia to F. S. Nitti (21 March 1920), in Valeri, *Da Giolitti a Mussolini*, 78.

332. G. D'Annunzio's interview with a Hungarian journalist, 140–41.

333. Letter from A. De Ambris to G. D'Annunzio (13 May 1920), in *Sindaclaismo Rivoluzionaro*, ed. De Felice, 183–84.

334. De Felice, "Introduzione," 81.

335. De Felice, *D'Annunzio Politico*, 124–25; Leeden, *The First Duce*, 171–72; De Felice, "Introduzione," 76.

336. Leeden, *The First Duce*, 171–77; Serge Noiret, "D'Annunzio a Fiume e i Socialisti Massimalisti: Il Ruolo di Nicola Bombacci (1919–1920)," in *D'Annunzio Politico: Atti del Convegno*, ed. De Felice and Gibellini, 175; De Felice, "Introduzione," 77.

337. Telegrams from F. S. Nitti to Mosconi, Sechi, and Savini (16 April 1920), in Valeri, *Da Giolitti a Mussolini*, 85, 86, 84.

338. Telegram from F. S. Nitti to Sechi (18 April 1920), in Valeri, *Da Giolitti a Mussolini*, 87.

339. Valeri, *Da Giolitti a Mussolini*, 55.

340. Ivan Jeličić, "Repubblica con Chi? Il Movimento Socialista Fiumano e il Giallo Sisa nel Contesto Post-Asburgico Fiumano," *Qualestoria* 2 (December 2020): 81.

341. Renzo De Felice, "Introduzione," 76–77.

342. Canziani, *A Fiume con D'Annunzio*, 63 (letter from G. Canziani to Lella [9 May 1920]); Telegram from General E. Caviglia to the Cabinet of the Ministry for Internal Affairs (7 May 1920), in Valeri, *Da Giolitti a Mussolini*, 93; Leeden, *The First Duce*, 146–47; Simonelli, "La Costruzione di un Mito," 170–71.

343. Ferdinando Cordova, *Arditi e Legionari Dannunziani* (Padova: Marsilio, 1969), 44.

344. G. D'Annunzio's message, reproduced in scanned form in *La Carta del Carnaro e Altri Scritti su Fiume*, ed. Fressura and Karlsen, 96.

345. De Felice, *D'Annunzio Politico*, 118–19, 131–32; Alatri, "La Storiografia," 22; Paolo Ungari, "Commento Giuridico alla Carta del Carnaro," in *D'Annunzio e il Suo Tempo*, ed. Perfetti, 52–53; De Vergottini, "Prassi e Utopia," 605.

346. Giuseppe De Vergottini, *La Costituzione secondo D'Annunzio* (Milano: Luni, 2020), 55.

347. Alceste De Ambris, "Verso il Futuro" (Comando di Fiume d'Italia, Bollettino Ufficiale 26 August 1920), in *Sindacalismo Rivoluzionario*, ed. De Felice, 303.

348. De Ambris, "Verso il Futuro," 303, 305.

349. De Felice, *D'Annunzio Politico*, 127–28; De Felice, "Introduzione," 88–89.

350. Guerri, *Disobbedisco*, 309.

351. Letter from G. D'Annunzio to A. Grossich (29 August 1920), in De Franchi, "Gabriele D'Annunzio e Antonio Grossich," 129.

352. De Felice, "Introduzione," 90.

353. Guerri, *Disobbedisco*, 311.

354. Gabriele D'Annunzio, "Lo Statuto Letto del Comandnante al Popolo," in *La Carta del Carnaro e Altri Scritti su Fiume*, ed. Fressura and Karlsen, 104.

355. D'Annunzio, "Lo Statuto Letto del Comandnante," 107.

356. Letter from G. D'Annunzio to A. Grossich (6 December 1920), in De Franchi, "Gabriele D'Annunzio e Antonio Grossich," 130.

357. D'Annunzio, "Lo Statuto Letto del Comandnante," 107.

358. D'Annunzio, "Lo Statuto Letto del Comandnante," 107.

359. Guerri, *Disobbedisco*, 312.

360. De Felice, *D'Annunzio Politico*, 82–83; Guerri, *Disobbedisco*, 333.

361. Alberto Pellegrino, "Lettere e Telegrammi di D'Annunzio e Riccardo Gigante," in *D'Annunzio Politico: Atti del Convegno*, ed. De Felice and Gibellini, 87; Peteani, "I Connotati," 45.

362. Guerri, *Disobbedisco*, 333.

363. Guerri, *Disobbedisco*, 439.

364. De Vergottini, *La Costituzione*, 67; Klinger, "La Carta," 275; Peteani, "I Connotati," 41.

365. De Vergottini, *La Costituzione*, 67, 69–70. See also Alatri, "La Storiografia," 28.

366. Letter from G. D'Annunzio to A. Grossich (6 September 1920), in De Franchi, "Gabriele D'Annunzio e Antonio Grossich," 130.

367. Enrico Serventi Longhi, "The Father of 'Sovereignism': D'Annunzio in Fiume between the Crisis of Liberalism and the Critique of Democracy," *Modern Italy* 27 (2022): 38.

368. Guglielmo Salotti, "Nuovi Studi sulla Carta del Carnaro," *Fiume: Rivista di Studi Fiumani* XIX–XX (1973–1974): 84–85.

369. Annibale, *La Questione di Fiume*, 71–75.

370. Gian Luigi Cecchini, "La Reggenza Fiumana nella Storia e nell'Ordinamento Giuridico Internazionale," in *Lo Statuto della Reggenza Italiana del Carnaro tra Storia, Diritto Internazionale e Diritto Costituzionale*, ed. Augusto Sinagra (Milano: Giuffré, 2009), 121–26.

371. Conference of Ambassadors, Paris, Minutes of Proceedings: Notes of a meeting held at Quay D'Orsay, Paris, 10 September 1920, Appendix F, The National Archives, FO 893/7; Annibale, *La Questione di Fiume*, 25.

372. De Felice, *D'Annunzio Politico*, 132.

373. On 27 October 1920, he was replaced by Corrado Zoli: Massagrande, "I Governi," 14.

374. First Decree of the Carnaro Regency, in Gerini, *Omaggio*, 84; Klinger, "La Carta," 328–29.

375. Serventi Longhi, "La Dittatura Sovrana," 161; Peteani, "I Connotati," 45.

376. De Felice, *D'Annunzio Politico*, 132.

377. Letter from the Managing Committee to G. D'Annunzio (17 September 1920), *La Vedetta d'Italia* (23 September 1920), in Massagrande, "I Governi," 36–37.

378. Letter from G. D'Annunzio to A. Grossich (20 September 1920), in De Franchi, "Gabriele D'Annunzio e Antonio Grossich," 130.

379. Resignation of the Managing Committee (21 September 1920), *La Vedetta d'Italia* (23 September 1920), in Massagrande, "I Governi," at 37–38.

380. Guerri, *Disobbedisco*, 346–47.

381. Serventi Longhi, "La Dittatura Sovrana," 161; Simonelli, "La Costruzione di un Mito," 226–27; see Massagrande, "I Governi," 11–14.

382. First Decree of the Carnaro Regency, in Gerini, *Omaggio*, 84.

383. Pellegrino, "Lettere e Telegrammi," 91; Simonelli, "La Costruzione di un Mito," 225.

384. Serventi Longhi, "La Dittatura Sovrana," 164.

385. Letter from G. D'Annunzio to M. Pantaleoni (8 December 1920), quoted in Carmelo Ferlito, "Principi Economici della Carta del Carnaro," *Storia Veritá* 52 (2008) (originally in Renzo De Felice, 'Il Carteggio Fiumano D'Annunzio-Pantaleoni," *Clio* X, no. 3–4 [1974]: 536–37).

386. De Felice, "Introduzione," 82–83.

387. Letter from A. De Ambris (in his personal capacity) to I. Bonomi (Minister of War) (June 1920) in *Sindacalismo Rivoluzionario*, ed. De Felice, 286–88.

388. Letter from G. D'Annunzio to A. De Ambris (17 July 1920), in *Sindacalismo Rivoluzionario*, ed. De Felice, 196–97.

389. Leeden, *The First Duce*, 189–94.

390. De Felice, "Introduzione," 91.

391. Simonelli, "La Costruzione di un Mito," 216–17.

392. Letter from A. De Ambris to G. D'Annunzio (16 November 1920), in *Sindacalismo Rivoluzionario*, ed. De Felice, 218–19.

393. Benedetti, *La Pace di Fiume*, 62.

394. Maxwell H. H. Macartney and Paul Cremona, *Italy's Foreign and Colonial Policy, 1914–1937* (New York: Howard Fertig, 1972), 87.

395. Macartney and Cremona, *Italy's Foreign and Colonial Policy*, 88; Cattaruzza, *L'Italia e la Questione Adriatica*, 109; Margaret Macmillan, *Peacemakers: Six Months that Changed the World* (London: John Murray, 2001), 313.

396. Cattaruzza, *L'Italia e la Questione Adriatica*, 90.

397. Lloyd George, *The Truth*, 896–97.

398. Harold Nicolson, *Peacemaking, 1919* (London: Constable, 1933), 183.

399. Cattaruzza, *L'Italia e la Questione Adriatica*, 108–9.

400. Leeden, *The First Duce*, 197–98; Valeri, *Da Giolitti a Mussolini*, 62.

401. Guerri, *Disobbedisco*, 378.

402. Draft letter from G. D'Annunzio [apparently to the Fiumans] (24 November 1920), in *Sindacalismo Rivoluzionario*, ed. De Felice, 228.

403. Moscati, *Le Cinque Giornate*, 26–33, 66–67; Benedetti, *La Pace di Fiume*, 69–83; Simonelli, "La Costruzione di un Mito," 244; Guerri, *Disobbedisco*, 379.

404. Albrecht-Carrié, *Italy at the Paris Peace Conference*, 101, 309 (note 60).

405. Letter from A. De Ambris to G. D'Annunzio (18 November 1920), in *Sindacalismo Rivoluzionario*, ed. De Felice, 220–23.

406. Letter from A. De Ambris to G. D'Annunzio (24 November 1920), in De Felice, *D'Annunzio Politico*, 224–27.
407. Letter from A. De Ambris to G. D'Annunzio (1 December 1920) *Sindacalismo Rivoluzionario*, ed. De Felice, 232–33.
408. Letter from A. De Ambris to G. D'Annunzio (24 November 1920), in De Felice, *D'Annunzio Politico*, 224–27.
409. Leeden, *The First Duce*, 200.
410. Giordano, "Sforza e D'Annunzio," 112.
411. Serventi Longhi, *Il Faro*, 134–35.
412. Moscati, *Le Cinque Giornate*, 37.
413. Moscati, *Le Cinque Giornate*, 52.
414. Simonelli, "La Costruzione di un Mito," 246.
415. Moscati, *Le Cinque Giornate*, 73; Macartney and Cremona, *Italy's Foreign and Colonial Policy*, 89.
416. Moscati, *Le Cinque Giornate*, 38–39, 84.
417. Cattaruzza, *L'Italia e la Questione Adriatica*, 131.
418. Susmel, *La Cittá di Passione*, 358.
419. De Felice, *D'Annunzio Politico*, 12–14.
420. Cerutti, "Ricerca del Consenso," 150.
421. Cattaruzza, *L'Italia e la Questione Adriatica*, 132.
422. Moscati, *Le Cinque Giornate*, 55–62.
423. Peteani, "I Connotati," 46–47.
424. Simonelli, "La Costruzione di un Mito," 246.
425. Pupo, *Fiume Città di Passione*, 146.
426. De Felice, *D'Annunzio Politico*, 96–102.
427. Moscati, *Le Cinque Giornate*, 137–38; Guerri, *Disobbedisco*, 484–85.
428. Peace Agreement between General C. Ferrario, Captain N. Host-Venturi and Mayor R. Gigante, Abbazia (31 December 1920), clause 16.3, in Moscati, *Le Cinque Giornate*, 144–46.
429. Moscati, *Le Cinque Giornate*, 144.
430. Massagrande, "I Governi," 9.
431. Reproduced in Moscati, *Le Cinque Giornate*, 147–48.
432. Moscati, *Le Cinque Giornate*, 147.
433. Annibale, *La Questione di Fiume*, 76–77.
434. Pellegrino, "Lettere e Telegrammi," 108–9.
435. Proclamation to the people of Fiume (27 April 1921), in Pellegrino, "Lettere e Telegrammi," 119–20.
436. Pellegrino, "Lettere e Telegrammi," 114.
437. Macartney and Cremona, *Italy's Foreign and Colonial Policy*, 90–91.
438. Cattaruzza, *L'Italia e la Questione Adriatica*, 157.
439. Macartney and Cremona, *Italy's Foreign and Colonial Policy*, 93–94; Cattaruzza, *L'Italia e la Questione Adriatica*, 168–69.
440. Letter from G. D'Annunzio to R. Gigante (15 March 1934), in Pellegrino, "Lettere e Telegrammi," 118.
441. Cattaruzza, *L'Italia e la Questione Adriatica*, 84; Alatri, "La Storiografia," 26.

442. Perfetti, "D'Annunzio, Ovvero la Politica," 378.

443. Alatri, "La Storiografia," 26.

444. Perfetti, "D'Annunzio, Ovvero la Politica," 378.

445. *Scritti Politici di Gabriele D'Annunzio*, ed. Paolo Alatri (Milano: Feltrinelli, 1980), 45 (editor's remarks); Payne, *A History of Fascism*, 92; Macartney and Cremona, *Italy's Foreign and Colonial Policy*, 95; Federico Carlo Simonelli, *D'Annunzio e il Mito di Fiume: Riti, Simboli, Narrazioni* (Pisa: Pacini, 2021), 258.

446. Alatri, "La Storiografia," 25.

447. Amoretti, "Gabriele D'Annunzio," 290.

448. Cattaruzza, *L'Italia e la Questione Adriatica*, 84; Cecchini, "La Reggenza Fiumana nella Storia," 101–2.

Chapter 5

Fiume's Radicals

INTRODUCTION

Part of Italian historiography has tended to downplay D'Annunzio's investment in Fiume's radical politics and in the values expressed in the *Charter*. From this perspective, his engagement with these was haphazard, contingent, or opportunistic, and his only abiding interest was to cause the collapse of Italy's parliamentary democracy and seize power in the Italian capital.[1] A more balanced view concedes that in 1919 D'Annunzio was able to respond to the unease that many youths felt with respect to the social world and cultural schemes they had inherited from previous generations. In Fiume, D'Annunzio facilitated a movement of moral and political contestation of the bourgeois social order, *Fiumanesimo*, which exceeded the poet's own contributions to it.[2] The innovative character of the *Charter* shows D'Annunzio's willingness to make his own the concerns and aspirations of those legionnaires that have come to be known in Italian scholarship as *'scalmanati'* ('unruly ones').

Among the ranks of the nationalists that had joined D'Annunzio's legionnaires there were those on the conservative Right of the political spectrum, some of whom vaguely hoped the occupation might prompt a political crisis in Italy and lead to a government of national unity.[3] Alongside them, however, there was also a substantial contingent of young national revolutionaries with more fluid and less traditional political affiliations. Nello explains that much of the generation coming of age during the war and in the years immediately preceding it felt alienated from the political institutions of the liberal state—whose uninspiring, pedestrian realities they saw as evidence that unified Italy had never realised the radical democratic aspirations of the likes of Mazzini and Garibaldi. Many of these young men also rejected the positivistic and utilitarian ethos of their fathers, to which they opposed one drawing variously on irrationalist, voluntarist, neoromantic, and neo-idealist tendencies. The experience of war fought in the name of the nation—not as a normative ideal whose value could be rationally articulated but as fact of life driving conflicts—and, specifically, the experience of trench life were deemed to have brought about a spiritual renewal that emphasised heroic virtues, inter-class solidarity and levelling, and democratic forms of social stratification ('democratic' because resultant from courage and skill in action rather than from accident of birth). These were to be harnessed in order to topple liberal institutions, class hierarchies, and conventional political ideologies, so as to bring to full fruition the unfinished revolution that had led to unification and to purge Italian society from all that was holding it back in the international contest for national greatness. Many youths who were drawn to this vision—whether they had fought in the war or had felt cheated by their young age of their chance to do so—enthusiastically flocked to Fiume, finding D'Annunzio's vitriol against the Versailles powers as resonant with their convictions as the libertarianism of the *Charter* congenial to their sentiments and heartily responding to D'Annunzio's rituality of power.[4]

This chapter provides an overview of sundry radical and subversive forces at large in D'Annunzio's Fiume. Without an appreciation of these forces, it is difficult to grasp how profoundly different D'Annunzio's occupation was from the Italian occupation that preceded it, between November 1918 and September 1919. This overview also helps put in their social and political context some of the most normatively significant and fascinating outcomes of the occupation—the League of Fiume (discussed at the end of this chapter) and the *Carnaro Charter* (to which I devote the central part of book).

RADICALS AND SUBVERSIVES

There is more than a grain of truth in Sitwell's observation, as an eyewitness, that 'in a curious way, D'Annunzio [in Fiume] united idealists with criminals'.[5] The moderate and conservative elements among the legionnaires were very concerned about, and sometime conflated, the immoral, criminal, and subversive forces present in D'Annunzio's Fiume. A good example is Major Reina, of the Sardinian Grenadiers, instigator of the Ronchi march. D'Annunzio fell out with Reina when the latter and other like-minded officers campaigned for acceptance of the *modus vivendi* and advocated the removal from D'Annunzio's side of some of his close collaborators, characterised as 'courtesans'.[6] Reina lamented the town being swamped, as he saw it, with 'adventurers', 'delinquents', degenerates', and 'undesirables' given to all manner of crime and immorality: 'from murder to theft,' he declared, 'there is no vice that is not blatantly paraded, from cocaine to pederasty'. The commandant only made things worse by 'keeping a depraved demeanour' himself.[7] Against this spectacle of criminality and immorality, Reina proudly asserted his normalcy and common sense: he was, he claimed, a simple soldier who knew trench life and wanted to give Italian people peace, unlike D'Annunzio, the war hero, with his daring flights and his eye fixed on a universal revolution.[8]

In a letter to the poet, who had sent him away from Fiume but later recalled him, Reina wrote, 'You were in favour of projects for an anarcho-militarist coup in Rome, and for this reason you protected Vecchi, Marinetti, Keller, Giunta. . . . Thankfully none of these planned follies was executed, but this is mainly thanks to those who, for many months, always tried to put the brakes on this.'[9] Indeed, about a month into the occupation, Nitti was writing to Badoglio about D'Annunzio's followers in Fiume reportedly planning an expedition to Italy.[10] A few days later, reports of the Italian military identified 'subversive elements' that had flocked to Fiume and hijacked the occupation to turn it into a movement threatening Italian political institutions and leadership.[11] General Caviglia, under whose orders the attack of the bloody Christmas was coordinated, later argued that 'Fiume's conditions of abnormality and illegality' had made it attractive to both Italian and foreign agitators and outlaws.[12] Moreover, according to Badoglio, 'many of D'Annunzio's followers outside Fiume were engaged in subversive propaganda',[13] making him conclude that 'in the Fiume enterprise, under a veneer of patriotism, lurked a veritable politics of rebellion and anti-statism'.[14]

There is truth in these reports.[15] Subversives of all political creeds did flock to Fiume. An intelligentsia of futurists, syndicalists educated *Arditi*, and others saw in D'Annunzio's occupation an opportunity to experiment with new political and social forms, and more or less vaguely aspired to use it as a launchpad for revolutionary projects of social and political renewal that were to invest Italy as a whole. These political ideologues and activists had particular sway on the volunteers who had been too young to take part in the war and had not been part of regular troops. Keller and others trained a number of these young volunteers in combat techniques and initiated them into *arditismo* (the spirit of the *Arditi*), constituting them into a special company. This was known as 'The D'Annunzio', or '*Arditi* of the Guard', or, again, '*Disperata*'—quite untranslatable, but best rendered as 'The Furious and Hopeless One' (in the feminine). This company's lack of formal military discipline and their youthful antics did much to establish the perception of Fiume as hotbed of danger and lawlessness.[16]

ARDITI

The *Arditi* of the Guard were young men initiated into *arditismo* rather than *Arditi* proper. True *Arditi*, as already mentioned, were World War I shock troops. They had been established in 1917. Many of them, who after the war had become vocal supporters of Italy's rights over both Fiume and Dalmatia,[17] enthusiastically embraced D'Annunzio's occupation. It is quite impossible to grasp the meaning of D'Annunzio's project without understanding the *arditismo* that fuelled it. In Fiume, the *Arditi*'s *eclát* far exceeded their relatively small numbers, and the other legionnaire corps found inspiration in their distinctively swaggering style.[18]

Being an *Ardito* during wartime was a risky affair: one out of five would lose their life in combat.[19] The *Arditi* took (and were widely given) credit for turning the tide during the war effort and making Italy's victory possible after the 'shameful' defeat of Caporetto. As a military 'aristocracy' enjoying certain privileges in exchange for their willingness to perform suicidal (in some cases in the literal sense of the word) surprise attacks, they had grown deeply invested in warfare as a way of life and had difficulty adjusting to the prospect of a return to the commonplace and drab realities of postwar life. Because of the way in which the experience of war had become a cardinal source of meaning in their life, the *Arditi* were deeply polemical towards 'defeatist' neutralism and its representatives—especially Socialism and the Church—as well as all draft dodgers and pacifists.[20]

At the same time, their self-understanding also involved opposition against those who had profiteered from (rather than fought in) the war—a bourgeoisie who, as they saw it, had enriched itself by exploiting the sacrifice of common men who had died for the nation. Indeed, their rhetoric tended to conflate draft dodgers and pacifists with those who had profiteered from the war, through the figures of the 'enriched draft-dodger'[21] and the neologism of '*panciafichisti*' (best rendered as 'purported pacifists who fill their bellies with figs').[22] In line with the *Arditi*'s critique of economic privilege, the postwar political programme of the *Arditi* Association included socially progressive demands such as the minimum wage, land reform, redistribution, and expropriation, alongside opposition to all dictatorships, abolition of the Upper House, introduction of divorce, and commitment to an international revolution of all 'proletarian Nations'.[23]

The *Arditi* Association came into being on 1 January 1919, after rumours had spread of plans to demobilise these corps.[24] Broadly, the *Arditi* were committed to the idea of a national revolution that would sweep away the political elite and constitutional forms of the prewar status quo and advocated the employment of assault combat techniques in civic life.[25] Their opposition to parliamentarism was grounded in the neutralist stance of the majority of members of Parliament at the outbreak of war, and the conviction that it did not represent the interventionist will of the people.[26] After Nitti replaced Orlando as Italy's prime minister, the *Arditi* threatened a revolution if a constitutional assembly failed to be called: the monarchy had exhausted its usefulness, and Nitti, they claimed, was a creature of the old system, marred by corruption and elitism.[27] It is apparent that many of these positions were well aligned with D'Annunzio's political rhetoric between 1918 and 1920. Nonetheless, the *Arditi* Association itself was mainly preoccupied with developments within Italy in 1919 and 1920 and does not appear to have contributed much to the Fiuman adventure,[28] unlike the individual *Arditi* who enlisted as legionnaires.

REVOLUTIONARY LEFT

Giulietti, a trade unionist close to Anarchist circles, founder and secretary of the Federation of Sea Workers, was one of D'Annunzio's close and most trusted associates in Fiume. His organisation had been one of the first to provide funding for the Fiume cause. On 10 October 1919, under his leadership, the *Persia* (a ship that Giulietti's federation suspected of carrying weapons intended to be used against the Bolsheviks) was seized and diverted from the Strait of Messina to Fiume. This episode marks the first apparent shift to the Left in D'Annunzio's Fiume politics—an orientation that became obvious after the appointment of De Ambris as head of D'Annunzio's cabinet.[29]

Given the youthful D'Annunzio's socialist sympathies (albeit laced with ambivalence due to his self-conscious individualism and elitism),[30] his role in enabling a movement capable of speaking to the revolutionary Left is not as unlikely as one might be inclined to believe from *clichés* about his association with fascism and nationalism. D'Annunzio openly flirted with the revolutionary Left because of its potential for subverting what he saw as the tired institutions of the liberal state.[31] At one point he went so far as to declare: 'I'm all for communism without dictatorship; no wonder, for my whole culture is anarchic. . . . I want to make of this town a spiritual island from where an eminently communist action will radiate for the liberation of all oppressed nations.'[32] In practice, however, it seems clear that D'Annunzio and De Ambris's (unsuccessful) overtures to the Socialists during the Fiuman period always envisaged a coup on their own terms. D'Annunzio showed little interest in supporting popular or workers' insurrections unless they could be brought under his own ideological direction.[33]

Antonio Gramsci is on record for defending D'Annunzio's cause against its detractors,[34] and Bombacci (who, together with Gramsci, would found the Italian Communist Party) supported it even more directly, as did the

Anarchist leader Enrico Malatesta.[35] In March 1920 D'Annunzio's emissaries in Rome were reporting that an unofficial representative of the Moscow government declined to parley with them: he was under surveillance and, in any case, had said he could not trust D'Annunzio's political showmanship and the support he attracted from nationalist and moderate forces. Having been informed, however, of the project to institute a new political order based 'on new social forms albeit unlike those of Moscow' (namely, what would be the Carnaro Regency), the Russian declared himself ready to recant his position if facts told against his own prejudices.[36] Lenin himself, reportedly, stated that Italian Communists should have appropriated the Fiume cause and used it to prompt a revolution of the proletariat in Italy, for D'Annunzio was the only revolutionary force in Italy.[37]

Republicans—an interventionist party then at the extreme Left of the political spectrum—had also immediately responded to Fiume's self-determination aspirations in 1918. While there was no consensus among Republicans on their assessment of D'Annunzio's occupation, there were many of them in D'Annunzio's legions. Many Republicans in Italy also applauded the proclamation of the regency (despite their disappointment at the failure expressly to style it a 'republic')[38] and fully approved of the content of the *Charter*.[39]

Within two years of the bloody Christmas, the credentials of *Fiumanesimo*—whose legacy was being perpetuated in De Ambris's anti-Fascist National Federation of Fiume Legionnaires[40]—with both the Socialist and Communist Left became apparent. Communists' and Socialists' overtures to the poet sought to bridge the rift caused by the war between interventionists and neutralists, with the goal—never realised—of creating a broad anti-Fascist movement that would have D'Annunzio as its spiritual leader.[41]

FUTURISTS

The urge to shake the status quo, which was characteristic of both *Fiumanesimo* and Bolshevism, also permeated other more or less contemporaneous political movements, including futurism.[42] The futurists had been proudly interventionist, seeing war and bloodshed as an opportunity for sweeping away the decay of Western civilization and for engendering its rebirth,[43] and had been courting the *Arditi* as a potentially formidable destabilising political force.[44] They championed a political praxis based on action and daredevilry, on (in their words) 'violence and courage', rejecting rationalism, deliberation, and dialogue.[45] Their political programme was a mixture of libertarianism, anti-socialism, anti-clericalism, economic liberalism tempered by workers' rights, nationalism, imperialism in foreign affairs, militarism, opposition to classical education and the cult of antiquity, and championing technophilia, technical education, progress, and innovation.[46]

An official Futurist Party was founded in 1918. The party intended to demolish all that smacked of tradition and the past and to create the conditions for new ways of life and new modes of thinking, but it also committed itself to concrete political demands that brought it close to the revolutionary Left. These included expropriation of poorly cultivated lands and future socialisation of the land, high taxation on capital gains, freedom to take strike action and to associate, and the minimum wage.[47] Even before forming into a party, the futurists had distributed their manifesto widely among the *Arditi*, and they in turn had assisted the establishment of the Futurist Party.[48] Largely populated by well-educated men and intellectuals, the Futurist Party quickly came to hold sway over the *Arditi*, whose class background and educational attainment was more diverse.[49]

The futurists held out the *Arditi* as paragons of the new man. Futurist Mario Carli had been the founder of the *Arditi* Association, and in 1919 the demarcation between (political) futurism and *arditismo* was not easy to draw.[50] Carli—who rejected 'mediocre common sense' as a basis for action and advocated imposing by dint of 'fists and stabs the beauty of an original image'[51]—claimed that, with their irreverence, free use of violence, and opposition to hierarchy, the *Arditi* represented the quintessential futurists.[52]

Because of his subversive propaganda, Carli had been under arrest when D'Annunzio occupied Fiume but he managed to escape and join the occupants.[53] In his 1920 book *In Fiume with D'Annunzio*, he declared, with more than a little of the futurists' trademark self-consciousness: 'To the young town . . . I brought my futurist virility and decisiveness, which saw in Fiume a luminous anticipation of what is to become, my joyful and colourful aggressiveness, the spirit of a new humanity, rebellious and imaginative, which went to cling to the edge of the Carnaro to take off and conquer Italy and the world.'[54]

Himself a member of the *Arditi*, Carli admired Lenin[55] and actively sought to join forces with Fascism,[56] Socialism,[57] and Bolshevism.[58] In Fiume he published a magazine (*La Testa di Ferro*) in which he openly conversed with Anarchists and professed Bolshevik sympathies.[59]

Marinetti, the controversial founder of futurism who a decade before the occupation had decried D'Annunzio's decadent sensibility, aestheticism, and romanticism as the antithesis of his own movement—similarly applauded the occupation and made his way to Fiume in September 1919.[60] He is reported to have led a demonstration of 'hundreds of shirtless soldiers' when, a few weeks into the occupation, the Italian Parliament had reiterated Fiume's Italian identity but fallen short of declaring its annexation.[61] Marinetti's stay was short—he was expelled, according to Badoglio, because of his 'excessive republican propaganda'.[62] His radical political views clashed with the mainstream conservatism of legionnaires such as Reina, a feud that threatened to erupt into public disturbances.[63] But the problem was also that Marinetti and his collaborator Vecchi—who saw D'Annunzio as politically naïve and soft on traitors—had come to Fiume to recruit the legionnaires for their own political objectives and to carry out exploits of their own.[64] According to Serventi Longhi, the main problem was Marinetti's and Vecchi's histrionic personalities, which sought to overshadow emergent leaders within the legionnaires' community, also tending to undermine D'Annunzio's own hold on it.[65]

Carli too—who had been previously asked by the command to tone down his propaganda[66]—was asked to leave Fiume in the summer of 1920.[67] The command was then keenly aware of the need not to further alienate more moderate and conservative elements in Fiume, particularly given the change in leadership of the Italian government. An agreement with Giolitti seemed possible at this time: not only was he more amenable than his predecessor to the nationalist designs in the Adriatic that mattered to D'Annunzio, but he was also seeking to exploit for his own purposes (namely, containing workers' agitations) the very nationalist zeal of ex-servicemen that the Fiume occupation had glamourised.[68] Under these circumstances, Carli's extremist and republican views were a liability.[69]

Both Marinetti and Carli, in any case, left Fiume with a keener awareness of the revolutionary potential of having artists in charge of government.[70] Carli even envisaged that D'Annunzio might become president of Italy once the republican form of government had been adopted and contemplated that the constitutional laws passed in Fiume during the occupation might be extended, *mutatis mutandis*, to Italy.[71]

FASCISTS

Mussolini also visited D'Annunzio in Fiume.[72] He was among those who had promised D'Annunzio men and funds to support the Fiume expedition and occupation and would be reprimanded by the poet for failing to do so. In Fiume they probably discussed a project foreshadowed in a letter sent by Mussolini two weeks earlier, envisaging a *coup d'état* in Italy, which would overthrow the monarchy, followed by elections for a Constituent Assembly. Nothing, however, came of this. Mussolini—an aspiring politician with a party to grow—would quickly realise that it was more expedient for him to preserve, rather than dismantle, the outer institutional forms of the status quo.[73]

Initially Mussolini's dynamic movement (with its declared sympathy for the Fiume cause, its socially progressive political programme,[74] and its lack of dogmatism over Dalmatia) had struck De Ambris as a natural ally.[75] As De Ambris himself noted, the original political programme of Mussolini's *Fasci* appeared progressive inasmuch as it included abolishing Italy's anachronistic Upper House, summoning a Constituent Assembly, setting up National Labour Councils with legislative powers, introducing the minimum wage and the eight-hour working day, establishing workers' control over the industrial sector, managing public services by capable workers' associations, improving social laws, instituting a national Army with purely defensive functions relying on short national service, partially expropriating wealth, and carrying out wholesale expropriation of the goods of religious congregations.[76] Shortly after the declaration of the regency in September 1920, De Ambris was therefore hoping that Mussolini's Fascists—who at the time were still officially antimonarchical—could play a role as armed militias in the progressive revolutionary movement he was seeking to launch from Fiume. This would be a popular and military mobilisation that would have as its leader D'Annunzio—the only man, for De Ambris, capable of uniting disparate classes and sectors of society. The *Charter* would be the movement's manifesto, and revolution in Italy would be its goal.

But Mussolini effectively derailed the plan. Indeed, the promulgation of the *Charter* had caused an ideological rift between Mussolini and D'Annunzio, though the former took care to disguise it for a time. By this time Mussolini had seen that his opportunities lay to the Right: in the latter half of 1920, his movement turned reactionary, at the same time as D'Annunzio's political project in Fiume had become more radical. Fascists would soon receive funds from land and factory owners to violently crush disorders caused by widespread protests and occupations carried out by workers, who had felt emboldened by the winds of change blowing in from Russia, and were supported by maximalist Socialists.[77]

De Ambris made further unsuccessful attempts to convert Mussolini and his forces to a progressive revolutionary project in December.[78] By that time, however, Mussolini favoured the Rapallo Treaty and had become an informer of the Italian government on Fiume.[79] Foscanelli, who was acting as minute taker at a meeting between Mussolini and De Ambris, testifies to Mussolini's manifest lack of interest and reports that at the end of a tense meeting he was instructed by agreement of the interlocutors to destroy the record.[80] It is not surprising, therefore, that the Fascists also failed to mobilise in support of D'Annunzio during the bloody Christmas.[81] D'Annunzio, who had accepted a Fascist Party card in 1920, when Mussolini had signified his full support for the Fiuman cause,[82] never renewed it thereafter.[83]

Before D'Annunzio left for Italy, at De Ambris's instigation he instructed all legionnaire officers that they should constitute themselves into an association that would take the *Charter* as its political programme, refusing to entertain any relationship with the 'traitors' of Fiume.[84] The expression was intended to apply to Mussolini's Fascists, if no one else. This became obvious in the explicitly anti-Fascist stance adopted by De Ambris's soon-to-be-constituted National Federation of Fiume Legionnaires.[85] As late as 7 April 1921 D'Annunzio was still giving Mussolini the benefit of the doubt and wrote to De Ambris telling him that the Fascist leader had assured him he was supportive of the *Charter* principles.[86] But a little over one month later the poet, commenting on De Ambris's candidature in Parma, praised his 'wise nostrils', which had 'smelt the corruption of death' and kept him from tying himself to 'dead men'. By this D'Annunzio meant that De Ambris had insisted on not participating in the so-called national block, which had seen Mussolini join forces with Giolitti's Liberals during the elections to oppose the forces of the Left.[87] By this time, De Ambris had fully persuaded both himself and D'Annunzio that Mussolini was irredeemably on the side of the forces of reaction.[88] In 1922 D'Annunzio was privately decrying the savagery and violence of Fascist thugs,[89] for all that many ex-legionnaires took part in Mussolini's march on Rome that year.[90]

Guido Keller's relationship with Fascism is instructive, if not necessarily emblematic, of the complex and contradictory entanglements between Mussolini's movement and D'Annunzio's Fiume legionnaires. In July 1922 Keller was writing to D'Annunzio that he found 'Mussolini's dead calf's head' chilling.[91] Yet later that year he was raving about how 'Fiume's aristocratic myth, once disciplined within the Roman legions, gave forth the miracle'. He revealed to D'Annunzio that he had been covertly involved in the march on Rome; that he was now being openly courted to become a member of the Combat Squads (the Fascist Party's armed militias); that other high-profile legionnaires, such as Host-Venturi and Colseschi, were also becoming involved with the party; and that he now intended to claim his place in the sun.[92]

In the same letter Keller also asked D'Annunzio, in cryptic terms, to lend his public support for the regime: 'I await your Ordinance. . . . Orpheus's lyre remains dumb. Or Calypso has bewitched the daring companions?' At the time of receiving this letter D'Annunzio had pointedly avoided—and, thereafter, would consistently continue to avoid—putting his oratorial and artistic skills (Orpheus's lyre) at the service of Mussolini and his movement. Keller's reference to Calypso, the nymph that, through her charms, detained Odysseus from his journey back to Ithaca for seven years, seems an allusion to D'Annunzio's deliberate (and splendid) seclusion at the Vittoriale after the closing of the Fiume adventure. D'Annunzio was clearly less than enthused by Keller's news in this letter, and exactly nine months later Keller was writing to him to announce his journey to Turkey, having 'left Rome in accordance with the warnings in your letters'.[93] Despite this, D'Annunzio did not take as clear and public a stand against Mussolini and Fascism as he should have, and as he might have if the movement had not kept making public professions of devotion to him.[94]

By December 1922 Mussolini's head of police had instructed all provincial prefects to repress the activities of 'anarchic' organisations guilty of public order disturbances in D'Annunzio's name.[95] In 1924 De Ambris declared that the 'dead and the inevitable atrocities of every revolution can be justified only if the revolution is truly one', bringing about new institutions and a new moral order. This the Fascist leader had failed to do,[96] having found the old bourgeois constitutional structures quite congenial to his own political project.[97] De Ambris and his National Federation of Fiume Legionnaires, as well as D'Annunzio's own appeals, did much to discourage the *Arditi* from being lured into Fascism after the Futurist Party had been dissolved, with mixed results.[98]

In 1924, after the Federation of Fiume's Legionnaires itself resisted absorption into Fascism, *carabineri* were dispatched to its congress (held in Ronchi) to intimidate federation members and coerce them to abandon their unorthodox political positions.[99] The federation, which had already allied itself with the *Arditi* Association, then merged with it under the name of Dannunzian Spiritual Union (while dissident *Arditi* created the Right-wing National Federation of Italy's *Arditi*, aligned with Fascism).[100] The Dannunzian Spiritual Union, taking note of D'Annunzio's intention to withdraw from politics, declared to find inspiration in his thought rather than his person and started organising as a clandestine association in the face of increasing Fascist repression.[101] The fact that D'Annunzio (at a time when the regime continued to celebrate him and to accede to his financial requests to pacify him) had been one of 250 signatories of Giovanni Gentile's 1925 *Fascist Intellectuals' Manifesto Addressed to Intellectuals of All Nations*[102] must have done nothing to reassure the union. While the manifesto made much of individual rights and freedom, the union knew from their own experience that the reality under Fascism was a very different one. By 1926 the Dannunzian Spiritual Union had been stifled alongside all other anti-Fascist organizations.[103]

FIUMANESIMO AND COUNTERCULTURE

We have seen that the military accounts stress the activist and more deliberate aspects of the legionnaires' subversive politics around the time of the occupation. But concentrating on these alone may give a misleading impression. At Fiume there were, certainly, radical political activists. But D'Annunzio's followers also included many legionnaires who simply disengaged from Italian political institutions and leadership; those whom the experience of war had left with a diffuse sense of unease about returning to normal life, or to a world they had inherited from their fathers but did not feel as their own; [104] and those who had come to despise all forms of constituted order and prudential virtues.[105] For these, Fiume may have represented a righteous cause that spoke to their inchoate sense of justice and to their desire to contest the status quo. But it was also, and perhaps mainly, a prized, once-in-a-lifetime opportunity to experiment with, or prolong beyond the end of the war, forms of life that were not possible during the ordinary social order of peacetime.

Carli lamented that the vast majority of legionnaires failed to grasp what *Fiumanesimo* was all about;[106] but we might as well say that *Fiumanesimo*, in addition to a set of definite and coherent political coordinates, was a diffused and heterogenous mood of oppositional and unconventional stances, which a much larger number of legionnaires than Fiume's intellectual and political *avant-garde* contributed to define. Some elements making up this mood were libertarianism, utopistic aspirations to abolish work, unorthodox takes on Catholicism, a gift ethics replacing market logics, the myth of the Orient, anticolonial solidarity in opposition to Anglo-American imperialism, cult of youth, and a devaluation of the quotidian.[107]

This mood of contestation of the status quo easily took the form of trashing both constituted power and bourgeois morality and making merry in the process.[108] D'Annunzio encouraged this iconoclastic and playful attitude, among other things by using disrespectful nicknames for his opponents in his public speeches. Nitti was, as we know, 'Cagoia'; Giolitti was *'boia labbrone'* ('thick-lipped executioner'); and Caviglia was *'Chiunque il quale'* ('Whoever that'—from a grammatical mishap in one of the general's written announcements he had sent around in Fiume). Salaris notes that such moves on D'Annunzio's part were continuous with those of contemporaneous artistic *avant-gardes*, such as the Dada Club's pictorial ridiculing of political and military hierarchies.[109]

D'Annunzio, of course, had also made a career of preaching the virtues of overman-ism and rule breaking for the gifted and daring. And according to the town's religious authorities, his delusions of grandeur were perilously infectious.[110] A manifestation of *Fiumanesimo*, then, was also a commitment to certain lifestyle choices, such as sexual freedom (already, in its heterosexual form, a rallying cry of futurism).[111] Some of the high-profile personalities that joined D'Annunzio in Fiume, such as Marinetti, were ideologically committed to free love and the abolition of marriage.[112] But for most legionnaires it was a matter of practice rather than theory. All the sources seem to agree that sex was rife in town during the occupation,[113] in part because the young women of Fiume enjoyed comparative freedom, characteristic of Central European secular port towns.[114] The inherent precarity of the occupation must have also created a general mood of impending change that encouraged risk taking; and the deprivations of the war, coupled with the town being flooded with young soldiers, no doubt also favoured the emergence of a market in sexual services.

Free sex was accompanied by drug use, partying, unconventional military attires, theatrics, nudism, cult of the body, gambling, etc.[115] Not even the local religious communities were immune, with a group of Capuchin monks unsuccessfully petitioning for the abolition of celibacy.[116] The pro-Yugoslav press was quick to rhetorically exploit this state of affairs, condemning the degeneracy of D'Annunzio and his legionnaires, stereotyped as criminally inclined southern Italians, unrestrained by law and morals, and intent on savagely 'raping' the town.[117] British military sources also reported that 'official dinners given to D'Annunzio in Fiume were followed by considerable debauchery, during which much damage had been done to property'. They gave credit to hearsay to the effect that the legionnaires lived 'very luxuriously, requisitioning whatever they wanted from private individuals' (certainly a false rumour, as far as the bulk of the body of legionnaires was concerned), and that businesses paid 'the most extortionate taxes . . . levied at random, and chiefly on those who opposed the annexation.'[118] Amidst such exaggerated reports, Fiume became a mecca for all manner of 'dreamers, libertarians and idealists'.[119]

Fiume's counterculture found expression not only in individual lifestyle choices but in the creative, and often humorous, solutions the command or the legionnaires found to logistical problems they were facing—ranging from day-to-day concerns (such as transportation and supply of goods) to more strategic questions (such as maximising propaganda for the Fiume cause).[120] Here acts that mainstream normative orders classify as illegal or immoral were resignified as permissible, praiseworthy, and heroic. Thus, the legionnaires did not hesitate to mitigate the effects of the blockade through acts of piracy,[121] as well as raids on the supplies of Italian troops stationed in the area surrounding the town. On one memorable occasion, the legionnaires seized forty-six horses from a military stable and returned an equal number of underfed ones.[122] These stunts were organised by the *Coup de Main* Office, created as a division within D'Annunzio's already mentioned special secretariat.[123] Indeed, such theatrics might be the very means by which membership of the legionnaire community was sought: Martini reports that a group of *Arditi*, 'armed with goodwill', had managed to join the occupation by pretending to be in distress at sea and proceeding to hijack a vessel at gunpoint.[124]

This is all consistent with the fact that the logic of the whole enterprise—for all its initial backing by powerful military and industrial networks—was, from its inception, one of resistance to officially constituted power structures. As we know, General Pittaluga had the command of the Allied troops in Fiume at the time of D'Annunzio's advance into town at the head of his legionnaires in September 1919. Choosing to let D'Annunzio through essentially unopposed, despite clear orders to the contrary, the general addressed the Fiumans with the following words: 'There are moments that are superior to any order and any Government, and this is one of those moments'. Susmel commented, 'It is official Italy that gives way to the Italy of Garibaldi.'[125]

THE LEAGUE OF FIUME

One of the most interesting political initiatives to emerge from this climate of oppositional politics was the League of Fiume—or, in the words of Toeplitz (from D'Annunzio's Office of Exterior Relations), *'l'Anti-Société des Nations'*. This aimed to unite all oppressed peoples around the world and is reputed to have given Wilson three sleepless nights.[126] The League of Fiume is argued to have been the first time the Third World had become involved in a flurry of intense diplomatic activity (albeit short lived and ultimately unsuccessful) to coordinate a global movement of liberation from colonial rule.[127]

The main driving force behind the league was Léon Kotchnitzky, musician and man of letters, Soviet sympathiser, and determined not to let the occupation be hijacked by reactionary nationalists.[128] Kotchnitzky was a fierce critic of all enemies of D'Annunzio's cause, from reformist Socialists ready to collaborate with the Liberal mainstream to the Italian political, bureaucratic, and military establishment.[129] But his most impassioned opposition was directed against the 'pseudo-League of Nations', 'this funny and powerless academy, with its well-paid sinecures',[130] which he believed to be but a tool for 'Capitalist states' to assert and reinforce their global hegemony. Prime among these states—whose financial and colonial interests had dictated the exclusion of Russia and Germany from the League[131]—was Britain, whose imperial rule over Ireland, Egypt, and India Kotchnitzky vocally denounced.[132]

Arriving in Fiume in late autumn 1919 in order to interview D'Annunzio for *Independence Belge*,[133] Kotchnitzky became D'Annunzio's minister for exterior relations (an office formally instituted only in January 1920, but which had been operative since the previous November).[134] Kotchnitzky's vision was to unite all oppressed peoples against powerful economic and imperialistic forces. 'Oppressed peoples' encompassed those of Europe (Dalmatians, Croats, Catalans, the Irish, German populations under foreign rule, etc.), through the Muslim world (Algeria, Egypt, Palestine, Afghanistan, etc.), to the Asia-Pacific and elsewhere (India, China, Hawaii, Puerto Rico, etc.), as well as oppressed races (the Chinese in California and Blacks in the United States) and countries unfairly treated by the negotiations in Paris (from Russia and Germany, through Siam and Turkey, to the Vatican).[135] Fiume, as a Latin and Western town strategically positioned on the threshold of the Slav and Muslim Orient, was ideally placed to take centre stage in this initiative.[136] In March 1920 Kotchnitzky proposed to D'Annunzio the constitution of a 'League of Fiume' in the form of an international association under D'Annunzio's personal leadership, with no connection to either D'Annunzio's command in Fiume or to the National Council. The role of the league would be to promulgate the new moral and political doctrine known as *Fiumanesimo* to 'the whole universe', in part because the Fiumans and legionnaires themselves were not morally, politically, and intellectually ready to work towards its realisation and would sometimes even attempt to thwart it.[137]

The diversion of the *Persia* and its cargo to Fiume had already given D'Annunzio an opportunity to remark on how Fiume and other movements of national liberation shared similar goals.[138] Not long afterwards—and well before Kotchnitzky proposed the formal constitution of the league in the spring of 1920—D'Annunzio declared, in a speech to the population of Fiume, that he aimed to unite under a single banner 'all the insurrections of the spirit against those who devour raw flesh and milk helpless people'. He singled out the British empire as the most egregious example: 'the voracious empire that has appropriated Persia, Mesopotamia, the new Arabia, much of Africa, and is never sated . . . the greedy empire that eyes Constantinople, that conceals its possession of at least one third of China's vast lands, that acquires all the islands south of the Equator with enormous riches, and is never sated'.[139] On that occasion he referred to the Fiume cause as 'the greatest and the most beautiful that is today opposed to a deranged and cowardly world. Today [that cause] . . . embraces white folks and peoples of colour; it reconciles the New Testament and the Quran'.[140] The oration prompted Martini to claim that Fiume had become the symbol of 'all the sacred revolts against the absurdities, calculations, and bullying clearly expressed in the Paris Conference.'[141]

At this time, however, the idea was not yet to constitute a formal league as such—D'Annunzio rather spoke of a 'wholly new crusade'.[142] Alongside idealistic motivations, it seems clear that the poet was alive to the political expediency of rhetoric about a movement of global liberation, hoping that it might facilitate the goal of Fiume's annexation. Well before discourse on the League of Fiume became part of his propaganda, D'Annunzio had written to Badoglio (in what appears to be a case of wishful thinking) that Britain was relenting in its opposition to Fiume's annexation because it feared that 'our sparks will light the fires of revolt in Egypt, in Arabia, in India, and that they will exasperate the Irish Sinn Fein.'[143]

After Kotchnitzky's proposal in March 1920 that this movement of liberation should be organised and led by a formally constituted league, D'Annunzio started his propaganda in favour of the nascent organization, contrasting it with the League of Nations—a 'plot of brigands and privileged swindlers'.[144] In the spring of 1920 many delegates of various groups from around the world met with the command in Fiume or its emissaries in Italy.[145] The three main lines of activity that the office entrusted with coordinating the league pursued were to create an international movement of resistance against Britain (through networking with Egypt and Ireland), to challenge the League of Nations (with the assistance of Hungarian Bolsheviks and Turks), and to undermine the Yugoslav state and Serbia's hegemony within it.[146]

The league, however, quickly floundered. This was due to a failure to secure the necessary funding, to political reasons (for example, some purported members of the league were not disposed to treat the United States as an enemy), and to D'Annunzio's need to navigate the treacherous ideological divisions in Fiume itself.[147] Not only did the National Council and some legionnaires look askance at the command's turn to the Left, but, specifically, Kotchnitzky's determination to work with Hungarian Bolsheviks was met with opposition.[148] The radical rhetoric of the Exterior Relations Office also hindered negotiations with the Italian government for a solution to the Fiume crisis.[149]

Kotchnitzky resigned in early July,[150] when a rapprochement was taking place between the poet and the more moderate and conservative elements among Fiume's legionnaires, including Giurati. D'Annunzio's internationalist idealism lost ground to a political realism that made him willing to instrumentalise the league chiefly in the service of regional goals, seeking to form a coalition of Balkan states opposed to Serbia's hegemony, with a view to weakening the newly born state of Yugoslavia.[151] Interestingly, as early as April 1920 Kotchnitzky had already foreseen that without the willingness and means to develop the league into a global affair, it might only serve local purposes in the Balkans.[152]

When he resigned, on the pretext of sickness, Kotchnitzky also alluded to the change in the command's foreign policy: if for a time it had not been useless to have a foreigner such as him head the Exterior Relations Office, this was no longer so, and Fiume's propaganda should now change to better reflect concerns that were essentially national.[153] Concrete efforts had been ongoing within the command since early 1920 to support, specifically, Croat nationalists based outside Fiume in their efforts to sabotage the creation of the new pan-South Slav state with Serbia and Slovenia.[154] It was, according to De Felice, partly because the Treaty of Rapallo made this prospect of anti-Serbian revolution evaporate that D'Annunzio resisted it.[155] In any case, the command's anti-Serbian plots in the Balkans turned out to be no more successful than the anti-imperialist internationalist project dear to Kotchnitzky.[156]

Given the speedy floundering of *l'Anti-Société des Nations*, it is legitimate to ask whether D'Annunzio was ever genuinely committed to it. His fervent nationalism, in particular, could be taken as evidence that his adherence to Kotchnitzky's project was merely opportunistic, for it seems hard to reconcile with the internationalist spirit of the League of Fiume. But nationalism comes in many forms, including anticolonial ones,[157] with which it might be argued D'Annunzio's brand of nationalism had something in common. Apart from this, we must recall D'Annunzio's longstanding claim that Italy's distinctive genius, and hope for redemption, lay in her devotion to beauty,[158] and how his brand of imperialism maintained that force was justified to the extent that it was generative of beauty.[159] This belief was echoed in the pages of the magazine of the Fiume-based association Yoga (founded by Guido Keller and Giovanni Comisso). Here, too, the Latin race was recurrently credited with being the repository of spiritual and aesthetic values, in contrast with the philistinism of much of the rest of Europe.[160] The preoccupation with fostering spiritual values and with the ennobling valence of art was also present among the futurists.[161] In short, the version of nationalism that D'Annunzio and Fiume's intellectual elite insisted on was based on a claim to Italian culture's privileged access to higher and nonmaterialistic values. Who, then, would be better placed than a spiritually renovated Italy to lead the insurrection of all oppressed people against the deadening and philistine forces of capitalistic imperialism? This explains how a nationalistic vision of Latin grandeur could, in Fiume, be reconciled with the internationalistic logic of a global revolution—or the paradox, to use Leeden's words, of D'Annunzio becoming 'one of the first leaders of what we call today the Third World revolution . . . in the name of his own peculiar brand of cultural imperialism.'[162]

CONCLUSIONS

The startling confluence of sundry revolutionary and subversive forces in D'Annunzio's Fiume was made possible in part by the plasticity and capacity of his political thought. This confluence, in turn, contributed to the climate that made such projects as the League of Fiume and the *Charter* thinkable and possible, if not ultimately successful.

In his biography of the poet, Woodhouse claims that D'Annunzio treated Kotchnitzky's 'wild dreams as such'.[163] Bonadeo seems to come closer to understanding D'Annunzio's psychology, where he remarks that the idea of the league naturally and irresistibly appealed to the poet. Like the war, and like the Fiume endeavour itself, the league offered him a unique opportunity to make his life conform with the spiritual and transcendental values he aspired to—it 'both inspired and held out the promise for a heroic struggle'.[164] As Leeden argues, the league in fact 'was of a piece with the design of the

Republic of the Carnaro', as both involved a commitment to forces and principles of the radical Left.[165]

D'Annunzio saw the league and the regency as two sides of the same coin. This can be garnered from a long speech he delivered in September 1922, in which he quoted freely from his Fiuman oratory. In the speech D'Annunzio reminisces about the foreign delegates that came to Fiume to discuss the league, the 'men of remote lineages [who] increased the capacity of my bosom and the agility of my thought.'[166] He also recalls his address to the Fiumans on the eve of the declaration of the regency, where his emphasis had been as much on what the constitution of Fiume into a sovereign entity would do for the town itself as on how it would galvanise a movement of global resistance. The commandant on that occasion had encouraged the town to look past its limited, self-regarding horizon and to embrace its destiny as a beacon for all oppressed nations, from Montenegro through Egypt to Ireland:

> And you yourselves will not see [your own light]? And you, who are in communion with numberless multitudes shaken by the self-same spasm, you think you can shrink yourselves to your 'corpus separatum'. . . . Dare [instead] to establish here . . . the ways of the new spirit, the new forms of life, an order of justice and freedom according to the inspiration of the past and divination of the future.[167]

The next chapter will analyse in detail what these 'ways of the new spirit', these 'new forms of life', and this forward- as well as backward-looking 'order of justice and freedom' consisted in, as envisaged in the *Carnaro Charter*.

NOTES

1. Paolo Alatri, "La Storiografia sull'Impresa Dannunziana a Fiume," in *D'Annunzio e il Suo Tempo*, vol. 1, ed. Francesco Perfetti (Genova: Sagep, 1989), 25–26.
2. Renzo De Felice, *D'Annunzio Politico, 1918–1938* (Roma and Bari: Laterza, 1978), xi.
3. Renzo De Felice, "Introduzione," in *Sindacalismo Rivoluzionario e Fiumanesimo nel Carteggio De Ambris—D'Annunzio*, ed. Renzo De Felice (Brescia: Morcelliana, 1966), 63.
4. Paolo Nello, "Natura e Funzione del Mito Dannunziano del Primo Fascismo," in *D'Annunzio e il Suo Tempo*, ed. Perfetti, 141–49.
5. Osbert Sitwell, *Discursions on Travel, Art and Life* (London: Grant Richards, 1925), 234.

6. Roberto Chiarini, "L'Impresa di Fiume nelle Carte del Maggiore Carlo Reina," in *D'Annunzio Politico: Atti del Convegno (Il Vittoriale, 9–10 Ottobre 1985)*, ed. Renzo De Felice and Pietro Gibellini (Milano: Garzanti, 1987), 55–56.

7. Quoted in Chiarini, "L'Impresa di Fiume," 53.

8. Chiarini, "L'Impresa di Fiume," 61.

9. Quoted in Nino Valeri, *Da Giolitti a Mussolini: Momenti della Crisi del Liberalismo* (Firenze: Parenti, 1957), 52–53. Incidentally, there is more than little irony in Reina's complaining about D'Annunzio's 'protecting' Keller, given Keller's own advocacy in Reina's defence, recorded by Kotchnitzky. Léon Kotchnitzky, *La Quinta Stagione: O, I Centauri di Fiume*, trans. Alberto Luchini (Bologna: Zanichelli, 1922), 176–77.

10. Letters from F. S. Nitti to General P. Badoglio (10 October 1919), in Pietro Badoglio, *Rivelazioni su Fiume* (Roma: Donatello de Luigi, 1946), 195–96 (documents 39 and 40 in the appendix).

11. De Felice, *D'Annunzio Politico*, 31–32 (citing at length Nunes Franco's report).

12. Quoted in De Felice, *D'Annunzio Politico*, 24.

13. Badoglio, *Rivelazioni*, 69.

14. Badoglio, *Rivelazioni*, 68.

15. At one point D'Annunzio had two legionnaires arrested who were planning to kill Nitti. Michael A. Leeden, *The First Duce* (Baltimore and London: John Hopkins University Press, 1977), 97.

16. Kotchnitzky, *La Quinta Stagione*, 66–67; Federico C. Simonelli, "La Costruzione di un Mito: Rituali, Simboli e Narrazioni dell'Impresa di Fiume (1919–1921)" (PhD diss., Universita' degli Studi di Urbino Carlo Bo, 2014–2015), 49, 146, 200, https://ora.uniurb.it/bitstream/11576/2630991/1/phd_uniurb_257536.pdf.

17. Ferdinando Cordova, *Arditi e Legionari Dannunziani* (Padova: Marsilio, 1969), 40–41.

18. Kotchnitzky, *La Quinta Stagione*, 65.

19. Günter Berghaus, *Futurism and Politics: Between Anarchist Rebellion and Fascist Reaction 1909–1944* (Providence, MA, and Oxford: Berghahn, 1996), 101.

20. Cordova, *Arditi e Legionari Dannunziani*, 13, 15.

21. Cordova, *Arditi e Legionari Dannunziani*, 50 (expression lifted from an article in *l'Ardito* [3 August 1919]).

22. Cordova, *Arditi e Legionari Dannunziani*, 13.

23. Mario Carli, "Associazione fra gli Arditi d'Italia: Programma e Statuto del Dopoguerra," art. 3, in Cordova, *Arditi e Legionari*, 217–21.

24. Cordova, *Arditi e Legionari Dannunziani*, 13–14.

25. Simonelli, "La Costruzione di un Mito," 145, 215.

26. Cordova, *Arditi e Legionari Dannunziani*, 18.

27. Cordova, *Arditi e Legionari Dannunziani*, 41–42.

28. Cordova, *Arditi e Legionari Dannunziani*, 51.

29. Leeden, *The First Duce*, 116–17; Guglielmo Salotti, "I Rapporti D'Annunzio-Giulietti: Dall''Idillio Fiumano' al 'Pactum Sine Nominem'," in *D'Annunzio Politico: Atti del Convegno*, ed. De Felice and Gibellini, 23; Badoglio, *Rivelazioni*, 68–69.

30. Jared M. Becker, *Nationalism and Culture: Gabriele D'Annunzio and Italy after the Risorgimento* (New York: Peter Lang, 1994), 39–41. Even as a teenager, D'Annunzio's poetry showed a preoccupation with poverty and the working classes. Alessandro Agrí, "Gabriele D'Annunzio e l'Ora Sociale: Dalla Carta del Carnaro al Patto Marino (1920–1924)," in *D'Annunzio Legislatore: Costituzioni, Visioni, Utopie dell'Impresa Fiumana*, ed. Giordano Bruno Guerri (Milano: Silvana Editoriale, 2022), 142.

31. Serge Noiret, "Les Communistes, D'Annunzio et l'Entourage Dannunzien (1921–1922)," in *D'Annunzio e il Suo Tempo*, ed. Perfetti, 200.

32. De Felice, *D'Annunzio Politico*, 61 (quoting D'Annunzio's words, as reported in a letter from R. Vella, published in *L'Umanitá Nuova* [9 June 1920]).

33. Compare Federico Carlo Simonelli, "L'Ordinamento dell'Esercito Liberatore: Una Rilettura," in *D'Annunzio Legislatore*, ed. Guerri, 126.

34. Claudia Salaris, *Alla Festa della Rivoluzione: Artisti e Libertari con D'Annunzio a Fiume* (Bologna: Il Mulino, 2002), 66.

35. Paolo Simoncelli, Relazione, in *Lo Statuto della Reggenza Italiana del Carnaro tra Storia, Diritto Internazionale e Diritto Costituzionale*, ed. Augusto Sinagra (Milano: Giuffré, 2009), 42.

36. Léon Kotchnitzky and Giovanni Bonmartini, Report of Activities with the Representatives of the Republic of Russian Soviets CPPC (14 March 1920), Fondazione Il Vittoriale degli Italiani, Archivio Fiumano, Kotchnitzky, Léon, 1–129.

37. Salaris, *Alla Festa della Rivoluzione*, 41.

38. Paolo Cavassini, "I Repubblicani e la Questione Fiumana tra 'Diciannovismo' e Intransigenza: Appunti per una Ricostruzione," in *Fiume 1919–2019: Un Centenario Europeo tra Identitá, Memorie e Prospettive di Ricerca*, ed. Giordano Bruno Guerri (Milano: Silvania Editoriale, 2020).

39. Guglielmo Salotti, "Nuovi Studi sulla Carta del Carnaro," *Fiume: Rivista di Studi Fiumani* XIX–XX (1973–1974): 89.

40. Noiret, "Les Communistes," 234–35; Francesco Perfetti, "D'Annunzio e il Sindacalismo Rivoluzionario dopo Fiume," in *D'Annunzio Politico: Atti del Convegno*, ed. De Felice and Gibellini, 213–14; Alessandro Agrí, 'La Reviviscenza della Carta del Carnaro dopo il Natale di Sangue," in *La Cittá di Vita Cento Anni Dopo: Fiume, D'Annunzio e il Lungo Novecento Adriatico*, ed. Davide Rossi (Padova: Wolters Kluwer—Cedam, 2020), 332–33.

41. Noiret, "Les Communistes," 202.

42. De Felice, *D'Annunzio Politico*, 153–55.

43. Günter Berghaus, *Futurism and Politics: Between Anarchist Rebellion and Fascist Reaction 1909–1944* (Providence, MA, and Oxford: Berghahn, 1996), 56–57, 61.

44. Cordova, *Arditi e Legionari Dannunziani*, 1–12.

45. Roberto Vivarelli, *Storia delle Origini del Fascismo: L'Italia dalla Grande Guerra alla Marcia su Roma*, vol. 1 (Bologna: Il Mulino, 1991), 322–23; John Woodhouse, *Gabriele D'Annunzio: Defiant Archangel* (Oxford: Clarendon Press, 1998), 325.

46. Berghaus, *Futurism and Politics*, 68–73.

47. Berghaus, *Futurism and Politics*, 96–99.
48. Berghaus, *Futurism and Politics*, 103, 106.
49. Cordova, *Arditi e Legionari Dannunziani*, 19–20.
50. Cordova, *Arditi e Legionari Dannunziani*, 43.
51. "L'Ardito Futurista—Manifesto" (November 1919), points (2) and (5) of Lyrical Programme section, in Cordova, *Arditi e Legionari Dannunziani*, 214–16.
52. Salaris, *Alla Festa della Rivoluzione*, 33.
53. Cordova, *Arditi e Legionari Dannunziani*, 44.
54. Quoted in Salaris, *Alla Festa della Rivoluzione*, 34.
55. Giordano Bruno Guerri, *Disobbedisco: Cinquecento Giorni di Rivoluzione. Fiume 1919–1920* (Milano: Mondadori, 2019), 190.
56. Simonelli, "La Costruzione di un Mito," 171.
57. Cordova, *Arditi e Legionari Dannunziani*, 46–47.
58. Berghaus, *Futurism and Politics*, 137–38.
59. Claudia Salaris, "Artisti e Libertari a Fiume," in *Fiume 1919–2019*, ed. Guerri, 222.
60. Berghaus, *Futurism and Politics*, 135.
61. Badoglio, *Rivelazioni*, 63.
62. Badoglio, *Rivelazioni*, 65.
63. Guerri, *Disobbedisco*, 114.
64. Berghaus, *Futurism and Politics*, 136–37.
65. Enrico Serventi Longhi, *Il Faro del Mondo Nuovo: D'Annunzio e i Legionari a Fiume tra Guerra e Rivoluzione* (Udine: Gaspari, 2019), 86.
66. Guerri, *Disobbedisco*, 190.
67. Salaris, *Alla Festa della Rivoluzione*, 100, 182–83; Cordova, *Arditi e Legionari Dannunziani*, 76 (note 38).
68. Simonelli, "La Costruzione di un Mito," 174–75.
69. Salaris, *Alla Festa della Rivoluzione*, 100, 182–83; Cordova, *Arditi e Legionari Dannunziani*, 76 (note 38).
70. Salaris, *Alla Festa della Rivoluzione*, 82–83, 101.
71. Salaris, *Alla Festa della Rivoluzione*, 123.
72. Badoglio, *Rivelazioni*, 67.
73. Leeden, *The First Duce*, 86–87; De Felice, "Introduzione," 62.
74. Stanley G. Payne, *A History of Fascism* (Madison, WI: University of Wisconsin Press, 1995), 91.
75. De Felice, "Introduzione," 56.
76. Alceste De Ambris, "Precisiamo il Nostro Concetto Rivoluzionaro: Il Manifesto dei Sindacalisti e la Costituzione Fiumana," *La Gioventu Sindacalista* (1 September 1921), in *Sindacalismo Rivoluzionario*, ed. De Felice, 334.
77. De Felice, "Introduzione," 96–108; Guerri, *Disobbedisco*, 356–59.
78. De Felice, "Introduzione," 114; Simonelli, "La Costruzione di un Mito," 217–18; Umberto Foscanelli, *D'Annunzio e l'Ora Sociale* (Milano: Carnaro, 1952), 160–64.
79. Guerri, *Disobbedisco*, 397–99.
80. Foscanelli, *D'Annunzio e l'Ora Sociale*, 162–64.

81. Cordova, *Arditi e Legionari Dannunziani*, 64, 113; Guerri, *Disobbedisco*, 483–83.
82. Guerri, *Disobbedisco*, 304.
83. Foscanelli, *D'Annunzio e l'Ora Sociale*, 172–73.
84. De Felice, "Introduzione," 116–17; Cordova, *Arditi e Legionari Dannunziani*, 114.
85. Foscanelli, *D'Annunzio e l'Ora Sociale*, 172.
86. Letter from G. D'Annunzio to A. De Ambris (7 April 1921) in *Sindacalismo Rivoluzionario*, ed. De Felice, 247.
87. Letter from G. D'Annunzio to A. De Ambris (11 May 1921) in *Sindacalismo Rivoluzionario*, ed. De Felice, 248.
88. De Felice, "Introduzione," 119–24; Letter from A. De Ambris to G. D'Annunzio (undated), in *Sindacalismo Rivoluzionario*, ed. De Felice, 246.
89. Foscanelli, *D'Annunzio e l'Ora Sociale*, 175–76.
90. Guerri, *Disobbedisco*, 504.
91. Letter from G. Keller to G. D'Annunzio (8 July 1922), Fondazione Il Vittoriale degli Italiani, Archivio Generale, Keller, Guido, LIX, 4.
92. Letter from G. Keller to G. D'Annunzio (5 November 1922), Fondazione Il Vittoriale degli Italiani, Archivio Generale, Keller, Guido, LIX, 4.
93. Letter from G. Keller to G. D'Annunzio (5 August 1923), Fondazione Il Vittoriale degli Italiani, Archivio Generale, Keller, Guido, LIX, 4.
94. Guerri, *Disobbedisco*, 501; Stefano Trinchese, "D'Annunzio nella Politica Italiana del Primo '900 (Riflessioni Storiografiche)'," in *Lo Statuto della Reggenza*, ed. Sinagra, 210–11.
95. Woodhouse, *Gabriele D'Annunzio*, 365.
96. Letter from A. De Ambris to C. Suckert Malaparte (January 1924), in De Felice, "Introduzione," 142–44.
97. Cordova, *Arditi e Legionari Dannunziani*, 117.
98. Cordova, *Arditi e Legionari Dannunziani*, 64–71.
99. Foscanelli, *D'Annunzio e l'Ora Sociale*, 174.
100. Cordova, *Arditi e Legionari Dannunziani*, 71–73.
101. Guerri, *Disobbedisco*, 512.
102. Guerri, *Disobbedisco*, 513.
103. Cordova, *Arditi e Legionari Dannunziani*, 64, 183; Foscanelli, *D'Annunzio e l'Ora Sociale*, 174.
104. De Felice, *D'Annunzio Politico*, 28–29.
105. Salaris, *Alla Festa della Rivoluzione*, 14.
106. Salaris, *Alla Festa della Rivoluzione*, 128–29.
107. Salvatore Cingari, "Virtuosa Gioia: Di Alcuni Aspetti Utopistici nella Carta del Carnaro," *Giornale di Storia Costituzionale* 10 (2005): 156.
108. Giordano Bruno Guerri, *D'Annunzio: L'Amante Guerriero* (Milano: Monadori, 2009), 277.
109. Salaris, *Alla Festa della Rivoluzione*, 50.
110. Guerri, *D'Annunzio*, 282.
111. Salaris, *Alla Festa della Rivoluzione*, 177–79.

112. Guerri, *Disobbedisco*, 106.

113. Raoul Pupo, *Fiume Città di Passione* (Bari: Laterza, 2018), 106–7; Giovanni Comisso, *Le Mie Stagioni* (Milano: Longanesi, 1963), 22, 38–39, 46, 49, 70, 92.

114. Francesca Rolandi, "A Never Requested Triumph? Reframing Gender Boundaries in Fiume and Sušak After 1918," *Italia Contemporanea Yearbook 2020* (2021): 28.

115. Salaris, *Alla Festa della Rivoluzione*, 154; Guerri, *D'Annunzio*, 283; Ledeen, *The First Duce*, 102–4; Comisso, *Le Mie Stagioni*, 68–69.

116. Salaris, *Alla Festa della Rivoluzione*, 180.

117. Rolandi, "A Never Requested Triumph?," 30–32.

118. Fiume: Diary of the British Military Mission, Fiume (3–9 November 1919), The National Archives, WO 106/853.

119. Guerri, *D'Annunzio*, 274.

120. Leeden, *The First Duce*, 157–60.

121. Guerri, *D'Annunzio*, 287, 301; Guerri, *Disobbedisco*, 214–15; Silverio Annibale, *La Questione di Fiume nel Diritto Internazionale* (Rovigno, Fiume, and Trieste: Centro di Ricerche Storiche Rovigno, 2011), 100.

122. Leeden, *The First Duce*, 157–58; Kotchnitzky, *La Quinta Stagione*, 72–75.

123. Serventi Longhi, *Il Faro*, 96.

124. Mario Maria Martini, *La Passione di Fiume: Diari, Cronache, Documenti* (Milano: Sonzogno, 1919), 131.

125. Edoardo Susmel, *La Cittá di Passione: Fiume negli Anni 1914–1920* (Milano: Treves, 1921), 244–45.

126. Salaris, *Alla Festa della Rivoluzione*, 19.

127. Marco Cuzzi, "Tra Autodeterminazione e Imperialismo: La Lega di Fiume," in *L'Italia e la "Grande Vigilia": Gabriele D'Annunzio nella Politica Italiana Prima del Fascismo*, ed. Romain H. Rainero and Stefano B. Galli (Milano: FrancoAngeli, 2007), 164; Marco Cuzzi, "'La Nostra Bandiera è la più Alta': La Politica Esteriore di D'Annunzio e la Lega di Fiume," in *Fiume 1919–2019*, ed. Guerri, 324.

128. Salaris, *Alla Festa della Rivoluzione*, 17.

129. Kotchnitzky, *La Quinta Stagione*, 62–63.

130. Kotchnitzky, *La Quinta Stagione*, 62.

131. Kotchnitzky, *La Quinta Stagione*, 144, 149–50.

132. Kotchnitzky, *La Quinta Stagione*, 150.

133. Serventi Longhi, *Il Faro*, 115.

134. Cuzzi, "Tra Autodeterminazione e Imperialismo," 134–35.

135. De Felice, *D'Annunzio Politico,* 75; Salaris, *Alla Festa della Rivoluzione*, 43.

136. Kotchnitzky, *La Quinta Stagione*, 153.

137. Léon Kotchnitzky, "Project of Constitution of the League of Fiume" (confidential Report for G. D'Annunzio, 22 March 1920), Fondazione Il Vittoriale degli Italiani, Archivio Fiumano, Kotchnitzky, Léon, 1–129.

138. Leeden, *The First Duce*, 117.

139. Gabriele D'Annunzio, "Orazione al popolo di Fiume" (25 October 1919), in Martini, *La Passione di Fiume*, 208.

140. D'Annunzio, "Orazione al popolo di Fiume," 209.

141. Martini, *La Passione di Fiume*, 192.
142. Gabriele D'Annunzio, "Italia e Vita" (24 October 1920), quoted in Cuzzi, "Tra Autodeterminazione e Imperialismo," 133.
143. Letter from G. D'Annunzio (16 October 1919), in Badoglio, *Rivelazioni*, 74–75.
144. G. D'Annunzio's interview with a Hungarian journalist, *La Vedetta d'Italia* (14 April 1920), in *La Carta del Carnaro e Altri Scritti su Fiume*, ed. Marco Fressura and Patrick Karlsen (Roma: Castelvecchi, 2009), 138.
145. Leeden, *The First Duce*, 178.
146. Cuzzi, "'La Nostra Bandiera è la più Alta'," 319.
147. Leeden, *The First Duce*, 179–80; Cuzzi, "Tra Autodeterminazione e Imperialismo," 152; Cuzzi, "'La Nostra Bandiera è la più Alta'," 319–20.
148. Cuzzi, "Tra Autodeterminazione e Imperialismo," 149.
149. Letter from L. Kotchnitzky to G. D'Annunzio (19 July 1920), Fondazione Il Vittoriale degli Italiani, Archivio Fiumano, Kotchnitzky, Léon, 1–129.
150. Cuzzi, "Tra Autodeterminazione e Imperialismo," 153.
151. Marco Cuzzi, "Una Costituzione Incompiuta: La Lega di Fiume," in *D'Annunzio Legislatore*, ed. Guerri, 102; De Felice, *D'Annunzio Politico*, 77–78; Leeden, *The First Duce*, 180–86, 190–97; Cuzzi, "'La Nostra Bandiera è la più Alta'," 321–22; Lorenzo Salimbeni, "La Lega dei Popoli Oppressi," in *La Cittá di Vita Cento Anni Dopo*, ed. Rossi, 136–42.
152. Confidential documents from L. Kotchnitzky to G. D'Annunzio (18 April 1920), in *La Carta del Carnaro nei Testi di Alceste De Ambris e Gabriele D'Annunzio*, ed. Renzo De Felice (Bologna: il Mulino, 1973), 123.
153. Letter from L. Kotchnitzky to G. D'Annunzio (3 July 1920), Fondazione Il Vittoriale degli Italiani, Archivio Fiumano, Kotchnitzky, Léon, 1–129.
154. Cuzzi, "Tra Autodeterminazione e Imperialismo," 139–40.
155. De Felice, *D'Annunzio Politico*, 80.
156. Cuzzi, "Tra Autodeterminazione e Imperialismo," 163.
157. Julian Go and Jake Watson, "Anticolonial Nationalism From Imagined Communities to Colonial Conflict," *European Journal of Sociology* 60, no. 1 (2019); Muhammed Noor Al-Abbood, "Anti-Colonial Nationalism and the West: Toward a Critique of Recent, Western-Based, Anti-Nationalist Scholarship," *Dirasat: Human and Social Sciences* 32, no. 1 (2005).
158. Guerri, *D'Annunzio*, 135–36.
159. Vivarelli, *Storia delle Origini*, 516 (note 71).
160. Salaris, *Alla Festa della Rivoluzione*, 69.
161. Salaris, *Alla Festa della Rivoluzione*, 87.
162. Leeden, *The First Duce*, 10.
163. Woodhouse, *Gabriele D'Annunzio*, 347.
164. Alfredo Bonadeo, *D'Annunzio and the Great War* (Madison and Teaneck: Farleigh Dickinson University Press; London: Associated University Presses, 1995), 136.

165. Leeden, *The First Duce*, 179.

166. Gabriele D'Annunzio, "Messaggio del Convalescente agli Uomini di Pena" (21 September 1922), in *Scritti Politici di Gabriele D'Annunzio*, ed. Paolo Alatri (Milano: Feltrinelli, 1980), 295.

167. D'Annunzio, "Messaggio del Convalescente," 297.

Chapter 6

The *Carnaro Charter*

INTRODUCTION

The *Carnaro Charter* continues to divide scholars in Italy. Villari dismisses its purported 'light-touch socialist and libertarian utopias' and 'provocative civil and political rights' as a diversionary tactic, which overshadowed—quite possibly with a view to facilitating the advent of Right-wing totalitarianism—the constructive German democratic liberties enshrined in the *Weimar Constitution*.[1] Instead I will argue that the *Charter* is more progressive than its better-known sibling, the *Weimar Constitution*, in several key respects. De Ambris could justly claim in 1922 that the *Charter* secured an assortment of civil and social rights that was 'richer than any other'.[2]

Like the constitutions that followed a typology inaugurated by the *Weimar Constitution*, the *Charter* is a lengthy document, setting out both the fundamental political principles governing the state and the organisation of its institutional apparatus.[3] It has been argued that the effectiveness of the latter—contemplating a directorial collegial executive without accountability to the legislature—is open to question.[4] In any case, the institutional structure of the regency was never put to the test because during the short period between its proclamation and dissolution the regency was governed by a provisional government.

Despite its provisions remaining essentially dead letter during that period, the *Charter* is one of the most original modern constitutional texts ever designed and promulgated,[5] and certainly the most literary.[6] Its legal and political significance was acknowledged by contemporary Italian scholars, particularly for its novel introduction of a corporatist representative system, which gave expression to the philosophies of part of the radical and revolutionary Left in early twentieth-century Europe.[7] As Ambrosini wrote in 1925, after much abstract syndicalist theorising, the *Charter* was the first instance of concrete implementation of syndicalist principles into a legal document intended to have practical application.[8]

THE MULTILAYERED AUTHORSHIP OF THE *CHARTER*

D'Annunzio accepted in its entirety De Ambris's radical constitutional design, even at the cost of alienating the remaining moderate elements among the legionnaires.[9] On the formal plane, it is of interest that D'Annunzio's text replaces the Arabic numerals in De Ambris's draft with their Roman equivalent, a move clearly calculated to gives aesthetic expression to the asserted Latin heritage of Fiume.[10]

In more substantive terms, some have found D'Annunzio's changes so well conceived as to hypothesise he was assisted by a legally trained man in revising De Ambris's draft.[11] Conversely, others have claimed that all that D'Annunzio cared about was the literary form of the document, as understanding its actual substance was beyond him;[12] that his changes were few and of limited social and political significance;[13] and that his contributions were confined to 'clauses guaranteeing a beautiful life, the free development of spiritual man as a gift to a world of brothers'.[14] But a reading of De Ambris's and D'Annunzio's versions side by side shows the poet's changes to be fairly numerous, and in some cases substantive. Indeed, the fact that D'Annunzio added but did not subtract from De Ambris's version makes me incline towards the view that De Ambris's draft was itself the product (as he himself claimed) of intellectual exchange with D'Annunzio. The draft De Ambris sent to D'Annunzio in March 1920 may already have been, as it were, 'co-authored'.[15]

D'Annunzio's text in the preamble of the *Charter* is heavily indebted to considerations made by the irredentist Edoardo Susmel in his historical study *Fiume Attraverso La Storia*, published first in Fiume in 1918 and then in Milan in 1919. Susmel wrote:

Fiume is the outermost stronghold of Latin civilization, the last Italian watch-tower of the Julian Alps. Fiume has been through long centuries the centre radiating Italian culture in the Carnaro Gulf. Volosca, Abbazia, Laurana, Moschiena, Alborna, Cherso, Veglia, Arbe have maintained their Italian character thanks to [Fiume]. And it is for this extremely important historical and national function that Fiume must stay . . . the great luminous beacon of Italian civilization in Dante's Carnaro.[16]

Now compare D'Annunzio's words in the preamble:

> Fiume is the outermost Italian custodian of the Julian Alps, is the outermost citadel of Latin culture, is the last bearer of Dante's mark. Through her, from

> century to century, from event to event, from battle to battle, from passion to passion, Dante's Carnaro remained Italian. From her the spirit of the Italian character radiated and radiates towards shores and islands, from Volosca to Laurana, from Moschiena to Albona, from Veglia to Lussino, from Cherso to Arbe.

D'Annunzio was notorious for plundering other people's work and refashioning it in more beautiful guise. This instance is significant because, by showing the new Constitution's intertexuality, it complicates the question of its authorship and diffuses its ownership—for all that, as we have seen, the *Charter* was never approved by either the people of Fiume or the National Council in a formal vote.

There is also a diachronic dimension to the multilayered authorship of the *Charter*. The *Charter* did not purport to set Fiume's constitutional arrangement in stone: in addition to providing for constitutional amendments when one-third of the electorate petitioned for it, it went so far as mandating an institutionalised process of constitutional revision every seven years.[17] While the Constitution remained therefore rigid (for these provisions make changing it more difficult than for ordinary laws), it also invited regular updating on the part of the Fiuman polity. This is significant in terms of D'Annunzio's and De Ambris's concession of their fallibility,[18] and is also interesting, specifically, with regard to the willingness of D'Annunzio-the-artist to permit others to 'interfere' with what was after all an instance of his creative output.

GROUNDS FOR THE LEGITIMACY OF FIUME'S ANNEXATION

The preamble critiques 'foreign iniquity, bullying and greed', which force Fiume to give itself a Constitution by frustrating its legitimate annexation to Italy. De Ambris's version makes the legitimacy of Fiume's annexation rest on a *de jure* basis: it is a will 'reaffirmed' on the basis of the town's 'ancient privileges' and the inalienable right to self-determination. D'Annunzio, on the other hand, puts the legitimacy of annexation on prepolitical foundations.

D'Annunzio appeals, specifically, to cultural-historical, geographical, and moral justifications for Fiume's annexation to Italy. The cultural-historical justification refers to its century-old Italian identity and its role in spreading Italian culture throughout the eastern Adriatic coast. The geographical claim (which D'Annunzio calls Fiume's 'terrestrial right' and in an earlier draft its 'natural right')[19] is based on Fiume's being contained within the so-called Julian Alps. These are said to delimit the Italian territory not only as a matter of tradition and history but also as a matter of scientific principle. The significance of morphology to determining national boundaries is not an invention of D'Annunzio's but a *topos* of Fiuman irredentist discourse. The Monenevoso mountain, specifically, was said to mark 'from time immemorial the natural boundary of Italy', its ridge being a 'watershed of two distinct regions', as well as the site of the Roman wall, within which Fiume was contained.[20] The attempt to give Fiume's choice of annexation to Italy a prepolitical, natural basis is most apparent in this appeal to morphological considerations. It seems significant, however, that D'Annunzio felt the need to back up the purported imperatives of morphology (what he calls 'science') with 'tradition' and 'history'.

Finally, D'Annunzio's third ground for the legitimacy of annexation—namely, the right to self-determination—has a less juridical and more moral character in D'Annunzio's text than in the version of the legally trained De Ambris. While De Ambris, in characterising the (legal) right to self-determination as 'inalienable', implicitly references natural law (that is, the moral order) as a basis of that right, D'Annunzio is more explicit. He terms that right as 'just', as Fiume's 'human right' to be in control of its destiny, and as a right that some of Fiume's own 'unjust adversaries' (namely, the United States) have themselves 'declared'. Despite the fact that he was not trained as a lawyer, we may suppose that D'Annunzio's terminology here ('declared') is deliberate, stressing that the right to self-determination preexists (as a matter of morality/natural law) its formal recognition/declaration at (positive) law by the international community.

TERRITORY AND TERMINOLOGY

Both D'Annunzio's and De Ambris's texts make Fiume and its *corpus separatum* the territorial nucleus of the new state, while leaving the state's boundaries to be progressively expanded through the consensual accession of other territories and communities. As D'Annunzio's version clarifies, the prospect of accession might appeal to such communities both for economic reasons (the status of the town as a freeport) and political ones, specifically, 'the liberality of its new statutes.[21] An earlier draft speaks of the liberality of 'the Constitution',[22] suggesting that by 'statutes' D'Annunzio intended the *Charter* itself rather than any other laws (such as the Italian criminal code adopted by the National Council, which was indeed more liberal than its predecessor in Fiume). This interpretation is confirmed contextually: elsewhere in D'Annunzio's draft manuscript we see the term 'Constitution' crossed out and replaced by 'statutes', in contexts where the signified is not in doubt.[23]

It seems likely that D'Annunzio favoured the term 'statutes' for two reasons. First, it implies continuity with the Italian tradition of *'statuti comunali'*—namely, the fundamental laws of mediaeval and early modern Italian autonomous 'city-states'. Fiume's own 1530 fundamental law was a 'statute'. Secondly, this terminology ('statutes') distances Fiume's *Charter* from the Allies: after all, the paradigmatic (written) 'Constitutions' were the French (1791) and US (1789) ones. Ramaioli has recently argued that D'Annunzio's mediaevalising terminological choice also signalled a specific—premodern—conception of law. This emphasises law's nature as a spontaneous, bottom-up form of governance rather than the kind of deliberate exercise of *pouvoir constituant* (as an act that both founds and legitimates a new institutionalised normative order) implied by the term 'Constitution.'[24]

Yet the expression 'Constitution' survives in a few provisions of the *Charter*. This does not appear to have been through oversight, as D'Annunzio changed the term 'statutes' back to De Ambris's original 'Constitution' on at least one occasion.[25] The rationale for preferring 'Constitution' to the more open-ended 'statutes' in these cases may have been complete avoidance of doubt in respect of matters (such as constitutional reform, or the distribution of competence between the central and local governments)[26] where any interpretive ambiguity might have brought the new constitutional order to a standstill.

FORM OF GOVERNMENT

De Ambris's draft declares the 'Republic of Fiume' a 'direct democracy, whose basis is productive labour', a formula reworked by D'Annunzio as follows: 'The Italian Regency of Carnaro is an honest government of the people, whose foundation is the power of productive labour'.[27] D'Annunzio's reference to popular government seems more accurate than De Ambris's use of the expression 'direct democracy', given that, as we will see, the constitutional order followed by and large the principle of representation, albeit with direct democracy correctives. This is one of the changes that, it has been suggested, D'Annunzio might not have made unless an adviser familiar with constitutional theory had pointed out to him De Ambris's inaccurate terminological choice.[28] It is possible, however, that by 'direct democracy' De Ambris had in mind the fact that, as we will see, political parties were not to mediate the relationship between citizens and the organs of the state in Fiume's regency. It has been argued that the *Charter* espouses the view that party control over the list of candidates for the legislature emasculates ordinary citizen's political rights.[29]

We have already seen the reasons for the terminological change from 'republic' to 'regency'. D'Annunzio seems to have agonised over the precise terminology. Revisions to article 2 (which describes Fiume's territory as encompassing the town, its *corpus separatum* and that of any community acceding to it) show that the poet first used the term 'confederation', then changed it to De Ambris's preferred term 'republic', and only later replaced it with 'regency'.[30] In any case, it is interesting that the term 'regency' is already in use in D'Annunzio's draft manuscript, sometimes in the original version of the relevant provisions, without evidence of any terminological revision.[31] It suggests the apocryphal nature of the story, oft-repeated in Italian literature, that only at the eleventh hour did D'Annunzio instruct the press charged with printing the *Charter* to replace 'republic' with 'regency'.

PRODUCTIVE LABOUR

Intriguing and novel is the reference, in both De Ambris's and D'Annunzio's versions, to productive labour as a social pillar of the constitutional order. A preoccupation with productive labour is in keeping with De Ambris's syndicalism it may appear remarkable that D'Annunzio, given his more ambivalent political allegiances, opted to retain this aspect of the Constitution. True, in D'Annunzio's formulation, labour is depersonalised and even spiritualised: it is the 'power of productive labour', rather than productive labour as such, that sustains the constitutional order. While this rarefies De Ambris's more definite 'productive labour' (as a social category), it does not follow that the reference to labour in the poet's text is hollow and rhetorical. Indeed, in both texts the foundational status of productive labour is expressly said to justify affording 'greater' (in De Ambris's text) or 'higher and overriding' (in D'Annunzio's reformulation) rights to those who engage in it.[32]

This mention of preferential treatment for productive labour early on in the Constitution foreshadows two later passages in the *Charter*. First, the part of the document devoted to the legislative power. In accordance with a corporatist conception of the organisation of powers, the state's law-making body is composed of two houses, one elected through adult universal suffrage, and the other made up of representatives of the different professions and labour categories.[33] Secondly, the preferential political treatment afforded to productive workers is apparent in the denial (following judicial process) of political rights to nonworking citizens, unless physically incapable of work.[34]

Other drafting choices in the *Charter* convey the preeminence of the concerns of productive citizens more subtly. For example, the provision listing the different categories of judges places 'labour judges' before those in charge of important civil and criminal matters. This was a very deliberate choice, as shown through the drafting history of the manuscript: D'Annunzio had initially reversed De Ambris's preferred order, only to change it back to how his collaborator had originally envisaged it.[35]

Contrast the clear valorisation of productive labour in the *Charter* with the disdaining treatment afforded to labour by the narrative voice in

D'Annunzio's 1895 novel, *The Virgins of the Rocks*: 'The world is a representation of a few superior men's sensibility and thought, who have created it, enlarged it and embellished over time and will continue to enlarge it and embellish it in the future. The world, in its present form, is a magnificent gift granted by the few to the many, by the free ones to those enslaved: by those who think and feel to those who must labour.'[36] The passage of time, D'Annunzio's wartime experiences, and, above all, the different functions of the *Charter* and the novel easily account for the chasm between the novel and the constitutional document in their treatment of productive labour. Indeed, *The Virgins of the Rocks* is by far the most fantasy-like of D'Annunzio's novels, complete with a literal spirit guide speaking to the main character, and entirely set in a dream-like location that feels outside time; much of the plot unravels within an enclosed garden and palace that isolate it even further from reality. As more or less pure personifications of virtues or affective principles, even the eponymous virgins themselves are more like allegories than real human beings. Significantly, *Fire*, the much more realistic novel published by D'Annunzio five years after *The Virgins of the Rocks*, had already clearly moved away from the idea that labour is for those who cannot think or feel.[37] Yet none of this, not even the fact that the main character in *The Virgins of the Rocks* literally hears voices in his head, has prevented specifically this novel from being regularly treated as the ultimate literal statement of D'Annunzio's political manifesto. The disparity between the treatment afforded to labour in the novel and in the *Charter* brings home the absurdity of such moves on the part of D'Annunzio's critics and the distortive effect they have on appraising his political thought.

Although the 1948 *Constitution of the Italian Republic* departed from the corporatist models contemplated in the *Charter* (and later practiced, in a different form, during the Fascist years), its first article declares that 'Italy is a democratic Republic founded on labour'. The likeness between this expression and the opening articles of the *Charter* has gone unnoticed, despite the fact that there are no other obvious constitutional documents that could have provided a model, inspiration, or antecedent for the postwar text. The Soviet Constitution of 1936, for example, opens with the expression that the USSR 'is a socialist State of workers and peasants', explicitly stressing the working *classes* rather than the polysemic expression 'labour', and declaring the state as belonging to the working classes rather than making the latter foundational to the former.[38] Leftist parties in postwar, post-Fascist Italy would indeed have favoured a formulation closer, in structure, to this Soviet model ('Italy is a democratic Republic of workers'), on the basis of the claim that the working classes were the best insurance against a return to the Fascist dictatorship enabled by the dominance of the bourgeoisie.[39] The compromise formulation that eventually made it into article 1 of the 1948 Constitution ('a democratic Republic founded on labour') makes it unlike any other existing constitutional documents. This idiosyncratic language cannot but derive from D'Annunzio's *Charter*: 'an honest government of the people, whose foundation is the power of productive labour.'[40]

POPULAR SOVEREIGNTY, DISCRIMINATION, AND RACE

Both De Ambris's and D'Annunzio's versions of the *Charter* stress that sovereignty belongs to all citizens regardless of sex, race, language, class, and religion, though D'Annunzio's version uses the word *'stirpe'* (lineage, ancestry) instead of 'race'.[41] It might seem unlikely that D'Annunzio's linguistic move here was consciously motivated by anything other than aesthetic considerations. All the same, his terminological preference has an intriguing effect: it anticipates the deconstruction of the concept of race (as something referencing objective biological realities), while at the same time acknowledging its status as an organising principle of inequality,[42] and hence its constitutional significance as a prohibited ground of discrimination.

The way in which D'Annunzio's formulation of this constitutional provision performs, with respect to race, this sophisticated political move, probably despite his own conscious intentions, mirrors the way in which D'Annunzio's other writings have a way of undermining his own suspect racial politics, revealing the ideological tensions that characterise his political thought. Consider the example of his 1889 novel *Pleasure*, which contains an unsavoury, to say the least, portrait of a Japanese character. This and other passages have made some commentators declare that at 'no point in the novel is the assignation of disgust to the realm of alterity challenged or undermined'.[43] But this is untrue. The heavily caricaturised description of the Japanese character concludes with the unexpectedly flattering remark that he had an 'ironic refinement at the corners of his mouth'.[44] Furthermore, later in the novel the protagonist's paramour embarrasses the Asian man through her facetious flirting at a social gathering; at this point, D'Annunzio writes, 'Everyone was laughing freely, as if that foreigner had been invited just so as to give the others a reason to have fun'.[45] Is the narrative voice, here, inviting the reader to join in the fun, or rather to interrogate the justice of the situation?[46] If the intention had been the former, a consummate stylist such as D'Annunzio would have controlled the reader's response much more effectively by ending the sentence at 'freely'.

Why does all this matter to the *Charter*? Because the ideological tensions within D'Annunzio's literary work are instructive. They suggest that his preference for using, in the *Charter*, the word *'stirpe'* rather than 'race' (with all its baggage of pseudo-scientific pretentions) may be, if not quite an exercise in *ante-litteram* political correctness, less than entirely accidental.

SEPARATION OF POWERS

The same article that declares the principle of popular sovereignty without discrimination also provides for a principle of separation of powers. The rationale for this shifts from the idea, in De Ambris's version, that breaking up state power is conducive to social harmony, to the view, in D'Annunzio's reelaboration, that 'through the harmonious interplay of diverse elements, social life is made richer and more vigorous.'[47] D'Annunzio's personal sensibility partly explains this bias towards the vision of a vibrant, rather than merely a peaceful or harmonious, society. But it also fits that it should be the poet, rather than the lawyer, who shows an explicit concern with quasi-aesthetic political values (a vibrant social life) rather than purely pragmatic ones (a peaceful coexistence). While similar concerns are not unknown in political philosophical thought (they were expressly thematised, amongst others, in Mill's writings on democracy),[48] their explicit articulation in a constitutional text is much more unusual. What made it possible is the unconventional genesis of the *Charter*, which, rather than issuing from negotiations in a Constitutional Assembly, was the result of a draft reworked into final form by a poet not formally bound to account to others for his textual choices.

RIGHTS

Similar reasons explain the text of the next article. According to De Ambris's draft, the state 'aims to protect the independence, freedom and common rights, to promote a higher moral dignity and greater material prosperity of all citizens'.[49] The expression 'common rights' is slightly indeterminate, as a tradition of eighteenth and nineteenth century sources use it either to refer to natural rights (the rights common to all humans)[50] or (less frequently) the rights that reflect a political community's fundamental (positive) legal principles and are vested in each and every citizen.[51] Either way, it seems clear that by 'common rights' De Ambris meant the important rights that Fiumans had, either by virtue of general moral imperatives anchored to ideas of human personhood or by virtue of the specific brand of political morality enshrined in Fiume's legal system (primarily, the *Charter* itself). Significantly, alongside the traditional civil and political rights captured in the expression 'freedom and common rights', De Ambris, as an exponent of the radical Left, also mentions the state's concern for its citizens' 'material prosperity', a formula that prefigures socioeconomic rights.

D'Annunzio's version of this provision shows some notable differences. Gone from D'Annunzio's formulation is the qualifier 'moral' before 'dignity', which might have smacked a little of the priestly class to D'Annunzio's Nietzschean sensibility. More significantly, 'independence, freedom and common rights' (as objects of state protection) become 'all freedoms and popular rights'.[52] Perhaps surprisingly, D'Annunzio's formula points towards a less metaphysical, more historicised understanding of rights than De Ambris's text. If, as we have seen, 'common rights' chiefly suggested the philosophical idea of natural rights inherent to human personhood, usage of the expression 'popular rights' tended to connote rights won by peoples from political and social élites through political struggles or negotiation in specific historical contexts.[53] The way in which 'popular rights' points to such a historicised understanding in nineteenth-century usage is particularly apparent in the contributions of those who opposed such rights and claimed that they conflicted with natural law.[54] However, such a historicised understanding was also shared by those who supported popular rights, where it could go hand in hand with the idea of a moral or natural law–based justification for popular claims to new rights,[55] and where 'popular rights' could also encompass the idea of social rights.[56] D'Annunzio's 'popular rights', in short, conveys a less esoteric understanding of rights than originally envisaged in De Ambris's 'common rights'. The poet's reformulation of the provision is also more ambitious in announcing a more definite commitment to such rights: where De Ambris spoke of the state aiming to protect them, D'Annunzio provides that the state 'protects defends preserves' them (no comma or *copula* in the original).[57]

While D'Annunzio retains, alongside the concern with protecting rights, the goal of promoting prosperity, he drops the qualifier 'material' before it. No doubt, this signals his preoccupation with spiritual and aesthetic values alongside those prized by socialist materialism. D'Annunzio's concern with such values, and his belief in their connection with the idea of human flourishing, is made clear in a whole new passage he inserts in De Ambris's original provision. The state, he writes, 'seeks to lead the days and works back to that feeling of virtuous joy which is to renew the people finally freed from a monotonous regime of impositions and lies'.[58] The passage appears to gesture, intriguingly, towards a form of state perfectionism that is free from either coercion or moralism.

SEX EQUALITY

We have already seen that sex, alongside lineage/ancestry, language, class, and religion, had been declared a prohibited ground of discrimination with respect to the exercise of political rights in the article that made sovereignty reside in all the people without distinction. In his letter to D'Annunzio accompanying the draft of the *Charter*, De Ambris states that 'civil and political equality' between the sexes in Fiume 'was for the great part already recognised by legislation currently in force'; but women's participation in the cause of Fiume (which D'Annunzio testifies to in his speeches)[59] demanded that such equality be made complete.[60]

The preexisting legislation De Ambris refers to had been enacted not long before D'Annunzio's Ronchi march, when women had obtained the right to vote in civic elections. At the time, they had pressured the National Council—which was due to be dissolved and reelected in accordance with the recommendations of the Inter-Allied inquiry—to hold a referendum, resulting in a new electoral law securing the right to vote for all qualifying men and women over twenty years of age.[61] After D'Annunzio's occupation of the town, elections had been held, to which numerous female voters had taken part, and three female councillors had been elected.[62]

This extension of the franchise did not occur in a vacuum. Rolandi points out that, as a cosmopolitan port town with 'a Central European tradition', Fiume was characterised by 'significant liberty from family restrictions among Fiuman women, a relative tolerance of premarital relations and a very strong female presence on the job market.'[63] All the same, the extension had not been uncontroversial. Father Macdonald, whose account is obsessively fixated with the role played by 'loose' women in the annexationists' cause, unsurprisingly claimed that it 'was an arbitrary infringement of the existing constitution'.[64] Despite the fact that Croat women in Sušak were no less involved in political activism than their Italian counterparts in Fiume, the Croat-language daily *Primorske Novine* (printed in Sušak) also attacked Fiume's new electoral law as a ruse designed to garner support for Fiume's Italian political elite. The National Council, the publication claimed, went to the lengths of courting the votes of disreputable women: no other members of the female sex could have any interest in, or time for, politics and the public sphere.[65]

After D'Annunzio's occupation of Fiume, even more measured Croat voices found it hard to divorce their remarks on Fiuman women's expression of their political colours from commentary about their presumed sexual morals.[66] Indeed, Fiuman women, animated by irredentist sentiments, had played a conspicuous role in the events that preceded and facilitated D'Annunzio' entry and continued to shape the fate of the town during the occupation,[67] right up to the resistance during the bloody Christmas.[68] During the occupation, some women contributed to moulding Fiume's political and intellectual *milieu*;[69] meanwhile, female legionnaires carried out humanitarian and educational work[70] and might even be appointed to military positions.[71] While the National Council's willingness to concede women the vote may have been due less to idealism than political expediency,[72] D'Annunzio's Fiume appears to have been genuinely receptive to women's political and civic participation. There is little reason to believe that D'Annunzio and De Ambris were being merely opportunistic in enshrining the principle of sex equality in the *Charter*.

The *Charter* mentions sex again in relation to military service. Although only able-bodied men were admitted to combat roles, military service was required of both men and women between seventeen and fifty-five.[73] To be more precise, it was required of 'firm women'—in a concession to gender stereotypes, made as a revision to the original draft of article XXXXVII.[74] Other provisions mandating equal treatment without discrimination on the ground of sex are the article that declares the principle of equality before the law,[75] and the article that provides for voting rights and the right to stand as a candidate for election upon reaching the age of majority, set at twenty.[76]

In D'Annunzio's draft manuscript, the expression 'without distinctions as to sex' is a later addition to the guarantee of voting rights.[77] But it is unlikely that this indicates D'Annunzio's initial reluctance to accept the principle of sex equality that De Ambris had stated explicitly in his version of the same article. The addition is written in pencil, like the main text, suggesting that it may have constituted an immediate correction to an initial oversight. Furthermore, D'Annunzio's version of the *Charter* as a whole goes even further than De Ambris's own in reasserting the principle of sex equality.

Specifically, in D'Annunzio's version, but not in De Ambris's original text, the provision that guarantees freedom of access to all forms of employment (encompassing all trades, professions, crafts, and arts) also expressly prohibits sex-based distinctions.[78] The right to freedom of trade and employment has an old pedigree—article 18 of the 1793 *French Declaration of the Rights of Man* already listed it as a negative freedom enjoyed by citizens. But the import of the *Charter* provision echoes rather the British *Sex Disqualification (Removal) Act* 1919, which had become law only a few months before the promulgation of the *Charter*.

The guarantee to freedom from discrimination in choice of and access to employment is particularly significant in terms of feminist politics, for well-rehearsed reasons. That it should be D'Annunzio, rather than the radical De Ambris, who spelt it out in the *Charter* is hard to reconcile with the charge of misogyny sometimes moved against the poet.[79] It may of course be that, even if it does not appear in De Ambris's original text, the addition made by D'Annunzio was nonetheless a result of the two men's discussions during D'Annunzio's work of revision rather than owing its paternity entirely to D'Annunzio. Either way, I think it is a mistake to regard D'Annunzio's receptivity to questions of sex discrimination in the *Charter* as incongruous with his gender politics.

Once again, a look at D'Annunzio's literary production is instructive. Consider Tullio, the antihero of the 1892 novel *The Innocent One*. Tullio is a philanderer who, in the book's first part, starts having doubts about his wife's fidelity to him. Previously, he had partially rationalised his own infidelity on the ground that by making his long-suffering wife Giuliana endure his cheating, he made her soar to peaks of heroic virtue, which in turn intensified his own admiration and, possibly, his love of her. Now, however, in a more honest moment, Tullio reflects:

> Knowing her guilt, could I forgive her?—But what guilt? What forgiveness? You have no right to judge her, you have no right to raise your voice. Too many times she kept quiet: this time it's your turn . . . the happiness you dream of rests entirely on obliterating the past. Why then, if she truly isn't innocent, could you not put to rest her guilt as much as yours? Why, if you exact her forgetfulness, would you not yourself forget? Why, if you desire to be a new man, severed from the past, wouldn't you look upon her as new woman, too, in the self-same position as you? This kind of double standard would be the worst of your inequities.[80]

Giuliana did have an extramarital affair, and it turns out she is pregnant. Tullio is haunted by the thought that the baby will be male; his own offspring with Giuliana is female, and the birth of a healthy baby boy would mean that an 'impostor' will carry on his name, inherit his wealth, and claim the love of his family. Tulio comes to abhor the foetus Giuliana carries, but that abhorrence is not automatically extended to the mother, towards whom Tullio's feelings veer from alienation and indifference (in moments when Tullio is consumed by self-preoccupation) to compassionate pity and tenderness (when he is able to appreciate her suffering).

Tullio's logic is perverse, which is why it makes for interesting fictional treatment: the blameless baby is made to bear the brunt of Tullio's violent hate. The key point is that the full extent of Tullio's hatred for the baby is conveyed partly through the disparity in his treatment of Giuliana and her son. Her share of responsibility for their predicament is effectively cancelled out by Tullio's own original sins—which all but drove her to seeking intimate solace outside marriage. Thus, when, as the baby is growing more and more hauntingly present through the steady enlargement of her belly, she asks Tullio if he hates her, he is overcome with pity and tenderness. 'I have no grudges against you, I never will,' he says. 'I don't forget that I owe you reciprocation. I forget nothing.'[81] Tullio's own past philandering, that is, made him incur a debt towards his wife, one that he cannot very well blame her for having exacted in kind. Thus, the whole conceit of *The Innocent One*—the needless and abhorrent sacrifice of a perfectly innocent baby—is partly built on insisting on the moral bankruptcy of gendered double standards. If Tullio did not hold on to his determination not to hold Giuliana responsible—if he were oblivious, that is, to the injustice of the double standard—the book would be much less powerful. For rather than being akin to a so-called rough hero—that is, a male character who transgresses moral norms but, through some redeeming qualities, is able to win the reader's (partial) approbation[82]—Tullio's case would then be one of wholesale moral inversion.

Not only does *The Innocent One* convey the injustice of holding men and women to different standards of sexual purity, but it also challenges the reduction of women's role to child-bearing. This comes across particularly clearly when Giuliana has given birth to the baby after a labour that nearly killed her. Tullio's relatives are gathered around the baby cot and doting on the newborn, whom they assume to be legitimate. Tullio knows better and feels only ill-disguised hatred and repugnance for him. As he and his brother leave the room, he notes, 'Giuliana is extremely ill; I don't understand how anyone could spare a single thought for anyone other than her, at this time'.[83] Tullio, who is also the narrator, concedes that he says this 'as if to justify' his odd behaviour before the baby, but it does not follow that his concern is opportunistically manufactured for the specific purpose of dissimulation. Tullio's stance here distances itself from Judaeo-Christian views that women rightfully pay through their labour for Eve's original sin and upends the misogynistic hierarchy of concern that would place the value of a new life over that of the woman who carried it. Indeed, the whole book refuses the notion that women redeem themselves through reproduction: both because Giuliana has done nothing that requires redeeming (her adultery being more Tullio's fault than her own) and because, if she had, her pregnancy and birth giving would logically provide just the grounds for blaming her rather than excusing her.

In sum, not only does *The Innocent One* resist reducing women to their reproductive capacities, but it also suggests that D'Annunzio was able to appreciate the injustice of gendered double standards. Other novels of D'Annunzio's are suggestive in their own right about his commitment to a nonmisogynistic gender politics. It is interesting, for example, that heterosexual sex is generally presented not as something that is done to women but an activity where male and female partners are equally agentic. In *Pleasure* we read: 'They felt an unspeakable joy in tearing apart all veils, in revealing all secrets, in violating all mysteries, in possessing each other's depths, in penetrating each other'.[84] And in *Fire*: 'She is sure of herself, she is master of her own power. When she finally feels free, she will show herself as a leader. She is made to subdue men, to excite their curiosity and their dreams. Her instinct already leads her, as courageous and cautious as experience'.[85] In the context of such clues in D'Annunzio's *oeuvre*, the poet's emphasis on the principle of sex equality in the *Charter*—even in connection with rights where De Ambris himself had failed to state it—is not, therefore, incongruous.

D'Annunzio's version of the statement of the principle of equality before the law in the *Charter* is also notable for performing a move highly unusual for a legal document. After stating that all citizens 'of both sexes' are equal before the law (a conventional formula also used in De Ambris's draft), it adds that men and women 'feel equal' before it. It is futile to ask oneself what this provision might have meant at law. Rather, the provision seems to signal D'Annunzio's desire to write a constitutional text that spoke not so much to the Fiumans but for them. Indeed, in the speech that preceded his informal promulgation of the *Charter* to the citizens of Fiume, D'Annunzio spoke of the enactment of the *Charter* as the 'people who give themselves their own re-birth into a higher form of life.'[86]

No doubt it was rhetorically and politically expedient for D'Annunzio to present the *Charter* as an act of self-government of the citizens of Fiume rather than a top-down imposition. After all, the way in which the question of legitimate authority has traditionally been approached sets considerable store by the idea of the people's appropriation of the authority's will.[87] Yet we have little reason to suppose that D'Annunzio here is being purely engaged in linguistically mediated strategic action rather than communicative action properly so called.[88] The utterances we are considering—both the extratextual one that the people 'give themselves' the *Charter* and the intratextual one that the citizens 'feel equal' before the law—are not purely instrumental. They are genuine 'dramaturgical' statements oriented towards reaching understanding, making an implicitly validity claim that appeals to the speaker's sincerity.[89] In simpler terms, D'Annunzio may well have been in good faith, both in claiming that the *Charter* was an expression of the popular will and in purporting to make it speak for (not just to) the Fiumans. It is pertinent to recall that, many years before, D'Annunzio had elaborated a belief in politically engaged artists' ability to cathect with, and articulate, the feelings of the multitudes.

LIBERAL FREEDOMS AND THEIR LIMITS

Article VII (article 4 in De Ambris's draft) of the *Charter* protects freedom of thought, religion, press, assembly, and association but states that religious convictions cannot be invoked to seek exemption from legally prescribed duties. Behind this qualification to the right to freedom of religion is certainly a concern that the survival of the city-state, given its small population, might be dependent on making no allowance for conscientious objection to military service. De Ambris and D'Annunzio's concern that an adequate number of well-trained bodies should be readily available for the defence of the city-state was made more pressing by their own choice not to maintain a professional, standing army during peacetime.[90] Indeed, the same concern easily explains the imposition, noted earlier, of the duty to perform military service on both men and women,[91] for all that such a gender-neutral duty is also consistent with the *Charter*'s general commitment to gender equality.

Conscientious objection to military conscription had emerged as an issue in the last few decades of the nineteenth century, when more and more countries adopted the Prussian model of universal military service. In the years leading to and during World War I, Anglo-American and some Nordic and northern European countries institutionalised systems of conscientious objection; other countries, such as France, were far less accommodating.[92] It is clear, in any case, that by the end of World War I, conscientious objection had emerged in European public consciousness as a problem to be managed. The problem loomed large enough for De Ambris and D'Annunzio themselves that they decided to include a clause in the *Charter* according to which those who refused to perform military service for the defence of the land would be deprived, following due process, of political rights.[93] A contextual reading suggests that the self-same preoccupation with conscientious objection to military duty motivates the provision that religious freedom is not a legitimate reason for excusing oneself from legally prescribed duties. It seems significant, too, that the provision is more narrowly formulated than constitutional limitation clauses making religious freedom subject to state laws.[94]

Article VII also provides that the law may criminalise the abuse of constitutional freedoms, so long as it does not violate their core (what De Ambris's text calls the 'essential principle' and D'Annunzio, less clearly, the 'perfect principle' of these freedoms).[95] Constructing a limitations clause around the concept of an inviolable core to liberal freedoms provides an original and interesting alternative to other coeval constitutional documents. The 1919 *Weimar Constitution*, for example, generally admitted restrictions of rights (such as personal freedom, the privacy of the home and correspondence) so long as they were legally prescribed[96] or subject to the general laws (as in the case of freedom of expression and religion)[97]—though in some cases it specified in great detail for what purposes a certain right, such as freedom of assembly, could be legally limited.[98]

D'Annunzio's text places more emphasis than De Ambris's on the impermissibility of draconian laws unduly impinging on liberty by insisting that laws that restrict the abuse of freedoms must not interfere 'in any way' with the core of these freedoms. Another difference is that in D'Annunzio's reformulation, instances of abuse of constitutional freedoms are apparently contemplated that are less serious and hence do not justify criminalisation: only 'when' abuses of constitutional freedoms 'tend towards an illicit goal' or 'disrupt the balance of civil life' are they liable to punishment.[99]

De Ambris's text did not make room for this possibility, speaking rather of 'abuse of freedoms for goals that are illicit and contrary to civil life'.[100] At the cost of overinterpreting these differences, De Ambris's wording seems underpinned by a neutralist perspective on the exercise of liberal freedom, so that either it infringes the harm principle and can thereby be outlawed or it counts as legitimate exercise of freedom. Conversely, D'Annunzio seems more inclined towards a liberal perfectionist position:[101] alongside harmful exercises of freedom which are subject to criminalisation, other exercises of freedom can be classified as objectionable ('abuses'), despite not reaching the threshold of harm, and hence not being liable to being dealt with coercively. A different interpretation maintains that D'Annunzio's wording envisages emergency situations when an individual's abuse of freedom becomes necessary to prevent harms to the common good.[102] But this is less satisfactory, for if an exercise of freedom normally unjustifiable is necessary to preserve the common good, it is hard to see why it should be classified as an 'abuse' at all.

Be that as it may, the qualification to the idea of an abuse of freedom (which must either involve illicit goals or disruption of civil life before triggering coercive legal intervention) was almost certainly intended to offer greater guarantees than the Italian Constitution in force at the time did. The 1848 *Statuto Albertino* guaranteed the freedom of the press so long as it was not abused, but without offering any guidelines on what abusing it might involve,[103] and made the restrictions on other freedoms (such as the privacy of the home, or personal freedom) subject only to the requirement of their being legally prescribed.[104] Albeit relatively open ended, the language used in the *Charter*'s promulgated text (*illicit* goal, *balance* of public life) points towards moral limitations on the laws that restrict liberal freedoms. The use of the word 'illicit' (rather than illegal/unlawful) imports a moral evaluation into the assessment of whether or not legally prescribed restrictions on freedom are consistent with the *Charter*. After all, restrictive laws might arbitrarily select as unlawful some of the goals that individuals pursue, subjecting them to coercive intervention without sound justification. While the *Statuto Albertino* authorised such outcomes, in the *Charter* individual goals must be morally impermissible ('illicit') before they can be outlawed.

This approach, pointing towards substantive, rather than merely formal, standards of justification in the restrictions of freedoms throws into relief the affinities between D'Annunzio and De Ambris's project and some of its most idealistically driven and ideologically charged constitutional antecedents, such as the 1789 French *Declaration of the Rights of Man and of the Citizen*. The *Declaration* makes much of the requirement that the restrictions of freedoms must be prescribed by law.[105] But the combined effect of articles 2 (on the preservation of the 'imprescriptible rights of man' as the aims of 'every political association') and 4 (whereby 'natural rights' can only be restricted to 'ensure to the other members of society the enjoyment of these same rights') is to impose significant substantive moral limits on the legal limitation of freedom.

Finally, article LXI of the *Charter* introduces a noteworthy novel principle—namely, the provision according to which victims of wrongful judicial decisions or abuses of power (including *corporazioni* or *comuni*, as well as citizens) were entitled to damages. Its only historical antecedent was apparently an eighteenth-century law enacted by the grand duke of Tuscany.[106]

POLITICAL RIGHTS

Deprivation of political rights—understood as the right to vote and to stand for elections[107]—was admissible only following due process and in circumscribed circumstances. One, as we have seen, was the refusal to perform military service. The second and third cases involved those who did not pay taxes and those who were 'incorrigible' in burdening society despite not suffering from incapacitation to work.[108] To contemporary eyes, this may sound like *avant la lettre* neoliberal punishing of the 'undeserving poor', but there is evidence that it was in fact intended as a socially progressive measure that would appeal to socialists by depriving the leisure classes of political rights.[109] Foscanelli notes that the paradigmatic targets of the provision were the likes of Andrea Sperelli—the self-indulgent aristocratic protagonist of *Pleasure*, whose chief occupations are sports, art collecting, and going to concerts.[110] 'Incorrigible' was an addition by D'Annunzio—it appears in the form of a revision to his own draft manuscript.[111] The effect is to lessen the severity of the provision, which applied only to those 'parasites'[112] who had proven unreformable.

The fourth case justifying deprivation of political rights involved those condemned to 'dishonourable punishment'.[113] The reference to 'dishonourable punishment' is somewhat ambiguous. Nineteenth-century Italian scholarship on criminal law and criminal justice was more or less unanimous in considering the category of dishonourable punishment (as a specific class of penalties distinct from capital punishment, pecuniary punishment, and afflictive punishment) moot in post-Enlightenment European states.[114] In the Italian Penal Code of 1889 (which the legally educated De Ambris no doubt was familiar with) the category of dishonourable punishment had been expressly abandoned as such.[115] But some speculated that certain forms of punishment—namely, interdiction from public office or from certain professions—were in fact instances of (or an anachronistic legacy of the old category of) dishonourable punishment.[116] Presumably these very penalties (interdiction from public office or from certain professions) were what De

Ambris and D'Annunzio had in mind by 'dishonourable punishment' as one of the grounds for depriving citizens of political rights.

SOCIOECONOMIC RIGHTS

The next article of the *Charter*, article VIII, protects two more traditional liberal rights: the privacy of the home and *habeas corpus*, which, interestingly, is just so designated—that is, by using the Latin expression originating in English common law. Alongside these, however, it includes an array of socioeconomic rights whose express inclusion in constitutional documents was only to become commonplace after World War II. The novelty of the *Charter* in this respect should not be overstated. The French *Declaration* of 1793 was the first to have acknowledged that education, work, and assistance should be provided to the needy; and after a period when such principles were quietly forgotten, they were reaffirmed in the French 1848 Constitution.[117] Some constitutions enacted after World War I started introducing the idea that such obligations were correlative to (a new class of) individual rights.[118] What is notable in the *Charter* is the wide range of socioeconomic rights it guarantees.

Given De Ambris's syndicalism, it is hardly surprising that the *Charter* enshrines robust protection for socioeconomic rights. Other factors, however, are also pertinent. First, Habsburg legislation had already provided for social security rights in Fiume for several decades prior to the war, and the attitude of employers towards workers' demands had also been traditionally conciliatory rather than antagonistic.[119] Thus, D'Annunzio and De Ambris were intervening in a context where the bar had already been raised. Secondly, social security asserted itself as an urgent priority as a result of the devastation to Fiume's economy caused by the combined forces of war, the demise of the Habsburg Empire (the local economy having been largely dependent on investment by Hungarian entrepreneurs), and the blockade that Italy had imposed to force D'Annunzio to desist.[120] Thirdly, in working on relevant provisions in the *Charter*, De Ambris could count on the assistance of other men who were strongly invested in a politics of socioeconomic entitlements (particularly Clemente Marassi, who would be appointed rector for work).[121] Fourthly, D'Annunzio himself appeared genuinely committed, after de Ambris's arrival in Fiume, to the so-called social question. The last few months of the occupation saw a flurry of activity, showing that the twofold objective of securing adequate salaries to the employed and assistance to the unemployed were high priorities in the political agenda of Fiume's command. This was consistent with the principles announced in the *Charter* and cannot be convincingly explained away by appealing to reasons of political expediency.[122] Lastly, the times were ripe, as suggested by the fact that in the immediate postwar period the *Carnaro Charter* was not alone in constitutionalising socioeconomic rights.

Notably, the *Weimar Constitution* included some provisions aimed at permitting a partial restructuring of the economy along moderately socialist lines (articles 151, 155, 156, 157, 165), at establishing a public schools system (articles 142–149), at mitigating the consequences of involuntary unemployment (article 163), and at setting up a 'comprehensive' insurance system 'for the maintenance of health and capacity to work, for the protection of maternity, and for provision against the economic consequences of age, infirmity, and the vicissitudes of life' (article 161). This amounted to a very advanced constitutional protection for socioeconomic rights at the time.[123] The *Carnaro Charter* similarly provides for primary school education;[124] for old-age pension; and for economic support in the event of 'illness, disability and involuntary unemployment',[125] for those incurring permanent disabilities during military service and for their families in need, as well as for the survivors of those who die while defending the state 'if they are in difficult straits'.[126] However, the *Charter* also goes beyond the *Weimar Constitution* in several interesting respects.

First, article VII of the *Charter* expressly states that these socioeconomic rights are 'guarantee[d]' to 'citizens of both sexes'. Secondly, its list of socioeconomic rights also includes a guarantee to 'remunerated work with a minimum wage sufficient to living well'—something that the *Weimar Constitution* could not bring itself to reference other than in the vaguest and most noncommittal way, by declaring that 'the organisation of the economy must be compatible with the principles of justice, aiming at the conditions of humane existence for all' (article 151). De Ambris, however, maintained that if society goes so far as to require of its members to die in its defence, then it is only fair for it to ensure that they have the wherewithal without which all guarantees to other rights are empty.[127] In the same spirit, and thanks to an addition made by D'Annunzio to De Ambris's draft, the support given to those who are injured during military service was to be 'liberal'.[128]

Thirdly, D'Annunzio's additions to De Ambris's text show a less bureaucratic conception of the right to education than we find in the *Weimar Constitution*. According to the latter, 'in all schools moral training, a sense of civic responsibility, personal and vocational efficiency in a spirit of national German feeling and international conciliation shall be aimed at. . . . Civics and manual training form part of the school curriculum . . . [and] every pupil shall receive a copy of the Constitution' (article 148). Contrast this with article VIII of the *Charter*, guaranteeing primary education 'in bright and wholesome school buildings' and 'physical education in open-air, well-furnished gymnasia', with the latter, additionally, being singled out as a discrete, self-standing right rather than an appurtenance to the former. In thus reenvisaging the right to education, D'Annunzio is channelling his artist's ability to cathect with the characters he is writing about: here school pupils. Children, D'Annunzio intuits, might greet their newly found right to education as something less than an unqualified blessing. But they could at least be made to experience its value in a material context conducive both to a pleasurable exercise of that right and to their ability to flourish not only intellectually but also physically.

Primary school education for all regardless of sex features specifically as an entitlement alongside other positive rights in article VIII, making it clear that its provision was intended to be *gratis*. The *Charter* also provides, however, for broader state intervention in education, with a whole section devoted to 'Public Education'. This encompassed all levels, from primary schools instituted by local authorities through to a free university.[129] De Ambris's draft had not mentioned art other than in generic terms,[130] but D'Annunzio specifically requires the institution of schools of music, fine arts, and decorative arts, which he expressly states must reject academicism, pursue innovation, and reward genuine talent, 'supporting the best in [students'] self-discovery and in discovering the new relations between impervious matter and human feeling.'[131]

MINORITY RIGHTS AND LOCAL AUTONOMIES

The provisions on public education are also interesting because they show D'Annunzio's and De Ambris's attempt to grapple with minority (specifically linguistic, cultural, and religious) rights. This is highly significant, given the centrality of school language policy to attempts at assimilating minority communities.[132] By way of background, one should recall Nationalist arguments about the 'denationalisation' of Dalmatia, effected through the denial of educational provision in Italian, as well as the Fiumans' own complaints about forcible de-Italianization during the period of Croat rule and during the last period of Hungarian rule. Fiuman annexationists themselves, despite decrying repressive measures targeting their language and culture, had called, shortly after D'Annunzio's arrival, for the town's epuration by sending packing its foreign elements—perceived to be both hostile and a drain on scarce resources.[133] In such a xenophobic context, where the rights of minorities seemed to matter only when one was targeted as a member of one, it is significant that De Ambris maintained that to ignore the Slav ethnicity and language of part of the population of the *corpus separatum* would be seriously unjust and imprudent,[134] and that linguistic heritage was the 'sacred right of every race.'[135]

This concern for minorities in De Ambris's design was connected with the regime of strong local autonomies contemplated in the *Charter*,[136] which is of a piece with the internal regulatory autonomy afforded to other entities, such as Fiume's university and *corporazioni*.[137] In deliberate contrast to the kind of Napoleonic bureaucratic centralization that had characterised Italy since the late seventeenth century, the *comuni* of the regency were given the 'amplest' legislative and administrative autonomy compatible with the 'spirit' of the *Charter*[138] with respect to all matters not expressly reserved for the regency legislature and executive.[139]

The model provided for in the *Charter* envisages a horizontal distribution of power on the basis of differentiated subject matter jurisdiction rather than a vertical relationship between central and local/nonstate law-making entities.[140] Decentralisation was favoured for the usual reasons of greater efficiency, of encouraging citizens' participation in political life, and of being more equitable towards those unable to afford travelling to a centralised political and bureaucratic hub.[141] Yet this decentralisation also was specifically intended to provide protection for minorities, much more so that there tended to be a fairly sharp division between the Slav rural communities of the hinterland of the *corpus separatum* and the Italian ones based in Fiume's old town.[142]

De Ambris's original text had provided that primary education should be imparted in the majority language of each local authority. Only if enough minority students requested it would the local authority be required to also deliver teaching in the language of the minority, which should in any case be one of the subjects taught at primary schools.[143] D'Annunzio's changes strengthen these minority rights while also attempting to reserve a special role for Italian culture. Specifically, the *Charter* in its final form requires parallel delivery of primary education in both the majority and minority language.[144] The protection of local cultural manifestations at primary school level is also apparent in D'Annunzio assigning 'pride of place' to 'the teaching of choral chants based on the most spontaneous rural poetry and instruction in decoration modelled on the most refreshing examples of peasant art'.[145] Considering that the rural population of the *corpus separatum* was almost exclusively Slav, this provision effectively works as a guarantee of specifically Slav manifestations of cultural identity. At the same time, the *Charter* states that the teaching of Italian is 'distinctly favoured' in all schools and that in middle schools it is compulsory to teach all the minority 'idioms' spoken throughout the regency.[146] This implies that after primary education, teaching would be delivered exclusively in Italian.

This tension, within the internal organisation of the regency, between minority and cultural rights on the one hand and a reassertion of Italian privilege on the other hand[147] has a parallel in occupied Fiume's international policy. As we have seen, D'Annunzio and part of Fiume's intellectual elite strove to reconcile an aspiration towards internationalism with a belief in the superiority of the Latin cultural legacy, which convinced them that Fiume had a special role to play in championing the international cause of anticapitalism and anti-imperialism.

Indeed, the provisions on the teaching of languages and the language of instruction in public schools are preceded by a very lengthy article, where D'Annunzio on the one hand extols culture as the supreme law of the nation[148] and on the other hand rationalises the importance of preserving and strengthening specifically Fiume's *Latin* cultural roots. This would be both the most effective form of resistance against foreign usurpation and conducive to the emergence of the 'free man'.[149] According to D'Annunzio,

> The Roman rhythm, the fatal rhythm of fulfilment must lead again along the consular way the other restive lineage who deceive themselves that they can obliterate the great vestiges or falsify history. In land of the Latin type, in land loosened by the Latin plough, the other lineage will sooner or later be fashioned by the spirit that created Latinity: which is nothing other than a disciplined harmony of all the forces that contribute to form the free man.[150]

For his part, De Ambris had indicated his faith that the encounter of Slav and Italian cultures in the regency (which, it must be remembered, might expand to encompass 'allied communities' and 'islands of Venetian tradition' that freely chose to join it)[151] would eventually see the latter win out. But he also maintained that this must happen spontaneously, not through coercion, whether legalised or otherwise.[152] In any case, according to a report prepared by the Information Office for D'Annunzio, non-Italian Fiumans welcomed the *Charter*'s regime of minority protection, although they did not believe it would be possible to put it into practice.[153]

The provision relating to public education also addresses minority religious beliefs. D'Annunzio considerably expatiates on De Ambris's concise statement that public schools must be accessible regardless of religious creed and without interference with anyone's freedom of conscience.[154] In the poet's formulation, 'public schools welcome followers of all religions, believers of all faiths, and those who are able to live without an altar and without God.'[155] The choice of words is surprisingly modern. 'Welcome' shifts the emphasis from accommodation of diversity to treating it as valuable; and the passage about atheists inverts the conventional asymmetry between religion and its other, which constitutional or human rights documents invariably create when they single out religion (rather than atheism) as deserving of special protection. This inversion, in D'Annunzio's text, is accomplished by the subtle value judgement conveyed by the expression 'those who are able to live without . . .

God', which implies that atheism is an achievement. Margiotta Broglio notes the vastly different approach taken in the coeval *Weimar Constitution*, where religious instruction was part of the compulsory curriculum.[156]

In the same article, D'Annunzio also addresses the practical implications of schools welcoming all faiths and beliefs—and he does so with considerable foresight, judging by subsequent European litigation on religious symbols in schools[157] and US litigation on classroom prayers.[158] Neither religious symbols nor politically partisan pictures,' states article LIV, 'suit the clear walls of airy schools. . . . There is perfect respect for freedom of conscience. And everyone can make their tacit prayers.' In other words, D'Annunzio here clearly distinguishes—as has become commonplace in human rights law[159]—between freedom of religious belief and its manifestation. Restrictions on manifestation of belief (that is, the ban on symbols, and the requirement that prayers be said tacitly) strive to create a climate of religious and political neutrality in public schools, in the interest of guaranteeing 'perfect respect for freedom of conscience' for all. The solution reminds one of what has become known as the French doctrine of *laicité*, which—although it was not to crystallise in its current form until several decades later—had its basis laid down with the Act of 9 December 1905, introducing the separation of the church from the state. Even D'Annunzio's detractors grudgingly acknowledge that the provisions relating to schools are 'fairly advanced', albeit only to go on to assert as fact what is in fact pure speculation—namely, that such provisions must be credited to 'some or other of D'Annunzio's collaborators'![160]

Having banned religious and politically partisan symbolism from classrooms, D'Annunzio-the-aesthete cannot resist, however, prescribing the adoption of a kind of iconography that might, through the power of affect, speak to all (and hence, presumably, perform an integrative function among students of disparate religious and political convictions): 'But there will recur on the walls those simple inscriptions that excite the soul and, like the themes of a heroic symphony, do not lose their power of rapture even when repeated. But there will recur on the walls great pictures of those masterpieces that interpret with utmost lyricism men's perpetual aspiration and perpetual supplication.'[161]

PRIVATE PROPERTY

The article dealing with socioeconomic rights is followed by one addressing private property. According to De Ambris, a conception of property as an absolute right had been consigned by wartime legal developments and the necessities of modern life to the dustbin of history.[162] Syndicalist thought insisted that the institution of private property must be conceived as much in terms of duties and responsibilities as rights, an idea that had a distinguished—specifically a Mazzinian—pedigree.[163] In line with this, De Ambris's version of the relevant article states that property, rather than an 'absolute right or individual privilege', has a social function; hence, property over the means of production or exchange can only be vested in those that, through their labour, make their property beneficial to society.[164] The wording is rather indeterminate as to economic theory. On the one hand, the idea that labour provides a title to property and the idea of a beneficial social function of private property rights are—for Anglophone readers at least—distinctly reminiscent of Locke.[165] On the other hand, 'means of production' is immediately suggestive of Marxist theory and may invite an interpretation of the passage about labour providing title to property along the lines that property of the means of production should vest exclusively in the working classes—for they alone 'labour', in the sense of toiling.

This key distinction between those who labour and those who do not was used to justify confining the enjoyment of fundamental rights to the former in the first Soviet Constitution of 1918.[166] With respect to property rights, the Soviet Constitution had been transparent: 'Financial policy . . . facilitates the fundamental purpose of expropriation of the bourgeoise. . . . To this end it sets forth as its task the supplying of the organs of the Soviet power with all necessary funds for local and state needs . . . without regard to private property rights'.[167]

Although the wording in the *Charter* provision on private property seems more definite than its Weimar equivalent (according to which the use of private property must benefit both the owner and the common good),[168] it is much more indeterminate than its Soviet counterpart. This was deliberate. As De Ambris explained to D'Annunzio, the chosen formula 'opens the door to the most daring social transformations, yet without artificially forcing into being that which at this premature time would be doomed to fail'.[169] In short, De Ambris—whatever his ultimate visions on the organisation of the economy as a revolutionary syndicalist—deliberately did not go so far in the *Charter* as the first Soviet Constitution did in 1918. Rather, it has been argued that his vision on the reformability of the institution of private property mirrors a conception advanced by Mazzini, who regarded resistance to reforming property laws as denying 'progress', and abolitionist advocacy as denying 'an element of human nature'.[170]

A contextual reading indicates that the intention of the *Charter*'s provision dealing with property was, at least for the time being, less to collectivise property to the benefit of the working classes than to ensure it was held only by 'productive citizens'. This is an expression to be found in the provision on *corporazioni* (trade unions and employers' associations), of which must be members, in De Ambris's formulation, all those 'citizens who contribute to material prosperity and civil development . . . through continuing manual and intellectual labour'.[171] Among other things, these 'productive citizens' had a privileged role in political life because they alone elected the members of one of the houses of the legislature.[172] It will also be recalled how the opening articles of the *Charter* extolled 'productive labour' as the foundation of the political order.

Importantly, such 'productive citizens' also included—alongside workers, teachers, civil servants, and others—employers managing their companies 'on a personal, direct and continuous basis',[173] or, in D'Annunzio's apparently even more demanding formulation, employers who, in addition to owning a company, also are, 'in accordance with the spirit of the new statutes—cunning managers and assiduous growers thereof'.[174] De Ambris, in his letter to D'Annunzio accompanying the first draft of the *Charter*, had noted the failures of Soviet Russia's policy to deprive all but manual workers of civil and political rights. He had been clear that entrepreneurs who are directly involved in their business perform an important social function and qualify as 'productive workers'.[175] Read in this context, the article on property rights is less indeterminate than appears at first blush. The goal was not to dispossess capital but to ensure that privately held assets were made productive. Indeed, this becomes apparent in the *Charter*'s official (that is, D'Annunzio's) formulation, which adds to De Ambris's draft the clause that 'no property can be reserved to an individual almost as it were part of him; nor is it admissible that such a purported, indolent[[176]] owner should let it lie fallow or manage it poorly, to the exclusion of others.'[177]

In sum, the *Charter's* provision on private property was not attempting to emulate Soviet Russia—rather it sought a third way between socialist abolitionism and liberal hypostatisation of private property[178] (which, it has been argued, was characteristic, among others, of the Italian legal order at the time).[179] Despite this, the radical import of the provision should not be underestimated. Indeed the final two paragraphs of article IX were by some even taken to suggest that private ownership of the means of production could only be justified if the owner *intensively* exploited them (it was not enough to put them to use); and then only over such means as were useful to society.[180] These paragraphs stated that 'labour is the only legitimate title of dominion over any means of production and exchange' and that 'only labour is master of matter made maximally fruitful and maximally profitable to the general economy'. No wonder that D'Annunzio's rector of finances, the *laissez-faire* economist Maffeo Pantaleoni, was alarmed by the provision on private property. He urged the poet to drop it, because 'it runs counter to any modern economic activity: we won't find a cent [in capital investment] if it stays the way it is.'[181]

THE CONSTITUTIONAL FOUNDATIONS AND NORMATIVE COMMITMENTS OF THE REGENCY

The 'General Part' of the *Charter* concludes, in De Ambris's draft, with the provision that 'the constitutional foundations' of the state are made up of three 'elements': citizens, *corporazioni* (trade unions and employers' associations), and *comuni* (local communities governed by local authorities).[182] As we will see, De Ambris maintained that political parties are artificial associations, in contrast to *corporazioni*, which, as communities of workers sharing the same interests, emerge organically within society. Similarly, he believed that *comuni* were historical entities that had emerged through a natural and spontaneous process, out of the human need for organised life.[183] The naturalness, thus conceived, of both *comuni* and *corporazioni* explains why they—and not other forms of collective organizations—are placed, alongside individual citizens, at the foundation of the new constitutional order.

It has been recently argued that the centrality of *corporazioni* to the constitutional order is one of the *Charter*'s deliberately mediaevalising moves, intended to recover their primary role as intermediate social formations enabling individual self-development.[184] The terminological choice *'corporazioni'* may well have gestured towards the social role played by their mediaeval equivalent, but this should not distract us from De Ambris's exquisitely modern appreciation of the political importance of trade unions and employers' associations in the context of the twentieth century's mass politics and economic relations of production.

De Ambris's provision about the 'constitutional foundations' of the new juridico-political order—with its use of technical legal language—is transformed by D'Annunzio into an oracular pronouncement of unmistakably Hegelian flavour: 'Three kinds of spirits and powers concurrently contribute to order move increase universality: the citizens, the *corporazioni*, the *comuni*.'[185] The same Hegelian philosophy is echoed in the article that introduces the *corporazioni*, according to which the 'state is the people's common will and common effort towards an ever higher degree of material and spiritual vigour', and citizens engaged in productive work are 'a single working substance, a single ascending wholeness' with the state.[186]

Directly following the article on the constitutional foundations of the regency is a provision that largely accounts for the characterisation of the *Charter* as 'too pagan' in clerical circles and by the Italian Popular Party.[187] In article XIV, D'Annunzio takes it upon himself to set out the

> three religious commitments placed above all others in the universality of sworn communes: Life is beautiful and worth living in a dignified and magnificent way by the man remade whole by freedom; the whole man is he who daily reinvents

> his own virtue so as to offer his brothers a new gift; work, however humble, however obscure, if well-executed, tends towards beauty and embellishes the world.[188]

Leeden noted that it is ironic that article XIV was written by D'Annunzio rather than De Ambris, for 'these three sentences conjure up the Karl Marx of the *Economic and Philosophical Manuscripts* of 1844.'[189] Others have suggested that the passage echoes instead some of Mazzini's writings.[190] It has been argued that D'Annunzio here shows his awareness that politics in the modern world must be turned into a religion, complete with its own liturgy,[191] something that might have escaped the philistine Mussolini without D'Annunzio's example.[192] Indubitably, D'Annunzio appropriated the language and symbolism of religion to great effect—not only in the provisions of the *Charter* but also in his speeches and the festivals he instituted in Fiume, particularly in 1920.[193] But stressing purely the instrumental function of these uses of religious imagery—almost as if the poet was simply involved in a process of deliberate manipulation of his audience, by conjuring up a sense of the mysterious and ineffable[194]—comes at the risk of distortion. Such a reading of article XIV, specifically, obscures the idealistic dimension that transpires from the constitutional text as a whole, which, as I will argue later, is consistent in foregrounding intrinsic, noninstrumental values.

Conversely it would be easy to dismiss article XIV—the least recognisably legal of the *Charter* provisions—as the flights of fancy of an artist who allows himself to get carried away, mistaking legal documents for philosophical manifestoes. Admittedly, D'Annunzio here legislates a so-called imperfect obligation. While on its face article XIV does set out a general obligation (albeit not formulated in terms of an ought) and so may technically qualify as a rule, it is twice removed from ordinary legal rules. First, because it lacks a sanction in case of a failure to comply; secondly, because it demands compliance for what is intrinsically not susceptible to monitoring for compliance. Yet there is nothing terribly unusual in constitutions declaring the values that a polity is committed to, and article XIV shows a particularly sophisticated, complex, and attractive take on values.

The provision as a whole speaks, without expressly naming it, to personal well-being ('life is beautiful', 'the whole man'), implying that the establishment of the new constitutional order has human flourishing as its ultimate object. D'Annunzio is aware that personal autonomy is central to personal well-being: for if well-being is the state enjoyed by the 'whole man', who is able to live a 'beautiful' life, it is 'freedom' that makes man 'whole'. But not any exercise of freedom is as good as any other. In keeping with the *Charter*'s emphasis on the utmost importance of productive work, D'Annunzio suggests that applying oneself to work (however 'humble' or 'obscure') that is well done (and that, for being well done, adds to the beauty of the world) is particularly worthy of the 'man remade whole by freedom'. Thus, in addition to articulating the connection between a self-determined life and human flourishing, the provision also seems to intuit that the latter is largely a function of success in the pursuit of one's worthwhile comprehensive goals.[195]

The reference to freedom remaking man 'whole' gestures towards a post-conventional understanding of morality, along the lines of what will be, several decades later, Foucault's observations on self-fashioning, as a process that critically and imaginatively engages with traditional moral codes.[196] For D'Annunzio, we flourish into a kind of self-made 'virtue' through 'freedom'. But even if self-made or self-invented, virtue is not whatever happens to suit us; it can only qualify as virtue if it constitutes a 'gift' to others, who are conceptualised as 'brothers'. This presupposes both fraternity and generosity (as an attribute of genuine gift giving) as normatively desirable. This explains why Revedin is broadly correct where he says that for D'Annunzio the wholeness of the 'whole man' is his dependence on an ethics of responsibility (as opposed to one driven by profit and success).[197] Additionally, D'Annunzio's formulation implies that the common good determines what counts as virtuous dispositions: to be virtuous (and lead to our flourishing), these dispositions must be productive of the kinds of gifts that will be welcomed as such (rather than as liabilities) by the polity-brotherhood to which we belong. Thus, D'Annunzio here seems implicitly committed to a view more clearly articulated a few decades later by Arendt: even as we reject conventional and heteronomous moral codes, this does not result in a normative free-for-all, for communicability remains a *sine-qua-non* no less of aesthetic than moral judgement.[198]

Finally, the social function of productive labour here is couched in an aestheticizing language (entirely suited, of course, to D'Annunzio's decadent sensibility): work well done has the effect of beautifying the world. In light of the observation just made about D'Annunzio's presupposing certain well-established and familiar values (fraternity and generosity) in his articulation of the normative commitments of the regency, it seems clear that here too D'Annunzio is choosing poetic language to convey, in part, moral points. To the extent that productive labour, if well done, adds to beauty, 'beauty' is best understood in the same encompassing way as the ancient Greeks understood it for most of antiquity, embracing 'virtues and truth, action and thought—moral beauty as well as aesthetic beauty.'[199] Steeped as he was in Hellenic culture,[200] there can be little doubt that D'Annunzio assimilated its conception of beauty. Work that is well done, even the humblest, adds to beauty, then, in the sense that it contributes to a social environment that caters to material, social, cultural, spiritual, and aesthetic needs, thus enabling human flourishing. It seems highly likely that the self-same understanding of beauty was implicit, at least in embryonic form, in D'Annunzio's oft-ridiculed[201] slogan that he was 'the candidate of Beauty' when he had stood for political office many years previously.

CORPORAZIONI

The centrality of trade unions and employers' associations (*corporazioni*) to the *Charter* has been read as a way of emphasising communitarian concerns alongside individual rights.[202] It derives, according to De Ambris, from the empirical fact that these associational forms were becoming a mainstay of social organisation.[203] We saw how D'Annunzio reworks De Ambris's provision on the 'constitutional foundations' of the state (namely, citizens, *corporazioni*, and *comuni*) into one about the 'spirits and powers [that] concurrently contribute to order move increase universality'.[204] Similarly, in the provision about the compulsory enrolment in *corporazioni*, the subject of this obligation shifts from De Ambris's 'productive citizens'—that is, those contributing to 'material prosperity and civil development through continuous manual and intellectual labour'—to D'Annunzio's 'perfect citizens'—namely, 'the assiduous producers of common riches and assiduous creators of common greatness'.[205] As De Ambris explained, the compulsory enrolment of each worker or employer in the appropriate *corporazione* was not intended as lifelong bondage. Rather, it aggregated producers on the basis of their common aptitudes, preferences, and needs and of the social necessities that created demand for certain forms of employment.[206] De Ambris's defensiveness should be considered in the context of eighteenth- and nineteenth-century antipathy towards mediaeval corporations, which viewed them as one of the oppressive and stultifying structures of the *ancien régime*.[207]

De Ambris's draft had provided that the *corporazioni* have full autonomy to regulate their internal affairs and the right to hold property.[208] In D'Annunzio's version, the right to hold property becomes their full legal personality, while the internal autonomy of each *corporazione* becomes a right to regulate 'its own autonomy according to its wisdom and its experience'.[209] This formulation has Platonic echoes. It recalls the dialogue between young Socrates and the Stranger in the *Statesman*, which keeps returning to the analogy between governing a city-state and the governance of a particular profession (specifically, sailing), emphasising the importance of experience and wisdom in such governance.

D'Annunzio assigns each *corporazione* a number of responsibilities with respect to training and development of its members ('embraces small labourers to encourage them and set them on the path to improvement'), promoting technical innovation ('takes care to perfect the technique of arts and crafts; seeks to discipline work directing it towards models of modern beauty'), welfare provision ('consecrates the duties of mutual assistance; determines the provisions to be made for sick and weakened companions'), and cultural-symbolic tasks, including promoting the dignity of its category of workers, designing its own imagery and songs, developing its own rituals and ceremonies, participating 'as magnificently as possible' in the town's festivals, and 'pay[ing] respect to its own dead, honour[ing] its leaders, celebrat[ing] its heroes'.[210] Curiously perhaps, the incurably individualist poet here seems to appreciate better than the revolutionary syndicalist the importance of communities and their forms to individual flourishing and social stability. But D'Annunzio's individualism, far from being of the free-floating variety, had always been premised on treating the past, its forms of knowledge, and its aesthetic achievements as sources of meaning and inspiration, both for his artistic production and for orienting his practical thought (even as this was applied to cultivating the art of breaking with bourgeois convention). For someone whose engagement with tradition was at one time so self-conscious and so second nature, it must have not taken much to become alive to communitarian concerns that seek to ground the individual in communities and their cultural forms.

The *raison d'être* of the provision on *corporazioni* was not only to discipline relations of production and commerce within a specific organisational framework but also, as we will see, to shift the balance of political power away from citizens as such towards productive workers organised in trade unions and employers' associations. All of this was far from uncontroversial. Pantaleoni, the rector of finances (who, as we saw, had strongly opposed the provision on private property), wrote to D'Annunzio to 'implore' him to rid the *Charter* of its provision on *corporazioni*. It would, Pantaleoni maintained, 'hand the town over to workers' trade unions', who would proceed to treat all employers as criminals in need of surveillance, leading entrepreneurs to depart for greener pastures, with catastrophic consequences for Fiume's economy. Pantaleoni warned D'Annunzio that the moment he was no longer around, the current design meant that a few trade union bosses would be in charge and that, instead of creating a unique space for well-ordered freedom, the poet had chosen to build a 'regulatory prison'.[211]

The ten *corporazioni* were as follows. Workers of the agricultural, industry, trade, and transports sectors belonged to a single *corporazione*, alongside very small craftsmen or farmers relying on few and seasonal workers. Technical and administrative personnel of any private company in the agricultural and industrial sector constituted a category of their own, as did their counterparts in the commercial sector. All employers, with the qualifications just noted about small craftsmen and farmers, belonged to yet another corporation, as did all civil servants. The sixth corporation encompassed teachers of public schools and students enrolled in *'istituti superiori'* (which was probably meant to encompass both university and high school students), but it also included, thanks to D'Annunzio's additions to De Ambris's text, all those who worked in the fields of fine, decorative, and dramatic arts. The seventh *corporazione* was a residual category covering all self-employed workers whose job was intellectual in nature but who did not fall into the previous categories. Another category was devoted to cooperatives, represented by their managers.

D'Annunzio also added to De Ambris's original catalogue a separate *corporazione* for all seamen—no doubt in return for the support to the Fiume cause provided by the Federation of Sea Workers.[212] Its founder, Giulietti, was very close to the poet throughout the Fiume period.[213] It has been argued, however, that the reason for this addition may be rather of an artistic-aesthetic order—D'Annunzio, on this account, would have been keen on having no less and no more than ten *corporazioni*.[214] Indeed, initially D'Annunzio only envisaged nine *corporazioni*: article XVIII in the manuscript of the *Charter* expressly mentions 'nine' *corporazioni*, but subsequently a revision was made to the text, in the form of a label bearing the word 'ten', pasted onto the original.[215]

THE TENTH *CORPORAZIONE*

The provision setting out the tenth *corporazione* is perhaps the most frequently cited passage of the whole *Charter*. It is worth quoting in full:

> The tenth [*corporazione*] is artless, nameless, wordless. Its fulfilment is awaited as that of the tenth Muse. It is reserved to the mysterious powers of the people, as they labour and rise. It is rather like a devotional icon, dedicated to anonymous genius, to the coming of the newest man, to the transmutation of works and days into their ideal equivalent, to the accomplished emancipation of spirit from pitiable heaving, from blood, sweat, tears.[216]
>
> It is represented, in the civic sanctuary, by a burning lamp whereupon are engraved Tuscan words from the age of *Comuni* [that is, mediaeval Italian city-states]—a wonderful allusion to a spiritualised form of human labour: 'Effortless effort.'[217]

This passage continues to be regarded as posing formidable interpretive challenges.[218] Recent suggestions are to the effect that the tenth *corporazione* is devoted to extolling 'work as such';[219] that it represents 'almost pure aesthetic longing';[220] that it functions as a revolutionary *avant-garde* directing the (new) people towards the 'realization of . . . an aestheticising utopia';[221] and that it is a home for an 'elite of workers' endowed with 'keen genius', who 'spontaneously emerged from all the workers of the [other] nine *corporazioni*', and whose task is 'to guide every kind of human work towards progressive improvement.'[222] Even Foscanelli, who insisted that the *Charter* was an eminently practical legal document (not a literary one), maintains that in this provision D'Annunzio allowed himself a foray into purely aesthetic territory. Foscanelli draws an analogy between this provision and a passage in a poem from the 1904 collection *Alcyone*. Here D'Annunzio describes an elderly former mower, who is able to smile while reminiscing about the hard work of his youth, but only because he is no longer forced to toil for a salary.[223] The implication of Foscanelli's analogy seems to be that, in the same way in which the distance of time cancels the old mower's memories of hardship, the poet's imagination removes him from the immediate realities of work and allows him to craft an aesthetically pleasing but impractical fantasy.

The correct interpretation is far less obscure than commentators have made it out to be. The tenth *corporazione* embraces novel forms of productive labour as yet unknown to us ('dedicated to the anonymous genius, to the coming of the newest man') but which D'Annunzio foresees will be less taxing on human physical energies ('the transmutation of works and days into their ideal equivalent, the accomplished emancipation of spirit from pitiable heaving'). The initial version of this provision, where the poetic 'works and days' was a more straightforward 'human work',[224] confirms that the idea here is that the full mechanisation of material production will eventually relieve workers of the necessity of physical toil. Indeed, the theme of machines succouring workers is already present in D'Annunzio's poetry from nearly two decades before.[225] A more pertinent literary reference than *Alcyone*, therefore, is *Maia* (1908), where D'Annunzio had envisioned a humanity free from the hardships of labour.[226]

The reference to the tenth Muse corroborates this interpretation. The nine Muses of Greek mythology are best known for inspiring artists, especially poets, who leave behind a record of calling upon them in their work. But D'Annunzio's reference to the tenth Muse is not—in contrast to what is commonly thought[227]—an indication that the tenth *corporazione* is reserved to poets or other inspired, free-spirited creators such as himself. The correct interpretation of the tenth Muse starts from the observation that the ancient Greeks assigned the Muses a much broader jurisdiction than is generally supposed. Not only did the Muses inspire work of genius such as poetry, but they also discovered and were protectors of many of the arts; and, at least until the end of classical period, the Greeks understood the arts broadly as work that, rather than stemming from pure inspiration, was governed by rules, including the work of artisans and scholars.[228]

Where does this leave D'Annunzio's tenth Muse and the tenth *corporazione*? The tenth Muse was a fairly recurrent Dannunzian conceit. On at least one occasion, well after his Fiume experience had come to an end,

D'Annunzio will refer to the tenth Muse as 'the Ronchi Muse',[229] apparently to underscore the generative import of the march on Fiume, leading one year later to the 'act of life' (as he liked to call it) that was the regency. But more usually she appears, variously, as a symbol of modernity and dynamic creativity. This may be in benign terms—for example, when conceived in contrast with the traditional nine Muses of Greek mythology.[230] But it may also be in more sinister forms. For instance, she is sometimes used to draw attention to the beauty of technological warfare[231] or to portend the potential for creative innovation unleashed through wartime destruction and sacrifice in the name of war.[232] It is apparent from these uses that the tenth Muse in D'Annunzio's literary imaginary is usually allied to technology, innovation and creativity. Clearly, then, she is the perfect figure to associate with the tenth *corporazione*. The *corporazione* gestures towards those future forms of labour that will be less physically demanding precisely thanks to the technological advancement enabled by modernity, which the tenth Muse herself symbolises.

It may seem that D'Annunzio oscillates between this utopian vision of a future in which people are no longer under the yoke of physically demanding labour and a more idealised one in which the value of productive labour has been so fully internalised by each productive citizen that, because work is no longer experienced as a heteronomous imperative, it feels effortless ('effortless effort'). In fact, there is a connection between these two visions that is explicitly articulated in the Syndicalist Manifesto, from which De Ambris quotes in an article dating from 1 September 1921. As the manifesto explains, physical work is joyful when it is 'sport': chosen rather than compelled. With full automation, physical effort in productive work will become sport-like, because it will be so negligible that it will be genuinely possible to undertake it willingly, and therefore joyously. Most human effort will then be redirected towards the pleasures of intellectual labour.[233]

Ungari is correct, then, in stating that the tenth *corporazione* is meant for 'those who are not here yet, it belongs to the future'.[234] Ricotti also makes a valuable point, where he notes that D'Annunzio's prophecy that technological advancement will relieve humans from physical toil has religious-ideological implications. Toiling is, according to Christianity, a consequence of original sin; to that extent, the *Charter* envisions labour in ways that set it free from religious necessities.[235]

The provision on *corporazioni* is in line with the *Charter*'s determination to treat productive labour as of utmost importance—not just politically (as in the provisions relating to the makeup of the legislature) but also socially/ethically (as in the provisions about the social functions of productive labour, its adding to the 'beauty' of the world). Indeed, a veritable cult of productive labour transpires here as the centrepiece of the town's new civic religion: the tenth *corporazione* 'is represented, in the civic sanctuary, by a burning lamp'. Additionally, implicit in the passage 'the mysterious powers of the people, as they labour and rise' recurs the Hegelian notion we have already encountered elsewhere, referencing the folk's spirit rising to ever-higher stages of development through participation in the totality of the state.

Kotchnitzky must have had the provision on the tenth *corporazione* in mind when he deplored the decadent aestheticism of the *Charter*, so nineteenth century, so much the product of 'two generations of Aestheticists, Parnassians, Symbolists, Ruskinians, Wildeans'.[236] But he also maintained that any such flaw was more than redeemed by the way in which the document made the valorisation of labour the centrepiece of the new social and political order.[237]

THE LEGISLATIVE POWER

In its adoption of universal suffrage regardless of sex, the *Charter* went far beyond not only Italian electoral laws but what the vast majority of European states provided at the time in terms of eligibility to vote (by 1920, only Soviet Russia, Finland, and Weimar Germany provided for female universal suffrage). The *Charter* provides for a bicameral legislature, elected through proportional representation. The two houses had both separate and shared legislative competence. The first house deliberated on crime, security, national defence, fine arts, secondary public education, and the relationship between the central and local governments.[238] The second house deliberated on commerce, labour law, transports, public works, trade agreements, tariffs, banks, industries, professions, and vocational education.[239] Merged into a single legislative body, the two houses deliberated on interstate relations, finance and treasury, university studies, constitutional amendments, etc.[240]

In D'Annunzio's version of the relevant provision, the houses, merged into a single legislature, are also entrusted with deliberating 'on the enlarged freedom'.[241] Here D'Annunzio seems to charge the legislature with making laws that are adequately protective of the rights and freedoms listed in the *Charter*. The implication is that the law makers were intended to be—as we will see, together with the courts—custodians of constitutional rights and freedoms, not simply political actors on whose lawmaking the Constitution imposes certain outer limits. There seems to be, in other words, a model that blends political and legal constitutionalism, and the emphasis is firmly on the political branch of government to err on the side of more rather than less liberty. There is a not so distant echo between this provision about 'enlarged' ('*ampliata*') freedom and the oath sworn by the old imperial delegate (the captain) upon taking office in Fiume. The text of the oath is recorded on the first page of the first book of the statute of 1530. The captain promised to both preserve and increase (*augebit*) the statutes, grants, and privileges of the town.[242]

De Ambris described the regency as 'the Republic of Trade Unions', brought into being by a 'Constitution that shrinks the State—as central power—to its most basic expression and entrusts local and technical bodies with the majority of its social and political functions'.[243] The system is more elaborate than that envisaged in Sidney and Beatrice Webb's coeval *A Constitution for the Socialist Commonwealth of Great Britain* (1920). The Webbs proposed the abolition of the House of Lords and a division of labour between two parallel branches of the House of Commons (the Political Parliament and the Social Parliament), both to be elected by universal suffrage of all citizens in separate elections. The former would be entrusted with 'political' matters and the latter with social and economic administration.[244] As the Webbs explain, 'both have the function of expressing the desires and formulating the will of the community as a whole'.[245]

In the *Charter*, on the contrary, the bicameral legislature was designed to empower two distinct political subjects—the citizen and the worker. This solution was broadly consonant with other projects of reform being advocated in Italy at the time by different social and political actors, both radical and fairly mainstream.[246] These projects culminated in the appointment of a special commission to consider a reform of the Senate, though its recommendations—to the effect that the Upper House should be made representative of organised economic interests—failed to be implemented.[247] In De Ambris and D'Annunzio's own project for Fiume, the worker was to be represented alongside the citizen: specifically, the first house was elected through universal suffrage of all citizens as a single electoral body,[248] while the second had a specified number of seats allocated to each of the first nine *corporazioni*.[249]

According to De Ambris's original design, the members of each *corporazione* would elect five representatives, except for employers and blue collar workers, each of whom were entitled to fifteen representatives.[250] D'Annunzio reduced both the workers' and employers' representatives to ten and allocated the remaining ten seats to the representatives of the seamen,[251] for whom, as we have seen, he had created a discrete trade union. This redistribution of political power in favour of this category of workers arguably reflects the poet's closeness to Giulietti[252] but also his appreciation of Fiume's nature as a port town, and it points towards a vision where sea commerce was to play a key role in the new state's economy. Overall, the effect is that employees elected twice as many representatives as those elected by employers,[253] providing evidence that D'Annunzio's commitment to workers' interests was more than lip service.

It has been argued that the way in which representation of both citizens and productive workers was built into the design of the legislature was intended to join liberalism with the logic of social relations of production and thereby to transcend class conflict.[254] Others have argued that postwar efforts to redesign representative systems so as to make workers alongside citizens the subjects of political prerogatives tended to undermine traditional state institutions. This is because these institutions were conceived to give effect to the will of the people as citizens—something that the will of the worker, as a political subject, is arguably antagonistic to.[255] Indeed, De Ambris was quite candid that in the long term the worker would fully replace the citizen as the only political subject. The *Charter*'s bicameral legislature was a transitional compromise, not an arrangement that resolved the problem of political and economic governance. The *Charter*, De Ambris says in his letter to D'Annunzio, must be 'mindful of the fact that democratic forces retain considerable power, while the *corporazioni* of productive workers are . . . too imperfect and incomplete to take charge of the State yet.'[256] The *Charter* did 'not purport to destroy the old democratic scion; but it graft[ed] the new conceptions onto it.'[257] However, when productive work became sufficiently well organised, the citizen centred by 'purely democratic constitutions' (an 'abstract entity' that overlooked individual means, talents, ambitions, and education) would 'vanish like stars at sunrise'.[258]

POLITICAL PARTIES AND PARLIAMENTARY DEMOCRACY

The *Charter* makes no mention of political parties. This omission is consistent with the key constitutional role played by trade unions and employers' associations, given that their independence from political parties was a central tenet of De Ambris's syndicalist thought.[259] Indeed, Stendardi and Costa maintain that the explicit mention of only three 'spirits and forces' of the community—citizens, *comuni*, and *corporazioni*—rules out political parties as contributors to the polity's civic and social life, primarily because of the way they tended to predetermine and control their members' exercise of political liberties.[260] The attempt was to establish a state that rejected as much the dictatorship of one class over the others, as the hegemony of political parties in parliamentary democratic systems.[261]

It has also been argued that the existence of parties did not sit comfortably with the ideological unity that the new constitutional order sought to create.[262] But the *Charter*'s and D'Annunzio's own libertarian streak suggest rather the opposite: the role of parties was to be diminished because of how political party ideologies constrained individual liberty, not in the name of greater 'thought control'. As Ballinger puts it, the *Charter* 'institutionalized the vision of an aesthetic society in which individuals no longer organized themselves by parties or ideologies but by corporations and communes, distinct bodies united through the ritualistic functions of art, and in particular music'.[263]

D'Annunzio and De Ambris saw the role of political parties as redundant at best and damaging at worst. Ferrero argues that during much of the history of postunification Italy parties had failed to perform their role. Parliamentary opposition and majorities, rather than mapping onto divisions along party lines, were shifting affairs, with majorities being built on an ad hoc basis through a prime minister's personal networks, his readiness to accord favours to agreeable members and their entourage, and his amenability to commit to contradictory policy goals.[264] These practices went by the name of *'trasformismo'*—transformism. A byproduct of this was also that ministers saw themselves as 'presiding over private fiefdoms' and tended to ignore other members of cabinet.[265] It has been argued that by the time D'Annunzio entered politics in the late 1890s, the salient political fault line in Parliament was not between Left and Right but between representatives who were amenable, in exchange of favours and concessions, to support the government and those who were not—either for contingent reasons, or principled ones, as in the case of the Extreme Left.[266]

For Rossi, the critique of parliamentary democracy in vogue at D'Annunzio's time was essentially a critique of corrupt and opportunistic political leaders and parties rather than of the institution of Parliament itself.[267] Certainly, one is sometimes apt to see critics impeach less parliamentarism per se than 'Giolittian parliamentarism',[268] after the name of the renowned political leader who had turned *trasformismo* into an art form. But the problem was also with the way in which the system itself seemed unfit for purpose, in the sense that it lacked inbuilt mechanisms to deter malfeasant parties, governments, and representatives. Meanwhile, the increasing ideological radicalization accompanying the emergence of mass political parties—resulting from the introduction of male universal suffrage (for those over thirty) in 1912—brought into even starker relief the inadequacies of these old techniques of government.[269]

Ferrero was himself a supporter of parliamentary democracy, which he saw as defective but indispensable.[270] But his lucid critical assessment of it is worth exploring in detail, because it illuminates some of the genuine reasons for concern that underlay the vitriolic attacks of such critics as D'Annunzio himself. Transformism (though Ferrero does not use this term) presupposed a prime minister backed by the monarchy and able to rely on a personal network of powerful interests. This kind of leadership would corrupt and undermine the workings of Parliament[271] while exploiting the legitimacy the institution afforded, so that 'the more the powers of popular sovereignty theoretically grew, the more the organ of such sovereignty—Parliament—must be deprived of authority and power'.[272] The result was that Giolitti's prewar Italian democracy was more akin to an oligarchy, however benevolent it may have been:[273] 'thirty million men, governed by thirty people to the benefit of three-hundred-thousand families.'[274] To this extent, argues Ferrero, prewar Italy actually never had a proper representative system, for it lacked both a true opposition and popular government.[275]

But the problems with parliamentary institutions ran deeper. The popular will was 'at the mercy of the most fleeting impressions; it is the queen of the universe but runs the risk, every day, to fall prey to a few daring men, who either flatter or terrorise it.'[276] The risks were compounded, within Italy's institutional arrangement, by a bicameral legislature where a 'nearly futuristic' house elected on the basis of *'suffragio universalissmo'* coexisted with an anachronistic Senate appointed by the king. This—unlike an elected Upper House, 'which might express the popular will in a more mediated, reflexive, and pondered way'—lacked all credibility and conviction to temper any excesses of the Lower House.[277]

Despite these risks instinct in a system based on popular sovereignty and representative democracy, Ferrero believed that there was no escaping it.[278] The political-philosophical principles that provide legitimacy to the government by justifying its authority could not be made and remade at will, and by necessity developed over long periods of time.[279] The potentially destructive tendencies of a divided, inchoate, fickle popular will might be disciplined by parties, if each of these was held together by a distinct conception of the good or, as Ferrero put it, 'by spiritual principles endowed with comparative stability'.[280]

Ferrero's diagnosis illuminates—much more clearly than D'Annunzio's more impressionistic critiques—the sources of political malaise and loss of faith in parliamentary institutions that characterised so much of Italian public opinion in the first two decades of the twentieth century. Ferrero's arguments about the anachronistic design of the Italian Parliament go some way towards explaining the innovative choices De Ambris and D'Annunzio made in designing the bicameral legislature of the regency. These choices, however, are the exact opposite of what Ferrero recommended. Whereas Ferrero urged parties to do their work and to commit to distinct and coherent conceptions of the good, D'Annunzio and De Ambris sought to do away with parties and to aggregate political subjects around the interests and needs of their category of productive work.

REPRESENTATIVE DEMOCRACY

Ferrero's argument that the popular will continued to function as the only credible source of legitimate authority helps explain why D'Annunzio's and De Ambris's aversion for the liberal-democratic institutions of the bourgeois state did not result in the *Charter* dispensing with representative democracy and the citizen. Practical considerations about the viability of any alternatives also seem to have played a role. This can be grasped by considering the influences of Plato on D'Annunzio's political thought.

D'Annunzio's critique of democracy and universal suffrage in his political writings preceding the Fiume experience are implicitly indebted to Plato's political philosophy, and specifically the philosopher's arguments that wisdom is not a possession of the multitudes but of a few select ones. We have already seen that in his writing 'The Electoral Beast' D'Annunzio had predicted and advocated for a resignification of class terminology: in the future a 'nobleman' would not be defined by lineage and wealth but by desire and capacity for self-rule, and correspondingly a 'plebeian' would be understood as a person lacking in will and imagination and thereby in freedom.[281] This seems a reelaboration of Plato's argument that the possession of wisdom (not lineage) should be the criterion for identifying kingship and the right to rule. While Plato's *Republic* articulates what a state governed by such philosopher-kings would look like, a lesser-known dialogue, *The Statesman*, qualifies the arguments made in *The Republic*. One of *The Statesman*'s arguments is that because men, unlike bees, do not come into the world readily identifiable as clearly superior to their fellow human beings, whatever can be said in favour of the rule of philosopher-kings is not directly applicable to the real world. In the real world, argues the Stranger in the *Statesman*, rather than giving free rein to purported philosopher-kings, it is best to be governed by strictly applied laws that are based on experiential knowledge (trial and error), are informed by the advice of knowledgeable people, and have secured popular approval.[282]

There is no doubt that D'Annunzio had studied the *Statesman*. Not only, as I mentioned earlier, are there echoes of this dialogue in the provisions of the *Charter* regarding *corporazioni*, but in *The Virgins of the Rocks*—a novel that is frequently (but mistakenly) taken to set out D'Annunzio's political manifesto—he also directly quotes from the dialogue. This occurs as the book's hero is imagining the life of one of his ancestors at the time he was supposed to have met, as a youth, Leonardo da Vinci, who had painted the young man's portrait. D'Annunzio writes: 'And perhaps the beardless knight that walked away with his own people seemed to [Leonardo] to have been made King by nature "like he who in a beehive was born leader of the bees."'[283] D'Annunzio does not indicate where the quote originates, but there can be no doubt about his intention to reference *The Statesman.* This much is made clear both by of the unique metaphor of bees and beehives and by the extended discussion of Socrates in the preceding pages of the novel: for much of what we know about Socrates has come down to us from Plato's dialogues, and the young Socrates is in fact one of the interlocutors in *The Statesman.*

In short, *The Virgins of the Rocks* shows that D'Annunzio was well aware of *The Statesman*'s key argument against entrusting government to purported philosopher-kings and for incorporating democratic processes into law making. In Plato's dialogue, that argument hinges precisely on the metaphor of the beehive: men are not quite so readily identifiable as natural leaders in the same way as queen bees are. D'Annunzio's familiarity with Plato's arguments must have played a role in the *Charter*'s choice to discount the option of an intellectual avant-garde leading the polity (an arrangement that one might expect from D'Annunzio's earlier, more elitist political writings), in favour of quite an opposite model: what Leeden aptly describes as a 'decentralized parliamentary republic'.[284] After all, like the Stranger in *The Statesman,* D'Annunzio was interested, when collaborating with De Ambris on the *Charter,* in a system of government designed for the real, rather than ideal, world.

At the same time, having one of the two houses of the legislature represent the interests of productive workers organised within the framework of *corporazioni,* and entrusting to it the regulation of commerce, labour law, public works, trade agreements, banks, industries, professions, vocational education, etc., is a concession to the strength of the starting point of *The Statesman*'s key argument. Here the Stranger asks the young Socrates if entrusting the governance of the art of navigation to strict laws, rather than to the wisdom and ad hoc judgement of skilled sailors, would not be a recipe for disaster. The Stranger here uses the metaphor of sailing to make a general point about the desirability of being governed by the evolving judgement of wise, technically expert men, able to respond to the changing exigencies of their trade or art, rather than by preexisting and strictly applied laws made in popular assemblies. The Stranger later recants, as we saw, that conclusion and recommends democratic law making after all; but clearly the U-turn is rather too complete. If it is true that all-knowing leaders (philosopher-kings) are hard to come by, it does not follow that we cannot entrust relevant matters to the governance of those possessed with specialist knowledge. In a state where all workers must enrol in a *corporazione* and each *corporazione* has an obligation to develop professional knowledge and skills, there are some fairly reliable ways of identifying people with such knowledge. This seems, therefore, to be the logic that underlies the distinct competences and representational mechanisms of the bicameral legislature contemplated in the *Charter,* where a technical house complements a democratically representative one.

In Fiume, D'Annunzio may well have thought of himself as acting like one of Plato's philosopher-kings, wielding a kind of discretionary power unrestrained by law. But when it came to working out a system of government for the future of the town in ordinary times, D'Annunzio and De Ambris did not renounce democratic institutions and representative processes. Rather, the *Charter* rethinks these processes and institutions in light of concerns as different as De Ambris's syndicalism (his belief that the citizen is an abstraction) and D'Annunzio's grappling with classical philosophical dilemmas about the best form of government.

CORPORATISM

One might expect that the importance assigned to productive labour in the regency's institutional makeup owes its paternity to the syndicalist De Ambris. But De Ambris was speaking the truth when he said to D'Annunzio that the first draft of the *Charter* was trying to give expression to the poet's vision, as previously discussed between them: D'Annunzio had been favouring a change in Italy's representative political system in a corporatist direction well before his work with De Ambris.

There is an instructive passage, in this connection, in a public speech D'Annunzio was due to deliver in Rome on 24 May 1919. At the eleventh hour D'Annunzio had been prohibited from doing so, partly on the advice of the British ambassador, who impressed on the Italian government the need to restrain the poet's 'intemperances of language'.[285] The speech was published, in censored form, by a number of newspapers.[286] D'Annunzio here does not advocate dispensing with representative democracy. Rather, he encourages the Italian people 'to dare to move, without hesitation or compromise, away from a lying representative system, towards an honest form of representation . . . elevating the true producers of national wealth and the true producers of national power against the [current] inept and parasitic political caste.'[287] The reference to 'true producers of national power' foreshadows the *Charter*'s productive workers.

Alongside Plato, some nineteenth- and twentieth-century Italian political writing was another likely influence on D'Annunzio's conviction that political representation must be reoriented in a corporatist direction. As early as 1878, Giacomo Savarese had suggested that political representation should occur via the mediation of groupings that spontaneously form as society organically stratifies itself.[288] Syndicalists such as Oliviero Olivetti and Sergio Pannunzio (an influence on De Ambris) argued that parties were artificial associations rather than spontaneous ones; hence, they advocated a bicameral legislature giving separate representation to the interests of workers organised in *corporazioni* and to the interests of the nation as a whole. These should take priority over the sectional interests of individual citizens and political parties.[289] The jurist Alfredo Rocco also theorised a corporatist model of representation, where workers' organisations would replace the divisions of the party system; the model became part of the Nationalists' political programme in 1914.[290]

An especially well-worked-out theorisation of corporatism had appeared at the turn of the century. Federico Persico had argued that all the systems that followed the postrevolutionary French model took as their political subject an undifferentiated citizen. This was abstracted from the kinship, neighbourhood, religious, cultural, and artistic groups that in fact shaped the distinctive identity and interests that each person possesses. In assuming this fictive subject, Parliaments were unable to be truly representative.[291] Because different experiences of socialisation produce individuals with varying aptitudes for politics, the individual citizen was not the appropriate bearer of political rights.[292] Rather, representation should be conceived, as it was when it first emerged in the Middle Ages, as a prerogative of communities. At this time, Aristocrats did not attend Parliament in accordance with a logic of representation (the magnates had a personal right to attend Parliament); representation, rather, emerged as an institutional device to allow for the political participation of towns, corporations, and universities, who sent their deputies to Parliament to assert an interest as members and spokespersons of their communities.[293] Because in the modern world our different interests are met though labour in its various forms, the social function of work is the most politically important: organised work, then, becomes the pivot on which modern political representation should turn.[294]

Gomez Homen argued that Persico's work was the main theoretical antecedent of Fascist corporatism.[295] But despite propaganda to the contrary, for much of the Fascist period (including the years in which Gomez Homen was writing) corporatism meant little more than a mixed economy and the coercively imposed, bureaucratic management of employment disputes. Only later did Fascist corporatism encompass a reform of the system of political representation; and even then the reform was rendered meaningless because members of the relevant 'representative' organ were appointed top down.[296]

Persico's influence is much more apparent in D'Annunzio and De Ambris's corporatism than in Mussolini's. D'Annunzio's mediaevalising suggestions in the *Charter*—particularly his terminological choices in connection with the representative organs—may suggest his knowledge of Persico's theory. Persico had argued that political representation emerged in the Middle Ages so as to enable the political participation of collective bodies rather than, as was generally assumed, simply as a device to replace direct democracy once the size of the state had increased to such an extent that it made the latter impractical.[297]

I argued earlier that in the *Charter* the empowerment of the worker as a distinct political subject was meant to give effect to a different form of representation, not to displace representative politics. Additionally, it is hard to see how the representative organ envisaged in the *Charter* could be regarded as anything other than a Parliament. Indeed, in contrast with the view that the most distinctive aspect of the *Charter* is its antiparliamentary character,[298] I would argue that only traces of D'Annunzio's antiparliamentarism survive in the *Charter*. First are his injunctions (absent in De Ambris's draft) that the meetings of the citizens' house should be conducted with 'exquisitely concise brevity'[299] and that the deliberations of the workers' house should adopt 'the laconic style'.[300] The unrealistically low number of meetings the Legislature should hold each year (once for the citizens' house and twice for the workers' house) also betokens an antiparliamentary sensibility.[301] Secondly, D'Annunzio's vocabulary for the legislative (and indeed the executive) branch of government eschews the familiar appellatives used by De Ambris ('House of Representatives', 'National Assembly', etc.).[302] These smacked of the institutions and experiences of modern parliamentary democracies; D'Annunzio prefers an archaic vocabulary derived from the experience of mediaeval Italian city-states (*'Consiglio degli Ottimi', 'Consiglio dei Provvisori', 'Arengo'*).[303] Thirdly, Kotchnitzky argued that the separation of legislative competence between the two houses effectively assigned a greater role to the new political subject—the worker—and a reduced role to the political subject of parliamentary democracies, the citizen.[304] None of these, however, negates the character of the law-making body as a (representative) Parliament.

DIRECT DEMOCRACY CORRECTIVES

Despite the *Charter*'s reliance on representative politics, a number of ways to build the people's active involvement into lawmaking are provided for. The people in the regency would have the right to propose new laws, so long as the initiative was supported by at least one-quarter of those entitled to vote in the elections of the legislative body responsible for legislating on the relevant subject matter.[305] Similarly, if at least one-quarter of the electoral body requested it, any law passed by the legislature could be subjected to a referendum in order to approve or reject it.[306] Finally, the people had a right to petition the legislature that they had elected,[307] as an individual entitlement.[308] Rossi notes that such measures were rarely incorporated into constitutional designs at the time, and their presence in the *Charter* is therefore evidence of a genuine commitment to direct democracy.[309] Indeed, even in modern-day Europe it is extremely rare to find all the mechanisms of direct democracy that the *Charter* recognises figuring simultaneously within the same constitutional system.[310]

It has been argued that the institutionalisation of these mechanisms of direct democracy gestures towards the practice of political power that had become established in Fiume during the occupation. This was characterised by the immediacy of a 'continuous and even obsessive dialogue' between the leader and the population, paving the way to the kind of twentieth-century populist politics that largely dispenses with the mediation of political parties.[311] Be that as it may, the partial sharing of law-making responsibilities between the people and their representatives provided for in the *Charter* is consonant with its attempt to disperse power. It also is in accordance with D'Annunzio's vision of a constitutional order ushering in the 'man remade whole by freedom'[312]—at least on the plausible assumption that the poet shared in the belief that direct involvement of citizens in governing functions was conducive to a vibrant citizenry.[313] A politically disengaged citizenry, after all, would not be compatible with the *Charter* definition of the state as 'the common will and effort of the people towards an ever-higher degree of material and spiritual vigour'.[314] From this perspective, the mechanisms of direct democracy provided for in the *Charter* must be seen as essential, rather than incidental, to the new regime.

THE EXECUTIVE POWER

The design of the executive was inspired by the Swiss directorial model.[315] The executive was organised in a nonhierarchical, decentralised way. The legislature would elect each member of the executive[316] and had to do so from candidates outside its own ranks, for 'no citizen [was] allowed to exercise more than one power . . . at the same time.'[317] The executive was made up of seven ministers (D'Annunzio calls them 'rectors')—each house electing two, and the other three being elected by the merged legislature, on the basis of their substantive competence.[318] On all nonroutine matters, the ministers decided collectively, by voting. This point is much clearer in De Ambris's formulation (which D'Annunzio had originally retained)[319] than in D'Annunzio's later inapt rewording.[320] The later rephrasing has led some commentators to the conclusion (implausible as a matter of legislative intention, but certainly justified on a literal reading of D'Annunzio's wording) that the executive power only had competence with respect to a circumscribed set of extraordinary matters.[321]

The minister of external affairs held the premiership, but that only meant representing the state internationally, chairing the meetings of the executive, and having the decisive vote in the event that preferences among the other ministers were evenly distributed.[322] Considering that interfacing with other states would have logically befallen the minister of external affairs anyway, and that the deliberations of an executive made up of an uneven number of ministers would never result in a draw, effectively the distinctive function of the premiership was reduced to chairing duties! Indeed, D'Annunzio is explicit in declaring that the premier was merely first among peers,[323] and his subtle rewording of the *Charter*'s text rhetorically demotes the premiership even further: De Ambris speaks of a minister holding the 'Presidency and External Affairs',[324] while D'Annunzio has a minister of external affairs, who, it is later clarified, also 'assumes the title of Premier'.[325]

Not only was executive power decentralised in terms of its perfectly even distribution among the members of the executive, but measures were also put in place to depersonalise it. This should give serious pause to all those scholars and popular commentators, as much in Italy as in the English-speaking world, who subscribe to the notion that D'Annunzio was a Fascist or protofascist. Specifically, the ministers were in office for just one year, with the possibility of reelection only for one further one-year term, and then becoming eligible again only after one year out of office.[326] The shortness of these terms of office echoes the models adopted in the Graeco-Roman world.[327] De Ambris clarified that the short duration was meant to avert the risks apparent in presidential systems, where power is concentrated in one man for a very long time, who might wield it against the wishes of the nation. He cited President Wilson as a case in point.[328]

All public officials could lose office, either as a result of judicial proceedings that deprived them of political rights or if a simple majority of the electoral body voted for it.[329] They were also civilly and criminally liable, as determined by the Court of Reason,[330] for any damage caused to private citizens or public bodies through their 'transgressions, abuse, carelessness, cowardice or ineptitude'.[331] These are D'Annunzio's words, which set a rather more demanding standard of conduct than De Ambris had contemplated in his original draft, where he used the expression (probably more practical than D'Annunzio's own) 'abuse or negligence in the performance of their duties.'[332] These provisions also apply to members of the legislative branch of government, challenging the liberal principle of parliamentary privileges and immunities in the name of greater symmetry between the rulers and the ruled.[333]

However, no mechanism was provided for the executive to lose the confidence of the legislature. De Vergottini notes that, alongside the goal of providing better protection for individual rights, postwar constitutional reforms typically sought to rationalise the relationships between the legislative and executive functions, with a view to securing stable governments; but this problem was bypassed in the *Charter*.[334] Indeed, given the way in which the ministers came to hold their office through election, and the short duration of their term, it seems clear that De Ambris designed an executive that might be insulated from the destabilising consequences of a vote of no confidence, to which systems based on proportional representation are especially vulnerable. This is confirmed by De Ambris himself, who argued that the *Charter* protected the executive from 'parliamentary cabals and treachery',[335] and in D'Annunzio's explicit statement that the ministers' 'office is stable and continuous'.[336] To this extent, the *Charter* sets up a form of government that, on paper at least, should be able to carry out its business. Even so, it is legitimate to query the practical effectiveness of such a decentralised, nonhierarchical executive functioning in accordance with democratic principles. If, as we may suppose, De Ambris and D'Annunzio themselves wondered about it, the fact that they took the plunge at least speaks to their idealism.

THE JUDICIARY

As with the legislature, D'Annunzio proceeded to relexicalise De Ambris's terminological choices in the provisions relating to the judiciary. And, like the executive, much of the judiciary would also be elected rather than appointed.

Judges in charge of minor civil and criminal affairs ('local judges' in De Ambris's text, 'good men' in D'Annunzio's) would be elected by the people; the *corporazioni* elected the judges in charge of employment disputes ('labour judges'); the highest court—'Supreme Court' for De Ambris, 'Court of Reason' for D'Annunzio—was elected by the two houses merged into a single legislature.[337] The legislature, however, was not vested with the power to revoke the court's members from office.[338] Only juries and judges in charge of disputes not reserved to the good men or labour judges were appointed—the latter by the Court of Reason.[339] D'Annunzio styled these judges *'giudici togati'* (literally, 'gown-wearing judges'); for De Ambris they were superior—literally, 'second-degree'—judges. They were the only category of judges to be chosen exclusively among law graduates.[340]

In contrast, only a majority of the Court of Reason itself had to be made up of law graduates.[341] Indeed, in De Ambris's original design it was only a minority (two out of five).[342] Though one might expect a law graduate such as De Ambris to consider a law degree a prerequisite to holding the highest judicial office, De Ambris's choice not to require law degrees for all members of the court actually suggests his acumen as a student of law and political institutions. This is because the Court of Reason's first task was to decide on the constitutionality of legislative and executive acts. Constitutionality review is a quasi-political task for which the technical skills in application of the law possessed by Continental European 'career judges'—who enter their role shortly after graduation and are promoted on the basis of seniority—are not necessarily an asset.[343] From this perspective, the way in which De Ambris designed the membership of the Constitutional Court (deemphasising the need for career judges) appears prescient.

Yet the *Charter* did require that at least some members of the court be law graduates. This can be explained by the fact that constitutionality review was not the only task of the Court of Reason, which also functioned, among other things, as an appellate court of last instance.[344] In this respect, De Ambris's design departs from what was to become the prevalent model of (centralised) constitutionality review in Europe, which tends to assign appellate functions and constitutionality review functions to separate bodies. The prevalent European model is in line with the principle of the separation of powers: in Europe this has tended to be understood less in terms of checks and balances than as a sharp division of roles between the legislative, executive, and judicial (law-applying) branches of government. This is largely due to the legacy of the French revolution: the *parlements* (appellate courts) having been known, during the *ancien régime*, to commit all manner of abuse, the European understanding of the separation of powers was historically conditioned by a perceived need to confine the courts to the strict application of the law as made by the people's elected representatives. This, in combination with the understanding that the politically charged task of constitutionality review was akin to law making rather than law applying, resulted in a tendency across much of Continental Europe towards a centralised model that entrusts constitutionality review to Constitutional Courts made up of political appointees rather than to appellate courts of last instance populated by career judges[345] (though pressures towards decentralisation have emerged in recent years).[346]

The historical roots of the centralised model of European constitutionality review just described (from which the *Charter* departs) date from 1920, the very year that the *Charter* was promulgated. The *Constitutional Charter of the Czechoslovak Republic* of 29 February 1920 and the Austrian Constitution of 1 October 1920 were the first to provide for a specialised body entrusted with the task of constitutionality review.[347] Both the Czechoslovak and the Austrian Constitution specifically provided for the annulment of acts found to be unconstitutional[348] and detailed the modes of initiating review. Neither empowered individuals to challenge an act's constitutionality. In Austria it was either a minister that set in motion the abstract review process or the court itself that could initiate so-called concrete review.[349] In Czechoslovakia, abstract review was triggered either by legislative bodies or by the Supreme Court, and then only within three years of a law's promulgation.[350]

De Ambris's draft of the *Charter* predates the promulgation of the Austrian Constitution by several months. One might suppose that he was aware of, and presumably inspired by, the February Czechoslovak Constitution. However, the *Charter* does not specify how constitutionality review could be initiated, nor its effects. Omissions on such key matters—clearly settled, instead, in the Czechoslovak Constitution—cast some doubt on the idea that De Ambris's project was at all indebted to concurrent legal developments in Europe. Indeed, the different mechanisms provided for in the Czechoslovak Constitution and the *Carnaro Charter* with regard to appointment to the bodies entrusted with constitutionality review (election by the legislature in the *Charter*,[351] as opposed to presidential appointment and judicial delegation in the Czechoslovak Constitution)[352] suggest that De Ambris may well have been working independently.

If so, then, in contrast to what is normally supposed, 1920 did not see two but as many as three parallel instances—none derivative of the other two—of constitutionality review being inaugurated into European Constitutions. However, of the three, only the Austrian model proved historically significant. The experiment of the regency being quickly nipped in the bud, Langášek's remark about the limited historical significance of the Czechoslovak Constitutional Court and its groundbreaking power of constitutionality review[353] apply *a fortiori* to De Ambris and D'Annunzio's Court of Reason.

EMERGENCY POWERS

The institutional arrangements governing the separation and allocation of powers in the regency could be exceptionally suspended and all legislative and executive power be concentrated in a single figure, the commandant.[354] For those who are concerned with tracing the origins of Italian Fascism to the Fiume experience, or at any rate to argue that D'Annunzio's Fiume paved the way for the advent of Fascism, it might be tempting to pin their case in part on this feature of the *Charter*. Even recent analyses purport to find in the relevant provisions of the *Charter* distinctly authoritarian roots. It is argued that the office of the commandant could be extended 'indefinitely', that the 'extreme danger' that could trigger the state of exception was predicated on a 'very malleable' understanding thereof, that all of this aligned with D'Annunzio's 'political agenda . . . based on the notion of permanent war', and that this 'normalisation of the state of exception and of plebiscitary principles unravelled the idea of law itself'.[355] Such readings insist on a purported 'dictatorial conception of the [political] power of the Regency'.[356]

However, appealing—whether expressly or implicitly—to the *Charter* provisions on the commandant as evidence of D'Annunzio's authoritarian, dictatorial, or proto-fascist inclinations proves both too much and too little. It proves too much because, as Agamben's historical analysis of the state of exception has documented, the existence of emergency powers was well known in Europe generally, and in Italy specifically, well before this time, and it became commonplace at the end of the war.[357] While this, as Agamben has argued, may well have compromised for good parliamentary democracy in the West, it has hardly led to anything comparable to Fascism or Nazism in Europe as a whole.

The argument also proves too little because the *Charter* imposed greater limits on the use of emergency powers than many of its European contemporary equivalents or antecedents. An obvious comparison is with the *Weimar Constitution*. Its article 48 is reputed to have facilitate Hitler's ascent to power, because it gave constitutional legitimacy to the more or less continuous 'regime of presidential dictatorship' during the previous three years, when emergency decrees where issued 'on more than two hundred and fifty occasions'.[358] Article 48 allowed the president of the Reich to take unspecified measures to restore 'public order and security' when they were 'seriously disturbed or endangered', including by abrogating the rights to free speech, freedom of assembly, freedom of association, personal liberty, private property, and privacy of the home and correspondence.[359] The article was used, among other things, 'to imprison thousands of communist militants and to set up special tribunals authorized to pronounce capital sentences.'[360]

Contrast this with the corresponding articles in the *Charter*. De Ambris's original draft, in describing the exceptional circumstances ('great danger')[361] that justified the appointment of a commandant was no less vague than the *Weimar Constitution*'s reference to serious disturbances of public order and security. Yet the heading to the provision—'Of the Commandant'—suggests the intention may well have been to limit the applicability of the provision to the case of war. And this is just what D'Annunzio's reformulation makes clear. Only in the event of war, or the threat of an impending war, could ordinary institutional arrangements give way to the power of a commandant. The *Charter*, as revised by the poet, speaks of 'extreme danger that sees [the regency's] safety secured in the dedicated will of one only', capable to 'lead' the people 'towards fighting and victory'.[362] The terminological choices ('commandant', 'safety', 'fighting', 'victory') point unequivocally towards a state of war. It is also noteworthy that 'extreme' was a later addition, further indicating an intention to meaningfully circumscribe the scope of the provision.[363]

The commandant was a military and political leader with full legislative and executive prerogatives, while the members of the ordinary executive would be demoted to the role of his secretaries during his time in office.[364] It is significant that the relevant article specifically omits to mention judicial powers among those that were delegated to the commandant. Similarly, it is significant that the article makes no mention of the commandant's ability to derogate from fundamental rights. While this, in itself, does not rule out the use of the commandant's legislative powers to set up special courts or to adopt rights-restricting measures, it seems at least to discourage such measures. Indeed, article XXXXIX specifically declares that during wartime (the very occasion that might result in the appointment of a commandant) or during military service, 'the citizen does not lose any of his civil and political rights; and may exercise them when they can be reconciled with the demands of active duty.' Given this contextual reading, dismissing the *Charter* as not a 'serious' constitution because of its ability to 'disappear' during times of emergency[365] is quite misleading. It seems clear that the appointment of the commandant was not intended to trigger an automatic suspension of the whole constitutional order, particularly not of fundamental rights.

Perhaps the most significant difference between the *Charter*'s model and those adopted elsewhere in Europe is the sharper division drawn by the former between ordinary political arrangements and the state of exception. Not only is this accomplished by the *Charter* limiting the state of exception, as we have already seen, to wartime but also in several other ways. First, the *Charter* creates a *special office* to which political and military powers would devolve rather than allowing the leader of the executive to appropriate those powers. Secondly, the *Charter* provides for a disjunction between the identity of wartime and peacetime leaders; it is not contemplated that the commandant would by default be the leader, or indeed even a member, of the existing executive. Thirdly, the *Charter* requires the legislature to authorise the commandant to take office in the first place. Specifically, the commandant was appointed by vote of the legislature, which selected him among all the citizens with political rights.[366] Fourthly, the *Charter* puts temporal limits on the state of exception. The commandant's term of office was to be categorically no more than six months in De Ambris's formulation[367] and indicatively so according to D'Annunzio's final draft. This provides that, upon appointing the commandant, the legislature would decide on the 'more or less short duration' of the office, while being 'mindful that in the Roman Republic the dictatorship lasted six months'.[368] Upon expiration of the term, the commandant could be reconfirmed in office, deposed, replaced by someone else, or—as D'Annunzio adds to De Ambris's draft, in a nod to the ancient Greek institution known as 'ostracism'—'even' banished.[369] The closest to this that the *Weimar Constitution* provided for was to empower the legislature to annul the exceptional measures taken by the president.[370] Unlike the *Charter*'s model of the state of exception, however, this oversight measure—alongside the other features of the Weimar model—paradoxically set up a dynamic where the state of exception could (and did) become normalised as part of ordinary politics.

It will be remembered that D'Annunzio had been appointed commandant of Fiume by the National Council in 1919 and had been acting in that capacity ever since. The *Charter*'s provision devoted to the commandant indirectly ratified that status quo until Fiume could give itself the institutional arrangements the *Charter* provided for (which, in the event, never happened at all). To that extent, the relevant provisions in the *Charter* can be seen to have been self-serving for D'Annunzio. Yet it does a disservice to our understanding of the Fiume experience to ignore the features of Fiume's model of the state of exception that set it apart (arguably as more protective of liberal and democratic principles) from the solutions devised elsewhere before, during, and after Fiume's occupation.

Some of these features may well have been necessitated by other aspects of the *Charter*'s institutional design of power allocation. The nonhierarchical, collegial model chosen for the peacetime executive perhaps would have made it an exercise in futility to provide for it to assume emergency powers along the lines of the state of exception model prevalent elsewhere. But the fact that the radical or progressive features of Fiume's constitutional design during peacetime all but forced on the drafters of the *Charter* a solution that more sharply distinguished between ordinary politics and the state of exception confirms the attractiveness of that design rather than diminishing the significance of its distinctive treatment of the state of exception.

In light of widespread claims about Fiume providing a small-scale laboratory for fascism, one might expect the provisions in the *Charter* relating to the commandant to be especially useful in shedding light on how the practice and theory of power in Fiume might have facilitated a kind of proto-fascist politics centred on the illiberal leadership of a 'strong' man. It gives pause for thought that Fiume is actually an outlier in the history of modern Europe's treatment of the state of exception. The specific model the *Charter* settled for hindered, rather than enabled, the normalisation of the state of exception as ordinary politics that Agamben has so eloquently decried as a defining feature of virtually all major postwar and contemporary European legal systems. Stendardi and Costa are among the few who appreciated this when writing, in 1971, that the *Charter* provisions about the commandant seem designed to avert, rather than facilitate, the danger of authoritarian *coups*.[371]

ARCHITECTURE, ARTS, AND CRAFTS

The *Charter* ends with three articles that are absent from De Ambris's draft and that bear the unmistakable marks of D'Annunzio's paternity. These, alongside the article dealing with public education (which we have seen is central to the *Charter* regime of minority protection), have been dismissed in some commentary as addressing 'contingent' matters of no 'great significance'.[372] They are actually among the most original contributions ever to constitution making, anywhere, and key to appreciating the unique kind of sociopolitical organisation legally envisioned in the *Charter*. These provisions turn art and culture into legal principles constitutive of the society inaugurated by the new constitutional order. Gelpi plausibly remarked that they call for a contextual reading,[373] in light of the prescription that the state 'seeks to lead the days and works back to that feeling of virtuous joy which is to renew the people finally freed from a monotonous regime of impositions and lies'.[374]

The first, very lengthy, article concerns the institution a body of *edili*, 'men of pure taste, exquisite attention to detail, and state-of-the art [not merely 'modern', as in a previous draft[375]] education.' Their tasks were—according to a provision that has been argued to foreshadow the principle of sustainable development[376]—to ensure the health, safety, and upkeep of public buildings and private houses; to 'prevent streets from being disfigured by indecent or ill-placed factories'; to organise civic festivities (keeping in mind the ancients' ability to perform 'miracles of joy' simply through the use of light, flower garlands, and choreography); to instil in the people a 'love for beautiful lines and colours' by helping them rediscover and practice the traditional crafts that turned everyday objects into things of beauty; and to encourage builders and entrepreneurs to respond to the demand of new materials (such as concrete and glass) 'to be elevated to harmonious life in the creations of the new architecture'.[377] The regency was too short lived to see the institution of a full-blown *edili* committee, but two well-known artists, Adolfo de Carolis and Guido Marussig, were entrusted with designing the regency's official iconography and monuments, to develop the curriculum for a school of decorative arts, and to protect the town's artistic and cultural heritage.[378]

This concern with beautifying daily life and business, in both their traditional and modern manifestations, is far from being tangential to the creation of the new constitutional order. In the same way that 'the spirit of the old civic freedoms manifested itself not only in lines, reliefs, and stone joinery, but in the very imprint on men's tools',[379] so the 'man remade whole by freedom'[380] cannot possibly prosper in a world that relegates aesthetic value to an afterthought: 'a people cannot but have the architecture deserved by its robust bones and noble forehead'.[381] In this respect, a point made by the Socialist Adelchi Baratono in 1923 remains as pertinent as it is generally overlooked. Baratono argued that the valorisation of culture and beauty in the *Charter* was of a piece with its valorisation of labour, for there could be no real dignity and parity between manual and intellectual labour unless manual labourers could partake, and see themselves as partaking, in the creation of that which is worthwhile and beautiful.[382]

All this brings home the political valence of D'Annunzio's devotion to beauty; indeed, this abiding preoccupation with beauty and its cult can be seen as D'Annunzio's most enduring political commitment throughout his life. I have already noted that little in *The Virgins of the Rocks*, widely regarded as the definitive statement of D'Annunzio's political thought, should in fact be treated as such, when contrasted with the much more straightforward manifesto that is the *Charter*. Nonetheless, the concerns with protecting architectural and environmental heritage from developmental encroachment is entirely consistent across the two texts. Before leaving Rome, the protagonist in the novel, Claudio Cantelmo, observes:

> The contagion spread all over the place, rapidly. In the incessant agonism of business, in the exclusive, indiscriminate exercise of purely useful activities, any sense of decorum was lost, respect for the Past was laid to rest. The struggle for profit was fought with implacable determination, without inhibitions. Pick-axe, trowel and bad faith were the weapons. And within a matter of weeks, with unimaginable rapidity, huge and empty cages grew on foundations filled with debris, shot through with rectangular holes, surmounted by faux cornices, encrusted with horrendous stuccoes. A sort of immense white tumour protruded from the flank of the old City and sucked its life away.[383]

Yet the concern with the cultural and aesthetic legacy of the past has profoundly different ideological implications in the novel and in the *Charter*. In the novel, degradation of architectural heritage and disregard for taste are seen as inseparable from processes of political democratization and emancipation (all of which are condemned in the name of preserving and asserting the greatness of a privileged, deserving, and select few). Conversely, in the *Charter* the emancipation of the masses is a central *desideratum* and treated as not only reconcilable with but also enabled by both the cultivation of aesthetic values and genuinely representative politics. Indeed, the solipsistic and elitist withdrawal favoured by Cantelmo (which in any case fails to pay off in the novel) had already been abandoned by 1898, where the hero of D'Annunzio's next novel, the public intellectual Stelio Effrena, successfully engages the multitudes by conveying his trust 'in the sovereign dignity of the spirit, in the indestructible power of Beauty, in all the high values regarded as base by latter-day barbarism.'[384]

MUSIC

The last two articles are devoted to music: the first to justify its importance as a 'social and religious institution',[385] and the second to practically ensure that music would be duly practiced and cultivated in the new state. Music too, D'Annunzio tells us, is integral to the process of the people's political rebirth: 'If the rebirth of a noble people is a lyrical effort . . . if every new order is a lyrical order . . . Music, as a ritual language, exalts that act of life, that work of life.'[386]

Music also portends the 'kingdom of the [human] spirit', which not even the new constitutional order has inaugurated, for its advent awaits the technological development that will free people from the toil of manual labour. D'Annunzio tells us that while we wait for that future, 'Music finds its movements and its fullness in the tools of work and profit and play, in the roaring machines that obey, too, a rhythm as precise as poetry'; whereas music's 'pauses' correspond to 'the silence of the tenth *corporazione*.'[387] It will be remembered that the vision of a future where manual labour would become less taxing had already surfaced where D'Annunzio spoke of the tenth *corporazione*: this was reserved precisely for those as yet unrealised forms of production that would emancipate humans from the demands of physical toil.[388] It fits that tenth *corporazione,* dedicated to what remains currently unfulfilled, should be silent.

Having rationalised the centrality of music to civic life in the penultimate article, in the final article D'Annunzio provides that each local authority will set up musical bands and choirs subsidised by the state. He also provides for the construction of a performance venue capable of accommodating an audience of at least ten thousand, with a large pit for the orchestra and choir. Musical performances, he adds, will be '"completely gratuitous" as said by the Church fathers of God's graces.'[389] The vaguely blasphemous effect of the comparison echoes a line in the previous article, declaring that 'not only does a great people create its god in its own image, but it also creates hymns for its god.'[390] Apparent in these remarks is a Nietzschean rejection of a transcendental (rather than human) source for values.[391] Although it may convey a serious meta-philosophical point, the comparison between the theological doctrine of Grace and concerts accessible free of charge is outlandish: it is its own gratuitousness (rather than the gratis basis on which access to the concerts is prescribed to be offered) that stands out most to the reader. The pompous Latin formula that follows upon the heels of the comparison and closes the *Charter*—'Thus it is established and ordained. I swear'[392]—only compounds D'Annunzio's deliberate irreverence. For all its levity, the provision does establish a constitutionally protected positive and substantive right for the citizens of Fiume to enjoy certain manifestations of art and culture. Such cultural rights are considered 'third-generation' human rights in contemporary reflection, suggesting the prefigurative character of the *Charter*.[393]

It has been speculated that the Venetian pianist Luisa Baccará, at the time D'Annunzio's lover, might have played a role in determining D'Annunzio to add these articles to the *Charter*.[394] Marinetti claimed their legitimate paternity:

'Music—clarifying, elevating, purifying proletarian masses. I expressed this concept fifteen days ago in my manifesto "Beyond Communism". Ten days before D'Annunzio's Statute of Fiume, who turns this self-same concept into something academic and banal.'[395] But D'Annunzio's devotion to music as a superior art form is well documented:[396] 'Only to music it is today granted to express the dreams that were born in the depths of modern melancholy, the vague thoughts, the limitless desires, the anxieties without a cause, the inconsolable despairs, all the darkest and most angsty apprehensions that we have inherited from the likes of Obermann and René.'[397]

Marinetti's petty accusation of plagiarism fails to see that the last two articles of the *Charter* are far from enlarging on anything so crudely literal as his own purification of the proletariat. For the same reason, I cannot agree with Ricco that in the *Charter* the key function of music is a pedagogical one.[398] For D'Annunzio, music expresses, touches, moves, resonates with, intensifies: it does not teach, as such, nor is it redemptive in the instrumental sense Marinetti thinks it to be. The *raison d'être* of music in the *Charter* is not any purported beneficial consequences it might produce. Music is rather conceived as contributing noninstrumentally to the good life.

The provisions on music and on the role of the body of men whose task it was, essentially, to ensure that aesthetic concerns would be taken seriously in the life of the town make apparent a broader orientation that pervades the *Charter* as a whole—namely, its refusal to treat intrinsic values as subordinated to instrumental ones. This very orientation frustrated involved observers such as Pantaleoni. D'Annunzio's rector of finance wrote to him that if Fiume's independence was to succeed, it would be because the international community felt that is would be '*useful* to the world', notably through the investment opportunities that it opened up for foreign capital. This meant the town's status as freeport should be immediately brought into operation. Whether or not Fiume's independence was, in addition to its utility, also 'beautiful or right', these were 'properties that the political world cares nothing for.'[399] Writing to De Ambris less than five months after the end of occupation, however, D'Annunzio stated, with uncharacteristically quiet pride, that in Fiume they had 'founded a new order on the claims of the soul.'[400]

CONCLUSIONS

D'Annunzio resigned his political powers and those of the provisional government of the regency on 28 December 1920. On 31 December Host-Venturi and Fiume mayor Riccardo Gigante signed the peace agreement with the representative of the Italian government. On the same evening, the Municipal

Council headed by Gigante ratified the agreement, taking note of the resignation of the commandant and of the provisional government and fixing a date for elections of a Constituent Assembly. In the interim, the agreement provided that the Municipal Council itself assumed 'all the functions and full State powers formerly exercised by the National Council, recalling into force the relevant constitutional norms.'[401] For all intents and purposes, the regency and the *Charter* had been an interlude struck out of the record by this return to the constitutional *status quo ante*.

The short-lived experience and disastrous end of the regency and its *Charter* explain the limited scholarly attention the *Charter* attracted for many decades. The Fascist regime attempted either to relegate the *Charter* to constitutional history's cabinet of curiosities,[402] where the libertarian and egalitarian elements of the *Charter*, which made for such a stark contrast with Fascist autocracy, could be safely contained, or to appropriate its innovations by praising it as an embryonic expression of principles later fully elaborated by Fascism,[403] glossing over those stark differences. The literary language of the *Charter*, the Fascist regime's dislike for a document deemed to exhibit anarchic tendencies, and paradoxically, the association of the regency with Fascism itself in later historiography all contributed to the modest attention the *Charter* received until recently.[404]

Much has been said about Mussolini appropriating the liturgy of power elaborated by D'Annunzio in Fiume to shore up support for the Fascist regime. This obscures the point that D'Annunzio's own symbolism of power was not—despite what some scholarship continues to give the impression of[405]—empty form practiced for the merely instrumental goals of unifying the legionnaires ideologically and regaining the Fiumans' approbation. It has been said that Dannunzian liturgy in Fiume was capable of 'acquiring autonomous significance throughout its existence purely as forms'.[406] But the civic liturgy practiced in occupied Fiume could only do its illocutionary work on condition that the audience believed in the social and political renewal and higher forms of human flourishing that D'Annunzio's rhetoric promised. It could not have been experienced as a source of meaning otherwise, in the same way that a Mass, however aesthetically pleasing, cannot carry its audience with it and be experienced as a Mass unless the audience buys into Christianity. Nor do we have any good reason to think that D'Annunzio was a rogue priest preaching a religion that was useful, but ultimately meaningless, to him. Nowhere is D'Annunzio's and his collaborators' belief in the myths they themselves spun more apparent than in the *Charter*, and in its attempt at creating the conditions of possibility of a world that belongs to the 'man remade whole by freedom'.

NOTES

1. Lucio Villari, *La Luna di Fiume—1919: Il Complotto* (Milano: Ugo Guanda, 2019), 129–30.

2. Alceste De Ambris, "D'Annunzio e il Proletariato," *L'Internazionale* (3 December 1922), in *Sindacalismo Rivoluzionario e Fiumanesimo nel Carteggio De Ambris—D'Annunzio*, ed. Renzo De Felice (Brescia: Morcelliana, 1966), 351.

3. Paolo Ungari, "Commento Giuridico alla Carta del Carnaro," in *D'Annunzio e il Suo Tempo*, vol. 1, ed. Francesco Perfetti (Genova: Sagep, 1989), 51.

4. Giuseppe De Vergottini, *La Costituzione Secondo D'Annunzio* (Milano: Luni, 2020), 36.

5. De Vergottini, *La Costituzione,* 63; Giuseppe De Vergottini, "Prassi e Utopia nel Disegno Costituzionale Dannunziano," *Rivista AIC* 3 (2019): 603; Michael A. Leeden, *The First Duce* (Baltimore and London: John Hopkins University Press, 1977), 163–64.

6. Compare Vittorio Frosini, "D'Annunzio e la Carta del Carnaro," *Nuova Antologia* 2041 (January 1971): 81.

7. Renzo De Felice, *D'Annunzio Politico, 1918–1938* (Roma and Bari: Laterza, 1978), 105–11; Guglielmo Negri, "La Carta del Carnaro tra De Ambris e D'Annunzio," in *D'Annunzio e il Suo Tempo*, ed. Perfetti, 57–59.

8. Gaspare Ambrosini, *Sindacati, Consigli Tecnici e Parlamento Politico* (Roma: A.R.E., 1925), 109, quoted in Renzo De Felice, "Introduzione," in *La Carta del Carnaro nei Testi di Alceste De Ambris e Gabriele D'Annunzio*, ed. Renzo De Felice (Bologna: il Mulino, 1973), 7.

9. De Felice, *D'Annunzio Politico*, 134.

10. De Ambris's and D'Annunzio's versions have been published side by side in *La Carta del Carnaro e Altri Scritti su Fiume*, ed. Marco Fressura and Patrick Karlsen (Roma: Castelvecchi, 2009), and previously in *La Carta del Carnaro nei Testi di Alceste De Ambris e Gabriele D'Annunzio*, ed. Renzo De Felice (Bologna: il Mulino, 1973).

11. Ungari, "Commento Giuridico," 53.

12. Fulvio Senardi, "Introduzione," in *Il Punto su D'Annunzio*, ed. Fulvio Senardi (Bari: Laterza, 1989), 56.

13. De Felice, *D'Annunzio Politico*, 114.

14. George L. Mosse, "The Poet and the Exercise of Political Power: Gabriele D'Annunzio," *Yearbook of Comparative and General Literature* 22 (1973): 38.

15. See also Francesco G. Muggia, "Preface" to Cinzia Guazzi, *La Reggenza Italiana del Carnaro nella Storia del Diritto Costituzionale* (Genova: Centro di Cultura Giuliano Dalmata, 1982), republished as "Studio di Cinzia Guazzi Edito dal Centro di Cultura Giuliano-Dalmata: Congiungimento nella Carta del Carnaro tra Pensiero Dannunziano e Progresso di Fiume," *L'Arena di Pola* (8 January 1983), 3.

16. Edoardo Susmel, *Fiume attraverso la Storia: Dalle Origini fino ai Nostri Giorni* (Milano: Treves, 1919), 3.

17. *The Carnaro Charter*, art. LV (D'Annunzio's text).

18. Nicolino Flaminio Costa and Gian Galeazzo Stendardi di Montebenichi, "La 'Carta del Carnaro'," in Gabriele D'Annunzio, *Reggenza Italiana del Carnaro: Disegno di un Nuovo Ordinamento dello Stato Libero di Fiume* (Milano: Perelli, 1973), 47.

19. Manoscritto Primitivo della "Carta del Carnaro" (Preamble), Fondazione il Vittoriale degli Italiani, Archivio Personale, 588.

20. Susmel, *Fiume attraverso la Storia*, 4.

21. *The Carnaro Charter*, article 1 (De Ambris's draft) and I–II (D'Annunzio's text).

22. Manoscritto Primitivo della "Carta del Carnaro" (article I), Fondazione il Vittoriale degli Italiani, Archivio Personale, 588.

23. Manoscritto Primitivo della "Carta del Carnaro" (art. VIII, heading to art. LV), Fondazione il Vittoriale degli Italiani, Archivio Personale, 588.

24. Federico Lorenzo Ramaioli, "Res Publica Fiumana: Elementi Medievali nella Concezione Giuridica della Fiume D'Annunziana," in *D'Annunzio Legislatore: Costituzioni, Visioni, Utopie dell'Impresa Fiumana*, ed. Giordano Bruno Guerri (Milano: Silvana Editoriale, 2022), 158–62.

25. Manoscritto Primitivo della "Carta del Carnaro" (art. XXII), Fondazione il Vittoriale degli Italiani, Archivio Personale, 588.

26. *The Carnaro Charter*, art. XXII, LV (D'Annunzio's text).

27. *The Carnaro Charter*, art. 2 (De Ambris's draft) and III (D'Annunzio's text).

28. Ungari, "Commento Giuridico," 53.

29. Costa and Stendardi, "La 'Carta del Carnaro'," 50; Paolo Bargiacchi, "Attualita' della Carta Costituzionle del Carnaro," in *Lo Statuto della Reggenza Italiana del Carnaro tra Storia, Diritto Internazionale e Diritto Costituzionale*, ed. Augusto Sinagra (Milano: Giuffré, 2009), 54.

30. Manoscritto Primitivo della "Carta del Carnaro" (art. II), Fondazione il Vittoriale degli Italiani, Archivio Personale, 588.

31. Manoscritto Primitivo della "Carta del Carnaro" (art. LII), Fondazione il Vittoriale degli Italiani, Archivio Personale, 588.

32. *The Carnaro Charter*, art. 2 (De Ambris's draft) and III (D'Annunzio's text).

33. *The Carnaro Charter*, art. 20, 23 (De Ambris's draft) and XXVIII and XXXI (D'Annunzio's text).

34. *The Carnaro Charter*, art. XVII (D'Annunzio's text).

35. Manoscritto Primitivo della "Carta del Carnaro" (article XXXVII), Fondazione il Vittoriale degli Italiani, Archivio Personale, 588.

36. Gabriele D'Annunzio, *Le Vergini delle Rocce*, in *Romanzi e Novelle*, vol. I (Milano: Mondadori, 1942), 405.

37. Gabriele D'Annunzio, *Il Fuoco*, in *Romanzi e Novelle*, vol. II (Milano: Mondadori, 1942), 857.

38. *Constitution of the Soviet Union* 1936, art. 1.

39. *Fondata Sul Lavoro* (Roma: Senato della Repubblica, 2018), 34–38, https://www.senato.it/application/xmanager/projects/leg18/file/repository/relazioni/libreria/novita/XVIII/FONDATA_SUL_LAVORO.pdf.

40. *The Carnaro Charter*, art. III (D'Annunzio's text).

41. *The Carnaro Charter*, art. 2 (De Ambris's draft) and IV (D'Annunzio's text).

42. On the concept of organising principles of inequality, see generally Davina Cooper, *Challenging Diversity* (Cambridge: Cambridge University Press, 2004).

43. Edwad S. Brinkley "Homosexuality as (Anti)Illness: Oscar Wilde's the Picture of Dorian Gray and Gabriele D'Annunzio's Il Piacere," *Studies in 20th Century Literature* 22, no. 1 (1998): 76.

44. Gabriele D'Annunzio, *Il Piacere*, in *Romanzi e Novelle*, vol. I (Milano: Mondadori, 1942), 44.

45. D'Annunzio, *Il Piacere*, 49.

46. It is worth noting that D'Annunzio was a keen admirer of Japanese art and crafts. In Fiume he also celebrated Japan's combining a bold programme of modernisation with respect for its cultural traditions as a welcome check on Western imperialism, and as a source of inspiration for Italy. Giordano Bruno Guerri, *Disobbedisco: Cinquecento Giorni di Rivoluzione. Fiume 1919–1920* (Milano: Mondadori, 2019), 194.

47. *The Carnaro Charter*, art. 2 (De Ambris's draft) and IV (D'Annunzio's text).

48. John Stuart Mill, *Considerations on Representative Government* (London: Parker, Son and Bourn, 1861).

49. *The Carnaro Charter*, art. 3 (De Ambris's draft).

50. Antonio Rosmini, *Filosofia del Diritto*, vol. 2 (Milano: Boniardi-Pogliani, 1843), 254; Pietro Esperson, *Condizione Giuridica dello Straniero secondo le Legislazioni Italiane ed Estere* (Roma, Torino, Firenze: Fratelli Bocca, 1890), 110; Gabriel Bonnot de Mably, *Dei Diritti e dei Doveri del Cittadino*, trans. G. M. (Milano: Stamperia Patriotica, 1797), 121; Pietro Castiglioni, *Della Monarchia Parlamentare e dei Diritti e Doveri del Cittadino Secondo lo Statuto e le Leggi del Piemonte*, vol. 1 (Milano: Guglielmini, 1859), 72.

51. Filippo Serafini, *Istituzioni di Diritto Romano Comparato al Diritto Civile Patrio*, vol. 1 (Firenze: Giuseppe Pellas, 1892), 61.

52. *The Carnaro Charter*, art. V (D'Annunzio's text).

53. Giuseppe Panattoni, "Diritti Fondamentali e Loro Dichiarazione in Inghilterra, America, Germania, Francia e Italia," *La Temi: Giornale di Legislazione e Giurisprudenza* 7 (1848): 387–96 (especially 389–91).

54. Giacomo Margotti, "Il Gran Libro dei Diritti del Popolo," in Giacomo Margotti, *Memorie per la Storia de' Nostri Tempi dal Congresso di Parigi nel 1856 ai Giorni Nostri* (Torino: Unione Tipografico-Editrice, 1865), 268–70.

55. John Rae, *Contemporary Socialism* (New York: Scribner, 1891), 350–51, 419–20.

56. Rae, *Contemporary Socialism*, 11, 126, 349.

57. *The Carnaro Charter*, art. V (D'Annunzio's text).

58. *The Carnaro Charter*, art. V (D'Annunzio's text).

59. Gabriele D'Annunzio, *Italy or Death, from the Vedetta d'Italia of September 10th and 12th 1919*, trans. Henry Furst (Fiume: La Vedetta D'Italia, undated), 21–22.

60. Letter from A. De Ambris to G. D'Annunzio (18 March 1920), in *La Carta del Carnaro e Altri Scritti su Fiume*, ed. Marco Fressura and Patrick Karlsen (Roma: Castelvecchi, 2009), 127.

61. Leeden, *The First Duce*, 68, 81; Rolandi, "A Never Requested Triumph? Reframing Gender Boundaries in Fiume and Sušak After 1918," *Italia Contemporanea Yearbook 2020* (2021), 24–26; Edoardo Susmel, *La Cittá di Passione: Fiume negli Anni 1914–1920* (Milano: Treves, 1921), 227, 238.

62. Rolandi, "A Never Requested Triumph?," 24.

63. Rolandi, "A Never Requested Triumph?," 28.

64. J. N. Macdonald, *A Political Escapade: The Story of Fiume and D'Annunzio* (London: John Murray, 1921), 91.

65. Rolandi, "A Never Requested Triumph?," 18–20.

66. On the occasion of witnessing one of D'Annunzio's dialogues with the crowd, the writer Valdimir Nazor's remarked: "At the bottom of his voice I can ever more discern the bleating of an old faun . . . while the woman, who will dance the Charleston and Foxtrot with the Arditi until late tonight on that same tiled surface, joins in the shouts of Eia, eia, alala! [D'Annunzio's invented Italianised version of 'Hip Hip, Hooray'] with her own shriek of: Bello come un Dio! Bello come un Dio!" Thea Pičić, *Rijeka Ili Smrt! D'Anunzijeva okupacija Rijeke, 1919–1921 / Rijeka or Death! D'Annunzio's occupation of Rijeka, 1919–2019* (Rijeka: Naklada Val, 2019), 129 (from Vladimir Nazor, *Eseji i Ćlanci* [Zagreb: Hrvatski izdavalački bibliografiski zavod, 1942], 38).

67. Pičić, *Rijeka o Morte,* 27, 57, 89, 101–2; Guerri, *Disobbedisco*, 149, 154; Carlo Leo, "I Letterati a Fiume tra Vitalismo e Trauma: Il Caso di Mary Vitali," in *Fiume 1919–2019: Un Centenario Europeo tra Identitá, Memorie e Prospettive di Ricerca*, ed. Giordano Bruno Guerri (Milano: Silvania Editoriale, 2020), 243; Federico Carlo Simonelli, *D'Annunzio e il Mito di Fiume: Riti, Simboli, Narrazioni* (Pisa: Pacini, 2021), 264.

68. Claudia Salaris, "Artisti e Libertari a Fiume," in *Fiume 1919–2019*, ed. Guerri, 226. Comisso reports that after Italian soldiers entered Fiume in December 1920, he was dining with his comrades, ready for battle, when an officer's female lover appealed to the men not to fire on other Italians. To Comisso's accusation that her words proved she herself was not a true Italian, she replied, 'But we're the ones who must then dress your wounds.' Giovanni Comisso, *Le Mie Stagioni* (Milano: Longanesi, 1963), 96–97.

69. Margherita Keller Besozzi (Guido Keller's cousin) in her published writings advocated female emancipation and sexual autonomy. Salaris, "Artisti e Libertari," 223–24.

70. Leonardo Tosoni, "Carta del Carnaro: Diritti di Libertà e Prospettive di Giustizia Sociale nella Fiume Dannunziana," *Historia Constitucional* 22 (2021): 866–67.

71. Margherita Incisa di Camerana was reputedly the world's first female officer. In Fiume, she was an *Arditi* lieutenant, fully taking part in drills and marches, and later married Elia Rossi Passavanti, Commandant of *La Disperata*, and seventeen years her junior. Léon Kotchnitzky, *La Quinta Stagione: O, I Centauri di Fiume*, trans. Alberto Luchini (Bologna: Zanichelli, 1922), 67; Raoul Pupo, *Fiume Città di Passione* (Bari: Laterza, 2018), 107.

72. Dominique Kirchner Reill, *The Fiume Crisis: Life in the Wake of the Habsburg Empire* (Cambridge, MA: Harvard University Press, 2020), 49.

73. *The Carnaro Charter*, art. XXXXVII (D'Annunzio's text).

74. Manoscritto Primitivo della "Carta del Carnaro" (art. XXXXVII), Fondazione il Vittoriale degli Italiani, Archivio Personale, 588.

75. *The Carnaro Charter*, art. 4 (De Ambris's draft) and VI (D'Annunzio's text).

76. *The Carnaro Charter*, art. 12 (De Ambris's draft) and XVI (D'Annunzio's text).

77. Manoscritto Primitivo della "Carta del Carnaro" (art. XVI), Fondazione il Vittoriale degli Italiani, Archivio Personale, 588.

78. *The Carnaro Charter*, art. 9 (De Ambris's draft) and XII (D'Annunzio's text).

79. See, for example, Mario Praz, *The Romantic Agony*, trans. Angus Davison (Birkenhead, UK: Fontana Library, 1960), 420–21; Mira Liehm, *Passion and Defiance: Film in Italy from 1942 to the Present* (Berkeley: University of California Press, 1984), 19; Joe Galbo, "Sex, Geography, and Death: Metropolis and Empire in a Fascist Writer," *Society and Space* 14, no. 1 (1996): 35.

80. Gabriele D'Annunzio, *L'Innocente*, in *Romanzi e Novelle*, vol. I (Milano: Mondadori, 1942), 434.

81. D'Annunzio, *L'Innocente*, 554.

82. Adriana Clavel-Vazquez, "Sugar and Spice, and Everything Nice: What Rough Heroines Tell Us about Imaginative Resistance," *Journal of Aesthetics and Art Criticism* 76, no. 2 (2018): 201–12.

83. D'Annunzio, *L'Innocente*, 588.

84. D'Annunzio, *Il Piacere*, 89.

85. D'Annunzio, *Il Fuoco*, 756.

86. Gabriele D'Annunzio, "Il Donatore in Ginocchio," in *La Sola Ragione di Vivere*, ed. Emanuele Merlino (Firenze: Passaggio al Bosco, 2020), 131–32.

87. Joseph Raz, "The Problem of Authority: Revisiting the Service Conception," *Minnesota Law Review* 90 (2006): 1040.

88. See generally Jűrgen Habermas, *The Theory of Communicative Action*, trans. Thomas McCarthy (Cambridge, UK: Polity Press, 1987).

89. Habermas, *The Theory of Communicative Action.*

90. *The Carnaro Charter*, art. XXXXIX (D'Annunzio's text).

91. *The Carnaro Charter*, art. XXXXVII (D'Annunzio's text).

92. Jeremy K. Kessler, "A War for Liberty: On the Law of Conscientous Objection," in *The Cambridge History of the Second World War*, vol. 3 (*Total War: Economy, Society and Culture*), ed. Michael Geyer and Adam Tooze (Cambridge: Cambridge University Press, 2015).

93. *The Carnaro Charter*, art. 12 (De Ambris's draft) and XVII (D'Annunzio's text).

94. See, for example, *Weimar Constitution* 1919, art. 135. In the following article, the *Weimar Constitution* goes on to provide, specifically, that civil and civic rights and duties are neither contingent upon nor limited by the exercise of religious freedom.

95. *The Carnaro Charter*, art. 4 (De Ambris's draft) and VII (D'Annunzio's text).

96. *Weimar Constitution* 1919, art. 114, 115, 117.
97. *Weimar Constitution* 1919, art. 118, 135.
98. *Weimar Constitution* 1919, art. 123.
99. *The Carnaro Charter*, art. VII (D'Annunzio's text).
100. *The Carnaro Charter*, art. 4 (De Ambris's draft).
101. See generally Joseph Raz, *The Morality of Freedom* (Oxford: Oxford University Press, 1986).
102. Alessandro De Servi, "L'Abbozzo di uno Stato Nuovo: La 'Carta del Carnaro'," in *L'Italia e la "Grande Vigilia": Gabriele D'Annunzio nella Politica Italiana Prima del Fascismo*, ed. Romain H. Rainero and Stefano B. Galli (Milano: FrancoAngeli, 2007), 178.
103. *Statuto Albertino* 1848, art. 28.
104. *Statuto Albertino* 1848, art. 26–27.
105. *Declaration of the Rights of Man and of the Citizen* 1789, art. 7, 8, 10, 11.
106. Umberto Foscanelli, *D'Annunzio e l'Ora Sociale* (Milano: Carnaro, 1952), 149.
107. *The Carnaro Charter*, art. XVI (D'Annunzio's text).
108. *The Carnaro Charter*, art. 12 (De Ambris's draft) and XVII (D'Annunzio's text).
109. Foscanelli, *D'Annunzio e l'Ora Sociale*, 126, 152–53.
110. Foscanelli, *D'Annunzio e l'Ora Sociale*, 154.
111. Manoscritto Primitivo della "Carta del Carnaro" (art XVII), Fondazione il Vittoriale degli Italiani, Archivio Personale, 588.
112. *The Carnaro Charter*, art. VII (D'Annunzio's text).
113. *The Carnaro Charter*, art. 12 (De Ambris's draft) and XVII (D'Annunzio's text).
114. Joseph-Louis Ortolan, *Elementi di Diritto Penale*, vol. II (Napoli: Stamperia Del Vaglio, 1857), 213–14; Francesco Carrara, *Programma del Corso di Diritto Criminale: Parte Generale*, third edition (Lucca: Giusti, 1867), 395–96; Amerigo Lecci, *Il Sistema delle Pene nel Codice Italiano* (Roma e Napoli: Unione Tipografico-Editrice Torinese, 1891), 220–21.
115. Lecci, *Il Sistema*, 40, 168.
116. As reported, but contested, by Lecci, *Il Sistema*, 219–21.
117. Giovanni Michele Palmieri, "Sulla Tutela dei Diritti dell'Uomo e delle Libertá Fondamentali nella Carta del Carnaro," in *Lo Statuto della Reggenza*, ed. Sinagra, 171–74.
118. Palmieri, "Sulla Tutela," 175.
119. Giuseppe Parlato, "Il Rettorato del Lavoro a Fiume (Settembre–Dicembre 1920)," in *D'Annunzio e il Suo Tempo*, ed. Perfetti, 69, 83, 77; Leeden, *The First Duce*, 21.
120. See generally Parlato, "Il Rettorato."
121. See generally Parlato, "Il Rettorato."
122. See generally Parlato, "Il Rettorato," especially 68–70, 86, 88.
123. Davide Rossi, "La Carta del Carnaro, Antidoto Contro le Tossine del Parlamentarismo," in *La Cittá di Vita Cento Anni Dopo: Fiume, D'Annunzio e il*

Lungo Novecento Adriatico, ed. Davide Rossi (Padova: Wolters Kluwer—Cedam, 2020), 271.

124. *The Carnaro Charter*, art. VIII (D'Annunzio's text).

125. *The Carnaro Charter*, art. VIII (D'Annunzio's text).

126. *The Carnaro Charter*, art. XXXXVIII (D'Annunzio's text).

127. Letter from A. De Ambris to G. D'Annunzio (18 March 1920), in *La Carta del Carnaro e Altri Scritti su Fiume*, ed. Fressura and Karlsen, 128.

128. *The Carnaro Charter*, art. XXXXVIII (D'Annunzio's text).

129. *The Carnaro Charter*, art. LI–LIII (D'Annunzio's text).

130. *The Carnaro Charter*, art. 37 (De Ambris's draft).

131. *The Carnaro Charter*, art. LI (D'Annunzio's text).

132. Angela Lupone, "L'Univeralismo della Carta del Carnaro (ovvero del Gioco Armonioso delle Diversitá)," in *Lo Statuto della Reggenza*, ed. Sinagra, 133.

133. Pičić, *Rijeka or Death*, 167–68.

134. Letter from A. De Ambris to G. D'Annunzio (18 March 1920), in *La Carta del Carnaro e Altri Scritti su Fiume*, ed. Fressura and Karlsen, 131.

135. Letter from A. De Ambris to G. D'Annunzio (18 March 1920), in *La Carta del Carnaro e Altri Scritti su Fiume*, ed. Fressura and Karlsen, 132.

136. About this regime, see Tosoni, "Carta del Carnaro," 860–62.

137. Carlo Ricotti, "Dannunziana Massonica Autonomista," in *La Carta del Carnaro: Dannunziana Massonica Autonomista* (Roma: Fefé, 2019), 40–41.

138. *The Carnaro Charter*, art. XXIIII (D'Annunzio's text).

139. Ricotti, "Dannunziana Massonica Autonomista," 18–19; Anton Marino Revedin, "Immaginazione al Potere (l'Avanguardismo Costituzionale dello Statuto del Carnaro)," in *Lo Statuto della Reggenza*, ed. Sinagra, 194.

140. Ramaioli, "Res Publica Fiumana," 166.

141. Costa and Stendardi, "La 'Carta del Carnaro'," 65.

142. Letter from A. De Ambris to G. D'Annunzio (18 March 1920), in *La Carta del Carnaro e Altri Scritti su Fiume*, ed. Fressura and Karlsen, 131–32; Ester Capuzzo, "Da Corpus Separatum a Provincia: Amministrazione e Legislazione a Fiume nel Primo Dopoguerra," in *Fiume 1919–2019*, ed. Guerri, 32.

143. *The Carnaro Charter*, art. 127 (De Ambris's draft).

144. *The Carnaro Charter*, art. LII (D'Annunzio's text).

145. *The Carnaro Charter*, art. LIII (D'Annunzio's text).

146. *The Carnaro Charter*, art. LII (D'Annunzio's text).

147. Salvatore Cingari, "Virtuosa Gioia: Di Alcuni Aspetti Utopistici nella Carta del Carnaro," *Giornale di Storia Costituzionale* 10 (2005): 155.

148. *The Carnaro Charter*, art. L (D'Annunzio's text). ('The Italian Regency of the Carnaro puts the people's culture at the top of all its laws.')

149. *The Carnaro Charter*, art. L (D'Annunzio's text). The reference to the 'free man' echoes Seneca's reflections about a so-called liberal education—one that, as he intended the term, liberates or frees the mind. Seneca, Letter 88 [On Liberal and Vocational Studies], in *Letters to Lucilius* (ca. 63 AD).

150. *The Carnaro Charter*, art. L (D'Annunzio's text).

151. *The Carnaro Charter*, art. II (D'Annunzio's text).

152. Letter from A. De Ambris to G. D'Annunzio (18 March 1920), in *La Carta del Carnaro e Altri Scritti su Fiume*, ed. Fressura and Karlsen, 132; Alceste De Ambris, "La Costituzione di Fiume: Commento Illustrativo di A. De Ambris" (1920), in *La Carta del Carnaro*, ed. De Felice, 96–97.

153. Guerri, *Disobbedisco*, 312–13.

154. *The Carnaro Charter*, art. 39 (De Ambris's text).

155. *The Carnaro Charter*, art. LIV (D'Annunzio's text).

156. Francesco Margiotta Broglio, "Tra Laicitá e Credenze Religiose 'Supreme'. Fiume 'Stato Libero' e il 'Vaticano Cittá Libera'. Il Diritto Ecclesiastico della Reggenza di Fiume," in *D'Annunzio Legislatore*, ed. Guerri, 58.

157. *Lautsi and Others v. Italy* (2012) 54 EHRR 3; see also Anna Lucia Valvo, "Valenza Internazionale dello Statuto della Reggenza Italiana del Carnaro: Un Paradosso che il Tempo non Ha Risolto," in *Lo Statuto della Reggenza*, ed. Sinagra, 216.

158. *Engel v. Vitale* 370 US 421 (1962).

159. European Convention on Human Rights, art. 9.

160. Villari, *La Luna*, 133–34.

161. *The Carnaro Charter*, art. LIV (D'Annunzio's text).

162. Alceste De Ambris, "La Costituzione di Fiume: Commento Illustrativo" (1920), 93.

163. Alessandro Agrí, *La Costituzione della Reggenza Italiana del Carnaro* (Torino: Giappichelli, 2023), 139–43.

164. *The Carnaro Charter*, art. 6 (De Ambris's draft).

165. Jukka Gronow, *On the Formation of Marxism: Karl Kautsky's Theory of Capitalism, the Marxism of the Second International and Karl Marx's Critique of Political Economy* (Leiden: Brill, 2016), 228–29.

166. Thomas E. Towe, "Fundamental Rights in the Soviet Union: A Comparative Approach," *University of Pennsylvania Law Review* 115 (1967): 1252.

167. *Constitution of the Russian Soviet Federated Socialist Republic* 1918, chapter 16 (as translated at https://www.marxists.org/history/ussr/government/constitution/1918/).

168. Alberto Gelpi, *Gabriele D'Annunzio Legislatore Costituente* (Roma: Ugo Pinto, 1957), 21.

169. Letter from A. De Ambris to G. D'Annunzio (18 March 1920), in *La Carta del Carnaro e Altri Scritti su Fiume*, ed. Fressura and Karlsen, 128.

170. Tosoni, "Carta del Carnaro," 871.

171. *The Carnaro Charter*, art. 13 (De Ambris's draft).

172. *The Carnaro Charter*, art. 14, 23 (De Ambris's draft).

173. *The Carnaro Charter*, art. 13(4) (De Ambris's draft).

174. *The Carnaro Charter*, art. XIX (D'Annunzio's text).

175. Letter from A. De Ambris to G. D'Annunzio (18 March 1920), in *La Carta del Carnaro e Altri Scritti su Fiume*, ed. Fressura and Karlsen, 129.

176. The original Italian uses the word 'infingardo', which can mean either 'illusory' or 'slothful'.

177. *The Carnaro Charter*, art. IX (D'Annunzio's text).

178. Federico L. Ramaioli, "Lo Statuto della Reggenza Italiana del Carnaro tra Innovazione e Tradizione: A Cento Anni dalla Costituzione di Fiume," *Fiume: Rivista di Studi Adriatici* XLI (2020): 90–92.
179. Tosoni, "Carta del Carnaro," 870.
180. Foscanelli, *D'Annunzio e l'Ora Sociale*, 150.
181. Quoted in De Felice, *D'Annunzio Politico*, 137.
182. *The Carnaro Charter*, art. 10 (De Ambris's draft).
183. Agrí, *La Costituzione della Reggenza*, 183.
184. Ramaioli, "Res Publica Fiumana," 163–65.
185. *The Carnaro Charter*, art. XIII (D'Annunzio's text) (no commas in original).
186. *The Carnaro Charter*, art. XVIII (D'Annunzio's text).
187. Guglielmo Salotti, "Nuovi Studi sulla Carta del Carnaro," *Fiume: Rivista di Studi Fiumani* XIX–XX (1973–1974): 87.
188. *The Carnaro Charter*, art. XIV (D'Annunzio's text).
189. Leeden, *The First Duce*, 168.
190. Tosoni, "Carta del Carnaro," 873–74.
191. De Vergottini, *La Costituzione*, 41.
192. Mosse, "The Poet," 35.
193. Leeden, *The First Duce*, 148–51.
194. Nino Valeri, *Da Giolitti a Mussolini: Momenti della Crisi del Liberalismo* (Firenze: Parenti, 1957), 39.
195. See generally Joseph Raz, *Engaging Reason: On the Theory and Value of Action* (Oxford: Oxford University Press, 1999).
196. Carlos A. Ball, "Sexual Ethics and Postmodernism in Gay Rights Philosophy," *North Carolina Law Review* 80, no. 2 (2002): 385–93.
197. Revedin, "Immaginazione al Potere," 195.
198. Hannah Arendt, *Lectures on Kant's Political Philosophy* (Chicago: The University of Chicago Press, 1992), 61–72.
199. Wladyslaw Tatarkiewicz, "Classification of Arts in Antiquity," *Journal of the History of Ideas* 24, no. 2 (April–June 1963): 231.
200. Carlo Diano, "D'Annunzio e l'Ellade," in *L'Arte di Gabriele D'Annunzio*, ed. Emilio Mariano (Milano: Mondadori, 1968), 51–67.
201. For example, Alexander Stille, "The Candidate of Beauty," review of *Gabriele D'Annunzio: Defiant Archangel*, by John Woodhouse, *London Review of Books*, July 2, 1998.
202. Augusto Sinagra, Relazione, in *Lo Statuto della Reggenza*, ed. Sinagra, 9.
203. Alceste De Ambris, "La Costituzione di Fiume: Commento Illustrativo" (1920), 98.
204. *The Carnaro Charter*, art. 10 (De Ambris's draft) and XIII (D'Annunzio's text).
205. *The Carnaro Charter*, art. 13 (De Ambris's draft) and XVIII (D'Annunzio's text).
206. Alceste De Ambris, "La Costituzione di Fiume: Commento Illustrativo" (1920), 99.

207. In France and elsewhere in Europe, this antipathy had led, even before the French Revolution, to laws abolishing not only traditional corporations but also novel forms of trade unionism. Agrí, *La Costituzione della Reggenza*, 7–10, 29–31.

208. *The Carnaro Charter*, art. 14 (De Ambris's draft).

209. *The Carnaro Charter*, art. XX (D'Annunzio's text).

210. *The Carnaro Charter*, art. XX (D'Annunzio's text).

211. De Felice, *D'Annunzio Politico*, 137–38.

212. De Felice, *D'Annunzio Politico*, 115; Salotti, "Nuovi Studi," 95; Palmieri, "Sulla Tutela," 164.

213. Guglielmo Salotti, "D'Annunzio, Giulietti e la 'Questione Marinara'," in *D'Annunzio e il Suo Tempo*, ed. Perfetti, 132.

214. Patrizia Paradisi, "Guerra e Poesia: 'Energeia', la Decima Musa di D'Annunzio," *Il Nome nel Testo: Rivista internazionale di Onomastica Letteraria* XVIII (2006): 138.

215. Manoscritto Primitivo della "Carta del Carnaro" (art. XVIII), Fondazione il Vittoriale degli Italiani, Archivio Personale, 588.

216. The original translates literally to 'sweat of blood'. D'Annunzio clearly reworked the Italian expression 'sudare sangue', which literally means 'to sweat blood'. This expression refers figuratively to activities that require inordinate efforts, as with the English 'blood, sweat and tears'.

217. *The Carnaro Charter*, art. XIX (D'Annunzio's text).

218. Pupo, *Fiume Città di Passione*, 126; Guerri, *Disobbedisco*, 321–22.

219. Palmieri, "Sulla Tutela," 164.

220. Carmelo Ferlito, "Principi Economici della Carta del Carnaro," *Storia Veritá* 52 (2008).

221. William Klinger, "La Carta del Carnaro: Una Costituzione per lo Stato Libero di Fiume (1920)," *Quaderni* (Centro di Ricerche Storiche-Rovigno) XIV (2002): 310.

222. Agrí, *La Costituzione della Reggenza*, 96.

223. Foscanelli, *D'Annunzio e l'Ora Sociale*, 156.

224. Manoscritto Primitivo della "Carta del Carnaro" (art. XIX), Fondazione il Vittoriale degli Italiani, Archivio Personale, 588.

225. Foscanelli, *D'Annunzio e l'Ora Sociale*, 111.

226. Gelpi, *Gabriele D'Annunzio Legislatore Costituente*, 18.

227. Agrí, *La Costituzione della Reggenza*, 92–93; Egidio Grego, "Utopie e Diritti nel Costituzionalismo Dannunziano," in *La Sola Ragione di Vivere*, ed. Merlino, 49; De Vergottini, *La Costituzione*, 21; Davide Rossi, "La Carta Fiumana 'non Pretende di Distruggere il Vecchio Tronco Democratico, ma Vi Innesta Sopra le Concezioni Nuove'," in *D'Annunzio Legislatore*, ed. Guerri, 35; Lucy Hughes Hallett, *The Pike: Gabriele D'Annunzio: Poet, Seducer and Preacher of War* (London: HarperCollins, 2013), 540.

228. Tatarkiewicz, "Classification of Arts," 231.

229. Paradisi, "Guerra e Poesia," 127–28.

230. Paradisi, "Guerra e Poesia," 129–30.

231. Paradisi, "Guerra e Poesia," 134.

232. Gabriele D'Annunzio, "Discorso Pronunciato a una Cena di Amici all'Alba del 25 Maggio 1915," in *Scritti Politici di Gabriele D'Annunzio*, ed. Paolo Alatri (Milano: Feltrinelli, 1980), 132.
233. De Ambris, "Precisiamo il Nostro Concetto Rivoluzionaro: Il Manifesto dei Sindacalisti e la Costituzione Fiumana," *La Gioventu Sindacalista* (1 Septmeber 1921), in *Sindacalismo Rivoluzionario*, ed. De Felice, 328–29.
234. Ungari, "Commento Giuridico," 55.
235. Ricotti, "Dannunziana Massonica Autonomista," 38.
236. Kotchnitzky, *La Quinta Stagione*, 158.
237. Kotchnitzky, *La Quinta Stagione*, 159–62.
238. *The Carnaro Charter*, art. XXX (D'Annunzio's text).
239. *The Carnaro Charter*, art. XXXIII (D'Annunzio's text).
240. The legislature would meet every seven years in an extraordinary session specifically for the purpose of reforming the *Charter*. *The Carnaro Charter*, art. LV (D'Annunzio's text).
241. *The Carnaro Charter*, art. XXXIV (D'Annunzio's text).
242. Unabridged text of the captain's oath, in Susmel, *Fiume attraverso la Storia*, 120, 124.
243. From a publication in the Fiume periodical *La Conquista* (uncertain date), quoted in Renzo De Felice, "Introduzione," in *Sindacalismo Rivoluzionario*, ed. De Felice, 92–93.
244. Sidney and Beatrice Webb, *A Constitution for the Socialist Commonwealth of Great Britain* (London and New York: Longmans, Green & Co, 1920), art. 111–31.
245. Webb and Webb, *A Constitution for the Socialist Commonwealth of Great Britain*, art. 111–21.
246. Leeden, *The First Duce*, 40; Agrí, *La Costituzione della Reggenza*, 114–19.
247. Agrí, *La Costituzione della Reggenza*, 117–19.
248. *The Carnaro Charter*, art. XXVIII–XXIX (D'Annunzio's text).
249. *The Carnaro Charter*, art. XXXI (D'Annunzio's text).
250. *The Carnaro Charter*, art. XXII (D'Annunzio's text).
251. *The Carnaro Charter*, art. XXXI (D'Annunzio's text).
252. Salotti, "D'Annunzio, Giulietti," 132.
253. Costa and Stendardi, "La 'Carta del Carnaro'," 61.
254. Grego, "Utopie e Diritti," 45. See also de De Vergottini, *La Costituzione*, 112.
255. Negri, "La Carta," 59.
256. Letter from A. De Ambris to G. D'Annunzio (18 March 1920), in *La Carta del Carnaro e Altri Scritti su Fiume*, ed. Fressura and Karlsen, 128.
257. Letter from A. De Ambris to G. D'Annunzio (18 March 1920), in *La Carta del Carnaro e Altri Scritti su Fiume*, ed. Fressura and Karlsen, 129.
258. Letter from A. De Ambris to G. D'Annunzio (18 March 1920), in *La Carta del Carnaro e Altri Scritti su Fiume*, ed. Fressura and Karlsen, 128–29.
259. De Felice, "Introduzione," 27, 29.
260. Costa and Stendardi, "La 'Carta del Carnaro'," 57.

261. Serge Noiret, "Les Communistes, D'Annunzio et l'Entourage Dannunzien (1921–1922)," in *D'Annunzio e il Suo Tempo*, ed. Perfetti, 208.

262. De Vergottini, *La Costituzione*, 114.

263. Pamela Ballinger, "Rewriting the Text of the Nation: D'Annunzio at Fiume," *Quaderni* XI (1997): 130.

264. Guglielmo Ferrero, *Da Fiume a Roma: Storia di Quattro Anni (1919–1923)* (Milano: Athena, 1923), 33–36, 57–58. See also Rossi, "La Carta del Carnaro," 217.

265. H. James Burgwyn, *The Legend of the Mutilated Victory: Italy, the Great War, and the Paris Peace Conference, 1915–1919* (Westport, CT, and London: Greenwood, 1993), 13.

266. M. F. N. Giglioli, "'Il Deputato della Bellezza': Gabriele D'Annunzio's Aesthetic Politics in the Fin-de-Siècle Crisis," *Journal of Modern Italian Studies* 18, no. 4 (2013): 512–13.

267. Rossi, "La Carta del Carnaro," 214.

268. Letter from L. Kotchnitzky to P. Hymans (22 November 1919), Fondazione Il Vittoriale degli Italiani, Archivio Fiumano, Kotchnitzky, Léon, 1–129.

269. Burgwyn, *The Legend*, 10.

270. Ferrero, *Da Fiume a Roma*, 120.

271. Ferrero, *Da Fiume a Roma*, 33.

272. Ferrero, *Da Fiume a Roma*, 34.

273. Ferrero, *Da Fiume a Roma*, 36.

274. Ferrero, *Da Fiume a Roma*, 35.

275. Ferrero, *Da Fiume a Roma*, 125, 138.

276. Ferrero, *Da Fiume a Roma*, 68.

277. Ferrero, *Da Fiume a Roma*, 69.

278. Ferrero, *Da Fiume a Roma*, 120.

279. Ferrero, *Da Fiume a Roma*, 93–94.

280. Ferrero, *Da Fiume a Roma*, 129.

281. Giordano Bruno Guerri, *D'Annunzio: L'Amante Guerriero* (Milano: Monadori, 2009), 109 (citing passages from the 1892 article "The Electoral Beast").

282. Aleardo Zanghellini, "The Foundations of the Rule of Law," *Yale Journal of Law & the Humanities* 28 (2016): 225–27.

283. D'Annunzio, *Le Vergini delle Rocce*, 426–27.

284. Leeden, *The First Duce*, 164.

285. British Delegation: Telegram from R. Rodd to A. Balfour (24 May 1919), The National Archives, FO 608/39.

286. Quoted in Roberto Vivarelli, *Storia delle Origini del Fascismo: L'Italia dalla Grande Guerra alla Marcia su Roma*, vol. 1 (Bologna: Il Mulino, 1991), 536–37.

287. Quoted in De Ambris, "D'Annunzio e il Proletariato," 349.

288. Pier Filippo Gomez Homen, *Antecedenti Teorici del Corporativismo Fascista* (Palermo: Sandron, 1929), 23

289. Klinger, "La Carta," 280–88, 305, 307.

290. Klinger, "La Carta," 278.

291. Gomez Homen, *Antecedenti Teorici*, 89.

292. Gomez Homen, *Antecedenti Teorici*, 100.

293. Gomez Homen, *Antecedenti Teorici*, 110–11.
294. Gomez Homen, *Antecedenti Teorici*, 114.
295. See generally Gomez Homen, *Antecedenti Teorici.*
296. Gianpasquale Santomassimo, *La Terza Via Fascista: Il Mito del Corporativismo* (Roma: Carocci, 2006), 22–23, 32–34, 44, 47–48; Foscanelli, *D'Annunzio e l'Ora Sociale*, 143.
297. Gomez Homen, *Antecedenti Teorici*, 110.
298. Davide Rossi, "D'Annunzio, la Carta del Carnaro e la Crisi dello Stato Liberale, tra Rappresentanza e Antiparlamentarismo," *Giornale di Storia Costituzionale* 38, no. 2 (2019): 142; Rossi, "La Carta del Carnaro," 226, 230.
299. *The Carnaro Charter*, art. XXX (D'Annunzio's text).
300. *The Carnaro Charter*, art. XXXIII (D'Annunzio's text).
301. Ricotti, "Dannunziana Massonica Autonomista," 26.
302. *The Carnaro Charter*, art. 20–26 (De Ambris's draft).
303. *The Carnaro Charter*, art. XXVII–XXXIV (D'Annunzio's text).
304. Kotchnitzky, *La Quinta Stagione*, 163.
305. *The Carnaro Charter*, art. LVI (D'Annunzio's text).
306. *The Carnaro Charter*, art. LVII (D'Annunzio's text).
307. *The Carnaro Charter*, art. LVIII (D'Annunzio's text).
308. Ricotti, "Dannunziana Massonica Autonomista," 26–27.
309. Rossi, "La Carta del Carnaro," 230.
310. Palmieri, "Sulla Tutela," 161.
311. De Vergottini, *La Costituzione*, 86–87.
312. *The Carnaro Charter*, art. XIV (D'Annunzio's text).
313. Mill, *Considerations on Representative Government.*
314. *The Carnaro Charter*, art. XVIII (D'Annunzio's text).
315. De Servi, "L'Abbozzo," 186.
316. *The Carnaro Charter*, art. XXXV (D'Annunzio's text).
317. *The Carnaro Charter*, art. LIX (D'Annunzio's text).
318. *The Carnaro Charter*, art. XXXV (D'Annunzio's text).
319. Manoscritto Primitivo della "Carta del Carnaro" (art. XXXVI), Fondazione il Vittoriale degli Italiani, Archivio Personale, 588.
320. *The Carnaro Charter*, art. 28 (De Ambris's draft) and XXXVI (D'Annunzio's text).
321. De Servi, "L'Abbozzo," 187–88.
322. *The Carnaro Charter*, art. XXXV–XXXVI (D'Annunzio's text).
323. *The Carnaro Charter*, art. XXXV (D'Annunzio's text).
324. *The Carnaro Charter*, art. 27 (De Ambris's draft).
325. *The Carnaro Charter*, art. XXXV (D'Annunzio's text).
326. *The Carnaro Charter*, art. XXXVI (D'Annunzio's text).
327. Negri, "La Carta," 63.
328. Letter from A. De Ambris to G. D'Annunzio (18 March 1920), in *La Carta del Carnaro e Altri Scritti su Fiume*, ed. Fressura and Karlsen, 130.
329. *The Carnaro Charter*, art. 45 (De Ambris's draft) and LX (D'Annunzio's text).

330. *The Carnaro Charter*, art. XXXXII (D'Annunzio's text).

331. *The Carnaro Charter*, art. LVI (D'Annunzio's text).

332. *The Carnaro Charter*, art. 46 (De Ambris's draft).

333. Guerri, *Disobbedisco*, 324.

334. De Vergottini, "Prassi e Utopia," 601.

335. Letter from A. De Ambris to G. D'Annunzio (18 March 1920), in *La Carta del Carnaro e Altri Scritti su Fiume*, ed. Fressura and Karlsen, 130.

336. *The Carnaro Charter*, art. XXXVI (D'Annunzio's text). See Negri, "La Carta," 62.

337. *The Carnaro Charter*, art. 30–31, 34 (De Ambris's draft) and XXXVIII–XXXIX, XXXXII (D'Annunzio's text).

338. Costa and Stendardi, "La 'Carta del Carnaro'," 64.

339. *The Carnaro Charter*, art. 32–33 (De Ambris's draft) and XXXX–XXXXI (D'Annunzio's text).

340. *The Carnaro Charter*, art. 32 (De Ambris's draft) and XXXX (D'Annunzio's text).

341. *The Carnaro Charter*, art. XXXXII (D'Annunzio's text).

342. *The Carnaro Charter*, art. 34 (De Ambris's draft).

343. Mauro Cappelletti, "Judicial Review in Comparative Perspective," *California Law Review* 58, no. 5 (October 1970): 1047–49.

344. *The Carnaro Charter*, art. 34 (De Ambris's draft) and XXXXII (D'Annunzio's text).

345. Cappelletti, "Judicial Review," 1040–41.

346. Victor Ferreres Comella, "The European Model of Constitutional Review of Legislation: Toward Decentralization?," *I.CON* 2, no. 3 (2004): 470–74.

347. Tomáš Langášek, *Ústavní Soud Československé Republiky a Jeho Osudy v Letech 1920–1948* (*Constitutional Court of the Czechoslovak Republic and Its Fortunes in the Years 1920–1948*) (Plzeň: Vydavatelství a nakladatelství Aleš Čeněk, s.r.o., 2011), https://www.usoud.cz/en/constitutional-court-of-the-czechoslovak-republic-and-its-fortunes-in-years-1920-1948 (excerpts).

348. J. A. C. Grant, "Judicial Review of Legislation under the Austrian Constitution of 1920," *The American Political Science Review* 28, no. 4 (August 1934): 674–75; Langášek, *Ústavní.*

349. Grant, "Judicial Review," 673.

350. Langášek, *Ústavní.*

351. *The Carnaro Charter*, art. XXXXII (D'Annunzio's text).

352. Langášek, *Ústavní.*

353. Langášek, *Ústavní.*

354. *The Carnaro Charter*, art. XXXXIII (D'Annunzio's text).

355. Enrico Serventi Longhi, "The Father of 'Sovereignism': D'Annunzio in Fiume between the Crisis of Liberalism and the Critique of Democracy," *Modern Italy* 27 (2022): 39–40.

356. Enrico Serventi Longhi, *Il Faro del Mondo Nuovo: D'Annunzio e i Legionari a Fiume tra Guerra e Rivoluzione* (Udine: Gaspari, 2019), 154.

357. Giorgio Agamben, "State of Exception," trans. Kevin Attell, in *The Omnibus Homo Sacer* (Stanford: Stanford University Press, 2017), 175–84.
358. Agamben, "State of Exception," 178.
359. *Weimar Constitution* 1919, art. 48.
360. Agamben, "State of Exception," 178.
361. *The Carnaro Charter*, art. 34 (De Ambris's draft).
362. *The Carnaro Charter*, art. XXXXIII (D'Annunzio's text).
363. Manoscritto Primitivo della "Carta del Carnaro" (article XXXXIII), Fondazione il Vittoriale degli Italiani, Archivio Personale, 588.
364. *The Carnaro Charter*, art. 34 (De Ambris's draft) and XXXXIV (D'Annunzio's text).
365. Raffaele Cadin, "E se la Carta del Carnaro fosse un Magnifico Pretesto per Costituzionalizzare la Dittatura?" in *Lo Statuto della Reggenza*, ed. Sinagra, 63.
366. *The Carnaro Charter*, art. 34 (De Ambris's draft) and XXXXIII–XXXXIV, XXXXVI (D'Annunzio's text).
367. *The Carnaro Charter*, art. 34 (De Ambris's draft).
368. *The Carnaro Charter*, art. XXXXIII (D'Annunzio's text).
369. *The Carnaro Charter*, art. 34 (De Ambris's draft) and XXXXV (D'Annunzio's text).
370. *Weimar Constitution* 1919, art. 48.
371. Costa and Stendardi, "La 'Carta del Carnaro'," 53.
372. Costa and Stendardi, "La 'Carta del Carnaro'," 71.
373. Gelpi, *Gabriele D'Annunzio Legislatore Costituente*, 39.
374. *The Carnaro Charter*, art. V (D'Annunzio's text).
375. Manoscritto Primitivo della "Carta del Carnaro" (art. LXIII), Fondazione il Vittoriale degli Italiani, Archivio Personale, 588.
376. Lina Panella, "Lo Statuto della Reggenza Italaina del Carnaro: Considerazioni di un'Internazionalista," in *Lo Statuto della Reggenza*, ed. Sinagra, 182.
377. *The Carnaro Charter*, art. LXIII (D'Annunzio's text).
378. Valentina Raimondo, "Gli Artisti che Hanno Contribuito ai Simboli Danniunziani," in *Fiume 1919–2019*, ed. Guerri, 275.
379. *The Carnaro Charter*, art. LXIII (D'Annunzio's text).
380. *The Carnaro Charter*, art. XIV (D'Annunzio's text).
381. *The Carnaro Charter*, art. LXIII (D'Annunzio's text).
382. Guglielmo Salotti, "La Valorizzazione del Lavoro nella Carta del Carnaro," *Clio* 27 (1991): 94–103.
383. D'Annunzio, *Le Vergini delle Rocce*, 432.
384. D'Annunzio, *Il Fuoco*, 625.
385. *The Carnaro Charter*, art. LXIV (D'Annunzio's text).
386. *The Carnaro Charter*, art. LXIV (D'Annunzio's text).
387. *The Carnaro Charter*, art. LXIV (D'Annunzio's text).
388. *The Carnaro Charter*, art. XIX (D'Annunzio's text).
389. *The Carnaro Charter*, art. LXV (D'Annunzio's text).
390. *The Carnaro Charter*, art. LXIV (D'Annunzio's text).

391. Martha C. Nussbaum, "Skepticism about Practical Reason in Literature and the Law," *Harvard Law Review* 107, no. 3 (1994), 740: 'As Nietzsche showed, it is only to someone whose faith in his own human capacities has been eroded by the teachings of an other-worldly faith that the news of the death of God brings nihilism and the abandonment of evaluation and selection.'

392. *The Carnaro Charter*, art. LXV (D'Annunzio's text).

393. See also Giuseppe Franco Ferrari, "La Carta del Carnaro: Un Centenario in Sordina," *Nomos: le Attualitá del Diritto* 3 (2020): 13, https://www.nomos-leattualita neldiritto.it/wp-content/uploads/2021/02/Ferrari-3-2020-REV-2.pdf.

394. Frosini, "D'Annunzio e la Carta del Carnaro," 85–86.

395. Filippo Tommaso Marinetti, *Taccuini 1915–1921* (Bologna: Il Mulino, 1987), 493, quoted in Renato Ricco, "'Esaltatrice dell'Atto di Vita, dell'Opera di Vita': Il Ruolo della Musica nella Carta del Carnaro di Gabriele D'Annunzio," *Forum Italico* 49, no. 2 (2005): 441.

396. See Ricco "'Esaltatrice dell'Atto di Vita, dell'Opera di Vita'," 438, 441.

397. D'Annunzio, *Scritti Giornalistici*, vol. II *(1889–1938)* (Milano: Mondadori, 2003), 250, quoted in Ricco, "'Esaltatrice dell'Atto di Vita, dell'Opera di Vita'," 441.

398. Ricco, "'Esaltatrice dell'Atto di Vita, dell'Opera di Vita'," 439–41.

399. Quoted in De Felice, *D'Annunzio Politico*, 137.

400. Letter from G. D'Annunzio to A. De Ambris (11 May 1921), in *Sindacalismo Rivoluzionario*, ed. De Felice, 250.

401. Peace Agreement between General C. Ferrario, Captain N. Host-Venturi, and Mayor R. Gigante, Abbazia (31 December 1920), in Giuseppe Moscati, *Le Cinque Giornate di Fiume: X Anniversario del Natale di Sangue* (Milano: Carnaro, 1930), 148.

402. Ungari, "Commento Giuridico," 56.

403. Alessandro Agrí, "Tommaso Mirabella e la Carta del Carnaro (1920–1940)," *Rivista di Storia del Diritto Italiano* 93, no. 2 (2020).

404. Rossi, "La Carta del Carnaro," 231–33.

405. Serventi Longhi, *Il Faro*, 136–43.

406. Ballinger, "Rewriting the Text," 143.

Chapter 7

Same-Sex Desire in D'Annunzio's *Oeuvre*

INTRODUCTION

'The Italian Regency of Carnaro is an honest government of the people, whose foundation is the power of productive labour'.[1] Labour, as we have seen, is central to the conceptual and normative economy of the *Charter*. But the *Charter* was itself labour. For D'Annunzio, it was a labour of love. The partners in that love affair were D'Annunzio himself and the body (indeed, the bodies) of legionnaires, who quickened his imagination, causing him to deliver their offspring in the form of the *Charter*. The point of departure of the rest of the book is D'Annunzio's claim to the effect that the *Charter* was the product of the (sublimated) erotic bond that tied him to the legionnaires. I take this idea entirely seriously, and this implicates me in a wide-ranging investigation into D'Annunzio's homoerotic investments, and the work that homoerotic affect did in occupied Fiume, including, but not limited to, D'Annunzio's public speeches.

D'Annunzio was 'strenuously heterosexual,'[2] though he had hardly any business to be. As Italy's response to Swinburne or Verlaine, one would expect him by rights to have been as incurably same-sex attracted as either of those two verse-spinning gentlemen. But whatever his sexual preferences and practices, D'Annunzio engaged with same-sex desire in his writings, and he deployed it quite deliberately, though not necessarily cynically, to elicit affective responses to the Fiume cause that were key to sustaining the occupation. We will see this through an examination of the use of homoerotic rhetoric in D'Annunzio's Fiume speeches to the legionnaires.

D'Annunzio's speeches are fairly eloquent: we need not dig very deeply to unearth their homoerotic undercurrents. Yet because this is uncharted interpretive territory, and my argument is likely to raise some eyebrows, I will show that D'Annunzio's preoccupation with same-sex desire predates the Fiume experience. It was an abiding one in his creative prose work. Indeed, as we will see, D'Annunzio's treatment of same-sex desire in his novels—which has attracted minimal scholarly attention—speaks directly to the productive and generative function that his Fiume speeches also appear to assign to it. The novels help us understand what D'Annunzio meant when he said that the *Charter* was born of his and the legionnaires' mutual love.

I will also look at the way in which D'Annunzio's homoerotic rhetoric articulated with some prominent legionnaires' own homoerotic preoccupations. The writings of some of D'Annunzio's key supporters within the *'scalmanati'* camp demonstrates that the poet was speaking a language of desire that phenomenologically resonated with them. This suggests that homoerotic affect was constitutive of the shared intentional attitudes[3] on which the existence of the regency's collective political and legal project depended.

Ever envious of his more illustrious colleague, Marinetti described D'Annunzio as suffering from 'a pederast's childish conceits'.[4] But this part of the book is not about reclaiming D'Annunzio for the queer literary canon, and even less is it about D'Annunzio's sexual orientation. Leeden has doubted Julian's suggestion that D'Annunzio was bisexual,[5] and D'Annunzio's best-known (today) Italian biographer states that he 'denied himself' homosexual experiences.[6] At the same time, D'Annunzio declared that 'moral orders follow degrees of latitude, rules and codes are transitory, truth is slippery and precarious, the only measure of energy is risk, and renunciation and obedience are the ears of abjection';[7] he pronounced himself 'often inconsolable' over being, by necessity, unable to try out absolutely everything, whether good or bad, which caused humans to feel intensely; and, when identifying examples of such lifestyles or experiences, he listed possibilities (such as a miraculous recovery from a bodily affliction or the meditative practices of certain Eastern monks) that were not within his reach.[8] Same-sex sexual conduct, however, would have been wholly within his reach; and it stands to reason that a sensualist such as D'Annunzio must have been more than a little intrigued by its potential for affording him with as yet untried sensations.

The point is that we simply cannot know, either way, whether or not D'Annunzio ever had same-sex sexual relationships or consciously experienced same-sex desire. My belief is that D'Annunzio was primarily, and powerfully, sexually attracted to women (there is certainly enough evidence of that). His same-sex desire appears to have been much less potent, but just because of this, it was also much more easily sublimated, aestheticized, and idealised. This explains D'Annunzio's treatment of both heterosexual and same-sex desires in his books: the former as an uncontrollable drive that risks shattering the self and his (creative) aspirations, and the latter (largely) as a much less unwieldy force, capable of being channelled in the service of those self-same aspirations. The radical irreducibility of same-sex desire to different-sex desire in D'Annunzio's thought also explains D'Annunzio's deployment of the former in the Fiume speeches he addressed to the legionnaires and, consequently, the phenomenological role that sublimated homoeroticism played in constituting and sustaining the occupation and the regency.

I will start by discussing elements in D'Annunzio's biography that are suggestive of what I call homoerotic preoccupations. Here a broad and impressionistic discussion serves my purposes well enough: it enables me to show that, despite the startling near-absence of commentary about it, an inquiry into D'Annunzio and same-sex desire is far from implausible, and indeed a matter that calls for interrogation. I will go on to discuss in much greater detail the role played by same-sex desire in D'Annunzio's novels and in one of his plays. It is simply reasons of space that prevent me from looking further into D'Annunzio's literary production. But the texts I do analyse are eloquent and largely consistent in their idealised treatment of same-sex desire as a force that—unlike heterosexual desire—can be sublimated into uniquely fruitful and generative bonds. In the next chapter I will turn to an analysis of D'Annunzio's speeches to show that he enacted this very sublimation in Fiume, enlisting same-sex desire in the production of certain forms of political affect uniting the legionnaire community around the values of the *Charter*. Finally, in the chapter that follows I will show how some prominent legionnaires experienced same-sex desire, as well as responded and contributed to its deployment by the poet in the constitution of an idealised political community.

D'ANNUNZIO'S HOMOEROTIC PREOCCUPATIONS

D'Annunzio is well known for his sometimes scandalous heterosexual love life, but plenty of elements in his biography suggest a queer sensibility and a candid appreciation of the male form. First, consider D'Annunzio's gender (re)presentation. When D'Annunzio, still a teenager but already a published author, made his social debut among Rome-based *literati* in the early 1880s, he was described by other men as 'a little one, with curly hair and sweet feminine eyes', 'the embodiment of the ideal of the romantic poet', 'a gentle and beautiful adolescent'.[9] Much later, anti-Italian propaganda in the foreign press during World War I routinely portrayed the poet as cross-dressing, wearing perfume and face powder.[10] Importantly, these assessments or representations were not entirely discontinuous with D'Annunzio's own gender performance and self-conception. As a young man he was proud of his white and delicate hands,[11] and throughout his life he apparently never felt the least need to cultivate outward virility in his gender presentation.[12] He unashamedly loved luxury and all the trappings of a decadent sensibility—incense, perfumes, and flowers (notably, heavy-scented tea roses, mimosa, and narcissus); in Fiume his troops, inspired by his example, bedecked themselves in blooms, and *Arditi* brandished blossoming boughs.[13] Duncan also draws attention to a fragment dating from 1927 in which D'Annunzio reports having sex with a female partner while she was fantasising about lesbian sex, which prompted the poet to follow her lead and identify with her female lover.[14]

We should, of course, not make too much of all this. Gender ambiguity may have come with the territory of being a writer (or at least Symbolist or Decadent writer) in D'Annunzio's time. Borelli notes that we owe to Spackman the insight that *fin-de-siècle* male writers tended to perceive themselves as uncommonly sensitive, imaginative, sensuous, and feminine.[15] Yet to the extent that in D'Annunzio's time one (not the only) way of representing homosexuality was in terms of gender transitivity,[16] it is also important not to dismiss the implications that this kind of gender performance and self-conception may have had for D'Annunzio's own sexual self-understanding.

Apart from his gender investments, D'Annunzio is known to have consorted with famously same-sex-attracted personalities. During the years preceding the war, while the poet was based in France, Robert de Montesquiou—the famously affected homosexual socialite reputed to have inspired both Wilde's Dorian Gray and Proust's Charlus—became the poet's patron and appears to have all but worshipped him.[17] In the same period, D'Annunzio was also intimate with cross-dressing artist Romaine Brook, Ida Rubinstein's lover, and might have had an affair with her.[18] Later in life (in the 1930s) he became acquainted with Radclyffe Hall, praising *The Well of Loneliness* and even inviting her to write his biography.[19] The suggestion that his motives were not innocent and had to do with a lesbian fetish[20] is sheer speculation. Rather, D'Annunzio appears to have felt a genuine affinity with homosexual artists. On 9 August 1935—a year when Hall came to visit him but was unable to see him[21]—D'Annunzio sent her a fascinating message at the Hotel Catullo, from his estate on Lake Garda. Written in French, the message addresses Hall in English as 'Daring comrade, darling little sister'. D'Annunzio goes on to present Hall with one of his books and an ancient medal '*honoris causa*', before closing with, '*Je pourrais, hélas, vous embrasser paternellement. Mais je vous embrasse fraternally.*'[22] The most famous lesbian writer of her day, notorious for writing on same-sex desire, was, for the poet, a comrade and a sibling, and someone who deserves both a medal and the kind of kiss bestowed on a spiritual brother: a more eloquent message of *ante-litteram* allyship is hard to imagine.

D'Annunzio's interest in male beauty is also apparent from numerous writings, as I will discuss at length when analysing his novels and drama work.

Here I provide three clues suggesting that an appreciation of male beauty was more than literary conceit for D'Annunzio. First, in October 1920, D'Annunzio complemented his and De Ambris's constitutional innovation with a project of reform of the Fiuman Army, in accordance with a radical vision of nonhierarchical organisation. Addressing the topic of games and ceremonies in the new Army regulations, D'Annunzio took care to provide that the officer in charge should stage every spectacle so that nudity will show off to best advantage 'glimpses of strength and rhythmical movements'.[23] Secondly, alongside Ida Rubinstein's legs, the poet wrote that he ranked the 'body of a genuine *Ardito* returning from the Piave front' among the most essentially beautiful things in the world.[24] Lastly, let me turn to D'Annunzio's treatment of Michelangelo.

In 'The Splendour of Sensuality', D'Annunzio's discussion of Michelangelo's art may have privileged female (Aurora, Leda) or heterosexual (Venus and Cupid) subjects.[25] But Michelangelo's women are notoriously male bodied.[26] And it is a headless male torso—in the massive physique style within the iconography of heroic nudity—that the poet chose to place in an alcove 'Sacred to the Godly Buonarroti' in the courtyard of the old nucleus of buildings of the Vittoriale, his fabulous residence overlooking Lake Garda, where he retired after Fiume. Similarly, it is a copy of Michelangelo's so-called Dying Slave that D'Annunzio chose to place opposite his bed.[27] Salaris notes that D'Annunzio gilded the strap binding the young man's chest and draped a luxurious textile around his hips, which intensifies the subject's sexual ambiguity.[28] In my estimation, D'Annunzio's changes rather heighten the subject's masculinity: the gilding on the strap draws attention to unequivocally male pectoral muscles, while the draping conceals the legs' position, which, in recalling a conventional representation of Venus in Greek sculpture (known as *Venus pudica*) imparted a distinctly androgynous character to the sculpture as conceived by Michelangelo; this androgynous element disappears as a result of D'Annunzio's treatment of the sculptural masterpiece. D'Annunzio himself may have intended neither to tone down nor sharpen the statue's masculinity: an erudite tour guide from the Vittoriale—who could name the sources of his information—told me during my visit there in 2023 that the cloth conceals what the poet regarded as an aesthetic infelicity in the hips or legs. Be that as it may, it is apparent that D'Annunzio treated this male nude with loving attentiveness and gave it pride of place in his bedroom. The significance of this is augmented by D'Annunzio's statement (accompanying the gift of his residence and its contents to the Italian state) that 'every house I furnished, every room I studiously assembled, . . . every object I chose . . . have always been for me a means of expressing myself, a means of revealing my spirit'.[29]

In sum, many elements emerge in D'Annunzio's biography that are suggestive of a certain queer sensibility and even of homoerotic interests, broadly intended. These include an apparent preoccupation with male beauty, as well as queer attachments and identifications, both social and aesthetic. And because, as we have seen, aesthetic values were central to D'Annunzio's politics (when he stood for political office, he was, in his own words, the 'Candidate of Beauty'),[30] these queer attachments cannot have failed to also shape his political vision.

HOMOEROTICISM IN *THE MARTYRDOM OF ST SEBASTIAN*

Becker has argued that D'Annunzio's queer sensibility, to the extent that he concedes he had one, was due to the influence of the French Decadent movement. The sexual ambiguity tropes of *décadentisme* resurfaced in D'Annunzio's earlier writings, but 'by the 1890s all that changes'. At this point, the poet favours and advocates, as an antidote to the sexual perversity and effeminacy that are symbolic of the degeneration of the polity, a national 'cult of virility', albeit one that generally remains tinged with homoeroticism, perhaps as a kind of decadent legacy.[31]

Becker rightly draws attention to the homoeroticism in D'Annunzio's writings—something that is all too rarely picked up on—but his points about effeminate degeneracy as opposed to a cult of virility are overstated. The kind of male comradeship that D'Annunzio's later writings celebrate need not be read as subservient to nationalistic or imperialistic goals. In the novels, at least, it is treated as valuable in itself: as contributing noninstrumentally to a kind of generativity that gives purpose to life and, as such, as an ingredient of a life well lived. This will become apparent in my analysis of the novels later in this chapter. Additionally, any celebration of heroic masculinity in D'Annunzio coexists with his own nonaligned gender performances (discussed earlier), as well as, in his literary production, with a more enduring commitment than Becker's analysis suggests to homoerotic representations that depart from the 'cult of virility' model. On the latter point, Duncan rightly notes that Becker flattens 'D'Annunzio's numerous male characters who fall short of the virile ideal', where Becker claims that they are ultimately nothing more than reiterations of tropes of effeminacy, degeneracy, and abnormality.[32]

Nowhere is this more apparent than in *Le Martyre de Saint Sébastien*. The play was published in 1911, two decades after D'Annunzio's purported turn to the cult of virility. Yet Sebastian is ephebic, androgynous, and the indisputable hero of the tale. A 'trope for artists linked to the aestheticist movement,' including Wilde and Beardsley,[33] St Sebastian is 'a sort of vermillion thread that runs through [D'Annunzio's] entire career of art connoisseur'[34] and something of a personal obsession of his. A quarter of a century before *Martyre* was written, during a *plein air* amorous rendezvous with a woman journalist a few years his senior, a teenage D'Annunzio had indulged a fantasy of impersonating the saint as he leant languidly and naked against a tree trunk.[35] About a decade after penning the drama, D'Annunzio took part in a carefully staged ceremony in Fiume's St Vito's church, where Fiuman women gave him a gold and silver bayonet, to be used to 'engrave victory upon the flesh of [their] enemies'—blessed by the chaplain of the *Arditi* at the end of Mass. The appointed date for the ceremony, not by coincidence, was St Sebastian's feast day in 1920.[36] D'Annunzio's speech likened St Sebastian's martyrdom to the sacrifice the legionnaires were called on to perform for the sake of Fiume.[37]

D'Annunzio's retelling (in archaic French) of the religious myth of Sebastian is something of an Italian response to Wilde's *Salomé*.[38] Written during D'Annunzio's French period (he had emigrated to escape debtors), it was staged in Paris in 1911, boasting music by Debussy, scenery by Bakst, and Ida Rubinstein (whom D'Annunzio liked to call 'brother')[39] playing the title role. Meeting Rubinstein—with her inspiringly androgynous 'lithe and slender body, long straight limbs and absolutely flat chest'—was the catalyst determining the poet to embark on the dramatic project, which he had been toying with for some time.[40]

Shortly before the Paris performance in 1911, the archbishop of Paris forbade all French Catholics from attending a play that 'disfigures the history of the martyr';[41] for good measure, the Church also officially blacklisted all of D'Annunzio's works.[42] Fifteen years later, when the drama was performed in Milan, it was the turn of the archbishop of Milan to ban the play,[43] and a Mass was scheduled specifically to coincide with the performance, attended primarily by pious young men.[44] It is unsurprising that the Church would so vehemently oppose a drama quite transparently intended to exaggerate not only the aesthetic but even the erotic dimensions of Sebastian's legend. Throughout *Martyre*, D'Annunzio repeatedly equates Sebastian and his story with the pagan myth of that archetype of male beauty, Adonis,[45] who had been the object of an ancient Greek cult in his own right. Gullace is quite right in observing that any element of Christian piety in the play is entirely subordinated to a pagan celebration of physical beauty—a treatment of Sebastian that was a legacy of Renaissance paintings, albeit magnified in D'Annunzio's drama.[46] It is because of this Adonis-like beauty that the people in *Martyre* are prepared to pay quite as much attention to the saint as they do. Thus, when young virgins convert to the Christian faith someone accuses, 'It is you, Sebastian, you who charm and intoxicate them'.[47] Others among the converted plead, 'Sebastian, Christ's archer, most beautiful of all mortal sons, pierce our hearts with your looks',[48] and they make sense of Sebastian's own faith in the same earthly terms: ‘How beautiful, nonetheless [Christ] must be if you love him of such a love!’[49]

Sebastian being said to outdo in beauty Antinoo—‘the adolescent from Bitinia, Hadrian’s favourite’[50]—invites direct consideration of the specifically homoerotic appeal of Sebastian’s beauty. The Emperor Diocletian himself takes a personal interest in Sebastian purely because of his looks. In a somewhat hermetic passage that conflates different queer references, Hadrian likens Sebastian to both Hyacinthus, beloved of Apollon, and the queer Roman emperor Elagabalus, who took the name of the sun god of whose cult he was hereditary high priest in Emesa: ‘Hail, beautiful youth! Hail, hyacinth-haired archer! I salute you, leader of the Court of Emesa, whom Apollon loves, who pleased the Sun-God!’[51] The analogy to Elagabalus is reinforced later, when some call for the defiant Sebastian to be thrown into Rome’s Greatest Sewer (Elagabalus’s remains had met a similar end):[52] for Sebastian has rejected the pagan gods in the name of the one true God, moving the emperor to rage and to condemn him to die. Yet Sebastian’s beauty is such that the emperor has second thoughts: he ‘observes the beardless hero with a queer fire in his keen pupils’ before declaring, ‘But how beautiful he is! Too beautiful.’[53]

As the contest between the saint and Diocletian escalates, the ‘emperor seems intoxicated by [Sebastian’s] every gesture: he leans towards the beardless one, he speaks to him in a subdued and ardent voice.’[54] Diocletian’s desperate effort to persuade the beautiful youth to make the choice that will spare him death references Hadrian’s deification of Antinoo: ‘I, I shall make a god of you. Everything is permitted to the Emperor. Hadrian deified the Youth from Bitinia with the melancholy mouth.’[55] Alexander the Great, notorious for his boundless love for Hephaistion, also gets a mention: ‘I shall give you all the boons of my Asian lands, Asia as deep and warm as a lion’s throat, as Alexander’s heart.’[56]

Not only does same-sex desire overtly structure the dramatic dynamic between the saint and the emperor, but it is also used as the prototype of religious rapture. Effectively, for Sebastian the choice is whether to give himself up to the emperor’s desire or to God’s own. This is apparent when a woman feels ‘pulled’ by a growing sense of faith. Sebastian tells her, ‘It is Him, Him. Because from the high sky he plunges and grasps like the shining eagle, He grasps, lifts, abducts in the wing-beat of his greatness.’[57] The reference here is clearly to the myth of Ganymede, snatched by the enamoured Zeus, changed into an eagle. Consistent with this, at the end of the play, right before the gates of Heaven open to receive Sebastian, it is the pagan god of love Eros that the Syrian Choir invokes upon the dead one.[58]

In this transparently sexually charged context, when Sebastian incites his executioners, the archers—in the name of the love they must show him—to blow harder on the fire he must tread on and to shoot harder the arrows that will transfix him, the homoerotic implications are not exactly subtle: 'Let me know your love, let me have the measure of it by fire';[59] 'From the deep, from the deep I call forth your love, Archers!';[60] 'Which of you would I choose still? He who aims straighter than everyone else, with his roughest arrow, and who shoots it so hard as to wound the bark of the tree, piercing me with the whole rod. That one, I will know for sure, loves me, loves me forever.'[61]

HOMOEROTICISM IN D'ANNUNZIO'S NOVELS

In *Martyre* the use of homoerotic tropes has a purely aesthetic and dramatic function. This is largely true of D'Annunzio's earlier novels too; but in the later ones, the treatment of same-sex desire is more complex, adumbrating an ethicopolitical conception of male-to-male love that also informs D'Annunzio's deployment of homoerotic rhetoric in his Fiume speeches. Derek Duncan's seminal essay 'Choice Objects: The Bodies of Gabriel D'Annunzio' rightly argues for the salience of same-sex desire to D'Annunzio's novels, where it manifests itself less as modern homosexuality than as a 'crisis in late nineteenth century heterosexuality'.[62]

Duncan argues that women have a 'functional role' in D'Annunzio's novels—almost a foil to men's homosocial bonds. To this extent, according to him, studies of gender in D'Annunzio's novels rather miss the point in focusing on women.[63] This is unclear to me. Scholarly engagement with D'Annunzio's novels on a feminist critical terrain—from Spackman's[64] to Barisonzi's[65]—has proved productive. Additionally, at least in D'Annunzio's first novel, *Pleasure*, any homosocial/homoerotic content is fairly marginal compared to the centrality of heterosexual concerns and the importance of female characters. More broadly, while it is true that D'Annunzio's protagonists are always male, their male comrades or nemeses—in both of whom the protagonists tend to have intense homoerotic investments—are generally absent (either somewhere else or dead) and mostly voiceless. The protagonists' female lovers, on the other hand, are very much present, agentic, and voluble. Rather than having to decide whether D'Annunzio's novels are ultimately about women or homosociality, therefore, we may be content with accepting that they centrally concern both.

I suggest that it is the tension between heterosexual and same-sex desire, and their different amenability to productive sublimation that offer the most interesting insight into both gender relations and the role played by homoeroticism in D'Annunzio's novels. D'Annunzio was not an outlier in centring desire in his literary writings. Interest in desire in the late nineteenth and early twentieth centuries was part of a bourgeoning interest in the unconscious (a concept first elaborated in the late eighteenth century).[66]

At that time, 'discourse of desire was ubiquitous' in Italy, and desire was viewed negatively both in 'the positivistic mind-set of the ruling class' and in the aestheticist movement known as *decadentismo*, whose most prominent exponents were Giovanni Pascoli and D'Annunzio himself.[67] This negative view of desire as 'an animalistic and obscure drive', to which men fall prey, according to Borelli, was at least partly based on a Darwinian model:[68] the reproductive drive effectively reduced humankind to a species, no less brutish than nonhuman animals.

Borelli argues that this problematisation of desire defines D'Annunzio's life and artistic project—and that it does so specifically by informing a debate, in which the writer participated, about whether the artist and intellectual should be socially and politically active or rather deliberately disengaged and devoted to the cult of beauty.[69] Thus, the male protagonists in D'Annunzio's novels attempt (mostly unsuccessfully) to free themselves from 'the tyranny of erotic desire'. They sublimate it either into art and the contemplative life (in D'Annunzio's earlier novels) or through political engagement and/or a life of action, which replaces desire with the will in the name of Nietzschean values of self-affirmation (in later novels).[70] The later novels, particularly, would attempt a rehabilitation of desire by associating it with the passions and the will to power, but not quite successfully, as 'sexual desire . . . remains tainted with the mark of the beast'.[71]

Borelli's analysis centres desire, but she does not interrogate sexual object choice, for she argues that it is heterosexual desire that is salient in D'Annunzio's novels: woman is invariably the object of desire.[72] Duncan's study of D'Annunzio's novels also 'deliberately avoid[s] foregrounding sexuality in terms of object choice' and rather analyses how these texts problematise the *fin-de-siècle* crisis of masculinity, while conceding that this crisis implicitly articulates with the development of homo/heterosexual definition that was underway in D'Annunzio's time.[73]

Like Borelli, I too foreground desire, but unlike her and Duncan, I centre sexual object choice. My analysis of D'Annunzio's novels adds a crucial dimension to Borelli's own. I argue that if we attend to the ways in which males are sometimes disavowed, but more often acknowledged, even quite explicitly, as objects of erotic desire in D'Annunzio's novels, we can come to appreciate D'Annunzio's views on the productive function of the sublimation of desire. This, in turn, enables us to grasp how the sublimation of homoerotic desire was enacted in Fiume through, among others, D'Annunzio's speeches to the legionnaires, in ways that were distinctly productive. Indeed, if we accept D'Annunzio's own claims, the sublimation of same-sex desire in Fiume was productive of the *Carnaro Charter* itself.

MALE BEAUTY IN D'ANNUNZIO'S NOVELS

D'Annunzio's novels objectify beauty as an aesthetic and erotic attribute of males. In *Perhaps So, Perhaps Not*, even more handsome than the gorgeous Isabella is her teenage brother Aldo, with his 'extraordinarily beautiful face',[74] his elegant movements, and a brow so perfect that people simply cannot tear their eyes away from it, and which makes him look like one of the 'young Immortals.'[75] In *Pleasure*, male beauty features as the paradigmatic case of beauty in a passage where the main character, Sperelli, reflects that his desire for exclusive possession of a lover is not unlike his desire to enjoy, to the exclusion of all others, things of perfect beauty. This reflection is brought home by Sperelli's imagining how, if he possessed them, he would secret away Myron's Discobolus, Polykleitos's Doryphoros, or the Aphrodite of Knidos, in that order.[76] It is, in other words, athletic male nudes that first come to Sperelli's mind when he fancies owning the ultimately desirable work of art.

In *Fire*, the writer Stelio Effrena discusses Venetian art in a public speech. Dwelling at length on a painting by Giorgione (*The Concert*), depicting a monk, a cleric, and a young layman, Effrena offers an interpretation of the painting. According to this, the monk, nearing middle age, is overcome with regret and anguish at the realisation of all the pleasures he has denied himself by following his vocation. The older cleric, unperturbed, seeks to appease him.

> But here is also, emerging from the warm shadows like the very personification of desire, the youth with a plumed hat and uncut flowing hair: the burning flower of adolescence, whom Giorgione seems to have created under the influence of an echo of that wonderful Hellenic myth from which sprang the ideal form of Hermaphroditus. . . . [The Youth] knows he is the master of that life that escapes the other two. . . . His look is aslant and intense, as if to seduce something, unknown, that seduces him; his closed mouth is like a mouth carrying the burden of an unbestowed kiss; . . . but if I think of his hidden hands, I imagine them busy in the act of tearing the leaves of the laurel bay to perfume his fingers.[77]

The suspicion that Effrena's words about the way the beautiful youth's hidden hands pluck at the laurel bay may be a metaphor for masturbation is reinforced when we are told that 'those in the audience who were young thought that they saw a representation of their unspeakable desire, a revelation of their innermost dream of relentless and endless pleasure.'[78] It is significant that, at the end of the novel, laurel bay is associated with masculine vigour when, at Wagner's funeral, two Italian soldiers are said to carry armloads of the plant: 'Muscular and powerful, selected amongst the strongest and handsomest, they looked like they had been modelled in the ancient

Roman mould.' The laurel itself has a more than vaguely phallic character with 'straight robust dusky branches, hard leaves powerfully veined, rough around the edges, as vivid as the bronze of fountains, rich with an aroma of victory.'[79]

MALE BEAUTY AS A FEMALE ATTRIBUTE IN D'ANNUNZIO'S NOVELS

Frequently, women themselves are erotically attractive in D'Annunzio's novels because they physically resemble males. In *Fire*, the heroine Foscarina's 'brow was as beautiful as a beautiful manly brow.'[80] In *Pleasure*, a minor character that opens the list of the protagonist's partners in debauchery 'had a youth's superb head, all golden and shimmering'.[81] Another's temptingly lascivious looks are the result of her dressing like a man, putting up dandy affectations, and looking for all the world like a 'genderless schoolboy'.[82]

More significantly, one of the three main characters in *Pleasure*, Donna Maria, is virginal and ethereal in everything but her heavy mass of hair, whose 'locks, in the front, had the density and shape of those which cover, helmet-like, the head of the statue of Antinoo in the Galleria Farnese'.[83] Not only does this passage use a male term of comparison to convey what is most sensually flesh-like about Donna Maria, but it selects one that would have immediate resonance for cultivated devotees of same-sex desire. And lest there should be any doubt about the significance specifically of Maria's hair to her erotic appeal, we are told of her boarding school days, when her girl-friends literally fought over the chance to comb and pet the plaited, 'beautiful black snake that reached [her] feet'.[84] These recollections of youthful 'passion and jealousy' prompt Maria's would-be paramour, Sperelli, to reflect that of all his female friends, none possessed 'such a vast and dark forest in which to get lost'.[85] Later, he reminisces about 'amorous dreams he dreamt around that beautiful, virgin hair that once reduced female pupils to love-sickness',[86] as well as the 'voluptuous deceits' he 'had savoured' 'in its shadow'.[87] Like her hair, Maria's mesmerising, musical voice participates of the male principle: 'It was an ambiguous voice, I daresay bisexual, double, androgynous; two-toned. The male tone, low and as if shrouded, sometimes softened, clarified itself, feminised itself'.[88]

In *The Triumph of Death*, the main character's beloved, Ippolita, has a 'masculine shadow, only just visible, veiling her upper lip';[89] narrow hips that 'made her look like a youth';[90] and nipples that are curiously penis-like in their 'extraordinarily erectile' quality.[91] The whole rear of her body, from nape to calf, also recalls the 'resemblance to a youth'; and in this youth-like beauty is discernible 'one of those fragments of the ideal human type, which

Nature sometimes throws into the numberless mediocre moulds in which the species perpetuates itself.'[92]

In *Perhaps So, Perhaps Not*, the irresistibly seductive Isabella 'was as thin slim quick as a youth trained to sprint', with broad shoulders, deep chest, powerful glutes, and a linear bone structure.[93] Her voice is at times 'masculine, almost violent' or 'as uneven and ambiguous as some [boys'] voices broken by the trials of puberty'.[94] For her part, her little sister Lunella has lush locks and a 'beautiful pouty mouth' like Antinoo.[95]

'QUEER' REFERENCES IN D'ANNUNZIO'S NOVELS

Alongside a candid appreciation of male beauty as both a male and female attribute, D'Annunzio's novels contain references to poets, artists, philosophers, and personalities whose homoerotic leanings today we openly admit or investigate, and which we have little reason to assume cultivated men in D'Annunzio's own time were oblivious to.

In *Pleasure*, Andrea Sperelli and Donna Maria, wandering about Rome's protestant cemetery, make their way to Percy Bysshe Shelley's and Edward John Trelawny's adjacent graves.[96] The celebration of male love on Trelawny's tombstone—from Shelley's own poem 'Epitaph'—is reported in full, including the line, 'Let not their bones be parted, for their two hearts in life were single-hearted'.[97] Later, Andrea and Maria go in search of the grave of another romantic poet who had early on become a symbol of queer investments[98] and whose queerness (actual or imputed) became iconic in Victorian times:[99] John Keats. For the avoidance of doubt, D'Annunzio reminds us that Keats is the poet who wrote *Endymion*.[100] With the poem's title immediately conjuring up countless visual representations of the eponymous sleeping shepherd as a legendary example of male beauty (objectified through Selene's female gaze), the Keats-*Endymion* coupling here redoubles the homoerotic allusiveness of this reference.

The Virgins of the Rocks includes a lengthy reference to Ludwig II of Bavaria, portrayed as a flawed yet tragic hero worthy of admiration for his uncompromising determination to live in a solipsistic, make-believe world filled with the music of Wagner, and the heroic myths it evokes, where 'he quenches his angsty thirst for the divine',[101] 'King of himself and of his dream'.[102] No mention of Ludwig's rumoured all-male orgies appears, for obvious reasons, but we can legitimately doubt that D'Annunzio had no inkling of them.

In the first five pages of the first book of this novel, the main character and narrative voice, Claudio Cantelmo, also reflects on the influence of Socrates on his outlook on life. Here, references to male beauty and to sublimated, or chastely manifested, same-sex desire are not only copious but explicit and integral to illustrating the exalted philosophy of life that Cantelmo attributes to Socrates. The most obvious such reference is to Plato's *Symposium* and Alcibiades, 'marvellous outlaw',[103] who had tried to seduce the philosopher in exchange for sharing his wisdom:

> 'When I hear this man's [Socrates's] speeches, my heart leaps higher than the *korybantes'* hearts [when they perform their orgiastic dances]', said the son of Cleinias [Alcibiades]—exquisitely savage, wild animal crowned with ivy and violets—weaving the most dazzling praise with which a man was ever deified on earth, at the end of a symposium which had received, from the mouth of the philosopher who resembled Silenus, the wisdom [about love] into which he had been initiated by Diotima.[104]

Cantelmo's reflections also dwell on the beauty of Socrates's disciples and the spiritualising effect of contemplating it:

> A queer melancholy filled me when reading [Plato's Socratic] Dialogues during my adolescence, when I wished to picture to myself that circle of eager and restless disciples gathering about [Socrates]. I used to admire the handsomest ones, attired most elegantly, on whom his round and protruding eyes . . . dwelt more frequently. . . . I was moved by the fate of that extraordinarily beautiful youth from Elis, Phaedo, who, captured in his own State as a prisoner of war and sold to a keeper of brothels, had fled that place of shame to Socrates, by whom he was redeemed and thanks to whom he partook in the festivities of pure thought.[105]

And: 'At the beginning of Xenophon's *Symposium*, [Socrates], with the others, regards at length, in complete silence, Autolycus' perfect beauty, as if recognising the presence of something exceeding the human.'[106] Finally, D'Annunzio embellishes on a passage of Plato's *Phaedo* to argue that the sensory (visual and tactile) experience of male beauty reveals to Socrates no less than the ultimate truth about life beyond death:

> [In Plato's *Phaedo*, we are told that Socrates, about to die,] laid a hand on [Phaedo's] head, caressing his hair and pressing it against his neck, being used to toy in that fashion amongst that thick youthful forest. He did not speak yet, so intensely moved and streaked with delight was he. Through that beautiful, living yet impermanent thing, he conversed one last time with the earthly life in which he had achieved his own perfection, in which he had realised his ideal of virtue; and he felt perhaps that nothing existed beyond, that his finite existence was sufficient unto itself, that prolonging it into eternity was but an impression produced—like the halo of star—by the extraordinary splendour of his humanity. Never had the hair of that youth from Elis held a value more sublime. Being

about to die, he was finding delight in it one last time; and he knew, too, that tomorrow it would be shorn. Eventually he said—and his disciples had never known such a sound in his voice—'Phaedo, tomorrow you will cut off your beautiful locks.' And the be-locked one: 'So it seems, Socrates'.[107]

Mythical figures central to the legacy of same-sex eroticism passed down to us from Graeco-Roman antiquity are also cited. In *Fire*, the main character, writer Stelio Effrena, engaged in gallant conversation, indulges in the following fancy: the pomegranate—a symbol he has chosen to associate himself with—represents him so fully that if 'he had lived at the time when men, unearthing Grecian marbles, found in the soil the roots, still moist, of old stories', a painter would never have dreamed of portraying him without that fruit. This is because the artist's 'paganising' conception of Effrena would be no different from his conception of 'Hyacinth, Narcissus, or Cyparissus'.[108] These three figures have in common the fact of their indissoluble association with the plant which is their namesake (and into which they change following an accidental death), explaining why Effrena cites them. But they have something else in common: they are all objects of same-sex desire—his own, in the case of Narcissus, and Apollon's in the case of the other two. Here, in implicitly claiming continuity between the Latin values that his art instantiates and the legacy of classical Antiquity mediated via the Italian Renaissance, it is same-sex myths that are invoked by Effrena as paradigmatic of that legacy.

HOMOSEXUAL CHARACTERS IN D'ANNUNZIO'S NOVELS

When D'Annunzio was writing his novels, the establishment of homosexuality as a psychological type (the transition to thinking of homosexuality in terms of identities rather than acts) was underway but not yet as taken for granted as in later decades.[109] The main characters in D'Annunzio's novels, as we will see shortly, manifest same-sex desire in ways that do not connote their sexual subjectivities as specifically and recognisably homosexual, or indeed indisputably queer. Their same-sex desire does seem to have something to do with the kind of aesthetic (hyper)sensitivity they share with D'Annunzio himself; but this psychological trait hardly casts them as distinct psychosexual (notably, homosexual) types. Explicitly or recognisably homosexual secondary characters, however, do make their appearance twice in D'Annunzio's novels.

In *The Triumph of Death*, we encounter a young married coupled, ostensibly heterosexual, who appear to have tied the knot as a result of family pressure. They and their families are gathered in a sanctuary to ask for the miracle that will allow the couple to consummate their marriage, for the bride is still intact. Yet from their demeanour, it seems apparent that consummation is ardently desired far more ardently by the families than the couple—especially the husband, who, alone among all his relations, makes no invocation to the Virgin Mary, merely 'keeping the Image fixed in his eyes, from which two rivulets of silent tears flowed.'[110] The couple's description strongly suggests their homosexuality. The wife, specifically, is the portrait of a butch lesbian in feminine garb, while the husband is 'less tall than she, almost beardless, extremely pale, with an expression of deep sadness, as if eaten away by a secret disease. And both appeared to carry in their looks the fatality of a primitive mystery.'[111] These last words—applicable to both spouses—seem to allude to congenital homosexuality rather than impotence on the husband's part. Yet impotence is the explanation for the lack of consummation that is assumed by everyone present: 'It was softly rumoured that they asked for the genital potency to be restored to the youth, who had perhaps had it destroyed by an evil spell.'[112] It is notable that there is no implication of negativity attaching to this case of homosexuality; rather, one senses a certain understated and implicit sympathy for the way cultural and family expectations make the young man's life miserable.

We find the second explicitly homosexual character in *Perhaps So, Perhaps Not*. Here we encounter, briefly, one Beppe della Luzza, described by a 'zealous' detective as 'lowest of the low', whom Dante, in the *Divine Comedy*, would have placed in the circle of Hell where fire rains down on the damned[113]—a punishment specially reserved for sodomites. Della Luzza appears alongside one Stefano Feri, a renowned pimp: together they are responsible for temporarily abducting and, apparently, trafficking Isabella Inghirami, one of the novel's key characters. Indeed, the detective speaks of Della Luzza and Feri in one breath as 'the two procurers'.[114] Thus, while Della Luzza is indubitably portrayed as a despicable character, he is no more so than his heterosexual counterpart, Feri. This has the effect of neutralising the relevance of sexual orientation to the palpably negative judgement about their character, which rather attaches to their corruption and exploitative behaviour.

SAME-SEX DESIRE IN *THE INNOCENT ONE*

So far we have established that, consistent with D'Annunzio's queer sensibility, both a preoccupation with male beauty and queer citations are pervasive in both *Martyre* and the novels. Additionally, on those rare occasions when homosexuality itself is addressed, it is without attaching any negative value judgements to it as such. In the rest of this chapter I engage in a more detailed examination of same-sex desire in the novels. Through this analysis, we can track the ways in which, from a mere aesthetic or dramatic device in earlier works, a more philosophical treatment of homoerotic desire emerges in D'Annunzio's later fiction—in accordance with a conception of same-sex desire that will inform D'Annunzio's oratorial practice in Fiume.

D'Annunzio's references to same-sex desire are often deftly exploited to add covert layers of psychological complexity to his characters, incidentally delivering (possibly despite the author's own intentions) astute social commentary. In *The Innocent One*, philandering Tullio ends up killing his wife Giuliana's adulterine baby, who is intruding into their rekindled marital bond. Tullio abhors the baby as much in himself as for being fathered specifically by Giuliana's lover, the decadent writer Filippo Arborio. Duncan, who rightly draws attention to Tullio's obsession with Arborio, attributes it to Tullio's insecurities about his own defective masculinity, which Tullio sees reflected in Arborio's own gender ambiguity.[115] I suggest, instead, that Tullio's hatred of Arborio is a textbook case of defensive projection,[116] where Tullio's disgust at his own repressed same-sex desire for Arborio is violently acted out against both Arborio and his baby.

Tullio's fascination with Arborio precedes their introduction: 'Had I not come under the spell of this extraordinary artist, whose books as it were sublimated him into a pure spiritual essence?' Tullio had also previously caught a glimpse of the writer's 'fine and seductive figure', known to be attractive to women.[117] D'Annunzio, no doubt deliberately, infuses Arborio with physical features typical of himself (the 'slim body') and Arborio's work with characteristics that—to listen to D'Annunzio's critics—are immediately recognisable as a trademark of D'Annunzio's own literary production: 'His novels—full of a complicated psychology, sometimes extremely insightful, often false—perturbed sentimental souls, kindled restless imaginations, taught with utmost elegance disdain for common life'.[118] As in a hall of mirrors, Tullio himself feels an affinity for Arborio-the-writer and whatever springs of Arborio's imagination: 'Did I not find in some of his literary creatures certain strange resemblances with my own intimate being?'[119]

Eventually, Tullio properly meets Arborio in a fencing hall:

> The din and gleam of blades, the sundry elegant or awkward postures of the fencers, the rapid movement of all those arched legs, the warm and acrid exhalation of all those bodies, the throaty screams, the violent ejaculations, the laughing outbursts reconstruct with unusual vividness in my memory the scene going on around us as we faced each other . . .[120]
>
> Later, we met again in the changing room. The low-ceilinged room was already full of smoke and a potent, nauseating, bodily odour. Everyone there, naked, in wide white capes, rubbed their chest, arms, shoulders, slowly,

> smoking, chatting loudly, giving vent to their beastliness in dirty talk. The noise of showers vied with that of vulgar laughs. And once or twice, with a vague sense of repulsion, with a start as if I had been jolted by a violent push, I caught a glimpse of Arborio's slim body, to whom my eyes kept returning against my own will.[121]

The psychological dialectic between protested revulsion and reluctant attraction in that most intensely erotically charged homosocial environment—the changing room—leaves little doubt about how Tullio's budding hatred for Arborio, albeit prompted by marital jealousy, is compounded by his own unresolved same-sex impulses. Tullio's mind had already become preoccupied—again, very much against his will—with images of Giuliana and Arborio locked in sexual acts before this meeting;[122] now the images start recurring more insistently.[123]

Tullio's unilateral love-hate relationship with Arborio becomes increasingly self-sustaining: what Arborio did with Giuliana almost takes a backseat to Tullio's own phantasmatic construction of Arborio as, 'like one of his characters, . . . queer, double, cruelly curious, made sterile by the habit of analysis . . . constantly busying himself with converting the warm and spontaneous movements of the soul into clear, glacial notions, used to treating every human subject as a pure object of psychological speculation, incapable of love . . . a sensualist, cynical, wicked.'[124] It is uncanny and ironic (but the irony was surely intended by D'Annunzio) that this characterisation reads very much like the sort of things D'Annunzio's detractors said (and say) about him.

At the same time, Tullio acknowledges that the 'complicated and ambiguous' Arborio 'belonged to my same race and his brain shared with mine certain constitutional peculiarities.'[125] The self-referential structure of Tullio's attraction/revulsion for Arborio/D'Annunzio does not mean that it is merely a proxy for Tullio's inner conflict about his own identifications. Rather, a dialectic is instituted between Tullio's identification with Arborio and his desire for him, which manifests itself as a longing to ravish him. As Tullio recounts, his hatred made Arborio's figure 'so intensely alive that I felt, looking at it, a *veritable bodily sensation*, a physical orgasm, sometimes similar to the wild thrill that had occasionally seized me on the field, standing before my adversary stripped of his shirt, at the signal of attack.'[126]

Tullio's narcissistic desire for Arborio is unlike, and interferes with, Tullio's love for his brother Federico. Tullio's brotherly love ('How I love Federico! I have never loved him so much'),[127] like his love-hatred for Arborio, is not devoid of erotic undercurrents. Thus, Tullio is capable of swooning over Federico's blushing ('Oh, the flush on his face so manly!').[128] Yet Federico—unlike Tullio, Arborio, and Arborio's characters (not to mention

D'Annunzio)—is wholesome, wholly uncomplicated, wholly good, wholly virile. Indeed, Federico's alterity from his brother could not be starker, making identification on Tullio's part impossible and his desire for Federico nonnarcissistic (or not in a simple sense). Because Federico's superiority is manifestly indisputable, Tullio's love is left the only logical outlet in a desire to submit: 'I wished that Federico would not only love me but dominate me; I wished to cede my birth-right as firstborn to him, so much more worthy than me, and submit to his counsel, treat him as my guide, obey him . . . he had a strong arm and would defend me.'[129] But the possibility of sublimating (incestuous) same-sex desire into a relationship of authoritative guidance and submission is not enough to distract Tullio from his powerful narcissistic preoccupations with the desired-abhorred Arborio. The baby—a stand-in for his biological father—is thus killed, leading to the relational and emotional dead-end that is the novel's denouement.

I am not sure that D'Annunzio consciously intended to portray two possible outlets (sublimation as against destructive acting out) of same-sex desire and to make a commentary about the consequences of each, though that seems the text's effect. However, neither am I purporting to unveil D'Annunzio's unconscious same-sex desire through a psychoanalytic reading of *L'Innocente*. D'Annunzio's language and imagery, and his ironic strategies (that is, the attribution to Arborio and his books of charges D'Annunzio's critics were wont to make against him) are simply too revealing to be anything but deliberate. My argument is that D'Annunzio consciously and deftly used same-sex desire as one of Tullio's own unacknowledged longings, in order to give psychological texture to his character's motivations; but then the treatment of same-sex desire took on a logic of its own. This logic is structured by the tension between the unrealised possibility of Tullio wholly giving himself up to the (possibly productive) sublimation of desire for his brother and his actual giving way to destructive acting out of his narcissistic desire-revulsion for Arborio. This logic is similar, though not identical, to that which, as we will see, will be more explicitly and consciously thematised by D'Annunzio's treatment of same-sex desire in his later works of prose fiction.

SAME-SEX DESIRE IN *THE TRIUMPH OF DEATH*

Federico's unalloyed goodness and his sibling status enable a wholesome sublimation of Tullio's desire (albeit one that ultimately fails to distract him from his narcissistic same-sex longing for Arborio). Likewise, in *The Triumph of Death* the main character, Giorgio Aurispa, is able safely to rhapsodise about 'the supernatural fascination'[130] he feels for his uncle Demetrio, in accents that fall just short of outright romantic passion. For, after all, Demetrio's suicide (that most iconic of homosexual deaths: 'Did he have a secret that ate at his heart?')[131] places him conveniently out of reach: 'Never before have I perceived his being more intensely than after his death. . . . He now exists for me alone, immune from any other contact, communicating to me alone. He exists pure and intense as never before.'[132]

Giorgio's memories—five years after his uncle's suicide—of sharing the pleasures of music in an intimate setting with Demetrio, a violinist, read remarkably like one's remembering the thrill of being initiated into love making:

> [Demetrio's] left hand, proud and frenzied, ran across the strings, along the handle, pressing them with his thin fingers, while beneath the skin the play of muscles showed so clearly as to look almost pitiful. . . . Sometimes he pressed the chin more forcefully, he bowed his head, lids half-closed, all concentrated in his inner delight. . . . [Giorgio in his memory] lived again those long hours of warm intimacy and oblivion, when he and Demetrio, alone, in the lukewarm room into which no noise penetrated, played the music of their favourite masters.—How they forgot themselves! What unique and high raptures the music they themselves produced let them experience! Not infrequently, they fell under the spell of a single melody, for the whole afternoon; and they were unable to step out of the magic ring that encircled them.[133]
>
> [Giorgio] saw again the violinist when he improvised [and Giorgio] accompanied him on the piano with unbearable anxiety, trying to follow his lead, to anticipate it, aways afraid of spoiling the rhythm, getting the tone wrong, hitting a false chord, missing a note.[134]

Some will think that, in purporting to read these passages as Giorgio's confession of his erotic attraction for Demetrio, I am overinterpreting. But my claim is intertextually and contextually plausible. Intertextually, the conceit of music making as love making recurs in *Perhaps So, Perhaps Not*, where gorgeous Aldo 'sat holding the cello tight [between his legs] as if to possess it, and turned the screw inside the eyed frog of the bow with patently orgasmic pleasure, as if he were not stretching the white hair but the bundles of his most sensitive nerves'.[135] Contextually, the impression that Giorgio, when picturing his uncle playing the violin, is really reminiscing about first love and love making is heightened when we are told about Giorgio exploring Demetrio's apartments after his death. Giorgio finds his own translation of a poem by Tennyson, to which Demetrio had made music. The translation is of the following passage from *The Princess* (1847), which now seems to describe Giorgio's own state of mind about the loss of his uncle and expressly references 'first love':

Tears, idle tears, I know not what they mean,
Tears from the depth of some divine despair
Rise in the heart, and gather to the eyes,
In looking on the happy Autumn-fields,
And thinking of the days that are no more.
. . .
Dear as remembered kisses after death,
And sweet as those by hopeless fancy feigned
On lips that are for others; deep as love,
Deep as first love, and wild with all regret;
O Death in Life, the days that are no more.[136]

The experience of recollection in those surroundings is so emotionally charged that Giorgio indulges in a fantasy to kill himself, using the same gun as his uncle, lying on his very bed: 'Demetrio's body has left the imprint where I myself shall lie.'[137] It is significant that a study whose main purpose was not—unlike mine in this part of the book—to unearth the homoeroticism coursing through D'Annunzio's novels notes that Giorgio's 'emulating Demetrio's suicide is a supreme act of both failed mourning and erotic union'.[138]

Giorgio does not, however, go through with it. The novel then unfolds as the story of his uncontrollable but fruitless, as he sees it, passion for Ippolita. She is not worthy of him; even if she were, he cannot—for no lover can—ever fully possess his beloved; and yet he cannot let go of her dominion over him and be his own master again.[139] This eventually leads Giorgio—whose thoughts grow increasingly more obsessive, morbid, fanatical, and misogynistic—to commit a murder/suicide, but not before regretting not having ended life beautifully in Demetrio's room, with Demetrio's gun. He mentally addresses his dead uncle in these terms: 'Why did I choose to tempt life again and [in tying myself to Ippolita,] cover myself with shame in your eyes? How could I lose myself seeking assurance in the possession of another soul, when I possessed yours, when you lived in me?'[140]

Here the fungibility between same-sex love and different sex-love is fully articulated: both aspire to a complete merging with the beloved. Because, however, sexual intercourse promises but invariably fails to realise that union, while condemning the lover to its fruitless repetition, sublimated same-sex desire in D'Annunzio's novels tends to have the edge over consummated different-sex desire. Nor does that sublimation, it turns out, require being enforced by such circumstances as the death of the beloved (as in Demetrio's case). For Giorgio, at one point, recalls another male 'kindred spirit', Adolfo Astorgi, a comrade of adventures 'with whom he had been able to live for some time in complete communion'.[141]

SAME-SEX DESIRE IN *GIOVANNI EPISCOPO*

There is also erotic tension between the eponymous protagonist of *Giovanni Episcopo* and his tormentor, Wanzer. Episcopo, a timid office clerk, becomes enthralled to the overbearing and despotic Wanzer after the latter accidentally hurts him by hitting his forehead with an object he was aiming at someone else. Wanzer takes Episcopo home and is continuously present during his recovery, after which he installs himself as a complete authority in Episcopo's life, who is too afraid to rebel. Eventually, Episcopo will kill Wanzer after the latter has interfered with his family life. Wanzer had already seduced Episcopo's wife and caused her to flee, but it is the imminent danger he poses to Episcopo's young child that sets the father off and causes him to snap out of his passivity.

Episcopo's painful inability to stand up for himself are attributable to a personality where a certain constitutional softness (the flip side of which is a keen capacity for empathy) shades into lack of self-respect and cowardliness. These personality traits explain much else that happens to him in the novel, including his agreeing to marry a disreputable woman, his tolerance of her blatant infidelity, his being tyrannized by her family, and his becoming emotionally dependent on her fairly harmless but manipulative, alcoholic father. Yet the novel also hints at Episcopo's unacknowledged same-sex attraction for Wanzer as playing a role in his submissiveness, his 'abjection', his '*absolute impossibility* . . . to escape the power of that man':[142]

> He dominated everyone in there, bullied everyone. . . . As soon as he appeared, even the angriest ones kept quiet; The shy ones smiled at him, caressed him. What was it about that man?
>
> I don't know. At the table I sat almost opposite him. Without wanting to, my eyes were riveted on him, incessantly. I experienced a strange feeling, I can't quite explain: an unaccountable mix of attraction and revulsion. It was like an evil, very evil charm sent my way by that strong, choleric, violent man . . .[143]

Episcopo goes on:

> Oh, Lord, who will be able to reveal this mystery to me, before I die? Are there, then, men on Earth who, meeting other men, can do with them what they please, can enthral them? . . .
>
> Before my tormentor I *never could will*. . . . Only one thing I knew: I was lost, irredeemably...
>
> I thought:—to die through those hands, one night, atrociously,—that is my fate, I'm sure.[144]

Despite Episcopo disavowing this fantasy purely as the object of his terror, we are left with the impression that part of Episcopo is, unconsciously, erotically invested in this thanatoid scenario as the logical outcome of his fetishisation of Wanzer's unalloyed male power and ruthlessness. Indeed, something like Episcopo's autassassinophilia[145] may be implied where he accounts for his ability to empathise with his wife's pitiful alcoholic father. Episcopo declares to feel a kind of 'brotherly compassion for every twisted, every sorrowful' soul in the 'innermost depths' of his 'substance'[146] and claims that he can see his own (unspecified) addiction (*'vizio'*) reflected in the old alcoholic's own addictions:[147]

> The man eaten away by vice . . . who . . . knows himself lost and does not want, cannot, save himself. . . . What pity, sir, what pity! Do you know anything more profound, more attractive, darker? Tell, tell: which of all human things is more sorrowful than the thrill you are seized by before the object of your most desperate passion? What is sadder than the trembling hands, the quaking knees, the twisted lips, one's whole being yearning in the implacable need to satisfy one sensation alone?[148]

Here Episcopo seems to confess how he himself might feel compelled to follow the imperatives of his own *'vizio'* (his irresistible urge to submit to Wagner's power) even unto death. Ultimately, even Episcopo's attraction for the woman he marries—a restaurant waitress who is the object of the lustful desires and crude remarks of all patrons—appears yet another element of his urge to yield to Wanzer's power: 'I recall the expressive gesture that Wanzer made and the greedy attitude his lips took on as they uttered an obscene sentence in dialect. And I remember that, getting out of there, I already felt infected by desire for that woman I had not yet seen.'[149]

Episcopo's desire for Wanzer is like Tullio's desire for Arborio in *The Innocent One*: a dark, irresistible drive with fatal consequences. In this, it is similar to how D'Annunzio's novels tend to portray different-sex desire. The conception of same-sex desire as capable of being integrated, generally through sublimation, into a well-ordered life, one ebbing with active and/or creative pursuits—a conception that first made its appearance in *The Triumph of Death*—is quietly forgotten in *Giovanni Episcopo*. It does, however, distinctly inform D'Annunzio's last three novels.

SAME-SEX DESIRE IN *THE VIRGINS OF THE ROCKS*

In *The Virgins of the Rocks* Claudio Cantelmo, disgusted with the philistinism of modern life in the Italian capital, retires to his country estate, with the intention of finding a bride who will bear him a son. Such a son will (as a matter of nurture, but also epigenetics) inherit and increase the perfection of the Cantelmo lineage and in turn transmit its spiritual, cultural, and life-affirming legacy. The bride will be chosen among three sisters who had been Cantelmo's childhood companions. Surprisingly, what drives Claudio to these momentous life choices is his love for a fifteenth-century ancestor, one Alessandro Cantelmo.

Claudio Cantelmo likes to think that Alessandro was bound to Leonardo da Vinci (on the basis of some commentaries penned by the latter) by the same kind of physical/intellectual attraction that drew together Socrates and his favourite pupils: 'Like Socrates, [Leonardo] favoured disciples endowed with rare refinements and beautiful hair. Like Socrates he excelled in the art of elevating human soul to the utmost degree of its vigour.'[150] The reference to the beautiful hair of Leonardo's pupils appears to have been inspired by Gian Giacomo Caprotti, an assistant, trainee, and model of Leonardo's, described by Giorgio Vasari in *The Lives of the Artists* (1550) as 'exceedingly graceful and handsome, blessed with beautiful, ring-like curls, which much delighted Leonardo'.[151] Today we speculate that Caprotti might have been Leonardo's lover, and D'Annunzio's erudition almost certainly also made him aware of the accusation of sodomy that had been made against Leonardo when he was twenty-four.[152]

D'Annunzio's likening of Leonardo to Socrates—against the backdrop (previously discussed) of his expatiating, in the same novel, on the homoerotic bonds between Socrates and his young followers—strongly suggests that he intended to allude to bonds of a like nature running between Leonardo and his pupils. This suggestion of a homoerotic tension between the Renaissance man of genius and his mentee Alessandro Cantelmo then spills over and colours the bond between Alessandro and his descendant Claudio himself. That is, Claudio Cantelmo's love for Alessandro, which determines him to embark on his search for a bride to produce a son that will carry on the Cantelmo legacy, also implies a homoerotic urge on his part: '"For you I shall be" I used to tell [Alessandro,] "for you, I shall be as I ought to be: because I love you, handsomest flower of my own blood: because I want to put all my pride in obeying to your law, my master."'[153]

Indeed, it is in an attempt to conjure up his beloved ancestor/master from the afterlife and back into this world that Cantelmo desires to father a child:

> You carried within you a power sufficient to subdue the Earth, but your royal destiny was not to find fulfilment during the time of your first appearance. . . . Your virtue . . . will necessarily rise again, one day, in your surviving descendance. Let it be tomorrow! Let your equal come forth from my own generative power! I call forth and await and make preparations for your re-born virtue with absolute faith, adoring your true image, my thoughtful master, who marked the

> page of the books of Knowledge by putting the blade of your naked sword into them![154]

Cantelmo's intense and genuine fascination with the three virgins is indubitable, but his motivations for courting them effectively reduce the value of heterosexual love making to the fulfilment of a same-sex love bond—a unilateral and phantasmatic (not to mention incestuous) one at that.

When it comes to picking a bride, Cantelmo's rational choice (which does not necessarily find fulfilment in the denouement) falls on Anatolia. In contrast with her neurotic, feminine[155] brothers, and with her two sisters, Maximilla and Violante—who are personifications, respectively, of virtuous and lustful femininity—Anatolia exudes virility. Cantelmo first meets her on a stone staircase in the vast garden encircling their palace, where her arm lends firm support to her brother's uncertain steps. Anatolia extends her hand towards Cantelmo and 'her gesture had a virile frankness', while its contact with his own hand communicates to him 'a kind of brotherly trust.'[156] Befittingly, Anatolia's hand is, unlike her brothers', 'ringless, not too white, not too elongated, but robust in its pure form, apt to gather and to sustain'.[157] Later we are told again of circumstances that confirm the 'virile power' she can conjure up in moments of crisis.[158]

Borelli remarks on the virility of Anatolia.[159] But having elected not to problematise D'Annunzio's sexual object choice in his novels, her analysis overlooks the point that preferring such a masculine bride is quite consistent with the way in which Cantelmo's motivations for having an heir have made heterosexual intercourse functional, for him, to a fantasy centred on same-sex desire. Having decided he needs to father a child out of love for his handsome master and admirable ancestor Alessandro, it is less than incongruous for Cantelmo to rationally incline towards virile Anatolia as the ideal partner in this project.

But Cantelmo is at loggerheads with himself. His desire for Anatolia is derivative of his same-sex desire for Alessandro—and this is unilateral, phantasmatic, intellectualised. His genuinely heterosexual desire for the sensual Violante, conversely, is physical, powerful, mutual, irresistible. Violante will not be pushed out of the picture, and the novel ends with fairly clear intimations that Cantelmo has failed to carry out his purpose. Cantelmo's error is, apparently, his failure to follow the example of Socrates and Leonardo, for whom the generativity of same-sex desire was in part enabled by a determination to live in the present. Cantelmo's same-sex desire is backward looking (far into the distant past when Alessandro lived), while the fruit it is supposed to bear (the birth of a son) is too forward looking and requires, for its realisation, the mediation of heterosexual desire. But heterosexual desire proves most resistant to harnessing for higher purposes.

SAME-SEX DESIRE IN *FIRE*

Rather than making, incongruously, the purpose of same-sex desire a procreative one (as in *The Virgins of the Rocks*), the main characters of D'Annunzio's last two novels appreciate that its generativity is a matter of pursuing an active (*Perhaps So, Perhaps Not*) or creative (*Fire*) life. *Fire* concerns writer Stelio Effrena's aspiration to produce a literary masterpiece, more or less frustrated by his sexual involvement with acclaimed theatre actress Foscarina. It is loosely autobiographical, D'Annunzio having drawn inspiration from his relationship with Eleonora Duse. There are some modest nods to same-sex desire in *Fire*. For example, there is an implication of homoeroticism in Effrena's awareness that his pleasure in sex with Foscarina is intensified by knowledge that she has had copious previous lovers. Effrena and Foscarina rationalise this in patriarchal terms—his jealousy and disdain at her lack of sexual purity unleash the sexual sadist within him: 'Ah, what had she done? She had armed a savage thirsty for laying ruin, and she had put him there, between herself and her friend.'[160] Yet the relevant passages also imply Effrena's titillation at touching the recesses of her flesh visited by other men—as if, through her, he might make love to them. Foscarina worries that Effrena 'would always see the shadow of other men on her caress',[161] and he acknowledges that 'his rough desire would feed off that impurity, that obscure baggage, those traces of lost loves'.[162]

We also briefly encounter, again, the imagery of masters and their youthful pupils endowed with copious hair: 'There stood the mystical doctor, close by, with his array [of followers] . . . [Stelio Effrena] descried their faces, intent and flushed, their hair thick and long, the mouth half-open in childish wonder or tight-lipped with a sort of sensitive vehemence'.[163] The rarefied homoeroticism here only becomes apparent intertextually, when keeping in mind the deployment of the same imagery in connection to Socrates and Leonardo in *The Virgins of the Rocks*.

Apart from these oblique references, *Fire* contains the most explicit treatment of same-sex desire and love in any of D'Annunzio's novels. Conveniently, this figures in the context of an embedded narrative, a fantasy one at that. This has the effect of distancing the subject matter of same-sex love sufficiently from both the author and reader as to allow for a direct, rather than oblique, treatment.

As Effrena and Foscarina are being rowed through Venice's canals on a gondola, he tells her a story he intends one day to write for his own pleasure and entertainment. It is the story of a cultivated mediaeval glass master from Murano, Dardi Seguso, who boasts that one day he will give Venice an extraordinary organ made of seven thousand glass pipes. The authorities hold him to his word and assign him a small island where he can undertake the work, threatening to behead him if he fails to deliver the organ. Much to her regret, the island is off limits to the courtesan with whom the glass master is wont to entertain himself. Her name—Perdilanza—vaguely recalls the nickname Effrena calls Foscarina by (Perdita). Dardi soon realises that he requires the services of a wind to help him blow molten glass paste into the shape of seven thousand organ pipes. The wind must be 'neither to strong nor too weak, docile, easy to manipulate'.[164] Thanks to a man who can propitiate winds before sea voyages, the glass master manages to capture a light wind that fits his requirements. He is Ornitio, carrier of migratory birds. Ornitio's attempts at escaping Dardi's island, to which he has been abducted, are thwarted by the glass master, who has quickly fallen in love with him. Ornitio eventually obliges with the task required of him and even comes to love the glass master back, mainly because he takes a fancy to the red thread tied around Dardi's neck (placed there to mark the spot where his head is to be severed, if he fails to keep his promise to deliver the organ). When the day of presenting the instrument comes, initial success is inadvertently cut short by lovelorn Perdilanza, who throws herself into the sea. Her body is carried by the tide into the organ's mechanics, jams them, and causes the sound to fail. Dardi is swiftly beheaded, and just as swiftly the head is recovered from the seawater by Ornitio, who carries it far across the sea, followed by his swallows, in an untimely migration that leaves Venice's summer skies deserted.[165]

Little is said about Ornitio, but enough to make us realise he is endowed with a charming youthful grace. Furthermore, he hails from Greece and knows by heart two odes 'unknown to humanists, which he carried one spring day from Mytilene to Chios', authored by Sappho[166]—a reference that seems deliberately chosen to underscore Ornitio's allegiance to same-sex love. The story thus frames Dardi and Ornitio's relationship in accordance with the 'exotic' and literary (for D'Annunzio's late nineteenth-century readers) model of Greek pederasty. For D'Annunzio's average middle-class reader, this would have put the explicit treatment of same-sex desire/love at a relatively safe distance—as do the facts that the story is far away in time, in an imaginary version of Venice, and that Ornitio himself, while definitely male, is not really human.

Yet this little trifle of a tale remains significant for two reasons in D'Annunzio's production. First, as already noted, it is a fully explicit treatment of same-sex desire, conveyed literally rather than through the usual oblique references that only spoke to a readership well versed in classical culture. Secondly, in D'Annunzio's novel, references to fruitful or admirable same-sex relationships tend to imply a sublimation of same-sex desire. This is true whether the relationship is between equals (as in his last novel *Perhaps So, Perhaps Not*, discussed shortly) or between a younger, less experienced male and his mentor (as in *The Triumph of Death*). Here, however, there is no implication of sublimation. Dardi and Ornitio can barely communicate: one speaks Greek and the other Venetian dialect and Latin. Their infatuation with each other has nothing to do with their powers of intellect, actual or potential. Dardi clearly fancies Ornitio for his grace and delicacy, and Ornitio for a physical detail (the red thread around Dardi's neck) that catches his unfathomable sprite-like imagination. Yet despite implied consummation, the relationship is fruitful (the seven-thousand-pipe organ is crafted with Ornitio's help), reciprocal, and suggests devotion beyond death.[167]

In the novel itself, the embedded narrative has an instructive function. Foscarina is convinced that the tale carries a message for her. The message, as we can work out from the novel denouement (in which Foscarina lets Effrena go and devotes herself to promoting his work through her acting), concerns hers and Effrena's obsessive sexual involvement: it drains his creative powers, whose use is the primary source of meaning in his life, and whose product is a source of value for others. This is apparent from the fact that in the tale within the tale, Dardi had banned Perdilanza from his island, so that he would be free to work; eventually her unwillingness to let go proves lethal to herself and Dardi and fatal to the happiness of both Ornitio and Venice (which experiences a swallow-less summer).

Otey has rightly argued that in *Fire* erotic desire figures as the wellspring of artistic inspiration but that successful art requires the artist to experience and subsequently transcend *eros*: this, she maintains, is manifest in how the novel ends with Foscarina leaving Effrena free to pursue his creative work and supporting him from a distance.[168] Otey maintains the story is a story of 'artistic victory',[169] not failure, because we have no reason to think that the process of presence/absence (of the beloved) and experience/transcendence of (desire) did not turn out to be fruitful for Effrena[170] and because he 'overcomes [the force of Eros] despite/through an admission of its indomitable nature and its primary importance as the source of all artistic drive'.[171]

Conversely, I maintain that the ending is open ended enough that the critics whom Otey takes issue with for reading failure in Effrena's story have a respectable case to make. We should not lose sight of the fact that ultimately it is Foscarina's act of heroic self-abnegation—not anything he himself does—that enables Effrena to devote himself to his art. And we should not gloss over the significance of same-sex desire in the story. The artistic talent that Effrena is seeking to harness 'is posited, not surprisingly, in the female artist's body',[172] Otey notes. Meanwhile, the existence of a different form of erotic desire in the novel fails to register altogether in Otey's reading. In the tale within the tale, it is the artistic cooperation of two erotically involved males—Drusi and Ornitio—that conclusively yields (rather than merely possibly so, as in Effrena's case after his separation from Foscarina) the awe-inspiring work of art that the artist-craftsman aspired to create. What the novel seems to say is that the generative power (artistically speaking) that is characteristic of heterosexual passion is an unknown quantity at best. But there is also a less indomitable kind of erotic desire, one whose harnessing for creative purposes is not a zero-sum game, for it requires no sacrifices comparable to those of Foscarina: this is same-sex desire.

SAME-SEX DESIRE IN *PERHAPS SO, PERHAPS NOT*

The destructiveness and/or fruitlessness of heterosexual desire is a recurrent motif in D'Annunzio's novels. It makes Andrea Sperelli in *Pleasure* remain attached to the 'wrong' woman and ruin his relationship with the 'right' one; it makes Giorgio Aurispa in *The Triumph of Death* feel robbed of self-ownership and self-direction; in the *Virgins of the Rocks*, it drives a wedge between Claudio Cantelmo and both his purpose and the 'virile' woman who could have helped him realise it; and in *Fire* it stands between Stelio Effrena and his work, with all its aesthetic and social value.

Similarly, in *Perhaps So, Perhaps Not*, heterosexual desire for Isabella Inghirami locks pilot Paolo Tarsis in an inward-looking, spiritually sterile relationship, in stark contrast to the active, adventurous, brimming-with-meaning life that he had led and might continue to experience in the company of Giulio Cambiaso, his wartime comrade and soulmate. Before Giulio's death in a flight accident, Tarsis reads in his comrade's eyes apprehension about Tarsis's future, due to his involvement with Isabella. Tarsis mentally reassures Giulio: 'Thus I shall do with the obscure beast that was growing within me and threatened to overpower me. I shall bind it and lift it up, and then brand it for its servitude. And I shall shrug [off my bondage] and give you my hand, and we'll set off for our new conquest, free'.[173] In the event, Tarsis proves himself utterly incapable of taming the beast:

> You [namely, heterosexual desire] are certainly love, because you feed off and grow out of that in my life which is most fiery, because I cannot strike you without fear that my own blood will pour out all over your wounds, because you are more me than the whole of me. . . . I had kept intact the depths of my senses so as to allow her to descend into them. Descend she does; and she re-awakens the monsters I sometimes saw in an orgy-filled night, on my exotic travels, when the male did not know if he enjoyed more shedding his seed or shedding blood. . . . I must look at you carefully, to discover if you are love or if you are hatred, or if you are two-faced.[174]

The dark, untameable beast of heterosexual desire could not differ more markedly from the 'loyalty, trust, equality and safety'[175] of Tarsis and Giulio's bond. Once Tarsis was with his comrade, travelling 'towards the unknown;

now he was in the unknown against his companion, and she against him, in an overt and covert struggle, relentless, to establish a mastery and a servitude.'[176] Unlike nearly all friendships, where asymmetries (humiliating for the weaker and more generous party) are the rule, Tarsis and Giulio's friendship 'was made of two equal statures, two even powers, two indomitable freedoms and faiths.'[177] Isabella's beautiful teenage brother, Aldo, has harsh words for his sister when she proposes to visit Tarsis, while he is keeping solitary vigil over Giulio's body after the accident: 'You are mad! Do you think he has any need for you?'[178]

Giulio's death means that the 'richest branch of [Tarsis's] own life is broken, the most generous part of himself destroyed'.[179] The nature of Tarsis and Giulio's bond, exceeding ordinary male friendship, is given away as Tarsis recalls 'those ancient words, well-known, uttered by a comrade to the ghost of his comrade: "Come closer, so that holding each other in an embrace, we may find enjoyment in jointly crying your death!"'[180] The quote refers to the best-known same-sex couple of Antiquity—Patroclus and Achilles—and specifically to the episode in the *Iliad* where Achilles dreams of Patroclus's ghost paying him a visit. Befittingly, when Tarsis watches over Giulio's body, it looks to Vana (Isabella and Aldo's sister) as if they share the same deathly pallor.[181] Later, when Tarsis flies his airplane in an attempt to follow in the tracks of Giulio's last, fatal flight, he distinctly feels Giulio's presence, until his 'shadow stood face to face before him, breathed into his own breath, was more alive than all living things in the contest over silence'.[182]

Vana, who had an impromptu and emotionally intense exchange with Giulio before he flew to his death, is in love with Tarsis, and is contemptuous of the purely sexual magnetism between Isabella and him. Her own love for Tarsis is of a different order because, by secretly visiting and comforting him the night of his vigil, she made her love partake of the love of the two men for each other, even enabled it, when she cried the tears Tarsis had been unable to shed.[183] Vana ends up committing suicide. After her death, Tarsis, mentally addressing Giulio, calls her (not without tenderness but ultimately underscoring the subservient function of Vana's love) 'the swallow of our spring.'[184] 'Our spring' has connotations of renewal and rebirth, but also romantic ones. Indeed, this language signals a shift in Tarsis's vocabulary, which so far has reserved the use of the word 'love' for heterosexual desire. What has changed?

Tarsis, finally able to partially detach himself from Isabella, has gone on a trip to inspect a statue made in honour of Giulio (for good measure, the statue resembles one of the Prisoners by Michelangelo,[185] that ultimate creator of heroic and erotic male nudes). In this context, Tarsis feels Giulio's presence clearer than ever: 'He felt him inside himself, as in their great hours of silence, when one and the other were a single, productive harmony; . . . he felt inhabited by him as if up to that point he had kept him hidden and fed him of his own veins'.[186] Tarsis thinks of the statue of himself that will also be forged, a twin to Giulio's, and reasons, 'How could they have failed, on the anniversary of your death, to engrave my name alongside yours?'[187] Finally, Tarsis is able to speak to Giulio explicitly in terms of their love: '—Me too.— Do you recall this word, said with a smile? It's the word of all those who love, it's the word of great love. You said that word to me, with your eyes in my eyes. How long I had to suffer, and what troubles, before I was able to repeat it to you! But it had to be that way.'[188]

Later, determined to undertake a flight westwards, as far as the fuel will take him, and then plunge to his death into the sea, Tarsis feels 'the memory [of his comrade] puls[ing] within him like a heart returned to its double state'.[189] This is clearly a reference to Aristophanes's myth of the origins of same-sex love, reported in that canonical text on same-sex desire, Plato's *Symposium.* Tarsis, yearning for 'a beautiful death',[190] asks of Giulio, 'Could you believe we would be reunited?'.[191] In the end, Tarsis chooses life and deftly manages to land the plane, which had started catching fire, on a beach in an utterly deserted part of Sardinia. This is not, in my opinion, a triumphant denouement of 'awe and celebration' and 'sacredness'.[192] Duncan is right that it is an indeterminate one,[193] at best. Tarsis too, like all other Dannunzian heroes, fails: in this case, he fails to make of his life the work of art that a beautiful death in the name of his love for Giulio would have made it.

It is significant that the one moment where Tarsis and Isabella experience a 'happiness unheard of', a 'celestial respite' from 'the science of torment'[194]—namely from the unrestrained pursuit of their carnal knowledge—involves Isabella's transfiguration into a male. And not any male, but Ornitio, no less, sprung forth from 'that delightful brackish tale by Gabriele D'Annunzio'[195]—the embedded narrative of *Fire*. This transfiguration of Isabella into Ornitio occurs after she demands—at the height of the couple's sexual involvement—yet more of his erotic attention, by thrusting her breast against Tarsis's mouth, at a time when he was caught up in thoughts of Giulio and his aerial exploits. It is a trigger, and Tarsis determines to take a break from love making and to return to flying. He takes Isabella on his flights, at her request. Day after day, the thrill of flying overpowers their lust. At this point Isabella 'had felt grow within her breast the wild heart of that young wind, carrier of migratory birds, Ornitio by name'.[196] She tells Paolo, who listens in delight, 'In memory of the glass master, I have returned of my own will to the love of man. You too, Paolo Tarsis, wear a scarlet thread around your neck, invisible';[197] and she 'really had the looks of a naughty boy, sparkling with joy and audacity.'[198] With Isabella capable of loving him with her newly found male heart, Paolo is, for a time, able to share with her a kind of pleasure that is unalloyed, outward looking rather than self-referential, and one that, unlike sexual pleasure, does not leave him 'wavering between the terror of annihilation and a more and more sterile desire'.[199]

CONCLUSIONS

In all of D'Annunzio's novels except *Pleasure* same-sex desire is an integral element of the narrative. Indeed, according to one reading it is also integral to *Pleasure*,[200] but that reading depends wholly on the controversial assumption that *Pleasure* is a self-conscious response to *The Picture of Dorian Gray*, and on rather greater interpretive latitude than I have allowed myself here.

In *The Innocent One* and in *Giovanni Episcopo* same-sex desire is unconfessed and repressed: in both cases the (admittedly overdetermined) outcome is deathly. In *The Triumph of Death*, *The Virgins of the Rocks*, *Fire*, and *Perhaps So, Perhaps Not*, a theme emerges of the productive, fruitful, constructive, creative, generative force of (mostly) sublimated same-sex desire, in stark contrast with the destructiveness of different-sex desire. In these novels, the difference between heterosexual and same-sex love is not that the former has no erotic content. The erotic tension between male characters is palpable. The difference is that male same-sex desire is capable of sublimation or, even when yielded to, homoerotic energy is capable of being redirected to creative and life-affirming goals, in a way that tends to be precluded to heterosexual desire. In heterosexual desire, lust—with all its baggage of death wish and mastery/subordination dynamics—remains the prevailing force. It is perhaps significant that in *Pleasure* Sperelli has been argued to make an attempt 'to fall in love with [Donna] Maria as a way of sublimating the incontrollable passion he feels for Elena'.[201] The attempt, there, clearly fails, in the same way that willing himself to love Anatolia proves fruitless for Cantelmo in the face of Violante's overpowering appeal.

Presumably, the dim view D'Annunzio took of different-sex desire had something to do with the way in which he experienced his own irrepressible heterosexual libido. D'Annunzio's work suggests that he was genuinely drawn to male beauty and capable of experiencing this attraction erotically. He may or may not have had homosexual experiences, but it seems clear that any attraction he felt for males was less 'raw' than his attraction for women. His knowledge of same-sex desire was filtered through specific aesthetic (literary and artistic) and philosophical-historical models (particularly Plato's *Symposium* and Greek pederasty). These both disciplined it and allowed for its sublimation into a form of love capable of being uniquely fruitful. I will argue in the next chapter that D'Annunzio portrayed and experienced the *Carnaro Charter* as a product of just this kind of love.

This is not to say that D'Annunzio's experience and representations of heterosexual love were culturally unmediated. Rather, whatever cultural resources were at his disposal to represent to himself the nature of heterosexual and same-sex desire had to be capable of being reconciled with how he experienced these forms of attraction. It seems obvious that D'Annunzio's heterosexual desire happened to be, quite simply, more powerful within him than any same-sex attraction he may have experienced. This made aestheticization, sublimation, and idealisation an option with respect to the latter in a way which was precluded to him in respect of the former, because of the sheer phenomenological intensity of heterosexual desire in D'Annunzio's lifeworld, in combination with D'Annunzio's cultural and ideological investment in ideas of self-mastery.

It is also worth noting that, if we read *Perhaps So, Perhaps Not* as autobiographical commentary, part of D'Annunzio appears to have been at least dimly aware that his tormented and destructive experience of heterosexual attraction was due to his own personal limitations, or at least to limitations deriving from his being a male in a patriarchal culture that he was unable or unwilling to transcend. This is most apparent in a passage where D'Annunzio is able to travel outside himself and speak through the voice of Isabella, who is being confronted with Tarsis's accusation of entertaining an incestuous relationship with her brother Aldo. The passage itself is eloquent enough:

> That sorrowful and choleric man [that is, Tarsis], similar to any other man in his need for reproach, contempt, punishment, seemed to her obtuse, thick. She would have liked to answer: '. . . Why are you like all others? Why is your jealousy so blind, so savage? I love you unto death. This much is certain. . . . And yet the crime of which you accuse me—I committed it. I committed it because I love Love, because it is not true that the perfection of love is in the conjunction of two; this men know, but do not dare confess. Love, like all divine powers, is truly exalted only in the trinity. This, in me, is no perverse doctrine, no cruel game, but a message witnessed through my martyrdom, with the most painful blood of my breast. Such love rejects happiness for an unknown but infinitely higher good, towards which the soul aspires, caught up in purest sorrow, the sorrow that despairs; while the couple requires a yoke and is always weighed down by it, bows under it towards the earth and the dust; and that is perhaps why it is fitting that the yoke should be guided by the miserly peasant. Ah, when will the lover be not a stupid enemy, but a thoughtful and sensuous brother? I know, I know: you will never understand.'[202]

Whatever we make of the apology of sibling incest contained in Isabella's words, the passage is of interest for the way in which it is critical of the unimaginative, stereotyped, predictable, oppressive ways in which men manage their desire for women. The point becomes even more apparent later:

> She couldn't stand that reproach, smacking less of anger than ill-disguised lust, that pain so narrow as any bodily pain, like a burn, a sprain, a cut. Once again she saw the man diminished, transformed into a boring, savage beast: she saw Love on four legs, stripped of its beautiful brow. 'Ah, don't injure me with the same words you would use with any other woman to shame her! Tell me one word that will reach inside me as I am, that may touch me as I am, that will shake me and trouble me and draw from my depths this unknown power that afflicts me . . .' And her brother's brow, and the hard melancholy of his keen pupils, and those lips so greedy and so unhappy, and all those traits of thought and divination, and all those flames of terrible precocity stood out [in the eyes of her mind] against [Tarsis's] brutal oppression, which even robbed her of the energy to respond.[203]

A nuanced analysis of such passages in D'Annunzio's book might disturb the line of criticism that sees him as cruel and misogynist,[204] but it would take me far beyond the remit of this work. What matters for the purposes of my discussion is that D'Annunzio's novels convey a dim view of the ability of heterosexual relations to do much good to either the lovers or the world. On the other hand, they suggest that same-sex love has just the potential for generating great and good things.

NOTES

1. *The Carnaro Charter*, art. 2 (De Ambris's draft) and III (D'Annunzio's text).
2. Andrea Mirabile, *Multimedia Archaeologies: Gabriele D'Annunzio, Belle Époque Paris, and the Total Artwork* (Amsterdam and New York: Rodopi, 2014), 12.
3. See generally David P. Schweikard and Hans Bernard Schmid, "Collective Intentionality," *Stanford Encylopedia of Philosophy* (2013, revised 2020), https://plato.stanford.edu/entries/collective-intentionality/.
4. Quoted in Claudia Salaris, *Alla Festa della Rivoluzione: Artisti e Libertari con D'Annunzio a Fiume* (Bologna: Il Mulino, 2002), 81.
5. Michael A. Leeden, *The First Duce* (Baltimore and London: John Hopkins University Press, 1977), 7.
6. Giordano Bruno Guerri, *D'Annunzio: L'Amante Guerriero* (Milano: Monadori, 2009), 285.
7. Gabriele D'Annunzio, *Cento e Cento e Cento e Cento Pagine del Libro Segreto di Gabriele D'Annunzio Tentato di Morire* (Milano: Rizzoli, 2010), 111.
8. D'Annunzio, *Cento e Cento*, 112.
9. Guerri, *D'Annunzio*, 49 (reporting the comments of Edoardo Scarfoglio).
10. Guerri, *D'Annunzio*, 237.
11. Guerri, *D'Annunzio*, 49.
12. Guerri, *D'Annunzio*, 286.
13. Guerri, *D'Annunzio*, 286; Léon Kotchnitzky, *La Quinta Stagione: O, I Centauri di Fiume,* trans. Alberto Luchini (Bologna: Zanichelli, 1922), 69; Léon

Kotchnitzky, article for *Hearst* magazine (April 1920), Fondazione Il Vittoriale degli Italiani, Archivio Fiumano, Kotchnitzky, Léon, 1–129.

14. Derek Duncan, *Reading and Writing Italian Homosexuality: A Case of Possible Difference* (Aldershot, UK: Ashgate, 2006), 22.

15. Elena Borelli, *Giovanni Pascoli, Gabriele D'Annunzio, and the Ethics of Desire: Between Action and Contemplation* (Madison and Teaneck: Farleigh Dickinson University Press, 2017), 80.

16. Eve Kosofsky Sedgwick, *Epistemology of the Closet* (Berkeley and Los Angeles: University of California Press, 2008), 45–47.

17. Guerri, *D'Annunzio*, 203, 208.

18. Guerri, *D'Annunzio*, 205–6.

19. John Woodhouse, *Gabriele D'Annunzio: Defiant Archangel* (Oxford: Clarendon Press, 1998), 377.

20. Woodhouse, *Gabriele D'Annunzio*, 377.

21. Woodhouse, *Gabriele D'Annunzio*, 377.

22. The message was auctioned in 2021 on Ebay (item no: 333987088644, seller: mittler72). Several elements about the content of the message make it, to my mind, stand well apart from forgeries of D'Annunzio's autographs that have appeared on the Italian market in recent years.

23. *Regulations of the New Liberation Army*, art. XXXIII. The regulations have been recently published in *La Sola Ragione di Vivere*, ed. Emanuele Merlino (Firenze: Passaggio al Bosco, 2020).

24. Quoted in Salaris, *Alla Festa della Rivoluzione*, 75.

25. Alfredo Bonadeo, *D'Annunzio and the Great War* (Madison and Teaneck: Farleigh Dickinson University Press; London: Associated University Presses, 1995), 39.

26. Ellie Rose Mattoon, "Delts Don't Lie" (19 July 2013), *Daily JStor*, https://daily.jstor.org/delts-dont-lie/.

27. The name of this sculpture was invented only in the nineteenth century: there is very little that suggests death in the naked man's languorous and intensely sensual posture and relaxed countenance.

28. Salaris, *Alla Festa della Rivoluzione*, 238.

29. Gabriele D'Annunzio, Deed of Donation (22 December 1923), Il Vittoriale degli Italiani, https://www.vittoriale.it/la-storia/atto-di-donazione/.

30. M. F. N. Giglioli, "'Il Deputato della Bellezza': Gabriele D'Annunzio's Aesthetic Politics in the Fin-de-Siècle Crisis," *Journal of Modern Italian Studies* 18, no. 4 (2013).

31. Jared M. Becker, *Nationalism and Culture: Gabriele D'Annunzio and Italy after the Risorgimento* (New York: Peter Lang, 1994), 169.

32. Duncan, *Reading and Writing*, 33.

33. Richard A. Kaye, "Losing his Religion: Saint Sebastian as Contemporary Gay Martyr," in *Outlooks: Lesbian and Gay Sexualities and Visual Cultures*, ed. Peter Horne, Reina Lewis, and Peter Norne (Abingdon, UK: Routledge, 1996), 88.

34. Mirabile, *Multimedia Archaeologies*, 10.

35. Guerri, *D'Annunzio*, 67; Giordano Bruno Guerri, *Disobbedisco: Cinquecento Giorni di Rivoluzione. Fiume 1919–1920* (Milano: Mondadori, 2019), 224.

36. Raoul Pupo, *Fiume Città di Passione* (Bari: Laterza, 2018), 102.
37. Marko Medved, 'D'Annunzio e la Chiesa Cattolica a Fiume: Tra Nazionalismo e Anticipazione della Politica di 'Mano Tesa'," in *D'Annunzio Legislatore: Costituzioni, Visioni, Utopie dell'Impresa Fiumana*, ed. Giordano Bruno Guerri (Milano: Silvana Editoriale, 2022), 69–70.
38. Giovanni Gullace, "The French Writings of Gabriele D'Annunzio," *Comparative Literature* 12, no. 3 (1960): 216.
39. Guerri, *D'Annunzio*, 206–7.
40. Gullace, "The French Writings," 212.
41. "French Catholics and D'Annunzio," *The Manchester Guardian*, May 19, 1911.
42. Paola Sorge "Introduzione: Le Martyre de Saint Sébastien: L'Opera Totale di Gabriele D'Annunzio," in Gabriele D'Annunzio, *Il Martirio di San Sebastiano* (Roma: Elliot, 2013).
43. Gullace, "The French Writings," 219.
44. "D'Annunzio's Drama of St Sebastian: Banned by the Church," *The Manchester Guardian*, March 10, 1926.
45. Gabriele D'Annunzio, *Il Martirio di San Sebastiano*, trans. Ettore Janni (Milano: Treves, 1927), 31, 209, 225, 230, 244, 266, 270. All references to relevant passages of the drama below refer to this (the 1927 Treves) edition.
46. Gullace, "The French Writings," 216.
47. D'Annunzio, *Il Martirio*, 86.
48. D'Annunzio, *Il Martirio*, 158.
49. D'Annunzio, *Il Martirio*, 167.
50. D'Annunzio, *Il Martirio*, 61.
51. D'Annunzio, *Il Martirio*, 205.
52. D'Annunzio, *Il Martirio*, 221.
53. D'Annunzio, *Il Martirio*, 219.
54. D'Annunzio, *Il Martirio*, 223.
55. D'Annunzio, *Il Martirio*, 232–33.
56. D'Annunzio, *Il Martirio*, 236.
57. D'Annunzio, *Il Martirio*, 65.
58. D'Annunzio, *Il Martirio*, 271.
59. D'Annunzio, *Il Martirio*, 99.
60. D'Annunzio, *Il Martirio*, 261.
61. D'Annunzio, *Il Martirio*, 262.
62. Duncan, *Reading and Writing*, 20.
63. Duncan, *Reading and Writing*, 25.
64. Barbara Spackman, *Decadent Genealogies: The Rhetoric of Sickness from Baudelaire to D'Annunzio* (Ithaca, NY: Cornell University Press, 1989), 211–12.
65. Michela Barisonzi, "The Death of the Angel: Games of Seduction and Moral Destruction in Gabriele D'Annunzio's *Il Piacere*," *MLN* 130, no. 1 (2015).
66. Borelli, *Giovanni Pascoli, Gabriele D'Annunzio*, xi.
67. Borelli, *Giovanni Pascoli, Gabriele D'Annunzio*, xii.
68. Borelli, *Giovanni Pascoli, Gabriele D'Annunzio*, 61.

69. Borelli, *Giovanni Pascoli, Gabriele D'Annunzio*, xii, 22.
70. Borelli, *Giovanni Pascoli, Gabriele D'Annunzio*, xxiii, xxv, 60, 85, 121, 132–33.
71. Borelli, *Giovanni Pascoli, Gabriele D'Annunzio*, 63.
72. Borelli, *Giovanni Pascoli, Gabriele D'Annunzio*, 61.
73. Duncan, *Reading and Writing*, 37.
74. Gabriele D'Annunzio, *Forse che Sí, Forse che No*, in *Romanzi e Novelle*, vol. II (Milano: Mondadori, 1942), 971.
75. D'Annunzio, *Forse che Sí, Forse che No*, 893.
76. Gabriele D'Annunzio, *Il Piacere*, in *Romanzi e Novelle*, vol. I (Milano: Mondadori, 1942), 278.
77. D'Annunzio, *Il Fuoco*, in *Romanzi e Novelle*, vol. II (Milano: Mondadori, 1942), 615–16.
78. D'Annunzio, *Il Fuoco*, 616.
79. D'Annunzio, *Il Fuoco*, 861.
80. D'Annunzio, *Il Fuoco*, 701.
81. D'Annunzio, *Il Piacere*, 108.
82. D'Annunzio, *Il Piacere*, 252–53.
83. D'Annunzio, *Il Piacere*, 165.
84. D'Annunzio, *Il Piacere*, 166.
85. D'Annunzio, *Il Piacere*, 166.
86. D'Annunzio, *Il Piacere*, 297.
87. D'Annunzio, *Il Piacere*, 358.
88. D'Annunzio, *Il Piacere*, 169.
89. Gabriele D'Annunzio, *Il Trionfo della Morte*, in *Romanzi e Novelle*, vol. I (Milano: Mondadori, 1942), 825.
90. D'Annunzio, *Il Trionfo della Morte*, 828.
91. D'Annunzio, *Il Trionfo della Morte*, 829.
92. D'Annunzio, *Il Trionfo della Morte*, 829.
93. D'Annunzio, *Forse che Sí, Forse che No*, 877–78.
94. D'Annunzio, *Forse che Sí, Forse che No*, 917.
95. D'Annunzio, *Forse che Sí, Forse che No*, 961.
96. *The Triumph of Death*, too, manages to slip in a reference to Shelley. D'Annunzio, *Il Trionfo della Morte*, 968.
97. D'Annunzio, *Il Piacere*, 358.
98. Caroline E. Kimberly, "Effeminacy, Masculinity, and Homosocial Bonds: The (Un)Intentional Queering of John Keats," *Érudit* (2004–2005): 36–37, https://doi.org/10.7202/011142ar.
99. James Najarian, *Victorian Keats: Manliness, Sexuality, and Desire* (Basingstoke, UK, and New York: Palgrave Macmillan, 2002).
100. D'Annunzio, *Il Piacere*, 359.
101. Gabriele D'Annunzio, *Le Vergini delle Rocce*, in *Romanzi e Novelle*, vol. I (Milano: Mondadori, 1942), 530.
102. D'Annunzio, *Le Vergini delle Rocce*, 531.
103. D'Annunzio, *Le Vergini delle Rocce*, 407.

104. D'Annunzio, *Le Vergini delle Rocce*, 407.
105. D'Annunzio, *Le Vergini delle Rocce*, 406–7.
106. D'Annunzio, *Le Vergini delle Rocce*, 408.
107. D'Annunzio, *Le Vergini delle Rocce*, 410.
108. D'Annunzio, *Il Fuoco*, 582.
109. But it should be borne in mind that it is an oversimplification to state that prior to the invention of modern homosexual identity, only acts were salient to thought about same-sex desire. The implication that same-sex acts or same-sex desire—at least under certain conditions—were connected to particular kinds of sexual subjectivities is apparent, or is at least latent, in a number of contexts from previous centuries. Samar Habib, *Female Homosexuality in the Middle East: Histories and Representations* (London and New York: Routledge, 2007); David M. Halperin, *How to Do the History of Homosexuality* (Chicago: University of Chicago Press, 2002).
110. D'Annunzio, *Il Trionfo della Morte*, 912.
111. D'Annunzio, *Il Trionfo della Morte*, 911.
112. D'Annunzio, *Il Trionfo della Morte*, 911.
113. D'Annunzio, *Forse che Sí, Forse che No*, 1169.
114. D'Annunzio, *Forse che Sí, Forse che No*, 1170.
115. Duncan, *Reading and Writing*, 30.
116. Gregory M. Herek, "Beyond 'Homophobia': A Social Psychological Perspective on Attitudes toward Lesbians and Gay Men," *Journal of Homosexuality* 10, no. 1–2 (1984).
117. Gabriele D'Annunzio, *L'Innocente*, in *Romanzi e Novelle*, vol. I (Milano: Mondadori, 1942), 410.
118. D'Annunzio, *L'Innocente*, 410.
119. D'Annunzio, *L'Innocente*, 410–11.
120. D'Annunzio, *L'Innocente*, 415.
121. D'Annunzio, *L'Innocente*, 416.
122. D'Annunzio, *L'Innocente*, 414–15.
123. D'Annunzio, *L'Innocente*, 509, 514.
124. D'Annunzio, *L'Innocente*, 510.
125. D'Annunzio, *L'Innocente*, 509–10.
126. D'Annunzio, *L'Innocente*, 509.
127. D'Annunzio, *L'Innocente*, 424.
128. D'Annunzio, *L'Innocente*, 426.
129. D'Annunzio, *L'Innocente*, 424–25.
130. D'Annunzio, *Il Trionfo della Morte*, 973.
131. D'Annunzio, *Il Trionfo della Morte*, 792.
132. D'Annunzio, *Il Trionfo della Morte*, 785.
133. D'Annunzio, *Il Trionfo della Morte*, 787.
134. D'Annunzio, *Il Trionfo della Morte*, 788.
135. D'Annunzio, *Forse che Sí, Forse che No*, 1064.
136. Alfred Lord Tennyson, "The Princess," Project Gutenberg, 2008 (updated 2013), https://www.gutenberg.org/files/791/791-h/791-h.htm.
137. D'Annunzio, *Il Trionfo della Morte*, 793.

138. James T. Chiampi, "'Un Dolore Pacato e Equale': Eternally Mourning Ippolita in 'Trionfo della Morte'," *Italica* 87, no. 4 (2010): 593.
139. D'Annunzio, *Il Trionfo della Morte*, 1020, 1041.
140. D'Annunzio, *Il Trionfo della Morte*, 998.
141. D'Annunzio, *Il Trionfo della Morte*, 968–69.
142. Gabriele D'Annunzio, *Giovanni Episcopo*, in *Romanzi e Novelle*, vol. II (Milano: Mondadori, 1942), 341.
143. D'Annunzio, *Giovanni Episcopo*, 340.
144. D'Annunzio, *Giovanni Episcopo*, 342.
145. Lisa Downing, "On the Limits of Sexual Ethics: The Phenomenology of Autassassinophilia," *Sexuality and Culture* 8, no. 1 (2004): 3–17.
146. D'Annunzio, *Giovanni Episcopo*, 361.
147. D'Annunzio, *Giovanni Episcopo*, 365.
148. D'Annunzio, *Giovanni Episcopo*, 360–61.
149. D'Annunzio, *Giovanni Episcopo*, 344.
150. D'Annunzio, *Le Vergini delle Rocce*, 427.
151. Giorgio Vasari, *Le Vite de' piu Eccellenti, Pittori, Scultori, ed Architetti* (Torino: Einaudi, 1986), 554.
152. Sander L. Gilman, "Leonardo Sees Him-Self: Reading Leonardo's Fist Representation of Human Sexuality," *Social Research* 54, no. 1 (1987): 149.
153. D'Annunzio, *Le Vergini delle Rocce*, 429.
154. D'Annunzio, *Le Vergini delle Rocce*, 429.
155. D'Annunzio, *Le Vergini delle Rocce*, 441.
156. D'Annunzio, *Le Vergini delle Rocce*, 451.
157. D'Annunzio, *Le Vergini delle Rocce*, 452.
158. D'Annunzio, *Le Vergini delle Rocce*, 560.
159. Borelli, *Giovanni Pascoli, Gabriele D'Annunzio*, 81.
160. D'Annunzio, *Il Fuoco*, 793.
161. D'Annunzio, *Il Fuoco*, 703.
162. D'Annunzio, *Il Fuoco*, 693.
163. D'Annunzio, *Il Fuoco*, 607.
164. D'Annunzio, *Il Fuoco*, 834.
165. D'Annunzio, *Il Fuoco*, 829–38.
166. D'Annunzio, *Il Fuoco*, 836.
167. This—the view that same-sex desire may be productive even if yielded to rather than sublimated—is not entirely unknown for D'Annunzio. Thus, Bonadeo notes that in 'The Splendour of Sensuality', D'Annunzio departs from the view that the unequalled heights reached by Michelangelo's art were due to sexual repression and sublimation and argues that he could have been an even better artist if he had let his desire have free rein and act as the wellspring of his inspiration. Bonadeo, *D'Annunzio and the Great War*, 39.
168. Jessica Otey, "D'Annunzio, Eros and the Modern Artist: Tragedy and Tragic Criticism Reconsidered," *MLN* 125, no. 1 (2010): 173–76.
169. Otey, "D'Annunzio, Eros," 180.
170. Otey, "D'Annunzio, Eros," 176–78.

171. Otey, "D'Annunzio, Eros," 180.
172. Otey, "D'Annunzio, Eros," 174.
173. D'Annunzio, *Forse che Sí, Forse che No*, 916–17.
174. D'Annunzio, *Forse che Sí, Forse che No*, 987–88.
175. D'Annunzio, *Forse che Sí, Forse che No*, 989.
176. D'Annunzio, *Forse che Sí, Forse che No*, 989.
177. D'Annunzio, *Forse che Sí, Forse che No*, 916.
178. D'Annunzio, *Forse che Sí, Forse che No*, 940.
179. D'Annunzio, *Forse che Sí, Forse che No*, 946.
180. D'Annunzio, *Forse che Sí, Forse che No*, 951.
181. D'Annunzio, *Forse che Sí, Forse che No*, 952.
182. D'Annunzio, *Forse che Sí, Forse che No*, 959.
183. D'Annunzio, *Forse che Sí, Forse che No*, 1056, 1062, 1082–83.
184. D'Annunzio, *Forse che Sí, Forse che No*, 1146.
185. D'Annunzio, *Forse che Sí, Forse che No*, 1144.
186. D'Annunzio, *Forse che Sí, Forse che No*, 1145.
187. D'Annunzio, *Forse che Sí, Forse che No*, 1145.
188. D'Annunzio, *Forse che Sí, Forse che No*, 1146.
189. D'Annunzio, *Forse che Sí, Forse che No*, 1171–72.
190. D'Annunzio, *Forse che Sí, Forse che No*, 1177.
191. D'Annunzio, *Forse che Sí, Forse che No*, 1170.
192. Borelli, *Giovanni Pascoli, Gabriele D'Annunzio*, 128.
193. See also Duncan, *Reading and Writing*, 36.
194. D'Annunzio, *Forse che Sí, Forse che No*, 1000.
195. D'Annunzio, *Forse che Sí, Forse che No*, 1000.
196. D'Annunzio, *Forse che Sí, Forse che No*, 1000.
197. D'Annunzio, *Forse che Sí, Forse che No*, 1000.
198. D'Annunzio, *Forse che Sí, Forse che No*, 1001.
199. D'Annunzio, *Forse che Sí, Forse che No*, 998.
200. Edward S. Brinkley, "Homosexuality as (Anti)Illness: Oscar Wilde's the Picture of Dorian Gray and Gabriele D'Annunzio's Il Piacere," *Studies in 20th Century Literature* 22, no. 1 (1998).
201. Piero Aragno, "Des Esseintes e Andrea Sperellli: Assenza a Presenza della Donna nell'Iter Edonistico di Due 'Vinti' Decadenti," *Annali di Italianistica* 5 (1987): 239.
202. D'Annunzio, *Forse che Sí, Forse che No*, 1126.
203. D'Annunzio, *Forse che Sí, Forse che No*, 1127–28.
204. Susan Bassnett, "Translating Gabriele D'Annunzio for the Twenty-First Century Reader" (6 March 2020), Decadence and Translation Network, Glasgow University, https://dandtnetwork.glasgow.ac.uk/translating-gabriele-dannunzio-for-the-twenty-first-century-reader/.

Chapter 8

Same-Sex Desire in D'Annunzio's Fiume Speeches

INTRODUCTION

D'Annunzio was a known Don Juan. Yet he kept company with and proclaimed affinity for notoriously same-sex attracted people; praised their artistic work; peppered his own work with references to a Graeco-Roman aesthetic and philosophical legacy thematising male beauty and same-sex desire; showed a candid appreciation of the beauty of the male form; performed his gender in ways that were liable to impugning his commitment to heterosexuality; wrote a play centred on the eroticisation of the martyrdom (an all-male affair) of a beautiful young hero; and pervasively used imagery, references, and conceits centred on male same-sex desire in his novels, culminating in a philosophical view about the unique generativity of (mostly) sublimated male same-sex desire. This much I have shown in the previous chapter.

While D'Annunzio's homoerotic preoccupations are of interest in their own right, they matter to this book because they help lend plausibility to my argument in this chapter. This is to the effect that D'Annunzio harnessed his queer sensibility to sustain support for the occupation. The discursive circulation of same-sex desire in D'Annunzio's Fiume was implicated, I argue, in the existence of an institutionalised normative order during the occupation, including after the proclamation of the regency.

My premise is a philosophical—notably, a jurisprudential—one. Like any institutionalised normative order, the one subsisting in Fiume during D'Annunzio's occupation existed as distinctive one, if it did, to the extent that it was effective. Effectiveness means that legal officials must treat and apply the norms of the system as binding, and there must be general (not invariable) conformity between the norms and the behaviour of the general population to whom these norms apply.[1] Kirchner Reill provides enough evidence of a functioning normative order in occupied Fiume, implying that the existence conditions for a legal order were satisfied. Strictly speaking, Kirchner Reill's evidence pertains to the institutions and norms left behind by the dissolved Habsburg Empire and the ways in which the National Council (even if we regard it as an insurrectional government) reinvented them. But until the regency was proclaimed, the command in practice shared normative powers with the National Council. The two officially recognised each other's authority, respected each other's competences, and (despite dissensions and even antagonism, especially in 1920) purported to be authoritative actors in the same normative system, not to be running two competing normative systems. After the regency was proclaimed, the provisional government of the regency took over normative powers from both the National Council and the command. But things went on very much as they had before. Preexisting laws continued in force (indeed, as we saw, the application of the *Charter* was even suspended until further notice). There is no evidence that Fiume at that point descended into lawlessness. I think we can safely conclude that throughout the occupation, the Fiumans' general conformity with the law encompassed Fiume's normative system as a whole, into which the command's ordinances were integrated.

The point that interests me is how the legionnaires may have come to share the requisite intentional attitude to conform with the law, thereby contributing to the successful existence of occupied Fiume's normative order.[2] The concept of conformity is agnostic about people's reasons for conforming: people, for example, may have prudential (self-interested) reasons for obeying the law. But sometimes people do become invested in the 'rightness' of a normative order, conforming with it because of it. To the extent that the legionnaires did, my hypothesis is that this had something to do with how D'Annunzio's public speeches to them sublimate same-sex desire in the name of the Fiuman cause, including by vindicating the legitimacy of the regency.

If I am right, same-sex desire must be seen as (in part) constitutive of the shared intentional attitudes on which the existence of Fiume's institutionalised normative order hinged during the occupation. Clearly, there were many contributing factors that ensured the general population's conformity with the rules of the Fiuman polity during the occupation—some Fiumans, for example, may have been made to obey or bullied into obeying by the legionnaires themselves. Yet the role played by D'Annunzio's speeches to the legionnaires deserves attention among these factors, especially when Fiume's normative order was reframed within the regency: D'Annunzio himself presented the *Charter* as the legionnaires' own offspring (not the Fiumans') and as a reciprocal labour of love between himself and them. We have good reason, therefore, to probe into the discursive circulation of same-sex desire between the commandant and the legionnaires as a factor contributing to legality (that is, the existence of an institutionalised normative order) in D'Annunzio's Fiume.

We have seen previously that a reason (according to Bonadeo, the main reason) why D'Annunzio became invested in the war, and its extension through the Fiume occupation, was that the conflict enabled him to channel his energies into the ideal and heroic life that eluded him as a civilian, when he fell prey to the irresistible demands of sexual desire.[3] In his 1915 oration at Quarto, D'Annunzio expressly celebrates the repression of carnal (heterosexual) desire in pursuit of a higher form of love: 'Blessed be those who shunned sterile loves to keep their virginity for this and last love of their life.'[4] A transvaluation occurs here, whereby the love that kills (love of nation) becomes the genuinely generative form of love, in contrast to the paradoxical sterility of the love that begets (heterosexual love). Similarly, in a lengthy entry in his *Taccuini*, dating from 1916, D'Annunzio describes the spiritual sterility and bitter regret he experienced during and after a (hetero)sexual encounter in Venice. He concludes with an appeal to Giuseppe Miraglia—the deceased pilot who had flown him in several missions in 1915[5]—to 'spirit [him] away on [his] wings once more'.[6] Male comradeship here is contrasted with heterosexual lust, almost as if the two are mutually exclusive options. Yet positioning Miraglia as the hero rescuing D'Annunzio-as-damsel-in-distress gives away the writer's subtle erotic investment in his homosocial bond with the defunct pilot.

This should not surprise us. It should be clear by now that, as D'Annunzio saw it, his existential dilemma did not concern a crude choice between a life ruled by eros and one free of it. Rather, as explained, even before joining the war D'Annunzio had elaborated a particular view about the generativity of (sublimated) same-sex desire. It is not eros itself but specifically heterosexual desire that D'Annunzio experienced as detracting from self-rule and from a life informed by the pursuit of higher (active or creative) values. Conversely, his novels generally (though not invariably) represent same-sex desire as capable of sublimation or, at any rate, of being harnessed successfully in pursuit of those very values. In light of this, if D'Annunzio conceived, as he did, of his relationship with his wartime comrades and, later, the Fiume legionnaires in terms of a spiritual bond between soulmates, we might expect him both to characterise and experience that bond as erotically inflected. I will show shortly that during Fiume's occupation D'Annunzio's spiritual love for his legionnaires—as a communion of soulmates and as an antidote to the lack of self-mastery that accompanies heterosexual desire—remains indeed haunted by palpably erotic investments.

D'ANNUNZIO'S FIUME SPEECHES AND THE RHETORIC OF LOVE

D'Annunzio's Fiume speeches are considered of interest primarily because they are seen as inaugurating a new way of doing politics. Here the immediacy of the relationship between the people/audience and the leader/speaker enables the latter to emotionally manipulate the former, consolidate or maintain his power, and secure endorsement for his programme. I have already noted that this kind of instrumental conception of D'Annunzio's Fiume speeches is unconvincing because it appears to distort the phenomenology, at least as far as I can reconstruct it, of those speeches. Neither D'Annunzio nor his audience appear to have experienced the speeches in the instrumental terms of manipulation, nor indeed lesser forms of 'linguistically mediated strategic action'.[7] Rather, what we see—and what the earnestness of D'Annunzio's rhetoric conveys—is a conception of public speeches as *loci* of genuine meaning making, where political, ethical, and aesthetic value is articulated, experienced, and instantiated.

When we turn to the content of the speeches—to whose meticulous drafting D'Annunzio devoted much of his time, considering it the real work demanded of him[8]—we find that it is distinctive, among other things, for its tireless reiteration of love-related *topoi*. Already before the occupation, D'Annunzio had exploited to great effect the imagery of burning love to inflame patriotic sentiment. At his famous Quarto speech, advocating Italy's intervention in the war, he had glorified as a 'fire of love, most bitter love, indomitable love' the patriotic sentiment of Garibaldi's followers in the Thousand-Expedition. These had sailed, precisely from Quarto, to conquer the Kingdom of two Sicilies in 1860, with a view to Italy's unification.[9] Similarly, the poet heavily relied on the vocabulary of love to legitimise Fiume's occupation, not only in virtually all of his public addresses but also in his private ones. He continued to do so even after the occupation had ended, as when he wrote to de Ambris that the *Charter* was 'a love pledge to Love.'[10]

In D'Annunzio's addresses to the citizens of Fiume, this love is de-eroticised. Thus, on the day of his triumphant arrival in Fiume, D'Annunzio proclaimed to the acclaiming crowd, 'In a cowardly and insane world . . . there is only one love, and that is Fiume!' and 'In this pilgrimage of love, I came to execute the promise I made last May to the people of Rome.'[11] Similarly, when D'Annunzio left Fiume on 18 January 1921, he declared to the Fiumans, 'I might have erred sometimes; you were always perfect . . . if you love me, if I am worthy of your love, you must protect the Fiume [that will always be in my heart] against any imposition, any snare, any revenge. Long live love.'[12]

Such uses of the vocabulary of love are continuous with the nationalist rhetoric of the time, establishing a link between love for Fiume and the love of Italy. At the end of the war, Italy was only just entering the sixth decade of its existence as a nation-state, and we know that completing the unification project had been one of the reasons for its joining the conflict. In these circumstances, waxing lyrical about *'amor patrio'*—the love of motherland—was scarcely the exclusive preserve of the nationalist Right. Many examples can be adduced to show that the vocabulary of love was commonplace in discourse into which matters of national pride entered.[13] In this context, D'Annunzio's use of that self-same conceptual economy to speak of patriotic values to Fiume's predominantly Italian population is fairly unremarkable. But it is quite a different story when D'Annunzio addresses his legionnaires. Here love assumes distinctly erotic connotation—homoerotic ones at that.

MORE THAN *PHILIA* AND *AGAPE*

Having reached literary fame at a young age with writings that captured and contributed to define the *fin-de-siècle* mood, it is no wonder that D'Annunzio had gained remarkable drawing power not only over women but also men, especially young men, well before the Fiume occupation.[14] His exploits as a war hero only added to his *éclat*. Kotchnitzky, who tells of the 'infectious' quality of D'Annunzio's over-the-top oratory style among young Fiumans,[15] was positive that thousands of young men would die for him without hesitation.[16] Kotchnitzky also relates an episode involving parleying between D'Annunzio and General Sailer, who chided D'Annunzio's soldiers for forming a defence line around the commandant, telling them that the poet was not their lover. An *Ardito* replied, 'Much worse than a lover!'[17]

D'Annunzio was aware of his appeal, and it would be surprising if he had not made the most of it during the occupation. It is still remarkable—if only because of his well-earned reputation as a heterosexual Don Juan[18]—that D'Annunzio's words would quite so unselfconsciously make love to the legionnaires in the way I will argue his public speeches do. By 'make love' I mean something that exceeds the ordinary ways in which virtually all political leaders may be said to 'court' the people's favour. The love-making metaphor is particularly apt because it underscores the relational dynamic of the parties to the speech: as Leeden points out, the poet 'virtually never gave a speech that was not, at least in part, a dialogue with the crowd, and the people filled the piazzas for well over a year to participate.'[19]

D'Annunzio's words of love to his legionnaires are no doubt deliberate. Yet they do not appear calculated to exploit the rhetoric of love in the service of political goals. The author regularly implicates himself within this rhetoric in a way that suggests artless personal investment rather than carefully instrumental deployment. Indeed, if his goals had been merely instrumental, D'Annunzio's rhetorical strategy was a risky one, because, as we will see, *eros* requires complete sublimation to effectively cement group ties and group members' commitment to collective goals. While D'Annunzio's speeches sublimate *eros* into words, the sublimation remains partial because those words remain words of sensual love.

We find an intriguing example of D'Annunzio's trading on the ambiguity of 'love' in a piece he published to celebrate the legionnaires' successful abduction of forty-six workhorses from the Italian army: 'You were luminous in the morning shadow, as if you had abducted the horses of the Sun. . . . It was less the harmony of youth than the enchantment of love. . . . [L]ove . . . that brought the gift stolen to hazard. . . . Strong and sinewy, well-built and sculptured, you were the sons of my spirit. . . . You only robbed so that you could give.'[20]

Here the legionnaires are said to have stolen in the name of love—a love that most resembles Christian charity. Befittingly, love transfigures them, making them 'luminous'. But D'Annunzio's own delight in the legionnaires' deed implies an amorous investment of the *erotic* variety, which straddles desire ('strong and sinewy, well-built and sculptured') and identification ('the sons of my spirit'). The legionnaires, then, are *agape*—the charity that motivates them to steal so that they may give; but they are also D'Annunzio's *eros* offering itself as a gift for his eyes to feast on, his imagination to claim as his.

Desire-based imagery when talking about the legionnaires is also employed by D'Annunzio in more private forms of communication, as in this letter to Giulietti, secretary of the Federation of Sea Workers:

> Every liberation effort must start from Fiume. . . . Here new forms of life are not only conceived, but enacted. Nowhere else on earth is there air of freedom as in this Quarnaro . . . I have *returned inside* the people that begat me. I am at one with his[[21]] substance. I live with simple soldiers, as a simple soldier. I eat their chow. I walk beside them. I sing their songs. . . . If you could witness some of the beautiful displays of humanity here, you would see that true new life does not begin with the bloodshed in which Lenin's doctrine loses itself. The Bolshevik thistle here is transmuted in Italian rose: a rose of love. . . . I have already upturned all our encumbering frameworks. I am wholly outside the ring of sterile institutions and worn-out laws.[22]

D'Annunzio here is addressing a trade unionist, indicating where his revolution is like and unlike the Bolshevik one. It is like it in its (purported) disregard of the laws and institutions of the liberal state, which have spent their usefulness. It is unlike it in being a revolution harnessing the power of 'love' rather than violence.[23] Love here manifests itself, specifically, as soldierly comradeship. D'Annunzio's allusions to this comradeship (sharing food, songs, etc.) is something an interventionist trade unionist might easily relate to workers' struggles. Yet D'Annunzio's comradeship is more than *philia* (brotherly love) and has suggestively homoerotic connotations. It is one where his 'substance' is commingled with that of the soldiers, and the commingling occurs via a return *'inside'* the people that generated him. By 'people' here D'Annunzio means ordinary folks—the kind of people from whom four decades of living as a literary celebrity among social and intellectual elites separate him. But note that 'people' in Italian is a masculine noun; indeed, the masculinity of the people here is reinforced by their being epitomised by the 'simple' soldiers D'Annunzio breaks bread and sings with. D'Annunzio's return to this male people—indeed his *return inside* (emphasis in original) the male people from whom he sprang forth ('that begat me'), which, literalised, suggests a kind of ejaculation played in reverse—results in a union that is two-in-one-flesh, hence marriage-like: 'I am at one with his substance'.

The union between D'Annunzio and the people/soldiers is also a union of passionate, rather than chaste, love. The image of the 'rose of love' here is key. While roses in the West have a complex symbology (their associations range from Aphrodite[24] to the Virgin Mary), in D'Annunzio they tend to feature as symbols of lust and eros, not virginal purity (as in his cycle 'The Romances of the Rose'). D'Annunzio's camaraderie with the legionnaires appears, thus, distinctly Whitmanesque in its passionate homoeroticism. Interestingly, in the speech delivered to the citizens of Fiume on the first day of the occupation, D'Annunzio had invoked precisely 'Walt Whitman's America' as a witness to the town's reconfirmation of the National Council annexation vote of 30 October 1918.[25]

WHITE TEETH

In several texts, D'Annunzio misses no opportunity to remark on the legionnaires' youth and beauty when he publicly addresses them. Simonelli argues, persuasively, that representations of legionnaires as young, handsome warriors, not to mention displays of their bodies, were functional to the ideology that legitimised the occupation, both in Fiume and in Italy. D'Annunzio's volunteers were the flower of youth, offering themselves for a noble cause, embodying the virile spirit of the nation—martial tropes already manifest in wartime discourses and born out of an unlikely confluence of futurist and romantic ideas.[26] We will see shortly how D'Annunzio's own contributions to this discourse are more complex than such accounts suggest, and even partially disruptive of it. Here, however, I am interested in drawing attention to how such references to the legionnaires' physical beauty are invariably to erotic effect. In part, this is because D'Annunzio's words were for the immediate consumption of the very subjects whose beauty he extolled in his speeches. Only vicariously were the speeches subsequently experienced by the general public, when they were published and circulated.

White teeth is an unlikely but recurrent trope used to convey to the legionnaires their own erotic appeal. It has recently been suggested that in D'Annunzio's speeches the crowd's teeth are a proxy for Hobbes's Leviathan, as a political monster constituted by the orator and his audience.[27] While D'Annunzio himself relied in some of his literary work on the metaphor of a 'formidable monster'[28] to represent the crowd addressed by a public speaker, teeth imagery in his Fiume speeches has—I think—little to do with this. Rather, white teeth clearly symbolise youth, health, vigour, and, hence, beauty.

When the poet swears that infamy will be the fate of those who might desert the Fiume enterprise, he contrasts this promise to 'the dirty leaflets'—part of the Italian government's antioccupation propaganda—'which yesterday rained on your contempt and on the youthful mirth of your white teeth'.[29] After revealing the Italian government's *naïve* calculations that they might soon desert him, he incites the legionnaires: 'Laugh, my sons. I have never seen so many white teeth, so many perfect sets of teeth worthy of young lions.'[30] And elsewhere: 'How much new sunshine did your white teeth chew on, during our gatherings and choral walks!'[31]

Such visions of white teeth echo the intensely sensual imagery of one of D'Annunzio's most celebrated poems, 'Rain in the Pine Forest', where a rain shower in the woodland drenches two lovers whose 'teeth in their sockets are like unripe almonds'. But white teeth, and specifically 'even, square white teeth, of extraordinary brilliance' also figure as a female-eroticised male attribute in *Pleasure*.[32] Ippolita's 'strong pure teeth' that 'gleamed in biting' sexually excite Giorgio Aurispa in *The Triumph of Death*.[33] Lastly, in *Perhaps So, Perhaps Not*, as lovers Paolo Tarsis and Isabella Inghirami while away idle hours making love in a seaside retreat, the man catches a glimpse, 'between her red lips parted by speech, of the pearlescence of gums and teeth, like the moistness of a freshly opened shell'.[34] These intertextual readings make manifest the erotic valence that white teeth invariably carry in D'Annunzio's aesthetic universe, and that they carry as an attribute of the legionnaires' in his speeches to them.

WHITMANESQUE ACCENTS AND THE THEBAN LEGION

One of the white teeth quotes reproduced earlier is pulled from 'The Intelligent Flame', an oration D'Annunzio delivered to the legionnaires in the autumn of 1920, to present to them the new Army regulations (*Nuovo Ordinamento dell'Esercito Liberatore*). The regulations were probably not intended to apply to the defensive militia of the regency, which, it will be recalled, would not have a standing army.[35] Rather, as Simonelli persuasively argues, they must have been meant to govern a new army of volunteers, whose chief task would be to 'liberate' Dalmatia alongside regular Italian troops, once the Yugoslavs had given them a pretext to launch an assault.[36]

The regulations owe much of their innovative content to Captain Giuseppe Piffer, although Keller had also sought to get D'Annunzio to introduce a reform of the Army.[37] They abolish the chain of command structure ('Every intermediate level of command between the Army and the Commandant is abolished')[38] and make the commandant the exclusive direct leader of each soldier.[39] The document stresses as much the personal relationship of absolute trust between the commandant and his soldiers as the Army's democratic self-governance in times of peace.[40]

In presenting the regulations to the legionnaires, 'The Intelligent Flame' metonymically addresses all of them as *'Arditi'*. We have already seen how the *Arditi* were looked up to for having turned the tide of war. Their *éclat* was even greater in the eyes of those younger legionnaires who, because of their age, had 'missed out' on the chance to take part in the war. *Arditismo* was also the mental orientation—more than mood less than outright ideology—that held together both Host-Venturi's Fiume Legion and the commandant's personal bodyguard, *La Disperata*.[41]

In 'The Intelligent Flame', the familiar image of vigorous young men's white teeth is followed by a Whitmanesque depiction of homosocial bonds, where desire shades into identification and identification into desire:

> Comrades, who will tell of the intoxication of our great days and great nights? Who will ever be able to sing in our accent, to walk our pace? . . . Everything burnt and burnt again, even my melancholy . . . I was like the comrade to my right, like the comrade to my left . . . I was in tune with everyone, and everyone with me . . . I had never felt my heart as broad and as light as when I sang with heavy-booted men. . . . We were one young god who broke the iron-wrought chain of adversities and walks towards himself with grass and mud stuck to his naked heels. . . . The will to revolt and the will to renew created in us a feeling of freedom. . . . We disobeyed no one because we obeyed love. . . . Comrades, over there—in the north, in the east—the spirit of new life labours amidst horrors. Here it wallows in ardour, is placated by love.[42]

In this passage, D'Annunzio's spiritual communion with the legionnaires is at one with their physical communion. This pattern of expressing spiritual values in terms of the physical and sensual reappears later in the same text, where the poet commends his legionnaires' inner beauty by paying homage to their handsomely athletic appearance: 'The *Ardito*'s step, supported by the suppleness of well-trained muscles, possesses an unspeakable spirituality that amazes the onlooker'.[43] It has been argued that the emerging nationalist politics of the times required mass mobilisation, effected through a kind of compact between the intellectual avant-garde, the producers, and the workers; from this perspective, the vigour of the proletariat became a symbol of the vigour of the nation.[44] The war itself had been largely manned by, and won at the cost of the loss of, multitudes of young male peasant and working-class bodies. In this context, D'Annunzio's celebration of his legionnaires' rude health may be seen as continuous with broader ideological and semiotic processes.

Yet D'Annunzio's celebration of the legionnaires' physicality is also erotically inflected, through its connection to his professions of love for the legionnaires. D'Annunzio begins the closing lines of this oration by calling for his soldiers' fidelity: 'Let everyone betray me, even those who kiss my hands. As long as my own soul doesn't. This I am; and I want my comrades to be this, too. Or I reject them. I know I have made many comrades here in my own image, and I glory in it. They are enough for me.'[45] The legionnaires here are fungible with the poet's own soul; their obligation of fidelity to the poet is no more and no less than an obligation of fidelity to oneself. The covert analogy here is to marriage, making one out of two. Like two lovers whom a shared life makes alike, the poet and his legionnaires also resemble each other ('in my own image').

The final twist arrives a few lines after: 'I don't care for a thick army. My legion is enough. . . . At the last battle I want no one with me but the "sweet Latin blood". Thus my Fiuman Legion will surpass in beauty the Theban Legion.'[46] The marital union that metaphorically serves as a model for the reciprocal devotion of the poet-commandant and his legionnaires turns out to be of the same-sex variety. This daring homoerotic reference to the Theban army of same-sex lovers might well have been lost on everyone in the audience who did not possess the requisite classical education. Perhaps D'Annunzio even banked on its opacity to all but the most learned of his men. Intriguingly, however, earlier in the oration, following the use of particularly visionary poetic imagery, D'Annunzio had denied speaking by soliloquy: 'To whom do I speak this language? To oblivious soldiers? To simple footmen? Can they understand? They do. Mine do. I know.'[47]

MAKING LOVE TO THE LEGIONNAIRES

The homoerotic subtext of D'Annunzio's Fiume speeches could be less rarefied than in the instances discussed so far. Phallic metaphors, for example, range from the oblique ('*Ardito* dusky and lean like his dagger')[48] to the fully explicit, as in D'Annunzio's observation that when the *Arditi* launched an assault they 'rose with the same vigour the Ancients imparted to the symbols of male fecundity',[49] a clear reference to the Roman *fascinum* and Greek *herma*.

Less crude, but even more eloquent, are D'Annunzio's express professions of love. In a 1919 speech to the legionnaires, he declares: 'It is unnecessary to tell you again how much I admire you and how much I love you. I have already told you a hundred times. And the other night, at your officers' mess, I was speaking to you too, who were not there. I had my heart, naked, in the palm of my hand. I do today, too. It's yours. You know it. And yours is mine. I know it.'[50]

Interestingly, Comisso reports that D'Annunzio could cause 'terrible jealousies' if he inadvertently showed more favour to one army unit than another.[51] This suggests that sublimated erotic investments were not simply a feature of D'Annunzio's oratory but a phenomenological reality for the legionnaires.

One year later, in the oration known as the 'Festival of all Flames', the poet calls the legionnaires his 'Army mates and [his] soulmates'.[52] In a passage that, according to the printed text of the oration, caused D'Annunzio's audience of legionnaires to acclaim in a manifestation of 'love respond[ing] to love',[53] the poet states, 'Even today, after feeling you living within me for so long, my own blood, my own flesh, my own soul, I cannot call you comrades without my heart trembling.'[54] Not by coincidence, right on the heels of this bold declaration of love, an injunction follows: '*Arditi*, the ancient said that flames are impenetrable. Black flames, you must be impenetrable.' Afterwards, D'Annunzio goes on to clarify that the legionnaires must be impervious, specifically, to the bogeys set up by the propaganda of the Italian government to persuade them to desert Fiume. But D'Annunzio's choice of word ('impenetrable') seems calculated to immediately restore the audience's masculinity at the point when his own earnestness—his verbal same-sex love making—had seemed to threaten it. Some intertextual support for this reading can be found where D'Annunzio, in an oration three weeks later, again uses the metaphor of the impenetrable fire, this time to describe the incorruptibility of the town of Fiume, which, D'Annunzio argues, will reject any settlement that compromises its Italian spirit.[55] In implicitly conjuring up an imagery of (female) Christian martyrs intent on preserving virginity at the cost of their death,[56] the metaphor of impenetrable fire here seems to have, as in the case of its use to describe the *Arditi* three weeks earlier, covert sexualised connotations.[57]

THE WINGED PAIR AND HEROIC COUPLES

The funerary oration D'Annunzio delivered for Lieutenant Aldo Bini and Sergeant Giovanni Zeppegno also references same-sex desire through the language of love and fire, though less D'Annunzio's own than that of the soldiers' for each other. As with other D'Annunzio speeches, its homoerotic subtext has gone unremarked in the literature.[58]

While flying in the sky over Fiume, Bini and Zeppegno had plunged to their deaths. D'Annunzio starts by reminding the crowds of his Whitsunday speech, where he had said that 'in a dim world Fiume alone appeared as the living city, the burning city, aflame, all sorrowful and raging . . . perfectly and wholly consumed by fire.' Today, too, he goes on to say that Fiume is 'the citadel of consumed love', a love whose exigencies defy even fate.[59] 'It was necessary,' he explains, 'that our renewed will to fight and resist should be consecrated by a flaming death', and adds, 'these two young Italians lit their own death by fire in the midst of the land of fiery fervour', converting 'their love into lasting fire'. It is apparent that here D'Annunzio refers to love for Fiume and its cause, which is ultimately love for the motherland Italy—a love that in D'Annunzio's conceptual imaginary is understood, it has been argued, as a 'community of shared suffering, of ideals, and of blood'.[60]

Some of the terminological choices, however, allude to erotic love by indirectly referencing the ardour of orgasm. The two young men 'exhaled and spent themselves over the heart of the town', and the women of Fiume, in tears, tried to quench the flames, but the fire was oblivious to the water and 'only felt the tears' as 'a sorrowful aroma that excites the flame'.[61] The erotic imagery is heterosexual up to this point. A later passage in the oration, however, conveys the young men's love for each other. 'Glory to the winged pair', says D'Annunzio, calling them 'firstfruits of fire, firstfruits of death, young couple bewinged and sworn'.[62] *'Coppia alata'* ('winged pair') in Italian strongly suggests an avian mating pair, not two sexually unrelated birds. Nothing in D'Annunzio's wordsmithery is left to chance. The homoerotic connotations of the term *'coppia alata'* ('winged pair') are thus best appreciated by considering that, had he been so minded, he would have used any number of alternative expressions to rule out those connotations.

The image of the winged pair used in the funerary oration had in fact been devised by D'Annunzio a few years before: it appears in his introspective prose poem *Notturno*, an 'extraordinarily popular evocation of the Great War in its immediate aftermath'.[63] The extent to which the winged pair conceit is homoerotically charged in *Notturno* deserves examination, because it helps us appreciate, from an intertextual perspective, the homoerotic subtext of the self-same conceit as redeployed three years later in the funerary oration in Fiume.

D'Annunzio drafted the prose poem in fragments while convalescing after an airplane accident in 1916. His daughter curated the fragments into an early edition, until the poem was published in its definitive, author-approved form, five years later. Though material was added for the 1921 version, D'Annunzio's annotation to that edition makes clear that the part in which the winged pair conceit is used dates from the original, 1916 draft.[64] The book is divided into three parts (or 'Offerings' as D'Annunzio calls them). The first is largely devoted to mourning Giuseppe Miraglia. We have already encountered him as the deceased aviator with whom D'Annunzio had flown several times and developed an intimate friendship. The conceit of the winged pair in *Notturno* appears where the poet laments his not having met his death together with Miraglia, whose plane had plunged into the sea not far from Venice:

> Now death, which should have taken both, took one, only one, against the pact, against the offering, against justice, against glory.
>
> At the summit of glory, for the winged pair, is the holocaust: that sacrifice in which the victim burns in its totality.[65]

The fantasy of dying with Miraglia is, admittedly, indulged in in the name of the patriotic values ('loyalty to the idea, gravity of purpose, tomorrow's silent sacrifice')[66] that cemented their bond: 'There is not today a nobler bond than this tacit compact that makes, of two lives and two wings, one speed, one prowess, one death.'[67] Yet the poet's yearning to be reunited with his pilot is unmistakably love-like. Frequently in his novels D'Annunzio speaks of physical passion as a desire to lose one's distinct identity and become one substance with the lover. In *Notturno*, speaking about Miraglia, he deploys a set of images that convey precisely that kind of merging:

> I am alive, but as definitely located in my own darkness as he in his. I breathe but I feel my breath pass through livid lips, as his were in the first few hours, [I feel my breath] part a mouth grown nearly lifeless . . .
>
> So, his death and my life are one.
>
> From his remote motionlessness comes to me that of him that I knew how to love; from my own motionlessness that part of me that was worthy of his love goes out to him. . . .
>
> [F]or both, flesh is abolished as our spirits conjoin anew.[68]
>
> There is a place in the soul, there, where the black river and the white river mingle.
>
> It is the place where our friendship survives.[69]

The purely spiritual nature of the bond allows D'Annunzio to explicitly compare it to the bond of lovers, which is found wanting by comparison: 'The most secret thrill of unspoken love is nothing compared to certain looks'[70] exchanged by the winged pair. Yet in spite of D'Annunzio's protestations of a purely spiritual bond and an aspiration for a purely spiritual merging with Miraglia, we have glimpses of attachment, not to say clinging, of the physical variety. These include not only Miraglia's 'livid and icy hand brushed by my lips before the lid [of the coffin] secreted him away from me'[71] but also a candid acknowledgement on the site of the burial: 'My woe is nonetheless entangled in his decayed flesh'.[72]

Indeed, D'Annunzio eventually concedes that in aviation, as in ancient Greece, 'The comrade *is* the comrade',[73] and the winged pair is none other than a reincarnation of the Greek heroic couple: 'the virile couple, the fighting couple, reborn in the creation of the human wing . . . led by a single will, like the young Greek's double spear.'[74] The young Greek's double spear might refer to the so-called *dory*, which was furnished with a point at one end and spike at the other. A spear of any kind, however, has phallic connotations, and one must wonder if D'Annunzio here is picturing a soldier-*erastes*'s initiation of his *eromenos* not only into fighting but also love making. The spear may be double because in a same-sex couple the phallus itself is redoubled. This may well be overinterpretation, but with D'Annunzio, any erotic allusion is more likely than not to be intended rather than the reader's projection.

It is true that the heroic couple in ancient Greece was not necessarily an erotic pair. Heroic couples are legion in the *Iliad* and in Greek mythology more generally. Twins or brothers figure prominently among them. Yet many of the most famous heroic couples were seen by the Greeks of the classical age as *erastes-eromenos* pairs, and same-sex sexual activity was pervasive in the armies of the Archaic age.[75] Besides, D'Annunzio had a fondness, specifically, for the *topos* of the Theban legion of same-sex lovers.[76] The Theban warriors swore to win or die together[77]—a vow that is exactly echoed in *Notturno*'s idealisation of the winged pair's compact and in their dying a single death.[78]

At one point D'Annunzio compares the winged pair specifically to the heroic couple of Odysseus and Diomedes, which is not a canonical homoerotic heroic couple. The comparison is in the line of *Notturno* where D'Annunzio speaks of the sacrifice of winged pairs who might die in action as their planes catch fire: 'As in the eighth bedlam, they are two "within one fire", but the fire is undivided'.[79] The image of the 'eight bedlam' and the quotation are drawn from Dante's *Divine Comedy*, according to which Odysseus and Diomedes, who had sinned because of their ingenious deceits during the occupation of Troy, ended up in Hell and suffered the punishment reserved to fraudsters: to burn perpetually in fires individually surrounding their bodies. In the case of Odysseus and Diomedes, however, because their fraud had been a joint enterprise, a single fire enveloped both, albeit bifurcating into separate tongues at the top.[80]

As mentioned, Odysseus and Diomedes are not renowned as an erotically involved heroic couple. Yet their iconography in the Graeco-Roman world from the fifth century BC to the second century AD regularly represents Diomedes as a beardless youth,[81] which is consistent with an *erastes/eromenos* relationship with Odysseus. This influenced later representations in European art, no more conspicuously so than in John Flaxman's 1793 illustrations for the *Iliad*. Flaxman's illustrations include a particularly affecting rendition of Achille's grief as he leans over the dead Patroclus, as well as a preliminary study of Achilles seeking to embrace the ghost of Patroclus. But they also include an engraving depicting Odysseus and Diomedes leading stolen horses to the Greek camp. In this illustration, Odysseus's mature and vaguely rugged manhood contrast with the young and athletic Diomedes's delicate facial features and graceful advance. This iconography of Odysseus and Diomedes is at the very least erotically suggestive—to say nothing of the fact that in the *Iliad* Odysseus's only spontaneous gesture of protectiveness has Diomedes as its beneficiary.[82]

Therefore we cannot assume that D'Annunzio's reference specifically to the heroic couple of Odysseus and Diomedes—rather than a more canonically homoerotic heroic pairing—neutralises the homoerotic subtext of his treatment of the winged pair in *Notturno*. Indeed, the communion with Miraglia that D'Annunzio longs for turns out to be physical after all: 'Blessed, the heroic couple [literally: 'the two comrade heroes'] whose unrecognisable bones are commingled in the litter like smoking embers!'[83] This is an unmistakable reference to one of the most famous homoerotically involved heroic couples in Greek mythology, Achilles and Patroclus. The *Odyssey* tells us that Achilles's 'white bones', cured 'in strong neat wine and seasoned oils', were placed in 'a gold two-handled urn, . . . mixed with the bones of dead Patroclus.'[84] Patroclus's visiting ghost had begged, 'Never bury my bones apart from yours, Achilles, let them lie together'.[85] Achilles had therefore instructed the Achaeans to enlarge Patroclus's tomb after he himself would join him in death.[86]

The frontispiece plate of the 1921 edition of *Notturno*, with artwork from De Carolis (whom, as we have seen, D'Annunzio had entrusted with designing the iconography of the regency), is also telling. It was probably designed under D'Annunzio's own directions, in the same way in which work he commissioned in Fiume was. The illustration portrays two naked males standing on either side of a doorway, which is dwarfed by their gigantic, muscular proportions. Through the doorway is nocturnal darkness into which rages the fire of the holocaust—a winged pair's ultimate sacrifice. But the insubstantial and ephemeral qualities of the fire are also suggestive of corpse candles: as such, the fire possibly references the fires enveloping the damned of the eight bedlam, including Odysseus and Diomedes, whose appearance Dante likens to fireflies.[87]

Before the doorway is a step heaped with strips of papers—those on which D'Annunzio wrote the fragments that became *Notturno* (he was then in bed, sightless and partially paralysed, and the strips of paper cut for him by his daughter made writing possible by physically guiding the tip of his pen). Only one strip bears a legible line: *'Et in tenebris'* ('Even unto darkness'). Clearly, this refers to the bond between the two men. Equally clearly, the men represent the winged pair. The one on the right has the wings of an angel, not folded, but arched towards his comrade. As with angels, his domain is not the Earth. He is, almost certainly, Miraglia, while the man on the right is D'Annunzio: his wings are not angel-like but a more modest affair growing out of his temples (a likely homage to the wings of D'Annunzio's imagination and creative genius). They shelter his eyes, rather like the bandages D'Annunzio was wearing while writing *Notturno*. The men are turned towards each other and their muscular arms, extended over the doorway, intertwine, suggesting interdependence but also, unmistakably, the sensuous comfort of a lover's touch. The man on the right (D'Annunzio) is also offering two flowers to the one on the left, recalling the line in *Notturno* to the effect that death is no barrier to Miraglia continuing to receive what in D'Annunzio was worthy of the aviator's love.

Beyond the symbolism, the overall aesthetic effect is as suggestively homoerotic as with Michelangelo's Sistine Chapel monumental male nudes, which are an evident source of stylistic inspiration for De Carolis in this illustration, almost certainly at D'Annunzio's own behest, given his abiding admiration for the Renaissance master. The least that can be said is that it is difficult to watch the cover of *Notturno*—the work where the winged pair conceit originates, before its redeployment in the funerary oration for Bini and Zeppegno—without the suspicion crossing our mind that the heroic couple depicted on it is of the erotically involved variety.

DELIVERING THE *CHARTER*

In the 'Festival of All Flames', the speech where D'Annunzio presents the *Carnaro Charter* to the legionnaires, homoeroticism is as subtle as unequivocal. The written version of this speech was produced from memory, and perhaps embellished, after D'Annunzio delivered an improvised one to the legionnaires gathered in the Phoenix Theatre.[88] It is in this speech that we see D'Annunzio not simply enacting (as in his other speeches to the legionnaires) the sublimation of same-sex desire but thematising its generative qualities, its ability to bear fruit, in a way that parallels that same thematisation in the later novels.

In the speech, D'Annunzio recalls how the previous night, when he had informally promulgated the *Charter* to the citizens of Fiume in the same Phoenix Theatre, the legionnaires themselves had been absent but had sent multitudes of flowers. The poet then indulges in a fancy that those blooms might be the self-same flowers his troops used to insert in the tubes of their rifles in their springtime morning drills (a practice recorded by Comisso)[89]—as if the legionnaires had pulled them out and now offered them to him, such that each flower 'conjured up the tube of a gun'. Each of the flowers proffered to D'Annunzio, thus, stands in for the soldier's gun, whence the poet likes to imagine it came; but these flowers are 'living creatures' too, no less than the 'hand that sweetly plucks them'.[90]

The conceit that each flower is a stand-in for its soldier's gun (D'Annunzio call them 'muskets') draws attention to the latter, with all the phallic connotations that firearms have. Those connotations are reinforced because this composite object that partakes both of the nature of guns (a hard, powerful, lethal thing) and flowers (a soft thing of delicate beauty) is also distinctly each soldier's own, and a living thing, like the flesh-and-bone hand that pulls on it. A self-consciously homosexual writer could hardly have produced a more loving account of young soldiers' endowments. 'But last night,' D'Annunzio goes on to add for good measure, 'the life of those flowers of yours almost seemed preternatural. They breathed like a young battalion resting by a fountain, after a march. I could feel its breath, its desire . . .'[91]

These passages are preceded by one in which D'Annunzio recalls another gathering of the legionnaires in the Phoenix Theatre, on the previous morning. Here we observe a careful use of imagery, including glimpses of young males' flesh, and metaphors that are especially at home with the vocabulary of erotic passion:

> But yesterday morning it was not a matter of uniforms, more or less open. The colours [of the different corps' uniforms] did not matter. There was only one dominant colour: that of smouldering embers. And at each new accent of the Commandant the smouldering embers burst into blaze. . . . [Some] recalled the incipit of a speech, already a thing of the past, by Gabriele D'Annunzio, delivered in September 1919: 'Coming into you is like going through fire, like penetrating the burning furnace, like breathing in the essence of the flame, without singing oneself, without consuming oneself.' . . . 'And what do I want, if not for you to burn'?[92]

At first blush, the mention of 'more or less open' uniforms appears to be a harmless, factual reference to the military attire of the *Arditi*. This included a black sweater and a coat open at the neck.[93] Yet the speech was delivered in the sweltering month of August, when sweaters would have been discarded. Thus, in mentioning the *Arditi*'s open uniform, D'Annunzio conjures up less the knit of a dark sweater than a vision of exposed flesh. The exposure would not have been confined to the *Arditi* either. As Kotchnitzky relates, the other legionnaires emulated their style, and 'one day infantrymen split the coat of their uniform, the collar opened, and out of it rose the bare neck, which will bronze in the seaside winds.'[94] The reference to necks bronzing 'in the seaside winds' immediately recalls D'Annunzio's sensuous poem 'Versilia', where a tree nymph, addressing a hunter eating some peaches, uses the exact same imagery: 'I spied on you from my scaly trunk, but you did not feel, man, my living lashes flutter against your suntanned neck . . . perhaps I like you. Your skin, which the sun has made dusky, has the scent of seawater. You have slim legs, as smooth as bronze.'[95]

This intertextuality between the writings of D'Annunzio and the homosexual Kotchnitzky is revealing of the homoerotic politics of the commandant's public speeches to the legionnaires. The erotic effect of D'Annunzio's oblique reference to exposed male flesh in the speech is magnified by the reference to *penetrating* the burning furnace, coming as it does right on the heels of D'Annunzio's likening the legionnaires to fire: 'the miracle of youths transfigured into flames: into veritable flames'.[96] As he had done with the image of 'more or less open' uniforms, D'Annunzio here references what is characteristic of the attire of Arditi—whose lapels bore flames of different colours, depending on their service branch[97]—to construct a powerfully suggestive metaphor.

These passages convey the erotic desirability of the legionnaires for a reason: they precede the key passage of the speech, where D'Annunzio describes the *Charter* as resulting from the intellectual intercourse between him and the legionnaires. Thanks to these preliminary parts of the speech, by the time D'Annunzio comes to characterise the *Charter* as an 'act of life', we have been primed to expect that the intellectual labour that generated it feeds off same-sex desire, rather like Socrates's and Leonardo's pedagogical labour does in *The Virgins of the Rocks*:

> We nurture the bloom of [Italy's] life and the bloom of its destiny in this soil, fertile as no other because sorrowful as no other. . . . And if we have behind us all our dead . . . we have before us those due to be born, more numerous than the killed.
>
> This act of life goes out to meet them. This work of life is performed for them.
>
> It is your own work, legionnaires. You made it. I bring it to light.
>
> The glory is wholly yours.[98]

In this passage, rife with images of fertility and birth, the *Charter* is an act of life because it has a generative quality: it will usher in a new, more radiant, and beautiful world for generations to come. But the *Charter* also is an 'act of life' in the sense that it is itself generated. It is the legionnaires' own work, and D'Annunzio simply brings it to light.[99] 'To bring to light' is a literal translation of, and its meaning corresponds exactly to, the Italian *'mettere in luce'*. But the Italian verb is cognate to the (today noncanonical) expression *'mettere alla luce'* (more frequently, *'dare alla luce'*), which means to give birth.

A Freudian reading here may see D'Annunzio inadvertently position himself on the terrain of the feminine vis-à-vis the legionnaires: he is to them as Anatolia is to Cantelmo in *The Virgins of the Rocks*, partner in intercourse and enabler of the act of life that will produce the offspring instantiating the legacy of the masculine. This is not in itself implausible: we have already learnt that D'Annunzio was able to make-believe a gender switch, as when he gave powerful voice to Isabella's antipatriarchal sentiments in *Perhaps So, Perhaps Not*, or when he followed the lead of his sexual partner's fantasies during intercourse to intensify her and his own pleasure.

But we also know that there is nothing ever inadvertent about D'Annunzio's use of words. Thus, what is at stake in this passage is probably not a Freudian slip: this is not D'Annunzio's unconscious fantasy of delivering the *Charter* like a mother delivers a baby, inadvertently conveyed through a telling word choice. Rather, in using an expression (*'mettere in luce'*) which recalls (but does not quite mean) the act of birth giving (*'mettere alla luce'*), D'Annunzio is deliberately alluding to the metaphor of childbirth. The point is to convey an idea by now familiar to us: the intellectual and creative generativity of same-sex desire, in this case resulting in no less than the elaborate political programme instantiated in the *Charter*.

'The Intelligent Flame', discussed earlier, also alludes to the metaphor of childbirth, and this time, even pregnancy, to refer to the genesis of the *Charter*. The *Charter* here is an 'act of life' that occurred 'nine months' after the (purported) betrayal around the *modus vivendi*.[100] But this speech also uses a different metaphor: 'In the gathering of 30 August [1920], introducing the new statutes [the *Charter*], I showed the legionnaires that I regarded the text as their own labour: labour prepared by them, rough-hewn by them in the manner of Michelangelo's sculptures, and led by me to polished form.'[101]

Instead of having recourse to analogies with heterosexual bodily generativity, this passage hints at the kind of aesthetic and intellectual generativity proper of the sublimation of same-sex desire, via the example of that ultimate sublimator, Michelangelo.

UNTIL THE LAST

Even *in extremis*, on 28 December 1920, before his resignation from power, D'Annunzio continued to address the legionnaires in the terms of romantic passion:

> For fifteen months I nourished you with myself, I gave you my sorrowful heart to devour, I made you captive of my own self-same aspiration.
>
> Lo, now you hand my heart back to me, you give me back my blood, you dye my dawn with your own blood.
>
> You seemed to me the creatures of my spirit. And now you look to me more beautiful than my own creatures. You surpass my dream . . .[102]

The same theme was picked up a few days later, when, on 3 of January 1921, D'Annunzio delivered his farewell and prepared to leave town. Describing the legionnaires processing the previous day towards the Corsala Cemetery, where the victims of the bloody Christmas were due to be interred, the poet's words rhapsodise about their beauty:

> The best sons of Italy went by, those whom the virile craftsman of the race fashioned in a happy hour, with his rich substance, with his most forceful vigour. The Latin youth went by, clad in iron helmets and coarse cloth, handsome as the handsomest Virgilian hero. The maned power went by, long locks seemingly ablaze on foreheads, like the fires of an imminent Pentecost.
>
> In what place of the world, under what sky today do human architectures live comparable to these?
>
> . . . One might have thought that, in a remote time, they were breathing heroism in the vault of the Sistine chapel. . . . Had they come into their own for me? Had they perfected themselves out of love for me?
>
> Were they intent on intoxicating me and devastating me on the eve of our farewell? Did they want to show that they truly were the creatures of my furious eagerness, of my cruel fate?[103]

The legionnaires fulfil D'Annunzio's dreams of heroic virtue so exactly that he can hardly bear parting from them and departing from the place that made such fulfilment possible. The key point is that he conveys all this through the metaphor of male physical beauty ('handsome as the handsomest Virgilian hero', incomparable 'human architectures'), the vocabulary of erotic passion ('love', 'intoxicating', 'devastating'), the idea of a generative male sexual power apparently dispensing with the services of the other sex ('the virile craftsman . . . fashioned . . . with his rich substance, with his most forceful vigour'), and the homoerotic imagery of Michelangelesque heroic nudes ('breathing heroism in the vault of the Sistine chapel').

Indeed, even D'Annunzio's funeral oration of the day before conjures up visions that convey a subtle homoeroticism, rarefied but not negated by the sombre occasion and the vocabulary of brotherhood: 'And perhaps this was the longing of a dying young *Alpino*, as one of our foot soldiers stooped over him: "Kiss me, my brother. Don't curse me. Only he who sent me to fight against you, let him be cursed."'[104]

THE SUCCESS OF D'ANNUNZIO'S HOMOEROTIC ORATORY

Within one year of the bloody Christmas Freud published *Group Psychology and the Analysis of the Ego*, where he made the groundbreaking argument that sexual instincts are at the root of group bonds[105] and that 'love relationships . . . constitute the essence of the group mind.'[106] The ability of group members to overcome narcissism and tolerate others cannot but be rooted in *eros*: 'Love for oneself knows only one barrier—love for others, love for objects.'[107] Conversely, collaborative relationships become eroticised because the *libido* 'chooses as its first objects the people who have a share' in satisfying 'the great vital needs', with the consequence that 'desexualised, sublimated homosexual love for other men . . . springs from work in common.'[108]

In groups whose organisational structure is not so high that it itself secures group's functioning and continuing existence through labour differentiation, group ties are supplied by the group members' *libido*. This is unconsciously diverted from its sexual aims towards a love object, the leader. Because the leader comes to replace the members' *ego* ideal—the mental faculty that, amongst other things, tests the reality of things—they are prepared to more or less blindly follow the leader. And because they all share the same love object, the members also come to identify with one another's ego, which results in group cohesion.[109] These psychic mechanisms are only possible to the extent that the leader becomes the target of object cathexis: 'all the ties upon which a group depends are of the character of instincts that are inhibited in their [originally sexual] aims.'[110] As a result of this inhibition, intergroup libidinal ties are unconcerned with 'genital organisation', and it is futile to try to classify them as either homosexual or heterosexual.[111]

The case of D'Annunzio's legionnaires is remarkable: it literalises Freud's explanation but also fails to be a central case of it. If D'Annunzio's oratory brings into focus the libidinal nature of the psychological dynamics that held the community of legionnaires together, in doing so it also undermined those very dynamics. Freud, who insists that hypnosis is a case of group psychology writ small, points out that hypnotists attempt to divert their patients' conscious attention from what they are trying to do so as to avoid eliciting their opposition.[112] We may hypothesise, then, that D'Annunzio's too earnest professions of love for the legionnaires and of admiration for their beauty may have brought to the surface of consciousness what was supposed to be unconscious. This may have broken the spell of sublimation, redirecting the legionnaires' *libido* away from the group and back towards its primal (sexual) aims. To the extent that 'direct sexual tendencies are unfavourable for the formation of groups',[113] not only did Fiume's oversexed climate detract from group cohesion, but D'Annunzio's speeches also made things worse. It was all very well for D'Annunzio to demand the channelling of erotic energy into sacrifice and dedication, but he should have done so *sans en avoir l'aire*: the erotic part of the equation should have remained covert.

Perhaps this is why the homoerotic affect that D'Annunzio deployed in his speeches was not effective across the board. Some legionnaires responded to it and continued to do their part in sustaining the normative order of occupied Fiume and the regency. By the last few months of the occupation, however, many others had left. D'Annunzio was under no illusion. In 'The Intelligent Flame' he rejects the deserters: he insists he has no need for 'a thick army' and orders those who are not fully committed to die for Fiume to leave.[114] Once again, however, he undermines the mystique of the Fiuman cause by giving away that it is ultimately a proxy for his and the legionnaires' libidinal bond: even if all Fiumans and Italians turn their back on him, he will continue so long as his own 'soul'—the legionnaires that have remained faithful—do not betray him.[115]

CONCLUSIONS

All the speeches to the legionnaires discussed in this chapter enact the sublimation of same-sex desire that D'Annunzio's novel thematise. But 'The Festival of All Flames' and 'The Intelligent Flame', which D'Annunzio delivered respectively when introducing the *Charter* and the New Army Regulations to the legionnaires, also thematise such sublimation in their own right. They do so where they present the *Charter* as a labour of love, and specifically of the love between the commandant and the legionnaires for each other. The legionnaires quicken D'Annunzio's imaginative commitment to giving shape to the new constitutional order. They do so because they share in his idealism—and they do because he has made them in his own image.[116] Having made the legionnaires in his own image means loving them in the romantic sense: again and again in his novels D'Annunzio insists that the essence of romantic love is complete possession of the other, or dominion over them (without necessarily denying reciprocity). But the possession of the other here is intellectual and spiritual rather than physical, and the fruit it bears is the *Charter*.

There is continuity between how D'Annunzio's speeches to the legionnaires were intended to function and the ways in which D'Annunzio's literary work describes the point of genuinely valuable public speaking. In *Fire*, the writer Effrena, shortly due to deliver a public address, has second thoughts about the point of these forms of public engagement and dismisses them to his friends as useless histrionics—unless, he provocatively claims, the speech manages to move the crowd to action, even violent action. Effrena's point is that the experience of truth or value is something that only the written word may facilitate, while it is precluded to the oral address. His favourite disciple, Daniele Glauro, quickly corrects his mentor, showing that his point is built on a false dichotomy.[117] Glauro claims Effrena's readers, in reading his work, 'have drunk your poetry, . . . breathed in the burning ether of your dream, . . . felt the claw of your chimera';[118] but Effrena's oral address, he argues, can have the self-same effect. The action to which Effrena's words can move his audience may well be 'an energic movement that turns them and directs them forever towards the Ideal', in the same way in which his writings 'have promised a more beautiful and more powerful life', 'have announced the transfiguration of the world into a new art', and 'have seduced [the readers] with your hope and with your joy'.[119]

Later, Effrena himself will recognise as much:

> He marvelled at that unknown power that flowed into him, abolishing the boundaries of the individual and imparting to a single voice the fullness of a choir.—Such, then, was the mysterious respite that the revelation of Beauty was able to grant to the daily existence of toiling multitudes; such was the mysterious will that could flood the poet in the act of responding to the uncountable soul inquiring about the value of life and longing to attain, for once, to the eternal idea.—In that hour he was nothing but the medium through which Beauty handed over to men . . . the divine gift of forgetfulness. . . . For one hour those men must look at the world with new eyes, must feel, think and dream with a different soul.[120]
>
> There was, then, tucked away in the multitude, a beauty which only a poet or a hero could cause to flash. When that beauty revealed itself through the sudden clamour raised in a theatre, trench or public square, then a torrent of joy filled the heart of he who had been able to elicit it with his verse, harangue, or a wave of his sword.[121]

The content of D'Annunzio's speeches in Fiume makes it apparent that through them the poet sought to have his audience experience just such a transfiguration of reality as articulated in these passages of *Fire*, albeit for a more extended timeframe than the one-hour duration of Effrena's speech. We must, I want to argue, suspend cynicism if we want truly to appreciate the affective work that D'Annunzio's speeches sought to do and did in Fiume, making the town, on virtually all the accounts of the legionnaires that remained faithful to D'Annunzio, the unique normative (social, political, and ethical) universe that it briefly was.

Simonelli may be right that 'there is no trace of official or private documents that provide evidence of public recognition of homosexuality in D'Annunzio's Fiume'.[122] There is, however, a wealth of evidence, from D'Annunzio's own speeches, of a highly homoerotically charged *milieu*, and one where homoeroticism was not disavowed but—at the instigation of D'Annunzio's himself—woven (sometimes subtly, other time rather more conspicuously) into the fabric of the legionnaires' interpersonal dynamics and collective self-understanding. The next and final chapter provides further details about this *milieu*.

NOTES

1. H. L. A. Hart, *The Concept of Law* (Oxford: Oxford University Press, 1961); Joseph Raz, *Practical Reason and Norms* (Oxford: Oxford University Press, 1999).

2. For the purposes of establishing general conformity with the law during the occupation, D'Annunzio's legionnaires must be regarded as part of the general population of the Fiuman polity. Like any visitors, they would have been expected and required to follow the rules: merely by virtue of being in town, they were no less addressees of the Fiuman polity's norms than the Fiumans. But the legionnaires were actually more than short-term visitors. Their residence was potentially indefinite, as they had vowed to stay on until annexation. Although they were not entitled to vote about the *modus vivendi* or the *Charter*, or in the elections of the National Council, some, perhaps many, were looking forward to becoming full members of the Fiuman polity. When the legionnaires had applied for 'pertinence' status, their applications had tended to be turned down by the National Council, determined to protect the town from excessive demands on its resources. Dominique Kirchner Reill, *The Fiume Crisis: Life in the Wake of the Habsburg Empire* (Cambridge, MA: Harvard University Press, 2020), 164–67. But after the promulgation of the *Charter*, these legionnaires could reasonably look to article XV as offering an avenue for achieving full civic membership. The article made explicit provision for the granting of citizenship on the basis of 'special merit' and may well have been designed having the legionnaires in mind.

3. See generally Alfredo Bonadeo, *D'Annunzio and the Great War* (Madison and Teaneck: Farleigh Dickinson University Press; London: Associated University Presses, 1995).

4. Quoted in Bonadeo, *D'Annunzio and the Great War*, 73.

5. Bonadeo, *D'Annunzio and the Great War*, 96.

6. Gabriele D'Annunzio, *Di Me a Me Stesso* (Milano: Andreoli, 1990), 73–78 (quoted in Bonadeo, *D'Annunzio and the Great War*, 119).

7. Jűrgen Habermas, *The Theory of Communicative Action*, trans. Thomas McCarthy (Cambridge, UK: Polity Press, 1987).

8. Federico C. Simonelli, "La Costruzione di un Mito: Rituali, Simboli e Narrazioni dell'Impresa di Fiume (1919–1921)" (PhD diss., Università degli Studi di Urbino Carlo Bo, 2014–2015), 149–51, https://ora.uniurb.it/bitstream/11576/2630991/1/phd_uniurb_257536.pdf.

9. Quoted in Stefano B. Galli, "Il Sentire Politico di Gabriele D'Annunzio per una 'Grande' Italia: Patriottismo, Nazionalismo, Interventismo," in *L'Italia e la "Grande Vigilia": Gabriele D'Annunzio nella Politica Italiana Prima del Fascismo*, ed. Romain H. Rainero and Stefano B. Galli (Milano: FrancoAngeli, 2007), 82.

10. Letter from G. D'Annunzio to A. De Ambris (11 May 1921) in *Sindacalismo Rivoluzionario e Fiumanesimo nel Carteggio De Ambris—D'Annunzio*, ed. Renzo De Felice (Brescia: Morcelliana, 1966), 250.

11. Mario Maria Martini, *La Passione di Fiume: Diari, Cronache, Documenti* (Milano: Sonzogno, 1919), 80.

12. D'Annunzio's farewell speech, *La Vedetta d'Italia* (19 January 1921), in Giuseppe Moscati, *Le Cinque Giornate di Fiume: X Anniversario del Natale di Sangue* (Milano: Carnaro, 1930), 193–94.

13. For example, shortly before the Ronchi march, Gherardo Marone (lawyer, academic, and man of letters, later an opposer of Fascism) described Harukichi Shimoi (Japanese Italianist and translator of Dante, D'Annunzio's friend and legionnaire in Fiume) as a 'young foreigner in love with our nation, come from afar in a pilgrimage of love', 'a living phenomenon of love'. Gherardo Marone, "Scimoi," in Harukichi Scimoi, *La Guerra Italiana Vista da un Giapponese* (Napoli: Libreria della Diana, 1919), 85, 86.

14. Giordano Bruno Guerri, *D'Annunzio: L'Amante Guerriero* (Milano: Mondadori, 2009), 183–84; Michael A. Leeden, *The First Duce* (Baltimore and London: John Hopkins University Press, 1977), 7; Giovanni Comisso, *Le Mie Stagioni* (Milano: Longanesi, 1963), 428.

15. Léon Kotchnitzky, *La Quinta Stagione: O, I Centauri di Fiume*, trans. Alberto Luchini (Bologna: Zanichelli, 1922), 24.

16. Kotchnitzky, *La Quinta Stagione*, 125.

17. Kotchnitzky, *La Quinta Stagione*, 126.

18. Leeden, *The First Duce*, 7.

19. Leeden, *The First Duce*, 96.

20. Quoted in Claudia Salaris, *Alla Festa della Rivoluzione: Artisti e Libertari con D'Annunzio a Fiume* (Bologna: Il Mulino, 2002), 144 (form *La Vedetta d'Italia* [28 aprile 1920]).

21. People—*popolo*—is a masculine noun in Italian.

22. Quoted in Salaris, *Alla Festa della Rivoluzione*, 37–38.

23. The *cliché* of love-invested Italians obviously spoke to Italian self-understandings. Keller also used it when reproaching a Serbian peasant for bullying his family and driving his sons away, who had then proceeded to consort with the *Arditi*:

'You, Serbian, ruled your family with the stick. We instead rule with love. And your race as it came in contact with ours melted like snow in the sun.' Giovanni Comisso, *Al Vento dell'Adriatico*, second edition (Torino: Fratelli Ribet, 1928), 103 (originally published as *Il Porto dell'Amore* in 1924).

24. Monica S. Cyrino, *Aphrodite* (Abingdon, UK: Routledge, 2010), 63, 96.

25. Martini, *La Passione di Fiume*, 80.

26. Simonelli, "La Costruzione di un Mito," 200–202; Federico Carlo Simonelli, *D'Annunzio e il Mito di Fiume: Riti, Simboli, Narrazioni* (Pisa: Pacini, 2021), 238–39.

27. Natalia Skradol, "Carnival of Exception: Gabriele D'Annunzio's 'Dialogues with the Crowd'," *Rhetorica: A Journal of the History of Rhetoric* 30 (2012): 82–84.

28. D'Annunzio, *Il Fuoco*, in *Romanzi e Novelle*, vol. II (Milano: Mondadori, 1942), 589.

29. Gabriele D'Annunzio, speech of 16 September 1919, in Martini, *La Passione di Fiume*, 94.

30. Gabriele D'Annunzio, "In Alto il Ferro" (2 October 1919), in Martini, *La Passione di Fiume*, 139.

31. Gabriele D'Annunzio, "La Fiamma Intelligente," in *La Sola Ragione di Vivere*, ed. Emanuele Merlino (Firenze: Passaggio al Bosco, 2020), 162.

32. Gabriele D'Annunzio, *Il Piacere*, in *Romanzi e Novelle*, vol. I (Milano: Mondadori, 1942), 50.

33. Gabriele D'Annunzio, *Il Trionfo della Morte*, in *Romanzi e Novelle*, vol. I (Milano: Mondadori, 1942), 838.

34. Gabriele D'Annunzio, *Forse che Sí, Forse che No*, in *Romanzi e Novelle*, vol. II (Milano: Mondadori, 1942), 984.

35. *The Carnaro Charter*, art. XXXXIX.

36. Federico Carlo Simonelli, "L'Ordinamento dell'Esercito Liberatore: Una Rilettura," in *D'Annunzio Legislatore: Costituzioni, Visioni, Utopie dell'Impresa Fiumana*, ed. Giordano Bruno Guerri (Milano: Silvana Editoriale, 2022), 124, 127.

37. Guido Keller, Report to Gabriele D'Annunzio ('copy no 2', project for a reform of the Army) (1919), Fondazione Il Vittoriale degli Italiani, Archivio Fiumano, Serie Corrispondenza, Keller, Guido.

38. *New Regulations for the Liberation Army*, art. I.

39. *New Regulations for the Liberation Army*, art. II.

40. Mauro Runco, "I Legionari Fiumani e la Riforma Militare di Giuseppe Piffer," in *La Sola Ragione di Vivere*, ed. Merlino, 82–83.

41. Simonelli, "La Costruzione di un Mito," 200.

42. D'Annunzio, "La Fiamma Intelligente," 162–63.

43. D'Annunzio, "La Fiamma Intelligente," 170.

44. Galli, "Il Sentire," 85.

45. D'Annunzio, "La Fiamma Intelligente," 171.

46. D'Annunzio, "La Fiamma Intelligente," 172.

47. D'Annunzio, "La Fiamma Intelligente," 170.

48. Gabriele D'Annunzio, speech of 29 September 1919, in Martini, *La Passione di Fiume*, 128–29.

49. Proclamation of 24 July 1920, *La Vedetta d'Italia* (24 July 1920), quoted in Simonelli, *D'Annunzio e il Mito*, 238.

50. Gabriele D'Annunzio, "In Alto il Ferro" (3 October 1919), in Martini, *La Passione di Fiume*, 137.

51. Comisso, *Le Mie Stagioni*, 73.

52. Gabriele D'Annunzio, "La Sagra di Tutte le Fiamme," in *La Carta del Carnaro e Altri Scritti su Fiume*, ed. Marco Fressura and Patrick Karlsen (Roma: Castelvecchi, 2009), 115.

53. D'Annunzio, "La Sagra," 116.

54. D'Annunzio, "La Sagra," 115–16.

55. Gabriele D'Annunzio, "Oration to the People of Fiume" (25 October 1919), in Martini, *La Passione di Fiume*, 201.

56. See Ida Magli, *Storia Laica delle Donne Religiose* (Milano: Longanesi, 1995). Note that towns and cities are always gendered feminine in the Italian language.

57. Note that in Italian the words *'amore'* (the noun 'love') and *'amare'* ('to love') are used more selectively (if not more sparingly) than their equivalent in English. These words admit of different meanings and connotations, but in declarative sentences that express a speaker's feelings for her interlocutor they almost invariably refer to romantic/erotic love. Italians living in Italy do not know of the supermarket cashier variety of love known to British people ('Thank you love'), nor of the 'love' that anglophone friends might exchange when closing their letters. We may speak of 'maternal love', but hardly ever will a mother say to her children, *'Ti amo'* ('I love you'), and it would not cross a child's mind to say it to its parents. Both would say, *'Ti voglio bene'* ('I care for you deeply'). These differences in usage must be borne in mind, if we want to grasp how D'Annunzio's professions of *amore* must have come across to, and affected, the legionnaires. In any case, there is reason to believe that in other languages too the central case of 'love' is sexual love. See Sigmund Freud, *Group Psychology and the Analysis of the Ego*, trans. James Strachey (London: Hogarth, 1949), 37–38, 71.

58. See, for example, Pamela Ballinger, "Rewriting the Text of the Nation: D'Annunzio at Fiume," *Quaderni* XI (1997): 144–45.

59. Gabriele D'Annunzio, speech of 7 October 1919, in Martini, *La Passione di Fiume*, 148.

60. Anton Marino Revedin, "Immaginazione al Potere (l'Avanguardismo Costituzionale dello Statuto del Carnaro)," in *Lo Statuto della Reggenza Italiana del Carnaro tra Storia, Diritto Internazionale e Diritto Costituzionale*, ed. Augusto Sinagra (Milano: Giuffré, 2009), 190.

61. Gabriele D'Annunzio, speech of 7 October 1919, in Martini, *La Passione di Fiume*, 149.

62. Gabriele D'Annunzio, speech of 7 October 1919, in Martini, *La Passione di Fiume*, 150.

63. Laura Wittman, *The Tomb of the Unknown Soldier, Modern Mourning, and the Reinvention of the Mystical Body* (Toronto: University of Toronto Press, 2011), 37.

64. Gabriele D'Annunzio, "Annotazione," in Gabriele D'Annunzio, *Notturno* (Milano: Treves, 1921), I.
65. D'Annunzio, *Notturno*, 36.
66. D'Annunzio, *Notturno*, 36.
67. D'Annunzio, *Notturno*, 35–36.
68. D'Annunzio, *Notturno*, 26.
69. D'Annunzio, *Notturno*, 27.
70. D'Annunzio, *Notturno*, 36.
71. D'Annunzio, *Notturno*, 26.
72. D'Annunzio, *Notturno*, 27.
73. D'Annunzio, *Notturno*, 35.
74. D'Annunzio, *Notturno*, 35.
75. Mara Vittoria Modesti, "Il Modello della Coppia Eroica in Alcuni Miti dell'Epoca Arcaica" (MA diss., Universita' ca' Foscari, Venezia, 2016–2017), 32–34, http://dspace.unive.it/bitstream/handle/10579/13152/841004-1214463.pdf?sequence=2.
76. Comisso, *Le Mie Stagioni*, 72; D'Annunzio, "La Fiamma Intelligente," 172.
77. Modesti, "Il Modello della Coppia Eroica," 171.
78. D'Annunzio, *Notturno*, 35–37.
79. D'Annunzio, *Notturno*, 36.
80. Dante, *La Divinia Commedia*, Canto 26.
81. Simona Garipoli, "Neottolemo o Diomede? Sul Giovane Imberbe al Fianco di Odisseo nell'Ambasciata a Lemno," *Engramma: la Tradizione Classica nella Memoria Occidentale* 109, (Settembre 2013), http://www.engramma.it/eOS/index.php?id_articolo=1384.
82. See Paul Robinson Coleman-Norton, "Odysseus in the Iliad," *The Classical Weekly* 21, no. 10 (19 December 1927): 73–74.
83. D'Annunzio, *Notturno*, 37.
84. Homer, *The Odyssey*, trans. Robert Fagles (New York: Penguin, 1996), Book 24, 78–84.
85. Homer, *The Iliad*, trans. Robert Fagles (New York: Penguin, 1990), Book 23, 100–101.
86. Homer, *The Iliad*, Book 23, 278–85. See Jonathan S. Burgess, "Tumuli of Achilles," *Classics@ Journal* 3, no. 1 (2005), https://classics-at.chs.harvard.edu/classics3-jonathan-s-burgess-tumuli-of-achilles/.
87. Dante, *La Divinia Commedia*, Canto 26.
88. Simonelli, "La Costruzione di un Mito," 210–11.
89. Giovanni Comisso, *Le Mie Stagioni* (Milano: Longanesi, 1963), 73.
90. D'Annunzio, "La Sagra," 113.
91. D'Annunzio, "La Sagra," 113.
92. D'Annunzio, "La Sagra," 111–12.
93. Ferdinando Cordova, *Arditi e Legionari Dannunziani* (Padova: Marsilio, 1969), 2.
94. Kotchnitzky, *La Quinta Stagione*, 65.

95. Gabriele D'Annunzio, "Versilia," in *Laudi del Cielo del Mare della Terra e degli Eroi*, book III: *Alcione* (Milano: Treves, 1908), 168.
96. D'Annunzio, "La Sagra," 111.
97. Cordova, *Arditi e Legionari*, 2.
98. D'Annunzio, "La Sagra," 116–17.
99. D'Annunzio, "La Sagra," 116.
100. D'Annunzio, "La Fiamma Intelligente," 164.
101. D'Annunzio, "La Fiamma Intelligente," 164.
102. D'Annunzio, "Siete Tutti Eroi" (28 December 1920), in Giuseppe Moscati, *Le Cinque Giornate di Fiume: X Anniversario del Natale di Sangue* (Milano: Carnaro, 1930), 132–33.
103. Gabriele D'Annunzio, "Comiato tra le Tombe" (3 January 1921), in Moscati, *Le Cinque Giornate*, 170–71.
104. Gabriele D'Annunzio, speech of 2 January 1921, Moscati, *Le Cinque Giornate*, 166.
105. Freud, *Group Psychology*, 37–40.
106. Freud, *Group Psychology*, 40
107. Freud, *Group Psychology*, 56.
108. Freud, *Group Psychology*, 57.
109. Freud, *Group Psychology*, 77–80, 93.
110. Freud, *Group Psychology*, 120.
111. Freud, *Group Psychology*, 123.
112. Freud, *Group Psychology*, 96–97.
113. Freud, *Group Psychology*, 120.
114. D'Annunzio, "La Fiamma Intelligente," 171–72.
115. D'Annunzio, "La Fiamma Intelligente," 171.
116. D'Annunzio, "La Fiamma Intelligente," 171–72.
117. D'Annunzio, *Il Fuoco*, 594–96.
118. D'Annunzio, *Il Fuoco*, 595.
119. D'Annunzio, *Il Fuoco*, 596.
120. D'Annunzio, *Il Fuoco*, 611–12.
121. D'Annunzio, *Il Fuoco*, 660.
122. Simonelli, *Annunzio a Fiume*, 239.

Chapter 9

Same-Sex Desire and the Political (Dis)Order of Occupied Fiume

INTRODUCTION

In a tantalising but truncated passage from *Group Psychology and the Analysis of the Ego*, Freud declares, 'It seems certain that homosexual love is far more compatible with group ties, even when it takes the shape of uninhibited sexual tendencies—a remarkable fact, the explanation of which might carry us far.'[1] Historical examples, such as the Theban legion, may bear this out, but they do not illuminate the causal explanation Freud must have had in mind, which no doubt turned on the way he theorised the psychic structure of same-sex desire vis-à-vis heterosexual desire. In any case, it seems interesting that some of the most high-profile and less instrumentally minded of D'Annunzio's collaborators were nonabstinent same-sex attracted men.

Leon Kotchnitzky, Henry Furst, Giovanni Comisso, and Guido Keller may not be broadly representative, but they are emblematic of D'Annunzio's Fiume intellectual and political elite. Kotchnitzky and Furst had definite positions in the Exterior Relations Office of D'Annunzio's command, and Kotchnitzky directly shaped the command's policy orientations through the League of Fiume initiative. Comisso also worked in the Exterior Relations Office,[2] but without holding equivalent high-level positions. Keller had rather an indeterminate role ('action secretary'), which seemed to have been designed specifically to let him have access to D'Annunzio without involving any day-to-day tasks and responsibilities. He was a particularly powerful influence on the poet. As we saw, he had been responsible for D'Annunzio's acquisition of a formal political leadership role in Fiume. Comisso mentions that at their first meeting he and Keller talked about the abolition of ranks within the Army:[3] something similar was later reflected in the new Army regulations. Leeden also maintains that many aspects of the *Charter* reveal Keller's unmistakable influence.[4]

Kotchnitzky, Furst, Comisso, and Keller belong to the unruly camp (*'scalmanati'*) of Fiume legionnaires, some of whom contributed to the derailment of the *modus vivendi* and to the turn to the Left of the Fiume endeavour. Of course, the category of the *scalmanati* is an *ex post facto* heuristic construct. There was no single block of unruly ones, no single concerted effort to bring the revolution to Fiume and from there to Italy and the world. Nonetheless, intellectually confident and politically radical (if sometimes also politically *naïve*) men such as Kotchnitzky, Furst, Comisso, and Keller are likely to have contributed more than most to periodically reorienting the command to the Left, when moderates and conservative forces gained ground.

As I will argue in this chapter, Kotchnitzky's, Furst's, Comisso's, and Keller's aesthetic-revolutionary sensibilities were partly shaped by their experience of same-sex desire. Furthermore, given their own homoerotic investments, the discursive circulation of same-sex desire effected through D'Annunzio's speeches to the legionnaires cannot have failed to resonate keenly with them. Because of these reasons, it is not out of place to speak of homoerotic affect being partly (if indirectly) constitutive of Fiume's political (dis)order during the occupation.

SAME-SEX DESIRE IN FIUME: COMISSO AND KELLER

In a diary entry shared in secret correspondence with the War Office, dating from 1920, Lieutenant Colonel Peck reports remarks made by one Mr. Leard ('a gentleman well known to the British Mission in Fiume and frequently referred to in this Diary'): 'D'Annunzio now lived in his palace with his women. . . . The immorality, unnatural and natural in the town, was deplorable.'[5] As we know, Peck's strengths in sourcing reliable informants left something to be desired. Mr. Leard, with his outlandish claims that a 'reign of terror existed in the town',[6] is a case in point. It is interesting, nonetheless, that this diary entry suggests that Fiuman displays of homoeroticism were sufficiently open as to preoccupy observers such as Peck or Leard more keenly than their 'natural' counterpart, which gets to be mentioned only after 'immorality' of the 'unnatural' variety has gotten its due.

Beyond suggestive glimpses such as this, we do not have very concrete evidence about the treatment of same-sex desire in Fiume during the occupation. Guerri located only one court case, dating from 1920, involving two teenagers (sixteen and eighteen years old) who were charged with sexual acts against nature. No cause was found to proceed, as the crime required publicity, while the acts had occurred in what were deemed to be private circumstances (camp beds at night time).[7] It is Giovanni Comisso's memoir (*My Seasons*) and his heavily autobiographical novel (*Harbour of Love*, otherwise known as *In the Wind of the Adriatic*) that provide, alongside Kotchnitkzy's *The Fifth Season, or the Centaurs of Fiume* (discussed later), the most significant testimony about the circulation of same-sex desire among the legionnaires.

In *Harbour of Love* there are many incidents and dynamics clearly governed by or implying same-sex desire. In the first chapter we find Keller (never explicitly identified by name) rhapsodising about a young male friend shortly due to join him and Comisso; Keller's attempts at warding off the newcomer's overly enthusiastic embraces; the latter—whose 'attitude resembled that of certain Oriental women at the height of boredom'[8]—revealing in his nudity 'muscles defined by an elegant weariness';[9] and Comisso's urge to touch them being thwarted by a young *Ardito*, 'not lacking in grace',[10] who had previously stamped his kisses on Comisso's face by way of introducing himself.[11] The second chapter introduces us to a fresh-faced but knowing boy being seduced by rather effete, artistically inclined, drug-using *Arditi*[12]—who will later prove to be brave soldiers.[13] The sixth treats us to male French-kissing involving the author and a cross-dressing Sicilian *Ardito*.[14] In the eighth chapter nothing comes of the sexual tension between the writer and a boy, more notable for healthy vigour than beauty, who is still plagued by clumsiness and lack of self-knowledge ('The Chrysalis' of the chapter title).[15]

In *My Seasons*, on the other hand, the most explicit mention of same-sex love recounts the comment D'Annunzio made upon seeing, from his office window, pairs of *Arditi* walk hand in hand towards the hills one morning. 'Look at my soldiers,' the commandant said, 'they advance in couples, like the Theban Legion'.[16] Much of the testimony in *My Seasons* about the circulation of same-sex desire in Fiume is more indirect. It consists of the writer conveying his own erotic response to the male form, frequently displayed nude or seminude, through careful language choices. Thus, we have the 'Michelangelesque' bodies of *Arditi* submitting to a nurse's hands-on ministering in the venereal disease ward of Fiume hospital.[17] We also have Keller forming D'Annunzio's bodyguard by recruiting (to the horror of regular officers) undocumented young volunteers, 'intoxicated and happy', 'all extremely handsome and proud', and stark naked (they were entertaining themselves diving from moored ships). Keller's recruits would go on to march and sing about town 'in shorts and bare-chested'.[18]

Male nudity or seminudity is even more recurrent throughout *Harbour of Love*: Keller wearing only 'short, rough canvas underwear';[19] Comisso and Keller experiencing sheer bliss while sunbathing in the nude;[20] *Arditi* sleeping 'semi-naked in tents, with tangled hair covering their eyes';[21] *Arditi*, their bodies 'brown and glistening', frolicking with boys in a mountain stream, striking the writer and Keller as the most beautiful men ever;[22] and Comisso and Keller bumping into each other in the pitch dark of a cave, with no clothes on, using their hands to fully ascertain each other's identity.[23]

During the spring and summer of 1920 Comisso and Keller rented a house in the hills, subsisting largely on fruit, honey, goat milk, and, in Keller's case (who aspired to free himself of the 'stupid' need to eat), rose petals. The nature of Comisso's feelings for Keller is clearly revealed in *My Seasons* by 'the immense void' and 'anxiety' Commisso declares to have felt when Keller used to disappear for a few days.[24] The physical dimension of their relationship is more subtly conveyed where he tells of waking up in the woods to the tickling of Keller's beard on his face after one of their rides in the hills on warm spring nights.[25]

Comisso comes out as same-sex attracted only late in *My Seasons*, when he confesses to his 'curious' (but, actually, frantic) anxiety when, in 1936, he lost his twenty-something domestic helper to the latter's marriage, after having made 'a companion' of him since his teens.[26] Even more explicitly, he later reveals how he was affected, in 1945, by the death of a young intellectual he had cohabited with and mentored. 'Everywhere I was haunted and am haunted by memories of him,' he writes on the book's last page, adding that his only comfort is that 'because of him, death will be sweet to me.'[27]

Keller's partiality to male beauty is disclosed in *Harbour of Love*, where his rage at something quite inconsequential is placated by the appearance of a 'young peasant boy of such grace and beauty' as to accomplish the miracle.[28] Comisso also remarks upon Keller's indifference to females: he happily left the graces of Fiuman women to southern Italian officers enjoying freedom from the strictures they must endure at home.[29] Even apart from this, Salaris makes rather a strong case for Keller's homosexuality.[30] Nonetheless, from Comisso's own account it transpires that Keller—despite his fondness for exposing his nudity—was not happy with giving way to erotic passion: 'He would have liked to feed exclusively on fruit and flowers to conquer his tyrant—sensuality.'[31] In this ambivalent relation with their unwieldy erotic drives (albeit homosexual for Keller and heterosexual for D'Annunzio), Keller and D'Annunzio appeared to have seen eye to eye. No doubt, this was an element in the intellectual affinity that brought them together and kept them intimate during the war and the Fiume endeavour.

According to *My Seasons*, at the end of the summer of 1920 Comisso left the mountain house he shared with Keller and relocated to town, thinking he had allowed Keller too much influence over him.[32] The move back to town marks the end of his and Keller's 'dreams',[33] of what had 'perhaps' been 'the happiest summer of their lives'[34] (a feeling even more poignantly conveyed at the end of *Harbour of Love*).[35] It also marks Commisso's mood shift (perhaps due to breakup depression) towards detachment from the deteriorating situation in Fiume.[36] Tellingly, returning to town is also a 'return' to heterosexuality: his landlady is a beautiful woman with whom he has physical relations, though his interest in watching her sexual activities with the *Arditi* rather betrays his continuing attachment to male erotic objects.[37]

It is characteristic of Comisso to observe or imagine heterosexual sex or relationships as a pretext to focus on males. 'I was tormented by a lecherous desire to picture him in a sexual match', he says of a boy in *Harbour of Love*.[38] In a ballroom, where white-clad Italian sailors dance with local peasant girls, he only has eyes for the former: 'Their eyes glistened in the brown faces and the teeth flashed white between the thick lips. The solid necks and the hands resting on belts expressed strength and grace. My race looked to me lordly and marvellous.'[39] When someone comments on the local women being 'consumed' by the *Arditi*'s sexual prowess, it is not the women that his titillated imagination conjures up but 'certain men's faces, reddish-brown, almost sunshine made flesh, picked out by shadows of lust, seen in the crowd in the last hours of daylight.'[40]

Without mentioning him by name, Comisso indicates in *My Seasons* that he had first noticed Keller at the Caffé Greco in Rome, where, after D'Annunzio's speech of 4 May 1919, his eye was caught by a group of Dannunzians deeply involved in animated conversation, among whom 'one with a black goatee and voluminous black hair, eagle-eyed'.[41] This portrait is unmistakably Keller (one only needs to compare it to Kotchnitzky's description of D'Annunzio's action secretary).[42] The two properly met some months later in Fiume when, on the stairs of a hotel, they quite literally checked each other out: Comisso 'watched this man of unusual face, in which shone the sharpest black eyes, which [in turn] scanned [him] from head to toe.'[43] They did not, as one might suppose, make their way to the nearest private place: rather, they instantly and eagerly fell to talking politics (talk about sublimation!), specifically that of the Fiuman command—just then, as the two saw it, overrun with the forces of reaction.[44]

A similar transposition/sublimation/feeding of erotic desire onto/into political discourse will also connote Keller and Comisso's last exchange in Fiume, recorded in *My Seasons*. Ready to depart after the bloody Christmas, Comisso had gifted his gun to a friend, telling him that he (Comisso) was a poor shooter from a distance, while at close quarters he would choose to embrace, rather than fire at, his enemy.[45] This being a very young Comisso, this professed choice to embrace an enemy could not remotely be an allusion to Christian brotherly love, which in any case hardly admits of drawing discriminations based on the distance or proximity of the object. It is, rather, desire that feeds the sentiment, much more so that the imaginary embrace between Comisso and his adversary is immediately followed by a real one with none other than Comisso's paramour Keller, who proclaims him endowed with 'true human wisdom.'[46]

Harbour of Love has a more ironic finale. After the devastation of the bloody Christmas, Comisso finds Keller in a hotel room attempting to light a stove. The two—especially Comisso—are overcome by emotion at the thought that it is all over; Comisso even rediscovers his long-lost ability to cry. As he turns towards Keller, giving in to an urge to embrace him, he realises his friend/former lover's signature mop of black hair is interwoven with grey strands. It is also teeming with lice eggs! As they violently scrub their scalps and anxiously inspect themselves in the mirror, the two curse the *Arditi*, with whom they had recently been in close quarters.[47] The closing paragraphs rob readers of the experience of *pathos* their expectations had been slowly been built up to; but they also are cleverly irreverent in demystifying the allure of the ever-so-desirable *Arditi*—to whose *éclat* both D'Annunzio's homoerotic speeches and Comisso's own writings had made more than their fair share of contributions.

A decade later, Comisso paid a visit to his former commandant. Characteristically for him at that time in his life, the poet invited him to wander about the grounds of his fabulous Lake Garda residence, but did not receive him[48] (indeed, Comisso would never meet D'Annunzio again after Fiume).[49] The special bond between Comisso and Keller had not escaped D'Annunzio, who wrote to the former, 'Rather than me, don't you owe a visit to Keller, still intact?'[50] D'Annunzio was alluding to Keller's remains, which he had had buried on his estate after the man had died in a car accident in 1929.

In 1932 Comisso wrote to D'Annunzio that Keller was still present to him: 'I meet him old and bent in the streets of Florence or Genoa, I see him again in my dreams, I find him anew in the postures, the words, the tastes of all those who were close to him . . . I owe him much: he taught me to shed many of my childish and bourgeois flaws.'[51] Of D'Annunzio himself he would say, after his death, that 'the Fiume years he created were the most sublime of my life, those that heaved my soul free from vast debris. . . . Intoxicated with life, we touched its most extreme possibilities.'[52]

DESIRE-SUSTAINED POLITICS: *YOGA*

Although Comisso did not hold a prominent position within D'Annunzio's command, he made a more significant contribution than most to Fiuman political discourse through his editorship of the magazine *Yoga*, published during the last few months of the occupation. *Yoga* served as the mouthpiece of the eponymous association Comisso had founded with Keller, and which predated the magazine itself by some months. The members of Yoga debated the abolition of money and prisons, free sex, the beautification of urban spaces, political leadership, army organisation, and radical neo-Luddism.[53]

The first few publications associated with Yoga had a futurist flavour, born of a contingent alignment of goals between Comisso/Keller and Carli. All three aspired to rescue D'Annunzio's Fiume from the forces of the mainstream, so that it could serve as the launchpad for wider-ranging social and political change.[54] *Yoga* the magazine, however, clearly shows that Keller and Comisso's normative and aesthetic vision departed from futurist technophilia and inclined towards physiocracy, advocating Italy's rejection of industrialization and its investment in the traditional productive activities of fishing and agriculture.[55]

At one point after founding the association and before establishing the magazine, Comisso and Keller had resolved to leave Fiume. They sent a letter to D'Annunzio to explain that soon they would fly off to Russia (Keller was an aviator) 'to incite barbarians to the destruction of Europe, sure that only out of such devastation could a new spiritual force arise to give new harmony to human life.'[56] D'Annunzio wished them good luck and told them that while they had spent the summer 'perching on trees, he was in the throes of creation of a new social order that he would promulgate on the anniversary of Fiume liberation'.[57] More correspondence followed, and D'Annunzio shared a draft of the proofs of the *Charter*. This convinced the two friends to stay on, bewitched by the commandant's vision in the same way as Calypso had bewitched Ulysses, for which reason Keller took to calling D'Annunzio 'Calypso'. The decision to publish a magazine came thereafter, with Keller and Comisso feeling a certain ambivalence towards D'Annunzio after meeting him in the modest offices that were the seat of the new regency, conveying to their youthful eyes of would-be revolutionaries an unwelcome impression of bureaucratic solicitude.[58]

Keller's pre-*Yoga* writings make clear his opposition to 'modern levelling revolutions, the national concept that derives from them',[59] and the consequent 'poisonous levelling bourgeois culture'.[60] The masses had embraced these revolutions as a way of nullifying aristocratic power, which had been leading them towards 'horizons [that were] negative for their rough-hewn structure'.[61] However, it was possible (in Fiume) to transcend bourgeois conditions into a new allegiance between the popular and aristocratic classes in the name of the will to power.[62] There are some indications that, in line with D'Annunzio's resignification of 'aristocracy' as capacity for self-rule (and, before him, Plato's resignification of 'kingship' as government directed by wisdom), by 'aristocratic' Keller meant something like spiritually elevated. For, elsewhere, he wrote to D'Annunzio that those in a privileged position to respond to D'Annunzio's vision and help spread it were either 'rough-hewn men' or those 'educated by music, by art'.[63]

The writings published in *Yoga* by Keller, Comisso, and their associates are somewhat less nebulous. They are supportive and occasionally constructively critical of the regency[64] and shared in D'Annunzio's and the *Charter*'s antimaterialism,[65] often reconceived in terms of antipositivism.[66] They reject parliamentary democracy,[67] nation,[68] and the other nonautochthonous (as they saw it) bourgeois political, economic, and social forms that the Italian establishment had embraced. They advocate the leadership of an intellectual (though not bookish) and creative elite. In the name of life, beauty, and individuality this might restore the country to more consonant forms of social, political, and economic organisation.[69] These would be more responsive to contemporary needs,[70] and they would be drawn from the creative wellspring that was the spirit of the Latin race—whose distinctive attributes were the result of adaptation to the natural conditions characterising the Italian territory.[71]

There are at least two ways in which the ideas propounded in *Yoga* articulate with same-sex desire. First, on a normative level, there can be little doubt that the obsessive insistence, on the part of two same-sex attracted men such as Keller and Comisso, on valuing 'individuality' was intended to cover sexual preference. Secondly, on the normative and epistemological planes, Comisso's and Keller's commitment to antimaterialism/antipositivism cannot be separated from their same-sex desire. In a suggestive passage, Comisso critiques 'the movement of thought on an analytical and sceptical basis' and the false promise that scientific knowledge, by dissolving what is mysterious and ineffable, will set us free.[72] By way of illustration, he explains how scientific knowledge and methods reduce the human body to an organism, similar in its nature and origins to any other animal. By contrast, in the past the human body was seen as a divine miracle, and at 'other times apprehended under the pure intoxication of harmony and beauty'.[73] The wording Comisso permits himself here—'intoxication of harmony and beauty'—clearly references, in an indirect and abstract way mediated by an unmistakably homosexual sensibility, ancient Greece and the Italian Renaissance. This sensibility appears to be one of the factors overdetermining Commisso's ethicopolitical vision as articulated in *Yoga*, and particularly his antimaterialist commitments. The scientific positivism imported from northern Europe is guilty of undermining aesthetic experience, specifically in the culturally determined ways that the homoerotically charged art of ancient Greece and the Italian Renaissance enables. That alone, for Comisso, appears to be a reason—though it is not in practice his only reason—to resist positivism. In this sense, same-sex desire is one of the factors that overdetermine Comisso's antimaterialism.

The same is true of Keller's own antimaterialism, which, as in Comisso, takes the form of opposition to analytic/scientific/positivist thought. Keller abhorred Germanic discipline, which he believed reduced the population to a 'mechanical value, like a zipline' and 'killed the virtue to be found in miracles';[74] he called for a 'discipline governed by feeling'.[75] In a lyrical piece of writing published in *Yoga*, Keller says that he would rather not know what 'these terrible men, as scientists are regarded by poets,' may have to say about the causes of such irrational and extrasensory experiences as *déjà vu*. For Keller, such experiences convey to us a sense of transcendence, the feeling that we can defy the materialist truth of our own mortality. As another such extrasensory experience, Keller mentions 'the soul [which] after an hour of lovemaking, lies regarding itself in the twilight of its languor.'[76] Given his sexual preferences, it is not an overinterpretation to suggest that, phenomenologically, it was specifically same-sex love that Keller had in mind when he credited love making for inducing the combination of physical torpor and hyperawareness that challenges scientific organicism, with its insistence on our finitude. Thus, Keller's antimaterialism too appears to have something important to do with same-sex desire. Acting upon same-sex desire enables, in its aftermath, a kind of transcendence that is threatened by scientific discourse and knowledge—which we had therefore better reject in the name of human flourishing. Same-sex eroticism is not the only transcendental experience that refutes, or is treated as a reason for refuting, scientific positivism and organicism, but it is paradigmatic enough that Keller gives it as the very first example of such experiences. As with Comisso, same-sex desire overdetermines Keller's normative and epistemological commitments.

SAME-SEX DESIRE IN FIUME: KOTCHNITZKY AND FURST

Léon Kotchnitzky and American writer Henry Furst were Communist sympathisers who were drawn to Fiume by the prospect of promoting radical Left revolutionary goals. Furst would sometimes argue about these with D'Annunzio to the point of exasperating him.[77] Neither Kotchnitzky's nor Furst's homosexuality are in doubt. Both seem to be examples of the kind of politically aware man (such as E. M. Forster) whose same-sex desire is one of the factors overdetermining his commitment to interclass solidarity and his admiration of workers' comradeship.

I have already had reason to mention Kotchnitzky—driving force behind the League of Fiume—on several occasions. By the time he joined D'Annunzio's special secretariat in Fiume in autumn 1919, he had been in Italy for eleven years, where he had undertaken his studies.[78] Kotchnitzky resigned from his position in the special secretariat during the events connected to the *modus vivendi*. Even before the Fiumans had voted in the referendum that D'Annunzio proceeded to annul, Kotchnitzky declared that they had made their will clear; he was uncomfortable with actions that were afoot to thwart the popular will.[79] Later, however, when De Ambris became the new head of cabinet and the Exterior Relations Office was formally instituted within D'Annunzio's command, Kotchnitzky assumed its direction.

Comisso conveys Kotchnitzky's homosexuality by stating that he 'did not particularly appreciate women's legs'.[80] One of the Belgian's letters to D'Annunzio enclosed 'a few withered violets, picked for you, the other day, in Rome, on John Keats's grave'[81]—an homage, among other things, to the scene in D'Annunzio's *Pleasure* taking place in the Protestant cemetery. As we have seen, in the relevant passage D'Annunzio studiously references the English Romantics' entanglements with same-sex desire.

As to Furst, who was educated at Yale and Oxford and had served two years in the British Army,[82] he was an idealist who dreamed of the advent of an egalitarian society without government. He had written to D'Annunzio to offer his services as translator and secretary, and the poet had welcomed him in Fiume. The commandant had made ample use of Furst's skills for the purpose of foreign propaganda, despite objections from some military quarters, who looked askance at his penchant for visiting homosexual *milieux* of ill repute.[83]

Kotchnitzky's account of D'Annunzio's Fiume is particularly evocative of the atmosphere during the occupation, though it is important to remind oneself that what the young Belgian experienced as the legionnaires' vitality, earnestness, idealism, and spontaneity may well have come across to different demographics in town as swagger, intimidation, fanaticism, and hooliganism. There are four references to homoerotic love in Kotchnitzky's account, which provide evidence of the circulation of same-sex desire in Fiume. All are coded and literary, but unmistakable.

The first occurs when Kotchnitzky paints a portrait of Furst—a friend of his, Keller's, and Comisso's.[84] Kotchnitzky does not mention Furst's sexual habits, but in a passage praising the American's professional skills and recording their friendship, he tells of their outings in the countryside, and of the local peasants calling them 'the Englishmen'. Kotchnitzky then alludes to the nature of his relationship with Furst through a literary analogy: the peasants who marvel at the foreigners admiring a landscape to them so familiar and unremarkable are not unlike 'the fishermen of one-hundred years ago who looked at two other "Englishmen" passing by: Byron and Shelley.'[85]

The second allusion to homosexuality is a reference to Boccaccio's irreverent collection of tales, *Decameron*, whose story 'V 10' deals with same-sex sexual activity and/or bisexual group sex.[86] Speaking of Comisso and Keller's rented mountain house, Kotchnitzky mentions that he and Furst used to spend whole nights there with the two Italians, 'improvising the most unusual *decameroni*'.[87]

The third literary allusion to same-sex desire is slightly more explicit, through a reference to Plato's *Symposium* and the myth narrated by

Aristophane within it. According to this, humans were first created as four-armed, four-legged, two-headed beings—either male-male, female-female, or female-male. Only later where these natural couplings split into halves, and ever since everyone seeks to be rejoined to their missing half, accordingly displaying a preference either for the same or a different sex. In reminiscing about the unforgettable Festival of Saint Vito, Fiume's patron saint, Kotchnitzky recalls how 'you could see soldiers, sailors, women, citizens spinning in dishevelled embraces to the rhythm of military fanfares, finding anew the triple diversity of primitive couples praised by Aristophanes'.[88]

Finally, in concluding his roundup of ten notable Fiume personalities (among whom Keller and Furst) in a section of the book called 'Fiume's Medals', Kotchnitzky teasingly reworks D'Annunzio's famous lines about the tenth *corporazione* in the *Carnaro Charter*:

> The tenth medal is made of bronze.
>
> The tenth medal bears no name, no motto, no profile: no figure, whether living or inanimate: it is the devotional vow, the divine and shining circle, the image of a star, the metal disc that hit the violet temple of the young Hyacinth.[89]

This time the literary reference is to Apollo's love for the youth Hyacinth, whom the god accidentally killed during a game of discus throwing, and out of whose spilt blood the hyacinth flower grew.[90] The medal bearing 'no name' seems an allusion to the status of sodomy as the nameless vice, while the 'devotional vow' might reference the kind of virtuous same-sex bonds instantiated in idealised *erastes-eromenos* relationships, or in famously steadfast and devoted male friendships that had become code for same-sex desire in the literary universe of cultivated European homosexuals in the nineteenth and early twentieth centuries.[91] For Kotchnitzky, homosexuality was apparently the tenth notable Fiuman personality deserving of a medal.

DESIRE-SUSTAINED POLITICS: KOTCHNITZKY AND D'ANNUNZIO

In addition to being indirectly referenced through literary allusions, same-sex desire colours Kotchnitzky's account of the Fiume endeavour in *The Fifth Season*. An example is in the last few pages of the book, where Kotchnitzky confesses that he sometimes feels a pang of intense nostalgia for D'Annunzio's Fiume. Kotchnitzky conjures up what was for him the quintessential character of occupied Fiume through the simple images of a crowd in the beflagged square, of D'Annunzio's voice addressing it through the clear air, and of 'handsome', 'bronze-voiced *Arditi*'.[92] Clearly, the political dimension (symbolised by the people in the crowded square and D'Annunzio's public speeches) and aesthetic/erotic one (symbolised by the handsome *Arditi*) are not readily separable in Kotchnitzky's recollection of the experience—at least not on the affective level.

Kotchnitzky's flattering portrait of Keller is also pervaded by homoerotic appreciation. Kotchnitzky has many words of praise for Keller's oratorial and logistical skills, his decisiveness, his integrity, and his commitment to the oppressed and marginalised.[93] But he also lovingly describes the 'immense mass of black hair, almost blue, the thick and dark beard, the warm look, the incredibly long eyelashes'; the profile that, rather than being aquiline, 'the eagle vainly attempts to imitate';[94] and the 'agile and handsome body', which Keller is fond of exposing naked to the sunshine.[95] The fact that Kotchnitzky considers it important to expatiate on these details alongside all the attributes that speak to Keller's political *bravura* once again suggests that his admiration for the latter shades into desire, and that desire feeds into his admiration.

This is even more apparent in Kotchnitzky's treatment of D'Annunzio himself. Kotchnitzky represents D'Annunzio as a potential object of (apparently) male love, when, wondering about his lack of true friends and confidants, he asks: 'Where are the companions of the darkest hours, the confessors of secret thoughts, . . . those who approach him neither out admiration, nor calculation, nor curiosity, nor even *love* [but] simply out of their own affection for him?'[96] More significantly, Kotchnitzky literally waxes lyrical about the unforgettable 'accents of [D'Annunzio's] voice', the bewitching 'measure of his inflections, melodious and yet distinctly uttered'.[97] Of himself Kotchnitzky confesses,

> I am utterly 'fiumanised', as they say. . . . I breathe in the glow that radiates from Gabriele D'Annunzio . . . by now I am nothing but an instrument without will, a tool that neither feels nor sees in the hands of the wondrous craftsman. . . . Such a deferent epigonism has nothing within it to lower or demean me; whether actor or spectator, comrade or observer, follower or daring witness I infinitely rejoice in seeing what I see, hearing what I hear, being who I am.[98]

Kotchnitzky assimilated with deliberation and self-awareness D'Annunzio's infectious style. This is especially apparent in a confidential note sent to the Belgian minister for foreign affairs one month after joining D'Annunzio's occupation. With respect to Belgian politicians' fears of Bolshevism and their suspicions of Fiume's connections with it, he wrote, *'Mais je connais la mentalité vaguement cagoyesque de certain hommes de gouvernement'.*[99] Apparently, Kotchnitzky assumed that the minister should understand (or he did not care that the minister would not understand) his own French rendition (*'cagoyesque'*) of an adjective based on D'Annunzio's irreverent nickname for Nitti (Cagoia).

Finally, as with Keller and Commisso, Kotchnitzky espouses an antipositivistic epistemological stance, which he uses to buttress his political commitment to securing an Italian future for Fiume. And, as with Commisso and Keller, this antipositivism is tinged with homoerotically suggestive images:

> Should we now appeal to figures, statistics, formal logic, oratorial tropes, to demonstrate that Fiume is Italian? It is unnecessary to argue, to persuade, to reason in order to resolve what is essentially an affective problem, where the relevant data are: subtlety of intuition, sensibility, passion; so much the worse for you, who toy with *expertises*, plebiscites, arithmetic and sociological formulae. . . . A stroll around the town is far more instructive. . . . Some handsome youths, dark eyes and slicked hair, tease a girl who quickly moves along, modelled by a typical Rialto fringed shawl; then three monks appear, and the girl and youths metaphorically 'touch wood' [in the quintessentially Italian ways], she by arranging her fingers into a pair of horns, they by ascertaining their own virility [that is, by grabbing their own testicles]. Wilson should have really sent his experts here, in the old town. But would they have understood?[100]

There is no doubting the integrity of Kotchnitzky's political commitments. When he felt he could no longer work towards the League of Fiume, and that the project was being irreparably hijacked by other elements in the command, he resigned and left town. It does not seem, therefore, that his desire—whether for Keller, the *Arditi*, Furst, D'Annunzio himself, or handsome dark-eyed slicked-haired groin-touching young Fiumans—distorted his political judgement. It rather sustained and intensified his political activism, insofar as D'Annunzio's Fiume offered a social *milieu* remarkably conducive to the sublimation of desire into political commitment. But Kotchnitzky only indulged in these desire-driven political activities while the circumstances appeared to justify his doing so.

On the eve of his departure he wrote to the poet that he had been a 'lifeless utensil, an inanimate object' for ten months; to be himself again he had to leave: 'There isn't enough light for me, in your shadow.'[101] Shortly before, Kotchnitzky had written to D'Annunzio to decry the political class 'whose pleasure it is to destroy' Italy's architectural heritage and to erect 'shitty' (*'stercoraire'*) monuments, urging the poet to continue to defend the ideals of culture and justice: 'your responsibility before the dead and the living is terrible.'[102] We have seen that D'Annunzio's conception of and concern with same-sex desire was mediated through Graeco-Roman and Italian Renaissance literary and figurative sources. Likewise, it is easy to intuit that Kotchnitzky's Italophilia and his devotion to D'Annunzio's cult of beauty as a central political value were in part impelled by the integrity of same-sex desire to the Graeco-Roman and Italian artistic heritage.

CODA: KELLER AND D'ANNUNZIO

Keller played a crucial role in the Fiume endeavour. Correspondence dating from 1919 shows that even before the occupation, Keller was something of a driving force in subversive plots with elements of the Army for actions (never undertaken) in Istria and Dalmatia, about which he kept D'Annunzio informed.[103] It is of interest that at this time Keller had already taken to calling D'Annunzio 'Commandant',[104] casting the poet into a role that he had yet concretely to assume (though the request from Fiume to lead its Army had already reached D'Annunzio one month before).

We know that Fiume became known for having institutionalised, through its *Coup de Main* Office, the practice of unlawful and forcible appropriation of provisions required for the occupation, often at the expense of regular Italian armed forces. But Keller had been the author of the original *coup de main*. It was thanks to him that the abortion of the Ronchi march was averted, when he forcibly 'requisitioned' the necessary means of transportation from an Army depot, after those whose use had been planned failed to materialise at the last minute.[105]

Although the extent of this is not generally and fully appreciated, Keller had a particular sway over D'Annunzio. As we saw, it was Keller who convinced the poet to assume political power in Fiume after the 'sacred entry'. Later, when D'Annunzio's choice of a new head of cabinet fell upon De Ambris, Keller appears to have influenced, if not completely determined, that decision. He wrote to D'Annunzio that it was necessary to 'come by degrees to the wisdom of the soldier and the workman', and De Ambris would be 'the ideal instrument'.[106]

There is a pattern, in Keller's correspondence with D'Annunzio during and after the occupation, of his attempts at prodding the poet into decisive, clear-cut, daring action, occasionally perhaps through subtle manipulation. Thus, when D'Annunzio was negotiating with the Italian government about a possible compromise that might see an end to the occupation—the *modus vivendi*—Keller wrote to D'Annunzio, 'Grave events are about to occur due to the overexcitement of misinformed souls. It is necessary to issue immediately a clear-cut and precise *ordre du jour*'.[107] Keller opposed the compromise, and in reality he may well have been among those responsible for spreading misinformation in order to thwart it. Here he may have attempted to get D'Annunzio to publicly commit himself to reject the compromise on the basis of possible disturbances that Keller may have been either exaggerating or himself have engineered.

As a rule, however, Keller was quite candid in letting D'Annunzio know what he thought best and in volunteering his advice. In a letter probably dating from the time of the immediate aftermath of the *modus vivendi*, he warned D'Annunzio of bitter rivalries within his command, as well as a general weariness—borne of an 'inability to pursue perfection'—which might lead to mutiny. He recommended reducing 'the military part to a minimum' and indicated which men could be trusted, and which ones were promising, so long as their 'prejudices of caste and Nation' were stamped out, and they were made to mingle with the indigenous environments of Fiume, which Keller believed to be an inextinguishable wellspring for D'Annunzio's programme.[108]

Particularly notable are Keller's attempts—which spanned several years—to get D'Annunzio to embark upon new projects in the interest of the Adriatic cause after the conclusion of Fiume's occupation. D'Annunzio declared that he now aspired to be 'a leader without partisans and a commander without followers'.[109] In response, no doubt, to a missive from Keller where the latter had rather gone overboard in pressuring him, D'Annunzio wrote, 'I wonder at your advice. My freedom can neither be understood nor grasped.'[110] Keller did not fail to convey his disappointment at such responses. In 1922 he wrote: 'My faith fades into monotony. My wing is too beautiful. Other skies. Others boundaries. I leave. The god is lost in Rome. The Magician [namely, D'Annunzio] in the enchantment of Myth.'[111] And seven years later: 'Your pleasure is perhaps to see me shorn of my wings and imprisoned—I live with burning-hearted youth—among the gold of your laurels [namely, at D'Annunzio's Vittoriale residence] I found twilight, not dawn . . . the secret of triumph is in the beauty of a conquered Adversary.'[112] There are instances, too, of Keller regretting his rash words to D'Annunzio and spending a sleepless night 'full of torment' reading and rereading D'Annunzio's own.[113]

If exchanges such as these quiver with unspoken recriminations—of betrayal, failure to understand, possessiveness—and with the bitterness and remorse reminiscent of the emotional dynamics between parting lovers or former lovers, it is because there was a distinctly erotic tension between D'Annunzio and Keller. Unlike the unilateral erotic investment on Kotchnitzky's part, this tension appears to have been bilateral, and it arguably explains why Keller seems to have had more influence over D'Annunzio than just about any other man.

In a letter penned in Fiume probably in late 1919, possibly under the influence of drugs, Keller writes to D'Annunzio that the better he learns to appreciate the poet's 'Spirit', the more he feels as if 'in the presence of platonic love for the creature of dreams made real though sheer force of will'. He then explains how he did his best to surround D'Annunzio in Fiume with men most endowed with 'beauty of form and intellect', rivals who became sick with Keller's own malady (his lovesickness). This, Keller clarifies, was all in a quest to excel among them and to be D'Annunzio's chosen one.[114] The imagery here echoes D'Annunzio's own homoerotic musings about Leonardo's and Socrates's disciples in his novels. Keller goes on to reveal how, being able to fully grasp the magnitude of D'Annunzio's spirit, he experienced a state of grace, which nonetheless resulted in self-loathing and an urge for self-destruction, due to his inability to give himself up to such grace and to translate it into words.[115] It all sounds so over the top that one almost suspects Keller having a laugh at D'Annunzio's expense, perhaps betting with Comisso that the poet's oversized ego would lead him to take the letter entirely seriously. Yet Keller's intentions probably were serious: this kind of metaphysical language and exaggerated style is characteristic of him, and any difference between this letter and Keller's other writings is merely one of degree.

Keller's professed 'platonic love' for D'Annunzio is corroborated in other correspondence. In a number of letters and messages Keller makes a point to reference Ornitio—the minor wind god that is the most explicit symbol of homoerotic love in D'Annunzio's novels. On one occasion he talks of his usual visit to Gardone, where D'Annunzio's Vittoriale residence is located, 'on the wind of Ornitio'.[116] On another, he refers to a visit he had paid (or intended to pay) there 'to renew the invitation for the feast of sunshine and sky' and says, even more cryptically, that 'Ornitio alone would have spoken amidst the foliage'.[117] On yet another occasion he sends D'Annunzio a photograph of himself naked, impersonating Triton; the gift is addressed to Ariel (a spirit of the air in Shakespeare's *The Tempest*) from Ornitio.[118] Lastly, in a letter sent from Turkey, Keller says to have entrusted Ornitio with a 'naked scimitar' for D'Annunzio, adding that he had got hold of an airplane which he would like to use to abduct the poet and encase him 'in a crystal at the top of the Himalaya'. He finishes this letter with, 'Will it [presumably, the peak of the Himalaya] be for me alone? Are you going to stay [at the Vittoriale]?'[119]

Another piece of recurrent imagery in correspondence between the two is a 'divine bunch of grapes',[120] with all its bacchic connotations of Roman decadence. Apparently, when D'Annunzio was in Ronchi, ready to depart for Fiume in the morning, but suffering from a high temperature, Keller had brought him some grapes. D'Annunzio had declined to eat them. In correspondence dating from the 1920s, up to 1926, D'Annunzio keeps urging Keller to bring him those grapes again;[121] in one such communication he complains that he is again afflicted with 'the high fever of Ronchi'.[122] Perhaps the grapes stand for cocaine, which both Keller and D'Annunzio are said to have consumed in Fiume. But it does not strain credibility to read the metaphor instead as erotically suggestive, particularly in the context of such lines from D'Annunzio as 'I embrace you with the consent of my woman, Melancholy' (implying that the two men's embrace might be such as to alarm a possessive female lover)[123] or 'I'm so tetchy tonight that it doesn't even please me to be with a nocturnal comrade like you. I don't know if you are the same Guido Keller as of that night'.[124]

More explicit is a letter from Keller where he reproaches D'Annunzio for having lost his faith in love. Warning the poet not to 'destroy love', Keller continues:

> Let us lie with abandon on the pillows before the Androgyne—look at him: it's Giorgio—let me kiss him as I used to do in the car of Ronchi, when we would drive up to the Vittoriale in the evening, under the stars. . . . If you 'love me faithfully' [here quoting D'Annunzio's words] the God of Miracles is in me and I shall know how to give you once again the grapes of Ronchi. . . . Do you doubt me? Then be generous and give me the Poison that Releases—I will know how to take it in Tiberius' Island next to Ephy Lovatelli's [illegible] and then vanish into the Vesuvius, carried by the wings of Hadrian and Giorgio.[125]

The reference to the grapes of Ronchi here is enmeshed within a veritable web of decadent images. On the one hand, these point to one of D'Annunzio's literary and artistic preoccupations, the Androgyne. On the other hand they involve unmistakably homoerotic reminiscences (Keller kissing one Giorgio under the stars) and employ the homoerotic *topoi* of Hadrian and Capri. For more than two decades homosexual expats from northern Europe had been flocking to Capri. These included, most notably, Ephy Lovatelli's intimate and notorious friend Jacques d'Adelswärd-Fersen. Two thousand years previously, the island had also been the chosen setting for the pleasure-filled pasttimes of boy-loving Emperor Tiberius. Hadrian had reigned almost one hundred years later, and his love for the beautiful Antinous was no less legendary than Tiberius's purportedly debauched romps. (Notably, D'Annunzio, in addition to referring to Antinous frequently in his *oeuvre*, installed a marble bust of the beautiful youth in the gardens of the Vittoriale.) Keller's letter is remarkable not only for compressing all of this homoerotic heritage and imagery into a single passage but also for treating D'Annunzio as a knowing audience and for making him figure as a witness to his homoerotic encounters with Giorgio.

The most direct piece of evidence that D'Annunzio may, after all, have experimented with same-sex sexual activities is in another undated letter from Keller. It was written from the Grand Hotel, presumably in Gardone, where Keller was waiting for D'Annunzio's message (probably to give him permission to visit him at the Vittoriale). The letter, titled 'September Moon', contains an explicit invitation for D'Annunzio: 'Let's seek out Enrico to eat him greedily together, as we wait for the Magic with some Mountain figs.'[126] Mountain figs might be an allusion to sexual favours to be obtained from local peasant women from the hills surrounding the lake: the feminised version of 'fig', in Italian, is a crude word for vagina. If that remains uncertain, the metaphor of Keller and D'Annunzio treating Enrico as food to feast on is unmistakably sexual in nature.

After Keller's fatal car accident, D'Annunzio ignored his wishes on the disposal of his remains and had them brought to the Vittoriale. There Keller rests with eight other 'heroes' and Fiuman legionnaires. Their tombs surround D'Annunzio's own, in the open air art deco mausoleum that commands a 270-degree vista over cypress-clad hills and the sparkling blue waters of Lake Garda.

CONCLUSIONS

The presence and activities of such men as Furst, Kotchnitzky, and Keller in occupied Fiume are not accidental. It is not the sexual freedom that occupied Fiume became famous for that explains their presence—if anything, it is the other way round: their presence contributed to characterise occupied Fiume as sexually free. Nor does the mere fact that Fiume was a laboratory for social experimentation and revolutionary politics explain their formal or informal (but either way significant) involvement in those social and political experiments. Rather, their presence and involvement can be best understood (partly) in light of the way in which D'Annunzio had discursively woven same-sex desire into the fabric of the endeavour.

Educated men such as Comisso, Furst, Kotchnitzky, and Keller were just the kind of audience who could descry and intimately respond to—with more self-awareness than most of those who came under the spell of D'Annunzio's words—the homoerotic subtext in D'Annunzio's Fiume speeches and prewar writings. While D'Annunzio's sensibility and theirs may not have been quite identical, they easily communicated, sharing certain affective and aesthetic commitments (compare Comisso and Keller's impassioned advocacy for an agrarian economy and D'Annunzio's horrors of factories, and his idealisation of the peasantry relative to the urban working classes; or consider D'Annunzio and Kotchnitzky rhapsodising about the beauty of the *Arditi*). This also means that, while D'Annunzio fancied he had made the legionnaires in his own image, and Kotchnitzky fancied that he was utterly Fiumanised in the sense of being an instrument of D'Annunzio's own will, in reality a process of mutual influences was at play.

Beyond whatever chance Furst's, Kotchnitzky's, and Keller's formal roles gave them of influencing the political course of the Fiume endeavour, men such as they and Comisso contributed not only to the mood of contestation by which Dannunzian Fiume became known but also to aesthetic and affective orientations to which D'Annunzio himself cannot have been insensible. Consider for instance Keller's creation of *La Disperata*—the *Arditi of the Guard* that he trained to become D'Annunzio's bodyguard. Comisso comments on the extreme beauty of the *Arditi of the Guard*, implying that it was one of Keller's conscious recruitment criteria. With D'Annunzio accepting their services and going about his tasks in closer physical proximity to them than with virtually any of the other legionnaires, the experience cannot have failed to consolidate and feed into D'Annunzio's own aesthetic idealisation of the *Arditi*, on which in turn are based some of the homoerotic investments transpiring from his speeches to the legionnaires.

It must be stressed that the homoerotically charged *milieu* to which Furst's, Kotchnitzky's, Keller's, and Comisso's sensibilities contributed, and which facilitated the discursive circulation of same-sex desire in D'Annunzio's Fiume speeches, had as its precondition D'Annunzio's own queer sensibility. This has been near-ubiquitously neglected in the literature. I have already enlarged on this, but one last piece of evidence will bring home its significance, by highlighting the very different rhetorical spaces inhabited by D'Annunzio and some of his ideological competitors—futurists Carli and Marinetti.

First, recall D'Annunzio's subtly but unmistakably homoerotic references to the *Arditi*'s open collars in 'The Festival of all Flames', discussed in the previous chapter. It is through this eroticisation of the bodies of the legionnaires—primarily via a vision of open uniforms exposing their bare necks—that the speech conveys the desire-based nature of the bond between them and the commandant, resulting in the 'act of life' that produces/is the *Charter*. Now compare D'Annunzio's use and purpose of homoerotic imagery in this speech to one that Marinetti addressed to the *Arditi*, as well as to several writings by Carli, also so addressed. All of these make reference to the open coats of the *Arditi*, but to altogether different effect from 'The Festival of all Flames'. Here is Marinetti:

> The open collar is prelude to an audacious stripping of your shirt the better to box, or to save a drowning man.
>
> Free neck of the strong man who creates. Neck free of idiotic ties. Athletic neck that makes society's collar burst.
>
> Beautiful, triumphant mafia of Italy's *Arditi* who love beautiful women and conquer them like trenches with a heroic gesture.[127]

And here is Carli (referring to the institution of the *Arditi* corps): 'It was necessary to gather and make recognisable through an emblem these one-hundred-thousand hidden forces, stifled within the buttoned-up coat. The coat was opened wide, and the heart of these brave ones opened up.'[128] Again, in the statute of the *Arditi* Association: 'The bold youths who opened wide their soldiers' coats to afford more breathing space to their brave hearts, will lead every new struggle . . .'[129]

In both Marinetti and Carli, any sensuality that the imagery of open collars or open coats might suggest is immediately tempered, if not quite nipped in the bud, through references to noble deeds and feelings (saving a drowning man, brave hearts). This is not surprising with respect to the father of futurism. A younger Marinetti may have been comfortable toying with explicit same-sex imagery when declaring of Wagner that 'willingly, out of love, I would lay myself down with him on a bed of clouds, so much am I enamoured with him, right down to the most hidden heart strings of my very being'.[130] But by 1918 Marinetti's homophobia had fully congealed and given proof of itself in *L'Isola dei Baci: Romanzo Erotico-Sociale*, a novella coauthored with Bruno Corra. This is notable as much for the deployment of tired *clichés* about homosexuality as for the authors' own self-consciously masculine posturing. No wonder that, just to be on the safe side, Marinetti quickly neutralises the homoerotic suggestiveness of the image of the *Arditi*'s open collars via an explicit mention of violent heterosexual conquest. The same rhetorical heterosexualising device is also apparent in Carli's Manifesto of the Futurist *Ardito*, where a description of the *Ardito*'s physical characteristics—including 'sensual and energetic mouth, ready to kiss furiously' and 'slimness of lean muscles, shot through with bundles of ultra-sensitive nerves'[131]—is followed by this injunction: 'Love frantically both speed and beautiful women.'[132]

Conversely, D'Annunzio's 'The Festival of All Flames', through a deft use of indefiniteness ('more or less open uniforms'), conveys a subtle homoeroticism that, paradoxically, hinges on its own inarticulation and is amplified by being further rarefied, through the use of metaphors involving flames and smouldering (m)embers, steadfastly avoiding its recuperation into either the respectability of conventionally noble deeds or heterosexuality. D'Annunzio's speech also complicates the crude gendered representation of martial virtues that had been characteristic of wartime rhetoric across Europe, which had insisted on the opposition between virile heroic soldiers and effeminate deserters. D'Annunzio does so by likening the legionnaires' bodies to both delicate flowers and incorporeal flames. D'Annunzio has been recently accused of participating in this pan-European wartime discourse,[133] but in fact the imagery of his Fiume speeches is startingly disruptive of its gendered tropes.

The practices established under his leadership in Fiume had a similarly disruptive effect. Kotchnitzky tells of the springtime mountainside or seaside drills in which D'Annunzio mingled with his youthful legionnaires and of their return when, adorned with an abundance of greenery and pink and white blooms, rank was forgotten in the Dionysian and bucolic mood.[134] Nor did D'Annunzio's office, as commandant in Fiume, renounce the 'aesthetic attributes' that coarser minds might consider unfit of heroic masculinity and authoritative leadership: from incense burning, through rare books, to roses in crystal vases, slowly shedding their petals.[135]

In his recent book, Simonelli quotes from a private letter sent by Carli to D'Annunzio to show that the counterpart to discourses of martial virility shared by the poet was a crude homophobia. Simonelli notes how D'Annunzio called Italian troops' withdrawal from Albania an act of 'self-emasculation' and reports what Carli, on the heel of that, wrote privately to the poet. Carli commented that 'these eunuchs [the Italian government who had ordered the withdrawal] want to castrate us, to make us all like them. But our balls choke-full of virility will spurt . . . their reserves of ammunitions on the backside of these vile pederasts'.[136] The implication is that D'Annunzio welcomed or partook in the joke, and hence its homophobia: Simonelli writes, 'The goliardic and derogatory reference to homosexuality remain confined to a private outburst. [But] it is worthy of note, despite recent representations of D'Annunzio's Fiume as a place of "free love".' Simonelli calls these representations a 'myth grafted onto the myth' of Fiume.[137]

But this amounts to indicting D'Annunzio's sexual politics for something someone else (Carli) said. Considering that homosexual men draw (at least) as much pleasure from their penises and testicles as heterosexual men do, D'Annunzio's metaphor of self-emasculation is no more homophobic than if he had said, 'shooting oneself in the foot'. In contrast with Simonelli's reading, what is most notable about the exchange is that the homophobia is wholly confined to Carli.[138] Far from indicating that D'Annunzio's discourse of martial virility has homophobic overtones, the exchange that Simonelli draws attention to confirms the point I made earlier: unlike the futurists Marinetti and Carli, D'Annunzio's celebration of virility does not partake in the mainstream gendered and heteronormative renditions of that discourse circulating during wartime. This fact helps explain the presence and important role played by such men as Kotchnitzky, Furst, Keller, and Comisso in the Fiume endeavour, as well as the intellectual, affective, and aesthetic synergies between them and the commandant. Curiously, these synergies made the discursive circulation of same-sex desire foundational to the political (dis) order of D'Annunzio's Fiume.

NOTES

1. Sigmund Freud, *Group Psychology and the Analysis of the Ego*, trans. James Strachey (London: Hogarth, 1949), 123.

2. Letter from L. Kotchnitzky to G. D'Annunzio (3 July 1920), Fondazione Il Vittoriale degli Italiani, Archivio Fiumano, Kotchnitzky, Léon, 1–129.

3. Giovanni Comisso, *Le Mie Stagioni* (Milano: Longanesi, 1957), 57.

4. Michael A. Leeden, *The First Duce* (Baltimore and London: John Hopkins University Press, 1977), 144.

5. Fiume: Diary of the British Military Mission, Fiume (12–18 January 1920), The National Archives, WO 106/853.

6. Fiume: Diary of the British Military Mission, Fiume (12–18 January 1920), The National Archives, WO 106/853.

7. Giordano Bruno Guerri, *Disobbedisco: Cinquecento Giorni di Rivoluzione. Fiume 1919–1920* (Milano: Mondadori, 2019), 102–3.

8. Giovanni Comisso, *Al Vento dell'Adriatico*, second edition (Torino: Ribet, 1928), 17.

9. Comisso, *Al Vento dell'Adriatico*, 16.

10. Comisso, *Al Vento dell'Adriatico*, 14.+

11. Comisso, *Al Vento dell'Adriatico*, 9–19.

12. Comisso, *Al Vento dell'Adriatico*, 20–39.

13. Comisso, *Al Vento dell'Adriatico*, 157–58.

14. Comisso, *Al Vento dell'Adriatico*, 98–99.

15. Comisso, *Al Vento dell'Adriatico*, 119–34.

16. Comisso, *Le Mie Stagioni*, 72.

17. Comisso, *Le Mie Stagioni*, 70–71.

18. Comisso, *Le Mie Stagioni*, 58.

19. Comisso, *Al Vento dell'Adriatico*, 73.

20. Comisso, *Al Vento dell'Adriatico*, 81.

21. Comisso, *Al Vento dell'Adriatico*, 104.

22. Comisso, *Al Vento dell'Adriatico*, 114–15.

23. Comisso, *Al Vento dell'Adriatico*, 116–17.

24. Comisso, *Le Mie Stagioni*, 74–75.

25. Comisso, *Le Mie Stagioni*, 75.

26. Comisso, *Le Mie Stagioni*, 398–99.

27. Comisso, *Le Mie Stagioni*, 502.

28. Comisso, *Al Vento dell'Adriatico*, 85–86.

29. Comisso, *Al Vento dell'Adriatico*, 93–94.

30. Claudia Salaris, *Alla Festa della Rivoluzione: Artisti e Libertari con D'Annunzio a Fiume* (Bologna: Il Mulino, 2002), 184–85.

31. Comisso, *Le Mie Stagioni*, 233.

32. Comisso, *Le Mie Stagioni*, 92.

33. Comisso, *Le Mie Stagioni*, 92.

34. Comisso, *Le Mie Stagioni*, 99.

35. Comisso, *Al Vento dell'Adriatico*, 155–56.

36. Comisso, *Le Mie Stagioni*, 93.

37. Comisso, *Le Mie Stagioni*, 92–93.

38. Comisso, *Al Vento dell'Adriatico*, 126.

39. Comisso, *Al Vento dell'Adriatico*, 67.

40. Comisso, *Al Vento dell'Adriatico*, 26.
41. Comisso, *Le Mie Stagioni*, 34.
42. Léon Kotchnitzky, *La Quinta Stagione: O, I Centauri di Fiume*, trans. Alberto Luchini (Bologna: Zanichelli, 1922), 173.
43. Comisso, *Le Mie Stagioni*, 57.
44. Comisso, *Le Mie Stagioni*, 57.
45. Comisso, *Le Mie Stagioni*, 101–2.
46. Comisso, *Le Mie Stagioni*, 102.
47. Comisso, *Al Vento dell'Adriatico*, 154–59.
48. Comisso, *Le Mie Stagioni*, 330.
49. Letter from G. Comisso to G. Maroni (8 March 1938), Fondazione Il Vittoriale degli Italiani, Archivio Generale, Comisso, Giovanni, VIII, 5.
50. Comisso, *Le Mie Stagioni*, 330.
51. Letter from G. Comisso to G. D'Annunzio (5 January [or July] 1932), Fondazione Il Vittoriale degli Italiani, Archivio Generale, Comisso, Giovanni, VIII, 5.
52. Letter from G. to G. Maroni (8 March 1938), Fondazione Il Vittoriale degli Italiani, Archivio Generale, Comisso, Giovanni, VIII, 5.
53. Comisso, *Le Mie Stagioni*, 84–85.
54. Simonetta Bartolini, *"Yoga": Sovversivi e Rivoluzionari con D'Annunzio a Fiume* (Milano: Luni, 2019).
55. Bartolini, *"Yoga,"* 59, 69–70; Anonymous, "Vogliamo Vivere," *Yoga*, November 20, 1920, in Bartolini *"Yoga,"* 187; Anonymous, "Valori Italici," *Yoga*, November 20, 1920, in Bartolini, *"Yoga,"* 213–16; [Giovanni Comisso,] "Stefano Radic," *Yoga*, November 27, 1920, in Bartolini, *"Yoga,"* 251; [Guido Keller,] "Arte Aumana," *Yoga*, December 4, 1920, in Bartolini, *"Yoga,"* 363–67.
56. Comisso, *Le Mie Stagioni*, 85.
57. Comisso, *Le Mie Stagioni*, 85.
58. Comisso, *Le Mie Stagioni*, 86–88.
59. Guido Keller, "Chi l'Onore?" (19 June 1920), Fondazione Il Vittoriale degli Italiani, Archivio Fiumano, Serie Corrispondenza, Keller, Guido.
60. Guido Keller, Report to Gabriele D'Annunzio ('copy no 2', project for a reform of the Army) (1919), Fondazione Il Vittoriale degli Italiani, Archivio Fiumano, Serie Corrispondenza, Keller, Guido.
61. Guido Keller, "Chi l'Onore?" (19 June 1920), Fondazione Il Vittoriale degli Italiani, Archivio Fiumano, Serie Corrispondenza, Keller, Guido.
62. Guido Keller, Report to Gabriele D'Annunzio ('copy no 2', project for a reform of the Army) (1919), Fondazione Il Vittoriale degli Italiani, Archivio Fiumano, Serie Corrispondenza, Keller, Guido.
63. Letter from G. Keller to G. D'Annunzio (undated), Fondazione Il Vittoriale degli Italiani, Archivio Fiumano, Serie Corrispondenza, Keller, Guido.
64. Bartolini, *"Yoga,"* 64–65, 74–75; Anonymous, "Orientazione," *Yoga*, November 27, 1920, in Bartolini, *"Yoga,"* 233–36; Anonymous, "Armonie," *Yoga*, Novembre 13, 1920, in Bartolini, *"Yoga,"* 139–43.
65. Bartolini, *"Yoga,"* 63; Anonymous, "Il Fior di Loto," *Yoga*, November 13, 1920, in Bartolini, *"Yoga,"* 107; Anonymous, "Vogliamo Vivere," *Yoga*, November

20, 1920, in Bartolini, "*Yoga,*" 185–87; Anonymous, "Movimento Yoga," *Yoga*, December 4, 1920, in Bartolini, "*Yoga,*" 306; Comisso, *Le Mie Stagioni*, 90.

66. [Giovanni Comisso,] "Delle Corporazioni," *Yoga*, November 13, 1920, in Bartolini, "*Yoga,*" 154; [Giovanni Comisso,] "Lo Spirito Italico e la Reazione Europea," *Yoga*, November 20, 1920, in Bartolini, "*Yoga,*" 165–67; [Guido Keller,] "Parole . . . ?," *Yoga*, November 27, 1920, in Bartolini, "*Yoga,*" 237–39; [Giovanni Comisso,] "L'Evoluzione del Principio Europeo," *Yoga*, November 13, 1920, in Bartolini, "*Yoga,*" 293.

67. Anonymous, "Parlamentarismo," *Yoga*, November 20, 1920, in Bartolini, "*Yoga,*" 173–75.

68. [Giovanni Comisso,] "L'Evoluzione del Principio Europeo," *Yoga*, November 13, 1920, in Bartolini, "*Yoga,*" 295.

69. Bartolini, "*Yoga,*" 67, 71; [Giovanni Comisso,] "Prospettive Italiche," *Yoga*, November 13, 1920, in Bartolini, "*Yoga,*" 99–101; [Guido Keller,] "Inizio," *Yoga*, November 13, 1920, in Bartolini, "*Yoga,*" 131; [Giovanni Comisso,] "Del Discutere. Dei Giovani. Del Governo," *Yoga*, November 13, 1920, in Bartolini, "*Yoga,*" 137; Anonymous, "Il Fior di Loto," *Yoga*, November 13, 1920, in Bartolini, "*Yoga,*" 107; [Giovanni Comisso,] "Imposizione del Principio Europeo," *Yoga*, December 4, 1920, in Bartolini, "*Yoga,*" 359–62; Comisso, *Le Mie Stagioni*, 76, 89.

70. Anonymous, "Ragguagli," *Yoga*, November 20, 1920, in Bartolini, "*Yoga,*" 162.

71. [Giovanni Comisso,] "Prolegomeni," *Yoga*, November 13, 1920, in Bartolini, "*Yoga,*" 91–93.

72. [Giovanni Comisso,] "L'Evoluzione del Principio Europeo," *Yoga*, November 13, 1920, in Bartolini, "*Yoga,*" 293.

73. [Giovanni Comisso,] "L'Evoluzione del Principio Europeo," *Yoga*, November 13, 1920, in Bartolini, "*Yoga,*" 293.

74. Letter from G. Keller to G. D'Annunzio (8 July 1922), Fondazione Il Vittoriale degli Italiani, Archivio Generale, Keller, Guido, LIX, 4.

75. Letter from G. Keller to G. D'Annunzio (undated), Fondazione Il Vittoriale degli Italiani, Archivio Fiumano, Serie Corrispondenza, Keller, Guido.

76. [Guido Keller,] "Parole . . . ?," *Yoga*, November 27, 1920, in Bartolini 2019, "*Yoga,*" 237.

77. Comisso, *Le Mie Stagioni*, 67

78. Letter from L. Kotchnitzky to P. Hymans (22 November 1919), Fondazione Il Vittoriale degli Italiani, Archivio Fiumano, Kotchnitzky, Léon, 1–129.

79. Letter from L. Kotchnitzky to G. D'Annunzio (17 December 1919), Fondazione Il Vittoriale degli Italiani, Archivio Fiumano, Kotchnitzky, Léon, 1–129.

80. Comisso, *Le Mie Stagioni*, 67.

81. Letter from L. Kotchnitzky to G. D'Annunzio (16 March 1920), Fondazione Il Vittoriale degli Italiani, Archivio Fiumano, Kotchnitzky, Léon, 1–129.

82. Fiume: Diary of the British Military Mission, Fiume (3–9 November 1919), The National Archives, WO 106/853.

83. Guerri, *Disobbedisco*, 98–99.

84. Comisso, *Le Mie Stagioni*, 66.

85. Kotchnitzky, *La Quinta Stagione*, 12–13.

86. Domenico Conoscenti, "Boccaccio, Dante e l'Omosessualitá nella Cultura del Trecento," *Allegoria* 59 (2009).

87. Kotchnitzky, *La Quinta Stagione*, 176.

88. Kotchnitzky, *La Quinta Stagione*, 52.

89. Kotchnitzky, *La Quinta Stagione*, 199.

90. Ovid, *The Metamorphoses*, book 10.

91. See Aleardo Zanghellini, *The Sexual Constitution of Political Authority: The "Trials" of Same-Sex Desire* (Abingdon, UK: Routledge, 2015), 128–29, 132 (discussing another instance—this one from the late nineteenth century—where homosexuality is obliquely referenced using these self-same semiotic strategies, namely, underscoring its namelessness, coupled with an allusion to devoted male friendships).

92. Kotchnitzky, *La Quinta Stagione*, 234.

93. Kotchnitzky, *La Quinta Stagione*, 174–77.

94. Kotchnitzky, *La Quinta Stagione*, 173.

95. Kotchnitzky, *La Quinta Stagione*, 173–44.

96. Kotchnitzky, *La Quinta Stagione*, 125 (emphasis added).

97. Kotchnitzky, *La Quinta Stagione*, 106–7.

98. Kotchnitzky, *La Quinta Stagione*, 57.

99. Letter from L. Kotchnitzky to P. Hymans (22 November 1919), Fondazione Il Vittoriale degli Italiani, Archivio Fiumano, Kotchnitzky, Léon, 1–129.

100. Léon Kotchnitzky, *La Quinta Stagione: O, I Centauri di Fiume*, trans. Alberto Luchini (Bologna: Zanichelli, 1922), 38, 45.

101. Note from L. Kotchnitzky to G. D'Annunzio (27 July 1919), Fondazione Il Vittoriale degli Italiani, Archivio Fiumano, Kotchnitzky, Léon, 1–129.

102. Letter from L. Kotchnitzky to G. D'Annunzio (19 July 1920), Fondazione Il Vittoriale degli Italiani, Archivio Fiumano, Kotchnitzky, Léon, 1–129.

103. Letter from G. Keller to G. D'Annunzio (30 July 1919), Fondazione Il Vittoriale degli Italiani, Archivio Fiumano, Serie Corrispondenza, Keller, Guido; various letters from G. Keller to G. D'Annunzio (1919), Fondazione Il Vittoriale degli Italiani, Archivio Generale, Keller, Guido, LIX, 4.

104. Letter from G. Keller to G. D'Annunzio (30 July 1919), Fondazione Il Vittoriale degli Italiani, Archivio Fiumano, Serie Corrispondenza, Keller, Guido.

105. John Woodhouse, *Gabriele D'Annunzio: Defiant Archangel* (Oxford: Clarendon Press, 1998), 330.

106. Letter from G. Keller to G. D'Annunzio (undated), Fondazione Il Vittoriale degli Italiani, Archivio Fiumano, Serie Corrispondenza, Keller, Guido.

107. Message from G. Keller to G. D'Annunzio (28 November 1919), Fondazione Il Vittoriale degli Italiani, Archivio Fiumano, Serie Corrispondenza, Keller, Guido.

108. Letter from G. Keller to G. D'Annunzio (undated), Fondazione Il Vittoriale degli Italiani, Archivio Fiumano, Serie Corrispondenza, Keller, Guido.

109. Letter (or telegram) from G. D'Annunzio to G. Keller (undated), Fondazione Il Vittoriale degli Italiani, Archivio Personale, Keller, Guido (28081).

110. Letter (or telegram) from G. D'Annunzio to G. Keller (undated), Fondazione Il Vittoriale degli Italiani, Archivio Personale, Keller, Guido (28080).

111. Message from G. Keller to G. D'Annunzio (23 April 1922), Fondazione Il Vittoriale degli Italiani, Archivio Generale, Keller, Guido, LIX, 4.

112. Letter from G. Keller to G. D'Annunzio (25 October 1929), Fondazione Il Vittoriale degli Italiani, Archivio Fiumano, Serie Corrispondenza, Keller, Guido.

113. Letter from G. Keller to G. D'Annunzio (25 April 1924), Fondazione Il Vittoriale degli Italiani, Archivio Generale, Keller, Guido, LIX, 4.

114. Letter from G. Keller to G. D'Annunzio (undated), Fondazione Il Vittoriale degli Italiani, Archivio Fiumano, Serie Corrispondenza, Keller, Guido.

115. Letter from G. Keller to G. D'Annunzio (undated), Fondazione Il Vittoriale degli Italiani, Archivio Fiumano, Serie Corrispondenza, Keller, Guido.

116. Letter from G. Keller to G. D'Annunzio (undated, forwarded by Gabriellino), Fondazione Il Vittoriale degli Italiani, Archivio Generale, Keller, Guido, LVII, 2, Cap. V B/8/h.

117. Photograph from G. Keller to G. D'Annunzio (8 June 1929), Fondazione Il Vittoriale degli Italiani, Archivio Generale, Keller, Guido, LIX, 4.

118. Message from G. Keller to G. D'Annunzio (undated; from Hotel Bella Riva, Fasano sul Garda), Fondazione Il Vittoriale degli Italiani, Archivio Generale, Keller, Guido, LIX, 4.

119. Letter from G. Keller to G. D'Annunzio (25 April 1924), Fondazione Il Vittoriale degli Italiani, Archivio Generale, Keller, Guido, LIX, 4.

120. Telegram from G. D'Annunzio to G. Keller (undated; from Castroreale Bagni), Fondazione Il Vittoriale degli Italiani, Archivio Personale, Keller, Guido (2376).

121. Letters from G. D'Annunzio to G. Keller (up to 1926), Fondazione Il Vittoriale degli Italiani, Archivio Personale, Keller, Guido (from 34768 to 34770).

122. Telegram from G. D'Annunzio to G. Keller (undated; from Castroreale Bagni), Fondazione Il Vittoriale degli Italiani, Archivio Personale, Keller, Guido (2376).

123. Telegram from G. D'Annunzio to G. Keller (undated; from Castroreale Bagni), Fondazione Il Vittoriale degli Italiani, Archivio Personale, Keller, Guido (2376).

124. Letter from G. D'Annunzio to G. Keller (12 September 1921), Fondazione Il Vittoriale degli Italiani, Archivio Personale, Keller, Guido (30266).

125. Letter from G. Keller to G. D'Annunzio (undated, "September Moon"), Fondazione Il Vittoriale degli Italiani, Archivio Generale, Keller, Guido, LIX, 4.

126. Letter from G. Keller to G. D'Annunzio (undated), Fondazione Il Vittoriale degli Italiani, Archivio Generale, Keller, Guido, LIX, 4.

127. Impromptu speech by Marinetti to 300 Arditi Officers in Riese (October 1918), in Ferdinando Cordova, *Arditi e Legionari Dannunziani* (Padova: Marsilio, 1969), 207.

128. Mario Carli, "Primo Appello alle Fiamme" (20 September 1918), in Cordova, *Arditi e Legionari*, 209.

129. Mario Carli, "Associazione fra gli Arditi d'Italia: Programma e Statuto del Dopoguerra," art. 3, in Cordova, *Arditi e Legionari*, 211–12.

130. Filippo Tommaso Marinetti, *La Grande Milano Tradizionale Futurista: Una Sensibilitá Italiana Nata in Egitto* (Milano: Mondadori, 1969), 21, quoted in Günter

Berghaus, *Futurism and Politics: Between Anarchist Rebellion and Fascist Reaction 1909–1944* (Providence, MA, and Oxford: Berghahn, 1996), 18.

131. Mario Carli, "L'Ardito Futurista: Manifesto" (November 1919), in Cordova, *Arditi e Legionari*, 214.

132. Carli, "L'Ardito Futurista: Manifesto," 216.

133. Mario Mondini, *Fiume 1919: Una Guerra Civile Italiana* (Roma: Salerno, 2019), 97.

134. Kotchnitzky, *La Quinta Stagione*, 68–69.

135. Kotchnitzky, *La Quinta Stagione*, 117–18.

136. Letter from M. Carli to G. D'Annunzio (9 August 1920), Fondazione Il Vittoriale degli Italiani, Archivio Fiumano, Serie Corrispondenza, Carli, Mario, quoted in Federico Carlo Simonelli, *D'Annunzio e il Mito di Fiume: Riti, Simboli, Narrazioni* (Pisa: Pacini, 2021), 239.

137. Simonelli, *D'Annunzio e il Mito*, 239.

138. Incidentally, Carli's homophobia paradoxically makes him relish a scenario in which he himself ejaculates on eunuchs/pederasts' glutes. This may suggest that Carli's homophobia was a case of projection. Alternatively, he was drawing on premodern Mediterranean conceptions of same-sex encounters, which absolve active/insertive partners from wrongdoing.

Conclusions

D'Annunzio's deeply polarising personality, his association in the popular imagination with the Fascist regime, and the temporal proximity and discursive entanglements of the occupation with it make telling the story D'Annunzio's Fiume not an easy task. In the final sections of these conclusions I will speak to these complexities. I start, however, by dwelling on some key insights this book has brought into focus.

TWO ITALIAN OCCUPATIONS, NOT ONE

While there has been some reliance on UK archival material relating to the Fiume question and to D'Annunzio's occupation, this has so far been limited by the broader scope and ambitions of the works in the context of which it has occurred. Neither biographies of the poet nor diplomatic history books on the Peace Conference called for the kind of close and systematic attention I paid to those archival sources in this book. My analysis of these sources has revealed three main insights that current literature on the Fiume question and occupation, the vast majority of which is in Italian, have not foregrounded.

Although reference has sometimes been made to the way in which Britain tended to favour Yugoslav interests, the extent of the British delegation's dogmatism regarding, specifically, Fiume has not previously been documented or fully appreciated. Nor has attention been drawn to the fact that information that reached London and Paris from British military sources in Fiume was often inaccurate, unreliable, and partisan. Woodhouse, as noted in the introduction, praises Lieutenant Colonel Peck's reports as 'models of sage objectivity', noting that 'eulogies of Peck are periodically to be found in the marginal jottings of his reports.'[1] But those marginal jottings owe their paternity to the British delegation representatives whose unmitigated anti-Italian bias I have been at pains to document—as I have Peck's own penchant for relying uncritically and exclusively on Yugoslav propaganda and other dubious sources.

It may be impossible, and quite beside the point, to attempt to trace a direct chain of influence on diplomatic decision making, from military reports through Foreign Office personnel to plenipotentiaries at Versailles. But there can be little doubt that both the British Mission's military reports and relevant Foreign Office staff (appointed as technical experts and nonplenipotentiary representatives in the political section of the British delegation at the Peace Conference) contributed to creating a certain mood, as it were, in the shadow of which the Adriatic question was apprehended. This mood, whose foundations had been laid out and continued to be buttressed by Seton-Watson, Steed, and Lord Northcliffe, cannot have failed to affect, at least in a diffused way, how the problem of Fiume was handled at Versailles by one of the greatest players at the Peace Conference. It has been argued that distrust of Italy became 'a natural part' of British foreign policy after Fiume,[2] but my research suggests that, rather than a consequence of the Fiume affair, such distrust was a structuring feature of how Britain approached the Fiume question at Versailles.

Let me now turn to the other two key points on which British archival materials shed light. First, the role of France in shaping the events that led to D'Annunzio's occupation; secondly, and relatedly, the fact that the occupation that preceded D'Annunzio's was less an Inter-Allied occupation than an Italian one. Leeden has underscored better than anyone the November 1918 contest between Italy and France for control of Fiume and clarified France's motives for appointing itself as the unofficial protector of the Yugoslavs.[3] British archival material throws light on the specific dynamics of this contest, in a way that helps us make sense of the timeline of events. The reactive character of Italian troops finally entering the town in November 1918 often fails to be emphasised, and the event to which they reacted is regularly misapprehended. It was not an attempted Yugoslav occupation but a French one. The Serb troops which are sometimes mentioned to have entered Fiume shortly before the Italian occupation turn out to have been under French command. I have drawn attention to the Villa Giusti and Belgrade peace agreements to show how their (mis)interpretation stayed the Italian hand for a while and determined the timing of the French occupation. General Franchet D'Esperéy's role in negotiating the agreement and his immediate despatch of Serb troops to Fiume show up that despatch as the French occupation by proxy that it was. Thereafter, the French established in Fiume a parallel military authority structure independent of the Italian Inter-Allied command.

Leeden argues that, after General Di San Marzano and Admiral Rainer's entry into Fiume, the town 'was effectively under Italian command' but the 'situation lasted only a couple of days'.[4] This is clearly not the perspective of the British, who repeatedly testify that between November 1918 and September 1919 the occupation was Inter-Allied only in name and provide evidence to make that statement quite credible. Appreciating the merely ostensibly Allied character of the occupation enables us to grasp the reasons behind the timeline of events that led to D'Annunzio's occupation. Despite all the plotting, nothing came of it until the reports of the Inter-Allied Commission on the July 1919 disturbances threatened finally to make the occupation a genuinely Inter-Allied affair. Grossich had been entirely transparent and public about Fiume intending to seek the assistance of an army of Italian volunteers in the event that the Italian occupation forces were made to leave. This is just what happened with D'Annunzio's entry. The July disturbances, which prompted this sequence of events, must then be appreciated both in the context of Italy's and France's rival claims over control of Fiume and the broader enmity between Italian and French occupation forces in the eastern Adriatic, which British sources eloquently describe.

Here is how the three insights I have just described come together. If the negotiations about Fiume at Versailles had not been so protracted (a situation that was partly of Britain's making), if the French had not precipitated the Italian occupation of November 1918 and maintained a parallel military authority structure independent of the Italian command, and if the Italian occupation had genuinely been an Inter-Allied affair from the start, the realisation of Italy's ambitions in Fiume would have panned out quite differently. Without Britain at Versailles, and without France and Italy quarrelling in Fiume between November 1918 and September 1919, there may have never been a Dannunzian Fiume at all, and no *Carnaro Charter*.

LAW

The limited interest—at least until recently—shown by legal historians and constitutional lawyers in D'Annunzio's Fiume means that the import of some of D'Annunzio's ordinances and certain *Charter* provisions has been seriously misunderstood. This is due to lack of legal-doctrinal knowledge on the part of historians, a failure to place these legal measures in the context of coeval legal developments in Italy and elsewhere in Europe, and confirmation bias in ideologically driven analyses. I have attempted to rectify some of these problems. With respect to the command's ordinances and other measures, my analysis has been to the effect of mitigating—not negating—their badness. To be clear, if you were a Croat or a non-Annexationist, there was much to feel indignant about, and at times intimidated by, during Fiume's two Italian occupations. But none of the measures taken by D'Annunzio were, considered in context, tyrannical in design, and even less so in execution.

As to the *Charter*, my analysis has rehabilitated certain of its provisions that have been, again, misread as proof of D'Annunzio's proto-Fascism, as well others that have been dismissed as ridiculous and useless. Notable examples of the former are the articles on the commandant or those relating to corporatism; the latter are composed of articles addressing aesthetic values. While legal scholars have started taking the *Charter* more seriously in the past two decades or so, there was still almost nothing—until this study and the nearly contemporaneous one by Alessandro Agrí[5]—approaching a comprehensive and detailed commentary of its provisions. I have undertaken to do my part to remedy this exegetical gap. The recourse to intertextual and comparative strategies of interpretation has proved especially illuminating. Through its innovative treatment of issues ranging from minority rights and gender, through private property and political representation, to emergency powers and aesthetic values, the *Charter* deserves, despite its short life, to be recognised as one of the most imaginative constitutional experiments of the twentieth century.

As its authors appeared to see it, the greatest innovation of the *Charter* was the attempt to make the productive worker, alongside and above the citizen, the central political subject of the constitutional order. This was in part a manifestation of the ascendance of Socialist (I am using the term in its broadest denotation) ideals in the first two decades of the twentieth century. But it was also bound up with a critique of representative democracy that had acquired broad currency in a disillusioned, postunification Italy. For the most part, this critique of representative democracy was directed at the 'representative' in the 'representative-represented' couplet. In other words, it was targeted at the dysfunctional behaviour of politicians and/or at the institutional design that failed to keep it in check (these are grievances that, more than one hundred years later, Italians still variously hold on to). But from a revolutionary Syndicalist viewpoint, and others, the problem was also with the other pole of the 'representative-represented' relationship. This was the *demos* in the concept of representative democracy, made up by all the individual citizens, holders of political rights. For revolutionary Syndicalists, the popular will enabled by universal suffrage was no less a fiction than the citizens to whose aggregation (the *demos*) this will was ascribed. The citizen *qua* citizen was a contrived abstraction. As such, the aggregation (via the mediation of artificial formations known as political parties) of individual citizens' wills into the popular will yielded only an empty concept.

Revolutionary Syndicalists, however, suggested that representation could be made to work. This required rethinking the subject of politics: if the citizen were replaced by the worker, a much thicker, much more definite and concrete will could be identified. This is because workers, organised in employment categories on the basis of the nature of their occupation or trade, actually shared (unlike disembodied, abstract citizens) common interests and concerns. This explains the *Charter* mandating the enrolment of all workers in *corporazioni* and its using *corporazioni* as the basis of representation in one of the houses of the legislature of the regency.

As we have seen, however, the other house retained the citizen as holder of political rights: De Ambris thought that it would have been premature to do completely away with representative democracy in favour of what we might call a full-blown representative *tektōnocracy* (a government of workers). Ferrero's critique of the democratic principle, and his own qualification to that critique, are particularly useful to help understand De Ambris's assessment that the time had not come yet for a more radical constitutional experiment. Ferrero conceded:

> What institution, principle, doctrine, or tradition can presume today—not even to rule over and direct—but to even guess the true will of these multitudes called ever now and again to rejuvenate, with a simple act of will, the principle of authority to which they will later have to obey? This will, which history today has known for the first time, is a huge power, opaque even to itself, imprecise, haphazard, swaying.[6]

And yet, for Ferrero, the divine right of kings had been swept away by the war, and there was no alternative to the democratic principle of popular sovereignty; for European states 'do not yet recognise, as a principle of [legitimate] authority, the dictatorship of any organised and self-aware minority: neither the proletariat, nor trade unions, nor the saviours of the nation'.[7]

By incentivising in various way productive work, the *Charter* attempted to eliminate the leisure classes. Its vision was one in which all citizens would eventually perform some form of work, thereby enjoying the full political rights accorded to productive workers. To that extent, even if the *Charter* had gone further than it did and made productive workers the *only* political subject, this would not have resulted in the dictatorship of an 'organised and self-aware minority' (to use Ferrero's expression). If everyone would eventually work and thereby belong to one *corporazione* or another, dispensing with the house that gave representation to the citizen and retaining only the house where workers, organised in *corporazioni*, were represented would not have resulted in a dictatorship of the minority via trade unions.

Yet De Ambris studiously avoided taking this further step. He was too aware of how controversial it would have been. Again, Ferrero's analysis brings this home. The representative parliamentary democratic 'forms that are the legacy of the war are weak and old, but they are the only ones that can survive',[8] he said. For beyond representative institutions, 'the popular will is sham'.[9] While Ferrero conceded that in the twentieth century Parliament must reckon with the wishes of trade unions, the media, and other 'forces directing society', it was not true, as Mussolini had claimed, that these forces had reduced the importance of Parliament: the popular will represented in democratic parliamentary institutions still stood as the only source of legitimacy.[10]

In contemporary societies, much of the general public—not to mention politicians, the courts, and even many academics—continue to regard, as Ferrero did one hundred years ago (despite his own misgivings), the popular will (operationalised through representative democratic mechanisms) as the foundation of legitimate government. Yet like De Ambris and many others one hundred years ago, the work of the best contemporary legal philosophers interrogates this conventional wisdom. For example, Dworkin's articulation of the conditions that must be satisfied for regarding democracy and the majority principle as intrinsically valuable also doubles as a theorisation of what makes political authority legitimate in the world as we know it. For Dworkin, these conditions are equality of political rights, protection of individual freedoms, and policies based on equal concern. Significantly, Dworkin's starting point is precisely that it is a puzzle why we should regard majoritarian decision making—that is, the popular will as operationalised in our contemporary representative democratic systems—as something valuable, and hence as a sound foundation for legitimate authority.[11]

Raz, for his part, argues that legitimate authority is, generally, a function of (and conditioned upon) the superior soundness of the authority's directives compared to the subjects' own decision making. While consent to the authority, where it actually subsists, legitimises it, consent is not morally obligatory and hence is at best a contingent basis for legitimate authority. The fixation of political philosophy with consent, for Raz, derives from the ill-conceived idea that in order for us to justify the legitimacy of authority, we must be able to see the will of the government/majority as our own (the popular) will. But this idea leads us into all manner of tortuous thinking and into blind alleys, for any explanation of the legitimacy of authority must face, rather than explain away, the nature of authority as a hierarchical, asymmetrical relationship.[12]

Contemporary political philosophical reflection on the relationship between legitimacy and the popular will from the likes of Raz and Dworkin indirectly shows the enduring relevance to European political thought of the intellectual contributions of those thinkers who were grappling with these self-same puzzles one hundred years ago (and who—as in the case of De Ambris in Fiume—sometimes imaginatively addressed those puzzles in the context of concrete institutional design). But contemporary theories such as those just discussed also complicate some of the assessments contemporary historians and jurists have tended to make about the legitimacy of the *Charter* and regency.

Generally, the *Charter* is critiqued for being a top-down initiative, with any popular input into it being limited to ratification through the problematic mechanism of the plebiscite. Some have responded that the circumstances in Fiume scarcely allowed for a more democratic genesis.[13] But it is not obvious that this is true; and the response rather misses the point. A more interesting line of argument might suggest that, because objections about the nondemocratic genesis of the *Charter* tend to impugn its legitimacy, we need to ask if consent to the constitutional structure is what matters most to the legitimacy of that structure. Dworkin argues that it is not: 'we must judge a political system by its capacity to improve the conditions of genuine political partnership' rather than assume that what matters is for a constitutional structure to have 'been created only in accordance with, or sustained by, the will and blessing of the people as a whole'.[14]

If Dworkin is right, then the legitimacy of the regency turns less on the extent to which the Fiumans happened to approve of the *Charter* than on the content of the *Charter* itself. Do the prescriptions of the *Charter* set up a form of government that satisfies Dworkin's partnership conception of democracy? It seems so. Or, in Razian terms, would the *Charter*'s prescriptions, if observed, have assisted the Fiumans in acting and living well and, specifically, better than they would have without their authoritative guidance? Looking (to name only one) at the *Charter* regime of minority protections and contrasting it with the worsening of interethnic tensions during the war and its aftermath, I would incline towards an affirmative answer. D'Annunzio's much-derided provisions concerning aesthetic imperatives and intrinsic value—today echoed in some so-called third-generation rights—make me lean towards the same conclusion. Such provisions may well assist a political community in acting and living well, better than they would without their authoritative guidance. It will be remembered that Pantaleoni in 1920 urged the poet to set aside his concerns for the beautiful in the *Charter* and think instead of the useful and lucrative. If we are hesitant to applaud the results of one hundred years of applying, now on a truly global scale, that logic of unrestrained economic growth, we should consider whether D'Annunzio was onto something where he sought to give constitutional status to the value of not 'thinking but through the belly'.

LOVE-LORE

Sedgwick famously argued that the tensions of homo/heterosexual definition more or less covertly inflect virtually every important aspect of Western culture.[15] There was enough in Comisso's *Harbour of Love*, which introduced me to the world of D'Annunzio's Fiume, to suggest that Sedgwick's claim might be borne out when it came to a fuller understanding of the Fiume endeavour, including in its legal dimensions.

Little did I expect, however, to find that D'Annunzio's Fiume speeches were saturated with same-sex tropes, that he all but explicitly claimed that the *Charter* was the child of his love affair with the legionnaires, and that his fiction too showed an abiding interest in male same-sex desire and its sublimation. Yet none of this turned out to be particularly incongruous, once put in the biographical context of his homoerotic investments. What remains remarkable is the low level of attention any of this has gotten in the literature. This ranges from 'a little and selectively' with respect to D'Annunzio's fiction to 'none at all' when it comes to his Fiume speeches.

Clearly, the perspective of mainstream historiography and literary criticism remains heteronormative. This is even more so in Italy than the English-speaking world: it is significant that the two (three, with the addition of this book) most prominent, and possibly the only, scholarly treatments of same-sex desire in D'Annunzio's works are in English. But it also seems likely that queer scholars and critics have not been exactly in a hurry to reclaim D'Annunzio as a cultural and political icon. This is for all the reasons (discussed in the last section of these conclusions) that also explain why avoiding bias and interpretive pitfalls is such a formidable task when it comes to writing the history of D'Annunzio's Fiume or to providing critical readings of his prose fiction.

Be that as it may, my research in this book shows that same-sex desire was channelled, consciously or unconsciously, by a number of legionnaires in ways that shaped their aesthetic-revolutionary sensibilities and, through them, affected the command's policy—albeit in mediated, nonlinear, diffused ways. To this extent same-sex desire can be said to have been constitutive of the political order of occupied Fiume. But D'Annunzio himself also saw homoerotic affect as foundational, specifically, to the new constitutional order of the regency, crediting his beloved legionnaires with the paternity of the *Charter* he himself begot. He also wooed the legionnaires at every opportunity in his public speeches, weaving a discursive practice that is all but brimming with homoeroticism, with mixed results.

If same-sex desire can be seen as constitutive of Fiume's political and normative order, none of it simply happened, as if by accident. Not only as I have pointed out earlier, D'Annunzio showed a preoccupation with same-sex desire and love, and queer investments, throughout his life; but by the time he became commandant in Fiume, he had also elaborated a belief in the intellectual and spiritual generativity of same-sex bonds. Generally—though not always invariably—this generativity was enabled by the sublimation of same-sex erotic desire. In Fiume, D'Annunzio thematised this sublimation when declaring that the *Charter*, which he had himself brought to light, was the legionnaires' own offspring; and he enacted this sublimation through the oral and written word, converting homoerotic into political passion, and infusing political discourse with homoerotic ardour and imagery.

We have seen that widely shared accounts of legal systems' existence maintain that it requires legal officials treating the norms of the system as binding, as well as a general population that is at least norm conforming, whatever their reasons for conforming.[16] With the regency, its idealism, its emphasis on intrinsic value, and its civic religion, D'Annunzio and De Ambris envisaged a higher-order level of political existence, one where laws are generally obeyed because they are good and seen to be good, not merely conformed with out of prudential or opportunistic reasons. The mixed reactions to the *Charter* coming from the National Council and the Fiumans, however, suggest that D'Annunzio and De Ambris's vision was mostly wishful thinking. If the regency had proved a less transitory affair, and if the Fiumans had shown the requisite conformity with its laws, many of them would probably have done so for all the usual mundane and prosaic reasons: fear of prosecution, preference for order over disorder, etc.

Unlike the Fiumans, the legionnaires whom D'Annunzio loved, and who loved D'Annunzio, may have responded to the regency and its laws in the way D'Annunzio wished them to; and they may have done so because the ways in which D'Annunzio's speeches sublimated same-sex desire into a vision of all that is beautiful, heroic, and virtuous resonated with them. But not all the legionnaires were as much in love with the commandant and his vision as he was with them—particularly, perhaps, after he gave the game away (not that it was a game for D'Annunzio) by drawing too much attention to the libidinal structure of the bonds holding together the legionnaire community. There were many fewer legionnaires at the end of the occupation than at its start. After the bloody Christmas, many of those who had been in Fiume defected to the very opposite of *Fiumanesimo* and the *Charter*: Fascism.

D'Annunzio himself, after leaving Fiume, retired from politics in the splendid isolation of the Vittoriale. The counterpart to his belief in the spiritual and cultural generativity of same-sex bonds had always been a recurring preoccupation (at least in the characters of his novels) with the way in which heterosexual erotism distracted from and enfeebled creative genius.[17] But now D'Annunzio professed a change of mind. Removed from the politically active, homosocial life he led in Fiume and during the war, D'Annunzio found himself performing a transvaluation: what he had consistently lamented as detracting from self-control and the pursuit of a higher form of life became the source of those very things. Heteroerotic passion was no longer an impediment to the realisation of ideal values but the wellspring of artistic invention, intellectual revelation, and self-discovery, free from the strictures of heteronomous convention. The animalistic passion quintessentially expressed (as he saw it) in female sexuality was divine in nature, and heterosexual experience conducive to the renewal of self-mastery (at least after the act).[18] It is at this time that D'Annunzio implausibly wrote, of Michelangelo, that he could have been an even better artist had he given way to sexual longing. But Bonadeo argues that these self-assured pronouncements appear to have been rationalisations, masking D'Annunzio's enduring anxieties about the destructive force of (hetero)sexual passion, always threatening to induce a loss of self.[19]

None of what I say in this section amounts to an argument that D'Annunzio was homosexual, let alone a practicing one. Those who are convinced of D'Annunzio's unreconstructed heterosexuality may, nonetheless, find it interesting to learn, as I have shown, that archival evidence from Keller's letters suggests episodical toying with same-sex desire. This, as well as the progressive and at times radical Left commitments of D'Annunzio's political manifesto, the *Charter*, should give pause to contemporary crypto-Fascists, who—impressionistically speaking—appear to be more or less the only nonacademic demographic in Italy who openly profess an interest in D'Annunzio's politics.[20]

NORMATIVELY COMMITTED SCHOLARSHIP AND HISTORICAL METHOD

D'Annunzio was a controversial figure during his lifetime. He has remained one, and writing about historical events of which he was the most high-profile protagonist has its hazards. The postwar years, with the memory of the Fascist dictatorship still vivid in the minds of both Italian laypeople and intellectuals, were not the context most conducive to objective treatments of D'Annunzio and the Fiume endeavour. Postwar Italian historiography contributed to solidifying the myth of D'Annunzio's own Fascism—ironically established by the Fascist regime itself and outwardly aided by the poet's opportunistic choices since he retired to Gardone at the end of the occupation. However mistaken, this ideological attribution, coupled with D'Annunzio's signature megalomania and his lifelong relish for the decadent and *outré*, makes it difficult to avoid bias and interpretive pitfalls, even for present-day historians or literary critics who choose to write about him.

My point is not that the history of Fiume, and history in general, should be a purely descriptive enterprise.[21] Moral judgements about the past can be important for their educative function,[22] and we fail to grasp the full significance of past events if we do not attend to their moral dimensions.[23]

The problem, therefore, is not with historians' formulating their moral judgements about D'Annunzio and his Fiume endeavour. The problem is, rather, when scholars let their moral indignation cloud the interpretation of events or the accuracy of their account.[24] There are many examples of this in recent scholarship on Fiume, even otherwise excellent scholarship. They are generally due to the researcher's precommitment to the view that D'Annunzio was proto-Fascist or had strong authoritarian tendencies. This affects the treatment afforded, for example, to the *Charter* or to events surrounding the *modus vivendi.*

Thus, Klinger claims that the regency lacked a system of checks and balances and was rather based on a rigid separation of competences presumed to work harmoniously together via ideological unity;[25] and Serventi Longhi maintains that D'Annunzio's version of the *Charter* rejects De Ambris's 'republican, Syndicalist, libertarian, and independentist . . . outlook' and replaces it with the poet's 'political mysticism'.[26] But we have seen that the *Charter* was one of three constitutions to inaugurate in Europe the practice of constitutionality review by a fully judicial body, which was not politically appointed. This is the paradigmatic mechanism of constitutional checks and balances. We have also seen that the republican, Syndicalist, libertarian, and independentist elements are as apparent in D'Annunzio's mysticised version as in De Ambris's more pedestrian draft of the *Charter*. The terminological change from 'republic' to 'regency' carried with it no substantive differences in the regency's republican—that is, its nonmonarchical—form of government.

Woodhouse's account of D'Annunzio's annulment of the referendum on the *modus vivendi* is another example. As we know, a majority of Fiumans were prepared—against D'Annunzio's expectations—to accept the compromise, whereby the Italian Army would take over from the poet's occupation forces, while the Italian government committed to territorial continuity between Fiume and Italy, and undertook not to consign the town into Yugoslav hands. D'Annunzio annulled the referendum citing irregularities. According to Woodhouse,

> The most probable explanation for D'Annunzio's dismissal of the popular vote was that he was fundamentally unwilling to let go of . . . absolute power. . . . Apart from the trappings of political and military power, he had constant supply of women to gratify his sexual appetites and he was able to engage in other self-indulgent practices for which no-one was in a position to reprove him. . . .[27]
>
> [The] prosaic prospect of losing supreme command and reverting to the banality of administrative governorship must have appalled D'Annunzio. Life was so exciting in so many new ways: to become even semi-respectable as a governor would put inhibiting limits on his dissolute, indeed debauched, life as the Duce of what was in effect a free state.[28]

It is to Woodhouse's credit that he clearly signals (through the use of the adjective 'probable') that his explanation is speculative. Yet much with the explanation seems wrong. First, D'Annunzio's power in Fiume was not absolute. The civil authorities kept doing their work (including by retaining control over the police), often coming into conflict with D'Annunzio's command, and clearly feeling at ease to voice their remonstrations. This was the case even after D'Annunzio unilaterally annulled the referendum.[29] Secondly, though D'Annunzio was enamoured with the trappings of military power, his attitude towards political power was much more ambivalent. More crucially, none of the different versions of the *modus vivendi* offered him an administrative governorship in lieu of supreme power.[30] If any concession to D'Annunzio's desire to remain in Fiume was at all contemplated during the negotiations, it was (reluctantly) that he might be allowed to stay in a military capacity strictly subordinate to the regular forces.[31] In the event, the final version of the compromise agreement did not even concede that. Fiume was permitted to maintain a 'local militia',[32] but D'Annunzio clearly understood that he and his legionnaires must leave (as made apparent in the open letter he wrote to the citizens of Fiume when he asked for a referendum).[33] The government was painfully aware that his continued presence in town would be highly destabilising. The whole *raison d'être* of the *modus vivendi* was to remove him from Fiume, not to appease him by assigning him an administrative post. Thirdly, Woodhouse himself correctly notes elsewhere that the poet was 'sublimely indifferent to public criticism';[34] and D'Annunzio self-consciously made a literary career out of preaching self-indulgence in the face of censure coming from conventionally minded folks. So the argument that his determination to stay in Fiume was in part due to a desire for immunity from criticism for his lifestyle is quite implausible.

A prejudiced apprehension of D'Annunzio's character also lies at the root of some claims made in recent English-language literature on D'Annunzio's Fiume, which range from the demonstrably wrong (in Fiume 'most legal and economic regulations were abolished')[35] to the speculative and unsubstantiated (D'Annunzio 'was uninterested in the masses and social rights, nor did he ever understand them').[36] The point of my critique is not to deny these scholars' commitment to epistemic values of truthfulness and to the "rules of evidence" that tend to promote them.[37] It is to draw attention to how difficult it may be to operationalise that commitment when dealing with controversial figures such as D'Annunzio.

Often, too, the evidence does underdetermine the matter. In this case, as a matter of practicing an ethics of respect towards the past agents whose behaviour we investigate, a principle of interpretive charitableness may generally be called for. If, for example, the evidence underdetermines the question of D'Annunzio's cruelty or insincerity in supporting the principles of the

Charter, it seems to me inappropriate to proclaim or imply that he was cruel[38] or insincere.[39] Checking the impulse to assume the worst helps us cultivate the imaginative skills[40] that are key to producing nuanced, careful, and truthful historical accounts.

Not long after the bloody Christmas, D'Annunzio wrote to De Ambris: 'And what do I care to be defeated in space, if I am destined to win in time?'[41] No doubt you hate—as I do—cruelty, Fascism, and insincerity; perhaps you have also convinced yourself that D'Annunzio (because of the plot line of *The Triumph of Death*, or because Fascists celebrated him as one of theirs, or whatever) was personally and politically cruel, chronically insincere, the John the Baptist of Fascism. In that case, you will think that, from D'Annunzio's own perspective, his prediction of a triumph, in this quote, was fulfilled during the *ventennio*. If, however, we make it a point to practice interpretive charitableness when the evidence underdetermines the matter, I think we are more likely to grasp what D'Annunzio meant, and what De Ambris took him to mean. If, in 1921, the revolutionary Syndicalist and the poet had been able to peer one hundred years into the future, they would have readily agreed with us that D'Annunzio's prediction proved to be a false prophecy. The 'man remade whole by freedom' failed to materialise in the intervening decades—never more signally so than during Italy's Fascist period.

NOTES

1. John Woodhouse, *Gabriele D'Annunzio: Defiant Archangel* (Oxford: Clarendon Press, 1998), 328.
2. Woodhouse, *Gabriele D'Annunzio*, 351.
3. Michael A. Leeden, *The First Duce* (Baltimore and London: John Hopkins University Press, 1977), 29–35.
4. Leeden, *The First Duce*, 30.
5. Alessandro Agrì, *La Costituzione della Reggenza Italiana del Carnaro* (Torino: Giappichelli, 2023), 219–59.
6. Guglielmo Ferrero, *Da Fiume a Roma: Storia di Quattro Anni (1919–1923)* (Milano: Athena, 1923), 68.
7. Ferrero, *Da Fiume a Roma*, 99.
8. Ferrero, *Da Fiume a Roma*, 101.
9. Ferrero, *Da Fiume a Roma*, 112.
10. Ferrero, *Da Fiume a Roma*, 112.
11. Ronald Dworkin, "The Partnership Conception of Democracy," *California Law Review* 86, no. 3 (May 1998).
12. Joseph Raz, "The Problem of Authority: Revisiting the Service Conception," *Minnesota Law Review* 90 (2006).

13. Achille Chiappetti, Relazione, in *Lo Statuto della Reggenza Italiana del Carnaro tra Storia, Diritto Internazionale e Diritto Costituzionale*, ed. Augusto Sinagra (Milano: Giuffré, 2009), 22.

14. Dworkin, "The Partnership Conception," 458.

15. Eve Kosofsky Sedgwick, *Epistemology of the Closet* (Berkeley and Los Angeles: University of California Press, 2008), 1.

16. H. L. A. Hart, *The Concept of Law* (Oxford: Oxford University Press, 1961); Joseph Raz, *Practical Reason and Norms* (Oxford: Oxford University Press, 1999).

17. Gabriele D'Annunzio, *Il Piacere*, in *Romanzi e Novelle*, vol. I (Milano: Mondadori, 1942), 146–47.

18. Alfredo Bonadeo, *D'Annunzio and the Great War* (Madison and Teaneck: Farleigh Dickinson University Press; London: Associated University Presses, 1995), 148–51.

19. Bonadeo, *D'Annunzio and the Great War*, 150–53.

20. Compare Christian Lamour, "The Scientific Discourse Circulated during a National-Populist Commemoration: Dannunzian Fiume and the 'Italo-Cosmopolitan' Field of History," *Modern Italy* 28, no. 1 (February 2023): 36, https://doi.org/10.1017/mit.2022.54. ('In Italy, a key denominator of the existing right-wing national-populist political parties . . . is their shared reverence for Gabriele D'Annunzio'.)

21. For an argument that it should be, see, for example, Robin G. Collingwood, "Lectures on the Philosophy of History (1926)," in *The Idea of History: With Lectures 1926–1928*, revised edition (Oxford: Oxford University Press, 1994), 402–4.

22. Adrian Oldfield, "Moral Judgments in History," *History and Theory* 20, no. 3 (1981); Edward P. Thompson, *The Poverty of Theory and Other Essays* (New York: Monthly Review Press, 1978), 234, cited in Rosalind Posel, "The Idea of a Hermeneutic History" (PhD diss., University of Natal, 1982), 183, https://ukzn-dspace.ukzn.ac.za/bitstream/handle/10413/8643/Posel_%20Rosalind_1982.pdf?sequence=1&isAllowed=y.

23. Isaiah Berlin, "Historical Inevitability," in *The Philosophy of History in Our Time*, ed. Hans Meyerhoff (Garden City, NY: Doubleday, 1959), 271, quoted in Posel, "The Idea," 171–72.

24. Oldfield, "Moral Judgments."

25. William Klinger, "La Carta del Carnaro: Una Costituzione per lo Stato Libero di Fiume (1920)," *Quaderni* (Centro di Ricerche Storiche-Rovigno) XIV (2002): 313.

26. Enrico Serventi Longhi, "The Father of 'Sovereignism': d'Annunzio in Fiume between the Crisis of Liberalism and the Critique of Democracy," *Modern Italy* 27 (2022): 39.

27. Woodhouse, *Gabriele D'Annunzio*, 338.

28. Woodhouse, *Gabriele D'Annunzio*, 344.

29. Letter from A. De Ambris to G. D'Annunzio (13 May 1920) in *Sindacalismo Rivoluzionario e Fiumanesimo nel Carteggio De Ambris—D'Annunzio*, ed. Renzo De Felice (Brescia: Morcelliana, 1966), 178–89.

30. *Storia Documentata dei Confini del Regno d'Italia*, vol. 4 (*Confine Italo-Jugoslavo*), ed. Vittorio Adami (Roma: Istituto Poligrafico dello Stato, 1931), 169–71;

Edoardo Susmel, *La Cittá di Passione: Fiume negli Anni 1914–1920* (Milano: Treves, 1921), 320–28.

31. Susmel, *La Cittá di Passione*, 325.

32. Susmel, *La Cittá di Passione*, 328.

33. Susmel, *La Cittá di Passione*, 380–81.

34. Woodhouse, *Gabriele D'Annunzio*, 3.

35. Natalia Skradol, "Carnival of Exception: Gabriele D'Annunzio's 'Dialogues with the Crowd'," *Rhetorica: A Journal of the History of Rhetoric* 30 (2012): 76.

36. Thea Pičić, *Rijeka Ili Smrt! D'Anunzijeva okupacija Rijeke, 1919–1921 / Rijeka or Death! D'Annunzio's occupation of Rijeka, 1919–2019* (Rijeka: Naklada Val, 2019), 9.

37. Mark Bevir, "Objectivity in History," *History and Theory* 33, no. 3 (1994): 334; Hayden White, "The Politics of Historical Interpretation: Discipline and De-Sublimation," *Critical Inquiry* 9, no. 1 (1982): 123.

38. Susan Bassnett, "Translating Gabriele D'Annunzio for the Twenty-First Century Reader" (6 March 2020), Decadence and Translation Network, Glasgow University, https://dandtnetwork.glasgow.ac.uk/translating-gabriele-dannunzio-for-the-twenty-first-century-reader/; Villari, *La Luna*, 16.

39. Paolo Alatri, "La Storiografia sull'Impresa Dannunziana a Fiume," in *D'Annunzio e il Suo Tempo*, vol. 1, ed. Francesco Perfetti (Genova: Sagep, 1989), 27; Budislav Vucas Jr., "La Carta del Carnaro nell'Opus di Ferdo Čulinović," in *La Cittá di Vita Cento Anni Dopo*, ed. Rossi, 307 (reporting Čulinović's opinion).

40. White, "The Politics of Historical Interpretation," 123.

41. Letter from A. De Ambris to G. D'Annunzio (11 May 1921), in *Sindacalismo Rivoluzionario*, ed. De Felice, 254.

Archival Sources

THE NATIONAL ARCHIVES (KEW, UNITED KINGDOM)

1918 Embargoes, FO 170/1134.
Fiume and the Adriatic: 51/1, FO 170/1247.
Fiume and the Adriatic: 51/2, FO 170/1248.
Croatia-Slavonia and Fiume (March 1919), FO 373/1/10.
British Delegation, Correspondence and Papers Relating to Austria-Hungary (Political), FO 608/8.
Italy: Aims in Dalmatia and Croatia, FO 608/15/8.
Adriatic, FO 608/27/9.
Adriatic, Italian Desiderata, FO 608/28/2.
Adriatic, Italian Desiderata, FO 608/28/4.
Adriatic, Italian Desiderata, FO 608/35/3.
Fiume, Statistics, FO 608/35/4.
Fiume, Administration, FO 608/35/5.
Fiume, Desiderata, FO 608/35/6.
British Delegation, FO 608/36.
Fiume, Desiderata, FO 608/36/2.
British Delegation, FO 608/38.
British Delegation, FO 608/39.
Italy, Rebellion, FO 608/41/1.
Conference of Ambassadors, Paris, FO 893/7.
La Question de Fiume, FO 925/33014.
Overseas: Italy, WO 32/5129.
Fiume: Diary of the British Military Mission, WO 106/853.
Brig-Gen Gordon Commanding British Troops in Fiume, WO 106/858.
Letter from G.H.Q. Italy to C.I.G.S. Brigadier General Gordon, WO 106/861.
Temporary Withdrawal from Fiume to Malta, WO 106/865.

Fiume, Zagreb, and Laibach, WO 106/1394.
Disturbances at Fiume (1919), WO 32/5004.
Inter-Allied Organisation of Fiume, WO 32/5129.

PARLIAMENTARY ARCHIVES (WESTMINSTER, UNITED KINGDOM)

Prime Minister, LG/F/43/7/13.
Prime Minister, LG/F/52/2/48.
Prime Minister, LG/F/55/4/39.
Prime Minister, LG/F/158/1/11.
Prime Minister, LG/F/200/1/20.
Prime Minister, LG/F/554/39.

FONDAZIONE IL VITTORIALE DEGLI ITALIANI (GARDONE, ITALY)

Archivio Fiumano, Kotchnitzky, Léon, 1–129.
Archivio Fiumano, Serie Corrispondenza, Keller, Guido.
Archivio Generale, Comisso, Giovanni, VIII, 5.
Archivio Generale, Keller, Guido, LVII, 2, Cap. V B/8/h.
Archivio Generale, Keller, Guido, LIX, 4.
Archivio Personale, Manoscritto Primitivo della "Carta del Carnaro," 588.
Archivio Personale, Keller, Guido.

Bibliography

Adami, Vittorio, ed. *Storia Documentata dei Confini del Regno d'Italia*, vol. 4. *Confine Italo-Jugoslavo*. Roma: Istituto Poligrafico dello Stato, 1931.

Agamben, Giorgio. *Lo Stato di Eccezione*. Torino: Bollati-Boringhieri, 2003.

Agamben, Giorgio. *The Omnibus Homo Sacer*. Stanford: Stanford University Press, 2017.

Agrì, Alessandro. "D'Annunzio Politico: La Carta del Carnaro (1920)." *Atti e Memorie dell'Accademia di Scienze, Lettere e Arti di Modena serie viii* XVII, no. I (2014): 161–88.

Agrì, Alessandro. "La Carta del Carnaro: Un Disegno Costituzionale Incompiuto." *Fiume: Rivista di Studi Adriatici* 27 (2013): 3–42.

Agrí, Alessandro. *La Costituzione della Reggenza Italiana del Carnaro*. Torino: Giappichelli, 2023.

Agrì, Alessandro. "Lo 'Stato di Fiume' e il Suo Diritto (1918–1924)." *Historia et Ius* 19 (2021): 1–54. http://www.historiaetius.eu/uploads/5/9/4/8/5948821/agri_19.pdf.

Agrí, Alessandro. "Tommaso Mirabella e la Carta del Carnaro (1920–1940)." *Rivista di Storia del Diritto Italiano* 93, no. 2 (2020): 219–77.

Al-Abbood, Muhammed Noor. "Anti-Colonial Nationalism and the West: Toward a Critique of Recent, Western-Based, Anti-Nationalist Scholarship." *Dirasat: Human and Social Sciences* 32, no. 1 (2005): 213–31.

Alatri, Paolo, ed. *Scritti Politici di Gabriele D'Annunzio*. Milano: Feltrinelli, 1980.

Albrecht-Carrié, René. *Italy at the Paris Peace Conference*. Hamden, CT: Archon, 1966.

Alosco, Antonio. "Il Percorso Socialista di Gabriele D'Annunzio tra Storia e Letteratura." *Forum Italicum* 54, no. 1 (2020): 377–90.

Aniante, Antoni. *Gabriel D'Annunzio: Saint Jean du Fascisme*. Paris: Mercure de France, 1934.

Annibale, Silverio. *La Questione di Fiume nel Diritto Internazionale*. Rovigno, Fiume, and Trieste: Centro di Ricerche Storiche Rovigno, 2011.

Aragno, Piero. "Des Esseintes e Andrea Sperellli: Assenza a Presenza della Donna nell'Iter Edonistico di Due 'Vinti' Decadenti." *Annali di Italianistica* 5 (1987): 237–44.

Arendt, Hannah. *Lectures on Kant's Political Philosophy*. Chicago: The University of Chicago Press, 1992.

Armistice Convention with Austria-Hungary. Protocol of Conditions of the Armistice between the Allied and Associated Powers and Austria-Hungary (3 November 1918).

Badoglio, Pietro. *Rivelazioni su Fiume*. Roma: Donatello de Luigi, 1946.

Badurina, Natka. "I Croati di Fiume." *Qualestoria* 48, no. 2 (2020): 45–72.

Baerlein, Henry. *The Birth of Yugoslavia*, vol. II. London: Leonard Parsons, 1922.

Ball, Carlos A. "Sexual Ethics and Postmodernism in Gay Rights Philosophy." *North Carolina Law Review* 80, no. 2 (2002): 371–464.

Ballinger, Pamela. "Rewriting the Text of the Nation: D'Annunzio at Fiume." *Quaderni* XI (1997): 117–55.

Barisonzi, Michela. "The Death of the Angel: Games of Seduction and Moral Destruction in Gabriele D'Annunzio's *Il Piacere*." *MLN* 130, no. 1 (2015): 124–44.

Bartolini, Simonetta. *"Yoga": Sovversivi e Rivoluzionari con D'Annunzio a Fiume*. Milano: Luni, 2019.

Bassnett, Susan. "Translating Gabriele D'Annunzio for the Twenty-First Century Reader." Decadence and Translation Network, Glasgow University, 6 March 2020. https://dandtnetwork.glasgow.ac.uk/translating-gabriele-dannunzio-for-the-twenty-first-century-reader/.

Becker, Jared N. *Nationalism and Culture: Gabriele D'Annunzio and Italy after the Risorgimento*. New York: Peter Lang, 1995.

Benedetti, Giulio. *La Pace di Fiume: Dalla Conferenza di Parigi al Trattato di Roma*. Bologna: Zanichelli, 1924.

Bevir, Mark. "Objectivity in History." *History and Theory* 33, no. 3 (1994): 328–44.

Bianchi, Nereo. "La Carta Costituzionale della Reggenza Italiana del Carnaro." *Fiume: Rivista di Studi Fiumani* 1, no. 1 (1982): 69–74; 1, no. 2 (1982): 46–50; 2, no. 1 (1982): 47–66.

Benussi, Cristina. "D'Annunzio e l'Adriatico: Dal Brigantino *Irene* all'Irredentismo." *Archivio D'Annunzio* 2 (2015): 163–76. https://edizionicafoscari.unive.it/media/pdf/article/archivio-dannunzio/2015/0/art-10.14277-2421-292X-AdA-2-15-11_vcYw6ip.pdf.

Berghaus, Günter. *Futurism and Politics: Between Anarchist Rebellion and Fascist Reaction, 1909–1944*. Providence, MA, and Oxford: Berghahn, 1996.

Berri, Gino. *La Gesta di Fiume: Storia di una Passione Inesausta*. Firenze: Bemporad, 1920.

Bonadeo, Alfredo. *D'Annunzio and the Great War*. Madison and Teaneck: Farleigh Dickinson University Press; London: Associated University Presses, 1995.

Bonnot de Mably, Gabriel. *Dei Diritti e dei Doveri del Cittadino*. Translated by G. M. Milano: Stamperia Patriotica, 1797.

Borelli, Elena. *Giovanni Pascoli, Gabriele D'Annunzio, and the Ethics of Desire: Between Action and Contemplation*. Madison and Teaneck: Farleigh Dickinson University Press, 2017.

Brinkley, Edwad S. "Homosexuality as (Anti)Illness: Oscar Wilde's the Picture of Dorian Gray and Gabriele D'Annunzio's Il Piacere." *Studies in 20th Century Literature* 22, no. 1 (1998): 61–82.

Burgess, Jonathan S. "Tumuli of Achilles." *Classics@ Journal* 3, no. 1 (2005). https://classics-at.chs.harvard.edu/classics3-jonathan-s-burgess-tumuli-of-achilles/.

Burgwyn, H. James. *The Legend of the Mutilated Victory: Italy, the Great War, and the Paris Peace Conference, 1915–1919*. Westport, CT, and London: Greenwood, 1993.

Burich, Enrico. *Fiume e L'Italia*. Milano: Ravá, 1915.

Canziani, Gastone. A *Fiume con D'Annunzio: Lettere 1919–1920*. Ravenna: Longo, 2008.

Cappelletti, Mauro. "Judicial Review in Comparative Perspective." *California Law Review* 58, no. 5 (October 1970): 1017–53.

Carrara, Francesco. *Programma del Corso di Diritto Criminale: Parte Generale*, third edition. Lucca: Giusti, 1867.

Carnaro Charter (*Statuto Italiano della Reggenza del Carnaro*) 1920 (Fiume).

Carteny, Andrea. "From the Lusanne Congress to the Rome Pact Until the Fiume League: Nationalists and Nationalism (1916–1920)." In *War, Peace and Nation-Building (1853–1918)*, edited by Aleksandar Rastović, Andrea Carteny, and Biljana Vučetić, 31–51. Belgrade: Institute of History, 2020.

Castiglione, Corrado. "Cent'anni di Me Ne Frego." *Il Mattino*, October 17, 2018. https://www.ilmattino.it/blog/batman_e_di_destra/manuale_politichese_giornalismo_politica_giornalese_corrado_castiglione-4045669.html?refresh_ce.

Castiglioni, Pietro. *Della Monarchia Parlamentare e dei Diritti e Doveri del Cittadino Secondo lo Statuto e le Leggi del Piemonte*, vol. 1. Milano: Guglielmini, 1859.

Cattaruzza, Marina. *L'Italia e la Questione Adriatica: Dibattiti Parlamentari e Panorama Internazionale (1919–1926)*. Bologna: Il Mulino, 2014.

Chiampi, James T. "'Un Dolore Pacato e Equale': Eternally Mourning Ippolita in 'Trionfo della Morte'." *Italica* 87, no. 4 (2010): 582–601.

Chiarotto, Francesca. "'Effetto Caporetto': Sconfitta Italiana e Vittoria Bolscevica nel Dibattio Pubblico Italiano." In *Il Trauma di Caporetto*, edited by Francesca Belviso, Maria Pia de Paulis, and Alessandro Giacone, 99–110. Torino: Accademia University Press, 2018.

Cingari, Salvatore. "Virtuosa Gioia: Di Alcuni Aspetti Utopistici nella Carta del Carnaro." *Giornale di Storia Costituzionale* 10 (2005): 147–64.

Clavel-Vazquez, Adriana. "Sugar and Spice, and Everything Nice: What Rough Heroines Tell Us about Imaginative Resistance." *Journal of Aesthetics and Art Criticism* 76, no. 2 (2018): 201–12.

Coleman-Norton, Paul Robinson. "Odysseus in the Iliad." *The Classical Weekly* 21, no. 10 (19 December 1927): 73–78.

Collingwood, Robin G. *The Idea of History: With Lectures 1926–1928*, revised edition. Oxford: Oxford University Press, 1994.

Comisso, Giovanni. *Al Vento dell'Adriatico*, second edition. Torino: Ribet, 1928.

Comisso, Giovanni. *Le Mie Stagioni*. Milano: Longanesi, 1963.

Conoscenti, Domenico. "Boccaccio, Dante e l'Omosessualitá nella Cultura del Trecento." *Allegoria* 59 (2009): 27–41.

Constitution of the Russian Soviet Federated Socialist Republic 1918.

Constitution of the Soviet Union 1936.

Convention Regulating the Conditions Under Which the Armistice, Signed between the Allies and Austria-Hungary, Is to Be Applied in Hungary (13 November 1918).

Cooper, Davina. *Challenging Diversity*. Cambridge: Cambridge University Press, 2004.

Cordova, Ferdinando. *Arditi e Legionari Dannunziani*. Padova: Marsilio, 1969.

Costa, Nicolino Flaminio, and Gian Galeazzo Stendardi di Montebenichi. "La 'Carta del Carnaro'." In Gabriele D'Annunzio, *Reggenza Italiana del Carnaro: Disegno di un Nuovo Ordinamento dello Stato Libero di Fiume*, 43–73. Milano: Perelli, 1973.

Cyrino, Monica S. *Aphrodite*. Abingdon, UK: Routledge: 2010.

D'Annunzio, Gabriele. *Cento e Cento e Cento e Cento Pagine del Libro Segreto di Gabriele D'Annunzio Tentato di Morire*. Milano: Rizzoli, 2010.

D'Annunzio, Gabriele. Deed of Donation (22 December 1923). Il Vittoriale degli Italiani. Accessed October 31, 2023. https://www.vittoriale.it/la-storia/atto-di-donazione/.

D'Annunzio, Gabriele. *Il Martirio di San Sebastiano*. Translated by Ettore Janni. Milano: Treves, 1927.

D'Annunzio, Gabriele. *Italy or Death*. Translated by Henry Furst. Fiume: La Vedetta D'Italia, ca. 1919.

D'Annunzio, Gabriele. *Lettera ai Dalmati*. Venezia: Squadra di San Marco, 1919. https://archive.org/details/digabrieledannvn00dann/page/n19/mode/2up.

D'Annunzio, Gabriele. *Notturno*. Milano: Treves, 1921.

D'Annunzio, Gabriele. *Romanzi e Novelle*, vol. I and II. Milano: Mondadori, 1942.

D'Annunzio, Gabriele. "Versilia." In *Laudi del Cielo del Mare della Terra e degli Eroi*, book III: *Alcione*. Milano: Treves, 1908.

"D'Annunzio's Drama of St Sebastian: Banned by the Church." *The Manchester Guardian*, March 10, 1926.

Dante. *La Divina Commedia* (ca. 1321).

Davidson, Jason. "Italy, British Resolve and the 1935–1936 Italo-Ethiopian War." *Cahiers de la Méditerannée* 88 (2014): 69–84.

Declaration of the Rights of Man and of the Citizen 1789 (France).

De Felice, Renzo. *D'Annunzio Politico, 1918–1938*. Roma and Bari: Laterza, 1978.

De Felice, Renzo, and Pietro Gibellini, ed. *D'Annunzio Politico: Atti del Convegno (Il Vittoriale, 9–10 Ottobre 1985)*. Milano: Garzanti, 1987.

De Felice, Renzo, ed. *La Carta del Carnaro nei Testi di Alceste De Ambris e Gabriele D'Annunzio*. Bologna: il Mulino, 1973.

De Felice, Renzo, ed. *Sindacalismo Rivoluzionario e Fiumanesimo nel Carteggio De Ambris—D'Annunzio*. Brescia: Morcelliana, 1966.

De Vergottini, Giuseppe. *La Costituzione secondo D'Annunzio*. Milano: Luni, 2020.

De Vergottini, Giuseppe. "Prassi e Utopia nel Disegno Costituzionale Dannunziano." *Rivista AIC* 3 (2019): 598–612.

Diano, Carlo. "D'Annunzio e l'Ellade." In *L'Arte di Gabriele D'Annunzio*, edited by Emilio Mariano, 51–67. Milano: Mondadori, 1968.

Dickie, John. "Review of John Woodhouse, Gabriele D'Annunzio. Defiant Archangel, Clarendon Press, Oxford, 1998." *Modern Italy* 3, no. 1 (1998): 142–44.

Downing, Lisa. "On the Limits of Sexual Ethics: The Phenomenology of Autassassinophilia." *Sexuality and Culture* 8, no. 1 (2004): 3–17.

Duncan, Derek. *Reading and Writing Italian Homosexuality*. Aldershot, UK, and Burlington, VT: Ashgate, 2006.

Dworkin, Ronald. "The Partnership Conception of Democracy." *California Law Review* 86, no. 3 (May 1998): 453–58.

Engel v. Vitale 370 US 421 (1962).

Esperson, Pietro. *Condizione Giuridica dello Straniero secondo le Legislazioni Italiane ed Estere*. Roma, Torino, Firenze: Fratelli Bocca, 1890.

European Convention on Human Rights (Council of Europe).

Ferlito, Carmelo. "Principi Economici della Carta del Carnaro." *StoriaVeritá* 52 (2008): 34–41.

Ferrari, Giuseppe Franco. "La Carta del Carnaro: Un Centenario in Sordina." *Nomos: le Attualitá del Diritto* 3 (2020). https://www.nomos-leattualitaneldiritto.it/wp-content/uploads/2021/02/Ferrari-3-2020-REV-2.pdf.

Ferrero, Ida. "Libertá Limitata in Tempo di Guerra: Memorie del Tribunale Territoriale di Torino (1915–1918)." *Italian Review of Legal History* 4, no. 4 (2018): 1–23.

Ferreres Comella, Victor. "The European Model of Constitutional Review of Legislation: Toward Decentralization?" *I.CON* 2, no. 3 (2004): 461–91.

Ferrero, Guglielmo. *Da Fiume a Roma: Storia di Quattro Anni (1919–1923)*. Milano: Athena, 1923.

Fondata Sul Lavoro. Roma: Senato della Repubblica, 2018. https://www.senato.it/application/xmanager/projects/leg18/file/repository/relazioni/libreria/novita/XVIII/FONDATA_SUL_LAVORO.pdf.

Foscanelli, Umberto. *D'Annunzio e l'Ora Sociale*. Milano: Carnaro, 1952.

Francisi, Giulio. "La Legislazione di Guerra e i Diritti della Popolazione." In *Parlamenti di Guerra (1914–1945): Il Caso Italiano e il Contesto Europeo*, edited by Marco Meriggi, 183–202. Napoli: FedOA—Federico II University Press, 2017.

Fressura, Marco, and Patrick Karlsen, ed. *La Carta del Carnaro e Altri Scritti su Fiume*. Roma: Castelvecchi, 2009.

Freud, Sigmund. *Group Psychology and the Analysis of the Ego*. Translated by James Strachey. London: Hogarth, 1949.

Fricano, Alessandro. "Cento Anni dalla Carta del Carnaro: Nuove Suggestioni Costituzionali." *Forum di Quaderni Costituzionali* 1 (2021): 667–76.

Frosini, Vittorio. "D'Annunzio e la Carta del Carnaro." *Nuova Antologia* 2041 (January 1971): 75–86.

Fuller, Joseph, ed. *Papers Relating to the Foreign Relations of the United States, The Paris Peace Conference, 1919*, vol. I. Washington: United States Government Printing Office, 1942.

Galbo, Joe. "Sex, Geography, and Death: Metropolis and Empire in a Fascist Writer." *Society and Space* 14, no. 1 (1996): 35–58.

Garipoli, Simona. "Neottolemo o Diomede? Sul Giovane Imberbe al Fianco di Odisseo nell'Ambasciata a Lemno." *Engramma: la Tradizione Classica nella Memoria Occidentale* 109 (Settembre 2013). http://www.engramma.it/eOS/index.php?id_articolo=1384.

Gentile, Emilio. "Fascism as Political Religion." *Journal of Contemporary History* 25, no. 2/3 (1990): 229–51.

Gerini, Giuseppe. *Omaggio a Gabriele D'Annunzio: Gabriele D'Annunzio e la Passione di Fiume*. Fiume: Termini, 1939.

Giannini, Giorgio. *La Giustizia Militare "Sommaria" nella Grande Guerra.* Centro Studi Difesa Civile, 2018. http://www.pacedifesa.org/wp-content/uploads/2020/11/Quaderno-n.1-2018-G.Giannini.pdf

Giglioli, M. F. N. "'Il Deputato della Bellezza': Gabriele D'Annunzio's Aesthetic Politics in the Fin-de-Siècle Crisis." *Journal of Modern Italian Studies* 18, no. 4 (2013): 500–520.

Gilman, Sander L. "Leonardo Sees Him-Self: Reading Leonardo's Fist Representation of Human Sexuality." *Social Research* 54, no. 1 (1987): 149–71.

Glefand, Lawrence E. *The Inquiry: American Preparations for Peace, 1917–1919.* New Haven, CT, and London: Yale University Press, 1963.

Go, Julian, and Jake Watson. "Anticolonial Nationalism From Imagined Communities to Colonial Conflict." *European Journal of Sociology* 60, no. 1 (2019): 31–68.

Gomez Homen, Pier Filippo. *Antecedenti Teorici del Corporativismo Fascista*. Palermo: Sandron, 1929.

Grant, J. A. C. "Judicial Review of Legislation under the Austrian Constitution of 1920." *The American Political Science Review* 28, no. 4 (August 1934): 670–76.

Gronow, Jukka. *On the Formation of Marxism: Karl Kautsky's Theory of Capitalism, the Marxism of the Second International and Karl Marx's Critique of Political Economy*. Leiden: Brill, 2016.

Guerri, Giordano Bruno. *D'Annunzio: L'Amante Guerriero*. Milano: Mondadori, 2009.

Guerri, Giordano Bruno, ed. *D'Annunzio Legislatore: Costituzioni, Visioni, Utopie dell'Impresa Fiumana*. Milano: Silvana Editoriale, 2022.

Guerri, Giordano Bruno. *Disobbedisco: Cinquecento Giorni di Rivoluzione. Fiume 1919–1920*. Milano: Mondadori, 2019.

Guerri, Giordano Bruno, ed. *Fiume 1919–2019: Un Centenario Europeo tra Identitá, Memorie e Prospettive di Ricerca*. Milano: Silvana Editoriale, 2020.

Gullace, Giovanni. "The French Writings of Gabriele D'Annunzio." *Comparative Literature* 12, no. 3 (1960): 207–28.

Gumbrecht, Hans Ulrich. "On Fiume's Place in the Genealogy of Fascism." *Journal of Contemporary History* 31, no. 2 (April 1996): 253–72.

"French Catholics and D'Annunzio." *The Manchester Guardian*, May 19, 1911.

Habermas, Jűrgen. *The Theory of Communicative Action.* Translated by Thomas McCarthy. Cambridge, UK: Polity Press, 1987.

Habib, Samar. *Female Homosexuality in the Middle East: Histories and Representations*. London and New York: Routledge, 2007.

Hallett, Lucy Hughes. *The Pike: Gabriele D'Annunzio: Poet, Seducer and Preacher of War*. London: HarperCollins, 2013.

Halperin, David M. *How to Do the History of Homosexuality*. Chicago: University of Chicago Press, 2002.

Härmänmaa, Marja. "Anatomy of the Superman: Gabriele D'Annunzio's Response to Nietzsche." *The European Legacy* 24, no. 1 (2019): 59–75.

Härmänmaa, Marja. "Gabriele D'Annunzio and War Rhetoric in the 'Canti della Guerra Latina'." *Annali d'Italianistica* 33 (2015): 31–51.

Hart, H. L. A. *The Concept of Law*. Oxford: Oxford University Press, 1961.

Haywood, Geoffrey A. *Failure of a Dream: Sydney Sonnino and the Rise and Fall of Liberal Italy, 1847–1922*. Firenze: Olschki, 1999.

Herek, Gregory M. "Beyond 'Homophobia': A Social Psychological Perspective on Attitudes toward Lesbians and Gay Men." *Journal of Homosexuality* 10, no. 1–2 (1984): 1–15.

Homer. *The Iliad*. Translated by Robert Fagles. New York: Penguin, 1990.

Homer. *The Odyssey*. Translated by Robert Fagles. New York: Penguin, 1996.

Jeličić, Ivan. "Repubblica con Chi? Il Movimento Socialista Fiumano e il Giallo Sisa nel Contesto Post-Asburgico Fiumano." *Qualestoria* 2 (December 2020): 73–93.

Kaye, Richard A. "Losing his Religion: Saint Sebastian as Contemporary Gay Martyr." In *Outlooks: Lesbian and Gay Sexualities and Visual Cultures*, edited by Peter Horne, Reina Lewis, and Peter Norne, 86–105. Abingdon, UK: Routledge, 1996.

Kessler, Jeremy K. "A War for Liberty: On the Law of Conscientous Objection." In *The Cambridge History of the Second World War*, vol. 3: *Total War: Economy, Society and Culture*, edited by Michael Geyer and Adam Tooze, 447–74. Cambridge, UK: Cambridge University Press, 2015.

Kimberly, Caroline E. "Effeminacy, Masculinity, and Homosocial Bonds: The (Un) Intentional Queering of John Keats." *Érudit* (2004–2005). https://doi.org/10.7202/011142ar.

Kirchner Reill, Dominique. *The Fiume Crisis: Life in the Wake of the Habsburg Empire*. Cambridge, MA: Harvard University Press, 2020.

Klinger, William. "La Carta del Carnaro: Una Costituzione per lo Stato Libero di Fiume (1920)." *Quaderni* (Centro di Ricerche Storiche-Rovigno) XIV (2002): 273–343.

Klinger, William. *Un'altra Italia: Fiume 1724–1924*. Edited by Diego Redivo. Rovigno, Fiume, and Trieste: Centro di Ricerche Storiche Rovigno, 2018. https://crsrv.org/wp/wp-content/uploads/2020/03/N.45-Klinger-Fiume.pdf.

Kosofsky Sedgwick, Eve. *Epistemology of the Closet*. Berkeley and Los Angeles: University of California Press, 2008.

Kotchnitzky, Léon. *La Quinta Stagione: o, I Centauri di Fiume*. Translated by Alberto Luchini. Bologna: Zanichelli, 1922.

Langášek, Tomáš. *Ústavní Soud Československé Republiky a Jeho Osudy v Letech 1920–1948*, (*Constitutional Court of the Czechoslovak Republic and Its Fortunes in the Years 1920–1948*). Plzeň: Vydavatelství a nakladatelství Aleš Čeněk, s.r.o., 2011. *Ústavní Soud*. Accessed November 1, 2023. https://www.usoud.cz/en/

constitutional-court-of-the-czechoslovak-republic-and-its-fortunes-in-years-1920-1948 (extracts in English).

Lamour, Christian. "The Scientific Discourse Circulated during a National-Populist Commemoration: Dannunzian Fiume and the 'Italo-cosmopolitan' Field of History." *Modern Italy* 28, no. 1 (February 2023): 35–50.

Latini, Carlotta. "Una Giustizia 'D'Eccezione': Specialitá della Giurisidizione Militare e Sua Estensione durante la Prima Guerra Mondiale." *Deportate, Esuli, Profughe* 5–6 (2006): 67–85.

Lautsi and Others v. Italy (2012) 54 EHRR 3.

Law on the Constitution and Functioning of Corporazioni, 5 February 1934 (Italy).

Lecci, Amerigo. *Il Sistema delle Pene nel Codice Italiano*. Roma e Napoli: Unione Tipografico-Editrice Torinese, 1891.

Leeden, Michael A. *The First Duce*. Baltimore and London: John Hopkins University Press, 1977.

Lenin, Vladimir I. *Materialism and Empirio-Criticism.* London: Wellred Books, 2021.

Liehm, Mira. *Passion and Defiance: Film in Italy from 1942 to the Present*. Berkeley: University of California Press, 1984.

Lloyd George, David. *The Truth About the Peace Treaties*, vol. II. London: Gollancz, 1938.

Lombardino, Andrea. *Lo Sguardo della Folla: Sighele, D'Annunzio e il Linguaggio della Modernitá*. Milano and Udine: Mimesis, 2020.

Lombardo, Renato. *Sui Fondamenti Culturali della Carta del Carnaro*: *Aristotele, Vico, Nietzsche*. Pescara: Tracce, 2011.

Macartney, Maxwell H. H., and Paul Cremona. *Italy's Foreign and Colonial Policy, 1914–1937*. New York: Howard Fertig, 1972.

Macdonald, J. N. *A Political Escapade: The Story of Fiume and D'Annunzio*. London: John Murray, 1921.

Macmillan, Margaret. *Peacemakers: Six Months that Changed the World*. London: John Murray, 2001.

Magli, Ida. *Storia Laica delle Donne Religiose*. Milano: Longanesi, 1995.

Manenti, Luca Giuseppe. "Geografia e Politica nel Razzismo Antislavo: Il Caso dell'Irredentismo Italiano (Secoli XIX–XX)." In *Fratelli al Massacro: Linguaggi e Narrazioni della Prima Guerra Mondiale*, edited by Tullia Catalan, 17–38. Roma: Viella, 2015.

Maranelli, Carlo, and Gaetano Salvemini. *La Questione dell'Adriatico*. Firenze: La Voce, 1918.

Marcuzzi, Stefano. *Britain and Italy in the Era of the Great War: Defending and Forging Empires*. Cambridge, UK: Cambridge University Press, 2020.

Margotti, Giacomo. *Memorie per la Storia de' Nostri Tempi dal Congresso di Parigi nel 1856 ai Giorni Nostri*. Torino: Unione Tipografico-Editrice, 1865.

Marone, Gherardo. "Scimoi." In Harukichi Scimoi, *La Guerra Italiana Vista da un Giapponese*. Napoli: Libreria della Diana, 1919.

Martini, Mario Maria. *La Passione di Fiume: Diari, Cronache, Documenti*. Milano: Sonzogno, 1919.

Marzari, Frank. "La Questione Etiopica." *Rivista di Studi Politici Internazionali* 39, no. 3 (1972): 393–438.

Massagrande, Danilo L. "I Governi di Fiume Indipendente, 1918–1924." *Fiume: Rivista di Studi Adriatici* 5 (2002): 6–50.

Mastriani, Francesco. *I Misteri di Napoli: Studi Storico-Sociali*, vol. 1. Napoli: Nobile, 1869.

Mattoon, Ellie Rose. "Delts Don't Lie." Daily JStor, July 19, 2013. https://daily.jstor.org/delts-dont-lie/.

Merdžo, Albert. "Nuove Conoscenze sulla Composizione Etnica della Popolazione di Fiume Attraverso i Secoli." *Quaderni* (Centro di Ricerche Storiche-Rovigno) XXX (2019): 255–305.

Merlino, Emanuele, ed. *La Sola Ragione di Vivere*. Firenze: Passaggio al Bosco, 2020.

Michels, Robert. *Political Parties: A Sociological Study of the Oligarchical Tendencies of Modern Democracy*. Translated by Eden and Cedar Paul. New York: Hearst's International Library, 1915.

Mileta Mattiaz, Olinto. "Ipotesi sulla Composizione Etnica in Istria, Fiume e Zara: Ieri e Oggi." *Ricerche Sociali* 11 (2002): 7–120.

Mill, John Stuart. *Considerations on Representative Government*. London: Parker, Son and Bourn, 1861.

Mirabella, Tommaso. *La Carta del Carnaro*. Palermo: Libreria D'Agata, 1940.

Mirabile, Andrea. *Multimedia Archaeologies: Gabriele D'Annunzio, Belle Époque Paris, and the Total Artwork*. Amsterdam and New York: Rodopi, 2014.

Modesti, Mara Vittoria. "Il Modello della Coppia Eroica in Alcuni Miti dell'Epoca Arcaica." MA diss., Universita' ca' Foscari, Venezia, 2016–2017.

Mondini, Mario. *Fiume 1919: Una Guerra Civile Italiana*. Roma: Salerno, 2019.

Moscati, Giuseppe. *Le Cinque Giornate di Fiume: X Anniversario del Natale di Sangue*. Milano: Carnaro, 1930.

Mosse, George L. "The Poet and the Exercise of Political Power: Gabriele D'Annunzio." *Yearbook of Comparative and General Literature* 22 (1973):

Muggia, Francesco G. "Preface." In Cinzia Guazzi, *La Reggenza Italiana del Carnaro nella Storia del Diritto Costituzionale*. Genova: Centro di Cultura Giuliano Dalmata, 1982. Republished as Muggia, Francesco G. "Studio di Cinzia Guazzi Edito dal Centro di Cultura Giuliano-Dalmata: Congiungimento nella Carta del Carnaro tra Pensiero Dannunziano e Progresso di Fiume." *L'Arena di Pola*, January 8, 1983.

Najarian, James. *Victorian Keats: Manliness, Sexuality, and Desire*. Basingstoke, UK, and New York: Palgrave Macmillan, 2002.

Nicolson, Harold. *Peacemaking, 1919*. London: Constable, 1933.

Nussbaum, Martha C. "Skepticism about Practical Reason in Literature and the Law." *Harvard Law Review* 107, no. 3 (1994): 714–44.

Oldfield, Adrian. "Moral Judgments in History." *History and Theory* 20, no. 3 (1981): 260–77.

Ortolan, Joseph-Louis. *Elementi di Diritto Penale*, vol. II. Napoli: Stamperia Del Vaglio, 1857.

Otey, Jessica. "D'Annunzio, Eros and the Modern Artist: Tragedy and Tragic Criticism Reconsidered." *MLN* 125, no. 1 (2010): 169–94.

Ovid. *The Metamorphoses* (ca. 8 CE).

Panattoni, Giuseppe. "Diritti Fondamentali e Loro Dichiarazione in Inghilterra, America, Germania, Francia e Italia." *La Temi: Giornale di Legislazione e Giurisprudenza* 7 (1848): 387–96.

Paradisi, Patrizia. "Guerra e Poesia: 'Energeia', la Decima Musa di D'Annunzio." *Il Nome nel Testo: Rivista internazionale di Onomastica Letteraria* XVIII (2006): 125–52.

Pareto, Vilfredo. *The Rise and Fall of the Elites: An Application of Theoretical Sociology*. Totowa, NJ: The Bedminster Press: 1968.

Payne, Stanley G. *A History of Fascism*. Madison, WI: University of Wisconsin Press, 1995.

Peace Agreement between General C. Ferrario, Captain N. Host-Venturi, and Mayor R. Gigante, Abbazia (31 December 1920).

Penal Code for the Army of the Kingdom of Italy 1869.

Perfetti, Francesco, ed. *D'Annunzio e il Suo Tempo*, vol. 1. Genova: Sagep, 1989.

Peteani, Luigi. "I Connotati del Regime Dannunziano a Fiume." *Quaderni del Vittoriale* 19 (1980): 39–47.

Peteani, Luigi. "Irredentisti Fiumani del Risorgimento." *Rivista di Studi Politici Internazionali* 17, no. 2 (April–June 1950): 283–89.

Peteani, Luigi. "Testimonianze sull'Italianitá di Fiume," *Fiume: Rivista di Studi Fiumani* II, no. 1 (1982): 1–4.

Pičić, Thea. *Rijeka Ili Smrt! D'Anunzijeva okupacija Rijeke, 1919–1921 / Rijeka or Death! D'Annunzio's occupation of Rijeka, 1919–2019*. Rijeka: Naklada Val, 2019.

Pireddu, Nicoletta. "'Il Divino Pregio del Dono': Andrea Sperelli's Economy of Pleasures." *Annali d'Italianistica* 15 (1997): 175–201.

Posel, Rosalind. "The Idea of a Hermeneutic History." PhD diss., University of Natal, 1982.

Praz, Mario. *The Romantic Agony*. Translated by Angus Davison. Birkenhead, UK: Fontana Library, 1960.

Pupo, Raoul. *Fiume Città di Passione*. Bari: Laterza, 2018.

Pupo, Raoul, and Fabio Todero, ed. *Fiume, D'Annunzio e la Crisi dello Stato Liberale in Italia*. Trieste: IRSML, 2010.

Rae, John. *Contemporary Socialism*. New York: Scribner, 1891.

Rainero, Romain H., and Stefano B. Galli. *L'Italia e la "Grande Vigilia": Gabriele D'Annunzio nella Politica Italiana Prima del Fascismo*. Milano: FrancoAngeli, 2007.

Ramaioli, Federico L. "Lo Statuto della Reggenza Italiana del Carnaro tra Innovazione e Tradizione: A Cento Anni dalla Costituzione di Fiume." *Fiume: Rivista di Studi Adriatici* XLI (2020): 83–100.

Raz, Joseph. *Engaging Reason: On the Theory and Value of Action*. Oxford: Oxford University Press, 1999.

Raz, Joseph. *Practical Reason and Norms*. Oxford: Oxford University Press, 1999.

Raz, Joseph. *The Morality of Freedom*. Oxford: Oxford University Press, 1986.

Raz, Joseph. "The Problem of Authority: Revisiting the Service Conception." *Minnesota Law Review* 90 (2006): 1003–44.

Regulations of the New Liberation Army (Statuto del Nuovo Esercito Liberatore) 1920 (Fiume).

Rhodes, Anthony. *The Poet as a Superman: A Life of Gabriele D'Annunzio*. London: Weidenfeld and Nicolson, 1959.

Ricco, Renato. "'Esaltatrice dell'Atto di Vita, dell'Opera di Vita': Il Ruolo della Musica nella Carta del Carnaro di Gabriele D'Annunzio." *Forum Italico* 49, no. 2 (2005): 433–46.

Ricotti, Carlo. *La Carta del Carnaro: Dannunziana Massonica Autonomista*. Roma: Fefé, 2019.

Rolandi, Francesca. "A Never Requested Triumph? Reframing Gender Boundaries in Fiume and Sušak after 1918." *Italia Contemporanea Yearbook 2020* (2021): 11–36.

Rosmini, Antonio. *Filosofia del Diritto*, vol. 2. Milano: Boniardi-Pogliani, 1843.

Rossi, Davide. "D'Annunzio, la Carta del Carnaro e la Crisi dello Stato Liberale, tra Rappresentanza e Antiparlamentarismo." *Giornale di Storia Costituzionale* 38, no. 2 (2019): 135–47.

Rossi, Davide, ed. *La Cittá di Vita Cento Anni Dopo: Fiume, D'Annunzio e il Lungo Novecento Adriatico*. Padova: Wolters Kluwer—Cedam, 2020.

Royal Decree 1561, 4 October 1917 (Italy).

Salaris, Claudia. *Alla Festa della Rivoluzione: Artisti e Libertari con D'Annunzio a Fiume*. Bologna: Il Mulino, 2002.

Salotti, Guglielmo. "La Valorizzazione del Lavoro nella Carta del Carnaro." *Clio* 27 (1991): 85–103.

Salotti, Guglielmo. "Nuovi Studi sulla Carta del Carnaro." *Fiume: Rivista di Studi Fiumani* XIX–XX (1973–1974): 78–102.

Sanders, M. L., and Philip M. Taylor. *British Propaganda During the First World War, 1914–18*. London and Basingstoke, UK: Macmillan, 1982.

Santomassimo, Gianpasquale. *La Terza Via Fascista: Il Mito del Corporativismo*. Roma: Carocci, 2006.

Sbordone, Giovanni. "Il Poeta e la Gazzetta: D'Annunzio nello Sguardo della Classe Dirigente Veneziana." *Archivio D'Annunzio* 2 (2015): 179–206. https://edizionicafoscari.unive.it/media/pdf/article/archivio-dannunzio/2015/2/il-poeta-e-la-gazzetta/art-10.14277-2421-292X-AdA-2-15-13.pdf.

Schmitt, Carl. *The Crisis of Parliamentary Democracy*. Translated by Ellen Kennedy. Cambridge, MA, and London: MIT Press, 1988.

Schweikard, David P., and Hans Bernard Schmid. "Collective Intentionality." *Stanford Encylopedia of Philosophy*, 2013 (revised 2020). https://plato.stanford.edu/entries/collective-intentionality/.

Senardi, Fulvio, ed. *Il Punto su D'Annunzio*. Bari: Laterza, 1989.

Seneca. *Letters to Lucilius* (ca. 63 CE).

Serafini, Filippo. *Istituzioni di Diritto Romano Comparato al Diritto Civile Patrio*, vol. 1. Firenze: Giuseppe Pellas, 1892.

Serventi Longhi, Enrico. "La Dittatura Sovrana di Fiume: Innovazioni Politiche, Sociali ed Economiche (1919–1920)." *Mondo Contemporaneo* 2 (May 2016): 139–67.

Serventi Longhi, Enrico. *Il Faro del Mondo Nuovo: D'Annunzio e I Legionari a Fiume tra Guerra e Rivoluzione*. Udine: Gaspari, 2019.

Serventi Longhi, Enrico. "The Father of 'Sovereignism': D'Annunzio in Fiume between the Crisis of Liberalism and the Critique of Democracy." *Modern Italy* 27 (2022): 35–47.

Serventi Longhi, Enrico. "The Triumph of the Noble People: Gabriele D'Annunzio and Populism between Literature and Politics." *Qualestoria* 2 (2020): 201–12.

Simonelli, Federico Carlo. *D'Annunzio e il Mito di Fiume: Riti, Simboli, Narrazioni*. Pisa: Pacini, 2021.

Simonelli, Federico Carlo. "La Costruzione di un Mito: Rituali, Simboli e Narrazioni dell'Impresa di Fiume (1919–1921)." PhD diss., Università degli Studi di Urbino Carlo Bo, 2014–2015.

Sinagra, Augusto, ed. *Lo Statuto della Reggenza Italiana del Carnaro tra Storia, Diritto Internazionale e Diritto Costituzionale*. Milano: Giuffré, 2009.

Sitwell, Osbert. *Discursions on Travel, Art and Life*. London: Grant Richards, 1925.

Skradol, Natalia. "Carnival of Exception: Gabriele D'Annunzio's 'Dialogues with the Crowd'." *Rhetorica: A Journal of the History of Rhetoric* 30 (2012): 74–93.

Sorge, Paola. "Introduzione: Le Martyre de Saint Sébastien: L'Opera Totale di Gabriele D'Annunzio." In Gabriele D'Annunzio, *Il Martirio di San Sebastiano*. Roma: Elliot, 2013.

Spackman, Barbara. *Decadent Genealogies: The Rhetoric of Sickness from Baudelaire to D'Annunzio*. Ithaca, NY: Cornell University Press, 1989.

Statuto Albertino 1848 (Italy).

Stelli, Giovanni. "Per una Storia di Fiume." *Fiume: Rivista di Studi Adriatici* 29 (2014): 3–30.

Stille, Alexander. "The Candidate of Beauty." Review of *Gabriele D'Annunzio: Defiant Archangel*, by John Woodhouse. *London Review of Books*, July 2, 1998.

Susmel, Edoardo. *Fiume Attraverso la Storia: Dalle Origini Fino ai Nostri Giorni*. Milano: Treves, 1919.

Susmel, Edoardo. *La Cittá di Passione: Fiume negli Anni 1914–1920*. Milano: Treves, 1921.

Tatarkiewicz, Wladyslaw. "Classification of Arts in Antiquity." *Journal of the History of Ideas* 24, no. 2 (April–June 1963): 231–40.

Tennyson, Alfred Lord. "The Princess." Project Gutenberg, 2008 (updated 2013). https://www.gutenberg.org/files/791/791-h/791-h.htm.

Tomes, Jason. "British Empire Delegation at the Paris Peace Conference" (24 May 2007). In *Oxford Dictionary of National Biography*. https://doi.org/10.1093/ref:odnb/95641.

Tooze, Adam. *The Deluge: The Great War and the Making of Global Order, 1916–1931*. London: Penguin, 2014.

Tosoni, Leonardo. "Carta del Carnaro: Diritti di Libertà e Prospettive di Giustizia Sociale nella Fiume Dannunziana." *Historia Constitucional* 22 (2021): 856–82.

Towe, Thomas E. "Fundamental Rights in the Soviet Union: A Comparative Approach." *University of Pennsylvania Law Review* 115 (1967): 1251–74.

Treaty of London (26 April 1915).

Valeri, Nino. *Da Giolitti a Mussolini: Momenti della Crisi del Liberalismo*. Firenze: Parenti, 1957.

Van Hout, Milou. "In Search of the Nation in Fiume: Irredentism, Cultural Nationalism, Borderlands." *Nations and Nationalism* 26, no. 3 (2019): 1–17.

Vasari, Giorgio. *Le Vite de' piu Eccellenti, Pittori, Scultori, ed Architetti*. Torino: Einaudi, 1986.

Viceroyal Decree 885, 20 June 1915 (Italy).

Villari, Lucio. *La Luna di Fiume—1919: Il Complotto*. Milano: Ugo Guanda, 2019.

Vivarelli, Roberto. *Storia delle Origini del Fascismo: L'Italia dalla Grande Guerra alla Marcia su Roma*, vol. 1. Bologna: Il Mulino, 1991.

Webb, Sidney, and Beatrice Webb. *A Constitution for the Socialist Commonwealth of Great Britain*. London and New York: Longmans, Green & Co, 1920.

Weimar Constitution 1919 (Germany).

White, Hayden. "The Politics of Historical Interpretation: Discipline and De-Sublimation." *Critical Inquiry* 9, no. 1 (1982): 113–37.

Wittman, Laura. *The Tomb of the Unknown Soldier, Modern Mourning, and the Reinvention of the Mystical Body*. Toronto: University of Toronto Press, 2011.

Wood, Jessica. "The Art of Dying in Trionfo della Morte." *Forum Italicum* 51, no. 2 (2017): 469–87.

Woodhouse, John. *Gabriele D'Annunzio: Defiant Archangel*. Oxford: Clarendon Press, 1998.

Woodward, Anthony. "Aestheticism and Politics: Gabriele D'Annunzio's Le Vergini delle Rocce." *English Studies in Africa* 42 (1999): 13–30.

Zanghellini, Aleardo. "The Foundations of the Rule of Law." *Yale Journal of Law & the Humanities* 28 (2016): 213–40.

Zanghellini, Aleardo. *The Sexual Constitution of Political Authority: The "Trials" of Same-Sex Desire*. Abingdon, UK: Routledge, 2015.

Index

About the Author

Aleardo Zanghellini is professor of law and social theory at the University of Reading, United Kingdom. His scholarship sits at the crossroads of law and the humanities (history, philosophy, and literary criticism). He is the author of *Imaginative Resistance, Queer Fiction and the Law: Same-Sex Desire and the Good Life in Heteronormative Orders* (Routledge, 2022), *The Sexual Constitution of Political Authority: The Trias of Same-Sex Desire* (Routledge, 2015), as well as a work of historical fiction on Edward II (*The Spellbinders*, Lethe Press, 2018).

www.ingramcontent.com/pod-product-compliance
Ingram Content Group UK Ltd.
Pitfield, Milton Keynes, MK11 3LW, UK
UKHW021032041026
15470UKWH00014B/1414

9 781683 934356